Order and Disorder after the Cold War

A WASHINGTON QUARTERLY READER

Order and Disorder after the Cold War

edited by

BRAD ROBERTS

The MIT Press
Cambridge, Massachusetts
London, England

Bruce D. Porter, "A Country Instead of a Cause: Russian Foreign Policy in the Post-Soviet Era," *TWQ* 15, no. 3 (Summer 1992); Gerrit W. Gong, "China's Fourth Revolution," *TWQ* 17, no. 1 (Winter 1994); Max Jakobson, "Collective Security in Europe Today," *TWQ* 18, no. 2 (Spring 1995); Ryuzaburo Kaku, "Perestroika in Japan," *TWQ* 15, no. 3 (Summer 1992); Zalmay Khalilzad, "Losing the Moment? The United States and the World After the Cold War," *TWQ* 18, no. 2 (Spring 1995); Kishore Mahbubani, "The United States: 'Go East, Young Man,'" *TWQ* 17, no. 2 (Spring 1994); Karin von Hippel, "The Resurgence of Nationalism and Its International Implications," *TWQ* 17, no. 4 (Autumn 1994); James C. Clad, "Old World Disorders," *TWQ* 15, no. 4 (Autumn 1992); Thomas G. Weiss, "The United Nations and Civil Wars," *TWQ* 17, no. 4 (Autumn 1994); Barry M. Blechman, "The Intervention Dilemma," *TWQ* 18, no. 3 (Summer 1995); Lincoln P. Bloomfield, "The Premature Burial of Global Law and Order: Looking beyond the Three Cases from Hell," *TWQ* 17, no. 3 (Summer 1994); Marc Dean Millot, "Facing the Emerging Reality of Regional Nuclear Adversaries," *TWQ* 17, no. 3 (Summer 1994); John Gerard Ruggie, "Peacekeeping and U.S. Interests," *TWQ* 17, no. 4 (Autumn 1994); George Weigel, "Religion and Peace: An Argument Complexified," *TWQ* 14, no. 2 (Spring 1991). Reprinted from *Resolving Third World Conflict: Challenges for a New Era* by permission of the United States Institute of Peace, Washington, D.C.; Phil Williams, "Transnational Criminal Organizations: Strategic Alliances," *TWQ* 18, no. 1 (Winter 1995); Peter J. Spiro, "New Global Communities: Nongovernmental Organizations in International Decision-Making Institutions," *TWQ* 18, no. 1 (Winter 1995); Gerald Segal, "Asians in Cyberia," *TWQ* 18, no. 3 (Summer 1995); Erik R. Peterson, "Looming Collision of Capitalisms?" *TWQ* 17, no. 2 (Spring 1994); James R. Golden, "Economics and National Strategy: Convergence, Global Networks, and Cooperative Competition," *TWQ* 16, no. 3 (Summer 1993); Murray Weidenbaum, "The Business Response to the Global Marketplace," *TWQ* 15, no. 1 (Winter 1992); Ernest H. Preeg, "The U.S. Leadership Role in World Trade: Past, Present, and Future," *TWQ* 15, no. 2 (Spring 1992); Joseph LaPalombara, "International Firms and National Governments: Some Dilemmas," *TWQ* 17, no. 2 (Spring 1994); Penelope Hartland-Thunberg, "A Capital-Starved New World Order: Geopolitical Implications of a Global Capital Shortage in the 1990s," *TWQ* 14, no. 4 (Autumn 1991); Paul W. Schroeder, "The New World Order: A Historical Perspective," *TWQ* 17, no. 2 (Spring 1994); Alberto R. Coll, "Power, Principles, and Prospects for a Cooperative International Order," *TWQ* 16, no. 1 (Winter 1993); John Stremlau, "Antidote to Anarchy," *TWQ* 18, no. 1 (Winter 1995); Jose E. Alvarez, "The Once and Future Security Council," *TWQ* 18, no. 2 (Spring 1995); Shahram Chubin, "The South and the New World Order," *TWQ* 16, no. 4 (Autumn 1993).

Library of Congress Cataloging-in-Publication Data

Order and disorder after the Cold War / edited by Brad Roberts.
    p.   cm. — (A Washington quarterly reader)
   Includes bibliographical references.
   ISBN 0-262-68088-2 (pbk. : alk. paper)
   1. International relations. 2. Security, International. 3. International economic relations.
I. Roberts, Brad. II. Series.
JX1395.073 1995
327.1'01—dc20
                                         95-35117
                                             CIP

Contents

Introduction

ORDER OR DISORDER—which will prevail in the international system that succeeds the Cold War? This question is at the core of the burgeoning debate about the nature of the world system at the end of the twentieth century and the place of the United States in that system.

A more orderly world seemed likely as the cold war confrontation collapsed in 1989. But the new world order touted by President George Bush seems little in evidence just a few years later. Rather, the new world *disorder* is a theme that resonates broadly in the community of analysts, scholars, and policymakers interested in global peace and security. The perception of disorder has been nourished by the foreign policy crises of recent years and reinforced by new media that bring these crises into people's homes. This perception has helped to stimulate a resurgence of isolationism in the U.S. body politic at a time when the domestic agenda is foremost in the national consciousness.

Probing beneath the headlines and rhetoric, what can be discerned about the sources of order and disorder in the post–cold war international system? The effort to find answers to this question has generated an expanding intellectual debate of weight and moment. Further inquiry into what public policies offer the most promise in terms of promoting order or minimizing disorder has generated a fertile debate about the purposes and priorities of U.S. foreign and security policies.

Some of the most important milestones in these debates have been published in *The Washington Quarterly*. A journal of international public policy issues published by the MIT Press for the Center for Strategic and International Studies of Washington, D.C., *The Washington Quarterly* has a broad intellectual purview. Its purpose is to stimulate readers to think afresh about statecraft, strategy, international security, and, more broadly, the international engagement of the United States. The breadth of the journal's agenda is well illustrated in the compendiums of its articles that have appeared in recent years: *The New Democracies: Global Change and U.S. Policy* (Cambridge, Mass.: MIT Press, 1990); *U.S. Foreign Policy After the Cold War* (Cambridge, Mass.: MIT Press, 1992); *U.S. Security in an Uncertain Era* (Cambridge, Mass.: MIT Press, 1993); and *Weapons Proliferation in the 1990s* (Cambridge, Mass.: MIT Press, 1995). A further reader will appear in late 1995: *The New World Economic Order.*

With a focus on order and disorder, the current volume has a very broad purview. The materials assembled here are intended to stretch thinking about the order and disorder theme by stimulating readers to see connections among issues and across disciplines. Toward this end, articles are organized into specific chapters.

Chapter I examines the roles of the major powers on the world stage. At times directly and at times obliquely, the articles identify the orientations and competencies of the major powers. The review is unsettling, because it raises profound questions about the leadership that one or all of the powers might provide at this time of uncertainty in the international system.

Chapter II evaluates new challenges to international order. The resurgence of nationalism, the growing prominence of civil wars, the dilemmas of intervention, and the limitations of the United Nations are featured. Weapons proliferation, transnational criminal organizations, the information revolution, religion, and nongovernmental organizations are also surveyed for their impact on order. A central theme is that the challenges must be clearly perceived. Some problems are systemic, while others are of our own making. In some are also to be found opportunities to deepen the sources of order.

Chapter III delineates the debate between geopolitics and geoeconomics as an organizing principle of international affairs. The clash of the advanced democracies in the marketplace, the limitations of the state system in governing the global economy, the growing prominence if not dominance of the private sector in that economy, and the vulnerabilities of the financial system are all evaluated in terms of their impact on global order. The picture that emerges is one in which geoeconomics is in the ascendant in a global system where matters of economics, politics, and statecraft interact in highly complicated ways.

Chapter IV comes to the core themes: Is the world moving toward a new order or toward increasing anarchy? What are the essential tasks of policy that will increase orderliness? Articles included here offer a sharp critique of the new world disorder fetish and of the perceived powerlessness of the international community in meeting the new challenges to order. They describe the missteps of policy, as seen from both inside and outside the United States. The cautionary note is strong: unless policymakers come quickly to a deeper understanding of the sources of order in the international system, they will squander—and perhaps eventually lose—the opportunities to consolidate the cold war victory. On the issue of leadership the articles go beyond the trite to identify specific means and ends.

Please note that authors have not been given the opportunity to update their articles subsequent to original publication. Although parts of some essays have necessarily been overtaken by events, each contribution makes arguments that remain relevant. Please note further that all biographies are current to the time of original publication. The views expressed here are those of the authors alone and should not be attributed to any institutions with which they are affiliated or to the publishers, CSIS and MIT Press.

It has been a pleasure to work with so creative and diverse a group of authors in publishing these materials. I admire their success—and discipline—in turning thoughtful reflection into a tool for broader discussion. I am grateful also to the talented individuals who have served in the editorial office of *The Washington Quarterly* during the period in which these articles were published, including particularly Yoma Ullman, James Rutherford, Denise Miller, and Lynn Northcutt de Vega. I hope that they, too, take satisfaction in the debate begun.

Brad Roberts
Washington, D.C.
May 1, 1995

I. The Major Powers in a Decade of Uncertainty

A Country Instead of a Cause: Russian Foreign Policy in the Post-Soviet Era

Bruce D. Porter

WITH THE DISSOLUTION of the USSR and the raising of the tricolor Russian flag over the Kremlin, it appears that a "thin hope" once expressed by Charles Bohlen, U.S. ambassador to the Soviet Union from 1953 to 1957, is being realized. Russia is finally beginning to "act like a country instead of a cause."[1] The transition to normalcy after more than seven decades of ideological rule will be neither easy nor quick, however. A multitude of contentious political, administrative, legal, and constitutional issues confront the new Russia: the structure of its government; its role within the Commonwealth of Independent States; the status and structure of the former Soviet armed forces; and the division of fiscal, capital, and bureaucratic assets among the states of the Commonwealth. Meanwhile, the dismantling of central planning has at least temporarily exacerbated a difficult economic situation and fueled growing popular discontent. Given such domestic challenges, Russia's leadership is likely to remain inwardly focused for some years to come, with international issues relegated to second rank in priority.

The foreign policy of Russia in the wake of the USSR's disintegration remains nonetheless a matter of considerable interest for the United States and its Western allies. Given Russia's immense geographical size (even without its empire), large population, abundant natural resources, sizable army, and still formidable nuclear arsenal, its international course over the next decade will profoundly influence world affairs. The independence of the former Soviet republics also introduces a host of new complexities and potential instabilities into the international system. It is important therefore to ask how *Russian* foreign policy is likely to differ from *Soviet* foreign policy. This article will offer some tentative answers to that question. Given the uncertainty of the current situation in Russia, however, it will not attempt to make precise predictions, but rather to map out the salient sources of change and continuity that bear on Russia's international behavior.

In order to limit the range of analysis within reasonable bounds, the discussion that follows will proceed from certain assumptions: first, that some kind of reform-minded government will remain in power in Moscow, even if key personalities or the govern-

Bruce D. Porter is the Lynde and Harry Bradley Research Associate in Strategic Studies at the Olin Institute of the Center for International Affairs, Harvard University.

mental structure change; second, that Russia will not undergo a civil war, a successful antireform coup, or a reimposition of totalitarian rule by either Old Guard Communist forces or by extreme nationalists; and third, that Russia's foreign policy will tend to become more "Russian" in nature, with the Commonwealth evolving toward more of an umbrella structure, as individual former republics move gradually toward full independence, with separate currencies, armed forces, controlled borders, and divergent foreign and economic policies. These assumptions are plausible at the present and conform to the trend of events since formation of the Commonwealth, but given the volatility of the current situation, they are only assumptions. Obviously a radical change of political direction, a civil war, or the recentralization of the Commonwealth would vitiate parts of the analysis laid out below.

Sources of Change in Russian Foreign Policy

Soviet foreign policy in the pre-Gorbachev era was an amalgam of four primary elements: Marxist–Leninist ideology; traditional Russian behavior and national character; the multinational character and federated structure of the Soviet Union; and the practical experience derived from 70 years of Soviet rule, with World War II and the Cold War of particular importance in shaping the self-image and international behavior of the Soviet leadership. The most dramatic source of change in the past two years has been the abandonment of Marxist–Leninist ideology and suspension of the Communist party (CPSU) that was its flamekeeper. But the other elements of this quartet are also undergoing change as a result of the "Second Rus-

sian Revolution." Russia's traditional behavior and national character may evolve over time as Russian society opens up, develops legal and constitutional norms, and establishes a market economy. The dissolution of the Soviet Union marks the end of Russia's multinational empire and promises to enhance the national content of its foreign policy. Finally, the European settlement that ended the Cold War relegates much of Soviet foreign policy experience to a closed chapter of history and may make possible a diplomatic revolution in Russia's relations with the outside world. The implications of these changes are generally quite positive, but they also introduce certain new complexities and unpredictable factors into world politics.

The Abandonment of Ideology. Marxist–Leninist ideology made the Soviet Union a revolutionary or challenging power within the world system—a cause instead of a country. It contributed to the anti-Western nature of Soviet foreign policy, justified its almost complete amorality and expedience, and caused Soviet leaders to exaggerate the threats posed to them by the outside world (which in turn led to the phenomenon of "self-encirclement"). Ideology motivated Moscow's interest in the Third World, including distant regions such as Africa and Latin America in which Imperial Russia had never shown much interest. It was the wedge with which the USSR attempted to extend its influence abroad by means of a network of contacts with other Communist parties and revolutionary regimes around the world. Although this network became less formalized after the dissolution of the Comintern during World War II, the Soviet leadership from Lenin to Konstantin Chernenko never entirely ceased thinking of itself as the vanguard of a world movement rather than the government of a mere country.

The formal abandonment of Marxist–Leninist ideology by Russia's political elite is therefore clearly the greatest single factor for change in post-Soviet Russian policy. Its probable consequences are already evident and include the following:

- a decline in expansionism and a dramatic decline in anti-Western and anti-U.S. rhetoric, sentiment, and policy;
- a greater willingness to pursue genuine cooperation with the Western industrial powers, whom Russian foreign minister Andrei Kozyrev has declared to be "the natural allies" of Russia;[2]
- a decline in Russian interest in third world countries not contiguous to or near its borders, a trend already evident in the Soviet withdrawal from regional disputes in southern Africa, Southeast Asia, and Central America;
- cooperation with the West in mediating regional conflicts, as recently demonstrated in the Persian Gulf War; and
- a deterioration of relations with Communist states adhering to the ideology, as had occurred in Soviet relations with Eastern Europe even before the autumn of 1989 and as is becoming increasingly apparent in Moscow's relations with the People's Republic of China (PRC), Cuba, and Vietnam.

The abandonment of Marxist–Leninist ideology has also resulted in an important institutional change: the end of the leading role of the Communist party in the formulation of foreign and security policy. The ideology justified one-party rule ("the dictatorship of the proletariat") and gave the Party whatever legitimacy or higher purpose it might claim. The Party's role as a shadow government in turn made it the dominant political institution of the USSR. Although the Ministry of Foreign Affairs was the primary operational or tactical arm of Soviet foreign policy, the Secretariat of the Party's Central Committee oversaw its functions and played a paramount role in the planning and formulation of the long-term strategic objectives of the Soviet Union. With the suspension of the Central Committee and CPSU following the August 1991 coup attempt, the role of state and governmental (as opposed to party) bodies in the formulation of foreign policy greatly increased. The Russian Ministry of Foreign Affairs (encompassing much of the former Soviet Ministry of Foreign Affairs) together with the president and leading officials of the Russian government will define Russia's foreign policy objectives; their thinking is certain to be based more on national interest than on ideological assumptions or objectives.

The Impact of Internal Reform on International Behavior. Richard Pipes, Barbara Jelavich, Adam Ulam, and other historians have pointed out numerous linkages between czarist foreign policy and Soviet foreign policy. Russia's historical legacy and national character will no doubt continue to exert influence on Russia's international behavior; as such, they will be examined as sources of continuity in a later section of this article. But there is no reason to assume that any nation's behavior is fixed and immutable. As Arrigo Levi, the former Moscow correspondent of *Corriera della Sera*, observed in 1969, "As soon as a totalitarian country is able to express itself freely, it not only discovers that it is different from

5

what it appeared to be, but it *becomes* different."[3] Internal political reform sustained over time may affect long-standing patterns of national character and behavior.

Traditional Russian behavior, even prior to the Soviet era, derived in part from the autocratic nature of the Russian imperial state and the absence of social counterweights (representative institutions, a middle class, a functioning "civil society") to the dominance of that state. Under Mikhail Gorbachev, Russia took several cautious steps in the direction of liberal democracy, the most important of which was the introduction of glasnost in public discourse. Today Russians can freely express their views on politics and current affairs without fear of retribution or penalty. Multiple political parties exist (although the proliferation of dozens of small, weak parties means that a true multiparty *system* has not yet emerged). At least some free elections have been held, including the election of Boris Yeltsin in June 1991 as president of the Russian Republic (now the Russian Federation). Religious freedom has advanced dramatically. If conditions of personal liberty prevail long enough, they cannot fail to have a long-term impact on the national character of the Russian people.

Also of great significance is the rise of an entrepreneurial class that is accumulating wealth and exerting influence on state officials. Russia is witnessing for the first time since the October Revolution the emergence of a propertied middle class (as opposed to an intellectual and technocratic middle class, which the USSR has long had). Such a class in other European countries has usually played a key role in the emergence of true liberal democracy. It is significant that Russia's new capitalists were in the forefront of popular opposition to the August coup—they had more to lose than anyone else. With several million Russian citizens now employed in a rapidly growing private sector, a long-missing counterweight to the dominance of the state is taking form.[4]

Such progress notwithstanding, Russia remains today an authoritarian state in many critical respects and, even on the most optimistic assumptions, it may take a decade or more before it can develop solid and enduring democratic institutions. In the interim, however, and even if full democracy does not emerge, it is probable that Russian society will exert increasing influence on the formulation of Russian foreign policy. The Russian Soviet, despite the tepid democratic sentiments of many of its legislators, represents one channel of public influence on the state. It has the right to challenge government decrees, confirm political appointees, and initiate legislation. Presumably, when new elections are held (most likely not before 1993), its influence will increase markedly.

The influence of mass public opinion is also on the rise. Several public polling organizations now exist in Russia, such as the National Center for the Study of Public Opinion, the Independent Institute for the Sociology of Parliamentarism, and the polling organization "Opinion." The results of these surveys are widely publicized by *Izvestia*, *Ogonyok*, and other Russian publications.

The growing openness of Russian society also makes Western intellectual influences stronger and more acceptable than in the past; this affects not only the intelligentsia, who have long followed Western developments closely, but journalists, educated laypeople, and even schoolchildren, whose teachers are now developing independent curricula of their own. Russian entrepreneurs want expanded links with the West, including an infusion of private Western capital; they will lobby for policies conducive to these ends. Assertive domestic constituencies thus cannot help but influence the direction and tenor of Russian foreign policy, even before a complete panoply of democratic institutions has been established. It is possible that public sentiment in Russia could take a hypernationalist turn, but at the present this appears unlikely. Greater public influence on foreign policy will probably work in the direction of moderation.

The Implications of a Decentralized Commonwealth. The demise of the Soviet Union means that Russian foreign policy will not only be less "Soviet" in nature but also less "Union." Even if the Commonwealth survives and achieves a measure of foreign policy coordination among its members, Russia's foreign policy will be more national in context, more overtly "Russian" than in the past 70 years. Moreover, as individual states of the Commonwealth acquire greater independence and diverge in their foreign policy paths, Russia will face a whole new set of issues regarding its relationships with those states. Already in February and March of 1992, Yeltsin faced the difficult issue of what role Russia should play with respect to the widening Armenian–Azerbaijani conflict over Nagorno–Karabakh; his decision to take a neutral stance was politically sound but did nothing to resolve a conflict likely to fester near Russia's borders for years to come. In Central Asia, interethnic conflict is now more muted, but the tension between Islamic fundamentalism and secular forces such as political modernization, industrialization, and the ris-

ing pan-Turkic movement will surely make for increasing turmoil over the next decade. The breakup of the Soviet Union will thus bring nearer to Moscow sources of instability that the former Soviet leadership had long sought to keep outside its territory. The announced intention of several former Central Asian republics to apply for membership in the Islamic Conference Organization portends the magnitude of this problem.[5]

Russia's greatest post-Soviet nightmare may be the possibility that former republics will eventually seek alliances or special relations with outside powers. One need only trace along the borders of the former Soviet Union on a map to see a large array of possible alliances with contiguous or nearby countries: Estonia and Latvia with the Scandinavian countries; Lithuania and Belarus with Poland; Moldova with Romania; Ukraine with Poland, Hungary, Czechoslovakia, or Romania; Azerbaijan with Iran; the Central Asian states with Turkey, the PRC, and of course the Islamic world.[6] Further afield, Ukraine is seeking to establish close ties with both Germany and the PRC, and it has signed a $7 billion oil and gas pipeline agreement with Iran.[7] All the former republics are discovering the potential of multilateralism in their foreign affairs.

Obviously the new Russian leadership would prefer that the former Soviet republics climb on the bandwagon with Russia rather than balance against it. For this reason, a priority objective of Russian policy will be to keep the Commonwealth as unified as possible, a tendency already seen in Yeltsin's efforts to have it retain a central army, single currency, coordinated foreign policy, and common economic space. The Commonwealth has already established a Council of Foreign Ministers, and Russia is likely to attempt to

7

ensure that it fields a foreign policy united to the maximum degree possible, even at the price of making concessions to the smaller states.[8] One Russian academic, Sergei Karaganov, has suggested that Russia must "provincialize itself," pursuing a less international agenda than, in the past: "Russia's external success will be 80 percent dependent not on relations with America or Europe—for all their importance—but on its ability to influence the policy of Ukraine, Belarus, Kazakhstan, and the other former republics of the USSR."[9] If Russia's influence wanes and the smaller Commonwealth states turn to outside powers for security, Moscow's own sense of insecurity will increase.

As the Commonwealth evolves, Russian nationalism will compel the Kremlin to regard itself as a guardian of the interests and security of Russians everywhere, including those residing beyond Russian borders proper. The Russian Federation has already announced that all Russians in the Commonwealth are automatically eligible for Russian citizenship, regardless of their residence. This was done partly to discourage the continuing large-scale migration of Russians from Central Asia and the Caucasus back to Russia, but also as a statement of long-term commitment to the new Russian diaspora created by the disintegration of the USSR. The presence of large Russian minorities in most of the former Soviet republics (and in Kazakhstan, a plurality) provides not only a potential source of contention between Moscow and the other Commonwealth states, but also a wedge of continuing Russian influence throughout the former Soviet sphere.

Shortly after the August coup, Yeltsin stated that Russia might seek border adjustments with the other Soviet republics to bring regions having a Russian majority into the Russian Republic. Although he later backed down and accepted the inviolability of existing borders, the incident highlighted the potential for nationalist disputes and border tensions among the Commonwealth states. The potential volatility of this problem manifested itself in a recent incident that received scant attention in the West: an armed uprising by the Russian-speaking population of the Dniester region of Moldova culminating in establishment of a pro-Moscow "Dniester Soviet Socialist Republic" shortly before the formation of the Commonwealth. There is abundant evidence that Soviet military officers supported the uprising, probably with tacit support from Moscow; Lieutenant General Gennadii Yakovlev, commander of the Fourteenth Army, even agreed to serve as chief of the Directorate for the Defense of the self-proclaimed Dniester government.[10] The Dniester conflict may be only a foretaste of one kind of unrest that will trouble the former Soviet Union over the next decade.

The Implications of the European Settlement. The Soviet Union's withdrawal from Eastern Europe, the reunification of Germany, and the end of the Cold War dramatically alter the context in which Russian foreign policy will operate in the future. Aside from ideological differences, the division of Europe has been the principal source of East–West tensions for the past 40 years. The end of that division has the potential for opening a transcontinental Era of Good Feelings in Europe, particularly if Russia's internal reformation continues. Russian foreign minister Kozyrev has argued that Russia today is surrounded not by hostile powers, but by "a civilized international community, that has learned to value human interests above all else and that is open to mutual association and cooperation."[11] Yeltsin, too, in his visit to the United Nations in January 1992 picked up Kozyrev's theme of the Western powers being Russia's "natural allies." Such statements would have been virtually blasphemous in the pre-Gorbachev period and go well beyond the pro-détente attitudes promulgated by the "new thinking" school of reformers after 1985. They represent a striking transformation in Russia's view of the outside world—what one Russian commentator has called "the new 'new thinking.'"[12]

The European settlement of 1989–1991, however, has also created new factors that may in the future complicate or forestall a Europe-wide Era of Good Feelings. The first is the possibility that an informal Russian–German axis may eventually be formed that would be regarded as threatening to other states in Europe. The second is the continuing political instability of Eastern Europe.

Ideally, the Russian relationship with Western Europe will advance at a similar pace for each country in the West. There is a significant possibility, however, that Russian–German cooperation will advance more quickly than Russia's relations with the rest of Western Europe. Russia and Germany (meaning largely Prussia prior to 1870) for more than two centuries have gone through cycles of conflict and alliance, and this pattern may continue in the future. There were numerous signs even prior to the Gorbachev era that Russia was rapidly shedding its postwar paranoia about German intentions; in the aftermath of reunification (for which German leaders give Russia substantial credit), Russian–German relations have become exceptionally warm. Yeltsin, accompanied by his foreign minister and a large delegation of top Russian officials, paid a three-day visit to Bonn in November 1991, and Helmut Kohl was the first Western leader officially invited to visit Russia after proclamation of the Commonwealth. Germany is the largest provider of financial assistance to Russia of any country in the world—and by a large margin. There is even a possibility that several years hence the Russian–German relationship could assume the form of a tacit alliance. Given the mounting apprehension in Europe over Germany's newfound assertiveness on the world scene, such an axis—even if its existence were informal and its intent benign—would doubtless be viewed with great alarm in the rest of the continent. No one wants a second Rapallo Treaty.

The problem of Eastern Europe is more imminent and in the short run at least, more serious. Soviet hegemony over the region enforced a *pax Sovietica* that no longer exists. Rising ethnic tensions trouble the region and may lead to future conflict. Economic recession may foster authoritarian or even neo-Fascist rule. The dissolution of the Council for Mutual Economic Assistance (COMECON) and the Warsaw Pact has left Eastern Europe with no effective framework for transregional economic or military cooperation, making it vulnerable to interstate squabbling or interference from outside powers. All these factors make Eastern Europe a potential arena for future East–West tensions. The general restraint shown by Russia and most of Western Europe toward the civil war in Yugoslavia suggests that local tensions can be contained, but there is no guarantee this restraint will always be exercised. Russia's interest lies in having a stable but weak Eastern Europe, one that will pose no threat to its security. It will seek to mediate or contain conflicts in the region, both so that they do not threaten its own territory and so that the former Warsaw Pact states have no incentive to rearm or to seek outside allies.

Another factor for change in Russia's relations with both Western and Eastern Europe is the fact that Russia's western frontier is now formally separated from its former Warsaw Pact allies by the newly independent states of Ukraine and Belarus and by the Baltic states. Politically speaking, this widens the *cordon sanitaire* between Russia and the West, but it also introduces new complexities and uncertain relationships into what was already a zone of political uncertainty.[13] The geographical distance between Moscow and Berlin has not changed, of course, and the Russian troops now deployed throughout this region are likely to remain there for years to come. Although the Russian Defense Ministry has finally agreed to begin withdrawing its troops from the Baltic states prior to 1994, Defense Minister Evgenii I. Shaposhnikov has stated his intent to negotiate permanent basing rights in those countries.[14] Moscow is also likely to seek permanent basing agreements in Ukraine and Belarus in order that it may retain some forces there indefinitely. Russian military power will thus remain an important factor in Central Europe for the foreseeable future.

Assuming that East European tensions remain localized and that a modicum of peace and cooperation prevails in Europe as a whole despite the potential complicating factors discussed above, then the locus of Russia's security concerns is likely to shift from its western to its southern and eastern borders, where numerous sources of instability, both old and new, are emerging. The Gorbachev revolution may lead to a more stable Europe but

a less stable Asia as the dissolution of the Soviet Union and growing perception of its weakness bring to the fore a host of agenda items previously relegated by their proponents to back-burner status: Islamic fundamentalism, Chinese border claims, Japanese claims on the Kuriles, and the myriad issues raised by the emerging independence of the former republics of Central Asia and the Transcaucasus. Benjamin Disraeli once said of Russia that it had two faces, "an Asiatic face which looks always toward Europe, and a European face which looks always toward Asia." The Europeanization of Russian foreign policy that began under Gorbachev may reverse this tendency, paradoxically leading Kremlin leaders to focus increasingly on South Asian and Far Eastern affairs.

Within less than three months of Yeltsin's assumption of power in December 1991, high-level Russian political or military delegations had visited the PRC, North Korea, Pakistan, Turkey, Iran, and Afghanistan; and Russia had hosted negotiations in Moscow with delegations from Japan and India, the latter set of which resulted in the signing of a political treaty with India replacing the 1971 Indo–Soviet Friendship Treaty.[15]

In the Far East, Russia's highest priority appears to be a postwar settlement with Japan, even if the price is yielding sovereignty over the Kurile Islands. Yeltsin has long shown flexibility on the issue: as early as January 1990, he proposed a five-stage plan that envisioned return of the islands to Japan by the year 2010, and in November 1991, he sent a special envoy to Tokyo who stressed Moscow's interest in settling the issue. The pace of Russo–Japanese relations has accelerated noticeably since December. Yeltsin has said publicly that he now wants a peace treaty no later than the year 2000, and there are numerous signs that this date could be moved up by several years. Russian and Japanese officials agreed that a new spirit of cooperation characterized the mid-February meeting in Moscow of a Russo–Japanese working group, the first such exchange since formation of the Commonwealth. Kozyrev's visit to Tokyo on March 20–22 will be followed by the Japanese foreign minister coming to Moscow in May and Boris Yeltsin visiting Tokyo in September. Japan's announcement of $100 million emergency food aid to Russia, and Russia's opening of four ports in the Kuriles to international freight and passenger traffic, are further signs of a warming relationship. Given their geographical proximity and complementary economic needs (Japan requires natural resources; Russia needs capital investment to develop Siberia), a Japanese–Russian détente is a logical step for both countries.[16]

During the Cold War, the United States maintained alliances with the former Axis powers both in order to contain the Soviet Union and to temper the historical tendencies of Germany and Japan toward expansion. With the Soviet Union dissolved and the former Axis powers now fully integrated into the world system, a partial reversal of the pattern may take place: Russia may seek close links with Germany and Japan in order to assist its own economic recovery in exchange for giving them international support in their increasingly troubled economic relations with the United States.

Sources of Continuity in Russian Foreign Policy

The forces favoring change in Russian foreign policy have captured headlines in the West during the past three years, and rightfully so. Realistically speaking, however, forces for change will be counterbalanced in some measure by deeply rooted traditions in Russian society and politics. Reform has never come easily in Russia. In 1969, an American observer of Russian affairs wrote the following:

> The more I look at the operation of the Soviet government, the more clearly I understand it is primarily the wording that has changed, and not the important qualities of style, attitudes, and the relationship of the governing to the governed. . . . For it was inevitable that Russia remain Russian. And the generations of Westerners who did not understand this, and who became passionate supporters or foes of the Revolution, were often grappling with illusory issues, far removed from the sober reality of daily Russian life.[17]

George Feifer's insight applies in some degree to the Second Russian Revolution as well. Despite the extraordinary changes of recent years, Russia remains Russia in important ways. The upheavals it has undergone have affected the structure of its political system but have not yet eliminated long-standing patterns of social behavior and societal interaction. Internal reforms may eventually change national character, as discussed earlier, but the process will take time. For this reason, it is important to take into account deeply rooted sources of continuity in any analysis of Russia's future behavior.

In the realm of politics, although communism has been abandoned, the remnants of its rule remain in place: the Russian parliament still consists largely of former Communist party officials; the judiciary is not yet independent; the major print and broadcast media, although no longer overtly censored, remain state property; channels for the redress of rights violations or the bringing of civil suits remain weak; an effective constitutional framework for protecting the rights of minorities does not exist; the duties and responsibilities of key government officials remain ill-defined, as do the limits on their power; and there are no effective institutional checks and balances to the exercise of arbitrary power (although in practice the current leadership has acted with restraint and shunned violence against its opponents). The result has been government by decree, with the ever-present possibility that a Yeltsin or his successor might slip gradually into the traditional role of a Russian boss.[18] Historical and bureaucratic inertia, in other words, will compete with the forces for change discussed above in the shaping of Russia's post-Soviet foreign policy.

Historical Sources of Continuity. Russian foreign policy from Peter the Great to the Bolshevik Revolution had certain historical characteristics that persisted with some modification in the Soviet era. In many instances, Marxist–Leninist ideology reinforced traditional Russian national behavior.[19] These national characteristics included (1) a chronic sense of geographical insecurity; (2) a corresponding commitment to high levels of military spending; (3) a compulsion to catch up with the West in military technology; (4) a persistent xenophobia paradoxically coupled with an almost obsessive need to be accepted by the West; and (5) a deep-rooted fear of and aversion to internal chaos, which partly accounts for the persistence of authoritarian rule in Russia. Liberalizing influences from the West, as well as changing internal

conditions, have already moderated some of these tendencies, as noted earlier. But over the short run at least, these historical characteristics will almost certainly continue to exert some influence on the evolution of Russian foreign policy:

(1) The Soviet Union's acquisition of a large nuclear arsenal did much to relieve its centuries-old sense of territorial insecurity. For this reason, Russia is almost certain to continue to place emphasis on maintaining a large strategic nuclear arsenal in the future. One evidence of this is that Soviet expenditures on strategic weaponry and nuclear modernization continued at a brisk pace during most of the Gorbachev years, even after conventional spending had begun to decline. More recently, strategic spending has also been reduced, but not so drastically as conventional spending. Gorbachev and Yeltsin had many differences, but they quickly found common ground on the need to maintain tight, central control of nuclear weapons, and the transition of control of those weapons between them took place judiciously. Even though other Commonwealth members have been promised advance consultation and effective veto power over the use of nuclear weapons, the actual technical means for using those weapons remain entirely in Russian hands.[20]

During the Cold War it was sometimes observed that the Soviet Union was a superpower in only one dimension, that of military power. Now that dimension has narrowed even further. Russia no longer has superpower ambitions, a European empire, or a capacity to sustain a global challenge to the status quo, but it does remain in a more narrow sense a *nuclear* superpower. A prominent figure in the Soviet nuclear establishment put it this way:

The nuclear world is . . . polarized and will remain so even after President Bush's latest initiative is implemented and President Gorbachev reciprocates, and even after the START Treaty takes effect. There will remain two nuclear superpowers whose superpower status will exist in the sphere of nuclear weapons alone. In all other respects the world is becoming monopolar. [21]

Although the overall level of Russian-controlled nuclear weapons will decline, the relative weight of nuclear weapons in Russian security strategy may actually increase. This suggests that U.S.–Russian arms-control negotiations may still play an important role (and the Russian Foreign Ministry has already established a large unit devoted to that issue). The West should recognize, however, that attempting to push the ceiling on strategic nuclear warheads too low (say below 1,000, as some analysts have argued) may actually feed Russia's traditional paranoia about territorial security and cause it to compensate through conventional strength.

(2) Security concerns, magnified by reduced borders and instability in the Caucasus and Central Asia, may motivate Russian leaders to maintain relatively high levels of defense spending—certainly not as high as in the Soviet period, but higher than any objective threat to Russian territory would justify. Whether or not this is feasible will depend of course partly on the success of the Russian economic recovery. Since December, Yeltsin has confirmed that the size of the former Soviet armed forces will be cut from 3.7 million to 3 million, and he has announced that Russia will form its own national army under Commonwealth auspices. But even if the eventual size of the Russian army

is cut by 50 percent, as intimated by Russian defense official Aleksandr Tsalko, it would still remain the largest single national army in Europe. This may be part of what Foreign Minister Kozyrev had in mind when he said in an interview, "it's too early to discard Russia as a great power."[22]

(3) Russia will continue to invest heavily in research and development and will seek the lifting of restrictions on technology sales imposed by the Coordinating Committee for Multilateral Export Controls (COCOM) as quickly as possible. Several Russian officials have already raised the latter issue in public statements. Moscow will also probably attempt to attain technical, and if feasible military, assistance from Germany and later Japan, as their relations improve. Again, the analogy of the Rapallo Treaty comes to mind.

(4) Desirous of joining the club of Western Europe, Russia will attend every international forum it can get invited to, seek actual or associate membership in every Western organization, and invite hosts of Western financial, technical, and scientific experts to assist with its internal problems. Yeltsin has even spoken of Russian membership in the North Atlantic Treaty Organization (NATO). But even as it draws nearer to Western Europe, Russia may act the part of an outsider, insisting on finding a third way, some economic path combining the best of both capitalism and socialism. In a pattern having antecedents in Peter the Great's borrowing from his archrival Charles XII, it may again find the Swedish political model of particular attraction.[23]

(5) Edward Keenan has suggested that Russian political culture is in essence a "conspiracy against chaos."[24] Fear of mounting public chaos fostered a tacit alliance between Gor-

13

bachev and Yeltsin in April 1991, despite their differences. Concern over rising social disorder (organized crime, public protests, disruption in factories, political uncertainty, ethnic turmoil) may lead Russian leaders across a broad spectrum to unite on the need for authoritarian solutions to domestic problems. Gorbachev shortly before his departure mused on the possible need for authoritarian government to shepherd Russia's transition to democracy. Many democratic-minded Russian activists are fearful of Yeltsin's sometimes manifested authoritarian streak (e.g., his tendency to rule by decree, his lack of respect for political opponents, and his ordering of the arrest of a man who stated publicly that the statue of Felix Dzerzhinsky should not be torn down). If authoritarian solutions of domestic problems do prevail, it is at least doubtful they will foster moderate behavior abroad.[25]

Institutional and Bureaucratic Sources of Continuity. Hannah Arendt once observed, "the most radical revolutionary will become a conservative on the day after the revolution."[26] One reason for this is the co-optation of political revolutionaries by the permanent bureaucracy and military establishment. Powerful entrenched interests—the military, the KGB, the government bureaucracy—remain intact in Yeltsin's Russia, despite reorganizations and decentralization. The central bureaucracy has been split up among the former republics, but within Russia its various components continue to operate largely with the same staffs as were in place previously. In fact, state institutions that were once subordinate to CPSU oversight are now more independent and may seek to flex newfound muscles. At a minimum they will act as interest groups seeking to limit or at least channel change in di-

rections favorable to their interests. Whereas the suspension of the Communist party represents an institutional source of change in Russian foreign policy, the strengthening of state institutions provides a source of continuity. The Russian Ministry of Foreign Affairs will inherit most of the personnel and assets of the Soviet foreign ministry, with the result that many of the same diplomats will represent Russian interests abroad who once represented Soviet interests. (It appears that even non-Russian employees of the ministry who are resident in the Russian Federation will be given the opportunity to remain on staff.)[27]

The General Staff of the armed forces will also form an important axis of continuity in foreign and security policy. During the past year, it lobbied hard against a breakup of the Soviet Union, and when that failed, against the breakup of the central army. Although these were rearguard actions, they reflect the inherent conservatism of the General Staff and senior officer corps. Younger officers may be more flexible (and officers such as Shaposhnikov owe their high positions to reform-minded politicians) but they will continue to act as a voice for certain traditional military interests, among them high military spending, heavy reliance on strategic nuclear forces, and emphasis on the so-called new technologies.

Technological and Economic Sources of Continuity. In 1990, the United States acquired over 100,000 international patents, while Western Europe and Japan were not far behind. Russia, by contrast, acquired only 500 or so patents. The crude reality is that Russian products and technology outside of the military sphere are only rarely competitive to Western standards. As Russia seeks to open its economy to the West and to earn hard currency through trade, it will find therefore that what it can most profitably offer the world are natural resources (e.g., petroleum, natural gas, diamonds) and weaponry. Exports of both are almost certain to remain high over the next decade.

Mercenary motives aside, there are other reasons to think that Russia will remain a major world arms supplier. Defense conversion—the conversion of the Russian capital plant from military to consumer ends—has proven enormously difficult, and despite much rhetoric, news coverage, and bureaucratic smoke, the amount of actual conversion that has taken place is small. Machinery designed to produce weaponry cannot easily be converted to other ends without massive investments; Ivan Materov, the minister responsible for defense conversion, has put the cost at $48 billion. Such massive investments will not be feasible until other fundamental economic changes occur. In the meantime, workers must be employed, and arms manufacturing will continue, if at a reduced level compared to the past. Second, a reduction in the size of Russia's army, as well as its adherence to conventional arms treaties, will result in large stocks of surplus weaponry, much of which will be obsolete by European standards but perfectly suitable for third world combat. The temptation to sell this weaponry to obtain badly needed hard currency will be very great.[28]

Because the third world countries with hard currency to spend are largely in the Middle East and Persian Gulf area, Moscow is likely to remain an arms supplier to this region for years to come. The reported arms deal between Iran and the Russian Federation in January 1992 is the first con-

crete evidence of this since the formation of the Commonwealth.[29] Oddly enough, this means that Russia will be competing with the oil-rich states for a share of the world petroleum market even while supplying them with arms in exchange for the hard currency they earn from oil sales. It also means that the Persian Gulf, true to Vyacheslav Molotov's famous dictum, will remain a continuing focus of Russian interests—less perhaps for strategic than for economic reasons.[30] By the same token, the Middle East is likely to remain one region of the Third World where U.S. and Russian interests will continue to intersect to a substantial degree. The visit of Russian vice president Aleksandr Rutskoi to Iran, Pakistan, and Afghanistan in late December 1991, immediately after formation of the Commonwealth, is one indicator of continuing Russian interest in the region.[31]

Conclusion

There is obvious tension between the political and social forces fostering change in Russian behavior and those that favor continuity. The manner in which that tension will be resolved is of great importance to the United States and its allies. Although it is difficult to know with any precision to what extent and in what instances continuity will prevail over change, the key variable will almost certainly be Russia's internal evolution. To the extent that political-economic reform continues and progress is made toward liberal democracy, positive change will occur. To the degree that there is internal reaction, forces of historical continuity will prevail instead. International influences will be distinctly secondary to what takes place internally, and Western statesmen would be well advised to keep in mind that

15

their capacity to affect change in Russia is limited. Russia must choose its own course and must feel that it is doing so.

Nevertheless, just as we have not reached the end of history, nor have we reached the end of statecraft. Richard Nixon's warning of March 1992 is well taken: it would be a tragedy if Western inaction tipped the delicate balance within Russia in the favor of reaction. Just as West Germany's extensive economic and political links with its allies in NATO and the European Community helped turn a once militaristic state into a model democracy, a web of cooperative economic and political links with the West may bring about a permanent change in the nature of the Russian state. This at least should be the conceptual thrust of Western strategy. The dire state of Russia's consumer economy poses the greatest threat to further reform by fueling popular discontent and encouraging demagoguery. Western assistance may forestall that threat until Russia can recover, but the nature of that assistance will be critical. Mere handouts not linked to continuing reform may create only a resentment-breeding dependence. Government to government assistance should be linked to continuing political and market reform and supplemented with assistance to private enterprises and institutions. The same linkage to reform should be applied to Russian admission to the various institutions that represent the "club" of the West. At every point, subtly but firmly, the West should link its own concessions to Russian internal reform.

Because of the risk that Russian relations with either Germany or Japan may develop at a much quicker pace than with the United States or other West European countries, it is important that the industrial powers conduct a unified and coordinated policy of increasing cooperation. The rapprochement with Russia should be broad as well as deep. An effective Western policy toward Russia will also require measures aimed at promoting stability on Russian borders. This means that assistance programs should not be aimed only at Russia proper but at other crucial Commonwealth states as well, such as those of Central Asia and the Caucasus. Some kind of coordinated program of assistance to the troubled polities of Eastern Europe is also imperative. Western obsession with the drama unfolding in the former Soviet Union has unfortunately led to relative neglect of this region's plight. Targeted Western assistance here may prove as important as aid to Russia in ensuring the long-term stability of Central Europe.

Alfred Lord Tennyson remarked to his son in 1888,

> Nihilism in Russia will never be laid at rest until an Emperor comes, bold enough to trust the people and chance the hatred of the nobles. . . . The Russians do not ask for much. Their men of thought, who are their men of action in domestic politics, ask for a graduated scale of liberty. Their moderation must have struck you.[32]

A century later, a Russian leader arose who was bold enough to trust the people and chance the hatred of the *nomenklatura*. The Gorbachev revolution brought leaders of thought and moderation once again to the fore in Russia, among them Boris Yeltsin who now heads the Russian Federation. The new Russian leadership has introduced a "graduated scale of liberty" at home, while changing long-standing patterns of behavior abroad. Its task, as well as that of the West, is to see that the positive forces for change now at work prevail over still deep-rooted historical forces of continuity. No one should underestimate the magnitude of that task, nor its paramount importance in world affairs today.

The views expressed in this article are the author's and do not necessarily reflect those of any institution with which he is affiliated.

Notes

1. Bohlen, "I do not think we can look forward to a tranquil world so long as the Soviet Union operates in its present form. The only hope, and this is a fairly thin one, is that at some point the Soviet Union will begin to act like a country instead of a cause." *Witness to History* (New York: W. W. Norton, 1973), p. 542.

2. Andrei Kozyrev, "Preobrazhennaia rossia v novom mire" (A transformed Russia in the new world), *Izvestia*, January 2, 1992.

3. Cited by Erik de Mauny, *Russian Prospect: Notes of a Moscow Correspondent* (London: Macmillan, 1969), p. 271.

4. In *The Rise of the Gulag: The Intellectual Origins of Leninism* (New York: Continuum, 1981), Alain Besançon discusses the significance for Russia of its failure to develop a strong civil society that could counterbalance the power of the state. See especially pp. 94–112.

5. TASS International Service in Russian, December 9–11, 1991. In mid-February 1992, Azerbaijan, Turkmenistan, Uzbekistan, Tajikistan, and Kyrgyzstan also joined the Economic Cooperation Organization (ECO), originally consisting only of Iran, Turkey, and Pakistan. The ECO plans to work toward creation of a common market of Muslim states. *Radio Free Europe/Radio Liberty Research Report* (hereafter *RFE/RL Research Report*), February 28, 1992.

6. For an early Russian assessment of the role the former republics will play in Europe, including the possibility of their forming alliances outside the Commonwealth, see Andrei Lipsky, "Joining the Battle for a Place in Europe's Sun," *Moscow News*, December 29, 1991–January 5, 1992. The Ukrainian–Polish link is developing rap-

idly. In late December 1991, a special envoy of Ukrainian president Leonid Kravchuk in Poland emphasized that Poland was Ukraine's window on the West: "For Ukraine, Poland is the most important political partner in the West." *Glasnost*, December 19–25, 1991.

7. *Izvestia*, February 4, 1992; Radio Kiev, February 4, 1992, cited in *RFE/RL Research Report*, February 14, 1992.

8. The Russian military clearly favors a closely unified commonwealth. See the commentaries by Aleksandr Holz and A. Klimenko in *Krasnaia zvezda*, December 26 and 28, 1991; the interview with General Evgenii I. Shaposhnikov in *Krasnaia zvezda*, February 22, 1992; and the poll of military officers in *Krasnaia zvezda*, February 14, 1992.

9. *Moskovskie novosti*, January 5, 1992.

10. *Report on the USSR*, December 13, 1991, pp. 35–36, and December 20, 1991, pp. 25–26.

11. Kozyrev, *Izvestia*, January 2, 1992.

12. Sergei Karaganov, *Moskovskie novosti*, January 5, 1991.

13. See Karl Feldmeyer's commentary in *Frankfurter Allgemeine Zeitung*, December 27, 1991.

14. Cited in *Baltic Independent* (Tallinn), December 20–26, 1991.

15. Delhi All India Radio Network, January 15, 1992 (FBIS); *Izvestia*, February 6 and 13, March 4, 1992; Moscow TASS and Radio Moscow, March 3, 1992 (FBIS); *Krasnaia zvezda*, March 3, 1992; TASS, December 20–23, 1991.

16. *Report on the USSR*, November 29, 1991; *Report on the USSR*, January 26, 1990, citing *Tokyo Kyodo* of January 16, 1990; *RFE/RL Research Report*, February 7 and 21, 1992; Interfax, March 2, 1992 (FBIS); Moscow TASS, February 4 and 14, 1992 (FBIS); *Tokyo Kyodo* in English, February 10 and 11, 1992 (FBIS); *Pravda*, February 12, 1992; *Izvestia*, February 13, 1992.

17. An Observer (George Feifer), *Message from Moscow* (New York: Alfred A. Knopf, 1969), p. 247.

18. In this regard, a statement by Sergei Stankevich, one of Yeltsin's advisers, may be prescient: "At all times, in all countries,

intensive reform efforts . . . were implemented only by leaders who were somewhat authoritarian." *Washington Post*, October 7, 1991.

19. In *A Study of Bolshevism* (Glencoe, Il.: Free Press, 1953), Nathan Leites analyzes the relationship between the strategic culture of the Bolsheviks and Russia's historical behavior.

20. At Minsk on December 30, 1991, the Commonwealth leaders agreed that the decision to use nuclear weapons would be made by the president of Russia "in agreement" with leaders of the three states— Belarus, Ukraine, and Kazakhstan—where nuclear weapons are now based. *Izvestia*, December 31, 1991. President Leonid Kravchuk of Ukraine claimed he would have technical means to prevent anyone from using the weapons on Ukrainian soil, although it was not clear what this meant. TASS, December 31, 1991, cited in *Radio Free Europe/Radio Liberty Daily Report*, January 2, 1991.

21. Vitali Goldansky, "Blessings in Disguise," *Vestnik*, December 1991, p. 18. Goldansky is director of the Institute of Chemical Physics of the Russian Academy of Sciences. *Vestnik* is a new journal published by the Foreign Policy Association headed by former Soviet foreign minister Eduard Shevardnadze.

22. Interview in *New Times*, no. 3 (January 1992), p. 21. According to Kozyrev, Russia is "destined to be a great power" despite its poverty and "whether within a Union or without it; within the Commonwealth or not." His sentiment captures the difficulty Russian intellectual and political leaders are having adjusting to Russia's decline in power. See Vera Tolz and Elizabeth Teague, "Russian Intellectuals Adjust to Loss of Empire," *RFE/RL Research Report*, February 21, 1992, pp. 4–8.

23. There were echoes of this in the state visit of Gennadii Burbulis, first deputy vice premier of the Russian Federation, to Stockholm in January 1992. Moscow TASS International Service, January 21, 1992 (FBIS).

24. Edward Keenan, "Muscovite Political Folkways," *Russian Review* 45 (April 1986), p. 145. The entire essay, pp. 115–181, develops this concept.

25. An excellent summary of Russian domestic criticism of Yeltsin and other self-styled "democratic" leaders is Julia Wishnevsky, "Russia: Liberal Media Criticize Democrats in Power," *RFE/RL Research Report*, January 10, 1992, pp. 6–11. See also Vera Tolz and Elizabeth Teague, "Is Russia Likely to Turn to Authoritarian Rule?" *RFE/RL Research Report*, January 24, 1992, pp. 1–8.

26. Hannah Arendt, "Reflections (Civil Disobedience)," *New Yorker*, September 12, 1970, p. 88.

27. Reported in the author's conversations with officials of the Russian Ministry of Foreign Affairs, Moscow, January 1992.

28. Boris Yeltsin, in an *Izvestia* interview of February 22, 1992, stated that the Russian Federation would continue to promote arms exports, partly in order to maintain employment levels in the armaments industry. Nikolai Paklin in *Izvestia*, January 16, 1992, also editorialized on the importance of Moscow remaining a reliable arms supplier to its former clients. (Materov's estimate of needed investments was reported by *Reuter*, January 30, 1992, cited in *RFE/RL Research Report*, February 14, 1992.)

29. Jack Nelson, "Arms Buildup Making Iran Top Gulf Power," *Los Angeles Times*, January 7, 1992.

30. On November 25, 1940, Molotov demanded of the German ambassador to the USSR that "the general direction of the Persian Gulf [be] recognized as the focal point of the aspirations of the Soviet Union." Jane Degras, ed., *Soviet Documents on Foreign Policy*, vol. 3 (London: Oxford University Press, 1953), p. 478.

31. TASS, December 20–23, 1991.

32. *Alfred Lord Tennyson: A Memoir by His Son*, vol. 2 (London: Macmillan, 1897), p. 349.

China's Fourth Revolution

Gerrit W. Gong

LIKE THE FAMOUS composite picture of the hag and the young woman (see figure 1), the People's Republic of China (PRC) can appear strikingly different if viewed from the inside out or from the outside in. Views from the outside often focus on China's aggregate superpower potential. This potential is the grist of International Monetary Fund and World Bank analyses based on purchasing power parity equivalents that rank China's economy third in the world—and the world's largest by 2010 if current growth continues. It underlies sobering scenarios in which China converts sustained economic dynamism into assertive definitions of national sovereign interest, defended and advanced by burgeoning power projection capabilities.

In contrast, views from the inside usually focus on China's myriad domestic dilemmas. For example, the 442.5 million metric ton grain harvest of 1992 was China's second largest in history; yet, because of excessive

A Rhodes scholar with master's and Ph.D. degrees in international relations from Oxford University, Gerrit W. Gong's State Department assignments included serving as special assistant to Ambassadors Winston Lord and James R. Lilley at the U.S. Embassy in Beijing from June 1987 to July 1989. He is currently director of the Asian Studies Program at CSIS.

Figure 1

Used with the permission of the University of Illinois Press from E. G. Boring, *American Journal of Psychology*, 42, 1930, 444–445. Copyright by Board of Trustees of the University of Illinois.

taxes, fees, and paper IOUs, peasant uprisings recently broke out in 11 provinces. Cash-starved members of Beijing University's political science department pursue lingerie production to supplement their own meager incomes; some 16 percent of China's population remain functionally illiterate, 75 percent of them women, largely from rural areas. To take a third example, because of the concentration of homes burning soft coal for cooking and heating, sulphur dioxide (SO_2)

pollution in some Chinese residential areas is worse than in neighboring industrial areas; according to World Health Organization statistics, Beijing exceeds the organization's sulphur dioxide standards 68 days a year, Shenyang 146 days a year.

These are the everyday realities that have belied for years long-term prognostications that China will fully realize its potential. Interlocking difficulties, they are rooted in the challenges inherent in bringing 1,152,428,417 individuals arrayed within 300,388,130 households in 22 provinces, 5 autonomous regions, and 3 special municipalities (each situation different) from the nineteenth century of agriculture into the twentieth and twenty-first centuries of industry and information.

But something new is now apparent. Whether one looks from the outside in or the inside out, a fourth revolution is engulfing China.

The domestic directions this fourth revolution takes will determine whether or not China becomes a regional and global engine of economic growth, a highly competitive producer able with skill and vitality to translate abundant human and natural resources into a stable, leading economy with compounded high rates of annual gross national product (GNP) growth and buoyant domestic demand.

The international directions this fourth revolution takes will also have regional and global ramifications; they will shape the structure of East Asia, as well as the pattern of relations among East Asia, North America, and Europe.

China's Fourth Revolution

This fourth revolution is not the result of dramatic social upheaval, sudden replacement of political system or

leadership, or abrupt change of ideology or approach. In contrast to earlier periods of revolutionary fervor, this fourth period of transformation is marked, not by revolutionary rhetoric and methods, but by gradualist and incremental policy changes. China's Communist party is being pulled into a future it cannot control; the locus of initiative and dynamism in economic and political decisions is shifting to provinces, townships, and individuals determined to chart their own destinies.

This is systemic change brought about by China's increasing conformity, not to the self-proclaimed standards of the Middle Kingdom, but to the patterns of information flow, political and economic decision making, resource allocation, and distribution of authority judged necessary to compete in the modern world. It is characterized by:

- the increasing market orientation of China's significant economic potential, in ownership, production, investment, and demand;
- the decentralization of decision-making structures and processes;
- a shift of legitimacy from ideology to rising standards of living and nationalism;
- the reorientation of some deep-rooted Chinese perceptions and patterns of social organization; and,
- most fundamentally, the unprecedented opening of the world and China to each other, and of China to itself.

These themes are worth briefly elaborating.

Market Orientation. Economically, China's fourth revolution is symbolized by China's increasing market orientation, the spreading as it were of

NON-STATE SECTOR
1978 22% 1992 = 52% of GROSS INDUST. OUTPUT.

China's Fourth Revolution

the capitalist revolution to a fifth of the earth's population. The government's role in the economy is shifting from central administrator toward market regulator; the public sector is shrinking. In 1978, 78 percent of China's industrial output was attributed to state-owned enterprises; by 1992, the non-state sector accounted for 52 percent of gross industrial output and more than 57 percent of non-agricultural employment. Government expenditure as a share of GNP has dropped from 41 percent in 1978 to 20 percent in 1992. In 1980, 80 percent of Guangdong's budget came from Beijing; in 1992, only 2 percent did.

Overall growth reached 12.8 percent in GNP in 1992 and continued at an annual rate of 13.9 percent in the first half of 1993. Trade has burgeoned with investment, as figure 2 illustrates. For example:

- From 1979 to 1982, China's direct foreign investment totaled $1.17 billion; in 1992 alone, it reached $11.2 billion.[1]
- In 1979, China had signed 36 contracts with two countries, valued at $51 million; by 1991, the number had grown to 8,438 contracts worth over $36 billion with 147 countries or regions. In 1992, signed contracts for 48,746 new projects pledged $57.5 billion in investment.
- Between 1978 and 1992, China's total trade volume rose over eightfold, from $20.66 billion to $165.6 billion, ranking China's trade volume eleventh in the world.

Throughout China, secondary and tertiary industries producing higher-value-added, finished goods and services are multiplying.

Disposable income has risen substantially for many and continues to outpace inflation, particularly in prosperous pockets in China's South and along its coasts. Although concentrated in Zhejiang, Guangdong, and Shandong provinces and in Shanghai municipality, 438 towns and townships across China now each boast 10 million yuan annual revenues ($1.75 million). Chinese local-currency Visa cardholders quadrupled last year, from 481,600 to 1.9 million; the value of their purchases more than quadrupled, from $2.15 billion to $9.3 billion.

New roads, rail lines, telecommunications systems, and other soft and hard infrastructure are proposed not only for the coasts and special economic zones, but increasingly to reach into what has heretofore been China's hinterland. These new infrastructural developments seek to link and unleash the productivity of strategic centers along the coast such as Beijing–Tianjin, Hong Kong–Guangzhou, and Shanghai, with Wuhan and Chengdu in the interior. Better access to interior areas such as Sichuan province, of which Chengdu is the capital, may link the capacities of Sichuan's 110,000,000 people with the outside world, as Guangdong's 65,000,000 population is already.

Decentralization and the Shifting Basis of Legitimacy. Depending on whether one emphasizes elements of continuity or change, China's fourth revolution is also its fourth period of structural modernization.

Sun Yat-sen's 1911 revolution was China's first structural modernization following the Opium Wars, which established sustained contact between China and the West. The 1911 revolution ended Qing rule and China's dynastic system. It made China into a constitutional republic.

In 1949, Mao Zedong's revolution transformed China into a people's republic.

In 1978, Deng Xiaoping's de facto

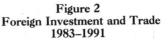

Figure 2
Foreign Investment and Trade
1983–1991

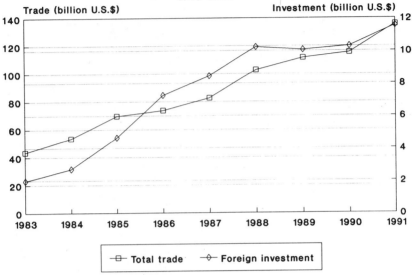

Source: China Statistical Yearbook 1992 (Beijing: State Statistical Bureau of the PRC, 1992), pp. 575, 588.

Note: Trade and investment are shown with different scales. Trade should be read against the left-hand scale, investment against the right-hand scale.

revolution was dedicated to making the People's Republic of China modern and strong by establishing socialism with Chinese characteristics.

Following the landmark Third Plenum in 1978, Deng established a new social contract. It premised the continued legitimacy of Communist party rule on reversing Cultural Revolution excesses and injustices, restoring order, reestablishing China's international prestige, and jump-starting productivity and thereby improving everyday standards of living, first in the countryside, then in the cities.

Deng's approach represented a farsighted, far-reaching strategy of reform from inside the party, within a socialist framework. It built less on revolutionary socialist idealism and

more on pocketbook issues and realpolitik.

Today's fourth revolution is now superseding even Deng's de facto transformation of China's system and orientation. This is a fourth revolution for China in part because it is not guided, structured, or conducted from the top. China is tired of revolution; its party is discredited, its Long March generation is fading, its system is bureaucratically feudalized. A popular Chinese expression quips, "Those above propose a policy; those below implement their own" (*shang you zhengce; xia you duice*).

Changes this sweeping cannot easily be said to begin at a specific point in time. Yet, especially to observers on the scene, the period from May 4 to

May 20, 1989, marks a new stage in the openness and interaction of China to and with itself, and to and with the outside world. This period coincides with the anniversary of the 1919 May 4th movement, the meeting in Beijing of the Asian Development Bank, the visit of Mikhail Gorbachev, and the declaration of martial law. It precedes the tragedy at Tiananmen, which history will record as a denouement, albeit a violent one.

May 1989 signals the real turning point. It represents a transition from the period of Deng's 1978 revolution, which still considered practical and legitimate the massive use of force to constrain economic and political change solely within an orthodox socialist system.[2]

During May 1989, in a dramatic way that endures for China and the world, internal Chinese political, economic, and social developments were self-consciously played on an international stage. And the reactions of a global audience were in some cases, correctly or not, taken as cues. This period was both culmination and cause of a new period of change. It brought together and highlighted the continuing juxtaposition of China's ongoing transformations in the countryside (where 75 percent or 900,000,000 of China's population officially reside), in industry (which experienced nearly 22 percent growth last year), and in information (which will require special adjustments for a nominally socialist country ruled by a single, dominant Communist party). It signaled the emergence of China's fourth revolution.

Social Reorganization. This fourth period of modernizing transformation includes changes that go to the core of China's psyche and its historical patterns of behavior. Always circumspect, as Sun Tzu's *Art of War* teaches, China has traditionally been a closed society, only loosely horizontally organized, with a penchant for camouflaging weaknesses and for deploying negotiating strategies built on its geopolitical position and past.

Regional satellite broadcasts of STAR TV and a group of literary journalists willing to pursue corruption in Beijing and accounts of cannibalism in Guangxi during the Cultural Revolution now illustrate a basic shift in China's information structure as China deals more forthrightly with the outside and, even more significantly, with itself.

An estimated 100,000,000 people have left China's countryside for its cities; hundreds of millions more are being encouraged to leave the land without leaving their homes (*litu, bulixiang*). They remain part of the countryside in name only, employed in light manufacturing and other rural enterprises linked to nearby cities, to more distant markets, and to the economies of the outside world.

Interaction with the World Outside. Finally, at the heart of this fourth period of transformation, and with a pace, scope, and reach unprecedented in its long history, is this change: China, increasingly including its interior, is becoming part of, and more like, the external modern world, which is itself in a continuous process of modernization.

This change includes but transcends cross-border and domestic flows of information by open conversation (progressively more mobile and well informed), telephone, television, satellite broadcast, fax, radio, and readily available printed materials. It reflects the information age reality that, in China as elsewhere, ideology is being superseded by the everyday convergence of the factors necessary

23

to be competitive in the political, economic, and social arenas.

This current transformation is the consequence of increasing portions of China's extensive interior interacting with global forces larger than even China. Competing on the world's economic terms is now drawing the productive capacities, and perhaps some of the minds and hearts, of growing numbers of China's citizens into a two-way flow of information and influence with the modern world.

This process now permeates China's coasts, cities, and their neighboring areas. It is increasingly penetrating China's interior villages and towns. This interaction of inside and outside is now two-way and irreversible. It recognizes the link between China's domestic social and political stability and its dependence on international trade to maintain current standards of living: in 1992, trade accounted for 37 percent of China's GNP, up from only 10 percent in 1978.

Two tempering caveats:

First, much of China's political, economic, and social continuity remains, even in the geographic areas of greatest change. Whatever their weaknesses, central leaders and institutions retain formidable abilities to determine personnel placement and advancement, to tax, and to favor or retard development.

The state sector remains substantial. It is heavily invested in over 10,000 state enterprises, employing 75 percent of China's urban labor force (some 108 million workers) but accounting for only 50 percent of the country's industrial production—an indicator of pervasive underemployment. In 1992, only one-third of China's state-owned companies were profitable; one-third were insolvent; and another third were suspected of large hidden losses. The 11 percent

($7.82 billion) of 1992 governmental expenditures that official subsidies absorbed understate their true costs, which include soft loans state banks have no prospects of recovering.

Whatever the interest in rising standards of living, substantial popular skepticism remains. Many feel their society is changing too quickly in a destabilizing way. For all those eager to interact with the outside, many others remain unaware, uninterested, or hostile to such possibilities.

Second, because there is (increasingly) no single "China," to speak of China's opening is to generalize about different openings of different parts of China to different parts of the outside world.[3] Coastal China is opening to the global economy, especially to Hong Kong, Taiwan, and Japan, as well as to China's interior; Xinjiang and the Northwest are opening to pan-Central Asian influences; Yunnan and the Southwest are opening to Southeast Asia, including Thailand and Myanmar.

Regardless of province or outside contact, the general trend is significant: few areas of China remain entirely isolated; almost all (including interior provinces establishing representative offices in Hong Kong and the special economic zones) are seeking ways to establish windows and doors to the larger outside, even if that world is initially only a neighboring province with more current ties or connections.

The Tasks Ahead for China

From the inside out, China must decide how to foster a globally competitive, market-oriented economy while retaining central control and governability. From the outside in, the world must consider how to deal with a diverse, independent China partly, but

*PROMPTED RESURGENCE
OF INVESTMENT WHICH HAD [?]
AFTER 1989.*

not fully, integrated into the international system.

Both from the inside out and the outside in, China must negotiate five crucial crossroads:

- promote a "socialist market economy" as a means of seeking stable and balanced economic growth;
- deal with Hong Kong, Taiwan, and the overseas Chinese communities;
- manage the post–Deng Xiaoping, watershed generational leadership succession;
- maintain legitimacy and governability in a political system dominated by a single Communist party;
- define a post–Persian Gulf War, post–cold war international role and identity appropriate for a regional power with global influence.

1. Promoting a "Socialist Market Economy." With his country sandwiched historically and geographically between the former Soviet Union and Eastern Europe on the one side, and Japan, South Korea, Taiwan, and the other dynamic East Asian economies on the other, no one understands the dilemmas of simultaneously maintaining political stability and promoting economic growth more acutely than Deng Xiaoping.

In theory, Deng once cited "practice as the sole criterion of truth." China was characterized as entering only "an initial stage of socialism." Today's theoretical task is to define the workings of a "socialist market economy."

In practice, Deng sought to let pragmatic experience establish a balance between the economic dynamism of the four modernizations and the political orthodoxy of the four cardinal principles. This is the dialectic of a large, complex, modernizing country: balancing growth with stability, order with dynamism, change with con-

stancy. Deng tipped the balance once more toward economic momentum by his visit to the South during the 1992 spring festival.

Perhaps it was as he took the endless walks around his garden when he was in exile during the Cultural Revolution and during the subsequent years of implementing his policies that Deng reached three conclusions of strategic importance for directing China's development:

- China must export in order to import the hard-currency-intensive, high technology necessary to modernize;
- a beleaguered Communist party can maintain at least some legitimacy by improving everyday standards of living and appealing to nationalism; therefore,
- China's domestic political stability is now linked to its ability to compete in an always-changing external world.

But there were two blind spots Deng and associates perhaps could neither anticipate nor avoid.

First, he underestimated how much economic improvement would stimulate jealous comparisons of increasing income differential and criticism instead of loyalty to the party. Some criticism reflected the reality that the economic playing field was not level; those with official ties had, made, and took opportunities to get rich first. Also, after essential stability in prices from 1949 to 1983, Deng's price reforms brought inflation. As the popular complaint at the time put it, "Under Mao, a dollar was worth a dollar; under Deng, a dollar is worth a dime."

Second, Deng could not have foreseen that allowing thousands of ordinary Chinese citizens to tie themselves by their own choice to the two-way flow of the world's goods and

25

services would inescapably link them to the world's modes of competitive production and introduce them to the world's ideas and ideals as well. This tying of China to the modern world establishes expectations and procedures with which Communist doctrine and the governing structure are seemingly finding it difficult to keep pace.

Herein lie China's dilemmas. In recent months, China's leaders have grappled with two contradictory economic imperatives. One is slowing an overheated economy. The other is seizing perceived historical opportunities for accelerated development. Such are the dilemmas inherent in implementing a "socialist market economy."

As figure 3 illustrates, in 1980, 1984, and 1988, as is common for developing economies, China moved through three cycles of high growth and high inflation (as indicated by inflated prices and excessive money supply). Under the direction of Vice Premier and Central Bank Governor Zhu Rongji, Beijing is trying to soften the landing and avoid a fourth retrenchment by tightening credit, controlling the money supply, and trying to bring the provinces into line.

Yet, something of the spirit of the Great Leap Forward lives, apparently, for Deng and other senior leaders impatient to make up missed historical opportunities and determined to build an economic momentum that will outlive them. Thus, the argument that the costs of missing economic oppor-

Figure 3
China's Economic Cycles
1978–1992

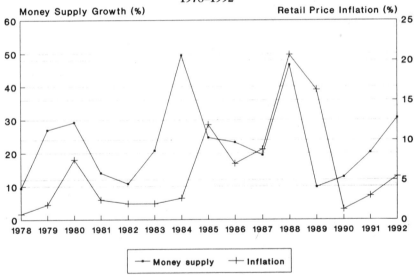

Source: China Statistical Yearbook 1992 (Beijing: State Statistical Yearbook of the PRC, 1992), p. 205; *IMF International Financial Statistics* (Washington, D.C., 1989, 1992, July 1993).

Note: Money supply growth and retail price inflation are shown with different scales. Money supply growth should be read against the left-hand scale, retail price inflation against the right-hand scale.

tunity were greater than the costs of an overheated economy contributed to growth-oriented amendments to China's constitution on March 29, 1993, and inspired the upward adjustment of the national target for average annual economic growth from 6 percent to 8 to 9 percent in the Eighth Five-Year Plan (1991–1995).

The difficulties are many. China's theoretical debate continues. From "economic laws" to "initial stage of socialism" to today's "socialist market economy," the doctrinal and practical arguments continue regarding ownership and means of production, whether in the context of stock markets or agricultural systems.

Structural economic reform can rationalize prices but is inevitably accompanied by increased income differential, "short-term behavior," and the "red-eye disease of jealousy."

Economic growth does not come without a price for a socialist system with a massive population living in a wide diversity of settings. Twenty percent of the earth's population now lives on 7 percent of the planet's territory; and, although China is now the world's second largest country, only 14 percent of its land is arable.

Significant regional disparities highlight differential growth between interior and coasts. For example, Guangdong, fueled by external capital and trade, enjoyed over 22 percent growth last year. Per capita income in rural, coastal Zhejiang was 1,015 yuan in 1991, almost 50 percent again the national rural average of 701 yuan, and almost three times that of a poor hinterland province such as Yunnan (329 yuan). In 1990, 119 of China's counties reported a per capita income of less than $43; one-fifth of China's peasants are without electricity; one-tenth are not served by public roads.

Particularly in the coastal areas, important blurring of rural and urban is now occurring. For example, of the 75 percent of collective industrial enterprises located in urban areas, one-half are owned by villages and rural townships. Since 1984, 273 new cities and 9,000 new towns have been established, largely based on a change of name for areas benefiting from expanded production capacities. Guangdong symbolizes this shift in the structure of employment; only 60 percent of its rural population are still engaged in agriculture, down from 90 percent in 1978.

The Chinese know speed of development is not merely a target or percentage; for this reason, China seeks the following economic priorities over the next five years:

- to reach its strategic target of doubling 1980 GNP;
- to see the return of sovereignty over Hong Kong;
- to enter the General Agreement on Tariffs and Trade (GATT);
- to draft more legislation to facilitate development of a socialist market economy.

2. Dealing with Hong Kong, Taiwan, and Overseas Chinese Communities. The spark of China's fourth revolution has come from within, but its fuel has come from East Asia, led by Hong Kong and Taiwan. Some 82 percent of foreign investment in China—$50 billion by the end of 1992—has come from Asia. According to Chinese statistics, Hong Kong, Macao, and Taiwan account for 67 percent; Japan for 13 percent; Europe and the Western Hemisphere for 13 percent; the countries of the Association of Southeast Asian Nations for 2 percent; others for the remaining 5 percent.

China's economic development has in many ways been driven by businessmen in Hong Kong, Taiwan, and among the overseas Chinese. Drawing on capital pools that may surpass $1 to $1.5 trillion, Chinese investors large and small across the region have driven the China boom for reasons of profit, prestige, and family ties.

Hong Kong manufacturers, for example, have invested more than $10 billion in the PRC, establishing some 25,000 factories in Guangdong province alone. Hong Kong has thus become a center of management and investment capital, employing some 3 million workers (four times its own labor force) across the Chinese border in the production of clothing, toys, and other export goods. The investors include:

- Li Ka-shing, of Hutchison Whampoa, Ltd., reputedly the world's richest Chinese with assets of $5.8 billion, who has signed deals to build a container port in Shanghai, shopping centers there and in Beijing, and an industrial park and highway in southern China. He also intends to buy a steel plant in Beijing.
- Peter Woo, son-in-law of the late shipping magnate Sir Y. K. Pao, who sees the future growth in the population centers in China's vast interior. Accordingly, he is investing in a $2 billion industrial park, rail, and port project to make Wuhan a hub in the economic flowering of the Yangtze River area. Woo also wants to build a container port near the mouth of the Yangtze at Ningbo, his father-in-law's home town.
- Gordon Wu, a Princeton-educated engineer and managing director of Hong Kong's Hopewell Holdings, who is forging another kind of tie. He has financed a $1.2 billion, 122-kilometer superhighway that links Guangzhou, the capital of Guang-

dong, with the special economic zone of Shenzhen, effectively opening more of the interior of already-dynamic Guangdong province to the ready ports and processing zones of the coast.

The economic success of China's fourth revolution may facilitate the transition of Hong Kong's 404 square miles and 5.8 million people from British colony to Special Administrative Region.

Today, leading Hong Kong businessmen stress three points. (1) China's most-favored nation (MFN) trade status is essential for investor confidence in Hong Kong; (2) good, long-term Sino–U.S. relations are vital to the region, particularly as Britain's role changes; and (3) although everyone favors China's democratization, Asian cultural contexts affect human rights standards. In this view, MFN should not be made contingent on Hong Kong's democratization.

Beijing must now balance the impact of Hong Kong's freewheeling lifestyle (South China eagerly tunes in to Hong Kong television) with the economic integration of Hong Kong as part of the Pearl River delta, even as Hong Kong prepares for a unique identity after July 1, 1997, as mandated by the 1984 Sino–British agreement.

With respect to Taiwan, it was to a delegation from the Center for Strategic and International Studies visiting Beijing in February 1984 that Deng Xiaoping first enunciated his formula of "one country, two systems." This idea explicitly recognizes that changes on the Taiwan side of the Taiwan Strait will occur outside the PRC's socialist system. It countenances them so long as China is preserved as one country.

Many developments affecting and

reflecting cross-strait relations will transpire in the upcoming months. Presidential elections are scheduled in Taiwan in 1996, although discussion continues about modalities and dates. A first round of unofficial talks was held in Singapore on April 27–29, 1993, between Chairman Koo Chen-fu of Taipei's Straits Exchange Foundation and Chairman Wang Daohan of Beijing's Association for Relations Across the Taiwan Straits. Preparation for a second is now under way. The 14th Kuomintang Party Congress in Taipei in August 1993 (at which three mainland China reporters participated for the first time) evidenced the political volatility in Taiwan between Taipei's one China policy and its desire for appropriate international recognition, including representation in the United Nations (UN).

Now over 4.2 million visits have taken place from Taiwan to the mainland, with over 40,000 visits the other way. Some 40,000 letters and 13,000 phone calls cross the strait daily. Taiwan-mainland indirect trade between 1987 and 1992 exceeded $20 billion; in 1992 alone, indirect trade totaled $6.28 billion, a 35 percent increase over 1991. Official Taiwan investment in the mainland now totals over $10 billion.

3. Managing Leadership Succession. China's rolling leadership succession continues, a watershed change in generational leadership at a time when economic and social directions remain to be charted. It remains impossible to measure, as with Mao, how much power and prestige Deng Xiaoping has held, and holds, until he is no longer there. He has been both check and balance.

A concerted attempt to guarantee leadership stability now gives senior leaders such as Jiang Zemin concur-rent positions within the party (general secretary), military (chairman of the Central Military Commission), and government (state president). In any case, leadership change will not come all at once by political fiat or sudden actuarial change, but will rather combine elements of Peking opera played out in the sometimes dark corridors of power. It is a continuous play of numberless acts.

The deaths of Wang Zhen and Li Xiannian reduced China's so-called "Eight Old Men" or "Eight Immortals" to six; led by Deng Xiaoping, they include Yang Shangkun, Chen Yun, Peng Zhen, Bo Yibo, and Xi Zhongxun. Their average age is 87.3 years. Yet China's leadership succession entails much more than waiting for the "old men" to pass away. The average age of China's seven-person ruling Politburo standing committee is only 64.7 years. Included in this elite group at the pinnacle of formal power are Jiang Zemin, 67 years old; Li Peng, 65; Qiao Shi, 69; Li Ruihuan, 59; Zhu Rongji, 65; Liu Huaqing, 77; and Hu Jintao, 51. But power and authority will no doubt become more diffuse and bureaucratically fragmented after Deng; no one in this successor generation commands Long March loyalty across the army, party, and government.

China's continued efforts to professionalize and invigorate its leadership are also evidenced by the fact that at 59 years the average age of the 20-member Politburo is even younger than that body's standing committee. Further, 70 percent of the members of the National People's Congress standing committee are new, averaging 64.5 years (2.9 years younger than the previous one), with 76.6 percent having graduated from college. All this argues for a more narrow scope of political debate and, possibly, a relatively smooth transition after Deng Xiao-ping.

Still, tensions are inevitable in collective leadership structures; the "core" leaders around whom consensus is expected to form will face surprises as power shifts generationally and among institutions (including the People's Liberation Army [PLA] and National People's Congress) and among levels and regions.

4. Maintaining Systemic Legitimacy and Stability. Those jockeying for power in China know that legitimacy requires both stability and a renewed motivating momentum. This is why Beijing must harness the potentially legitimizing but sometimes volatile forces of nationalism and ideology. This is why its bid to host the Olympic Games became so politicized.

Ordinary citizens throughout China want signposts for the future. Unbridled economic Darwinism is now manifest in the mad rush to make money in real estate, trading companies, and almost anything else. Alarming numbers of women and children are being bought and sold; the incidence of drug use and AIDS is rising; public security officials are receiving posthumous medals for stopping train robberies.

Some say China's socialist system will collapse from outside pressure, some say it is crumbling from the inside. Others posit it will be maintained and gradually transformed by incremental adjustments. Still others predict it will be overhauled through structural reform and liberalization.

As the popular Chinese expression puts it: "Let go and everything becomes chaos; grasp and it dies" (*yi fang, jiu luan; yi zhua, jiu si*). Oscillations will continue as forces of change shake old patterns and distributions of power, wealth, and opportunity, only to be reined in when they threaten the

core institutions and moral values of modern Chinese society. As in the past, China's governing system endures in part because no one wants chaos, although the future of that system remains full of unpredictable twists and turns.

5. Defining a Post-Gulf, Post–Cold War International Role and Identity. The measure of a country is not only its output of steel or very-large-scale integrated chips, its oil consumption or export volume. The measure of a country also requires an ongoing assessment of its history and culture, its self-concept and identity, and, therefore, the likely proclivities and aspirations of its leaders and people.

In this regard, the nationalism and rising standards of living that are becoming the basis of legitimacy for a fourth-revolution China underscore Beijing's traditional objective: to project global influence while asserting regional great power interests according to the dictates of sober realpolitik.

A noted Chinese strategist, the late Huan Xiang, once characterized Beijing's perspective on the international situation in an elegant 16-character description: "One world, two systems, political and economic multipolarity, competitive coexistence." How Beijing fits itself into this new environment will reflect and direct the regional and global implications of China's fourth revolution.

The post–cold war world suggests Beijing must shift from playing the margins of the power balance in the old bipolar system; it also requires Beijing to adjust to the competitive realities of market economies through the GATT, the Asia–Pacific Economic Cooperation, and other rules and groupings. Beyond the importance of high-tech weaponry, the post–Gulf war era highlights the even more critical role of advanced command, control, communications, and intelligence, of coordinated lift, logistics, and combined arms operations. It demonstrates the continuing utility of highly maneuverable, lethal military force, as well as the leverage of a permanent seat on the United Nations (UN) Security Council.

Given projected failure of domestic supply to meet overall oil demand, ongoing modernization needs and marketization interests in the PLA, issues of sovereign pride and privilege, and a sophisticated negotiating approach that seeks to maximize every possible asset, Beijing can be expected to take a firm posture regarding its various international interests. These include territorial claims (whether the Spratly Islands or various disputed borders); transfers or sales of weapons or weapons technology; and an expansive international diplomacy (including current ties in East Asia, expanding ties in the Middle East with countries as diverse as Iran and Israel, as well as developing ties in Europe, Latin America, and Africa).

A key issue remains the extent to which Beijing will see its security interests best advanced by abiding by established international rules and regimes, whether the Nuclear Non-Proliferation Treaty or the Missile Technology Control Regime.

Implications for the United States

Whether or not one accepts a shift toward the Pacific in the international center of gravity, current focus on U.S. domestic economic revitalization and thereby on geoeconomics only highlights the importance of U.S. ties to the Asia–Pacific and to China.

Concern for long-term U.S. competitiveness and the potential fragmentation of the world trade system into competing North American, European, and East Asian trading blocs underlies a recognizable shift by Japan, China, and other East Asian countries toward closer regional cooperation even while they jockey for leadership and position in East Asia. For this reason, U.S. policy toward China is inseparable from U.S. East Asian regional interests and relations.

As has been noted, the coming five years will mark a watershed for China's internal directions and international role. During this period, the attention of the international community's policymakers, including those of the United States, will naturally focus on the intensified interaction of developments and events in the PRC, Taiwan, and Hong Kong.

For example, the pace, scope, and process of Hong Kong's reversion to PRC sovereignty on July 1, 1997, including the "through train" issues of political representation and legal rights, are inextricably tied to the ticking of the actuarial clock for the aged leaders in Zhongnanhai, to China's other interlocking domestic dilemmas, and to Beijing's interaction with the world.

Likewise, Taiwan's ongoing efforts to distribute political and economic power in the second generation and to balance the realities of substantial de facto independence against the risks of pursuing de jure independence are now inseparable from developments in the PRC. Taipei and Beijing share an interest in balancing exchange and cooperation against Taiwan's continued determination to secure an international role and identity. Taipei contends that as a country of 21 million people with a dynamic political system and vibrant economy, with the world's largest foreign exchange reserves (some $82.3 billion), and as its 14th largest trading entity, Taiwan deserves

31

international "breathing space." Many in Taiwan feel Taipei is as well or better qualified than many other UN members and that, although nomenclature remains sensitive, Taiwan deserves representation in the United Nations and the UN family of institutions.

These interactions will demand comprehensive U.S. government policies to deal with the whole of China. They underscore the need for calibrated, high-level dialogue (not just visits) with Beijing and Taipei. U.S. policy-level decision makers should see for themselves the internal and interactive dynamics of the whole of China in regional and global context.

Systematic political dialogue with the PRC should include when necessary those at all levels in current leadership positions in Beijing and elsewhere, in the central offices and key ministries of the government, party, and army. This ongoing dialogue should also consciously be broadened to encompass other leaders and groups as a civil society emerges in China, including the National People's Congress, the provinces, and key urban centers.

The complexities of China's interactions also suggest an increasing need to broaden the communication web among actors within the region. Here, because of direct interests and historical ties to the PRC, Taiwan, and Hong Kong, the United States has a special role, as elsewhere in East Asia, as part of a two-track process. Governmental joint liaison, working groups, and commissions all have their contributions to make. In addition, nongovernmental efforts can bring together, in triangular or quadrilateral settings, key policy, business, and (in their private capacities) governmental decision makers to work through current issues and to anticipate future ones.

None of this suggests a shift in the official U.S. role. The United States has wisely eschewed setting negotiating timetables or conditions and has refused to mediate in cross-strait disputes. The nature and complexity of interactions within China, however, require an integrated analytical and policy response, as well as a means to draw on the best thinking, interests, and information from within and beyond government.

This process will remain ongoing. Success in various aspects of U.S. relations with the PRC, Taiwan, and Hong Kong can be expected to raise new challenges, whether in the political, economic, sociocultural, or security spheres.

In the economic arena, for example, the United States should patiently and persistently define and advance its own interests, not making undue concessions on GATT accession, implementation of intellectual property rights agreements, or market access memoranda of understanding. The PRC should not be unfairly singled out for stringent enforcement of bans on prison labor exports, mislabeled or transshipped imports, or dumping. But neither should the PRC be given unwarranted preferential treatment, especially not on the basis of vague future benefits promised to the United States.

As the past three years demonstrate, the broad mix of politics, policy, and philosophy inherent in the debate over China's MFN status demonstrates that it is too blunt an instrument to use for regulating overall U.S.–PRC relations. That is, unless Beijing chooses to violate the carefully developed guidelines the Clinton administration announced on May 27, 1993, which were intended to deal with economic and proliferation issues in alternative channels and thus condition Beijing's continued MFN status on broad improvement in human rights conditions alone.

Undermining China's socialist system or remaking it according to Washington's concepts should not be a U.S. policy objective. The interaction of global and domestic forces leading to a fourth revolution in China, as elsewhere, is a practical fact of everyday modern life, not of ideology.

Egregious violations of international conventions or law with respect to human rights are not strictly internal matters. Individual human rights cases should continue to be pursued by the public and private means most effective. Regardless of the institutional mechanism chosen to implement Radio Free Asia, U.S. interests are best reflected by the highest standards of professional, not polemical, international broadcasting.

Conclusion

Twin paradoxes remain at the heart of China's fourth revolution. Contrary to conventional wisdom that exchange automatically enhances mutual understanding, increased interchange has in some ways also heightened the realization in Washington and Beijing of how different their political and economic systems and their underlying patterns of organization and values really are.

But the parallel paradox for those in China eager to compete in the world is that they must do so on the world's terms. This represents a shift in the historical debate about whether or not China can modernize without altering its traditional values and structures. The everyday reality is that it must and is.

Thus, significant divergences between China's realities and those of the outside world still exist. But these are increasingly subject to strong, ongoing forces of modernization that lead toward their convergence. These forces will be noted in China's long and continuing history as part of a fourth period of structural modernization—as part of China's fourth revolution, both from the outside in and the inside out.

Although the views expressed here are his own, the author acknowledges with appreciation the research and administrative contributions of CSIS Asian Studies Program staff to this article, including the charts developed by Chi J. Leng.

Notes

1. All dollar amounts cited in this article are in current U.S. dollars.

2. Following the Tiananmen tragedy, the world's outrage significantly undermined the will and ability of Russian troops and others to preserve forcefully the Soviet and East European regimes when they began to fragment in the latter part of 1989. For example, in the former East Berlin and Dresden recently, the author was told that the former East German government's public support for the repression at Tiananmen was a significant catalyst in the Honecker regime's own loss of legitimacy and subsequent downfall.

3. Anne Simone Kleinman, CSIS Asian Studies Program, elaborates this theme in a paper entitled "Across China: Regional Pluralism and Developmental Imbalance."

Collective Security in Europe Today

Max Jakobson

AFTER EVERY GREAT war an attempt has been made to create a system of collective security for Europe: after Napoleon, the Holy Alliance; after World War I, the League of Nations; after World War II, the United Nations (UN). And now, after the Cold War, Europe once again is reaching toward something "better than a balance of power."

A grand design for a Europe united on the basis of common values was outlined in the Charter of Paris issued in November 1990 by the summit meeting of the Conference on Security and Cooperation in Europe (CSCE). Peace and security, according to the Charter, will be assured once all European nations have adopted the Western system of democracy and the market economy. The objective of Western policy is thus to integrate the countries of the former Soviet empire, including Russia itself, into the Western political and economic system and its institutions.

Max Jakobson, a former Finnish ambassador to the UN, is the author of several books, among them *The Diplomacy of the Winter War* (1961) and *The United Nations in the 1990s* (1993).

The Washington Quarterly • 18:2

This vision of the future of Europe reveals the enduring influence of eighteenth- and nineteenth-century German philosophy on political thought. To paraphrase John Maynard Keynes, politicians are often unaware that the opinions they express can be traced back to the books written by professors they have never heard of. The notion that democracies do not make war against each other was first put forward by Immanuel Kant, who wrote 200 years ago that "eternal peace" would be attained when in every state decisions on war and peace were made by the citizens rather than by a single ruler. The claim that the Western system of government has universal validity echoes Hegel's thesis of the "end of history." And present-day faith in the capacity of the market to transform the former socialist societies recalls Karl Marx's prediction that the capitalist system would force all nations to use the same method of production and thus create a world in its own image.

But Marx failed to grasp the strength of national, religious, and cultural factors, and similarly today universalist doctrines clash with the stubborn facts of particularism prevailing in the vast area formerly ruled from Moscow.

The nations of Central and Eastern Europe have in fact little in common except the fate they shared as victims of the conflict between German and Russian imperialism followed by forced integration into the Soviet system. Liberal democracy and the market economy have never had a strong constituency in these countries. Before World War II Czechoslovakia was the only democracy and advanced industrial state among them. All the others were agrarian countries ruled by authoritarian regimes. Once Soviet power was withdrawn, the uniformity imposed by Moscow broke down, and the old differences, rivalries, and feuds reemerged.

The validity of a universal model of development was explicitly rejected by President Boris Yeltsin in a speech made in February 1994, in which he explained why the leading market-oriented reformers had been left out of the Russian government. Russia is different, Yeltsin said, the national character of the Russian people is not like that of other Europeans. He promised that reform would continue, but reform *à la Russe*, not according to the recipes of the International Monetary Fund.[1]

One could argue, however, that on the contrary Russia is no different from other nations. No country has ever been able to acquire a system of parliamentary democracy and market economy off the peg, as it were, like buying a ready-made suit; everywhere it has required a long evolutionary process. In Russia such an evolution has hardly begun.

True, the Soviet Union is dead, but it is only brain dead; the organs of the old system continue to function. The military-industrial complex, the vast provincial bureaucracy, the military establishment—all these are still almost intact. The revolution that put an end to the Soviet Union as a state was like a neutron bomb in reverse: it destroyed the structures without removing the people in power. The great majority of the men—there are very few women among them—who run Russia today belong to the former Soviet *nomenklatura*. The switch from one system to another has hardly caused them severe pangs of conscience because for most of them the Soviet ideology was a mere facade for the exercise of power: democracy serves the same purpose.

Russia does have one foot in the open market, but the other foot is stuck under the heavy weight of old structures. The country is straddling two worlds, shifting its weight from one foot to the other in response to conflicting pressures, external and internal.

The West has showered upon the Russians good advice on how to solve their economic problems, but no outsider can help them tackle the root cause of their present misery—the collapse of public morality. Macroeconomic indicators may be pointing upward, but they do not measure the extent of criminal activity and corruption, the decay of social infrastructure, the consequences of ecological neglect, or the depth of despair and cynicism among the Russian population.

As the full extent of devastation, physical and moral, caused by Soviet rule has unfolded, the vision of a united Europe seems far removed from the brutal realities of the eastern half of the continent. Western societies themselves are racked by self-doubt and pessimism. The blueprints for a pan-European "security architecture" drafted in the first flush of post–cold war optimism have been swept away. Solid structures implied by the term architecture cannot be built on shifting sands.

The Case of Yugoslavia

Some of the fundamental issues Europe now faces have been cast into sharp relief by the conflict in the former Yugoslavia. The fighting itself, as well as the reactions of the rest of Europe, have conformed to a historical pattern of behavior that has proved resistant to new influences.

A useful reminder of the historical roots of the conflict is provided by the republication of the report of an international inquiry into the Balkan war of 1912–13 commissioned by the Carnegie Endowment for International Peace.[2] The similarity of the events described by the commission 80 years ago to what is happening today is striking. The deliberate use of military action for the extermination of civilian populations, the destruction of towns and villages, the atrocities committed by all sides against women and children, the total lack of willingness to compromise: in all these respects 1993–94 has been a repetition of 1912–13.

In his introduction to the new edition of the report, George Kennan concludes that

what we are up against is the sad fact that the developments of those earlier ages . . . had the effect of thrusting into the southeastern reaches of the European continent a salient of non-European civilization that has continued to the present day to preserve many of its non-European characteristics, including some that fit even less with the world of today than they did with the world of eighty years ago.[3]

This is an unfashionable opinion in our age of integration, which tends to gloss over ethnic or cultural differences between peoples, but as such it is a useful antidote to the tendency of political analysts and commentators to leap from a particular event to a general theory.

The Balkan peoples are, of course, not the only Europeans capable of aggressive behavior. As Kennan points out, we are dealing with relative distinctions. But there is nowhere in Europe a concatenation of historical, ethnic, and religious conflicts comparable to the viper's nest in the Balkans.

True, the former Soviet Union is a vast minefield of ancient ethnic feuds, minority problems, and territorial disputes. But the violence in that area is not related to what has happened in the former Yugoslavia: the Armenians and the Azeris, the Tajiks, and others hardly needed encouragement from the outside to start killing each other.

At the outset, the Western governments were inclined to look upon the fighting in the former Yugoslavia as one more chapter, not necessarily the last one, in the long history of savage strife between the Balkan peoples—a civil war not amenable to outside influence. It seemed little had changed in Europe since the days of Otto von Bismarck, chancellor of the newly united Germany, who in December 1876 made his famous remark that Germany had no interest in the Eastern Question, as the Balkan conflict of that time was called, "that was worth the healthy bones of a single Pomeranian grenadier." President Bill Clinton, in an unguarded moment, put it less eloquently: "Until these folks get tired of killing each other over there, bad things will continue to happen."[4]

Yet the Western governments, harassed by the media, did not succeed in keeping aloof. Recognition of the independence of Slovenia and Croatia was the first step on the slippery slope.

We shall never know what might have been achieved had the major powers made recognition conditional upon a prior peaceful settlement, under UN auspices, of borders, minority rights, and other contested issues. What we do know is that the reflexive application of the principle of national self-determination virtually forced the Muslim population of Bosnia-Herzegovina, a religious rather than a national or ethnic community that had never aspired to become a nation-state, to seek independence in order to avoid being left at the mercy of Serbian imperialist ambitions. The struggle between the peoples of the former Federation of Yugoslavia was thus transformed into a war between sovereign states: the UN could not stand aside.

What followed is a familiar story. The UN intervention has progressed from mediation to arms embargo, economic sanctions, humanitarian missions to protect the civilian population, finally selected air strikes by planes of the North Atlantic Treaty Organization (NATO)—anything short of the use of armed force of the kind that might risk substantial casualties.

What distinguishes the current Balkan war from earlier ones is the role of the media. Yet the pressure of public opinion has been ambiguous. People are revolted by television reports of atrocities and demand that something be done to stop them. But in no country are people urging their government to send their own soldiers to do the job. They say: Let the UN or NATO do something. This is a way of asking someone else to do what one is not prepared to do oneself. The initials of international organizations remain abstractions unless brought to life by the national will of the member states. This will is lacking.

Bismarck, once again, said it: "I have always found the word Europe on the lips of those politicians who wanted something from other powers which they dare not demand in their own names."[5]

Those who believe in a federal Europe claim that, once the mechanisms envisaged in the Maastricht treaty are in place, the European Union (EU) will have an effective common foreign and security policy. But institutional arrangements can only reflect reality, not change it. The reality is that, although politicians pay lip service to the idea of collective action in defense of common values or of the principle of collective security, nations will take up arms only when their own national interests are directly threatened. The Balkan crisis is not perceived to constitute such a threat.

The United States, too, has set a limit to its intervention: No ground forces. Americans prefer to use air power. This goes back all the way to the first U.S.–Soviet summit meeting, which took place during Foreign Minister Viacheslav Molotov's visit to Washington, D.C., in May 1942. After dinner in the White House, President Franklin D. Roosevelt outlined his vision of collective security after the war. He said the four major powers, the United States, Great Britain, the Soviet Union, and China (France was added later), should act together as "policemen" to keep the peace. Smaller nations were to be disarmed, and if any one of them defied the policemen, it should be bombed into submission.[6] This notion was subsequently written into the Charter of the UN.

It took almost 50 years before the Roosevelt–Molotov pact was actually consummated. Iraq was bombed into submission. But Operation Desert Storm may have been the last of its kind. In any case, bombing is a blunt instrument for use in a European civil war, like the one in ex-Yugoslavia. Air strikes can deter or punish, but as President Clinton said on April 20, 1994: "Air power will not settle this conflict. . . . It must be settled through negotiations."[7]

On an intellectual level, the critics of Western policy have made a persuasive case by arguing that not only humanitarian concerns but the fundamental national interests of the Western world are at stake in the Balkans, and that the failure to act forcefully has undermined Western credibility throughout Central and Eastern Europe, including Russia. But such a calculation of the long-term interests of the West fails to touch the emotional chords of people living in conditions of security and relative affluence. Without genuine public support a large-scale Western military intervention on behalf of Bosnia could have had disastrous political consequences in the West itself.

Western societies today simply have no stomach for the kind of large-scale military interventions that would have had to be mounted in the former Yugoslavia. Whether this is due to a general weakening of loyalty to the state, hedonistic individualism, or simply the small size of families, as Edward Luttwak has claimed,[8] remains for sociologists to analyze. The political consequences are already evident. Somalia and Haiti speak for themselves, as does the extreme sensitivity of the British and French governments to any action that might risk the lives of their peacekeeping forces in the former Yugoslavia. Politicians are haunted by the specter of body bags flown back from distant battlefields to grieving relatives. In a memorable scene on British television, the weeping mother of a soldier killed in Bosnia said to reporters: "And I was so happy when he joined the army—we thought it was a secure job." The spirit is no longer what it used to be in the days of Tennyson: "Theirs not to reason why/Theirs but to do and die" ("The Charge of the Light Brigade").

New Configurations in Europe

This, then, is the message of the Bosnian tragedy for the nations of Central and Eastern Europe: it has revealed the limits of the West's will to use force in defense of common values and collective security. That is why Russia's neighbors are now striving to be admitted to the institutions the West is committed to defend. They desperately wish to be accepted, to belong. They must take into account the possibility, as President Václav Havel of the Czech Republic has put it, "that in Russia forces still enamored of the imperial ambitions of the former Soviet Union would temporarily gain the upper hand: chauvinistic, Great Russian, crypto-communist and crypto-totalitarian forces."[9] Could they then rely on Western support?

It can be argued that fears of a resurgence of Russian aggressiveness are exaggerated. That Russia is weak today is obvious, and it is a fallacy to imagine that Russia could become strong again by reverting to a closed command economy and a militarized foreign policy—in other words, by methods that led to the downfall of the Soviet Union. The imperialist rhetoric emanating from Moscow only shows that Russian politicians have learned to shout when arguing a weak point. For a long time to come Russia will lack the strength to play an important role in world affairs.

But as a regional power Russia retains a massive preponderance over its European neighbors, and Russia's weakness in the global context has the paradoxical effect of sharpening the security concerns of these countries, because it tends to lessen Western interest in this region. They have not forgotten all that Yalta stands for.

During his visit to Prague in January 1994, President Clinton was asked by a Czech reporter whether it was conceivable, given the lessons of history, that NATO would fail to come to the aid of an East European country if it were invaded or subject to military aggression. Clinton replied, according to agency reports, that he thought it was "doubtful" that there would be no help. "I think your reading of our history is right," he said.[10]

One wonders what history he had in mind. The history the people in Prague remember is one of Western indifference to their fate. At the end of World War II the West acquiesced in Soviet hegemony over Central and Eastern Europe. The Cold War was not caused by what happened east of the line that cut across Germany, but by the fear that Soviet military power combined with Communist subversion posed a direct threat to Western societies themselves. The Soviet domain was never seriously challenged. Even in the dying days of the Soviet empire, President George Bush and other Western leaders preferred stability—helping Mikhail Gorbachev to stay in power—to encouraging East Europeans to seek their freedom. Now that the ideological contest is over and Russia is weak, the West might turn its back on what happens in those "faraway countries." Because joining the European Union is bound to be a long process, NATO membership appears to offer the countries of Central and Eastern Europe a shortcut into the Western fold.

The dilemma raised by the desire of the Poles and others to join NATO has been at the center of the Western debate for the past two years. It is not likely to be resolved in the near future. The past discussion has focused on the problem of how to reassure the Poles without upsetting the Russians. It is important to note which Russians would be upset. It is the "Westerners" who urgently advise the West not to extend NATO to Russia's borders. They fear that such a move would be used by the "red-brown coalition" of former Communists and ultranationalists as a pretext to demand a remilitarization of Russian policy.

At the same time, admitting some of the Central and East European countries—the former Visegrad states are usually mentioned as likely candidates[11]—would intensify the sense of insecurity among the nations left out. To draw a new line across the map of Europe would be tantamount to telling the Russians: These are ours, the rest is yours. The Baltic states, in particular, would feel abandoned: they have not forgotten the Ribbentrop–Molotov Pact of August 1939.

The first attempt to solve the dilemma was the scheme called the Partnership for Peace (PFP). Its reception has varied in accordance with the level of expectations in each of the countries concerned. Those who feared they might be left on the wrong side of a new line welcomed the PFP as better than nothing—a cup half full. But those who had hoped to be admitted to membership were disappointed—a cup half empty. The Poles in particular feel let down, like a suitor who is proposing marriage and is offered platonic friendship instead.

So now NATO says: Yes, the alliance will take in new members, the question is only when and how. New members must be producers of security, not only consumers; an enlargement must not create a new division in Europe; Russia, too, must understand that NATO's purpose is to ensure stability and thus to serve Russia's interests as well. A cynic reading the fine print might conclude that NATO membership will be available to the countries of Central and Eastern Europe when they no longer need it.

NATO or the EU?

The debate on the future of NATO has been an American one; the European members of the alliance have been reticent. This is understandable. Every European NATO member has an urgent need to cut military expenditures so as to lighten the oppressive burden of budget deficits. In these circumstances an extension of military commitments could hardly carry much conviction. But there is also a deeper reason for the reluctance of Western Europe to consider an enlargement of NATO. A military alliance is, after all, a mutual insurance society. It insures each member against the risk of being left alone to meet an aggression, but in return each must pledge itself to join in the defense of any other member that has become an object of aggression. Since the collapse of the Soviet Union the risk that these pledges would actually have to be redeemed has diminished to a point close to zero, but with every new member from the East it would rise again sharply. It would be difficult to persuade the parliaments of Western Europe that an enlargement of NATO would increase the security of existing members enough to offset the additional risk.

At their meeting on December 1, 1994, the NATO foreign ministers decided to begin "an extensive study" on the principles that should guide the process of enlargement and on the implications of membership. This reminds me of the old story about the Jewish scribe who was serving a cruel and capricious despot. One day he was told by his master: "You must teach my dog to read. You must do it in one year, or else." In desperation the scribe went to a wise rabbi for advice. After some thought the rabbi said: "A year is a long time. Many things may change. Your master may die. Or the dog might die." "But what if none of this happens?" "In that case," the rabbi said, "you will have to teach the dog how to read."

Many things may indeed change in the course of 1995. But in the end NATO must be prepared to face the choice between two incompatible policies: between showing confidence in the Yeltsin regime as a partner that can be trusted, and guaranteeing some of the Central and East European countries against Russian aggression. The code word "stability" is designed to blur the contradiction between the two policies. The fact remains, however, that if at the end of 1995 no definite decision is taken about enlargement, it will be said that Russia has been granted a veto over NATO policy; but if NATO begins to carry out an enlargement in practice, the repercussions within Russia may intensify the threat enlargement is supposed to avert.

A way out of this impasse was indicated by the NATO Council itself in its statement on December 1, 1994. It pointed out that an enlargement of NATO should be viewed as complementary and parallel to the enlargement of the EU. In fact, the predominant view in Europe is that the EU, not NATO, is the right instrument for the promotion of stability in Central and Eastern Europe.

No doubt there is an element of institutional rivalry in this. The institutions set up during the Cold War are all struggling to survive by producing new services for a changed market. "NATO is going to make itself relevant to the future," Secretary of State Warren Christopher said at the NATO Council meeting. Instead of traditional defense, NATO is now offering crisis management and peacekeeping; instead of security, stability. The CSCE is in the same business, and so is the Western European Union, which until recently was no more than a discussion group of NATO's European members.

But of course the differences in approach have deeper roots. They reflect divergent views of the threat Europe faces today. If it is a resurgence of Russian imperialism, then NATO is the answer. But if, as I believe, Russia will for a long time to come lack the strength to project its influence beyond the borders of the former Soviet Union, then the threat to the security of Russia's Western neighbors is not primarily a military one, but rather the danger of being sucked into the vortex of economic backwardness and social instability that is the legacy of 50 years of Soviet rule. Against this, NATO membership by itself would not provide sufficient defense. Only a gradual extension of the security concept represented by the EU can promote political stability and economic prosperity in the eastern half of Europe and thereby create a reliable and lasting basis for the security of both halves.

The first step in this direction has now been taken. Austria, Finland, and Sweden have joined the EU. This will shift the Union's geopolitical focus toward the North and the East. With Vienna inside, Budapest, Prague, Bratislava, and Ljubljana will be brought into its orbit. Through Finland, the EU will acquire a common border with Russia. From Helsinki, on a clear day, one can almost see the coastline of Estonia. The entire Baltic region will be embraced by EU members.

Thus a look at the map reveals what the logical next step must be: the Visegrad states, as well as Estonia, Latvia, and Lithuania, will have to be drawn into the EU's fold. Obviously, they have a long way to go before they will be able to carry the economic responsibilities of membership. But by engaging the prospective new member states in what is called a structured relationship, the EU has found a way of bringing them into the framework of political integration. The six countries now being prepared for membership are Poland, Hungary, the Czech Republic, Slovakia, Romania, and Bulgaria. The three Baltic states—Estonia, Latvia, and Lithuania—as well as Slovenia, are expected to enter this process by the end of 1995.

An enlargement of the EU would not alienate or isolate Russia. On the contrary, it would lend support and encouragement to the Russian modernizers who realize that the only way their country can lift itself out of its present misery is through integration into the Western economy. Significantly, Finland's decision to join the EU was welcomed by the Russian government. Had it joined NATO the reaction would have been different. But having gained membership in the EU Finland feels no urgent need to seek entry into NATO, although it has not excluded that option for the future.

The eastward widening of the EU is consistent with its original purpose. It has always claimed to be "Europe." During the Cold War it had no choice but to remain an exclusively West European institution. Now at last it has the opportunity to make good its claim to represent all of Europe.

For obvious reasons, Germany is the engine driving the EU forward in the new direction. If Europe remains divided, as it is today, Germany will continue to be a frontline state, ever exposed to the fallout from conflicts and disorders in the eastern half of Europe. Germany thus has an overriding strategic interest in promoting political stability in Central and Eastern Europe and the Baltic region, including Russia, an area that for centuries has been a German sphere of economic and cultural influence. This interest is shared by the four new members of the EU, which is why the German government worked hard to enable them to join.

The cost of widening will be enormous. The present members will have to provide the Central and East European countries with development funds to help them restructure their economies. They will also have to open their own markets to imports of food and other products from Central and Eastern Europe. A thorough overhaul of the EU's common agricultural policy will be necessary.

EU institutions will be strained to the utmost. Until now, the EU has revolved around the Paris–Bonn axis. This functioned smoothly as long as Germany was a West European state—an economic giant but a political dwarf. But after unification Germany is no longer a West European state: it is a European power, once again at the center of the continent, with Berlin as its future capital. This is bound to affect the political balance within the EU. The recent signs of closer cooperation between France and Britain on defense may foreshadow a realignment of forces. This trend is likely to be reinforced by uncertainties about the future of U.S. policy.

Understandably many people in Western Europe feel uneasy about Germany's *Drang nach Osten*. There is, however, a crucial difference between Germany's past imperialist eastern campaigns and its present *Ostpolitik:*

Germany today is acting within the framework of the EU. It is in the interest of the other member states to make sure Germany will continue to do so. This they can best achieve by joining Germany in an effort to widen the EU into a truly European institution.

Europe's Borders

Where does Europe end? General Charles de Gaulle spoke of Europe from "the Atlantic to the Urals"—a phrase of calculated ambiguity. Today, too, political leaders speak of Europe in ambiguous terms, although perhaps less by calculation than through indecision.

The answer to the question depends on the West's view of Russia and its future. The assumption underlying Western policy is that economic reform laced with Western aid will make Russia a democratic and peace-loving state content to live within its present borders. No doubt an improvement in the economy would strengthen the Yeltsin regime and, more broadly, stabilize the political situation. But will this resolve Russia's postimperial identity crisis?

The phenomenon itself is, of course, familiar to students of the rise and fall of great powers. The British and French, too, have had difficulties in reconciling themselves to the loss of empire. But in some respects the Russian case is unique. While the British and the French had to withdraw from overseas possessions populated by alien peoples, the Russian domain itself has shrunk in size, leaving 25 million Russians outside the Russian Federation, beyond borders that used to be merely administrative divisions. What makes this contraction all the more painful is that the Russians, again unlike the British and the

French, have no established national or geographic identity to fall back on. What is Russia if it is not an empire?

Actually the Russian withdrawal from the "inner empire"—the area now called the "near abroad"—is more apparent than real. The former Soviet republics belonging to the Commonwealth of Independent States (CIS) remain chained to Russia by the structures of the former Soviet military-industrial complex; most of their leaders are members of the old *nomenklatura*, and the Russian Army moves freely across their borders.

Is Russian domination within the CIS a form of imperialism that has to be resisted before it advances even further, or is it a natural and inevitable consequence of the interdependence between the members of the CIS—a process of "reintegration," as the Russians themselves prefer to call it?

The question presents Western policymakers with a dilemma they would prefer not to face. It was never an objective of Western policy to bring about the disintegration of the Soviet Union. The West on the contrary tried to help Gorbachev to keep the USSR together. The leaders of the Baltic independence movement were advised by the West not to rock the boat. President Bush even traveled to Kiev to lecture the Ukrainians on the evils of nationalism.

Yet, once the Soviet Union had fallen apart, the West rushed to recognize the former Soviet republics as sovereign states and to admit them to international organizations. Ironically, what Stalin proposed in 1945 has now come to pass: all 15 former Soviet republics have been granted a vote in the UN. As in the case of Yugoslavia, the principle of national self-determination has been applied indiscriminately; on demand, as it were, without

an examination of the credentials of each applicant. Clearly, some of them would not pass any reasonable test of viable statehood. As a result, the credibility of the UN and the CSCE is bound to be damaged by their inability to protect the integrity of their new members.

The Russian government has gone so far as to ask the CSCE to endorse its military operations in Tajikistan and the Caucasus, and even to pay part of their costs. Understandably the Western governments have refused to grant a "seal of good peacekeeping" to operations they cannot control or effectively monitor. But in terms of realpolitik, the Russian Army may be doing Europe a favor by stemming the Islamic tide along the southern rim of the CIS.

Ukraine is, of course, in a category of its own: a European nation of 52 million, partly Roman Catholic, with an influential lobby in the United States. Its leaders have skillfully used the nuclear weapons inherited from the Soviet Union to extract support from the West. Ukraine has become the fourth largest recipient of U.S. aid after Israel, Egypt, and Russia. Step-by-step, the West is committing itself to supporting Ukrainian independence. Yet Ukraine's future is clouded by the religious divide that cuts across its people, the presence on its territory of more than 10 million Russians, and the disputed status of Crimea.

The eastern border of Europe as a community of nations sharing common values—Immanuel Kant's Europe—will be determined by the ongoing battle between the integrating effects of technological and economic developments and traditional cultural and social structures and ways of life. In the long run the relentless march of integration may penetrate further east than either Napoleon or Hitler. But in a period of time more relevant to policymaking, I believe Europe is likely to stop at roughly the ancient cultural fault line between East and West. In practice this would mean that the lands of the former Austro–Hungarian empire as well as Poland and the Baltic states can be brought into the EU in a reasonable space of time. The rest will be shrouded in uncertainty.

Conclusion

Four years ago, when the Charter of Paris was issued, it was possible to believe that a dynamic, self-confident Western community would exercise, in countless different ways, a powerful influence on developments throughout the former Soviet empire. But today the West itself is in crisis. Victory in the ideological contest of the Cold War has had the paradoxical effect of making the Western nations more critical of their own system. Now that the rival system has collapsed they can no longer console themselves with Winston Churchill's famous dictum—that democracy is a poor way to govern a country, but less so than any known alternative. The advance of economic integration, particularly the liberalization of capital movements, has radically reduced the ability of national governments to direct economic policy; yet movement toward a more effective system of international decision making meets increasing resistance. As a result Western Europe finds itself uncomfortably living in no-man's-land between the two systems: the old one is no longer adequate, but the new one does not yet function.

The great project of widening the EU has been undertaken by governments with weak or uncertain support in their own countries. Public opinion

is preoccupied with domestic problems—high unemployment and the erosion of the welfare state. Western Europe will have to find ways to help itself before it will be able to help Central and Eastern Europe.

The Charter of Paris, like the Charter of the United Nations, provides the vision, but practical policies must be content with more modest goals. European security must be built from the ground up, step-by-step. Instead of dealing in categories, the specific characteristics of each nation must be taken into account. This has now been recognized by the EU, which decided at its summit meeting on December 9–10, 1994, that admission of new members will be decided case by case. If the pace of integration is forced, it could undermine rather than enhance stability in Central and Eastern Europe. Nationalism remains a vital force, for better and for worse. The European idea is too abstract and distant to inspire the kind of loyalty and solidarity that is necessary for the cohesion and orderly functioning of societies. Only a healthy nationalism can provide such a focus. Communities based on ethnic, linguistic, or historical bonds retain their intrinsic value: universal human rights include the right to be different.

Reconciling the diversity of the European reality with the needs of overarching continental unity is a task of infinite complexity. It cannot be compressed into the timetable of normal parliamentary politics. It can only be measured by generations.

Notes

1. President Boris Yeltsin's speech at a joint session of the two chambers of the Russian Parliament, February 24, 1994.

2. Carnegie Endowment for International Peace, *The Other Balkan Wars* (Washington,

45

D.C.: Carnegie Endowment for International Peace, 1993).

3. George F. Kennan, "Introduction: The Balkan Crisis: 1913 and 1993," to *ibid.*, p. 13.

4. Quoted by Max Kampelman in his testimony before the Senate Committee on Foreign Relations, February 23, 1994.

5. A.J.P. Taylor, *Bismarck: The Man and the Statesman* (London: Random House, Arrow Books, 1961), p. 167.

6. Ruth Russel, *A History of the United Nations* (Washington, D.C.: Brookings Institution, 1958), p. 97.

7. *Times* (London), March 15, 1994.

8. Edward N. Luttwak, "Where Are the Great Powers? At Home with the Kids," *Foreign Affairs* 73 (July/August 1994), pp. 23–28.

9. *International Herald Tribune*, October 20, 1993.

10. *International Herald Tribune*, January 13, 1994.

11. The Visegrad states: the Czech Republic, Hungary, Poland, and Slovakia.

Perestroika in Japan

Ryuzaburo Kaku

JAPAN STANDS TODAY at the crossroads of history, a fact little recognized among the politicians, bureaucrats, and senior managers of the Japanese establishment. The firmly rooted mind-set that has brought about the Japanese economic miracle is now outdated. Unless Japan changes drastically through perestroika-like reforms of its economic and political structures, it is doomed to become an orphan among the nations, crippled by mounting domestic crises and antagonism overseas. Few Japanese perceive the necessity of this change; moreover, there is no certainty that once the issues are confronted Japanese leaders will make the choice most appropriate for the nation and the world.

Only a new national agenda, which emphasizes a genuine globalization (as opposed to a merely commercial internationalization), can enable Japan to cope with the challenges of the future. The cornerstone of this strategy must be the transformation of Japan into a state based on the values of harmony with, and prosperity for, the world rather than only Japan. My proposed ethical state initiative would emphasize *kyosei*—the challenge and opportunity of living together with all of the peoples of the world. This would be a decisive turn away from a Japan committed to making only itself rich, toward a focus on the quality of life for individuals in Japan and elsewhere, and the alleviation of the global problems of employment, development, and the environment.

This is a task for which government is ill-suited to act alone. In the world of the twenty-first century, the private sector will have both the possibility and the responsibility of overtaking the public sector as the basic provider of wealth and stability around the globe. Leaders in government and industry must recognize these facts and genuinely lead accordingly. An international debate on these challenges would be of far greater benefit to the peoples of Japan, the United States, and elsewhere than the increasingly rancorous trans-Pacific dialogue on trade restraints.

Historical Foundations of Japan's Policy

There is now much criticism directed against Japan on the grounds that it is merely a mercantilist nation. Although there is some truth in this charge, the Japanese can legitimately be proud of the origins of their trade policy. In the late sixteenth century there was a man of means by the name of Suminokura Ryoi, whose son, Suminokura So-an, was involved in trade with the "southern barbarians" (the contemporary Philippines, Vietnam, Thailand, and Cambodia). In 1603, in collaboration with the great Confucian scholar Fujiwara Seika, Suminokura So-an

Ryuzaburo Kaku is chairman of Canon, Inc., a diversified global manufacturer of business machines and optical equipment.

drafted a set of rules to be applied when boarding a trade ship. Article 1 outlined the objective of trade itself, stating that trade must be carried out not just for one's own benefit but must also take into account the interests of others. Article 2 stated that despite the different skin color and culture of foreigners they should be considered as brothers.

These ideals must be seen in historical context. In 1600, England founded the East India Company. In 1602, Holland set up its own East India Company. France did likewise some time later. Certainly that was the age when the winds of mercantilism were blowing throughout the world. Yet the Japan embodied in the works of Suminokura So-an was not mercantilist and was instead trading on the basis of commendably fair principles. The noble ideals prevalent in 1603 are rather different from those espoused in contemporary Japan.

For 100 years, starting in the middle of the sixteenth century, Japan was in a state of chronic civil war. Toward the end of this destructive "warring states" period, three renowned generals succeeded in unifying Japan: Oda Nobunaga, Toyotomi Hideyoshi, and Tokugawa Ieyasu, who opened an entire new era under the shogunate he founded. Japanese lore has it that his commitment to building a heaven on earth in a pure and isolated Japan was the result of a transforming experience when, at one point in the wars, Ieyasu faced a choice between being taken captive and suicide and was advised by a monk as follows, "Onri-edo-gongu-jodo." This difficult Buddhist term may be translated roughly to mean that it is a dirty world, in which warriors all fight for their own personal gain and profit, and one must free oneself from that world and work toward

creating, as one might say, heaven on earth. Ieyasu was inspired by this advice and decided then to work toward building a pure world in Japan.

The guiding national principle of the Tokugawa government was to maintain peace, which dovetailed conveniently with the fundamental interest of the ruling Tokugawa family in sustaining its position as the preeminent feudal power. The role of the emperor was nominal, and actual power rested in the hands of the shogun. A rule-based system neutralized the political power of the clans through policies of government land control, currency regulation, military dominance, and purges of rival leaders.

To build the "heaven on earth," the Tokugawa government also imposed a policy of seclusion and isolation, which lasted from 1639 to 1853. Ieyasu's decision to close the nation's doors was a result of the mercantilist designs of the Europeans, who had sent ships to Japan. No trade was conducted. Only the Dutch were allowed to keep a commercial post at Dejima in Nagasaki. Also, population control was exercised in order to prevent an increase in the country's inhabitants in the midst of its underdevelopment.

During this period, Japan was poor but peaceful. Haiku poetry, drama, and Kabuki flourished, as well as painting, ukiyoe, and literature. With the blossoming of the arts, the Japanese enjoyed spiritual fulfillment. Japan's 250 years of peace are practically unmatched in any country's history.

But the tightly controlled "heaven on earth" fell prey to internal conflicts and international exposure. Within Japan, problems were stimulated by the development of clan monopolies, new market growth, a greater emphasis on material life, a weakening of currency control, and an economically disenfranchised samurai class.

International pressures also emerged. When Commodore Matthew C. Perry led the U.S. black ships into the Japanese harbor at Uraga-kō, Japan was forced open. The country was thrown into turmoil. Japan's leaders of that era coped relatively well with this turmoil, not by turning to foreign powers for assistance but by carrying out a virtually bloodless revolution.

The Meiji Restoration of 1868 marked the official end of the system the Tokugawa established, and the Japanese set about building a modern nation. The primary objective of this era was to catch up with the industrialized West. In propelling forward the development of Japan, the entire structure and raison d'être of the nation were transformed. The goal was a "wealthy and strong nation." Political and bureaucratic leaders undertook drastic reforms of the economy and political system, emphasizing industrialization and militarization. They abolished old feudal domains and dismissed the warrior class. The Meiji government redrew administrative boundaries, amalgamating the 273 feudal domains of the Tokugawa shogunate into 48 prefectures. It also drafted a constitution, opened a parliament, and established a new, centralized administrative system.

A characteristic feature of the Meiji era was the adoption of what Chalmers Johnson later called "developmental capitalism." This is to say that the public sector took the initiative in building industry because the private sector had neither the money nor the power to do so. The government built Western-style shipyards, ironworks, and arsenals, while it annulled restrictions on the sale of land.

A second characteristic was the promotion of economic development by widening participation in the economy. The Dajokan (Cabinet) Order of November 5, 1880, mandated the sale of state-owned enterprises to private individuals and corporations. For example, the Yawata steelworks, established by the government, were privatized after achieving a certain degree of development. A more flexible, longer-range industrial policy was also adopted, which became the formula for Japan's subsequent growth and development until the present. Yet these policies also resulted in the subordination of the people to bureaucratic leadership.

The third characteristic was a strong emphasis on education. During the Tokugawa period, education was based on a samurai-dominated class system in which separate schools were established for samurai and commoners. In the fifth year of Meiji, under the Decree of 1872, the foundation for compulsory education was laid, which resulted in a weakening of class distinctions and the adoption of a system of merit achievement. The establishment of middle schools provided access to higher education. As a result, illiteracy was systematically eradicated. A competent professional class with basic Confucian ideals of service and loyalty emerged.

The government also established a system of military conscription. This reflected a general commitment to strong and modern armed forces.

But over time the goal of a "rich nation, strong army" was perverted—in a way, by its very own success. The newly rich nation projected its economic power abroad. Economic expansion in Asia and elsewhere proceeded aggressively, nourishing imperialist ambitions. The newly strong army assumed untoward influence in Japan. The militarization of Japanese society and policy went deep, and the emphasis shifted from legitimate defensive purposes to improper offensive ones. The direct result of this policy was the war in the Pacific, Japan's decisive defeat, and the destruction of the country.

After the war, the task of rebuilding Japan was begun. Demilitarization and democratization reformed Japanese society. The effort to rebuild a rich nation has been relentlessly pursued ever since. With the exception of the prewar national objective of building a strong army, the Meiji era national policy remained intact, as it does to this day. But by 1968, exactly 100 years after the Meiji Restoration, the objective of making Japan rich and prosperous had been more or less achieved. In that year, the balance of payments finally went from deficit to surplus, and the nominal per capita gross national product (GNP) caught up, symbolically, with the Western world's average.

Japanese leaders have yet to understand that with the achievement of full national development after a 100-year struggle a new national policy must be devised. Instead, they have continued to work within old frameworks. The pursuit of national wealth has become single-minded. Prosperity has come to be measured in wholly economic terms, with emphasis on net inflows of currency and a concentration on the continued building up of gross national product. As a result, Japanese national policy since 1968 has proven disastrous even though surplus balances of payments have become permanent, Japanese acquisitions of overseas real estate and foreign corporations continue to mount, and per capita GNP continues to increase.

Internationally, Japan faces mounting criticism from a citizenry weary of Japanese investment insensitive to the feelings of the local people. Although many communities value the jobs provided by Japanese companies, most resist the growing dominance of Japan's economy in many major industrial sectors as well as the closed trading doors behind which the Japanese economy itself is shielded.

Domestically, Japan also pays a price for its success. Its social capital has not kept pace with its fiscal capital. Savings have been invested in speculative real estate. Land prices in the Tokyo metropolitan area have skyrocketed, triggering a hike in nationwide land values. Consequently, 3 percent of the entire world's land area accounts for 60 percent of its value. Wage earners are still unable to buy modest homes in a Tokyo suburb. This has broken what the Japanese were once proud of—a fair social structure in which differences in income were relatively small. Japan has a new rich and a new poor, that is, those who have land and those who do not. The morals of Japan have been badly corrupted by the ready availability of cash and favors.

This, then, is the Japanese crisis: Either Japan will remain fixated on an objective that is long outdated in historical terms, keeping its nose firmly to the grindstone of profit generation, deaf to the mounting chorus of frictions arising from this policy, or Japanese thinking about the nation's identity and its role in the world will begin to evolve, such that Japan will become a new kind of nation, based on new principles. The national objective of making the country prosperous was certainly entirely appropriate at the outset of the Meiji era, when Japan was still a poor, agricultural country. Now that Japan has caught up with the West, however, it must adopt quite different objectives.

A Second Meiji Reform—Japan's Perestroika

The time for reform is ripe. Reform has emerged as a real possibility—and certainly as a clear necessity—with the bursting of the Japanese bubble. The Japanese can no longer afford the luxury of ignoring new realities as the economy begins to suffer under the weight of accumulated frictions.

Japan's Meiji reform period provides a glimpse of how the country can survive in the next century and beyond. Japan must embark on a reform as ambitious as that of the Meiji era and its contemporary counterpart in the Gorbachev-era perestroika. The nation needs a new sense of purpose: a new philosophy should be adopted—*kyosei*—of living together in harmony with all of the peoples of the world. Japan should stop the policy of making only Japan rich and focus its priorities on its people, rather than industry, with the objective of offering them a better life. A more global sense of purpose and identity requires also a shifting of emphasis away from the public sector to private initiative. Moreover, it requires that the whole Japanese nation be involved in this process.

Political reform should include the following. The present centralized government should decentralize its power in order to vitalize local regions. The number of members of parliament should be reduced to curb excesses. Administrative reform should also be implemented. The present administration is inherited from the Meiji days. This means, for example, that the Ministry of International Trade and Industry still exists to protect and nurture only domestic indus-

tries; the Ministry of Agriculture, Forestry, and Fisheries exists to protect and foster only domestic agriculture and fisheries; and the Ministry of Finance continues to protect and nurture only the domestic financial sector. It is not surprising that they are unpopular outside Japan.

The interests of the producer should be deemphasized in favor of meeting the needs of the consumer. During the years when national policy gave priority to building industry, a high level of production was given paramount consideration. With this objective achieved, emphasis must now be placed on rewarding ordinary citizens. Policies in such areas as agriculture, education, taxation, and industry should also be changed to fit the principle of *kyosei*.

Rather than amassing ever larger international balance of payments surpluses, the virtual monopolization of which by Japan has created obvious international problems, money should be spent to improve infrastructure. Houses should be built, facilities improved, and social capital developed.

The education program must also be revised and renewed. Prior to Meiji, education was "liberal." The emphasis was on teaching music and the arts and stressing philosophy and ethics with the objective of raising members of a moral society. After the Restoration, education became a tool of the national obsession to catch up with the industrial countries and it provided an intensive curriculum in technology and practical skills and knowledge. This method continues today, with the result that Japan's educational system has become severely distorted toward competition for superior grades, which forces children to attend mind-numbing extracurricular cram schools from kindergarten onward. The abuse of education must be stopped and the emphasis on liberal studies renewed.

Moreover, the responsibility for economic leadership should be shifted from the government to the people. While Japan was in the process of modernization, the economy was managed effectively by the bureaucracy, although this situation generated an overly close connection between government and industry. Because this relationship continued long after the original objective of catching up with the West had been achieved, it is not surprising that the Ministry of Finance became involved in developments such as the recent scandals in the security industry. The need to realize true democracy will require a shift from public to private leadership.

The Private Sector in the Twenty-First Century

The prescriptions included here under my ethical state initiative have applications outside Japan as well. In fact, the emphasis on private leadership and on empowering individuals and non-governmental institutions is universally applicable in the kind of world in which we live at the turn of the millennium.

The world today is beset with a host of serious problems: underdevelopment, uneven development, environmentally destructive development, famine, and their international consequences in the form of regional instability, economic friction, terrorism, and war. Politicians and bureaucrats are charged with bringing stability and peace to the world, but their apparently waning capacity to resolve these and other world problems must be a source of deep concern. What sets these problems apart from their counterparts of decades or centuries past is their global character, yet politicians

are by definition nationally oriented. They are elected to give top priority to the interests of their constituencies. National interests must prevail in their thinking over global ones. Bureaucrats are charged with maintaining or expanding the interests of their respective ministries, something that often takes precedence over national priorities and always over global ones. What is occurring is a clash of national egos that is throwing the world into confusion.

It is a part of human nature that we are reluctant to be seriously involved in issues that are not in our immediate self-interest. Unlike saints, ordinary people cannot be expected to do things that are to their disadvantage. Today there is only one entity whose effort to create stability in the world matches its self-interest. That entity is a corporation acting globally. Of course, private enterprises are governed above all by the pursuit of profit and survival in the marketplace; also, their role in supporting national well-being by employing people is well understood. But their interests extend well beyond profits. Maintenance of the free market system and world peace are clearly in their interest as well. This is especially true of those enterprises that cross national borders—the growing majority of significant enterprises—and thus transcend political, cultural, and even racial differences. Today, the multinational corporation has given way to the truly global corporation that operates in a world virtually without borders. Corporations have the people, resources, and networks to create wealth around the world. As the only entities actually creating wealth, corporations must be involved in issues beyond the scope of business. Whereas politicians and bureaucrats are seemingly inefficient at working toward the realization of human values, corporations can play a growing, even dominant role in this area. International enterprises—companies with global operations—should, therefore, exercise leadership.

This has not, of course, been the traditional role for corporations. But a corporation should strive to become globally conscious by evolving through four stages. The first is existence as a "purely capitalistic corporation" that invigorates the economy but also exploits labor and leads to strained labor-management relations. Thus, past corporate behavior has emphasized raising profits for the benefit of shareholders by producing and marketing goods. The second stage is a "corporation sharing destiny" and is typified by companies in which management and labor work closely together to resolve tensions in industrial relations (this type has been criticized by some consumers because of its propensity to put corporate interests before others). The third stage is seen when a corporation goes beyond profit maximization to fulfill its corporate responsibilities to society, although with a worldview limited to one country or region, such that these activities often create frictions abroad. The fourth, and most highly evolved, type of company is a global corporation, one that contributes positively to the prosperity of the entire world through profitable business. In the spirit of *kyosei*, this corporation resolves industrial conflicts and social and international friction.

Global corporations should not just resolve trade friction. They have an obligation to establish manufacturing operations in developing countries, to transfer technology to them, and to help them to be self-sufficient. Localization, or integration with local communities, is the most important question facing global corporations in the twenty-first century (it is also the basic requisite for long-term development of overseas operations). It means reinvesting profits in the countries in which companies operate, thereby contributing to local employment, central and municipal government finances in host countries, foreign currency earnings through exports, and technological progress.

Global corporations can make another important contribution to the global future—to the environment. They play the critical role in countering the depletion of the world's natural resources and the destruction of the environment. Linked with this problem is the fateful question as to whether the deteriorating world will be able to feed its rapidly growing population and even to sustain life on earth. This is the vital imbalance between mankind today and in the future. Global corporations must be positively committed to the challenges of this overriding environmental issue.

Building the Global Corporation

All companies expanding into overseas markets should strive to become companies of the fourth type—the truly global, responsible corporation. The company that I lead, Canon Inc., has taken these tasks seriously. Essentially, Canon started in the second category outlined above, evolved to the third, and is now striving to attain the fourth. Canon adopted a kind of perestroika program of its own in 1976 in the form of a six-year policy aimed at making the company a *yuryo kigyo*, an "excellent company," or "an enterprise of the top ranks in all respects."

Yuryo kigyo reforms are based on five major strategies: a new corporate philosophy, research and development (R&D), diversification, management globalization, and organization. The new corporate philosophy is grounded

53

in the notion of *kyosei*, or mutual prosperity and harmony. It reflects the company's commitment to serve the human race and the world. This goal combines an abstract ideal with a practical program of creating a premier corporation.

Canon's second strategy was to strengthen research and development. "Technology diplomacy" was promoted to attract innovative technologies or jointly conduct research and development with other corporations. For this purpose, Canon's parent companies invested, on a nonconsolidated basis, more than 10 percent of sales in R&D. As a result, Canon was awarded more U.S. patents in 1987 than any other company and has remained in the top three.

The third strategy was diversification. Twenty years ago, cameras represented nearly all of Canon's products; by 1990, they accounted for only 15 percent of Canon's total revenues. Diversification allows Canon to keep up with changing times, thus ensuring its survival and promoting employment in perpetuity. At Canon, diversification has not been pursued through the usual route of mergers and acquisitions (nor have they been used as a means for growth). Canon has emphasized diversification within peripheral lines, enabling the use of existing marketing channels and technology, which is the safest kind of diversification. It has also pursued the riskier diversification of related lines, which capitalizes on either existing technology or marketing channels. An example is Canon's diversification into office machines. Canon has also pursued vertical integration in either an upstream or downstream direction (going upstream means adding value by producing components in-house rather than using outside sources, and going downstream means creating the ability

to provide service to customers instead of commissioning sales and service by outside companies). Canon has also explored diversification into non-related business, but reluctantly, given the high risks associated with new technologies and markets.

Canon's fourth strategy emphasizes management globalization. This entails the globalization and rationalization of marketing, production, and R&D. These goals are pursued under its commitment to *kyosei*. Although Canon competes with companies in the United States and Europe, it also works closely with Texas Instruments, Hewlett Packard, Apple, and Kodak, for example. It is currently working with Lepton in the field of semiconductor printing technologies, with ECD in solar cells, and with NeXT in computer technology.

In keeping with *kyosei* principles, Canon pursues joint ventures or capital participation in the United States only under certain conditions: that it remain a minority shareholder; that it provide what other parties require, such as capital and production technology; that it produce the benefits of R&D in the United States; and that it market them worldwide. In 1979, Canon established an Advanced Technology Department (ATD) in the United States, strengthening its own Products Technology Research Division and R&D operations. Today, Canon has two research laboratories in the United States and one each in Britain, France, and Australia.

Globalization does not mean mercantilism and monopolization. Effective globalization means effective localization. As developed at Canon, this means contributing to local communities through the company's business activities and becoming a premier corporate citizen welcomed by local residents. More specifically, this means reinvesting profits in the countries in which Canon operates, with the benefits specified earlier.

The fifth strategy of *yuryo kigyo* is organization. Canon's system is what may be called a centralized-decentralization, reflecting a management strategy based on efficiency and company size. In 1978, Canon switched to a new management approach, using a matrix system and making each product group and geographical region responsible for its own decision making and revenue development. The new management system required that each product group have its own exclusive factories to increase rationalization. For example, Toride was to manufacture only business machines, Kosugi, optical products, and Fukushima, Tamagawa, and Tochigi, camera products. As Canon diversified and expanded, it also trained an able body of overseas managers through the International Operations Headquarters, which took on the concerns of overseas marketing strategies and structures as well as managerial training of staff members appointed to positions abroad.

This strategy has served Canon well—it is becoming a stage four responsible corporate citizen without sacrificing its profit-generating abilities. Canon was first listed among *Fortune* magazine's world's biggest industrial corporations in 1975, and the growth index for companies listed continuously from 1975 to 1990 shows Canon with the highest growth rate.

With Canon's financial success, it has been able to develop itself into a globally conscious corporation. In 1980–1981, Canon expanded its *yuryo kigyo* policy and focused on global consciousness. Rather than simply operating as a stage two company servicing the needs of its employees, Canon made a commitment to work for the betterment of the entire human race. In the spirit of *kyosei*, it aimed to develop itself into an enterprise that conducted operations worldwide and was capable of contributing to global prosperity and the well-being of mankind. Specifically, Canon's goal was to increase profits, reinvest earnings, and expand employment opportunities throughout the world.

In 1985 Canon launched a program to discuss its future at all levels of the company. The result was the definition of new goals for the twenty-first century, the adoption of the *kyosei* philosophy, and our commitment to becoming a global corporation.

As argued above, integration with local communities is the basic requisite for long-term development of overseas operations. It is also the most important challenge facing corporations in the twenty-first century. Globalization has also required efforts to address the imbalances between current and future generations in terms of population, environment, and resources. At Canon plants we are doing everything in our power to avoid the emission of chlorofluorocarbons (CFCs) and carbon dioxide. Throughout the world we retrieve and recycle cartridges of personal copiers and laser printers. The company also invests in research on photovoltaic cells as part of the ongoing search for clean energy sources in the future.

This digression on Canon is made not simply to tout the virtues of a single firm. Rather, it points to the way in which reform can revitalize organizations and empower them to expand their scope of endeavors such that they are able to play a catalytic role in positive global change. Perestroika does not begin without a good deal of boldness, and it is not implemented without a good deal of upheaval. But without perestroika, the institutions of the state and of business are doomed to growing crisis if not eventual irrelevance. Canon's rebirth is merely a testament to the broader changes sweeping the international business community, changes that in many ways are far beyond those that decision makers in government have even begun to grasp. And unless the reforms at Canon and elsewhere are paralleled by a new vision of Japan's identity and purposes, they will be for nought.

Conclusion

The choice confronting Japan today is stark: face the pain of emerging as a more mature political and economic actor on the global scene, or struggle to cope with the growing domestic and international frictions produced by a national policy decades out of date. The courageous program of perestroika begun by Mikhail Gorbachev, like the Meiji reform of Japan in the nineteenth century, suggests some of the challenges confronting Japan today. Japanese politicians can continue to speak politely about national growth, but the Japanese political system is faltering under a chronic crisis of corruption and fatigue. They can continue to repeat the fine slogan, "Japan must contribute to the world," but their words are trite and meaningless unless a system is created to realize this high ideal.

Japan has been fortunate to find friends in the world who have helped it through difficult times. But continued deference and second-class political status is the least appropriate way to express Japanese gratitude for the assistance shown it in the years after the war. In those years, General Douglas MacArthur characterized Japan as a 12-year old youth—but today that youth has passed into young adulthood and must now attain its own identity and independence. This does not mean adolescent rebellion; rather, it means partnership and trust. The time for a new, modern, and better Japan to emerge is now.

If Japan can successfully reform itself, it will become a key and effective partner of the United States, Europe, and others in leadership for the twenty-first century. Cultural differences will prove an occasional obstacle to cooperation, but the concerns and objectives that bind the nations of the world together are today more important than the ones that divide us. Corporations in Japan and elsewhere can and must play a critical role because their survival is directly linked to world stability. Given the scale of the problems of waning prosperity, pollution, and instability already present in the 1990s, we must waste no time in resolving the major issues of the world together.

Losing the Moment?
The United States and the
World After the Cold War

Zalmay Khalilzad

THREE YEARS AFTER the collapse of the Soviet Union, the United States is heading toward squandering a once-in-a-lifetime opportunity to shape the future of the world because it still does not have a broadly agreed upon vision and a grand strategy for the new era. The United States cannot succeed in shaping the post–cold war world unless it knows what shape it wants the world to take, understands what it takes to mold international relations in accordance with that vision, and has the will to see the task through. Without a strategy, the United States will tend to lose the initiative in world affairs and be placed in a reactive mode.

The lack of vision endangers the completion of even modest tasks. An administration can neither evaluate specific policy decisions adequately, nor reach an effective consensus with respect to them, without first constructing a framework for guiding policy, setting priorities, and deciding what constitute vital U.S. interests. Absent such a framework it will be more difficult to decide what is important and what is not, to determine which threats are more serious than others, and to develop coherent approaches to respond to new challenges. Policy on many issues will be ambivalent and uncertain and will lack staying power. Short-term and parochial interests will take priority over longer-term, national interests.

Without a broadly agreed architectural framework, gaining widespread bipartisan support for policy also becomes harder, as has been evident in recent discussions of foreign and security policy. Sustaining popular support and staying the course for particular policies become harder if the costs of implementation increase but the commitment cannot be explained in terms of a national interest and a strategy on which broad agreement has been achieved.

The Search for a New Vision

Despite efforts by both the Bush and Clinton administrations, three years after the end of the Soviet Union, no

Zalmay Khalilzad is program director for strategy, doctrine, and force structure of RAND's Project AIR FORCE. From 1990 to 1993 he was assistant under secretary of defense for policy planning.

The Washington Quarterly • 18:2

grand strategy has yet jelled and there is no consensus on overarching national security objectives. It appears that the United States is still trying to get its strategic bearings.

With the disintegration of the Soviet Union, Secretary of Defense Dick Cheney's department put forward a new defense strategy—the "Regional Defense Strategy"—which emphasized precluding any hostile power from dominating a region critical to U.S. interests; strengthening and extending the alliances among democratic and like-minded powers; and helping reduce the likelihood of conflict by reducing the sources of instability.[1] The Regional Defense Strategy did not jell as the nation's grand strategy. There was an intense but brief debate when versions of the document were leaked. Although President George Bush appeared supportive of the concept as indicated in some of his statements, he did not try actively to build political support for it. Given the dangers involved in any systemic shift in power, President Bush managed the disintegration of the Soviet Union extremely well. But because of the deteriorating domestic economic situation during the last year of his presidency, he did not push for a broad political consensus on a new grand strategy. Besides, an election year may not be the best time for generating such a consensus.

In July 1994, a year and a half after coming to power, the Clinton administration published its *National Security Strategy of Engagement and Enlargement.* Like the Regional Defense Strategy of the previous administration, President Bill Clinton's document proposes strengthening and adapting the alliances among the market democracies. Similarly, it emphasizes regional threats. It goes further, however, in its emphasis on peacekeeping operations,

in highlighting the importance of economic issues and the global expansion of democracy, and in its concern about environmental issues. It also emphasizes a readiness to "participate in multilateral efforts to broker settlements of internal conflicts." Similarly, it states that "our forces must prepare to participate in peacekeeping, peace enforcement and other operations in support of these objectives." Other than globalizing democracy, the document does not have a unifying concept. It does not deal with some of the tough issues such as how to hedge against Russian reimperialism and Chinese expansionism. It also does not provide a clear sense of priorities.[2]

For most of his presidency, Clinton's handling of foreign and security policy has been controversial. Although the president has committed himself to building a "new public consensus" for "active engagement abroad" no determined effort toward achieving that consensus has been made so far.

Besides the problems with the content of what has been proposed and inadequate efforts to build consensus on a new grand strategy, two other broader factors have played a role in the absence of broadly agreed upon grand strategy. One is the fact that American culture is disinclined toward great strategic design. The task is made even harder by a second reason: an underlying and widely held belief that the world is more uncertain now compared to the cold war period—making both the development and broad acceptance of a grand strategy more difficult.

But this assumption of greater uncertainty is only partially and only retrospectively correct. The cold war world was not truly much more certain than the world of today—at least not to those who were players in the struggle. Even though the enemy was known, it was never easy to predict Soviet behavior and developments around the world. "Kremlinology" was an almost mystical science, and as developments showed, U.S. information and understanding of what was really happening in the Soviet Union were often well off the mark. Nor was there always a consensus over policy; there were major disagreements about issues such as arms control and Vietnam. Even so, during the Cold War the United States was relatively certain of its overall objectives and priorities among them. Now it is not. This is the critical difference between the Cold War and the current era.

The United States' Possible Visions

Given the opportunity costs, the United States should no longer delay the development of a vision and a national grand strategy. The shift in the tectonics of power confronts Washington with several options. The choice that the United States makes is not only important for setting the country's global direction for this new era, but also for the major impact it will have on the calculations of others.

As the victor in the Cold War, the United States can choose among several strategic visions and grand strategies. It could abandon global leadership and turn inward. Alternatively, it could seek to give up leadership gradually by reducing the U.S. global role and encouraging the emergence of a seventeenth- to nineteenth-century style balance of power structure with spheres of influence. Third, it could seek, as its central strategic objective, to consolidate its global leadership and preclude the rise of a global rival.

Neo-Isolationism

In the short run, abandoning global leadership and turning inward could be an attractive option. It would result in a significant reduction in defense expenditures—although how much money the United States would really save over either the short or the long run should it adopt such a strategy has not been seriously studied.[3] Such a policy would also mean that U.S. servicemen and servicewomen would be less likely to be put in harm's way in places like Bosnia or Iraq, Haiti or Somalia. The reduction in defense burden could help deal with the budget deficit and improve U.S. economic competitiveness, especially because, at the same time, many foreign competitors would have to increase their defense expenditures. Ignoring foreign issues would enable the United States to concentrate on and solve its many domestic problems more effectively.

Furthermore, in many cases, allies to whose defense the United States has been committed no longer need it (e.g., the Soviet threat to Western Europe has disappeared and the current threats to Europe are much smaller by comparison) and should be able to manage on their own (e.g., South Korea has over twice the population and many times the gross national product [GNP] of North Korea). The commitment of the United States to the defense of an ally like South Korea may only serve to enable its government to spend less on defense and focus more on strengthening its economy.

Realistically and over the longer term, however, a neo-isolationist approach might well increase the danger of major conflict, require a greater U.S. defense effort, threaten world peace, and eventually undermine U.S. pros-

59

perity. By withdrawing from Europe and Asia, the United States would deliberately risk weakening the institutions and solidarity of the world's community of democratic powers and so establishing favorable conditions for the spread of disorder and a possible return to conditions similar to those of the first half of the twentieth century.

In the 1920s and 1930s, U.S. isolationism had disastrous consequences for world peace. At that time, the United States was but one of several major powers. Now that the United States is the world's preponderant power, the shock of a U.S. withdrawal could be even greater.

What might happen to the world if the United States turned inward? Without the United States and the North Atlantic Treaty Organization (NATO), rather than cooperating with each other, the West European nations might compete with each other for domination of East-Central Europe and the Middle East. In Western and Central Europe, Germany—especially since unification—would be the natural leading power.

Either in cooperation or competition with Russia, Germany might seek influence over the territories located between them. German efforts are likely to be aimed at filling the vacuum, stabilizing the region, and precluding its domination by rival powers. Britain and France fear such a development. Given the strength of democracy in Germany and its preoccupation with absorbing the former East Germany, European concerns about Germany appear exaggerated. But it would be a mistake to assume that U.S. withdrawal could not, in the long run, result in the renationalization of Germany's security policy.

The same is also true of Japan. Given a U.S. withdrawal from the world, Japan would have to look after its own security and build up its military capabilities. China, Korea, and the nations of Southeast Asia already fear Japanese hegemony. Without U.S. protection, Japan is likely to increase its military capability dramatically—to balance the growing Chinese forces and still-significant Russian forces. This could result in arms races, including the possible acquisition by Japan of nuclear weapons. Given Japanese technological prowess, to say nothing of the plutonium stockpile Japan has acquired in the development of its nuclear power industry, it could obviously become a nuclear weapon state relatively quickly, if it should so decide. It could also build long-range missiles and carrier task forces.

With the shifting balance of power among Japan, China, Russia, and potential new regional powers such as India, Indonesia, and a united Korea could come significant risks of preventive or preemptive war. Similarly, European competition for regional dominance could lead to major wars in Europe or East Asia. If the United States stayed out of such a war—an unlikely prospect—Europe or East Asia could become dominated by a hostile power. Such a development would threaten U.S. interests. A power that achieved such dominance would seek to exclude the United States from the area and threaten its interests—economic and political—in the region. Besides, with the domination of Europe or East Asia, such a power might seek global hegemony and the United States would face another global Cold War and the risk of a world war even more catastrophic than the last.

In the Persian Gulf, U.S. withdrawal is likely to lead to an intensified struggle for regional domination. Iran and Iraq have, in the past, both sought regional hegemony. Without U.S. protection, the weak oil-rich states of the Gulf Cooperation Council (GCC) would be unlikely to retain their independence. To preclude this development, the Saudis might seek to acquire, perhaps by purchase, their own nuclear weapons. If either Iraq or Iran controlled the region that dominates the world supply of oil, it could gain a significant capability to damage the U.S. and world economies. Any country that gained hegemony would have vast economic resources at its disposal that could be used to build military capability as well as gain leverage over the United States and other oil-importing nations. Hegemony over the Persian Gulf by either Iran or Iraq would bring the rest of the Arab Middle East under its influence and domination because of the shift in the balance of power. Israeli security problems would multiply and the peace process would be fundamentally undermined, increasing the risk of war between the Arabs and the Israelis.

The extension of instability, conflict, and hostile hegemony in East Asia, Europe, and the Persian Gulf would harm the economy of the United States even in the unlikely event that it was able to avoid involvement in major wars and conflicts. Higher oil prices would reduce the U.S. standard of living. Turmoil in Asia and Europe would force major economic readjustment in the United States, perhaps reducing U.S. exports and imports and jeopardizing U.S. investments in these regions. Given that total imports and exports are equal to a quarter of U.S. gross domestic product, the cost of necessary adjustments might be high.

The higher level of turmoil in the world would also increase the likelihood of the proliferation of weapons of mass destruction (WMD) and means for their delivery. Already several rogue states such as North Korea and Iran are seeking nuclear weapons and long-range missiles. That danger would only increase if the United States withdrew from the world. The result would be a much more dangerous world in which many states possessed WMD capabilities; the likelihood of their actual use would increase accordingly. If this happened, the security of every nation in the world, including the United States, would be harmed.

At present, mainstream sentiment in the two major U.S. political parties rejects isolationism as a national strategy, even though both have elements favoring it. It is possible, however, that without a vision and grand strategy, the United States might follow policies that result in at least some of the consequences of a neo-isolationist strategy.

Return to Multipolarity and Balance of Power

Another option for the United States would be to rely on a balance of power to preclude the emergence of a "superpower" that could threaten U.S. security. This approach has some positive features, but it is also dangerous. Based on current realities, the other potential great powers are Japan, China, Germany (or the European Union [EU]), and Russia. In the future this list could change. A new great power—such as India, Brazil, or Indonesia—could emerge, or one of the existing ones—such as Russia or China—could decline or disintegrate and cease to be a great power.

Some argue that the world is inevitably heading toward a multiplicity of roughly equal great powers and that the United States should facilitate such a development. This approach starts from the assertion that, based on economic indices, the world already consists of several great powers and assumes that the diffusion of wealth and technology will continue. It is further assumed that, over time, the current economic powers will become political and military powers commensurate with their economic strength; they will be obliged to do so because, in the post–cold war world, others will not perceive threats in the same way and so will not be willing to run risks for them.[4]

In a balance of power regime, NATO would gradually decline in importance and would ultimately disappear, or it would be subsumed, as the Russians now advocate, into a broader but less muscular organization such as the Organization on Security and Co-operation in Europe (OSCE). The U.S. presence in Western Europe would end as the West Europeans built up their capability and a balance of power emerged on the continent. The United States could affect the pace of such a development by, for example, announcing that it intended to withdraw from Europe by a specific date— thus giving impetus to a European military buildup to balance Russia.

For such a balance of power system to work, either Germany would have to substantially increase its military power or the EU would have to strengthen its internal unity and become a kind of superstate. The United States would continue to have a vital interest in preventing the domination of Europe—including Russia—by a single power. So, if the Germans decided to build up militarily to a force that appeared to threaten the rest of Europe, the United States could play its part by forming alliances with any European country or countries that sought to prevent German hegemony and by maintaining adequate forces in the United States and perhaps in

Great Britain. Problems unrelated to any attempt to establish hegemony over Europe, however, such as instability in the Balkans, East-Central Europe, or North Africa, would be the responsibility of the Europeans alone and the United States would not get militarily involved in conflicts in these regions.

Similarly, the United States would be unlikely to get involved militarily on the territory of the former Soviet Union; in general, it would accept a Russian sphere of influence there. The other European great powers (and perhaps also the United States) would not want Russia to reincorporate Ukraine, however, because, combined, Russia and Ukraine would have a military potential so much greater than any European state as to threaten to destroy the possibility of achieving a balance of power. Western Europe and Russia would both have interests in East-Central Europe and would have to try to work out rules for regulating their interactions.

In East Asia, the United States would similarly become a balancer against either China or a Japan that had built up its military capability. In the event of a serious imbalance between Japan and China, the United States could play a balancing role with forces based in the United States or possibly in some of the smaller states in the region. As in the case of Europe, the United States would seek to prevent the emergence of regional hegemony by shifting alliances; it would cooperate with other powers to protect common interests and be prepared to protect specific interests in the region, such as the lives and property of U.S. citizens.

In the Persian Gulf, in this framework, the United States and other major powers would oppose the domination of the region by any one power, because such a power would acquire enormous leverage over states that depend on the region's oil. At the regional level, the United States and other major powers could rely on a balance between Iran and Iraq to prevent regional hegemony. Assuming the great powers were willing to pursue a joint policy toward the Persian Gulf, the fact that the United States is relatively less dependent on the Gulf than either Western Europe or Japan would give it a strong bargaining position when the time came to allocate the burdens required by such a policy among the great powers. On the other hand, one or more great powers might be tempted to abandon the great power coalition and to support a potential hegemon in the Gulf in return for favorable access to the Gulf's resources and markets. Finally, the United States would have to be the dominant power affecting important security issues in the Americas.

Aside from the question of inevitability, a balance of power system would have certain advantages for the United States. First, the U.S. government could reduce defense expenditures (probably not by as much as with a neo-isolationist strategy) and deploy U.S. military force less often to world hot spots, because it would let other great powers take the lead in dealing with problems in their regions. Second, the United States would be freer to pursue its economic interests, even when they damaged its political relations with countries that had been, but were no longer, allies; only in the particular case that required the United States to ally with another great power to ward off a specific threat would it be constrained.

It is possible that in a balance of power system the United States would be in a relatively privileged position as compared to the other great powers.

Given the relative distance of the United States from other power centers, it might be able to mimic the former British role of an offshore balancer. As in the nineteenth century, the United States and other great powers would compete and cooperate to avoid hegemony and global wars. Each great power would protect its own specific interests and protect common interests cooperatively. If necessary, the United States would intervene militarily to prevent the emergence of a preponderant power.

But there are also several serious problems with this approach. First, there is a real question whether the major powers will behave as they should under the logic of a balance of power framework. For example, would the West European powers respond appropriately to a resurgent Russian threat, or would they behave as the European democracies did in the 1930s? The logic of a balance of power system might well require the United States to support a non-democratic state against a democratic one, or to work with one undesirable state against another. For example, to contain the power of an increasingly powerful Iran, the United States would have to strengthen Iraq. The United States may, however, be politically unable to behave in this fashion. For example, after the Iraqi victory against Iran in 1988, balance of power logic indicated that the United States should strengthen Iran. However, because of ongoing animosity in U.S.–Iranian relations, the nature of Iran's regime, and moral concerns, the United States could not implement such a strategy. There are many other examples. To expect such action is therefore probably unrealistic.

Second, this system implies that the major industrial democracies will no longer see themselves as allies. Instead, political, and possibly even military, struggle among them will become not only thinkable but legitimate.[5] Each will pursue its own economic interest much more vigorously, thereby weakening such multilateral economic institutions as the General Agreement on Tariffs and Trade (GATT) and the liberal world trading order in general. This would increase the likelihood of major economic depressions and dislocations.

Third, the United States is likely to face more competition from other major powers in areas of interest to it. For example, other powers might not be willing to grant the United States a sphere of influence in the Americas, but might seek, as Germany did in World War I, to reach anti-U.S. alliances with Latin American nations. Similarly, as noted above, another great power might decide to support a potential hegemon in the Persian Gulf.

Finally, and most important, there is no guarantee that the system will succeed in its own terms. Its operation requires subtle calculations and indications of intentions in order to maintain the balance while avoiding war; nations must know how to signal their depth of commitment on a given issue without taking irrevocable steps toward war. This balancing act proved impossible even for the culturally similar and aristocratically governed states of the nineteenth-century European balance of power systems. It will be infinitely more difficult when the system is global, the participants differ culturally, and the governments of many of the states, influenced by public opinion, are unable to be as flexible (or cynical) as the rules of the system require. Thus, miscalculations might be made about the state of the balance that could lead to wars that the United States might be unable to stay out of. The balance of power system failed in the past, producing World War I and other major conflicts. It might not work any better in the future—and war among major powers in the nuclear age is likely to be more devastating.

Global Leadership

Under the third option, the United States would seek to retain global leadership and to preclude the rise of a global rival or a return to multipolarity for the indefinite future. On balance, this is the best long-term guiding principle and vision. Such a vision is desirable not as an end in itself, but because a world in which the United States exercises leadership would have tremendous advantages. First, the global environment would be more open and more receptive to American values—democracy, free markets, and the rule of law. Second, such a world would have a better chance of dealing cooperatively with the world's major problems, such as nuclear proliferation, threats of regional hegemony by renegade states, and low-level conflicts. Finally, U.S. leadership would help preclude the rise of another hostile global rival, enabling the United States and the world to avoid another global cold or hot war and all the attendant dangers, including a global nuclear exchange. U.S. leadership would therefore be more conducive to global stability than a bipolar or a multipolar balance of power system.

Precluding the rise of a hostile global rival is a good guide for defining what interests the United States should regard as vital and for which of them it should be ready to use force and put American lives at risk. It is a good prism for identifying threats, setting priorities for U.S. policy toward various regions and states, and assessing needs for military capabilities and modernization.

To succeed in the long term in realizing this vision, the United States should adhere to the following principles as guidelines for its policies. It must:

- maintain and strengthen the "zone of peace"[6] and incrementally extend it;
- preclude hostile hegemony over critical regions;
- hedge against reimperialization by Russia and expansion by China while promoting cooperation with both countries;
- preserve U.S. military preeminence;
- maintain U.S. economic strength and an open international economic system;
- be judicious in the use of force, avoid overextension, and develop ways of sharing the burden with allies; and
- obtain and maintain domestic support for U.S. global leadership and these principles.

Why are these principles important and how can the United States pursue them effectively? The remainder of this article will focus on these issues.

Maintain, Strengthen, and Extend the Zone of Peace

In the course of building up the Western alliance, the United States helped create a community of nations in Western Europe and East Asia that was held together by more than just the Soviet threat. These nations shared common values, most important among them democracy and a commitment to free markets. War among these nations became unthinkable. This commonality of interests was expressed in the creation of organizations such as NATO and the Group of

Seven (G–7), and in bilateral treaties such as that between the United States and Japan. Under U.S. leadership, this group of nations pursued a policy of containing the Soviet Union until its collapse; in the post–cold war era, it is clear that, given continued unity, these nations will be strong enough to overpower any threat from outside their ranks. Thus, this community of nations may be called the "zone of peace." Maintaining, strengthening, and extending the zone of peace should be the central feature of U.S. post–cold war grand strategy.

Maintaining the zone of peace requires, first and foremost, avoiding conditions that can lead to renationalization of security policies in key allied countries such as Japan and Germany. The members of the zone of peace are in basic agreement and prefer not to compete with each other in realpolitik terms. But this general agreement still requires U.S. leadership. At present there is greater nervousness in Japan than in Germany about future ties with Washington, but U.S. credibility remains strong in both countries. The credibility of U.S. alliances can be undermined if key allies such as Germany and Japan believe that the current arrangements do not deal adequately with threats to their security. It could also be undermined if, over an extended period, the United States is perceived as either lacking the will or the capability to lead in protecting their interests.

In Europe, besides dealing with balancing Russian military potential and hedging against a possible Russian reimperialization, the near-term security threat to Germany comes from instability in East-Central Europe and to a lesser degree from the Balkans. For France and Italy, the threats come from conflicts in the Balkans, Islamic extremism, and the spread of WMD

65

and ballistic and cruise missiles to North Africa and the Middle East. For example, at present the Germans fear that conflicts and instability in East-Central Europe might "spill out" or "spill in." Such crises could set the stage for a bigger conflict and/or send millions of refugees to Germany. The Germans are divided on how to deal with the threat from the east. For now, however, they are focused on integrating the former East Germany and favor a U.S.-led alliance strategy rather than filling the vacuum themselves, as indicated in their substantial defense cuts. This is in part because of their confidence in the United States and the common values and interests they perceive among the allies, and in part because an alliance-based policy is cheaper for Germany than a unilateral approach. But should the Germans come to believe that the alliance will not or cannot deal with threats to their interests, they might well consider other options.

In East Asia, too, Japan favors alliance with the United States to deal with uncertainty about Russia, future Chinese military capability, including power projection, and the threat of nuclear and missile proliferation on the Korean peninsula. For the same reasons as Germany, Japan currently prefers to work with the United States. But the loss of U.S. credibility could also change Japan's calculations; the test will be how well the United States deals with North Korea's nuclear program.

As long as U.S.-led allied actions protect their vital interests, these nations are less likely to look to unilateral means. This implies that the United States needs a military capability that is larger than might be required based on a definition of U.S. interests based on isolationism or the balance of power.

U.S. power and willingness to lead in protecting vital joint interests in Europe, East Asia, and the Middle East are necessary to preserve the zone of peace. In Europe these interests can be best served if NATO remains the primary entity to deal with the security challenge from instability and conflict to the south and the east and a possible revanchism in Russia. To perform this role, NATO must adapt by maintaining a robust military capability as a hedge against Russia's going bad; by preparing for the eventual membership of the nations of East-Central Europe in the alliance in coordination with EU expansion; and by developing the capability to deter and defeat threats from the south. NATO allies need to increase their ability to project power to perform these tasks. West Europeans have ample capability for self-defense but their capability for projecting power eastward or southward is far more limited. Even with increased European power projection capabilities, the United States would need to maintain a significant military force on the continent for an indefinite period—both because of military needs and to demonstrate its commitment and resolve.

Asia has no NATO-like multilateral alliance. The core security relationships are the U.S.–Japanese and U.S.–South Korean ties. Maintaining security ties with each other is important for both the United States and Japan, even though trade relations between the two have a greater potential to create mutual antagonism than trade relations between the United States and Germany. While North Korea remains hostile and militarily powerful and, in any case, in order to hedge against uncertainties in Russia and China, the United States needs to station sufficient force in the region to deter all three countries and, with reinforcements, defend critical U.S. interests while running only limited risks. At present the main military threat is a possible North Korean attack against South Korea. The United States and its Asian allies should explore the possibility of establishing multilateral security arrangements that can promote stability by increasing mutual trust and providing for effective burden sharing.

Within these constraints, it is in the U.S. interest and the interests of the other members of the zone of peace that the zone ultimately encompass the whole world. Unfortunately, this is not a near-term proposition. Many regions and states are not ready. The United States should seek to expand the zone selectively and help others prepare for membership.

The most important step that the United States and the other prosperous democracies can take is to assist others in adopting the economic strategies that have worked in North America, Western Europe, and East Asia and are being successfully implemented in parts of Latin America and elsewhere in Asia. Economic development and education are the most effective instruments for solving the problems of the nations outside the zone of peace.

Preclude Hostile Hegemony over Critical Regions

A global rival could emerge if a hostile power or coalition gained hegemony over a critical region, defined as one that contains economic, technical, and human resources such that a power that controlled it would possess a military potential roughly equal to, or greater than, that of the United States. It is, therefore, a vital U.S. interest (i.e., one that the United States should be willing to use force to protect) to avoid such a development. Although

this could change in the future, two regions now meet this criterion: East Asia and Europe. The Persian Gulf is critically important for a different reason—its oil resources are vital for the world economy.

In the long term, the relative importance of various regions can change. A region that is critical to U.S. interests now might become less important, while some other region might gain in importance. For example, Southeast Asia appears to be a region whose relative importance is likely to increase if the regional economies continue to grow as impressively as they have done in the past several years. The Gulf might decline if the resources of the region became less important for world prosperity because technological developments provided economically feasible alternative sources of energy.

At present, the risks of regional hegemony in Europe and East Asia are very small. This is due in large part to the alliance of the key states of these regions with the United States, which endorses the presence of U.S. forces and the credibility of U.S. commitments. It is thus vital that U.S. alliances in Europe and East Asia be maintained but adapted to meet the challenges of the new era. During the Cold War, the U.S. role in these two regions not only deterred threats from the Soviet Union but also contained rivalries. In Europe, it is not in the U.S. interest for the EU either to become a superstate or to disintegrate. The former could ultimately pose a global challenge—Western Europe's economy is bigger than the U.S. economy. The latter could encourage mutual suspicion and contribute to renationalization and a possible repeat of the first half of the twentieth century.

At this point, the United States is the preponderant outside power in the Persian Gulf. Its position there helps to discourage the rise of a rival and will put it in a strong position to compete should one arise. U.S. preponderance serves the interests of the members of the zone of peace because it helps diminish the threat of interruption of oil supplies from the region. But the threat of hostile regional hegemony remains. The United States, with support from its allies, needs to maintain adequate military capability to deter and defeat the threat of regional hegemony from Iraq or Iran. The United States should seek greater contributions from its NATO allies and Japan in meeting the security challenges in this region. Washington and its allies must also encourage regional cooperation among the GCC states and help them cope with the contradictory pressures—liberal and fundamentalist—for domestic change that beset them. Given the recent progress in the Arab–Israeli conflict, U.S. security ties with Israel can help in dealing with threats from Iran or Iraq in the Gulf.

Hedge against Reimperialization in Russia

Russia is still trying to find a place for itself in the world. Although still weakening militarily and economically, as heir to the Soviet strategic nuclear arsenal it is capable of conducting an all-out nuclear attack on the United States. Consequently, it requires special attention under any circumstances. In the near term—10 years—Moscow is unlikely to pose a global challenge. Even in its current weakened condition, however, Russia can pose a major regional threat if it moves toward reimperialization. This scenario has been dubbed "Weimar Russia," denoting the possibility that, embittered by its economic and political troubles and humiliations, Russia may attempt to recover its past glory

by turning to ultranationalist policies, particularly the reincorporation of—or hegemony over—part or all of the old "internal" empire. In the aftermath of the December 1993 parliamentary elections and Vladimir Zhirinovsky's strong showing in them, many Russians indicated a strong preference for reincorporation of the so-called near abroad—the states on the territory of the former Soviet Union. But, more recently, concerns about costs and negative international reaction have resulted in a shift in favor of hegemony—Russian geopolitical and economic domination of weak but nominally independent states.

To avoid Russian hegemony over the near abroad, to say nothing of creating the groundwork for future cooperation on a whole range of international matters, the United States and the other members of the democratic zone of peace have a substantial interest in helping Russia become a "normal" country, that is, a country that does not hanker for an empire and whose domestic life is not distorted by overmilitarization. Ideally, it would become a prosperous, free market, Western-style democracy. Whether Russia will succeed in becoming a normal state is difficult to predict, but the stakes justify a major Western effort. Even so, the key determinant is Russian domestic politics, over which, under the circumstances, the United States can have only limited influence, and the domestic trends are not very hopeful.

As the United States encourages Russia to join the zone of peace and cooperate on specific issues based on common concerns, it is in the U.S. interest that Russia's neighbors, such as Ukraine, Kazakhstan, and Uzbekistan, be able to make any attempt by Russia to recreate the empire very costly, thereby deterring it. And should deterrence fail, such an approach would help sap its energies, undermining its prospects for becoming an effective global challenge. This does not mean that the United States needs hostile relations between these countries and Moscow; good economic and political relations between Russia and its neighbors are not inconsistent with U.S. interests. But discouraging the emergence of a very robust Commonwealth of Independent States and consolidating Ukrainian, Kazakh, and Uzbek independence should be the primary U.S. objective in dealing with these countries.

The United States and its allies have lost some opportunities here because economic problems and pressure from Russia have reduced support for independence in some of the newly independent states. To discourage Russian reincorporation of Ukraine by force, NATO must make it clear to Russia, and must convince its own publics and parliaments, including the U.S. Congress, that such an action would lead to a cutoff of economic assistance to Russia, to NATO membership for the nations of East-Central Europe on a much faster track—perhaps at once—than would be the case otherwise, and possibly to material support to a Ukrainian resistance movement and Russian isolation from the West. Without such preparations now, there is danger that, in the face of a possible Russian takeover of Ukraine, NATO expansion to East-Central Europe would not be politically supported because it would appear to be too provocative. Unfortunately, at times in the past the United States has appreciated its stake in a situation too late to express its intentions clearly enough to deter an aggressor. A clear and strong Western posture now should also strengthen those Russians who do not consider reimperialization to be in their country's interests.

But this is not only a military matter. The key for Ukraine and others is to carry out economic and political reforms to increase internal stability and reduce their vulnerability to Russian interference and domination. The United States, the EU countries, and Japan have a stake in helping Ukraine and others adopt significant economic reforms. To encourage such a development, the G–7 states should be willing to meet some of the costs of the transition to a market-oriented system.

Discourage Chinese Expansionism

China is another major power that might, over the long term and perhaps sooner than Russia, emerge as a global rival to the United States. China's economic dynamism, now also being reflected in its military development, ensures that—if domestic turmoil can be avoided—China will become an increasingly important player on the global scene in coming decades. The country has had dramatic economic growth. Between 1978 and 1992 its GNP increased by 9 percent annually. In 1992, that rate increased to 12 percent. Its foreign trade increased from $21 billion in 1978 to $170 billion in 1992. According to the International Monetary Fund, Chinese output may have exceeded $1.6 trillion dollars in 1992. The World Bank gives an even higher estimate: $2.3 trillion. Militarily, China has been increasing its power projection capability—both naval and air—in part by purchasing advanced equipment from Russia. If China continues to grow at a higher rate than the United States, at some point in the next century it could become the world's largest economy.[7] Such a development would produce a significant shift in relative economic power, with important potential geopolitical and military implications.

China, however, faces significant political uncertainties in its domestic politics, including a possible succession crisis on the death of Deng Xiaoping and the centrifugal tendencies unleashed by differential economic growth among the provinces. Indeed, Chinese weakness, not excluding a possible civil war that could disrupt economic prosperity and create refugee flows, may cause significant problems for its neighbors and the world community.

Assuming these difficulties can be avoided, the world will have to deal with the fact that China is not a "satisfied" power. Among the major powers, China appears more dissatisfied with the status quo than the others. Beyond Hong Kong and Macau, which will be ceded to China by the end of the century, it claims sovereignty over substantial territories that it does not now control, such as Taiwan, the Spratly Islands and the South China Sea generally, and the Senkaku Islands between China and Japan. Although China has abandoned communism as a global ideology and seems to have accepted the economic imperative of the global economy, it is still seeking its "rightful" place in the world geopolitically. How will China define its role as its power grows beyond its territorial interests? China appears to be seeking eventual regional predominance, a prospect opposed by Japan, Russia, and several other rising regional powers such as Indonesia and India.

Even without regional domination, China might become interested in becoming the leader of an anti-U.S. coalition based on a rejection of U.S. leadership generally or as it is expressed in such policies as nonproliferation and human rights. This is evident in its

assistance to Pakistani and Iranian nuclear programs. It is also clear that China is not as opposed to the North Korean nuclear program as the United States is. Some Chinese writing on strategy and international security expresses hostility to U.S. preponderance and implies the need to balance it. But China recognizes the importance of the United States—as a market for Chinese goods and as a source for technical training and technology. Without U.S. help China is less likely to achieve its economic and military objectives.

China, however, is decades away from becoming a serious global rival either by itself or in coalition with others, and its internal political development is likely to influence the type of foreign policy it pursues. In particular, its degree of democratization is likely to determine how much money and effort China is willing to devote to improving its international standing in the light of its immense development tasks at home. This provides the United States with ample strategic warning. For the near term, economic considerations are likely to be dominant in Chinese calculations. Nevertheless, China by itself or as the leader of a coalition of renegade states could complicate U.S.-led efforts to deal with issues such as proliferation and stability in the Persian Gulf and Northeast Asia. Chinese economic success confronts the United States with a dilemma. On the one hand, it increases Chinese potential to become a global rival. On the other, it might produce democratization, decentralization, and a cooperative China.

The United States should continue to pursue economic relations with China and encourage its integration in global economic and security regimes. It should also use the leverage of economic relations, which are very important to China, to continue to encourage Chinese cooperation in restraining nuclear and missile proliferation in places like Korea and Iran. But Chinese cooperation is likely to remain limited. While the United States continues to cooperate with China, it should be cautious in transferring to it technologies that have important military implications. It should also ensure that China's neighbors, such as Taiwan and the member states of the Association of Southeast Asian Nations, have the means to defend themselves. Working with other powers, especially Japan, Korea after unification, and Indonesia, the United States should preclude Chinese regional hegemony by maintaining adequate forces in the region. Without a U.S. presence in the region, as Chinese power grows, some states in the region are likely to appease China and move closer to it, while others such as Indonesia, Japan, and Vietnam would seek to balance it.

Preserve U.S. Military Preeminence

A global rival to the United States could emerge for several reasons. Because the main deterrent to the rise of another global rival is the military power of the United States, an inadequate level of U.S. military capability could facilitate such an event. This capability should be measured not only in terms of the strength of other countries, but also in terms of the U.S. ability to carry out the strategy outlined here. U.S. tradition makes the prospect of defense cuts below this level a serious possibility: historically, the United States has made this error on several occasions by downsizing excessively. It faces the same danger again for the longer term.

The issue is not only what levels of resources are spent on defense but also on what, for what, and how they are spent. For the United States to maintain its military preeminence, in addition to meeting possible major regional contingencies (MRCs), it needs specific capability in three areas.

First, besides maintaining a robust nuclear deterrent capability because of concerns with Russian and Chinese existing or potential nuclear postures, the United States needs to acquire increased capability to deter, prevent, and defend against the use of biological, chemical, and nuclear weapons in major conflicts in critical regions. The regional deterrence requirements might well be different from those with regard to the Soviet Union during the Cold War because of the character and motivations of different regional powers. U.S. ability to prevent and defend against use is currently very limited. In the near term, therefore, to deter use of WMD against its forces and allies, the United States may have to threaten nuclear retaliation.

To counter the spread of WMD and their means of delivery (especially ballistic and cruise missiles), the United States should seek to develop the capability to promptly locate and destroy even well-protected facilities related to biological, chemical, and nuclear weapons and their delivery systems. Equally important will be the ability to defend against the use of these weapons, including both active and passive defense. Deploying robust, multilayered ballistic missile defenses is vital for protecting U.S. forward-deployed forces and extending protection to U.S. allies, thus gaining their participation and cooperation in defeating aggression in critical regions.

Second, the United States needs improved capability for decisive impact in lesser regional crises (LRCs)—internal conflicts, small wars, humanitarian relief, peacekeeping or peacemaking operations, punitive strikes, restoration of civil order, evacuation of noncombatant Americans, safeguarding of security zones, and monitoring and enforcement of sanctions. Given the end of the Cold War, the United States can be more selective in deciding when to become involved militarily. It has not been selective enough during the past three years. Getting involved in LRCs can erode U.S. capabilities for dealing with bigger and more important conflicts. Nevertheless, some crises may occur in areas of vital importance to the United States—e.g., in Mexico, Cuba, South Africa, or Saudi Arabia—and others might so challenge American values as to produce U.S. military involvement. The United States might also consider participating with allies in some LRCs because of a desire either to extend the zone of peace or to prevent chaos from spreading to a critical region and thereby threatening the security of members of the zone of peace.

At present, LRCs are treated as lesser included cases of major regional conflicts, in the same way that some thought about regional conflicts in relation to a global conflict during the Cold War. It has been suggested that the United States "underestimated and misestimated the MRC requirements during the Cold War."[8] It would be a mistake to treat LRCs the same way now, especially because in the future U.S. forces will be much smaller than in the past and will provide a smaller margin for error. Even small LRCs can impose substantial and disproportionate demands on the support elements of U.S. forces—such as airborne warning and control systems (AWACS), SEAD (suppression of enemy air defenses), airlift, and communications. To be prepared for its MRC commitments and to have some increased LRC capabilities, the United States needs more airlift and changes in the MRC-driven training and organization of U.S. forces.

Third, it is essential to retain a mobilization base to reconstitute additional military capability in a timely fashion if things go badly in any major region. Without such a capability the United States is unlikely to be able to take prompt action, given the amount of strategic warning it is likely to receive.

To discourage the rise of another global rival or to be in a strong position to deal with the problem should one arise, focusing U.S. military planning for the future on Korea and the Persian Gulf, plus increased ability for LRC operations, is inadequate. Over time, although the threat from North Korea will probably disappear, other larger threats could emerge. As an alternative, the United States should consider moving toward sizing its forces largely by adopting the requirement that they be capable of simultaneously defeating the most plausible military challenges to critical U.S. interests that might be created by the *two* next most powerful military forces in the world that are not allied with the United States. Such a force should allow the United States to protect its interests in Asia, Europe, and the Persian Gulf. Such a force-sizing principle does not mean that U.S. forces have to be numerically as large as the combined forces of these two powers. It means that they should be capable of defeating them given relatively specific near-simultaneous scenarios of great importance to the United States—a Gulf and Asia scenario; a Europe and Asia scenario; or Asian and Gulf scenarios nearly simultaneously. Such an approach would give the United States a flexible global capability for substantial operations.

U.S. superiority in new weapons and

their use would be critical. U.S. planners should therefore give higher priority to research on new technologies, new concepts of operation, and changes in organization, with the aim of U.S. dominance in the military-technical revolution that may be emerging. They should also focus on how to project U.S. systems and interests against weapons based on new technologies.

The Persian Gulf War gave a glimpse of the likely future. The character of warfare will change because of advances in military technology, where the United States has the lead, and in corresponding concepts of operation and organizational structure. The challenge is to sustain this lead in the face of the complacency that the current U.S. lead in military power is likely to engender. Those who are seeking to be rivals to the United States are likely to be very motivated to explore new technologies and how to use them against it. A determined nation making the right choices, even though it possessed a much smaller economy, could pose an enormous challenge by exploiting breakthroughs that made more traditional U.S. military methods less effective by comparison.

For example, Germany, by making the right technical choices and adopting innovative concepts for their use in the 1920s and 1930s, was able to make a serious bid for world domination. At the same time, Japan, with a relatively small GNP compared to the other major powers, especially the United States, was at the forefront of the development of naval aviation and aircraft carriers. These examples indicate that a major innovation in warfare provides ambitious powers an opportunity to become dominant or near-dominant powers. U.S. domination of the emerging military-technical revolution, combined with the maintenance of a force

of adequate size, can help to discourage the rise of a rival power by making potential rivals believe that catching up with the United States is a hopeless proposition and that if they try they will suffer the same fate as the former Soviet Union.

Although, based on the strategy proposed here, the United States needs increased capabilities in some areas, it can cut back elsewhere and do things differently to free up resources for them. The United States still has too many bases. The country does not have the most effective process for making informed decisions for allocating resources for various types of force elements—that is, those forces that are required for current and future objectives and operational requirements. As things currently stand there is too much duplication in some key areas and capabilities that are not as relevant now as they were before. This is especially true in the maintenance and support area. For example, the navy, the air force, and industry all provide maintenance for military aircraft engines. Greater centralization here could save significant resources. The Defense Department is still being forced to buy weapon systems that it says it does not need and will not be needed under the proposed strategy. The current acquisition system is very costly and can save resources if streamlined.

Preserve U.S. Economic Strength

The United States is unlikely to preserve its military and technological dominance if the U.S. economy declines seriously. In such an environment, the domestic economic and political base for global leadership would diminish and the United States would probably incrementally withdraw from the world, become inward-looking,

73

and abandon more and more of its external interests. As the United States weakened, others would try to fill the vacuum.

To sustain and improve its economic strength, the United States must maintain its technological lead in the economic realm. Its success will depend on the choices it makes. In the past, developments such as the agricultural and industrial revolutions produced fundamental changes positively affecting the relative position of those who were able to take advantage of them and negatively affecting those who did not. Some argue that the world may be at the beginning of another such transformation, which will shift the sources of wealth and the relative position of classes and nations. If the United States fails to recognize the change and adapt its institutions, its relative position will necessarily worsen.

To remain the preponderant world power, U.S. economic strength must be enhanced by further improvements in productivity, thus increasing real per capita income; by strengthening education and training; and by generating and using superior science and technology. In the long run the economic future of the United States will also be affected by two other factors. One is the imbalance between government revenues and government expenditure. As a society the United States has to decide what part of the GNP it wishes the government to control and adjust expenditures and taxation accordingly. The second, which is even more important to U.S. economic well-being over the long run, may be the overall rate of investment. Although their government cannot endow Americans with a Japanese-style propensity to save, it can use tax policy to raise the savings rate.

Another key factor affecting the global standing of the United States is its current social crisis: the high rate of violence in cities, the unsatisfactory state of race relations, and the breakdown of families. Although it faces no global ideological rival, and although movements such as Islamic fundamentalism and East Asian neo-Confucian authoritarianism are limited in their appeal, the social problems of the United States are limiting its attractiveness as a model. If the social crisis worsens, it is likely that, over the long term, a new organizing principle with greater universal appeal will emerge and be adopted by states with the power and the desire to challenge the erstwhile leader.

Use Force Judiciously; Avoid Overextension; Share the Burden with Allies

Overextension is a mistake that some of the big powers have made in the past. Such a development can occur if the United States is not judicious in its use of force and gets involved in protracted conflicts in non-critical regions, thereby sapping its energies and undermining support for its global role. And when the United States uses force in critical regions, its preference should be to have its allies and friends contribute their fair share. Having the capability to protect U.S. vital interests unilaterally if necessary can facilitate getting friends and allies of the United States to participate—especially on terms more to its liking. It is quite possible that if the United States cannot protect its interests without significant participation by allies, it might not be able to protect them at all. For example, in the run-up to the Gulf war, several allies did not favor the use of force to evict Iraqi forces from Kuwait. If the military participation of these allies had been indispensable for military success against Iraq, Saddam Hussein's forces might still be in Kuwait and Iraq might now possess nuclear weapons.

When it comes to lesser interests the United States should rely on non-military options, especially if the stakes involved do not warrant the military costs. It has many options: arming and training the victims of aggression; providing technical assistance and logistic support for peace-keeping by the United Nations, regional organizations, or other powers; and economic instruments such as sanctions and positive incentives. The effectiveness of these non-military options can be enhanced by skillful diplomacy.

The members of the zone of peace have a common interest in the stability of Europe, North America, East Asia, and the Persian Gulf. Japan, for example, imports oil from the Gulf and exports to and invests in the other critical regions. The same is true of Europe. The U.S. global role benefits these other members as well as the United States. But there is a danger (known as the "free rider" problem) that the other members of the zone of peace will not do their fair share. This was a problem during the Cold War and it is unlikely to go away. It is a potentially important political issue in the United States, which does face a dilemma: As long as the United States is able and willing to protect common interests, other countries may be happy to rely on it, thereby keeping their political opposition under control, accepting no risk for their youth, and continuing to focus on their economies. But on the other hand, the United States would not want Germany and Japan to be able to conduct expeditionary wars. The United States will probably therefore be willing to bear a heavier military burden than its allies, but fairness

and long-term public support require that this disproportion not be excessive.

A balance needs to be struck and a formula has to be found to balance each country's contribution of "blood and treasure." In the Gulf war a substantial degree of burden sharing was realized. But the allies can do more. For the long term, one possible solution is to institutionalize burden sharing among the G–7 nations for the security of critical regions, including sharing the financial costs of military operations. Questions of out-of-area responsibility are important in peacetime, both on a day-to-day basis and in times of crisis and war. Burden-sharing steps would not obviate a significant and perhaps disproportionate U.S. military role in major crises in critical regions, but this is a price the United States should be willing to pay.

Obtain and Maintain Domestic Support for U.S. Leadership

Some might argue that, given the costs involved, the American people will not support a global leadership role for the United States. It can also be argued that the public might not support the level of defense expenditure required to pursue a global leadership strategy because domestic priorities are in competition for the same dollars. Public opinion polls indicate that Americans are focused on domestic concerns. Such a perception discouraged a serious debate on national security issues in the last presidential debate.

According to a recent poll, however, Americans support both U.S. involvement in world affairs (90 percent) and also want more attention to domestic issues (84 percent). A majority of Americans support peace "through strength."[9] Whether the public would in fact support a global leadership

75

strategy as outlined here is not known. Such a role is indeed not without costs. The cost of sustaining U.S. leadership is, however, affordable. At present the burden imposed by U.S. defense efforts, approximately 4 percent of GNP, is lighter than at any time since before the Korean War. The burden will shrink further as the economy expands, and the costs of leadership can be kept at a sustainable level by avoiding overextension and by more effective burden sharing among the members of the zone of peace.

Moreover, a global leadership role serves the economic interests of the United States. For example, it can facilitate U.S. exports, as recently seen in U.S. contracts with Saudi Arabia for the sale of aircraft and the modernization of Saudi telecommunication systems. As discussed earlier, the costs of alternative approaches to U.S. global leadership can ultimately be higher. Rather than undermining domestic prosperity, such a role can in fact facilitate it. The economic benefits of U.S. leadership have not been focused on either analytically or in the statements made to the public.

Global leadership and building a more democratic and peaceful world should also appeal to American idealism, a defining American characteristic. For sustaining domestic political support, this appeal might well be as important as appeals to more selfish and material American interests. In fact, having such a lofty goal can be a spur to the kinds of social and educational reforms that are necessary, rather than being an alternative to them.

Conclusion

As a nation, the United States is in a position of unprecedented military and political power and enjoys a unique leadership role in the world. Maintaining this position and precluding the rise of another global rival for the indefinite future is the best long-term objective for the United States. It is an opportunity the United States may never see again.

In the long run, this situation will not last if Americans turn inward or make the wrong choices. The question is whether the country will accept its responsibility—for reasons of self-interest and historical necessity—and meet the challenge of the new era with vision and resolve. The time has come for President Bill Clinton to make a compelling case for U.S. leadership and to seek to shape public attitudes. Without a vision, a strategy, and bipartisan support, he will fail to win public approval for U.S. global leadership, and his country will fail to seize this historic moment.

This article is drawn from a larger RAND study, "From Containment to Global Leadership? America and the World After the Cold War." The author would like to thank Cheryl Benard, Abe Shulsky, Andrew Marshall, David Chu, Paul Davis, Brent Bradley, Kevin Lewis, Scooter Libby, Chuck Miller, Craig Moore, Chris Bowie, Dan Drezner, and Ken Watman for their comments on the earlier drafts.

Notes

1. Dick Cheney, *Defense Strategy for the 1990s: The Regional Defense Strategy* (Washington, D.C.: Department of Defense, 1993).

2. William J. Clinton, *A National Strategy of Engagement and Enlargement* (Washington, D.C.: The White House, July 1994).

3. Among the questions that would have to be addressed are: Would the defense of the United States include the defense of North America or the Americas generally? How far into the Atlantic and Pacific Oceans would the defensive perimeter extend? Would the United States need a robust anti-ballistic missile defense?

4. Henry Kissinger, *Diplomacy* (New York, N.Y.: Simon & Schuster, 1994), p. 809.

5. It is, however, an interesting question

whether the governments of modern industrial democracies would be able to convince their populations to support preparations for (let alone, actually fight) major wars against each other on purely realpolitik terms, or whether ideological or nationalist motives would have to be adduced.

6. The concept of a "democratic zone of peace" was used in U.S. Defense Department documents in 1992. See Dick Cheney, *The Regional Defense Strategy* (Washington, D.C.: Department of Defense, January 1993). The concept was also used by Max Singer and Aaron Wildavsky in their 1993 book, *The Real World Order: Zones of Peace/Zones of Turmoil* (Chatham, N.J.: Chatham House Publishers, 1993).

7. *Economist*, October 1, 1994, p. 70. According to the *Economist*, if current trends hold by the year 2020 the Chinese economy might well be 40 percent larger than the U.S. economy.

8. Kevin Lewis, "The Discipline Gap and Other Reasons for Humility and Realism in Defense Planning," in Paul Davis, ed., *New Challenges for Defense Planning* (Santa Monica, Calif.: RAND, 1994), p. 103.

9. Times Mirror Center for People and the Press, *The People, the Press and Politics* (Washington, D.C., September 21, 1994), p. 37.

The United States: "Go East, Young Man"

Kishore Mahbubani

FOR THE LAST CENTURY or more, in the passage of ideas across the Pacific, the flow has fundamentally been one-way. Poverty-stricken and backward Asian societies have looked to the United States for ideas and for leadership. Not surprisingly a deeply ingrained belief has settled in the American mind that the U.S. mission in East Asia is to teach, not to learn. The time may have come for this mind-set to change. The fundamental purpose of this article is to trigger a discussion that will help to bring this about.

In a major reversal of a pattern lasting centuries, many Western societies—including the United States—are doing some major things fundamentally wrong while a growing number of East Asian societies are doing the same things right. The results are most evident in the economic sphere. In purchasing power parity terms, East Asia's gross domestic product (GDP) is already larger than that of either the United States or the European Community, and it will exceed that of both combined in the year 2005. Such economic prosperity, contrary to American belief, results not just from free market arrangements but also from the right social and political choices. Although many East Asian societies have assumed some of the trappings of Western society, they have also kept major social and cultural elements intact, elements that may explain their growing global competitiveness.

In reaching their present stages of development, many East Asian societies had to engage in deep critical examination of their societies to understand why they had fallen behind the West. The United States could wait until the evidence of East Asian success becomes too strong and overwhelming to ignore before deciding whether it should emulate the East Asians in critical self-analysis. Alternatively, it could do the prudent thing and begin reflecting now on why and how it needs to question its fundamental assumptions about its social and political arrangements and, in the process, learn a thing or two from East Asian societies.

Psychologically, this will be a difficult and painful process for many Americans. The conviction that American society, for all its flaws and blemishes, is the best society in the world runs deep in the American soul. So, too, does the conviction that American society need not contemplate funda-

Kishore Mahbubani, permanent secretary in the Ministry of Foreign Affairs and dean of the Civil Service College, Singapore, last served overseas as Singapore's permanent representative to the United Nations (1984–1989).

mental changes in the new global era. Given these convictions, there is bound to be strong resistance to many of the suggestions made in this essay. At the very outset, I should also admit and stress that I do not have the answers to many of the questions I raise. The main contribution I can make is to suggest that Americans have to address some fundamental questions. Because East Asians have benefited a great deal from well-intentioned American advice, it may be useful for Americans to have an honest feel for what many East Asians really think about key trends in American society, especially thoughts they are reluctant to express out of traditional Asian diffidence or politeness. In short, if this essay works, it should both encourage Americans to open new windows in their minds and, hopefully, give them a new understanding of real East Asian thinking.

In reading this essay, it is absolutely vital for an American to be aware that no East Asian society—perhaps not even North Korea—desires to see a weak or incapacitated United States that is unable to sustain its current global responsibilities. In more ways than one, the American presence has been immensely civilizing for East Asians. It has opened East Asian minds to the most generous aspects of Western civilization. By imposing a geopolitical order, however subtly and benignly, the United States has also prevented the emergence of conflicts among traditionally suspicious East Asian neighbors. In short, East Asians have much to be grateful for to the United States and, perhaps most important, an even more vital interest in seeing a strong American presence in East Asia. Most East Asians have no desire to see the United States fall off a cliff. This article is, therefore, written with the clear intention of warning the United States that it is approaching a cliff of which it seems as yet blissfully ignorant.

Social Decay

In most Asian eyes, the evidence of real social decay in the United States is clear and palpable. Since 1960, the U.S. population has grown by 41 percent. In the same period, there has been a 560 percent increase in violent crimes, a 419 percent increase in illegitimate births, a 400 percent increase in divorce rates, a 300 percent increase of children living in single-parent homes, a more than 200 percent increase in teenage suicide rates, and a drop of almost 80 points in Scholastic Aptitude Test scores. A recent report by the United Nations Development Program also ranks the United States number one among industrialized countries in intentional homicides, reported rapes, and percentage of prisoners.[1] The number of prison inmates has gone up from 329,821 in 1980 to 883,593 in 1992. Hunger in the United States has increased by 50 percent since 1985. The American elite think they understand this phenomenon because they see it on TV. The reality is that they are still not conscious of this social decay, mainly because most of them have retreated into distant suburbs, enclaves, and townships to shut themselves out and away from it.

Asian and American reactions to these statistics can be strikingly different. Americans assume that the figures merely reveal that either economic growth has stalled in the United States or that its law and order mechanism has broken down. Hence the natural reaction is to suggest changes that only tinker with the established social framework. By contrast, many Asians see the figures as evidence that something fundamental has gone wrong in American society. In working so hard to increase the scope of individual freedom within their society, Americans have progressively cut down the thick web of human relations and obligations that have produced social harmony in traditional societies. Effectively, in tearing down such social constraints upon individuals, American society has carried out slash and burn tactics that have, as in natural forests, left sections of their society denuded of social obligations. It is therefore not surprising to Asians that virtual anarchy has resulted in so many American inner cities.

A clear American paradox is that a society that places such a high premium on freedom has effectively reduced the physical freedom of most Americans, especially those who live in large cities. They live in heavily fortified homes, think twice before taking an evening stroll around their neighborhoods, and feel increasingly threatened by random violence when they are outside. They have to carefully map out routes for travel, even in their cars, to ensure they take no wrong turn in Miami, New York, or Chicago. It is a telling indication of the American condition that in the capital city, Washington, D.C., out of four quadrants, a visitor is advised not to stray out of one, the Northwest. The murder rate in the city was 77.8 per 10,000 people in 1990, one of the highest in the developed world.

Both Western and Asian societies assume that criminal elements will always exist. Each society has to devise its own mechanisms to capture and punish them. No society can do without such safety nets. But in Asia, the clear assumption is that the tougher the punishment, the less the likelihood of recurrence. The benefit of the doubt is given to the victim, not to the criminal. In the United States, it

would not be a major caricature to suggest that the explosion of liberal values in the 1960s somehow led to the belief that criminals were victims of society. If they took to crime, society was to blame. Hence, society should punish itself, not the criminals. Ironically, this liberal hypothesis has proved true with a vengeance. The society that has let its criminals escape unscathed now lives in constant fear.

Reams have been written on why there has been a decline in law and order in America. This essay will not settle the debate. But to an Asian mind, what is striking about the debate is the failure of Americans to ask fundamental questions such as: Is there too much freedom in American society? Did American society sacrifice the interests of the community as it rapidly and unthinkingly tried to tear down rules, legal or social, that fettered the individual? Has the political system become paralyzed by the fear of ceding effective power to any authority? And, to touch a really sensitive nerve in the American body politic, have long-term American interests been truly served by media that, especially since the Pentagon Papers and Watergate, have tried to undermine public confidence in virtually every public institution while leaving their own powers neither checked nor balanced by any countervailing institution? I shall try to discuss some of these fundamental questions, while acknowledging that the full answers to them are too complex to be covered in one essay.

Freedom

Freedom has been an integral part of American society from its very beginnings. The original migrants fled from an oppressive feudal order and religious persecution. They were determined to create social and political structures that left them unfettered. Faced with a wide-open continent, waiting to offer its rewards to brave individuals with a strong frontier mentality, it made eminent sense for the settlers to create conditions that placed no restriction, for example, on men bearing arms. As the United States prospered, its democratic institutions also helped to ensure that the fruits of economic growth would be widely shared among all prospective voters, uplifting a far greater portion of human society than anything ever seen in the history of man. This democratic tradition provided a sense of hope to each and every American (but not, until recently, the blacks) that he or she could make it if he or she tried. Hence, the boundless optimism of the American spirit, the sense of certitude that no class barriers could hold a person back. This initial American experiment was remarkably successful.

It may take centuries for historians to understand how and why the United States exploded into the most prosperous society ever seen. Clearly, several factors were right: the drive of the new migrants, the classless social conditions, the boundless resources of a vast continent, the investment in education, especially in science and technology, and so on. Perhaps there may have been another important underlying force: the United States may simply have been the splendid end product of Western civilization as it climbed to its greatest heights of power and glory. The impulses that had become tired in Europe were allowed to burgeon in the United States. With the right soil, thousands of flowers bloomed.

But this dynamic impulse that carried Western civilization—and the United States—to great heights may have finally run its course. This should

not be altogether surprising. Civilizations rise and fall. Not one has discovered the elixir of immortality. History does not stop—or end—for any civilization. Most simply become victims of their successes. If a certain set of factors has propelled a civilization to great glory, it becomes virtually impossible for its citizens to conceive that these same factors—in different circumstances—could bring grief to them. This fatal flaw undermined Chinese civilization when Europe exploded with new energy. With East Asia now exploding, it is surprising that Americans do not ask whether they, in their turn, are trapped in inertia.

It is not difficult to find examples of areas where American society has become trapped by its past. For example, the frontier is gone but the frontier mentality lingers, not in the Marlboro advertisements only but in the guns that are freely owned by American citizens. The *Washington Post* has noted that firearms kill more teenagers than cancer, heart disease, AIDs, and all other diseases combined.[2] A former U.S. surgeon general, C. Everett Koop, warned in 1986 that "violence is as much a public health issue for me and my successors in this country as smallpox, tuberculosis and syphilis were for my predecessors in the last two centuries."[3] Despite this warning, one of his successors, Joycelyn Elders, had to reiterate his message when she told a panel of the House of Representatives' Government Operations Committee on November 1, 1993, that firearm injuries alone cost the country nearly $3 billion a year. She noted that for young people in America "it's easier to find a gun than a good friend, a good teacher, a good school."[4] There are currently more than 200 million guns on the streets of the United States. President Bill Clinton has noted that there are "more federally-licensed gun dealers than gas stations."[5] A *U.S. News and World Report* survey reported that 10,567 people were killed with handguns in the United States in 1990, compared to 87 in Japan. Yet 56 percent of people surveyed thought that banning guns kept firearms away from law-abiding citizens.[6]

In spreading the belief that possession of firearms is legitimate, the National Rifle Association has cleverly mined an element deep in the American mind: the belief that any restriction on the right of Americans to bear arms would be the beginning of a slippery slope leading to other restrictions on their freedom. There could be no more vivid example of how a nation can become trapped by its ideology, even when the myths that give it meaning become dysfunctional. The frontier myths, which encouraged individualism, may have finally become a liability for the United States.

Many Americans continue to believe that a society that places a premium on individual freedom will triumph. But the evidence is accumulating that socially cohesive and disciplined societies are developing a competitive edge in today's world. In 1993 the World Bank commissioned a study to identify the causes of East Asia's success. It reached some obvious conclusions. According to John Page, the leader of the research team, "People in these [East Asian] economies have simply studied harder, worked harder and saved more than people in other countries." He added that "they are the only economies in the world that have had sustained high rates of growth while simultaneously reducing the gap between rich and poor."[7] And while East Asians are working harder, studying harder, saving more, and investing more, Americans are working less, studying less, and saving and investing less.

While East Asia was prospering, the United States has gone from being the world's largest creditor country to being its largest debtor—all within a decade. A Swiss investment consultant, Jean-Antoine Cramer, has noted,

It took 150 years for the U.S. government to create a debt of $1,000 billion, and only 10 years to quadruple this debt. With a GNP of $5,600 billion, the situation is beyond repair. American consumers owe $7,000 billion, corporations $5,000 billion and the government $5,000 billion.[8]

Today East Asian savings are needed to finance American deficits. Many East Asians are puzzled by this American belief that the United States can perpetually live beyond its means and yet never come to grief. They wonder how an avowedly self-critical society can become the prisoner of such an irrational belief.

There are still many areas of excellence in the United States. For every IBM, there is a Microsoft. The United States will remain the leader in areas like biotechnology, medical devices, artificial intelligence, and high-performance computing. Outer space may well remain an American preserve, despite the National Aeronautics and Space Administration's obvious deterioration (perhaps another symbol of the current American condition). The U.S. military will also probably remain unchallenged for at least a decade or more. And universities in the United States will continue to attract the best and the brightest from all around the world. (In 1990–91 these included more than 180,000 East Asian students, nearly three times the number 10 years ago.[9] More than 1 in 10 American doctoral degrees granted in science and engineering in 1990 went to students from only three East Asian countries: the People's Republic of China, Taiwan, and Korea.)

The United States is far from becoming as decrepit a society as many East Asian societies once were. It retains many powerful centers of excellence. But elites do not cause civilizations and nation-states to rise and fall. They fall when leaders fail to mobilize their populations, especially the man in the street. It is ultimately these Americans—including those who occupy the lower rungs of society—who will determine how far and how fast the country will grow. An abundance of Nobel prize winners or Harvard MBAs cannot propel a society to success if the middle and lower classes have lost their drive and spirit of competitiveness. For an avowedly egalitarian society, it is surprising how little awareness American elites have of the real condition of their working class. The debate over the North American Free Trade Agreement in late 1993 revealed the significant gap in perceptions between the elite and working class. In the most explosive period of American economic growth, it was the rising levels of productivity of the American worker that fueled growth. Today, this same productivity is declining in relative terms while that of East Asians is rising.

It is at this micro level that one can see most clearly where the United States—in contrast to East Asia—is veering down the wrong path. After centuries of inertia resulting from oppressive feudal rule, the work ethic is coming back in full force in most East Asian societies. Japan has shown the way for a century or more. Chinese, Korean, and now Southeast Asian workers are showing that given the right conditions, they will work just as hard, if not harder, than their counterparts in most parts of the world.

Although it is dangerous to make straight-line projections in assessing the future of a society, certain demographic indicators can provide an accurate projection of things to come. This is especially true of educational statistics. More than one quarter of U.S. high school students drop out before completing their studies. A 1987 survey of elementary and secondary schools in six countries, including Russia, Japan, the United Kingdom, and the United States, compiled by 22 comparative education experts from the United States, Western Europe, and Japan, concluded that the U.S. students ranked last in "the study of their own language." In science and mathematics, American students ranked second to last while the Japanese came out top.[10] A survey by the U.S. Education Department noted that half of the American adults studied had such poor literacy levels that they were unable to fill out a bank deposit slip.[11] Clearly if these educational trends continue, the United States will find it difficult to compete with East Asian societies.

Again, the solution here appears painfully obvious to many Asians. The American educational system must move away from its tendency to encourage freedom over discipline in the classroom. Anyone who doubts this should pay a random visit to any city school in East Asia and compare the ambience there with a contemporary American city school. CBS News reported that in 1940 the top problems in American public schools as cited by teachers consisted of talking out of turn, chewing gum, making noise, and other fairly innocuous acts.[12] By 1980, these problems had been replaced by suicide, assault, robbery, rape, drug abuse, alcohol, and pregnancy. No East Asian society would tolerate the level of teenager violence prevalent in the United States. From 1985 to 1991, there was an 85 percent increase in the number of teens arrested for murder in the United States. The Justice Department reported that about 1 million children between the ages of 12 and 19 were raped, robbed, and assaulted, usually by their peers.[13] This social deterioration is so drastic that it cannot possibly be the result of a mere economic downturn or fewer resources for law and order. To Asian eyes, it suggests that something fundamental has gone wrong in the United States.

Many Asian cities from Shanghai to Bombay, Bangkok to Jakarta, have had and many still have sections that are far poorer than Harlem or Watts. But none of them have experienced the social breakdown seen in American ghettos. The reasons must be complex, but one simple glue that has held Asian society together is the family. Many (*not* all) of the poorest will work hard to save for future generations. By contrast, each American generation is today living for itself—and beyond its means. The accumulated debt is passed on to successive generations, not wealth. Many Asians would be horrified to do this to their children.

The disintegration of the American family means the disintegration of a fundamental building block of a society. *Half* of the marriages contracted between 1987 and 1990 ended in divorce. Fifty years ago, 5 percent of American births were to unmarried women. Lee Rainwater, a Harvard sociologist emeritus, testifying to the Finance Committee in fall 1993, foresaw that nearly 40 percent of all American births would be out of wedlock by the turn of the century.[14] Again, the causes are too complex to discuss in this short essay. But an outsider must conclude that the seductive notion that any social obligation is only a diminution of individual freedom has played a key role in undermining the family as an institution. Woody Allen seems to believe that no moral considerations are relevant when he has an affair with his adopted daughter. American society, by permitting all forms of lifestyles to emerge—without any social pressures to conform to certain standards—may have wrecked the moral and social fabric that is needed to keep a society calm and well ordered. A well-ordered society needs to plant clear constraints on behavior in the minds of its citizens. In the United States it is clear that many such fundamental psychological constraints have collapsed, with the acceptance of all forms of lifestyle as legitimate.

This is the area where American society can start to experience some benefits if it tries to draw closer to East Asia. Societies, like individuals, can learn through osmosis. Many Asian students who went to the United States in the 1950s and 1960s felt exhilarated. Never had they experienced so much individual freedom. They felt liberated from the tight social nets of Asian society. But they did not destroy these nets when they returned home. They only loosened them. It would take full-scale sociological studies to document all the differences between American and Asian families, but some differences are obvious. In the United States, family obligations, if any, are felt by the nuclear family. In Asia, it is the extended family. Language demonstrates this. Most Asian languages have precise words for cousins twice or thrice removed. Americans do not. A visit to an Asian airport or hospital can provide a visual understanding of the differences. When an

Asian travels or is hospitalized, it is not just his nuclear family who will see him off or visit. His extended family will do so too. Within these elaborate family networks, obligations of one to another are clear and often heavy. This is one key reason why there are relatively few homeless people on the streets. The family as an institution survives even in Asian squatter colonies. Among Asians who have become widely dispersed across continents, be they Chinese, Korean, or Sindhi, the extended family remains a strong source of support and comfort. The net effect of this is simple: few Asian individuals ever feel that they are on their own. When things get bad, they can collapse into the arms of family members, nuclear or extended.

Today, an American student sent to live in an East Asian society will have his sense of social obligations strengthened. He will feel the sense of discipline and the need to be sensitive to the concerns of family and society. If he is observant, he will notice that his own psychological map is different from his Asian host's. Americans find it quite natural to send their parents to old people's homes. Most Asians take care of their parents, no matter how old.

East Asian societies are by no means universally harmonious. They have their share of family and social breakdowns. But, relative to most societies in the world, they are disciplined and cohesive. Social order prevails. The deep value placed on family in Asian societies is not easily erased. Family cohesiveness is not always an unmitigated blessing. It breeds nepotism. It can also create a suffocating home environment. But it does generate, relatively speaking, greater social harmony. Overall, if Americans were to try to begin learning from Asians, their nation would become a better place.

The fundamental lesson that Asia can provide to the United States here is that societies can be better off when some boundaries of individual freedom are limited rather than broadened. The resultant increase in social and communal harmony can in turn be liberating for the individual.

The Role of the Media

Many Asians are puzzled that, in the face of such evidence, Americans have made no public move to learn from Asia. This hesitancy suggests a resistance, and that resistance is most evident in the minds of those who decide what information should be poured into American minds: the media. Until the media become convinced that something fundamentally wrong is happening in American society and that Asians may be able to help, the American public will remain ignorant of Asia and what it can offer.

Despite Allan Bloom's widely cited but little read book, most Americans will be astonished by the suggestion that there could be such a thing as a closed American mind.[15] The term is surely an oxymoron in the American context. This is a result of the absolute conviction in the United States that the American media will always open windows for American minds. Hence the belief that the American media are doing no harm to American society. Across the Pacific Ocean there is, however, a strong perception that the irresponsibility and unchecked power of the American media may be responsible in part for America's deteriorating social fabric.

There is today a gross mismatch of perceptions when a Western journalist arrives in East Asia. Subconsciously, he sees himself as the representative of a superior civilization, a white knight out to battle the dark forces of oppression that linger in Asia. By contrast, most East Asians would view him either as a dishonest or a misguided person, who is determined consciously or subconsciously to prove to his readers that East Asia, for all its merits, has not and cannot possibly reach the levels attained by the West. Certainly, the claims that a Western journalist's presence can only be good for East Asia is highly suspect.

In their writings, both on the domestic and external scene, most journalists assume a posture of being paragons of wisdom and virtue. Yet it is clear that many have double standards. For example, American journalists do not believe in the Christian rule: "Do unto others as you would have others do unto you." From their exposures of public figures from Gary Hart to Bill Clinton, there has developed an honorable tradition among journalists that the infidelities of a politician are public property, to be exposed in every detail. But those who participate in this tradition do not feel themselves bound by Jesus Christ's injunction: "Let him who has not sinned cast the first stone."

To the best of my knowledge, based on my limited stay in Washington, D.C., the average level of infidelities seemed about the same, whether in Congress or in the press corps. Power is a great aphrodisiac. Both politicians and journalists have equal difficulty resisting the temptations that flow their way. Yet although in the informal pecking order worked out in Washington, D.C. (as in any other tribal society), many a senior journalist enjoys far more effective power than a congressman, the actions of one group are deemed immoral and subject to public scrutiny, while those of the other are deemed private matters.

The same disparity applies to personal finances. Any aspiring politician, even the few unfortunates who may have entered politics to do a service to the nation, has to declare every penny of his or her financial worth. Yet none of the Washington journalists, many of whom enjoy far greater incomes, feel any moral obligation to declare all their financial worth; nor do they feel any need to declare how discussing the financial worth of an aspiring politician enhances their own. A full disclosure of income and wealth on the part of those who make and those who influence public policy decisions (including journalists) would probably indicate the great mismatch in financial muscle between the actual policymakers and those who seek to influence them. It may also help to illuminate why so many irrational public policy choices are made.

The greatest myth that an American journalist cherishes is that he is an underdog; the lone ranger who works against monstrous bureaucracies to uncover the real truth, often at great personal risk. I never understood this myth when I was in Washington. Cabinet secretaries, senators and congressmen, ambassadors and generals promptly return the phone calls of journalists there and cultivate them assiduously. Some of these powerful officeholders are good at seducing American journalists; but none would dare tell an American journalist on a major paper to go to hell. It is as inconceivable as trying to exercise dissent in the court of Attila the Hun. A key assumption of the American Constitution is that unchecked power leads to irresponsibility. It is therefore puzzling that many American journalists assume their unchecked power will do no fundamental harm.

But American journalism may have done harm to its society in many different ways: the unbridled free press could have, for example, served as the

87

opium of society. This statement is not quite as outrageous as Marx's dictum that religion is the opiate of the masses but it will probably be dismissed as quickly as Marx's statement was when he first uttered it. The American media pride themselves on the ability of their investigative journalism to uncover the real truth behind the stories put out by government, big business, and other major institutions. They could never stomach the proposition that they could serve as the opium of American society. But they may well have done so.

In the last 20 years, two parallel developments have occurred. First, American journalism has become much more aggressive. John F. Kennedy was the last U.S. president to be treated with kid gloves; his sexual peccadilloes were well known but never publicized. The parallel trend is this. The last 20 years have also seen increasingly bad government. President Lyndon Johnson felt that he could fight a war and create a good society without raising taxes. This unleashed fiscal indiscipline. No American politician, in the land of the free press, dares to utter any hard truths on the sacrifices needed to stop this rot. The consequence has been irresponsible government on a mind-boggling and historically unparalleled scale.

It would be impossible for me to prove absolutely that there is a causal connection between a more aggressive free press and increasingly bad government. It may have been purely a coincidence. After all, the American press has been second to none in exposing the follies of the American government. But have all their exposures served as opiates, creating the illusion that something is being done when nothing is really being done?

Most American journalists have no doubt that they are ultimately doing good because of their belief that any time they surface the truth in a society, this will automatically lead to a better society. This assumption is both dangerously simplistic and flawed. As far back as the nineteenth century, Max Weber warned that good intentions do not necessarily lead to good results. As he said, "it is not true that good can follow only from good and evil only from evil, but that often the opposite is true. Anyone who fails to see this is, indeed, a political infant."[16] In short, ferocious unchecked efforts by the American media to uncover the truth need not result in a well-ordered society. Metaphorically speaking, they may have the same effect as acid thrown on established physical structures—it corrodes; it does not build.

The inability of many American journalists to see this result perhaps reveals a certain flaw in the American mind: the inability to accept paradoxical truths. Throughout the Cold War, the well-intentioned argued in favor of disarmament as the way to end the Cold War. But it was the rapid arms buildup of the Reagan era that ended it instead, following an old adage, "To make peace, prepare for war." The domestic corollary for this, as Asian experience suggests, is that to have more freedom in society, one should sometimes increase the boundaries not of freedom but of order and discipline.

One final crucial point about the role of the media. In arguing against the unchecked and uncheckable power of the U.S. media, I am not suggesting that the Soviet *Pravda* or the Chinese *Peoples Daily* are the alternative choices. Far from it. Media that are known to be dishonest have no credibility. State censorship is not the answer. But given the crucial role that the media play in molding minds, it is absurd that control should be left solely in the hands of the media moguls, whose main concerns are personal profit, not social good. The U.S. media need a watchdog, with teeth, which will regularly judge whether the media promote the good of society or not. One can argue at length about the nature and powers of such a watchdog, but a society without one—as in the United States—is letting loose a powerful force that can, wittingly or unwittingly, damage society. This notion that the U.S. media, left on their own, will naturally do good should not be regarded as an a priori truth. It needs to be tested against experience.

Freedom for Whom?

Most Americans consider this suggestion that it is time for American society to begin reducing, rather than expanding, the boundaries of freedom unthinkable. No major speech by an American leader is complete without the regular ritualistic reference to freedom, which is mentioned in the same breath as democracy. For example, in his opening statement before the Senate Foreign Relations Committee on U.S.–Asia relations on March 25, 1987, Senator Alan Cranston said "capitalism flourishes in freedom."[17] He meant it as an obvious truism. Recent Asian experience suggests that there is room for doubt.

In a speech on September 21, 1993, Anthony Lake, President Clinton's national security adviser, said that, as "the world's most powerful and respected nation," America's ideals of freedom and democracy were being embraced by the rest of the world "as never before."[18] Many years earlier, President Ronald Reagan, in a foreign policy message to Congress on March 15, 1986, said, "the tide of the future is a freedom tide. If so, it is also a peace tide, for the surest guarantee we have of peace is natural freedom and

democratic government."[19] These statements demonstrate the deep-rooted assumption in the American mind that the expansion of freedom and democracy can only do good. Surely enough evidence has surfaced to question such an obviously facile assumption. Again, Asians see Americans trapped in rhetoric that may have been appropriate when they were fighting for the overthrow of a feudal order, but today, when the problem is not too many but too few constraints, Asians find it puzzling that the rhetoric cannot be changed to suit new circumstances.

Almost all American thinkers freely admit that democratic systems are flawed, although when this admission is made to Asians it is often done in a smug, condescending tone. Few fail to quote Winston Churchill's dictum that democracy is the worst form of government, except for the alternative. After saying this, most American thinking on democracy seems to stop. The idea that democratic systems may indeed create inherent problems for a society does not surface strongly in either *Washington Post* or *New York Times* editorials, the main contemporary intellectual fodder of many leading American minds. Certainly all conceivable alternatives to democratic government appear to have worse results in the long run, but this does not mean that democracies will naturally and inherently result in good for man and society. The longer history of democracy, stretching from Greek times, would indeed suggest that blind faith in democracies could be fatal. It may not yet be possible for humankind to discuss a better political arrangement, but this does not mean that democracy is not a highly flawed system, against which leaders must often struggle if they are to do good to their societies in the long run. This is not an argu-

89

ment against democracy per se. It is a warning that Americans, in universally prescribing the virtues of democracy to themselves and to the world, fail to provide adequate product label warnings. Democracy is no panacea. As shown by the Philippines, Zambia, or Russia in recent times, it can produce serious dangers. It is a highly combustible instrument, not a simple neat sword that automatically solves problems.

The dramatic inability of either the American or European democratic systems to persuade their respective populations that the long-term interests of the nation can only be protected by painful immediate sacrifices (either by French farmers or U.S. auto workers) reveals the traps that democratic systems can create. Perhaps this is only a short-term problem. Perhaps eventually democratic systems will correct themselves through electoral renewals. Perhaps. But in a world that is changing rapidly, especially with the emergence of billions of workers from China, India, Indonesia, and elsewhere, ready to compete with American workers on the level playing field of a global marketplace, the failure of the American political system to engineer change through short-term sacrifices could lead to catastrophic consequences later.

Asians are particularly troubled by the inability of Western thinkers to understand how democracy in America and Europe—even if it produced good for their own citizens—can adversely affect the lives and livelihood of the rest of the inhabitants of planet earth. Seduced by TV pictures of a few courageous Western individuals struggling against great odds to help starving people in desperate societies like Somalia or Ethiopia, many Americans and Europeans have come to believe that they represent the most compassion-

ate members of the human tribe. Unfortunately, the truth may be closer to the opposite. Billions of lives in poor countries could have been made easier as far back as 1989 if the Uruguay Round of the General Agreement on Tariffs and Trade had been successfully concluded on schedule. The inability of the most affluent societies of the globe to make relatively painless sacrifices to help the whole world (and their own societies too) shows, however, that democracy can result not in compassion for but cruelty to the vast majority of mankind. A few thousand French farmers, using the democratic system to suit their selfish ends, have effectively damaged the lives of hundreds of millions of farmers in poor societies. But because this connection could not be captured on TV, their cruelty was not displayed for all to see. This example alone should have provided an American philosopher sufficient grounds to raise questions about the moral worth of democratic systems. The fact that such questions do not surface demonstrates the ideological blinders that grip the minds of Western thinkers when they discuss democracy.

A warning against democracy's many hidden flaws and dangers is *not* an argument in favor of totalitarian or authoritarian systems. History amply demonstrates that governments that lose the mandate of their people hang on to power at their peril. Consent of the governed is absolutely vital for any government. This is democracy's key virtue: it provides a safe and easy mechanism for "throwing the rascals out." This key dimension of democracy—the need to obtain the consent of the governed—is an essential ingredient of any government. But the United States has stretched the definition of democracy so wide that it may have in the process lost another equally essential ingredient of government: it must allow the government to *govern*, leaders to *lead*, and encourage both to think in terms of long-term good, not short-term polls. This is another paradoxical political truth that evades American minds: to have good government, you often need less, not more, democracy.

Real Interests versus Hubris

Still, the history of mankind shows that national interests—not moral compassion—move nations to change course. This is also true of the United States, even though many Americans believe that their country is unique in injecting moral considerations into its foreign policy. When a nation's real interests are threatened, morality is thrown out of the window. Asians assume that Americans will put their national interests first, even though few Americans realize how much their national circumstances, and therefore those interests, have changed.

From its very creation, the United States did not really have to worry about the rest of the world. Two great oceans protected it. After World War II, the overwhelming power of the United States, despite Soviet competition, ensured that Americans could be immune to the global condition. The rest of the world could sink or swim, but the United States could always prosper alone. It is astonishing how few Americans realize that in many, many ways, the United States has effectively shrunk. It has become a normal nation-state, subject like any other to global winds and currents.

In early 1992, before the Carnegie Endowment produced its report *Changing Our Ways*, it sent its commission members to various cities, including Boston, to seek ideas on American reactions to new global conditions.[20]

Sitting in a room full of Boston luminaries invited to present ideas to the commission, I thought that I was making an obvious point: that in the deeply interconnected world we live in (an interconnectedness that ironically was largely a result of American science and technology), American workers and citizens were no longer immune. AIDS in Africa, Islamic terrorism in the Middle East, the increasing productivity of Asian workers: all these would affect American lives. America had to adapt. To my surprise, a former provost of a leading American university dismissed my remarks. The United States was a society that set global rules, he said, not one that bent to global trends.

It took many months before the real significance of this remark dawned on me. American society, like every other powerful society before it, has become a victim of hubris: it is convinced that it is invulnerable. What is even more shocking to an outsider is that this hubris persists even after we have seen the most rapid collapse of a great power ever witnessed in the history of man: the collapse of the Soviet Union. When a powerful gladiator sees one of his strongest competitors wilt and crumble, surely the thought must strike him that it could also happen to him. Why doesn't this thought occur to Americans? Asians, who have seen so many powerful empires and dynasties come and go, have no problem with such an idea.

It would be ironic if future historians were to record that euphoria in the West, including the United States, after the collapse of the Soviet Union accentuated Western blindness just when the eyes of the West most needed to be open. In Western Europe, it is hard to escape harsh realities: the turbulence of Islam in the Middle East, the hopelessness of Af-

91

rica, and the desperation of Russia are on their very doorstep. In the United States, apart from a rapidly growing Hispanic population, there is no harsh reality nearby to shake American senses. And so the party goes on.

Mental Ossification

The inability to raise fundamental questions about its society suggests that the American mind may have become, in its own unique way, as ossified as Asian minds were for centuries. The dangers of mental and cultural ossification were made painfully clear to me—an Asian born in the colonial era—from a very young age.

As a young boy in a Hindu family in the British colony of Singapore, one painful point that emerged from my British textbooks was that the vast country of India had crumbled so easily under the boots of a few thousand British soldiers only because Indian culture and civilization had become ossified. The Indian mind had become intellectually dead. Caught in a thick web of superstitions and taboos that fixed the way of life of a Hindu from birth to death, it had no room for creativity or movement.

Some 30 years later, it has come as a great shock to discover that the American mind has become, in its own way, equally ossified. The Hindus used to look back millennia for wisdom; American intellectuals feel obliged to quote the founding fathers of their republic to confirm that they are on the right path. These founding fathers are treated with almost the same reverence as Hindu gods. Just as Hindu society cannot contemplate the slaughter of millions of sacred cows, so too American society cannot conceive of creating any new set of social arrangements that might offer less

freedom and liberty. The concepts of democracy, human rights, freedom, equality, justice—to name a few—are to be worshiped. not challenged.

The alternative to worship is not rejection. All these ostensible political virtues can be stretched to do harm. Too much equality, as the twentieth-century Soviet Marxist experiment has shown, can bring a society down. Too much freedom, as this essay argues, can lead to crime and social anarchy in the United States. Too many human rights, which place criminal rights ahead of victims' concerns, can also produce social disorder. And so on. It is startling that the mere suggestion that these virtues should be practiced in moderation is considered too heretical a thought to be contemplated.

What makes the ossification of the American mind even more pernicious is that it rests on a massive delusion: that the open society—with its avowed denial that anything in it is beyond scrutiny—would prevent any ossification and that the persistence of alternative points of view would ensure that any truth vital to American interests would somehow surface and produce the right solution for society. The spectrum of views, from the left to the right, would somehow deliver new ideas.

The classic expression of this faith in the marketplace of ideas was formulated by Oliver Wendell Holmes, who said that

> When men have realized that time has upset many fighting faiths, they may come to believe . . . that the ultimate good desired is better reached by free trade in ideas—that the best test of truth is the power of the thought to get itself accepted in the competition of the market, and that truth is the only ground upon which their

wishes safely can be carried out. That at any rate is the theory of our Constitution.

These words are often quoted. But he also went on to say "it is an experiment, as all life is an experiment," suggesting that this faith in the market place of ideas could also be challenged.[21] Unfortunately, this is not done. Only someone standing outside can see that the apparent polar opposites of the American political spectrum are like two groups of sailors arguing over who should man the bridge, both equally ignorant of the fact that their boat is sinking. Much of American political debate ignores the real challenges faced by American society today because it is constrained by certain ideological blinkers.

The British colonial experience was immensely liberating for India. It opened an alternative window on the world for Indian intellectuals. Secular Indian culture, the biggest gift of Britain to India, cut a wide and deep swath through Indian taboos. Overall, it was a liberating experience, although many a secular Indian remains intellectually colonized by the West long after the British left.

The American reaction to British colonization was also initially liberating, albeit in a different way. For almost 200 years after the British left, the social, economic, and political arrangements worked out by a small elite group of white farmers and merchants suited American society well. With a vast continent in which to spread out and with only soft resistance from another ossified culture, the Mexican, and of course the helpless Indian tribes, the American spirit soon became convinced that there was no frontier it could not conquer. The landing on the moon vindicated this

conviction. Following its victories in World Wars I and II and now the Cold War, the United States of America stands utterly confident that while many a society may have to consider some fundamental tinkering with its social arrangements, the United States need not do so. The American Constitution, defying the logic of history, is supposed to be eternally valid.

The simple but stark truth is that no society has ever in history devised social arrangements that suit all times and all circumstances. The American Constitution, like all other documents of its kind, is susceptible to age. And the enormously intricate grid of checks and balances, designed to prevent the emergence of a long-dead despotic English monarch, has become dysfunctional at a moment when the United States, which stands on the verge of becoming a normal country, has to respond to events on the globe at the same pace as the rest of the world. A new race has begun. It is absurd that the United States insists on running this race with its legs hobbled when a whole new set of sprinters are emerging.

This does not mean that the U.S. Constitution should be thrown out, lock, stock, and barrel. Many of its essential features will remain valid for many more centuries. But like any other 200-year-old document, it contains anachronisms. This has to be so. There is a lot of wisdom in the American society's reluctance to tinker with the Constitution. Special interests could tear apart the document in a constitutional convention.

This is one fundamental lesson that Americans can learn from Asians: to move ahead, one has to shake off the debris of history. Certainly, the United States will have an easier time than, say, China or India. But no Chinese or Indian intellectual labors under the illusion that his society has achieved the best possible social arrangements, valid for all time. In their hearts, they know that many radical changes are necessary. Each society will have to weigh how much of its past it has to shake off without losing its unity and integrity. The United States, by contrast, wears its past as proudly as an emperor wears his imperial robe, disdaining the thought that this robe might have finally become a liability. It would be truly ironic if future historians were to record that generations of Chinese and Indian students, intellectually liberated in great American universities, went home to help their societies shed their past, while the United States continued to be a prisoner of its own history.

Until recently, virtually no Asian intellectual would have dared to suggest that the United States could begin learning from Asia, because both Asians and Americans assumed that the United States had discovered the secret of achieving a well-ordered society. Until recently, both also assumed that apart from retaining their cultural peculiarities, Asians would evolve in only one direction—that of emulating the political and economic arrangements of American society.

But the United States, whatever it may have been in the past, does not appear to be a well-ordered society today. One clear Asian vision of a well-ordered society is that spelled out by Confucius in the sixth century BC:

When the perfect order prevails, the world is like a home shared by all. Virtuous and worthy men are elected to public office, and capable men hold posts of gainful employment in society; peace and trust among all men are the maxims of living. All men love and respect their own parents and children, as well as the parents and children of others. There is caring for the old; there are jobs for the adults; there are nourishment and education for the children. There is a means of support for the widows, and the widowers; for all who find themselves alone in the world; and for the disabled. Every man and woman has an appropriate role to play in the family and society. A sense of sharing displaces the effects of selfishness and materialism. A devotion to public duty leaves no room for idleness. Intrigues and conniving for ill gain are unknown. Villains such as thieves and robbers do not exist. The door to every home need never be locked and bolted by day or night. These are the characteristics of an ideal world, the commonwealth state.[22]

Certainly, the United States enjoys a political stability that is the envy of many. No revolution or coup d'état waits in the wings. But underneath this political stability, American society is breaking down and falling apart in myriads of ways. Many Americans will acknowledge that their nation is failing in many spheres. But all these failings are confidently regarded as mere aberrations. The great magic of democracy is that, ultimately, the people's "will" will be done. Democratic society, like the eternally self-righting doll, will reform itself. American faith that this will be done is incredible in the face of many harsh new facts about American society. In confidence, it almost matches the bravery of the courageous Hindu Marathi warriors who went into battle against British soldiers fully convinced that their gods would protect them against British gunpowder. It took thousands of British rounds, with many Indian lives lost on countless battlefields, before the Indian mind woke up to realize that gunpowder was stronger than Hindu gods.

Today, many American citizens who live in cities or now even suburbs, live in little fortresses and leave their homes at night with some fear. Nothing can deprive people of their freedom more effectively than the fear of losing their own lives. It envelopes their minds and confines them to narrow spaces where they can be free of fear. Despite America's vast territory, each citizen is living and working within increasingly narrow confines to protect his or her personal well-being and that of their family. Even home is no longer a castle.

To any Asian, it is obvious that this enormous reduction of freedom in America is the result of a mindless ideology that maintains that the freedom of a small number of individuals (criminals, terrorists, street gang members, drug dealers), who are known to pose a threat to society, should not be constrained (for example, through detention without trial), even if to do so would enhance the freedom of the majority. In short, principle takes precedence over people's well-being. This belief is purely and simply a gross violation of common sense. But it is the logical end product of a society that worships the notion of freedom as religiously as Hindus worship their sacred cows. Both must be kept absolutely unfettered, even when they obviously create great social discomfort.

To make American society a less crime-ridden, more socially cohesive, and more disciplined society, Americans may have to do what Asians are obliged to do in their own society: peer into every nook and cranny to judge which social arrangement should be discarded and which should be kept. Social arrangements are particularly difficult to dismantle because they do not stand out clearly as physical structures do. They exist often as concepts in the mind, revealed only in patterns of behavior, whether it be on the street or on judicial benches, at home or in school. When Americans wake up each day and make choices, they do so on the basis of what they have been taught to do. As in any other society, they are also taught which areas contain "inalienable truths" and which, doubts.

One article is hardly likely to change the mainstream of American intellectual thought. My only hope is that it will lead more Americans to visit East Asia. When they do, they will come to realize that their society has swung much too much in one direction: liberating the individual while imprisoning society. The relatively strong and stable family and social institutions of East Asia will appear more appealing. And as Americans experience the freedom they feel walking on some city streets in Asia, they may begin to understand that freedom can also result from greater social order and discipline. And perhaps the best advice to give to a young American is "Go East, young man."

Nothing is inevitable in the history of man. The resources of a vast continental land mass are not enough to guarantee continued wealth and prosperity: witness the fate of Argentina and Brazil. The success of the United States in the last century or more was the result of a triumphant American spirit that was ready to overcome all challenges and cross all frontiers, in land, sea, or space. The loss of this great American spirit will be a loss not just for the United States but for all of mankind. The twenty-first century may well not experience the sweet pleasures of the presence of a benign world power that the second half of the twentieth century enjoyed.

But clearly this American spirit can only be revitalized if the American condition is seen to be improving, not declining. A new burst of energy and hard work may be required to blaze a new trail of hope and triumph in America. This is the area where, hopefully, East Asians can help. By demonstrating how well they have done—in part by extracting and transplanting the best elements that American culture and society had to offer—they can demonstrate what were the most positive features of American society. In the case of Europe, Islamic civilization had to preserve the Greek heritage for centuries before returning it to Europe. East Asia is ready to return the best aspects of American culture and society and also share the best features of its own cultural heritage with the United States. Both gratitude and self-interest dictate that this be done. But it can only be done if Americans approach East Asia in the right spirit.

The views expressed in this essay are the author's personal views and should not be read as a reflection of the views of the Singapore government.

Notes

1. "Profile of Human Development," *United Nations Human Development Report 1993* (New York, N.Y.: United Nations, 1993).

2. Quoted in "The Gun as Health Problem," *International Herald Tribune*, October 15, 1993, p. 8.

3. *Ibid.*

4. Quoted in "Violence in US adds $21 billion to Medical Bill," *Straits Times* (Singapore), November 2, 1993, p. 3.

5. Quoted in "Clinton Proposes Bigger Police Force, Tighter Gun Control in Anti-Crime Laws," *Straits Times* (Singapore), August 13, 1993, p. 4.

6. "Outlook," *US News and World Report*, April 19, 1993, p. 10.

7. Quoted in "East Asian Miracle No Miracle But Hard Work: World Bank," *Straits Times* (Singapore), September 27, 1993, p. 4.

8. Jean-Antoine Cramer, "World Politics and Finance" (Paper delivered at the conference on "Investment in 1993," sponsored by the *Financial Mail*, Johannesburg, October 29–30, 1992).

9. U.S. Department of Education, *Digest of Education Statistics 1992* (Washington, D.C., 1992).

10. Reuters News Report, "Education: Survey Flunks US and Great Britain, Lauds Japan," January 11, 1988.

11. Quoted in "Almost Half of US Adults Have Poor Literacy, Says Survey," *Straits Times* (Singapore), September 10, 1993, p. 5.

12. "The Victims of TV Violence," *US News and World Report*, August 2, 1993, p. 64.

13. "Wild in the Streets," *Newsweek*, August 2, 1993, p. 35.

14. Quoted in "One-Third of US Births in '91 Came from Unmarried Mums," *Straits Times* (Singapore), September 12, 1993, p. 3.

15. Allan Bloom, *The Closing of the American Mind* (New York, N.Y.: Simon and Schuster, 1987).

16. Max Weber, *Politics as a Vocation* (Philadelphia, Pa.: Fortress Press, 1965), p. 49.

17. Press release on Senator Alan Cranston's opening statement before the Senate Foreign Relations Committee on U.S.–Asia Relations, March 25, 1987.

18. Anthony Lake, "From Containment to Enlargement" (Address at the School of Advanced International Studies, Johns Hopkins University, Washington, D.C., September 21, 1993). Reprinted in *Dispatch* 4, no. 39 (U.S. Department of State) (September 27, 1993).

19. President Ronald Reagan's message to Congress on foreign policy, quoted in *New York Times*, March 15, 1986.

20. *Changing Our Ways*, Report to the Carnegie Commission (Washington, D.C., January 1992).

21. Justice Oliver Wendell Holmes, dissenting opinion in *Abrams v. United States*, 250 U.S. 616, 630 (1919).

22. Confucius, *The Record of Books*, book 9, "The Commonwealth."

II. New Challenges to International Order

The Resurgence of Nationalism and Its International Implications

Karin von Hippel

FEW ISSUES POSE a greater threat to the post–cold war international order than those emanating from nationalism and the quest for self-determination. Many of today's most intractable political problems and related humanitarian disasters, such as civil war, genocide, and ethnic cleansing or forced population transfers, stem from nationalist disputes. In order to understand why such claims are so potent today, it is important to analyze their development in international society over the course of this century. This article does so in four sections: the first defines terms as well as outlines the historical progression of ethnic claims; the second focuses on the dangers posed by irredentism, one of the relatively unexplored by-products of nationalism; the third lists all current claims; and the fourth con-

cludes with a discussion of policy implications.

Irredentism, Secession, and Self-Determination Defined

Prior to the discussion of the evolution of nationalist claims, clear definitions of several terms are imperative because the current definitions are not consistently applied. "Irredentism" refers to a historical claim made by one sovereign state to land and/or people outside its internationally recognized boundaries, justified on the grounds that the earlier separation was illegal or forced. The term is derived from the Italian movement at the end of the nineteenth century, *Italia irredenta* (unredeemed Italy), a campaign for the return of lands that Italy had lost to its neighbors during earlier wars. The definition that will not be used is the more restrictive one that refers to people only, and not also to territory. This article endorses the broader definition because so much of the nationalist debate is about land as well as people. It is rare indeed that a country would lay claim to a "people" without also including the territory in which they live. Moreover, this type of territorial claim is not encompassed in other definitions. The Spanish claim

Karin von Hippel has a Ph.D. in international relations from the London School of Economics and is currently researching democratization efforts in the Western hemisphere for an LSE project.

to Gibraltar is an example of an irredentist claim based primarily on territory, while the Armenian claim to Nagorno-Karabakh incorporates mostly the people, but also the region.

Irredentist claims have other features as well:

> The claimants share a sense of unjust deprivation and seek to use the contemporary climate of opinion to generate support for their attempts at recovery. Proximity lends plausibility—the claimants are nearby, the legal titleholders are not.[1]

Conversely, the inhabitants of the region often assert that a distinctive identity has developed, separate from the surrounding region, and that their right of occupation has been validated by some sort of treaty. Irredentist movements are rarely successful—witness the quick response to Iraq's seizure of Kuwait or the Argentine invasion of the Falklands. The irredentist campaign is normally a "top-down" phenomenon, initiated and/or maintained by the government, while the movement for the other major by-product of nationalism, secession, is conducted from the "bottom up," that is, from the grassroots level.[2]

"Secession" is used to describe the attempt of a region within a state, usually inhabited by a minority, to separate and become an independent state, or to form an autonomous region within the state, or, less frequently, to federate with another state. The latter form can overlap with irredentism, although the sentiment in such cases emanates from the inhabitants of the separatist region as well as from the claimant state. From 1945 to the end of the Cold War, the only clear-cut secession was the formation of Bangladesh in 1971. The repercussions of the disintegration of the Soviet empire

have recently generated a myriad of secessions and possible secessions in the former Soviet Union, its former satellite countries, and in the less-developed countries where much of the Cold War was fought.

The term "self-determination" will be defined against the backdrop of the formation of nationalist claims in general. The history of self-determination as it relates to the international order is well documented, yet several salient points need reiteration. The rise of self-determination coincided with the demise of the landed classes at the end of World War I. Just as the cessation of the Napoleonic Wars almost 100 years before marked the onset of industrialization and its by-products of urbanization, population explosion, and economic depression, so the end of the Great War in 1918 brought about equally powerful societal upheavals. A new order emerged from the chaos of war, one that shifted away from privilege and primogeniture toward egalitarianism and its natural corollaries of universal adult suffrage, representative government, state-sponsored education, and the redistribution of land and resources—although none of these was by any means fully achieved.

In their eagerness to build a new world at Versailles, the victors hastily applied the principle of self-determination drawn from Woodrow Wilson's Fourteen Points to the European countries ravaged by the war. Thus were born the separate nations of Austria, Hungary, Czechoslovakia, Poland, Yugoslavia, Finland, Estonia, Latvia, and Lithuania, while other countries, such as Italy, Belgium, and France, had their prewar borders restored.[3] But that was where the application of self-determination ended; Italy received land in South Tyrol, Japan acquired economic rights in the

Shantung peninsula, Poland inherited control of the Germans living in Silesia, and the British, French, and Japanese all pocketed ex-German colonies. Any further changes reflected the status quo ante as much as was possible.

Colonial agitation surfaced at this same time, primarily as a result of Wilson's push for self-determination as the mainstay of the League of Nations and the subsequent release of this idea onto the international stage. Only after World War II did the colonies as separate entities successfully challenge the existing order, but the harbingers of this change were evident as early as the second decade of the twentieth century. The protest that led to the Amritsar Massacre of 1919, Egyptian independence in 1922, and the Irish Free State declaration that same year built on the legacy of Wilson's encouraging words and could not help but inspire other colonies to seek independence.

Although the post–World War II map was initially redrawn in similar fashion to the Versailles document, with colonial outposts retained for the victors, this time the colonies did not succumb so willingly. The use of colonial troops in the war, who had accounted for notable Allied victories, served as the final catalyst for colonial emancipation after the war. The troops realized that they had been fighting for the liberation of Europeans but not for themselves. Moreover, the elite from the colonies could now articulate their demands in the political idiom of the West: they had been educated in the parent countries and were returning home with liberal ideas about freedom from oppression.

These demands found their voice at the United Nations (UN), the replacement for the defunct League of Nations. The concept of self-determina-tion was firmly enshrined in article 1 (2) and article 55 of the UN Charter, and in resolution 1514, which was passed in 1960 and covered all those non-self-governing territories not included in the Trusteeship System.[4] Paragraph 2 of resolution 1514 states unequivocally that, "all peoples have the right to self-determination," although paragraph 6 has caused considerable controversy by noting that any disruption in the "national unity and the territorial integrity of a country is incompatible with the purposes and principles of the Charter of the United Nations."[5] Paragraph 6 was built into the resolution as a guarantee that the international community would not support secessionist and irredentist tendencies and would apply the resolution only in colonial cases (as the title of the declaration indicates).[6] It has been suggested that,

> Most states voting for Resolution 1514's paragraph 6 probably did so in the belief that they were creating a sort of "grandfather clause": setting out the right of self-determination for all colonies but not extending it to parts of decolonized states and seeking to ensure that the act of self-determination occur within the established boundaries of colonies, rather than within sub-regions.[7]

Federations could occur, according to international law, but only at the wish of the resident population expressed through the ballot box, usually with the assistance of the UN. Surprisingly, most transitions were conducted rather peacefully, with some exceptions, notably Algeria and the Belgian Congo. Through resolution 1514, countless requests were made for recognition of the right to self-determination, primarily in Africa and Asia, with over 1 billion people receiving independence in the next three decades. In most cases, independence occurred within several years of the request. The international community had reached a working consensus over the interpretation of self-determination because of its inability to address the anomalies of the international system: but that interpretation applied only to the withdrawal of the European powers from their colonial outposts.

During the period of African and Asian decolonization between 1960 (when resolution 1514 was passed) and 1975, most hearings for self-determination received overwhelming support from the international community in the UN, among organizations such as the Organization of African Unity (OAU) and the Non-Aligned Movement (NAM), and from various governments. But by 1976, when the majority of colonies had received independence, and only Rhodesia, Namibia, and some small areas remained on the UN wish list, support for non-colonial requests (which fell outside the UN mandate) withered away. The OAU also contributed to this change because it attempted to maintain order by its determination to respect existing borders, no matter how unfair their origin might have been.

What was once considered the normal route to independence by application to the UN Special Committee of 24[8] for a hearing under resolution 1514 gradually became abnormal as former colonies evicted their landlords in droves. Yet this rapid pace of decolonization could not help but be contagious: similar cries for self-determination were heard from groups of people sharing a common heritage, language, and/or culture although not necessarily the same borders. As one author has put it,

One searches in vain . . . for any principled justification of why a colonial people wishing to cast off the domination of its governors has every moral and legal right to do so, but a manifestly distinguishable minority which happens to find itself, pursuant to a paragraph in some medieval territorial settlement or through a fiat of the cartographers, annexed to an independent State must forever remain without the scope of the principle of self-determination.[9]

The 180 plus independent countries represented at the UN today include over 8,000 distinct ethnic cultures, which explains why nationalism is so pervasive, especially when self-determination is a cornerstone of the UN Charter.[10] All of a sudden, those atypical claims not included in the UN mandate, that is, irredentist and secessionist claims that were mostly non-European, were pronounced to be topical and, significantly, without precedent. The cases of Goa, Biafra, East Timor, Kurdistan, Katanga, Western New Guinea, the Falklands, Belize, Tibet, the Western Sahara, Ceuta, Melilla, and Gibraltar all fell outside the traditional rubric of resolution 1514, and were, in general, largely ignored by the international community, especially by the newly created African and Asian states.[11] James Mayall summarized this situation when he wrote:

In human affairs there can be no such thing as a *tabula rasa:* However the political map is redrawn, there are going to be dissatisfied groups. It is the recognition of this stubborn fact, which has produced, at the international level, the pragmatic reconciliation between the prescriptive principle of state sovereignty and the popular principle of national self-determination.[12]

Based on the desire to avoid anarchy, the compromise over the interpretation of self-determination continued to be observed at the UN until perestroika shook up the political landscape.

What will emerge from the breakup of the former Soviet empire is difficult to predict. Membership at the UN has already shot from 159 before 1989 to more than 180 by 1994. Yet this rapid surge of new membership does not imply that all previous claims awaiting settlement at the UN will be quickly resolved; indeed, if anything they could be delayed while the organization tries to make sense of the residual effects of the post–cold war order. It is too early to state with certainty, but thus far it seems that the new states are the result of breakups in federations, and that in these cases nations have been formed out of preexisting states along national lines. Even in the proposed Vance–Owen peace plan, put together in early 1993, the attempted carve-up of Bosnia was calculated within the external boundary of the existing Bosnian state. New external borders were not created, and thus the proposed map resembled a complex jigsaw puzzle. The more recent proposals have also sliced up the Bosnian state, but thus far they have not been sanctioned by the warring parties either, and the external boundaries remain non-negotiable.

As such, the pieces of the former Soviet empire may be treated like the colonies of ex-European empires in an attempt to maintain some sort of cohesion in the international system. That is, the breakup of any empire will generate international support, although that support will almost always be proffered at a dilatory and cautious pace, with the redrawing of borders confined, when possible, within existing boundaries. Accordingly, even the recent secession of Eritrea could be construed as an inevitable side effect of the withdrawal of Soviet influence in the Horn region, an area where Soviet interest and involvement had been significant.

The international community is reluctant to support secessionist and irredentist efforts because almost every state has within it disaffected groups. Each country, therefore, fears that support given to a sector within another country would only encourage similar claims within that country's own borders; witness Spain's initial misgivings about recognition of Slovenia and Croatia, based on Spanish nationalism in the Basque and Catalan regions. Not surprisingly, the country that paved the way for recognition, Germany, is one of the few West European countries without aggressive, separatist movements. This non-nationalist status can be attributed to the democratic fervor spawned by German reunification. The ideals of self-determination were given greater weight in the larger German nation, and the fairly homogeneous population facilitated this process. When secession does occur, however, economic viability is a criterion often used by the international community in determining support for emerging microstates, though again, this is not uniform.

Even when the international community agrees to allow a new country to emerge from either a secession or by shaking off an aggressive, occupying state, further complications arise in the formation of the referendum required under international law. How can the true population be computed? What happens if the majority of the indigenous population leaves, claiming a fear of persecution (whether real

105

or artificially induced), as in the case of the Western Sahara, and the new inhabitants have an allegiance to the aggressor? Will their votes be representative? How are the questions to be drawn up? Such thorny situations interfere with referendums, both during and after their occurrence, often to the point where one side declares the results void.

The Challenge Posed by Irredentism

Irredentist claims in particular are so tenacious precisely because it is impossible to delineate a proper period of time after which an occupation becomes legal and distinct from the surrounding territory. As Martin Wight has aptly put it, "An act of violence and injustice, by lapse of time and some degree of acceptance, could give rise to rights."[13] And Lee Buchheit has added,

> Even if one arbitrarily relied on history to establish a nation as an entity that had once enjoyed a measure of self-government, it [is] unclear how far back into the past one should search for this characteristic.[14]

Does the fact that the Arabs and the Moors inhabited Spain for almost 800 years between 711 A.D. and 1492 entitle Morocco to lay claim to present-day Spain? What of the Japanese claim to the four islands north of Hokkaido, occupied by the Soviets in August 1945?

Irredentist claims are thus complicated because they are based on a historical memory, usually shared by the contenders for the geographical space. This collective memory, irrespective of whether it is held by the present population or their ancestors centuries ago, helps to define and distinguish a nation, despite the difficulties inherent in making such a definition. Alfred Cobban noted this problem when he explained,

> The best we can say is that any territorial community, the members of which are conscious of themselves as members of a community, and wish to maintain the identity of their community, is a nation.[15]

For reasons based on the emotional need to belong and on security, people prefer to associate with others, whether that unit be the family, neighborhood, city, or state. Further, the smaller the group, the greater the loyalty; allegiance to one's family is stronger than to one's tribe, neighborhood, or city, which in turn is stronger than loyalty to the state in which one lives. Aggression can occur when such ties are severed due to external causes that often result in increased competition, for example, religious or border disputes between neighbors, ethnic groups, and/or states, or famine. As Abba Eban reportedly said after the 1967 Arab–Israeli war, "Men use reason as a last resort."[16]

The complications linked to irredentist claims point to the need for more attention to be paid to these "extraneous" issues that have infiltrated the international arena and have, in a sense, superseded the traditional colonial-based claims. Unlike secession, irredentism remains a largely unexplored and ignored concern, precisely because it is so difficult to defuse. This does not imply that secessionist claims are easy to understand and resolve, but rather that irredentist claims must not be overlooked in studies of nationalism.

Secession and irredentism do coincide on the same territory on occasion. One example is the Western Sahara, where many Saharawis want self-determination, or secession, depending on the stance one takes on the legality of the Moroccan occupation, yet Morocco also has an irredentist claim. In general, however, the factors that lead to the birth of the two types of claims are not the same. In most texts, irredentism is usually referred to as a minor by-product of secession—which assumes that it is a similar phenomenon. Moreover, many researchers argue that it rarely occurs; hence the paucity of research on it. At present there is only one book dedicated to irredentism as a separate issue, and that was published in 1991.[17] Irredentism is often neglected precisely because many researchers define it in the narrow fashion mentioned at the beginning of this article.[18] This article, however, employs the wider definition, thereby accounting for the argument that irredentism is a very topical phenomenon, threatening the "new world order" in places far from Somalia.

Irredentist claims are also discounted because they are more anachronistic in character, as opposed to secession, which is based on the modern concept of self-determination. Historical claims are thus less likely to receive legal sanction by the international community; this point is verified by the sparse evidence available from the International Court of Justice (ICJ). At present, war is not an acceptable alternative to the Court, but the results of the Greater Serbia campaign and Armenia's struggle for Nagorno-Karabakh will have implications for other irredentist cases. Irredentist claims, such as those of the Irish Republic to Northern Ireland, Argentina to the Falklands (Malvinas), Morocco to the Western Sahara and Ceuta and Melilla, Spain to Gibraltar, Iraq to Kuwait, Syria to Lebanon, Somalia to Djibouti, Guatemala to Belize, Cuba to Guantanamo, and the People's Republic of China to Hong Kong and to border regions of the former Soviet Union, not to mention the many cross-claims within the pieces of the former Soviet Union, continue to frustrate normal diplomatic efforts, both at home and abroad—often to the point of bringing the nations involved to war.

Current Claims

Tables 1 through 4 demonstrate the plethora of nationalist claims that had not been resolved by mid-1994. Tables 1 and 2 list secessionist and irredentist movements, table 3 details ambiguous or minor claims to secession or irredentism, and table 4 records claims that have arisen from the collapse of communism and the former Soviet Union. It is useful to draw a distinction between irredentist claims where some form of legality as to the ownership of the territory exists, as in the case of Gibraltar, and claims where there is no comparable international recognition of a legal claim, such as in the case of Tibet. Such ambiguous claims have been put in the third table although the dividing line is fuzzy, especially in a case like the Western Sahara where the international community is split as to the recognition of the Western Sahara as a separate nation. Moreover, any public utterances over the disputes can imply some form of recognition by both parties. Thus the division into separate tables does not mean that an ambiguous irredentist/secessionist claim cannot transfer to become a fully fledged irredentist or secessionist effort at some point on the continuum, or indeed the opposite. Most claims travel on a random curve depending on a wide variety of external factors. It should also be under-

107

Table 1
Secession Efforts

Region	Sovereignty	Affiliation To
Aceh	Indonesia	
Assam/Manipur/Nagaland/Punjab	India	
Basque regions	Spain/France	
Bougainville	Papua New Guinea	
Cabinda	Angola	Zaire
Casamance	Senegal	
Catalonia	Spain	
Corsica	France	
Karen people	Myanmar (Burma)	
Kurdistan	Iraq/Iran/Turkey/Azerbaijan	
Mindanao	Philippines	
Northern Italy	Italy	
Oromo	Ethiopia	
Quebec	Canada	
Scotland	Britain	
Southern Sudan	Sudan	
Tamil Eelam	Sri Lanka	India
Zanzibar	Tanzania	

Table 2
Irredentist Efforts

Region	Sovereignty	Affiliation To/Also Claimed By
Belize	Belize and U.K.	Guatemala/Mexico
Ceuta (Sebta) & Melilla	Spain	Morocco
Falklands, South Georgia, & South Sandwich Is. (Malvinas Is.)	Britain	Argentina
Gibraltar	Britain	Spain
Golan Heights	Israel	Syria
Guantanamo	United States	Cuba
Hatay	Turkey	Syria
Kashmir	India	Pakistan/China
Kurile Is.	Russia	Japan
Kuwait	Kuwait	Iraq
Lebanon	Lebanon	Syria
Mayotte	France	Comoros
Northern Ireland	Britain	Republic of Ireland
Ogaden	Ethiopia	Somalia
Taiwan	Taiwan	China
West Bank & East Jerusalem (Palestine)	Israel	Jordan/Palestinian people
Spratley & Paracel Is.	China/Vietnam	Taiwan/Malaysia/ Philippines/Brunei

Table 3
Ambiguous/Minor Secession or Irredentist Efforts

Region	Sovereignty	Affiliation To/Also Claimed By
Aegean Sea Is.	Greece/Turkey	Greece/Turkey
Åland Is.	Finland	Sweden
Brittany	France	a
China	China	Taiwan
Cyprus	Greece/Turkey	Greece/Turkey
Diego Garcia	Britain	Mauritius
Djibouti	Djibouti	Somalia
East Timor	Indonesia	
Hong Kong	Britain	China
Irian Jaya (West Papua)	Indonesia	
Matthew & Hunter Is.	France	Vanuatu
Navassa Is.	United States	Haiti
Sabah	Malaysia	Philippines
San Andrés, Providencia & cayes	Colombia	Nicaragua
Senkaku (Diaoyutai) Is.	Japan	China/Taiwan
South Tyrol	Italy	Austria
Tibet	China	
Tromelin Is.	France	Mauritius
Tunb Is.	Iran	United Arab Emirates
Wales	Britain	
Western Sahara	mostly Morocco	Algeria/Saharawi people

Note: a. The absence of a name in this column indicates that the region wants to secede or have greater autonomy.

stood that when no country is listed in the third column of table 3, a claim is made by the inhabitants of the territory.

When only one name is listed, that does not preclude an alternative name given to the region by the claimant state, but rather it is the name most recognized and related to the particular dispute. Not included in these tables are some disputes that have advanced to levels of full-scale aggression, namely, civil wars in countries such as Rwanda, where the war is over control of the state. The very small island disputes and the numerous boundary disputes, the claims within South Africa from the homelands and from Lesotho and Swaziland, and the overlapping claims to Antarctica have also been omitted. These claims have

been left out because some are currently undergoing cataclysmic change and are thus indecipherable at present (except for Antarctica where no indigenous people are involved).

Table 4 incorporates the claims that are emerging from the collapse of communism and the former Soviet Union. This table is organized in a different fashion because the present status of most of the regions is insecure. One country excluded from this table is Poland, which does not at present harbor any nationalist impulses, although it is involved in many regional problems, especially with respect to Polish minorities. As former prime minister Hanna Suchocka stated,

> Poland is perhaps the only post-communist country that is not threatened with disintegration,

Table 4
Countries and Claims Deriving from the Collapse of Communism
and the Former Soviet Union

States	*Other Claimant States, Disputed Subregions, or Persecuted Minorities*
Albania	Greece[a]
Bulgaria	Ethnic Turks
Hungary[b]	
Bosnia-Herzegovina	Muslims, Croats, Serbs[c]
Croatia	
Slovenia	
Yugoslavia (Serbia & Montenegro)	Kosovo,[d] Vojvodina, Novi Pazar Sanjak
Macedonia (FYROM)[e]	Greece[f]
Czech Republic	
Slovakia	
Estonia	Ethnic Russians
Latvia	Ethnic Russians
Lithuania	Ethnic Russians
Armenia	
Azerbaijan	Nagorno-Karabakh[g]
Belarus	
Kazakhstan	
Kyrgyzstan	
Moldova	Dniester and Gagauzia[h]
Romania	Ethnic Hungarians, Transylvania region[i]
Russia	Chechen-Ingushetia, Kaliningrad, North Ossetia,[j] Siberia, Tatarstan, Volga region
Tajikistan	Kulyab, Leninabad oblasts
Turkmenistan	
Ukraine	Crimea, Northern Bukovina, Serpents' Is., Transcarpathia
Uzbekistan	
Georgia	Abkhazia, South Ossetia
	Karelia and Petsamo[k]

Notes: a. Ethnic Greeks in southern Albania are worried about their treatment by the government of Albania, and some want to federate with Greece.
  b. There are approximately 3,160,000 ethnic Hungarians living outside Hungary, and they fear persecution in the countries where they now reside. Of that total, 2 million are in Romania, 600,000 in Slovakia, 400,000 in Serbia, and 160,000 in Ukraine. The Hungarians claim a slightly higher total of 3.5 million.
  c. All three groups claim persecution, although the Serbs are largely recognized as being the dominant aggressors.
  d. Ethnic Albanians make up a minority in Kosovo and are worried about ethnic cleansing by Serbs.
  e. Most states recognize it as the Former Yugoslav Republic of Macedonia (FYROM).
  f. Greece recognizes the region as a separate state, but not the use of the name "Macedonia" for this part of the former Yugoslavia. Greece fears that such recognition will generate irredentist claims on the people living in the Macedonian area of northeastern Greece who also speak the Macedonian language.
  g. Nagorno-Karabakh wishes to join Armenia, and likewise, Armenia claims it.
  h. Dniester and Gagauzia oppose any Moldovan attempt to join with Romania.
  i. Disputed between Hungary and Romania.
  j. The Christian North Ossetians are fighting the Muslim Ingushetians.
  k. Disputed between Russia and Finland.

that is not making territorial claims on its neighbors and whose borders are not questioned by neighbors.[19]

Conclusions and Implications for the International Community

Because the nationalist claims listed in the four tables are mostly distinguishable from the colonial cases, and are therefore without precedent, the international community cannot easily create norms that apply to all cases. At present, any international laws concerning territorial claims favor the status quo, which for these cases means prolongation of the conflicts. Despite the seemingly insurmountable task of deciphering nationalist claims, it is essential that the international community focus more intensely on these disputes. It is only through international recognition and attention that a new country can legally emerge, or borders be restored in the case of unlawful aggression.

Irredentist and secessionist disputes are multiplying and intensifying rapidly, yet outside scholarly circles too little attention has been placed on identifying their causes, similarities, and differences, and on proper mediation techniques to employ before they progress into threatening conflicts. Since 1989 there has been significant debate among policymakers and in the press on many of the related issues, such as preventive diplomacy and humanitarian intervention, but the connection of most post–cold war concerns with nationalist disputes needs to be more closely examined. For example, in the United States, foreign affairs policy makers deal with nationalist disputes on a country-by-country basis, that is, Russian (or more often Soviet) experts analyze the problems in Russia and the former Soviet republics while Balkan experts apply their knowledge to the former Yugoslavia. Further, the United States only attends to conflicts late in their development, in a reactive as opposed to preventive fashion, and often only does so because of television coverage or some major humanitarian disaster. Although it is important to recognize the specifics of each case, it is also imperative that all irredentist and secessionist disputes—within their separate categories—be viewed through a similar lens because their commonalities are considerable, their genesis alike, and the issues to which they give rise interrelated. As stated earlier, the lessons from the Serbian campaign will resonate far beyond the surrounding territories.

The United States can play an important leadership role in pressuring the UN to become more active in its involvement, because the UN is the only venue where these issues can be fully addressed. Membership in the UN is, after all, contingent on international recognition and respect of borders, and on members signing the UN Charter and the Universal Declaration of Human Rights. In order for these documents to be worth their political weight, the UN must attempt to ensure compliance. As a first step, the mandates of the Policy and Analysis Unit of the Office of the Under Secretary General and the newly established high commissioner for human rights should be expanded to deal with the question of persecuted minorities.

Major structural changes, however, need to be instituted at the UN. In the past, the UN has been successful in promoting decolonization, and at times, in dealing with violations of human rights, despite the significant constraints imposed on the organization throughout the Cold War. Yet it has not attempted to incorporate regulations for responding to cases of persecuted minorities, especially when they occur within states. According to the UN Development Programme, between 1989 and 1992 approximately 82 armed conflicts were tallied, and of those, only three were between states, the rest occurred within states.[20]

The UN needs to develop a set of guidelines that lays the groundwork for determining which cases merit attention and how it can be directed in order to fill the gaps in international law and practice that are due to a fundamental failure to address these problems. Early and assertive mediation can be effective, and can serve to encourage others embroiled in sticky disputes. Even though many points need to be ironed out in the Palestinian–Israeli peace agreement over Gaza and Jericho, the mere sight of bitter enemies signing a peace accord and shaking hands in front of the entire world can be nothing less than inspirational for other groups entangled in intractable conflicts.

In addition to establishing guidelines for responding to situations in which minorities are being persecuted, especially in the cases of genocide or ethnic cleansing, or for when the international community should recognize or assist in the birth of a new state, the UN must focus on other related issues that are usually the result of nationalist conflicts in their most extreme form. What should the UN do in cases where the state completely breaks down and disintegrates into a civil war, where there is no peace to keep, such as happened in Somalia and is now happening in Rwanda? When should the UN intervene militarily by appealing to chapter VII of the UN Charter (which permits the Security Council to advocate intervention in the interest of international peace and security)?[21] Should chapter VII then be rewritten in a more precise manner? The UN Security Council has begun to address some of these issues; as recently as May 1994 it set out a list of factors to be considered in peacekeeping operations, including periodic checks on operations to see if they are being fulfilled. Yet other questions remain unanswered.

When should UN safe-havens, or possibly even in extreme cases, protectorates, be established, and how should they be defended? If safe-havens are created, like those at present in Bosnia, should a time frame be fixed so that all members of the UN are aware of the commitment they are making? How long should the UN be stationed in these regions? To be effective, should plans similar to the Marshall Plan be enacted, and the UN be prepared to remain in these territories for 40 plus years?

These difficulties lead to even thornier ones concerning the financing of UN operations, whether they be in the realm of peacekeeping or establishing and maintaining safe-havens and/or protectorates or for full-scale military interventions. As was blatantly apparent in the Somalia intervention, these operations are perceived to be prohibitively expensive, and fears of this expense have hindered willingness to get involved in Rwanda, although some would argue that the costs can easily be borne by the international community. According to Sir Brian Urquhart, "In 1992 the UN in all its peacekeeping operations throughout the world cost $2.4 billion—less than the cost of two days of Desert Storm or two Stealth bombers."[22] Further, as was also learned from Somalia, operations can become even more expensive if the international community waits until the last minute, and finds that it cannot eschew involvement anyway for humanitarian purposes. Had the UN acted in a preventive fashion early on as the Somalia crisis was developing, the costs would have been significantly lower. A similar scenario has developed in Rwanda because the massive scale of the violence and the incredible death tolls are hard to ignore.

Another issue to consider related to the financing of these operations is whether the United States should continue to put up the bulk of the costs of running the UN—currently at 25 percent—and of peacekeeping operations—at 30.4 percent.[23] The extent of the contribution by the United States has, in most cases, served to impede the smooth running of the UN, because funding is held up by a Congress whose members are often unwilling to become involved in expensive operations and have a difficult time explaining away these costs to their constituents. As Ambassador Madeleine Albright remarked in May 1994, "Our entire assessed share of U.N. peacekeeping costs in the current fiscal year—an amount we expect to exceed $1,000 million—is currently unmet."[24]

Burden sharing and increased involvement among all UN members are vital to avoid charges of U.S. imperialism, to ensure greater commitment among all members to the organization itself, and to broaden internal support of the UN's activities. Reforming UN finances in such a way as to distribute the burden more equally, especially among the wealthier members, is attractive to the United States in almost every way—except for the inevitable consequence that the United States would lose some control within the organization, which thereby would reduce its impact and influence internationally as well.

In addition to attending to the con-troversy over financing UN operations, the UN also needs to be prepared to act consistently in all international crises, difficult as that may be in the unpredictable realm of politics. Members of the UN have to realize that once decisions are made to become involved, the commitment and responsibilities that go with them should be binding. This is not to say that the UN should get embroiled in lots of Vietnams, but rather that if intervention is undertaken, vacillating policy-making, similar to what took place in Somalia, must be eschewed. Moreover, significant numbers of soldiers should be sent in from the start to maintain a cease-fire, complete and impartial disarming of participants in the conflicts must ensue, and tribunals should be set up immediately to begin prosecuting those who violate the cease-fire.

The lesson from recent interventions, including the Somalia and Bosnia operations, is that when intervention transpires, it cannot be of the Panamanian variety, but instead, political and strategic control of the country must be placed in the hands of the UN. Such aggressive involvement is not popular among most members of the international community as nationals will be risking their lives and the ventures will be costly. Yet the alternative, a return to traditional peace-keeping with small numbers of soldiers who are not allowed to fire in most circumstances, has been proven to be ineffective in civil wars or in situations in which there is no peace to keep, and can be more costly in the long run as larger-scale involvement is often inevitable because some conflicts degenerate into civil wars.

The conclusion drawn by many was that it was not wise to become entangled in civil wars, that such involvement only drew parties deeper into the conflicts. Yet it is almost impossible for the international community to stand aside as thousands are being slaughtered, as in Rwanda, where the death toll has reached half a million by some estimates. In other words, just because the UN has made a mess of many past interventions, this does not preclude success for future ones, especially if clear guidelines are established.

If errant members of the international community are fully aware of the risks they are taking when they embark on an aggressive course of action, and especially of the repercussions of their actions, they are more likely to abide by international law. Although the war continues in Sudan, the threat of intervention for humanitarian reasons has been forcing the president, Omar Bashir, to supply the southern regions with food. Thus, claimed certain Sudanese officials, "There is no humanitarian pretext here for intervention."[25] Yet measures are still inadequate for establishing peace in Sudan.

Once intervention in a civil war has been undertaken, the UN has to be fully committed to building a stable government in order to ward off a return to civil strife. Similarly, in the case of involvement in nationalist conflicts where there is less aggression, the UN must try to facilitate conflict resolution in the territory, possibly through expanding its peacekeeping operations. The United States can contribute here by sharing its experience and expertise in democracy building. Recent concerns about international peace and security have focused on democratization as one technique for enhancing global stability. The underlying assumption is that liberal democracies do not use force to resolve conflicts; instead they channel discontent through existing multilat-

eral structures, such as the UN, the General Agreement on Tariffs and Trade, the European Union, the Conference on Security and Cooperation in Europe, the Organization of American States, and other such organizations. Moreover, there is a growing belief that democratization can assist in undermining oppressive regimes. Democracies are also seen as the best available political structures for resolving ethnic conflicts. Minorities are normally given some representation in democratic systems by their right to vote, and the free press offers them a chance to air grievances.

For the United States to assist in instituting any lasting change, then, the various foreign policy organs of the government (including U.S. embassies in areas where ethnic conflict is severe), and organizations involved in democratization, like the Agency for International Development (AID), need to coordinate their efforts, expertise, and findings, and share them with the UN.[26] Strategies for eliminating or at least managing ethnic conflict within democratic structures can be compiled from the wealth of information already in circulation that deals with electoral, educational, legislative, municipal, civic, judicial, and military reforms. The results of such collaboration could then be disseminated in a high-profile public relations campaign to educate the U.S. public about the very real dangers that these conflicts pose.

Nationalist claims, anomalous leftovers from a past imperial age, exacerbate an already unstable international order and could undermine it if steps are not taken to confront such aggression. It is critical that the international community, prodded by the United States, concentrate on all nationalist disputes for political, economic, and humanitarian reasons. The risk that ethnic violence will spill over into neighboring countries lacking strong institutional structures is great, and the likelihood that large-scale wars will erupt increases.

The global market is also affected by these disputes as investments cannot be safeguarded in insecure regions. Lack of investment can, in turn, exacerbate many conflicts as citizens of such states find that neither their basic needs are being fulfilled nor can they purchase necessities, such as food and fuel. There are few states today that are self-sufficient, not reliant on other states for many of their essentials. Nationalist conflicts also create refugees, who are threatening to overwhelm the international system by their sheer numbers. The resultant problems affect every state, especially the wealthier ones, such as the United States, which are often called in at the last minute to sort out the problems once they have escalated. Early involvement in many disputes, on the other hand, can be an effective mechanism for defusing tension before the state completely implodes.

The author accepts full responsibility for the views expressed in this article, which is based on her doctoral dissertation, submitted to the Department of International Relations, London School of Economics. The author gratefully acknowledges the assistance of James Mayall, her thesis adviser.

Notes

1. Thomas D. Lancaster and James L. Taulbee, "Britain, Spain, and the Gibraltar Question," *Journal of Commonwealth and Comparative Politics* 23 (1985), p. 251.

2. See James Mayall, *Nationalism and International Society* (Cambridge: Cambridge University Press, 1990), pp. 59–61.

3. Alsace-Lorraine was finally returned to France after it had been lost in the 1871 Franco–Prussian War.

4. The Trusteeship System provided for a council to administer the transition to independence and to inspect all trust territories according to article 73 of the UN Charter.

5. General Assembly Resolution 1514, 15 UN GAOR Supp. 16, UN Document A/4684, 1960, pp. 66–67.

6. Declaration on the Granting of Independence to Colonial Countries and Peoples.

7. Thomas M. Franck and Paul Hoffman, "The Right of Self-Determination in Very Small Places," *New York University Journal of International Law and Politics* 8 (1976), p. 370.

8. The watchdog committee set up by the UN to monitor progress toward independence. Its official title is the Special Committee on the Situation with Regard to the Implementation of the Declaration on the Granting of Independence to Colonial Countries and Peoples. Originally created by General Assembly resolution 1654 (XVI) on November 27, 1961, as a committee of 17 members, it was expanded to 24 by resolution 1810 (XVII) on December 17, 1962.

9. Lee C. Buchheit, *Secession: The Legitimacy of Self-Determination* (New Haven, Conn.: Yale University Press, 1978), p. 17.

10. Ernest Gellner, *Nations and Nationalism* (Oxford: Blackwell Publishers, 1983), p. 44. Gellner noted only 159 countries in his study, as opposed to today's figure. He actually calculated the number of languages at 8,000 and argued that "a difference of language . . . entail[s] a difference of culture."

11. They were considered at the UN on an annual basis, but these hearings were primarily a formality.

12. Mayall, *Nationalism*, p. 45.

13. Martin Wight, *Systems of States* (Leicester, U.K.: Leicester University Press, 1977), p. 163.

14. Buchheit, *Secession*, p. 5.

15. Alfred Cobban, *National Self-Determination* (London: Oxford University Press for the Royal Institute of International Affairs, 1945), p. 48.

16. Cited in Edward O. Wilson, *On Human Nature* (Cambridge, Mass.: Harvard University Press, 1978), p. 117.

17. Naomi Chazan, ed., *Irredentism and International Politics* (London: Adamantine Press, 1991).

18. See Donald Horowitz, *Ethnic Groups in Conflict* (Berkeley, Calif.: University of California Press, 1985), especially the chapter entitled, "The Logic of Secessions and Irredentas," for an example of the use of the more restrictive definition.

19. *Economist*, Eastern Europe Survey, March 13, 1993, p. 18.

20. *Economist*, June 4, 1994, p. 67. The UNDP defined a conflict as one in which more than 1,000 were killed.

21. This clause was invoked in the Kuwaiti and Somali interventions, and in the short-term operations in Bosnia.

22. Sir Brian Urquhart, "Who Can Police the World?" *New York Review of Books*, May 12, 1994.

23. From Ambassador Madeleine Albright's testimony to a House Foreign Affairs subcommittee, May 17, 1994.

24. *Ibid.*

25. *Economist*, March 6, 1993, p. 63.

26. The major obstacle to greater coordination of efforts is bureaucratic politics. One possible solution would be to assign the role of coordinator to an office in an already established agency, such as the National Security Council, and hold that office accountable for compiling and managing all related information.

Old World Disorders

James C. Clad

ALTHOUGH THE RELENTLESS unraveling of established political order within the former Soviet Union, Yugoslavia, and other Central European states has seized Western attention in recent months, much more redrawing of the world's political map lies ahead—especially in regions we still describe, for want of a better word, as the Third World. The magnitude of this change can scarcely be overemphasized; by comparison to the fault lines opening beneath dozens of bogus "nation-states" created after World War II, Europe's ruptures will come to look like simple hairline fractures.

With every passing week the news from Europe makes us realize how much the old, bipolar confrontation propped up many rickety states or suppressed the ethnic discord within them. But we have yet to realize that most of the world's feeble sovereignties lie well outside Europe; after two waves of state-creation following World Wars I and II, a superabundance of cardboard governments now clutters the membership rolls of international organizations. Within them, as in Central Europe, ethnic discord threatens the state; within them, far more than in Europe, a collapse of even minimal civic standards augurs the rapid disappearance of the state.

One notion has sustained the exis-

tence of third world sovereignty—the European model of the nation-state. Self-determination for colonial peoples became global orthodoxy 40 years ago as the decolonization period began, meshing two, incompatible ideas. The first was the notion that separate peoples require a separate state. The second was insistence, by colonizer and colonized alike, that frontiers positioned during the colonial era should remain as markers for this new "national" identity, even if (as was invariably the case) they were drawn with little heed to achieving coincidence of ethnic geography with boundaries.

This contradiction hardly slowed the decolonizing momentum. Sovereignty alone, it was thought, would prove a transportable and expandable concept, adding scores of new building blocks to the international system. Transportable, yes, but not workable: like flying buttresses of stone holding up cathedral walls, superpower rivalry lent these entities a semblance of solidity. So did the dozens of conventions, protocols, and other instruments that characterize the international system of customary state relations.

But political priorities are another matter. And today, without great power rivalry, there is scant reason to care if territories such as Somalia, once described as a strategic patch of sand, have degenerated into warring sandboxes. If the resolution of the Yugoslav, Moldovan, Georgian, Azeri, and other Central European crises now depends (as American and European di-

James C. Clad, a journalist and former diplomat, is a senior associate at the Carnegie Endowment in Washington, D.C.

plomacy implicitly shows it does) on those who inhabit these lands, the Western powers are even more disinclined to intervene in the Third World to determine the outcome. Only one result is clear: the outcomes cannot square with a continuation of the original, decolonized state erected 20 or 30 years ago.

The remainder of this article looks beyond the fading of global confrontation to another, and far more compelling, reason for the lengthening of the roll call of "national" failures. The disappearance of the outside buttressing occurs at a moment when decay *within* these flimsy sovereignties dooms many to dismemberment or chaos.

In the Third World, as noted, few territorial lines correspond to national affinities. Frontiers too often cut across peoples rather than define them. The second wave of state-creation in our fast-ending century occurred just 35 years ago; it went far beyond the European and Middle Eastern focus of the first wave of the post–World War I era, which crested on the Wilsonian ideal of self-determination.

The entities spawned by the second wave, during the 1950s and 1960s, are now slipping into chronic failure. The demographics alone portend growing Malthusian distress in places like the Philippines, Kenya, and Bangladesh. Successive economic strategies—articulated by patronizing outsiders (Marxists or free-marketeers) or by local wise men (Tanzania's or Cambodia's own brand of indigenous socialism)—have failed.

One by one, the aid experts' prescriptions—privatization, smokestack industries, training, "basic needs," appropriate technology, or whatever—have been tried and discarded. Meanwhile, it is getting harder and harder

for indigenous elites to find excuses. Even the currently fashionable, free-market dogma cannot fill the gap. The international free-trading economy may have bestowed wealth on a lucky group of East Asian countries (and on lucky enclaves within those countries), but export-led industrialization cannot become a universal model.

The reason is simple. If the predominant local "civic culture" favors extraction rather than investment, whatever modest comparative advantage accrues from producing better bananas or hosting the cheapest sweatshop industries will do little to permanently deepen and broaden their economies. Some "national" economies, in any event, are permanently disadvantaged by an out-of-the-way position, by local costs, or by diminutive size. Most South Pacific or Caribbean microstates are already resigned to marginality, while other territories, large in size but slender in resource endowment (or the hard commodity of humankind), have experienced stagnation for two decades.

Meanwhile, third world poverty grows worse with the incessant pressure of numbers. The lure of out-migration to the West assumes a burning, immediate appeal, vitiating any remaining attraction of the original—albeit invented—postcolonial nationalism. Negative reactions in the West to third world migrants—bound to arise in the United States as well—augur poorly for these hopes. Nor is democracy the panacea. In a great swath of the non-Western world, little correlation exists between political participation and economic success. Asia's most voluble country, the Philippines, has recurrent elections and a vibrant if sensationalist free press; these survive robustly beside abject administrative failure and economic distress. Contrast this to the authori-

is a formidable but nonetheless crucial challenge.

Governments have begun to think of such preventive actions as the symbolic deployment of UN soldiers, for example, to Macedonia and Kosovo, or the expanded use of fact-finding, human rights monitors, and early warning systems. Longer-term economic and social development, reforms to distribute the benefits of future growth more equitably, and restructured global financial and trading systems could mitigate conflict. But effective prevention today and tomorrow would also include a trip wire consisting of the physical deployment of well-armed troops with contingency plans and reserve firepower for immediate retaliation in case such a trip wire were engaged. This would amount to an advance authorization for a chapter VII riposte, not simply a hope that best-case scenarios will prevail.

It is always easier to demonstrate that earlier investments would have been worthwhile when it is too late rather than when experts warn of impending disasters. The dilemma is that prevention is cost-effective in the long run but cost-intensive in the short run. Except for the military's ability to plan for worst-case contingencies to defend *raisons d'état*, governments and politicians are rarely anything but myopic. Blunting the edges of local conflicts requires so many resources that the most likely future scenario involves more wars and fewer efforts to mitigate their consequences rather than more efforts to forestall violence.

At a minimum, prevention requires that the UN and its member states at least avoid legitimating ethno-nationalism. The breakup of the former Yugoslavia without minority guarantees and the establishment of an international war crimes tribunal without resources to document or pursue criminals have fomented rather than attenuated ethno-nationalism.

Thus, prevention appears Pollyannaish and vacuous—two analysts have dubbed it "an idea in search of a strategy."[28] But what are the alternatives? Either there can be spreading chaos with accompanying policies and actions to contain the spillover, or there can be better military intervention than has taken place to date. Neither lacks moral and geopolitical consequences.

Other Actors and the UN's International Safety Net

The combination of military, civil administration, and humanitarian activities in UN operations in civil wars creates almost overwhelming problems of coordination, at headquarters and in the field. The UN secretary general is first among equals, with an emphasis on equals, a well-known structural handicap creating obvious problems between the UN secretariat and the autonomous main players of the UN system in civil wars (UNHCR, the UN Children's Fund [UNICEF], and the World Food Programme [WFP]).[29] The additional strains caused by weaknesses in the professional capacity to oversee the growing number of UN military operations exacerbates another serious and well-documented set of problems.[30]

What is unusual and emerges from the case of civil wars is the need to strengthen the UN by taking advantage of the potential contributions by other actors. In this regard, activities by nongovernmental and regional organizations are essential, as are those of the Washington-based financial institutions.

135

In the UN's operations in civil wars, nongovernmental organizations (NGOs) have made a significant contribution to the physical delivery of relief, to monitoring human rights, and to election monitoring. Given their closeness to the grass roots and their relatively low costs (on average, one of their staff costs less than half a UN international civil servant), the UN should subcontract for more services from international NGOs, as it has in Bosnia-Herzegovina and to a lesser extent in Cambodia, Central America, and Somalia. Also governments and other donors should expand resources made available directly through private agencies as well as strengthen incentives to make better use of local NGOs—if necessary, even at the expense of bilateral and intergovernmental aid programs and certainly of their traditional defense postures.

NGOs are increasingly worried, however, that the growing volume of aid for humanitarian relief is instead being subtracted from the stagnant public resources devoted to economic development and especially to the alleviation of poverty in poor countries. Eight donors expended more than 10 percent of their total bilateral assistance on humanitarian assistance in 1992 (the most recent year for which statistics are available) compared with just a couple as little as five years ago.[31] Because humanitarian emergencies routinely take place in the context of open warfare, UN or UN-blessed military forces compete with development assistance rather than with defense allocations. This creates more than a statistical problem—where the military is used for the delivery of humanitarian assistance, only the incremental costs are usually tabulated as overseas development assistance. The policy challenges in the West are urgent, namely how to simultaneously determine the most effective mix of military and humanitarian inputs in complex emergencies; maintain the scarce resources that donor governments at present devote to poverty alleviation; and downsize military spending.

Regional organizations are sometimes considered to be an alternative to the UN. In spite of considerable rhetoric, they are less substitutes for than complements to the organization.[32] Most existing regional institutions have virtually no military experience or resources. They normally also contain hegemons whose presence makes legitimate intervention in civil wars problematic. The regional institutions that were unable to make a difference in Somalia—the Organization of African Unity, the Arab League, and the Islamic Conference—are clear illustrations.

In fact, ill-founded reliance on Europe's regional institutions in the former Yugoslavia provides the best example of these difficulties. Even these well-endowed regional organizations failed the test: the EC and the CSCE were unable to develop a common foreign policy for recognizing independence with guarantees for minorities, and member governments dithered in NATO and the Western European Union (WEU) about possible military action. A military response to either the international aggression or the continued civil war in the former Yugoslavia would hardly have been an "out of area" operation. For two years, however, weakness rather than resolve characterized European diplomacy, which in turn slowed down and sometimes impeded reactions from the one entity best suited to make the decision to authorize outside military intervention, the UN Security Council.

The cases of Central America and

Cambodia suggest another approach. Regional groupings whose members are essentially small countries are less threatening and can be helpful on the diplomatic front. Thus the Contadora Group, the Lima Support Group, and the Central American presidents have helped in El Salvador and Nicaragua, and the Association of Southeast Asian Nations (ASEAN) in Cambodia. The conventional wisdom is for the Security Council to make political decisions on behalf of the international community and then subcontract downward to a regional institution like NATO—as in the case of the former Yugoslavia—for its support services. Cambodia and El Salvador suggest the plausibility of a different model, namely, the regional institution ensures agreement among the parties and then subcontracts upward to the UN for its military, civil administration, and humanitarian services.

Finally, the UN's involvement in the civil wars in Central America has led to the realization that international organizations approach security in a variety of ways, some of which can clash. This is one of the few regional conflicts where a page has been turned, but peace-building has focused largely on short- and medium-term objectives (cease-fire monitoring, resettlement, elections). As these specific activities are completed, the UN military and civilian staff charged with them withdraw. Their departure leaves largely untouched the deeper, long-term structural problems that were at the root of the wars in the first place and that require long-term development.

The disconnect between military and economic security is striking in El Salvador, for instance. It has been argued convincingly by two participants in the peace process that the UN system is confronting difficulties there

because its efforts in the politico-military field "could be on a collision course" with the stabilization program and other economic adjustment activities mandated by the International Monetary Fund (IMF) and the World Bank.[33] The Washington-based financial institutions are autonomous and not usually considered part of the so-called UN system. But they are clearly an essential component of the international community's arsenal to combat civil wars. Whatever else was implied when the UN secretary general wrote of an "integrated approach to human security" in his *An Agenda for Peace*,[34] intergovernmental organizations in the politico-military and the economic development realms should work in tandem rather than at cross-purposes. Institutional changes—for example, involving the Washington-based organizations in peace negotiations from the outset rather than after the fact, and creating a unified UN presence in postconflict countries rather than multiple sources of authority—are required to overcome the schizophrenia. And they are possible.

The Media

From a historical perspective, the media's capacity to influence foreign policy is not new. Before the Spanish Civil War, for example, William Randolph Hearst, the newspaper magnate, commented to Frederick Remington, the artist, "You furnish the pictures; I'll furnish the war." More recently, the media have played a role in galvanizing international measures regarding civil wars. Their current influence was foreshadowed by earlier crises: in Biafra in the late 1960s, in Bangladesh in the early 1970s, and in Ethiopia in 1973 and again in 1984. But media influence in post–cold war crises has sharply increased. Starting with northern Iraq in 1991 and continuing with Somalia and Bosnia-Herzegovina, observers have quipped that Ted Turner and his Cable News Network (CNN) rather than the UN secretary general or the U.S. president are in charge.

Although the connections between the media and political and humanitarian action in civil wars recur repeatedly, the chemistry of the interaction between public exposure and international engagement requires serious analytical review. There can be no doubt that interactions between and among the three key sets of outside actors responding to civil wars—the media, governmental policymakers, and the UN—have been speeded and sharpened by technological changes in the communications world.

Everyone seems to have a view on this issue, but there are more anecdotes than data. Understanding the interactions among the actors has a special urgency. There is widespread agreement that the media exercised decisive influence on political decision makers and on military and humanitarian organizations alike in Somalia and Bosnia. If the wrong conclusions are drawn about these operations and publicized by the media, these actions may come to represent the high-water mark of assertive post–cold war action by the UN in civil wars. Given the prospect of retreat from such challenges, better informed responses to questions like the following are urgently required.

Why was the December 1992 intervention in Somalia not followed by intervention in neighboring southern Sudan where even more civilians were in danger, or in Angola where soon after 1,000 people were dying per day? Was it a lack of TV coverage, or were other political factors more important? If policy, as the British foreign secretary Douglas Hurd claimed, is not driven by the media, how can one interpret the sudden spiriting away of the Bosnian youngster Irma Hadzimurotovic and other war-wounded Sarajevans to previously unavailable hospital beds in Britain and beyond?[35] Or again, as the president of United Press International claimed in an effort to delimit the responsibility of the media, why has the war in the Balkans dragged on despite relentless media coverage of the carnage?[36]

The media have speeded up the tripartite interaction in some instances and in others may have complicated it unnecessarily. In Somalia, for example, the media played a role in bringing about the military intervention that many (but not all) nongovernmental humanitarian agencies had sought, thereby bypassing the dissenting views of other NGOs. Moreover, media coverage of the U.S.-led intervention actually brought other operational problems in its wake; for instance, more aid workers were killed during the Unified Task Force (UNITAF) phase than in the preceding year. And media airing of indignities suffered by dead marines also played a role in the premature termination of the Western military presence.

As well as dramatizing needs, publicizing human rights abuse, stimulating action, and generating resources, the media have distorted the kinds of assistance provided, skewed the allocations of resources and personnel among geographical areas, ignored the role of local humanitarians, and focused international attention on the perceived bungling of various agencies. The influence of the media has also posed difficult choices for aid agencies regarding the amount of human and financial resources that they allocate to the cultivation of media relationships rather than to operations.

In purveying information, the media help set the agenda in the foreign policy arena. Here, too, viewpoints differ about the nature of the media as an institution. Some observers see the media as manipulators and as bound to convey shallow and misinformed conclusions; others view them as the helpless victims of circumstance and of the harsh economics of the industry itself.

If the media are disaggregated into broadcast (radio and television) and print (newspapers, journals, and specialists), significant differences appear between news and opinion sources, and between those with local or national perspectives and those with a global reach. Analysis must take into account the economic realities that drive the media to "tell a good story" ever more quickly and more compellingly than competitors, and the prevailing tensions that arise from the challenge simultaneously to inform, to entertain, and to persuade.

In short, the media are both an institution and a process, subject to influences over which they have little control as well as major players in their own right. They have clearly had an influence on the UN and civil wars, but a more basic understanding of their exact impact on both policy formulation and action is essential.

The U.S. Role

Charles Krauthammer's "unipolar moment" lasted no longer than Francis Fukuyama's "end of history."[37] "Superpower" is an inaccurate description for the United States, but its leadership is still the sine qua non of meaningful UN actions, particularly those involving significant military forces. The lack of vision and direction in the present administration's foreign policy is thus particularly unsettling. As has become obvious in Somalia, Haiti, Bosnia, and now Rwanda, if the United States does not participate in the toughest assignments, few others will.

Policymakers in Washington have steadily abandoned the pro-UN stance that formed part of Bill Clinton's campaign. Symptomatic of this shift was the contentious interagency debate beginning in mid-1993 about the wisdom of placing U.S. combat troops under UN command and control as had been recommended in those portions of a draft presidential decision directive leaked to the media. The same tension surfaced in September 1993 in the minority report of the U.S. Commission on Improving the Effectiveness of the United Nations.[38] It continued as the president delivered his maiden speech before the General Assembly in New York while heavy U.S. casualties were being sustained in Mogadishu. The Defense Department's 1993 *Bottom-Up Review* questioned the feasibility of multilateral military efforts in general and, in particular, the wisdom of sending U.S. troops as part of UN efforts to restore the elected government in Port-au-Prince.

After a year of fierce interagency feuding, ill-fated military operations in Somalia and Haiti, and dithering about the former Yugoslavia, PPD–25 was finally signed in early May 1994. The document not only justifies an abrupt change in policy but also appeared to be part of a historical pattern of U.S. about-faces.[39] The so-called policy reflects the extent to which Washington has washed its hands of responsibility and abandoned the mantle of leadership.

PDD–25 spells out strict guidelines now to be considered before the United States agrees to participate in any operation: its impact on U.S. interests, the availability of troops and funds, the necessity for U.S. participation, congressional approval, a clear date for U.S. withdrawal, and appropriate command and control arrangements. Moreover, Washington will not approve any new UN operation, with or without U.S. soldiers, unless other restrictive criteria are satisfied. The crisis must represent a threat to international peace and security (specifically including starvation among civilians), gross abuses of human rights, or a violent overthrow of a democratically elected government. Any proposed intervention must lay out clear objectives, the availability of troops and funding, and, most important, consent of the parties and a realistic exit strategy.

New operations will rarely, if ever, satisfy these conditions. More reactions like that to Rwanda's gruesome ordeal must be expected. In response to the slaughter of tens of thousands of civilians and the appearance of the largest number of refugees (250,000 according to some estimates) ever to materialize in a 24-hour period, the international community actually reduced its commitment from 2,700 troops to a few hundred. While the massacre continued, the Security Council debated how to send and finance African peacekeepers, and the United States blocked the first efforts to do so. Meanwhile, the president told graduating naval cadets in Annapolis that Rwanda was not relevant to U.S. interests, and France went forward with symbolic, controversial intervention. Rwanda's abandonment followed the retreat of U.S. and Canadian peacekeepers aboard the U.S.S. *Harlan County* headed for Port-au-Prince, the withdrawal of U.S. and other Western troops from Somalia, and the U.S. refusal to consider sending ground forces to Bosnia or pursu-

ing any other robust military effort in that hapless region.

Oddly enough, PDD–25 still maintains a provision for fighting two regional conflicts simultaneously. How can an administration elected with a promise to trim military expenditures justify maintaining a $250 billion annual budget for the Pentagon to cover that eventuality while at the same time renouncing participation in UN security operations?

With Pontius Pilate as the new model for the engagement of the United States in armed conflicts, the UN and those suffering in civil wars are in desperate straits.

Conclusion

Although humanitarians often argue that "compassion fatigue" is a facile excuse to avoid global responsibilities,[40] domestic political constraints are nonetheless very palpable throughout the West, where recessionary and budgetary requirements directly clash with the need for outside help in what seems like a never-ending series of crises around the world. I have argued elsewhere that triage, the French term to describe the wrenching process of selection, is the foremost challenge for policymakers who must balance these claims in the immediate future.[41] Not only are parliamentary financial pressures at loggerheads with the growing demands for assistance, but also the UN's brief as a world organization with a broad mandate, universal membership, and a global operational network means that virtually no crisis is not on its agenda. Like the surgeon on the battlefield, policymakers have to make tough decisions during this crisis of crises.

For those trying to make sense of the UN's possible contribution to the post–cold war security agenda, several lessons emerge to guide decisions about who needs no help, who cannot be helped, and who can and must be helped. Whether a civil war is located in the Third World or the former Second World is not important—except that appropriate Russian participation must be ensured. Moscow clearly will play a central role in the "near abroad," but NATO must be careful to ensure that Russia's participation in the "partnership for peace" is not perceived as a new Yalta for peacekeeping in the former Warsaw Pact.

With fragmentation likely to continue, hair-splitting about the distinctions between interstate and intrastate conflicts is worthwhile only for international lawyers. Attempting to mitigate the human suffering from civil wars is a growing and legitimate task for the international community. Great care is required, however, before making commitments because civil wars are a complicated terrain for the UN, or anyone else. It would be better to avoid commitments and maintain a tattered credibility rather than put collective toes in the water and pull back when the temperature is not quite right, as it rarely is.

Specifying in advance the criteria for an operation would be extremely helpful in measuring success or failure. Such an approach has an additional advantage: it requires decision makers to be perfectly clear in communicating with their publics about UN involvement in civil wars. At a minimum, governments voting for resolutions must also commit commensurate resources—military and humanitarian—to provide a realistic basis for mandates. Better training of the military, civilian administrators, and humanitarians is increasingly required for the coming generation of multifaceted

operations. The task of coordination, long a hobbyhorse of governments vis-à-vis the UN, has become even more imperative as a result of bringing together more complex UN efforts with military forces and an ever-growing number of NGOs. Real leadership as well as a more hierarchical and military-like structure are required for UN operations in active civil wars. The laissez-faire approach of the past toward the bevy of actors that flocks to the scene of disasters is simply impermissible when so many lives are at stake and so few resources available.

The Security Council's role at center stage should continue. Additional efforts are required from governments to ensure more transparency and better criteria governing intervention. Whatever the results of such multilateral diplomacy and discussions, however, moving toward a UN monopoly in decision making about enforcement should help deter abuse of populations and resort to purely unilateral agendas. The professional ineptitude of the UN in matters military, however, dictates an expansion of the coalition-type efforts used in northern Iraq rather than the establishment of any UN army or even a small rapid deployment force. Better working relationships with, and more subcontracting to, NATO should also be explored.

The concern to keep on the right side of governments cannot continue to dominate the attitudes of the UN secretary general and secretariat toward its operations. Slavish adherence to an outmoded notion of state sovereignty means that the UN's field personnel in civil wars have not done as much as they could have in terms of protecting human rights. What this points toward is the notion of a better division of labor in civil wars. Both local and international NGOs should play an expanded role in the physical delivery of assistance, while the Washington-based financial institutions should be integrated early into efforts to end civil wars.

Prevention is so intuitively attractive that the international community needs to begin operationalizing its practice. In spite of the difficulties in moving beyond rhetoric, the political and economic costs of outside intervention in civil wars so dwarf those of forestalling them that prevention is emerging as the diplomatic issue of the late 1990s. At a minimum, governments should avoid legitimizing ethno-nationalism.

The media influence governmental, nongovernmental, and intergovernmental responses to civil wars. Analysts often suffer from a professional malady that makes them routinely call for more research, but nonetheless in this arena the call is on target because there are more hypotheses than data and analysis.

Finally, there is simply no substitute for leadership from Washington. This essential condition for UN action in civil wars has disappeared from the White House but is surfacing elsewhere. The mid-June 1994 vote in the House of Representatives to order the president to circumvent the UN resolutions and end U.S. participation in the arms embargo against the Bosnian government may be a harbinger of a necessary shift in power from the White House to the Hill. Although the Senate's subsequent tie vote on the issue necessitates further negotiations in a congressional conference, the House directly rebuked the inept president and his team of advisers and began to assert leadership to fill the vacuum in Washington. This development may sadden Democrats, but it is nevertheless crucial with a Clinton administration so obviously bereft of a foreign policy. The demonstrated lack of resolve in the White House not only puts dictators and thugs at ease; it also exacerbates suffering by civilian victims of civil wars.

This article draws on the introductory and concluding chapters of the author's forthcoming edited volume, The United Nations and Civil Wars *(Boulder, Colo.: Lynne Rienner, 1995).*

Notes

1. See Thomas G. Weiss, David P. Forsythe, and Roger A. Coate, *The United Nations and Changing World Politics* (Boulder, Colo.: Westview Press, 1994).

2. See "Executive Summary: The Clinton Administration's Policy on Reforming Multilateral Peace Operations," unclassified document, May 3, 1994.

3. For discussions of these operations, see Samuel Makinda, *Seeking Peace from Chaos: Humanitarian Intervention in Somalia* (Boulder, Colo.: Lynne Rienner, 1993); Jarat Chopra, *United Nations Authority in Cambodia*, Occasional Paper no. 15 (Providence, R.I.: Watson Institute, 1994); Cristina Eguizábal et al., *Humanitarian Challenges in Central America: Learning the Lessons of Recent Armed Conflicts*, Occasional Paper no. 14 (Providence, R.I.: Watson Institute, 1993); and Larry Minear et al., *Humanitarian Action in the Former Yugoslavia: The U.N.'s Role 1991–1993*, Occasional Paper no. 18 (Providence, R.I.: Watson Institute, 1994).

4. For these and other gruesome statistics, see Sadako Ogata, *The State of the World's Refugees 1993: The Challenge of Protection* (New York, N.Y.: Oxford University Press, 1993).

5. "Moscow Counts on Itself to Stem Conflicts in CIS," *Peacekeeping Monitor* 1 (May–June 1994), pp. 4–5, 12–13.

6. Charles William Maynes, "A Workable Clinton Doctrine," *Foreign Policy*, no. 93 (Winter 1993–94), pp. 3–20.

7. Robert D. Kaplan, "The Coming Anarchy," *Atlantic Monthly*, February 1994, pp. 44–76. For other discussions of these challenges, see James N. Rosenau, *Turbulence in World Politics: A Theory of Change*

and Continuity (Princeton, N.J.: Princeton University Press, 1990); August Richard Norton, "The Security Legacy of the 1980s in the Third World," in Thomas G. Weiss and Meryl A. Kessler, eds., *Third World Security in the Post–Cold War Era* (Boulder, Colo.: Lynne Rienner, 1991), pp. 19–34; Lawrence Freedman, "Order and Disorder in the New World," *Foreign Affairs* 71, no. 1 (1992), pp. 20–37; James N. Rosenau, "Normative Challenges in a Turbulent World" and Charles W. Kegley Jr., "The New Global Order: The Power of Principle in a Pluralistic World," *Ethics and International Affairs* 6 (1992), pp. 1–40; Daniel Patrick Moynihan, *Pandaemonium: Ethnicity in International Politics* (New York, N.Y.: Oxford University Press, 1993); Joel Kotkin, *Tribes: How Race, Religion, and Identity Determine Success in the New Global Economy* (New York, N.Y.: Random House, 1993); Ted Robert Gurr, *Minorities at Risk: A Global View of Ethnopolitical Conflicts* (Washington, D.C.: U.S. Institute of Peace, 1993); "Ethnic Conflict and International Security," a special issue of *Survival* 35 (Spring 1993); and "Reconstructing Nations and States," a special issue of *Daedalus* 122 (Summer 1993).

8. See Ruth Sivard, *World Military and Social Expenditures 1993* (Washington, D.C.: World Priorities, 1993).

9. See Morton H. Halperin and David J. Scheffer, *Self-Determination in the New World Order* (Washington, D.C.: Carnegie Endowment, 1992).

10. *The Geneva Convention of August 12, 1949* and *Protocols Additional to the Geneva Conventions of 12 August 1949* (Geneva: ICRC, 1989).

11. See Thomas G. Weiss and Jarat Chopra, "Sovereignty Is No Longer Sacrosanct: Codifying Humanitarian Intervention," *Ethics and International Affairs* 6 (1992), pp. 95–117.

12. Gerald B. Helman and Steven R. Ratner, "Saving Failed States," *Foreign Policy*, no. 89 (Winter 1992–93), pp. 3–20.

13. See Paul Johnson, "Colonialism's Back—and Not a Moment Too Soon," *New York Times Magazine*, April 18, 1993.

14. John Gerard Ruggie, "Wandering in the Void," *Foreign Affairs* 72 (November/December 1993), pp. 26–31.

15. "U.N. Commander Wants More Troops, Fewer Resolutions," *New York Times*, December 31, 1993, p. A–3.

16. John Steinbruner, "Memorandum: Civil Violence as an International Security Problem," reproduced as Annex C in Francis M. Deng, *Protecting the Dispossessed: A Challenge for the International Community* (Washington, D.C.: Brookings Institution, 1993), p. 155.

17. See Thomas G. Weiss, "Intervention: Whither the United Nations?" *The Washington Quarterly* 17 (Winter 1993), pp. 109–128.

18. Adam Roberts, "Humanitarian War: Military Intervention and Human Rights," *International Affairs* 69, no. 3 (1993), p. 429.

19. Alex de Waal and Rakiya Omaar, "Can Military Intervention Be 'Humanitarian'?" *Middle East Report*, nos. 187/188 (March–April/May–June 1994), p. 7.

20. See Mohammed Ayoob, *The Third World Security Predicament: State-making, Regional Conflict, and the International System* (Boulder, Colo.: Lynne Rienner, forthcoming 1995).

21. See Boutros Boutros-Ghali, "Empowering the United Nations," *Foreign Affairs* 71 (Winter 1992/93), pp. 89–102; and *An Agenda for Peace* (New York, N.Y.: United Nations, 1992).

22. Boutros Boutros-Ghali, "An Agenda for Peace: One Year Later," *Orbis* 37 (Summer 1993), p. 332.

23. As quoted by Julia Preston, "U.N. Officials Scale Back Peacemaking Ambitions," *Washington Post*, October 28, 1993, p. A–40. For a further discussion of conceptual fuzziness, see Thomas G. Weiss, "New Challenges for UN Military Operations: Implementing an Agenda for Peace," *The Washington Quarterly* 16 (Winter 1993), pp. 51–66.

24. Deng, *Protecting the Dispossessed*, p. 134.

25. See Human Rights Watch, *The Lost Agenda: Human Rights and U.N. Field Operations* (New York, N.Y.: Human Rights Watch, 1993).

26. The author is grateful to Roberta Cohen for insights on this issue. See her "International Protection for Internally Displaced Persons," in Louis Henkin and John Lawrence Hargrove, eds., *Human*

Rights: An Agenda for the Next Century (Washington, D.C.: American Society of International Law, 1994), pp. 17–49. See also Charles H. Norchi, "Human Rights and Social Issues," and José E. Alvarez, "Legal Issues," in John Tessitore and Susan Woolfson, eds., *A Global Agenda: Issues Before the 48th General Assembly* (Lanham, Md.: University Press of America, 1993), pp. 213–311.

27. For a discussion, see Dick Thornburgh, *Reform and Restructuring at the United Nations: A Progress Report* (Hanover, N.H.: Rockefeller Center, 1993). See also other cautionary notes by Charles William Maynes, "Containing Ethnic Conflict" *Foreign Policy*, no. 90 (Spring 1993), pp. 3–21, and Stephen John Stedman, "The New Interventionists," *Foreign Affairs* 72, no. 1 (1992/93), pp. 1–16.

28. See Bruce Jentleson and Michael Lund, "Preventive Diplomacy: An Idea in Search of a Strategy" (paper presented at the International Studies Association, Washington, D.C., March 1994).

29. For a discussion, see Larry Minear and Thomas G. Weiss, *Mercy under Fire: War and the Global Humanitarian Community* (Boulder, Colo.: Westview Press, forthcoming 1995); see also their *Humanitarian Action in Times of War: A Handbook for Practitioners* (Boulder, Colo.: Lynne Rienner, 1993) and a series of edited essays with commentary in *Humanitarianism across Borders: Sustaining Civilians in Times of War* (Boulder, Colo.: Lynne Rienner, 1993).

30. For the history of peacekeeping, see Alan James, *Peacekeeping and International Politics* (London: Macmillan, 1990) and *The Blue Helmets* (New York, N.Y.: United Nations, 1990). For more analytical treatments, see Thomas G. Weiss and Jarat Chopra, *UN Peacekeeping: An ACUNS Teaching Text* (Hanover, N.H.: Academic Council on the United Nations System, 1992); William J. Durch, ed., *The Evolution of UN Peacekeeping: Case Studies and Comparative Analysis* (New York, N.Y.: St. Martin's Press, 1993); Adam Roberts, "The United Nations and International Security," *Survival* 35 (Summer 1993), pp. 3–30; Paul Diehl, *International Peacekeeping* (Baltimore, Md.: Johns Hopkins University Press, 1993); Marrack Goulding, "The Evolution of United Nations Peacekeeping," *International Affairs* 69 (1993), pp. 451–464; Mats

R. Berdal, "Whither UN Peacekeeping?" *Adelphi Paper* 281 (London: Brassey's for IISS, 1993); and David A. Charters, ed., *Peacekeeping and the Challenge of Civil Conflict Resolution* (Fredericton, New Brunswick: Centre for Conflict Studies, 1994). For a focus on the military, see John Mackinlay and Jarat Chopra, "Second Generation Multinational Operations," *The Washington Quarterly* 15 (Spring 1992), pp. 113–131, and *A Draft Concept of Second Generation Multinational Operations 1993* (Providence, R.I.: Watson Institute, 1993); William J. Durch, *The United Nations and Collective Security in the 21st Century* (Carlisle Barracks, Pa.: U.S. Army War College, 1993); *The Professionalization of Peacekeeping: A Study Group Report* (Washington, D.C.: U.S. Institute of Peace, 1993); and Dennis J. Quinn, ed., *Peace Support Operations and the U.S. Military* (Washington, D.C.: National Defense University Press, 1994).

31. See Judith Randel and Tony German, eds., *The Reality of Aid 94* (London: Actionaid, May 1994), especially pp. 30–32.

32. For a discussion of these issues, see Neil S. MacFarlane and Thomas G. Weiss, "Regional Organizations and Regional Security," *Security Studies* 2 (Fall/Winter 1992–93), pp. 6–37, and "The United Nations, Regional Organizations, and Human Security," *Third World Quarterly* 15 (April 1994), pp. 277–295.

33. Alvaro de Soto and Graciana del Castillo, "Obstacles to Peacebuilding," *Foreign Policy*, no. 94 (Spring 1994), p. 70.

34. Boutros-Ghali, *An Agenda for Peace*, para. 16. This theme is expanded in his *An Agenda for Development* (New York, N.Y.: United Nations, 1994).

35. See Michael Binyon, "Media's Tunnel Vision Attacked by Hurd," *Times* (London), September 10, 1993; Robin Gedye, "Hurd Hits Out Again at Media," *Daily Telegraph*, September 11, 1993; and Michael Leapman, "Do We Let Our Hearts Rule?" *Independent*, September 15, 1993.

36. Louis D. Boccardi, "Luncheon Remarks," at the "Forum on War and Peace in Somalia: The Role of the Media, An International Perspective," Columbia University, New York, February 16, 1994.

37. See Charles Krauthammer, "The Unipolar Moment," *Foreign Affairs* 15 (Summer 1992), pp. 113–134, and Francis Fuku-

yama, *The End of History and the Last Man* (New York, N.Y.: Free Press, 1992). This argument about the U.S. role was first made in Thomas G. Weiss, "When the U.S. Washes Its Hands of the World," *Christian Science Monitor,* May 25, 1994, p. 23.

38. U.S. Commission on Improving the Effectiveness of the United Nations, *Defining Purpose: The UN and the Health of Nations* (Washington, D.C., 1993).

39. See Robert W. Gregg, *About Face: The United States and the United Nations* (Boulder, Colo.: Lynne Rienner, 1993). See also Roger A. Coate, ed., *U.S. Policy and the Future of the United Nations* (New York, N.Y.: Twentieth Century Fund, 1994).

40. See Randel and German, *The Reality of Aid 94,* and Ian Smillie and Henny Helmich, eds., *Non-governmental Organisations and Governments: Stakeholders for Development* (Paris: Organization for Economic Cooperation and Development, 1993).

41. Thomas G. Weiss, "Triage: Humanitarian Interventions in a New Era," *World Policy Journal* 11 (Spring 1994), pp. 59–68, and "UN Responses in the Former Yugoslavia: Moral and Operational Choices," *Ethics and International Affairs* 8 (1994), pp. 1–22.

The Intervention Dilemma

Barry M. Blechman

WITH THE END of the Cold War and, with it, the risk that interventions abroad could result in confrontation, crisis, and even war between the nuclear-armed superpowers, Americans have begun to rethink the norms governing U.S. involvements in the affairs of other states. Contradictory impulses have dominated this debate. The typical American urge to export democratic and humanitarian values has encouraged activist policies and resulting involvements in many countries. But the traditional American antipathy toward "overseas entanglements" and, particularly, a distaste for military interventions, have diminished support for many individual expeditions that implied a serious risk of U.S. casualties or even significant expenditures.

The resulting policy dilemma caused difficulties for President George Bush and has bedeviled President Bill Clinton. Both administrations sought to escape from the dilemma by turning to the United Nations (UN), both to legitimate interventions and to spread the burden to a wider group of countries. As a result, the world organization's traditional peacekeeping functions have been transformed into more muscular "peace operations." But UN peace operations have had only mixed results, and the few clear failures have led to legislative initiatives that would severely curtail U.S. participation in UN peace operations and possibly cripple the organization's ability to sustain more than a traditional peacekeeping role.

Lost in the furor have been the facts that the UN has had more successes than failures in its expanded security role, and that the UN's apparent failures have not been completely its fault, to say nothing of the possibility that steps could be taken to greatly strengthen the UN's potential to contribute to international security through peace operations.

Contradictory Impulses

The belief that governments have a right, even obligation, to intervene in the affairs of other states seems to have gained great currency in recent years. Of course, modern communications have made people everywhere more aware of situations that seem to cry out for intervention, and more familiar with the personal tragedies that accompany these horrible calamities. Technology, too, has provided more ready means of intervention—whether for diplomats to mediate, for observers to monitor elections, for paramilitary forces to enforce economic sanctions, or for armed forces to carry out military

Barry M. Blechman is cofounder and chairman of the Henry L. Stimson Center in Washington, D.C.

The Washington Quarterly • 18:3

operations—removing in many cases the excuse of infeasibility. The governments of the great powers, and particularly the U.S. government, have the means to intervene today, whether they choose to do so or not.

Yet, far more than the physical means of awareness and intervention has changed. The norms governing intervention themselves have evolved. The sanctity once accorded to state boundaries has eroded considerably. The interdependence and penetrability of states need no elaboration. Serious crises anywhere in the world cause financial markets and currency rates to reverberate, affecting investors' confidence and the business climate overall. Companies large and small depend on foreign investors, components, markets, and technologies. Individuals are both affected more directly by turmoil in distant lands and more familiar with foreign countries. Ordinary citizens interact more frequently with people living abroad. People exercise rights to visit and conduct business in foreign countries routinely, almost without thinking about the legal boundaries that have been crossed.

Most important, however, profound changes have occurred in popular expectations. After decades of little more than formal intonation, the belief that governments can be expected to adhere to certain universal standards of behavior, even within their own borders, seems to have taken hold. This is certainly not to say that all people in all parts of the world already hold this belief. The view has penetrated populations to different degrees—most profoundly in Europe and North America, to a lesser degree in other parts of the world—but the trend is very clear, particularly among the economic and social elites that dominate politics in most countries.

What is the basis for the new view? Apparently, increasing numbers of people are willing to act on what must be an implicit belief that sovereignty does not reside with an abstraction called the state, and certainly not with self-appointed military or civilian dictatorships, but with the people of a country themselves. Even more, the view seems to hold, the power of all governments, even those popularly elected, is limited: individuals have inalienable rights that must be observed and protected by all governments. As a result, according to this increasingly powerful view, all governments can be held to certain standards of behavior involving basic human rights and democratic processes. In addition, when a country falls into such disarray that no governing body can end a humanitarian tragedy, the world community itself is accountable. When such events occur, the view continues, all people in other countries, and their governments, have not only the right, but the obligation, to intervene on behalf of both oppressed peoples and innocent bystanders.

Historically, when murderous civil wars or large-scale abuses of human rights occurred in a country, powerful governments with direct interests in that state sometimes intervened. Today, as a result of the greater currency of the views described above, great powers often feel compelled to intervene in domestic conflicts even when their direct stakes are limited. Sometimes, the officials of a great power hold to the views just described—and see intervention as a humanitarian responsibility. But at other times, if governments hesitate, and if the events in question are of sufficient magnitude, various constituencies exert political pressures for action—action to end the slaughter, to feed the refugees, to restore democracy, to at least save the lives of the children. Often, these days, private citizens and organizations become involved in these situations before governments even contemplate acting. Religious charities, humanitarian organizations, and activist political rights groups are involved on the ground in virtually all troubled nations. Their reports and activities reinforce, and sometimes help to create, popular pressures in foreign capitals for some kind of official action.

Thus, in the contemporary world, major powers react when troubles occur in even the most remote parts of the globe. Diplomats are dispatched, good offices tendered, observers emplaced, and political and economic campaigns of isolation launched. Sometimes, if exercised with persistence and skill, these peaceful means of conflict resolution work. More often, they do not: dictators stubbornly cling to power, powerful elites continue to oppress the masses, ethnic factions continue to revenge historic slaughters with the even greater slaughters made possible by modern weaponry.

Why do peaceful means fail? Many factors, no doubt, are responsible, but one stands out. In the contemporary age, intervening governments can only rarely use peaceful instruments of conflict resolution knowing that they could credibly threaten military intervention should peaceful means fail. This is the intervention dilemma. Even as the proclivity of major powers to intervene in domestic conflicts in foreign nations has grown, the natural reluctance of populations to pay the price of such interventions, if challenged, has also gathered steam. This reluctance takes two forms: pressures in many democratic states against the use of public funds for foreign operations; and, more pointed, popular opposition in democratic states to the use of military power in most circumstances.

Thus, increasingly, even while powerful political constituencies demand action by democratic governments to resolve domestic conflicts in foreign nations, even more powerful constituencies resist the use of the one form of intervention that often is the only realistic means of accomplishing the first constituency's demands—the threat or actual use of force. In an international system with no central authority, the absence of credible military threats curtails the effectiveness of all forms of coercive diplomacy and limits the effectiveness of even peaceful means of conflict resolution.

Formally, of course, countless treaties and agreements concluded over decades have proscribed the use of military force except in self-defense. Such morally based constraints no doubt continue to motivate many in their opposition to the use of force. Even more powerful, however, are more tangible constraints. Increasingly, the citizens of democratic nations appear unwilling to underwrite military interventions with either blood or treasure. When one looks at the history of the twentieth century, it is clear that the moral basis for restraint in the use of force has carried only limited weight. It has been the coupling of these ethical concerns with the current unwillingness to sacrifice either money or lives for government objectives that seems to have turned the tide against military interventions.

In the 1950s, for example, the populations of most European powers expressed clearly their unwillingness to support military operations in most parts of the world, the one possible exception being a direct attack on themselves. Even the French proved unwilling in 1958 to continue paying the very high price of France's colonialist military intervention in Algeria.[1]

The watershed for the United States came 10 years later in Southeast Asia. The popularity of U.S. military operations in Grenada, Panama, and Kuwait may seem to contradict this assertion, but a look at the complete record of U.S. military operations since the withdrawal from Vietnam makes it clear that popular support for military interventions seems to hinge on their brevity, bloodlessness, and immediate—and evident—success. The abrupt U.S. withdrawals from Beirut in 1983–84 and Somalia in 1993–94, following isolated, if dramatic, incidents in which U.S. forces suffered casualties, demonstrate clearly the U.S. public's opposition to interventions that appear to be either difficult or costly.

Nor is the phenomenon restricted to popular attitudes. Episodes like Beirut and Somalia seem to have impressed both the executive and legislative branches of the U.S. government, and both major political parties, profoundly. How else to explain the sudden termination of Operation Desert Storm short of its logical strategic objective of deposing the source of the problem, Saddam Hussein? And how else to explain the current bipartisan hesitancy to undertake even the most minor military tasks, such as restoring the democratically elected government in Haiti?

The unpopularity of military operations helps to explain why the United States and European governments came to believe in the early 1990s that interventions should be carried out through the UN. Trapped in the dilemma—popular pressures to intervene more frequently in the affairs of other states, but even more powerful forces poised to oppose the threat or use of military force—the U.S. and European nations turned decidedly away from unilateral actions and toward multinational activities sanctioned, and often managed, by the UN.

The greater cooperativeness of the Soviet Union that began in the late 1980s made the turn to the UN feasible, of course, but it did not necessitate this major shift in policy. Indeed, as the Soviet military threat receded and the United States emerged increasingly as the world's sole military superpower, one might have thought that the United States would have demonstrated a greater propensity to act unilaterally, or at least in coalition with its traditional allies. All else being equal, it is certainly less complicated to act in one of these modes than under the UN's aegis. Just the opposite has occurred, however, with both the Bush and Clinton administrations turning to the UN in virtually every relevant situation.

Figure 1 shows the number of peacekeeping and good offices missions carried out each year from 1947 through 1994, by or for the UN. As is well known by now, this number has doubled since the mid-1980s, rising from an average around 10 per year to more than 20 per year. More to the point, figure 2 shows that the increase is accounted for in large part by interventions in domestic situations—both civil wars and other kinds of internal conflicts. Indeed, the annual number of UN missions related to domestic conflicts has grown dramatically, rising from less than 5 per year through the 1980s, to an average of roughly 17 per year so far in the 1990s. (Figure 3 shows how missions related to domestic situations are divided between civil wars and other kinds of domestic conflicts.)

Governments turned to the UN for

Figure 1
UN Peacekeeping Operations and Good Offices Missions, 1947–1994

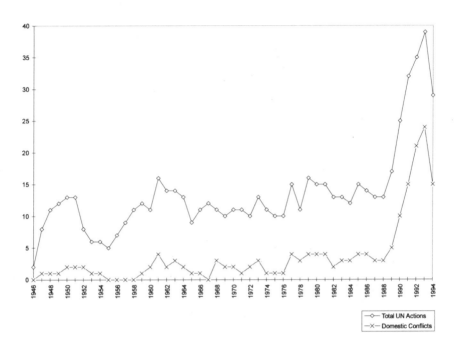

several reasons. First, the democracies have shared the goal of creating effective collective means of resolving conflicts since World War II. When the Soviet Union began in the mid-1980s to use its veto power far less frequently, achieving this goal appeared to be possible for the first time.

Second, on more practical grounds, acting through the UN is a means of sharing the burdens of maintaining international stability—both the tangible burden in money and lives, and the political burden of imposing one's will on others. The United States may pay close to one-third the cost of UN peacekeeping operations, but that is still better than the three-thirds costs of unilateral actions. Action through the UN, moreover, both legitimates and sanctions military interventions in the eyes of domestic and foreign audiences. As was demonstrated in the Kuwait case, for example, recourse to the UN's formal procedures for the exercise of collective self-defense was essential both to retain popular support in the United States and to hold together the coalition of nations that actually fought the war.

There is, however, a third reason for the turn to the UN, which, even if not perceived by decision makers, has also motivated more frequent recourse to

151

Figure 2
UN Activities: Interstate and Domestic Conflicts, 1947–1994

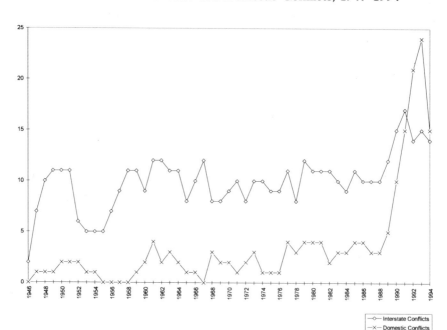

the world body. When government officials find themselves confronting the intervention dilemma—pressures to act, but a distinctly remote possibility of acting successfully due to the difficulty of credibly threatening the use of force—they have an additional incentive to turn to the UN.

Dealing with civil conflicts through the UN enables government decision makers to shift the locus of responsibility. Introducing the issue in the Security Council, cajoling action by the world body, is itself a means of satisfying those constituencies demanding intervention. Turning to the UN, in effect, says, "We are acting, we are drawing attention to the issue, we are writing resolutions, stepping up pressures, persuading others to join us, etc." At the same time, if UN diplomacy and political pressures prove inadequate and the situation remains unacceptable, it appears not to be the government's failure, but the failure of the world body. Government officials in many countries have been more than willing to practice such scapegoating, as if the UN were able to act more effectively or ambitiously than its key members permit.

Naturally, this attempt to sidestep the intervention dilemma by acting through the UN failed in many cases. The paper demonstration of action provided by activity in the UN Secu-

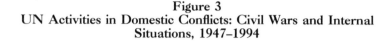

Figure 3
UN Activities in Domestic Conflicts: Civil Wars and Internal Situations, 1947–1994

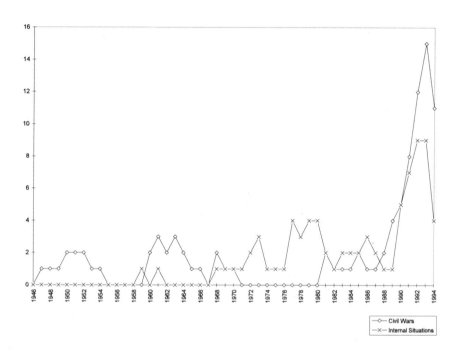

rity Council proved of only limited value in stanching political pressures for effective interventions in conflicts in foreign nations. At the same time, the cloak of respectability conferred by the UN proved of only limited utility in confronting the popular reluctance to undertake military tasks of any substantial difficulty or cost.

In most civil conflict situations, if political constraints make recourse to military force infeasible, the intervenor's leverage is limited. If a civil war is not ripe for resolution, if contending factions are not yet convinced that the price of continued warfare exceeds any

potential gain, mediators cannot succeed regardless of their skills. In such cases, only a willingness to separate the combatants forcefully and impose a settlement has even a chance of ending the war, and then only so long as the intervenor is willing to continue sitting on the belligerents.

Similarly, as has been seen repeatedly in recent years, neither political nor economic pressures are typically powerful enough to dislodge dictators who see everything to lose, and little to gain, by stepping down peacefully. If the use of military power is not a credible instrument of last resort, then

153

the intervenor's objective is often impossible from the outset. In many situations, without a credible threat of effective military action, UN diplomats and mediators are no more effective than national representatives in similarly constrained circumstances.

The UN has been a useful vehicle for taking limited military actions to help mitigate the more visible aspects of conflict situations—ensuring the delivery of humanitarian assistance, implementing cease-fires, and so forth—but the use of real force to impose solutions has almost always been ruled out. The prospect of significant financial costs and, particularly, loss of life, has proven just as powerful a deterrent to forceful interventions in foreign nations under the UN flag as under national insignia. As a result, in most UN peace operations, the rules of engagement have carefully specified constraints that both ensured that UN forces remained out of harm's way and made it impossible for them to enforce solutions. In the one case in which such constraints were eased, and casualties occurred, the haste with which even the world's greatest military power withdrew doomed the mission to failure and proved to many the weaknesses of the UN.

Emerging from the Dilemma

Currently, both the administration and most members of Congress who have addressed the issue are seeking to restrain the number and scope of military interventions by the UN. The greater emphasis now being placed on "realism" in deciding when and how to intervene, as spelled out in the administration's 1994 peacekeeping policy, is essentially an attempt to break out of the intervention dilemma by mustering pragmatism as the first line of defense against the political impulse to intervene. Rwanda was the first clear demonstration of the new policy. Following the brutal intensification of the civil war in that troubled country in April 1994, the United States worked to maintain realistic boundaries on the strengthening of the UN mission there.

A greater emphasis on realism in approving UN interventions is clearly appropriate at present, given the huge expansion in the organization's agenda over the past few years and its clear inability to carry out many of the tasks that have already been assigned to it. But the United States should not define a realistic intervention policy too narrowly, for failures to intervene are not without their own costs. By committing itself to making the changes that would make the UN an effective instrument for containing world conflict, the United States would make possible, eventually, a more ambitious definition of what is realistic.

The United States and most other great powers may not have significant, tangible interests in Rwanda, but they do have economic and political stakes in other places that have been, or might in the future be, rent by civil conflicts. The realism that long delayed military intervention in Haiti cost the United States dearly, for example, in terms of losses for Americans who do business in Haiti, in terms of the cost of dealing with Haitian refugees on the seas and in the United States, and, more important, in terms of the impact that U.S. timidity had on perceptions around the world of the nation's fitness to lead the world community.

In other cases, too, realism defined too narrowly could have profound long-term effects. The jury is still out on the effects of the U.S. and European failure to intervene decisively in the civil wars in the former Yugoslavia. The U.S. decision was right not to put troops on the ground there without a peace agreement, excepting the deterrent force in Macedonia, but the consequences of this realism are not yet clear. The potential for new conflicts in the Balkans, and for the broadening of old ones, remains high. Such contingencies could engulf the entire region in war and trigger even broader and longer-term conflicts among the great powers.

And, finally, there is a moral cost of nonintervention that should not be ignored. The impulse for intervention is not some fad, nor a plot foisted on innocent populations by a liberal clique, as some have maintained. It reflects the deeply held humanitarian values of democratic populations in the contemporary age. Five hundred thousand people may have died prematurely in Rwanda in 1994, many of them children. How do Americans feel about that tragedy? Could it have been prevented or, at least, restrained in its consequences? How would Americans feel if it were the case that an investment of a few hundred million dollars could have prevented one-half the Rwandan deaths? Every person evaluates such trade-offs, or potential trade-offs, differently. They not only have to judge the cost to Rwandans against the cost to themselves, but must also reach a judgment about the likely effectiveness of the intervention. There is no single right or wrong answer.

Civil conflicts and humanitarian tragedies affect every American by indicating a failure in fundamental human values. They also affect Americans more tangibly, by diminishing business activity, by disrupting financial markets, by stimulating population movements that impose economic burdens and political disruptions on neighboring countries, by posing risks of broader conflicts that would upset world peace and prosperity in momentous terms. If the United States could prevent such conflicts for free, and for certain, citizens would clearly want the government to act. Judging when it is realistic to act is a more tricky endeavor, which requires hardheaded assessments of options *and* interests.

The recent failures of the UN in a number of interventions—more properly, the failures of the members of the UN in a number of interventions— should cause Americans to be modest in their estimates of what is realistic. This is understandable. But the United States can, and should, push the boundaries of realism, by working to make the UN a more effective instrument for interventions in conflicts. If the United States had greater confidence in the UN's abilities, it would be more ambitious in what it considered realistic. Any number of reports have spelled out the reforms that are required.[2]

- Most important, the UN needs to be taken seriously as an institution and reorganized and professionalized accordingly. Necessary reforms go well beyond the symbolically important step of establishing an independent inspector general, the keystone of current U.S. demands for UN reform. To become an effective organization, the UN requires, at a minimum, a streamlined bureaucracy beginning at the most senior levels, the appointment of a deputy secretary general to manage the organization and coordinate its component agencies, the assignment of clear responsibilities to senior officials, and the imposition of a professional personnel system grounded firmly on merit.
- The financial aspects of peacekeeping and other UN military activities

155

need to be handled in a more routine manner. The budgets for peace operations should be placed in a single account and integrated into the regular UN budget. Their costs should be apportioned to member states on the basis of the same formula used for other organizational expenses.

• The UN also needs to be given the means of conducting military operations effectively. This includes the financial resources necessary to build an infrastructure capable of providing effective command, training, and logistical capabilities, and sufficient resources to carry out the mandates of individual missions effectively. Member states need to earmark military units for potential use in UN operations and to give them the specialized training and equipment they need to be effective. Consideration also should be given to permitting the Security Council, through an organization governed by the Military Staff Committee, to recruit a small quick reaction force composed of individual volunteers. Such a force would make it possible to establish the vanguard of a new peace force promptly after a Security Council decision to intervene.

UN reform has long been discussed, but little has been accomplished. The time is ripe for a far-reaching initiative. All that is required is a coherent U.S. position with the support of both the president and Congress, determined and persistent U.S. leadership, and a little common sense.

Finally, the executive branch would be in a better position to judge when interventions are realistic—and when they are not—if it worked more closely with Congress on these issues, long before it reached the point of decision.

Legislators necessarily know more than the executive about the beliefs of their constituents—about the balance in any one situation between the interventionary impulse and the bias against the use of military force. This is not to say that executive branch decisions should always be determined by opinion polls. Consultations with Congress can help to reveal not only what the public believes, but also what actions and policies might encourage positive changes in public opinion.

Closer coordination between the branches on these issues also has the potential to build political support either for interventions or for decisions not to intervene, whichever is relevant. Congress clearly believes that its financial powers are short-circuited when the administration supports the initiation of UN missions without real consultations and then hands the bill to the legislature. The leadership group and ranking members of key committees clearly should be consulted prior to U.S. approval of any UN mission. A more serious problem concerns those UN missions that will include U.S. combat forces. In these cases, any administration is well advised, in its own interest and in the interest of sustaining its policy, to seek formal congressional approval of the commitment of U.S. forces.

Although the consultative process between the branches on UN peacekeeping and potential military interventions improved during 1994, the accession of a Republican majority in Congress has led to legislative initiatives that would make it virtually impossible for the United States to make use of UN peace operations to advance its own interest in a more stable and humane world. Such legislation has already been passed by the House and will be taken up by the Senate later this year. It would be tragic if the House bill, particularly its provisions that would sharply cut back U.S. contributions to UN peace operations, were permitted to stand.

As the branch of government most directly attuned to currents in public opinion, and necessarily most responsive to them, Congress can play a special role in helping the executive branch to break out of the intervention dilemma. A more forthcoming position by the executive branch on the establishment of formal consultative procedures might help to avoid the passage of crippling legislation, enabling the United States to move beyond the current debate and on to more constructive actions to strengthen the UN's ability to carry out peace operations.

This article was prepared initially for a conference organized by the Aspen Institute.

Notes

1. France, of course, has continued to intervene in Africa in the years since, but only on a scale so small that the operations could be managed by highly specialized volunteer units.

2. See William J. Durch and Barry M. Blechman, *Keeping the Peace: The United Nations in the Emerging World Order* (Washington, D.C.: Henry L. Stimson Center, March 1992), and *Peacekeeping and the U.S. National Interest,* Report of a working group cochaired by Senator Nancy L. Kassebaum (R–Kan.) and Representative Lee H. Hamilton (D–Ind.) (Washington, D.C.: Henry L. Stimson Center, February 1994).

The Premature Burial of Global Law and Order: Looking beyond the Three Cases from Hell

Lincoln P. Bloomfield

IN THE FIVE years from 1945 to 1950 a monumental victory was won over tyranny, a major new challenge loomed, the democracies responded with strategies for the long haul, and a whole set of international institutions was set in motion to perform important pieces of the world's business.

In the five years from 1989 to 1994 a monumental victory was won over tyranny, new challenges loomed, the United Nations (UN) began to cope with them, the democracies were overcome in varying measure by self-absorption, moral flabbiness, and military vacillation, and the prospects were shaken for the kind of reformed international security regime their interests dictate.

How could that happen? What kind of international security system is realistically possible? What should be the U.S. role in such a regime?

A Funny Thing Happened on the Way to the New World Order

Reversing Iraq's assault on Kuwait in 1991 seemed to jump-start the process of collective security. But cross-border aggression was not the main challenge of the 1990s. Instead, the volcano of change spewed forth what Václav Havel called "a lava of post-communist surprises," generating a panorama of turbulence and strategic ambiguity as multinational states broke up, and other states simply broke. For leftover conflicts UN peacekeeping was the method of choice to monitor cease-fires and help with transitions in old cold war battlefields from Angola and Mozambique to El Salvador and Nicaragua, along with older trouble spots like the Western Sahara, Namibia, Suez, southern Lebanon, and Cyprus.

But the trickiest of the new threats arose not among states and their surrogates, but from mayhem within state borders. Renewed anarchy in Cambodia, man-made starvation in So-

Lincoln P. Bloomfield is professor of political science emeritus at MIT. Author of several books on foreign affairs, he has served in the U.S. Navy, State Department, and National Security Council.

The Washington Quarterly • 17:3

malia, mugging of newly won democracy in Haiti, and slow-motion genocide in Bosnia all violated not so much the "law" as the underlying moral order. It was behavior that article 2 (7) of the UN Charter bars the organization from touching because it is "essentially within the domestic jurisdiction of any state." Those new cases would also not have passed the cold war test of "strategic threat." But with the fear of superpower escalation gone, and with a potent assist from worldwide TV coverage, they powerfully assailed the conscience of the nations. Waiting in the wings were equally hairy scenarios of tribal warfare in Russia's "Near Abroad" and in some "states-but-not-nations" like Burundi, along with human rights outrages in Sudan, Myanmar, Iran, Syria, the People's Republic of China—you name it.

Working within a drastically altered strategic landscape, a born-again UN Security Council began a chapter of law-in-the-making with novel interventionary doctrines to deal with famine-producing anarchy, ethnic cleansing, and the deliberate creation of refugees. It was not exactly "peacekeeping" as in Cyprus, and certainly not "collective security" as in the Persian Gulf. It was an unprecedented "policing" function carrying such provisional labels as "peacemaking," "humanitarian enforcement," and "second-generation operations," led by a United States committed to a stance of "assertive multilateralism." The UN Charter's criterion of "threats to the maintenance of international peace and security" became stretched beyond recognition. But despite all the ambiguities, the early 1990s looked like an open moment for the liberal internationalists' dream of a system of global law and order, and

one equipped with a heart. The moment was brief.

Three Cases from Hell

The new era of multilateral intervention for humanitarian purposes began fairly successfully in Iraq after the defeated regime turned savagely on its disaffected Kurdish population in the North. In response to public outrage, the victorious coalition moved inside Iraqi territory and established protected aid channels to "Kurdistan," although not in the South where the regime was busily crushing Shi'ite dissidence. Successive UN resolutions mandated destruction of long-range ballistic missiles and weapons of mass destruction, along with unprecedentedly intrusive monitoring of missile testing and other sites. When Baghdad boggled at monitoring, UN threats backed by U.S. bombing of selected targets alternated with promises to unfreeze badly needed Iraqi oil revenues, and in February 1994 the International Atomic Energy Agency (IAEA) reported that all declared stocks of weapons-grade material had been shipped out. But compliance by Baghdad came only after credible threats of punishment. Indeed, these events also raise the question of whether an offending power has to be militarily defeated before the community will *enforce* its norms against intolerable national behavior.

Three other UN "peace-enforcement" operations did not pose that particular question but for other reasons brought the trend to a screeching halt. In Somalia, where anarchy was generating mass starvation, the UN was shamed into action by Secretary General Boutros Boutros-Ghali, and the Security Council for the first time launched a peacekeeping operation not requested by the "host government" (in this case there was no government at all). Humanitarian aid was authorized with a mandate to create "a secure environment" for its delivery. The primarily U.S. force used both diplomacy and military presence to stem the famine, but the UN mission became controversial when it actually used force to create the required environment. Willingness to back up a humanitarian operation with force if necessary may turn out to be the price of humanitarian intervention by the international community. But the reaction of risk-averse Americans to casualties fewer than New York experiences in a slow week suggests that the use of force, even to carry out a unanimously agreed mission, had better remain as a last resort, particularly if the situation on the ground gets murky—as it invariably does.

In splintered former Yugoslavia, the UN undertook another humanitarian mission of aid to refugees, in an environment in which Serb authorities escalated their noxious policy of "ethnic cleansing" to uproot and terrorize Bosnian Muslims. The Security Council authorized use of "all means necessary" to protect aid. But Britain and France, which had put a modest number of noncombatant peacekeepers on the ground, balked at facing down those blocking aid. In May 1993 the Council established six "safe havens" for embattled Muslim populations and authorized force to protect, not the people, but the peacekeepers. But once more the available enforcers of the community's rules were unwilling to stand up for their own norms.

It was only after a particularly murderous—and televised—mortaring of a Sarajevo market crowd that the North Atlantic Treaty Organization (NATO) finally stirred itself into a credible pos-

ture and Serb guns were pulled back. Nothing could more clearly illustrate both the "CNN effect" and the painful truth that bullies respond only to believable threats. But it was disgracefully late in coming and useless to the thousands already left dead and the hundreds of thousands left homeless.

In Haiti the issue was restoration of democratic rule in the face of official thuggery. To do so required at least a believable show of force. But a United States once burned wanted none of that and executed a humiliating retreat, leaving the Security Council incapable of enforcing its own decisions. (The equally involved Organization of American States [OAS], faithfully reflecting Latin America's deep resistance to anything resembling intervention, was not a credible alternative.)

In diplomacy as in war, success has 100 fathers but defeat—or even plain bad luck—is an orphan. In Bosnia a European Union suffering from tired blood and historical amnesia for far too long turned away from its responsibilities, and Washington—regrettably but in my view correctly—declined to act alone. In Somalia and Haiti humanitarian intervention was overtaken by a bloody endgame between claimants for power. In all three cases the Security Council and secretary general made some questionable judgments, and the responsible powers blinked when it came to taking casualties. Just when the international community had begun to act like one, its staying power and seriousness of purpose were suddenly in serious question.

Defining U.S. Interests

Debate about the future world role of the United States soon became hostage to the three "cases from hell." An administration without a settled strategy shared its internal uncertainties with a Congress that smelled blood in the water. Indispensable public support, already weakened by erratic leadership, was not edified by news media that tend to portray all events as random, and public confusion echoed back to a government that often bases policy on opinion polls. Pessimism replaced post–cold war euphoria as a shortlist of foreign situations of minimal strategic importance distorted the already complex process of redefining U.S. economic and political interests.

To regain its balance, the United States badly needs a coherent strategy toward the changed nature of conflict. To create one requires that present difficulties be assessed in the light of broad national interests. So far this has not really happened, and the great sucking noise one hears is the sound of fragments of doctrine rushing to fill the conceptual vacuum. Utopian internationalists keep themselves marginalized without a strategic perspective, while leftover strategists still misunderstand the power of global issues. Single themes like "new world order," "end of history," "clash of civilizations," have been attention-getting but are, like all sound bites, too simplistic. Isolationism as a policy is absurd, but the United States cannot and will not play the role of global policeman.

How then can a workable basis be found for policy toward the internal implosions and struggles that dominate our times? In February 1994 President Bill Clinton belatedly asserted U.S. national interests toward Bosnia.[1] But a rational longer-term policy will be based on three more fundamental national interests.

One primordial interest is the worldwide economic position of the United States, which requires at least minimal political stability around the shrunken globe.[2] U.S. global interests are negatively affected by any turbulence that threatens to create a dangerous whirlpool in the stream of international relationships. Global economic and other interests simply cannot be satisfied with a laissez-faire policy toward conflict.

A second interest grows out of the 200-year preference of Americans to show a benign and humane external face to the world. (By a curious coincidence, George Washington's farewell address embodies a similar dual prescription.) Cooperative attempts to maintain international "law and order" used to be entirely optional. Given the unprecedented role of TV, the growing role of whistle-blowing private groups, and the extraordinarily consistent public opinion favoring UN peacekeeping,[3] it is a delusion to think that demands for human rights or political justice can now be dismissed as a sideshow the United States can avoid at will.

The third fundamental U.S. interest is the most problematic. It stems from core values of political democracy and free enterprise, summarized in the Clinton administration's commitment to "enlargement of democracy." Haiti was seen by some as a test of this interest, and there will doubtless be others as feeble new democracies come under strain. But this policy will encounter the 200-year-old argument between active U.S. proselytizing versus simply keeping, in Henry Clay's words, "the lamp burning brightly on this western shore, as a light to all nations." History also suggests that democracies keep the peace better than tyrannies, and where a recognizable democratic process is throttled by its enemies—Grenada was an even clearer case than Haiti—it ought to engage U.S. interests.

The policy objective flowing from those interests is not complicated. It is to achieve a threshold level of "law and order" in the international community that enhances U.S. global purposes as well as embodying a fundamental concern for conflict limitation and, yes, justice. The wrong question to ask is "Should the United States be the world's policeman?" Even if a president sought that role, it would not long be tolerated by other countries, not to mention Congress and the American people. If the United States will not support forceful intervention in situations that do not obviously threaten its "vital" interests, the rational alternative is a far more focused effort to *prevent* conflicts, which I will come to shortly. The central questions then are: "How is the international community, global or regional, to deal with situations of destabilizing anarchy, clandestine weapons programs, or gross political criminality that exceed the bounds of tolerability on strategic or humanitarian grounds?" and "What role should the United States play in that quest?"

Is There Really an "International Community"?

Discussions of multilateralism assume the existence of an "international community," but some challenge that concept as a figment of the liberal imagination. In a little-remarked assertion in a much-discussed article Samuel Huntington stated that "the very phrase 'the world community' has become the euphemistic collective noun . . . to give global legitimacy to actions reflecting the interests of the United States and other Western powers."[4] Is he right? How different from a genuine community is today's international society?

According to political theory, a viable community rests on a minimum consensus of community-held values. It is endowed with core powers of taxation and policing, which depend on a relative monopoly of force. People generally accept rules because of a shared sense of commonality, whether ethnic, linguistic, religious, or ideological. They also benefit from a governance system that protects them from physical threats. People know what "compliance" and "enforcement" mean in familiar local settings. They know the cost of breaking the rules and consider believable the probability of enforcement action, whether by cops on the beat, sheriffs, tax-collectors, or armies.

Government works because there is a presumptive self-interest in abiding by the rules and a known penalty for noncompliance. Is international society today capable of behaving like a real rather than a rhetorical community, armed with enforceable "law and order" rules complete with credible incentives to comply and disincentives to misbehavior? The answer is "No—but."

When it comes to bottom-line law and order, the limiting realities are the world's infinite variety, decentralized power centers, fragmentary structures, and primary reliance on self-help with only a contingent possibility of community "police" assistance when threatened. The combined logic of economic interdependence, technology, and weaponry tells us that peace, security, and prosperity all require strengthened forms of "international governance."[5] But international society is still a bit like 1930s China, equipped with a "constitution" and functioning central apparatus, but with real power monopolized by provincial warlords, some benign and cooperative with the center, some decidedly not. The UN may simulate a government; but it cannot really act like one. World society is a partial and imperfect community when it comes to gut qualities of sovereignty, legitimacy, and power. Its characteristics all fall short of the definition of true community.

But does that really mean that all recent actions in the international system can be explained by U.S. pressure? Hardly. Enormous majorities in the UN voted to condemn the Iranian seizure of the U.S. embassy in 1979. Why? Because states of every religion and ethnic background have a deep interest in keeping inviolate the global diplomatic nexus. Large majorities condemned the Soviet invasion of Afghanistan in 1979 and the Iraqi invasion of Kuwait in 1991. Why? Because virtually all agree on the primordial rule of interstate relations that forbids invading, trashing, and obliterating the identity of a neighboring state. Thousands of troops from 57 non-Western countries help to staff 18 current UN operations in the field. Why? Because they decided their national interests are served by that kind of community policing.

At the UN Conference on Environment and Development in Rio in 1992 the great majority—opposed, incidentally, by the United States—voted goals and policies reflecting the conclusions of cross-cultural environmentalists. And over 140 states have voluntarily signed the Nuclear Non-Proliferation Treaty (NPT). Why? Because sensible people have noticed the twin realities of environmental interdependence and the unusability of nuclear weapons.

Even in the most neuralgic sector, UN human rights bodies have recently distanced themselves from their ideological and cultural biases and now publicize violations in Muslim, Ortho-

dox, Christian, Slav, Turkic, Jewish, and secular societies—including the United States. One reason has been Western pressure to apply what are arguably universal values. But equally influential is the revolution in mass communication that informs people about common standards of civility.

The evidence is obviously mixed, and several things are going on at once. But there are unmistakable signs that some broad common values and interests are cutting across "civilizations." It is this evidence of commonality that constitutes the foundation of a minimal "world community" for limited but crucial common purposes. To turn Marx on his head, the basic global *structure* is composed of states and significant non-governments, powerfully driven by their cultures. Common problems none can handle alone constitute the agenda of the *superstructure* of agencies of international cooperation and coordination. The global architecture is, so to speak, split-level, and one level is not going to replace the other.

So is there a genuine "world community"? Not really. Should we act as though it exists on matters of common concern? Of course. The goal is certainly not world government, which even if practical could become world tyranny. But the system already functions effectively in the sectors where states agree to pool sovereignty without actually saying so. Indeed, the UN's critics do not challenge (or even seem to know about) the networks that already monitor and to a degree regulate global trade, telecommunications, mail, health, air travel, weather forecasting, nuclear power, and refugee flows.

Most of the powers of governance will continue to be "reserved" to the member states on the model of the

U.S. Constitution, and we should not become distracted by theological arguments about sovereignty. The vexing question as we grope our way toward the next stage of history is how to achieve improved compliance with the limited but crucial rules agreed upon by the larger community.

Here, of course, is the central dilemma of the "international community." In a true community the actions required to cope with violations of its rules add up to a graduated continuum of responses—a kind of updated "escalation ladder," based on the principle that the earlier one achieves compliance, the cheaper and less hairraising the level of policing required. But in a world of sovereign states the center has no independent power, national interests change, today's terrorists and war criminals can become tomorrow's rulers, the UN inherits conflicts after they have got out of hand, ground rules are imprecise, aggression has never been universally defined, threats to peace are subjectively assessed, and ethnic cleansing and making refugees of one's own people are not adequately on the lawbooks.

This is not to say that nothing can be done now to improve matters. UN supporters have proposed new varieties of stand-by forces, whether oldfashioned "chapter 6½" peacekeeping units in blue berets, "chapter 6¾" peacemaking/peace-building protectors in flak jackets, or even a standing 10,000-man "UN Legion."[6] The end of the Cold War also revived discussion of the never-implemented article 43 agreements under which the great powers would make major forces available to the Security Council. Secretary General Boutros-Ghali's *Agenda for Peace* is a major, if premature, statement of both doctrine and plans for what he terms "peace enforcement."[7]

Some practical operational processes can also be reformed, such as headquarters operations, which need to be more efficient, and the UN information system, which is improved but still needs to be more autonomous and to have backup from national intelligence (as it reportedly had in Iraq from the U.S. Central Intelligence Agency and Britain's MI5). It is at least theoretically possible that such improved readiness would make it easier to respond to calls for UN intervention.

Proposals for improved "law and order" functions must also deal with other security sectors that raise similar questions of predictability and coherence in international—and U.S.—responses, most critically the violation of rules barring proliferation of weapons of mass destruction. North Korea's 1993 announcement that it was dropping out of the NPT inspection system pressed a hot button. A combination of threats and inducements to secure international inspection of suspected nuclear sites was improvised by the United States acting de facto for the NPT and UN community, with as yet uncertain results. The IAEA can turn as a last resort to the Security Council, but nothing is said about what happens next. (The same is true for other potential international crimes for which compliance arrangements are still embryonic—state-backed terrorism against civilian targets, international drug trafficking, electronic sabotage of transnational networks, illicit traffic in nuclear or toxic wastes, perhaps ultimately criminality in the "global commons" of outer space and the deep sea bed.)

Counterproliferation policy runs up against two special obstacles. First, the barn door is partly open, thanks to clandestine bomb-building by Israel,

India, and South Africa (before it turned back) and potentially by Pakistan, Iraq, North Korea, and Brazil. Second, it will always be argued—and it will always be true—that such arrangements are inherently discriminatory, leaving weapons and technologies of mass destruction in U.S., European, Russian, and Chinese hands and keeping others from their assumed benefits.

Common sense kept some countries from going nuclear, and the stigma of second-class membership can still be alleviated by attractive "carrots" and by including have-nots at the decision-making tables.[8] The line generally held during three decades, even as some famous scientists, along with President John F. Kennedy, confidently predicted at least 30 nuclear weapons powers by 1970 or 1980. And it is true that the current collection of treaty cheaters—Iraq, Iran, North Korea—constitutes an exceptional, small category of states committed to destabilizing the neighborhood, which is generally not the aim of those who already possess the offending capabilities.

Counterproliferation will feature ambiguities as ambitious states find the threat to go nuclear more bankable than crossing the threshold.[9] But some clandestine weaponeering may appear so threatening that states will decide not to wait for the stately processes of what Harlan Cleveland calls a "committee-of-sovereigns-with-a-staff." The Israeli air force engaged in do-it-yourself enforcement in 1981 to abort progress in Iraq's Osirak reactor, and in extremis such "unilateral enforcement" may have to be repeated. U.S. policy correctly assigns a high priority to counterproliferation, and if all else fails the United States may have to trade off higher later costs by

risking a confrontation with an isolated North Korea.

A Modest Midterm Scenario

The times are not propitious for upgrading the enforcement of international "law and order" beyond some useful but modest procedural fixes, but the issue is of course far more political than it is technical. Action is always subject to veto by the permanent members of the Security Council, and Russian and Chinese cooperation cannot be taken for granted in perpetuity. Nevertheless, conditions may return that make progress again possible, and it is useful to have a defined goal in mind as a target for discussion and planning. The following sketches a modestly reformed process that falls short of what happens in cohesive communities, but goes beyond what most people consider feasible today.

A more coherent international system will feature compliance procedures that resemble a process of *law enforcement*. It will look less like a traditional binary choice between war or peace and more like a step process that mimics domestic *policing*. Violations of agreed rules will take many forms along a broad continuum, matched by a continuum of community responses.

A state-backed bomb-thrower or electronic terrorist represents the lowest end of the law-breaking spectrum. Next come violations involving limited nuclear, chemical, biological, or missilery development, all potentially reversible. A more serious challenge comes from a pair of countries threatening or sporadically skirmishing against each other. And a major threshold is crossed when organized, uniformed military forces engage in "small wars." A similar threshold is crossed with an internal "small war" when civil strife afflicts the global conscience or imperils regional stability. At the extreme end lie the wars of conquest of other peoples' countries.

A step process of "community responses" begins with article 33 of the Charter, which enjoins states to settle disputes themselves before unloading them on the UN. Early-stage responses are exemplified by the diplomat with the briefcase and the observer with the binoculars and electronic sensors. At the next step up, failure to halt illicit work on weapons would bring a kind of SWAT team of technicians such as IAEA inspectors accompanied by UN guards in civvies (as in Iraq today) armed with state-of-the-art nonlethal weapons.[10] If fighting breaks out but can be halted, the truce would, as now, be monitored by nationally contributed, nonfighting, peacekeeping units—a low-cost tripwire, primarily symbolic but respected because the sides want to be separated, whatever their rhetoric.

Coercive enforcement starts with article 41 economic and communications sanctions. For the first 40 years international sanctions were applied only twice—on Rhodesia (ineffectively) and against South Africa (military only, but more effective because observed by the major powers). Recent UN sanctions against Iraq, Haiti, and Serbia were technically effective, those against Libya and Angola less so. But sanctions against Iraq, Haiti, and Serbia devastated the innocent. Sanctions should be targeted primarily on leaders' overseas bank accounts and travel rights, and compensation should be made to third countries that suffer from sanctions the way Turkey did in the Iraq case.

If diplomacy and peacekeeping fail, a well-armed blue-bereted "posse" would use whatever force is required to persuade the sides to separate and get relief supplies to civilians—the still unlabeled "peacekeeping plus" model of armed humanitarian intervention that for so long tragically failed on this count in Bosnia. As discussed below, the compliance force could be drawn from one already in existence such as NATO, an invigorated regional organization such as the OAS or the Organization of African Unity (OAU), or a future Asia–Pacific security organization.

The greatest need up to this point on the spectrum is for technical personnel who can monitor, recognize, and if necessary dismantle illicit weaponry and production; for "peace officers" on the lines of U.S. marshals, who can protect both relief operations and UN monitors; and for quick-reaction U.S. National Guard–type units that can be dispatched to protect the protectors—precisely the capabilities that never successfully functioned in the cases from hell.

The final point is the rare instance of coercive military force under article 42—son of Desert Storm, as it were. Overt armed aggression is mercifully rare. But we have learned the hard way that some few situations turn out to be genuinely nonnegotiable, and that doctrinal pacifism can give a green light to aggression and tyranny, whether to a Hitler planning the conquest of Europe, a Saddam Hussein coveting neighboring states, or Serbs and Croats murderously pursuing dreams of expansion. All act in the spirit of Bismarck who, asked if he wanted war, reportedly said "Certainly not, what I want is victory."

If the community leaves matters until this explosive point, it will confront the worst case: having to force compliance with Security Council directives through deployment by powerful states of UN-flagged national ships, tanks, and assault helicopters, whether under article 43 or not. If the aggressor is a nuclear-armed great power, the system will be back where it was at the height of the Cold War. As discussed shortly, this is one of many persuasive reasons to focus on conflict prevention.

A Role for Regional Organizations?

So far the reference point has been the UN Security Council. Given overload at the global center, calls are once more heard to "beef up" regional and subregional organizations so they can carry more of the burden of peacekeeping and perhaps even armed "peacemaking." Chapter VIII of the UN Charter flags regional organizations as the first port of call for dispute settlement, and some modest successes have been scored in this realm. But until now they have proved poor "law and order" agents for the community, either because a major regional country was battling the rest (Cuba in Latin America, Israel in the Middle East, South Africa in Africa) or because, as with NATO, the purpose of the organizations was something different. All these situations have changed and greater reliance on regional organizations is consistent with the larger trend toward decentralization of functions in both public and private sectors. They will, however, have to change significantly if they are to share the peacemaker's burden. Assuming that such changes are at least theoretically possible, what would a modestly improved system look like?

In Latin America, under the Bogota Pact and Rio treaty, the OAS is equipped, at least on paper, with a wide spectrum of functions ranging from conflict resolution to collective security. It has had modest success in fact-finding and dispute settlement, as have subregional groupings such as the Contadora Group in Central America. OAS peacekeepers served in the Dominican Republic (following U.S. intervention), but the organization has been notably allergic to anything resembling intervention by its own members (and to U.S. domination). Freed of cold war hang-ups that entangled the United States in Cuba, Nicaragua, and El Salvador, the OAS would take the lead in actively policing the region. The OAS would become the primary regional peacekeeper, with the Security Council invoked only in exceptional circumstances. Considering Latin America's oversize military establishments as well as the U.S. military's role in mentoring what turned out to be some of the region's most obnoxious military figures, regional military training would focus on peacekeeping units for ready deployment at the call of the OAS, much as Scandinavia has trained its splendid peacekeepers.

Much the same applies to the African region—not tomorrow but perhaps the day after. The OAU has played a role in a few regional situations and actually sent peacekeepers to Chad in 1981, but it has been irrelevant to most African conflicts. Individual countries have sometimes acted as subregional cop, for instance Tanzania in Uganda. Ethiopia's leaders have played an impressive role in trying to bring peace to Somalia, and a regional military force from the Economic Community of West African States worked hard to overcome anarchy in Liberia. In November 1993 the OAU secretary general announced tentative agreement on a mechanism for conflict management and a fund for such operations. With that kind of capability, the OAU could replace the UN (and the United States) for further policing duties in Somalia and take the lead in Burundi and in other regional outbreaks of anarchy, genocide, or famine. On any political calculus, subsidizing the proposed African fund would be more cost-effective for the West than direct involvement.

It is too early to envisage a midterm regional peacemaking role in the Asia–Pacific region, which is in the early stages of organization, and where the United States will have to act as strategic makeweight for some years to come. But in Europe a dual NATO role of deterrence and peace enforcement, prefigured in Bosnia in February 1994, could serve several important purposes.

As the world's premier military alliance, NATO should be a prime source for regional peacekeeping and regional peace enforcement (and has indeed already offered to do just that). NATO—that is to say, its members—failed its first important test in that department when it refused until tragically late in the day to use even a fraction of its incomparable military power to protect the delivery of humanitarian aid—or its own peacekeepers—in former Yugoslavia. Prudence dictates that NATO also retain its historic mission aimed at deterring any would-be hegemonic Eurasian power (implicitly Russia, with Germany again as subtext). As new uncertainties increase the pressure for inclusion of Central European states, it will be important to declare a genuinely dual role for NATO. Russia unilaterally—and helpfully—dealt itself into the peacekeeping game in Bosnia. It should be explicitly made a senior partner in regional peacekeeping missions to offset any new paranoia about encirclement—and to preempt any Russian imperial moves via "unilateral peacekeeping." NATO should be explicitly reconstituted a regional organization under chapter VIII of the UN Charter, its membership expanded, and its secondary mission clarified as the primary maintainer of peace and security in the Eurasian region.

Some who prefer an all-Europe team argue that the European Community (now Union), through the incorporeal Western European Union (also absent from Bosnia), should become the future peacekeeper of choice in the region. Others look to the not quite so incorporeal Conference on Security and Cooperation in Europe (CSCE). Like NATO, CSCE has agreed to supply peacekeeping troops to the UN, and in fact maintains an observer mission in Macedonia. But it had to withdraw its observers from Kosovo, 10 of its 52 members are involved in shooting wars, and it has no real power.

Making Preventive Diplomacy a Reality

If U.S. global interests require a generally stable external environment, and if the present UN and existing regional organizations cannot at this time consider expanding their police function to deal with destabilizing disorder and intolerable national behavior, and if the United States declines to be the global policeman, what is the alternative?

The question answers itself. The best available strategy is to head off violations before they take place. This is true whether the offender is a ruler contemplating a territorial grab, a pair of countries deadlocked over a disputed border, a rogue political force like the Khmer Rouge threatening to sabotage an international agreement, a majority regime abusing a minority, or a resentful people smarting under an unjust treaty. "Conflict prevention" and "preventive diplomacy" are now much in vogue. The challenge is to transform them from slogan to policy.[11]

In fact the record of quiet diplomacy to defuse potential crises is far from zero, often featuring unsung heroes whose triumphs are rarely trumpeted. Nor does one have to go further than chapter VI of the UN Charter to discover the comprehensive battery of devices available for resolving or moderating disputes before they become small wars. Even a modest revival of the 1920s vogue of compulsory arbitration treaties would be an improvement, and some have reappeared on the scene. But in the main, modern history is a dismal chronicle of missed opportunities to take effective preventive steps, followed by later painful costs.

No collective preventive/deterrent efforts were seriously undertaken prior to the war between Britain and Argentina over the Falkland Islands (Malvinas), or the buildup leading to Iraq's invasion of Iran in September 1980. In the Gulf, the application of purposeful disincentives by Washington and London, instead of self-deception and wishful thinking, might have brought about a different outcome. The glaring example of too little and too late is former Yugoslavia, where Germany insisted on premature recognition of Catholic Croatia and Slovenia, Washington reportedly discouraged an early compromise agreement to partition Bosnia,[12] and European politicians declined to counter unspeakable behavior on their own doorstep.

What, in concrete terms, can be done to strengthen preventive diplomacy? Three available approaches are publicity, deterrence, and proactive peaceful change procedures.

Publicity. In the age of global communications, publicity has already become a powerful diplomatic instrument, with the international spotlight a proven tool for noncoercive compliance through its powers of, so to speak, shame, embarrassment, and ridicule. Governments are resistant to open discussion of alleged misbehavior, official candor concerning which can be downright embarrassing. But intense commercial television coverage stimulated action in Ethiopia, Somalia, and eventually Bosnia, and there is now a UN high commissioner for human rights with modest powers of inquiry and reporting. It continues to be important for Amnesty International and other nongovernmental human rights groups to throw a healthy glare on egregious behavior regardless of governmental nervousness. And so that network news editors do not always set the action agenda, every UN observer mission should carry its own camcorder, with the UN making the videotapes available at cost.

Much recent attention has been devoted to crisis prevention centers and other techniques for diplomatic early warning. Such procedures can be useful, if only to force attention to incipient hot spots governments know about but would prefer to ignore.[13] But even with ample warning, the management of current crises invariably takes priority over longer-range planning or prophylactic diplomacy. Whistle-blowing does not always deter and is not always followed by action. What else might help?

Deterrence. Given its crucial importance for more general conflict prevention, deterrence should not remain the conceptual monopoly of nuclear strategists. Some modern disasters might have been averted by a credible and timely threat of sanctions for noncompliance by incipient aggressors, abusers, and proliferators. Conflict-prevention military units can be stationed on a threatened border before fighting breaks out (as is taking place on the Macedonian side of the Serbian–Macedonian border—but not along the preinvasion Iraq–Kuwait border). More forcefully, if the European powers (or the United States) had moved early to confront the latter-day vandals off Dubrovnik, or to actively protect relief supplies and UN peacekeepers at Sarajevo airport when first fired upon, or had consistently punished violations of their no-fly zone, things might have turned out differently. Even later, if the huffing and puffing in major Western capitals had added up to a credible threat, the radical Balkan expansionists might have been stopped earlier. But Serb and Croat leaders soon understood that the threats were hollow, and remained undeterred until the carnage was virtually completed. The policy prescription is embarrassingly obvious: democratic leaders should follow through on their threats to enforce the "law," or undemocratic ones will make fools and hypocrites of them.

Deterrence is one of the reasons to codify meaningful sanctions against human rights abuses. U.S. legislation has denied some aid to egregious violators, and occasionally reforms have followed (with due acknowledgment of the logical fallacy of *post hoc, ergo propter hoc*). But the community's rulebook needs a sharper set of teeth. The UN Genocide Convention, along with the Fourth Geneva Convention and its successors on laws of war, should be expanded to cover "slow-motion genocide" of the Yugoslav variety. Sanctions should be added to the declaration on human rights of minorities the General Assembly passed in December 1992. Future official murderers and rapists will be carefully calibrating the seriousness of the Bosnian War Crimes Commission and the International Criminal Court recently created by the UN.

The generation of refugees as an expression of deliberate policy constitutes a particularly ugly form of political behavior. Relief agencies do not like to discuss murderous activities by tyrants, and diplomats usually tiptoe around "host" government sensitivities. The consequence has been virtual immunity for those who torment and displace thousands of innocents while good people clean up after their crimes. The United States should push its proposal to extend the concept of war crimes, left vague by the Nuremberg trials, to cover peacetime humanitarian crimes such as ethnic cleansing and deliberate creation of refugees. The community must find ways to make the costs of forcible civilian displacement far more credible in advance before pieces of the old USSR devour each other, Sudan's rulers further decimate non-Muslim populations or, more remotely, Hungarian ultranationalists some day trigger a catastrophic drive for "greater Hungary."

Peaceful Change. In the best of all worlds, compliance begins with obedience to law. In our second- or third-best world, a more relevant process is that of peaceful change.

The law works in disputes where the parties are prepared to compromise or, if given a fair hearing, to accept an impartial third-party judgment. Except for a Hitler or a Saddam Hussein, where the only remedy may be counterforce, states generally comply with international law to the extent the rules are considered fair.

The problem arises when the reason for not accepting third-party adjudication or arbitrament is either mistrust of the dominant legal system or unvarnished insistence on winning. The International Court of Justice (ICJ) has had some successes in dealing with primarily legal questions, but a string of failures when the issue was really political, from disregard by Albania in 1949 of the Court's ruling in the Corfu Channel case, to the Nicaragua harbor-mining judgment of 1986, on which the United States, unlike even Communist Albania and Qadhafi's Libya, rejected the Court's jurisdiction. (The current argument before the Court between Bosnia and "Yugoslavia" is obviously not about law and will not be resolved there.)

Disputes that are not "justiciable" require not so much application of existing law as justice and equity. Article 14 of the UN Charter was drafted with the Versailles treaty's disastrous rigidity in mind, and the UN played a major role in the process of decolonization—a de facto peaceful change process. But the General Assembly was never intended to acquire "legislative" powers (except when asked by the foreign ministers to decide the disposition of the Italian colonies after World War II) and article 14 has been invoked only rarely.

Today pressures for changes in the map are being fueled by exploding national and ethnic passions—the pathological flip side of the world's glorious diversity. Some are purely racist, such as the rabid nationalism of Russian or Serb extremists. But some pressures for change reflect genuine grievances with a legitimate case for relief. Diplomats usually find such issues as welcome as a visit to a leper colony. But a long and lugubrious history argues

against their squeamishness and in favor of significantly greater activism toward justice in advance of disaster. The needful motto—indeed the updated definition of peace itself—could usefully be "The dynamic management of change without war."

The International Court of Justice should dust off its rarely used capacity to deal with disputes in the fashion lawyers call *ex aequo et bono*, meaning applying equity and common sense rather than the letter of the law. There are already a few examples of the type of small panels of Security Council members advocated by Louis Sohn to work out equitable resolution of clashing claims before they become full-blown Council debates. Such peaceful change devices should be applied to allegations of injustice by both sides in Kashmir, permanent stalemate in Cyprus, denial of Kurdish national rights in Turkey and Iraq, and arguments about ownership of rich resources in the Spratley Islands dispute between half a dozen Asian and Southeast Asian states, all of which have the potential to explode.

Inconsistency and Hegemonic Power

Intervention in civil wars and other forms of domestic mayhem is, with the best of motives, going to violate the fourth cardinal rule of diplomacy (never get between a dog and a lamppost), and at best appear inconsistent. The Security Council enforced its no-fly zones in northern Iraq but turned a blind eye until spring 1994 to violations in Serbia; forcibly protected famine relief in Somalia but not Bosnia; defended Kuwait but not Azerbaijan. Burundi was doubtless as deserving as Haiti, but as Boutros Boutros-Ghali said, "The United Nations cannot solve every problem," while Under

Secretary General James Jonah acknowledged that Rwanda but not Burundi got peacekeepers and money because "maybe they were first in line."[14] As with the rest of human life, consistency cannot be the major litmus test. It is not cynical but realistic to acknowledge that political triage is the likely prospect, and that the world is fortunate if the large matters—Iraqi aggression, starving children, the ozone layer, nuclear spread—are tackled by the community even while some lesser issues remain unresolved.

Another troublesome reality is the disparity between states' power, money, and influence. Even a modestly reformed international "law and order" system will appear to be dominated by the strong both in making and enforcing rules. There are times—Korea in 1950 and the Gulf in 1990—when the community agrees to meet aggression by naming one country as "executive agent" for the Security Council (the formula used in Korea). If in such extreme circumstances—cross-border aggression or domestic genocide—the system fails to respond, action on behalf of the community could be carried out by what I have dubbed a "coalition of the willing." Both U.S. leadership and coalition surrogates run counter to the principle/fiction of sovereign equality. But only a minority of states are in a position to give leadership based on advanced technology, capital, educated and trained armed forces, and a democratic process that protects the rights of individuals against governmental abuse. Others resent the unique influence of the United States. But the precondition for any enforcement system is the power and logistical reach the United States alone commands.

The real danger is not U.S. domination but its withdrawal from the game. The future could look a lot more dangerous if setbacks and scapegoating in Somalia, Haiti, and Bosnia reversed the recent U.S. turn toward cooperative security, or if premature intervention fatigue allowed new breaches of the "civil peace" to turn into serious security threats. Nothing is more important than to persuade would-be violators that failure to enforce the community's rules in Bosnia, plus erratic behavior in Somalia and Haiti, have not switched on a green light for arson in other tinderboxes.

In the turbulent wake of controversy over the cases from hell, Washington crafted a policy toward UN "peace operations." In part political damage-limitation with the help of rhetorical straw men ("We will never compromise military readiness to support peacekeeping . . . [or transfer] troops into a standing world army . . . the President will never relinquish his constitutional command authority over U.S. troops," etc.), the bottom line is continuity in policy toward selective involvement after "asking tough questions," getting the Pentagon to help pay, and demanding fairer assessments and more efficient management.[15] The United States in fact retains a unique role in providing logistical support (already anticipated in the so-called Prepo Afloat program of shipborne floating equipment for an armored brigade whose mission includes disaster relief and humanitarian operations). But U.S. domestic agonies over the cases from hell would seem to confirm the wisdom of traditional UN peacekeeping policy under which, except for enforcement, UN policing units on the ground were drawn from countries other than Russia and the United States. The concept of impartial peacekeeping and peacemaking by "neutrals" may still have high political value even if it is no longer clear what they are neutral about, and even

173

though they are backed by great-power logistics, air and sea cover, and Japanese money.

Conclusion

Definitive conclusions drawn from recent events are likely to be misleading. After all, no one predicted the fantastic changes of the past five years. Our age is a hinge of history, and the post–cold war order is a work in progress. Winston Churchill once observed that "The United Nations was set up not to get us to heaven, but only to save us from hell." There is nothing wrong with the basic norms and ground rules contained in the present UN Charter, which provides ample machinery for prevention, deterrence, and enforcement. The fault, pace Shakespeare, is not in our stars but in our leaders and those of us they represent.

Despite setbacks and loss of nerve, the innovative collective measures of the early 1990s could in time become habit-forming, particularly if politicians keep their nerve and eschew the "Principle of the Dangerous Precedent," which says that nothing should ever be done for the first time.[16] Once again, as in 1945, the future hinges on the political imagination and moral authority of those in power. Absent those qualities, there is no UN, no law, and no order.

This essay elaborates some concepts developed for the Commission on Global Governance (Geneva) and the project on Rethinking International Governance of the University of Minnesota's Hubert Humphrey Institute.

Notes

1. Broadcast of February 19, 1994, as reprinted in Douglas Jehl, "Clinton Says Serbs Must Fully Comply on Arms Dead-line," *New York Times*, February 20, 1994, p. A–1.

2. As the *Economist* put it, "because world trade moves in all directions it needs a worldwide . . . set of rules, and a global . . . enforcement service." "The Trade Winds Shift," November 20, 1993, p. 15.

3. A nationwide random sample polled in February 1994 by National Research, Washington, D.C., found an overwhelming majority in support of the concept of UN peacekeeping, with 81 percent supporting operations in the event of gross human rights violations and 83 percent in favor in case of large-scale atrocities. Steven Kull and Clay Ramsay, "U.S. Public Attitudes on UN Peacekeeping, Part I Funding" (Program on International Policy Attitudes, Center for International and Security Studies at Maryland, School of Public Affairs, University of Maryland, College Park, Md., March 7, 1994), p. 5.

4. Samuel P. Huntington, "The Clash of Civilizations?" *Foreign Affairs* 72 (Summer 1993), p. 39.

5. Elaborated in *Rethinking International Governance* by the present author and Harlan Cleveland (Minneapolis: Humphrey Institute, University of Minnesota, 1988).

6. The long half-life of such proposals is illustrated by some much earlier attempts in this realm. See, for example, the author's *International Military Forces: The Question of Peacekeeping in an Armed and Disarming World* (Boston: Little, Brown, 1964), and "Peacekeeping and Peacemaking," *Foreign Affairs* 44 (July 1966).

7. Boutros Boutros-Ghali, *An Agenda for Peace: Preventive Diplomacy, Peacemaking and Peace-Keeping* (New York, N.Y.: United Nations, 1992).

8. The arguments were explored in the author's "Nuclear Spread and World Order," *Foreign Affairs* 53 (July 1975).

9. Lewis A. Dunn, "Rethinking the Nuclear Equation: The United States and the New Nuclear Powers," *The Washington Quarterly* 17 (Winter 1994), pp. 5–25.

10. John Barry, "Soon, 'Phasers on Stun,'" *Newsweek*, February 7, 1994, pp. 24–26.

11. As the German foreign minister, Klaus Kinkel, put it: "There is preventive diplomacy, but in practice we often see too little

of it, too late." Quoted in Craig R. Whitney, "Europe Seeks Ways to Put Out Its Brushfires," *New York Times*, December 2, 1993.

12. According to David Binder in "U.S. Policymakers on Bosnia Admit Errors in Opposing Partition in 1992," *New York Times*, August 29, 1993.

13. Apart from closing a memory gap, this is probably a principal value of such systems as the CASCON computerized conflict analysis program developed by the author and Allen Moulton, already used experimentally by the UN, government agencies, and scholars. See the author's "Com-

puterizing Conflicts," *Foreign Service Journal*, June 1988.

14. Reported in the Boston *Globe*, October 28, 1993. According to Paul Lewis, Washington blocked efforts to send a UN force to Burundi. "Reluctant Peacekeepers: Many U.N. Members Reconsider Role in Conflicts," *New York Times*, December 12, 1993.

15. As described by National Security Adviser Anthony Lake in "The Limits of Peacekeeping," *New York Times*, February 6, 1994.

16. F. M. Cornforth, quoted by Peter J. Gomes in "Back in the Military Closet," *New York Times*, May 22, 1993.

Facing the Emerging Reality of Regional Nuclear Adversaries

Marc Dean Millot

DRAWING IN PART on the Clinton administration's experience during 1993 and early 1994 with North Korea's nuclear program, this article reviews nuclear proliferation from a strategic perspective. It first assesses the prospects for a nonproliferation policy aimed at preventing potential nuclear powers from acquiring a nuclear arsenal, either by denying them access to the relevant capabilities or by destroying their weapons programs. It concludes that neither approach is likely to succeed. Nuclear weapons capabilities are proliferating, and the United States will have to deal with some of the new nuclear powers as nuclear adversaries. Moreover, by placing overwhelming emphasis on the ideal of prevention, U.S. policy tends to deny the emerging reality of proliferation and obstruct thinking about its consequences, particularly the military threat to U.S. allies.

Next, the article reviews the current state of U.S. planning for conflict with regional nuclear adversaries. It finds the United States unprepared to fight a Major Regional Contingency (MRC) under the shadow of nuclear attack. It argues that this follows from the belief of many U.S. military officers that nuclear weapons are obsolete after the Cold War. The article goes on to discuss the potential effects of this situation for the United States, focusing on the deterioration of its security guarantees to its allies and the possibility that they too will "go nuclear."

Finally, the article examines an approach to proliferation proposed by former Secretary of Defense Les Aspin in a speech given shortly before his resignation and, unfortunately, overshadowed by it.[1] This approach recognizes that the United States and its allies are confronted by regional nuclear adversaries and places emphasis on improving U.S. ability to cope with the threat by military means. The article explains the actions the new secretary must take to realize Aspin's vision and places the new military strategy in the context of a more comprehensive and balanced national policy toward the emerging reality of nuclear proliferation.

Marc Dean Millot is a social scientist in The RAND Corporation's Washington, D.C., office.

The Washington Quarterly • 17:3

The Proliferation of Nuclear Weapons Capabilities Is Here and Now

The first serious obstacle to thinking about how to deal with the consequences of proliferation is the policy of nonproliferation as currently formulated. Its principal means are:

- the Nuclear Non-Proliferation Treaty (NPT), with its exchange of promises by the acknowledged nuclear powers to work toward nuclear disarmament and offer technical assistance in peaceful nuclear technology in return for a pledge by non-nuclear weapon states to forswear nuclear weapons and submit their peaceful nuclear programs to certain safeguards designed to monitor adherence to that covenant; and
- a system of unilateral and multilateral controls by Western nations on the export of nuclear weapons-related technologies.

In essence, the strategy underlying this traditional conception of nonproliferation has been to prevent nuclear proliferation by denying potential proliferators unobstructed access to the relevant technologies and materials.

Few would argue against the proposition that a world free of nuclear weapons capabilities would be to the United States' advantage. But the strong demand for nuclear weapons and the explosive spread of nuclear weapons capabilities suggest that the proposition should not constitute the guiding principle of U.S. policy toward proliferation.

The Demand for Nuclear Arsenals Remains Strong

The demand side of nonproliferation has always been strong. In terms of state behavior, there is nothing aberrant about nuclear weapons prolifera-

tion. The motivations are as diverse as those of humanity itself: fear; the drive for power, influence, and prestige; and the desire to assure security and control one's destiny. Some combination of these impelled the acknowledged nuclear powers—the United States, the Soviet Union, Great Britain, France, and the People's Republic of China—to acquire their arsenals.

These motivations have also driven other states down the same path. In a few of these cases, the policy of denial seems to have worked. Argentina, Brazil, and South Korea have renounced their nuclear weapons programs. In some cases, prevention has not been achieved. Israel, India, and Pakistan remain essentially unacknowledged nuclear powers. In other cases, nonproliferation has been advanced, but for reasons unrelated to either the NPT or export controls. Iraq was denied the nuclear option by a war with the United States. South Africa developed nuclear weapons without U.S. knowledge, but as it moved to settle its domestic problems, it gave up its nuclear weapons.

In still other cases, the prospect of nonproliferation remains quite unclear. Some days U.S. leaders have reason to hope that the Ukrainians will deny themselves the nuclear option, some days they have reason to be less hopeful.[2] In several cases, states continue to harbor the desire to acquire nuclear weapons. According to Lynn Davis, under secretary of state for international security affairs, Iran is one such state.[3] Libya and Algeria are also widely believed to want the bomb.

In at least one case, the prospect of nonproliferation is quite dim. In 1992, the Bush administration's director of central intelligence, Robert Gates, said that North Korea was between "a few months and a couple of years" from possessing a nuclear weapon.[4] In 1993, Director R. James Woolsey stated "there is a real possibility that North Korea has manufactured enough fissile material for at least one nuclear weapon."[5] The Central Intelligence Agency (CIA) reportedly now claims that the North "probably has developed one or two bombs."[6] Former Secretary Aspin estimated "maybe a bomb and a half at the outside."[7] At his confirmation hearings, Secretary of Defense William J. Perry conceded that North Korea could have as many as two weapons.[8] Meanwhile U.S. intelligence analysts argue over how many months will pass before the North could place nuclear warheads on the Nodong missile, a rocket capable of striking Japan.[9]

North Korea's program demonstrates how a dirt-poor pariah, isolated from the world by sanctions and multilateral technology controls, and sometimes operating under an International Atomic Energy Agency (IAEA) inspections regime pursuant to the NPT, can nevertheless prove quite capable of acquiring or developing nuclear weapons. It constitutes a threshold test for the policy of prevention. If North Korea can get the bomb, how can the United States be expected to deny other potential adversaries?

The Supply of Nuclear Weapons Materials, Technology, and Expertise Is Exploding

Looking to the "supply side," the prevention of nuclear proliferation by means of denial is becoming increasingly infeasible.

The Inexorable Advance of Technological Sophistication. Less than two weeks before he resigned, in a now largely forgotten speech given before the National Academy of Sciences, Secretary

Aspin explained that the industrial and technological basis of a nuclear weapons arsenal has come well within the reach of the states mentioned above.

[M]any potential aggressors no longer have to import the sophisticated technology they need. They are growing it at home. The growth of indigenous technology can completely change the nonproliferation equation. Potential proliferators are sometimes said to be, quote "several decades behind the West," end' quote. That's not much comfort nowadays. A would-be nuclear nation is . . . four decades behind the West. Then in 1993 it is at the same technology level as the United States was in 1953. By 1953, the United States had fission weapons. We were building intercontinental-range bombers, and we were developing intercontinental missiles. Realize too that most of the thermonuclear weapons in the United States' arsenal were designed in the 1960s using computers which were then known as "supercomputers." However, these same computers are no more powerful than today's laptop personal computers that you can pick up at the store or order through the catalog.[10]

The Trade among China and the Pariah States. The supply of nuclear weapons materials, technology, and expertise has expanded well beyond the reach of the United States and other Western countries that share its views on nuclear proliferation. Senator John Glenn (D–Ohio), who has spent a good part of his career working for nonproliferation, told the Senate Armed Services Committee:

We've seen the North Koreans and the Chinese, the People's Republic of China, out willing to

179

sell whatever to anybody in these areas of mass destruction. We know the connection with Pakistan through the years and what's developed there. We now see varying sales going on not only to Pakistan but Iran, Algeria, Libya and Syria.[11]

Reports in 1993 suggest that North Korea and Iran may be jointly developing the Nodong medium-range ballistic missile.[12] The United States has had its occasional successes in restraining Chinese sales, but it is proving unable to halt the expanding nuclear weapons cooperation among the pariahs.

The Many Sources of Former Soviet Nuclear Weapons-Related Capabilities. The breakup of the Soviet Union created an enormous potential source of nuclear weapons-related technology, materials, expertise, and even of weapons. We have no conception of its actual extent. In 1992, Secretary of Defense Richard B. Cheney told the House Foreign Affairs Committee:

There's such a demand for that kind of capability out around the world, they'll pay any price in Libya or Tehran or elsewhere, I have to assume that some of that capability in the form of technical experts with significant know-how will in fact find its way into capitals where we'd rather it not be. We . . . shouldn't be foolish enough to think it's not going to happen.[13]

And in late 1993 Aspin said:

[P]eople working on the nuclear weapons in the Soviet Union are now available for hire in other parts of the world. . . . It is possible that nuclear weapons or the materials that go into making nuclear weapons could find their

way into some kind of a nuclear black market.[14]

The Unavoidable Leakage of "Dual-Use" Technology from the West. The promotion of highly advanced, military-related—i.e., "dual-use"—technology is an important element of the Clinton administration's economic strategy.[15] The strategy explicitly integrates the military industrial capabilities of the Departments of Energy (DOE) and Defense (DOD) in domestic economic renewal:

For example, the Oak Ridge National Laboratory's once highly secretive Y–12 plant made components for nuclear warheads. . . . Now outside researchers have access to one Y–12 plant's engineering center, prototyping facility, and ultraprecision manufacturing equipment that were formerly reserved for military work.[16]

The entire Y–12 complex is to become a Center for Defense and Manufacturing Technology.

President Bill Clinton's second secretary of defense doubts that the export of such dual-use technologies should be controlled. In 1992, Perry succinctly stated his position during his confirmation hearings to be deputy secretary.

We have to draw a clean distinction between defense-unique systems, and between dual-use technology. [In] the former we can and should control the sale whenever we think that's going to damage our proliferation goals. But in the latter, the dual-use technology, I think it's a hopeless task, and it only interferes with a company's ability to succeed internationally if we try to impose all sorts of controls in that area.[17]

If the Y–12 complex exemplifies dual-use, rather than "defense-unique," technology, the barrier between potential proliferators and nuclear weapons-related capabilities is low indeed. During 1993, the administration decided to relax controls on a broad range of telecommunications technology and computer exports; to allow sales of supercomputers, satellite technology, and nuclear power plant parts to China, despite that country's nuclear weapons-related exports; and to reconsider exports related to space-launch vehicles and remote sensing satellites.[18] As President Clinton explained to a group of business executives, the administration is unwilling to pursue nonproliferation to the point where we "cut off our nose to spite our face."[19]

Denial Is not Working, and Cannot Work

In a very basic sense, reliance on the policy of nonproliferation based on the denial of nuclear weapons-related capabilities cannot provide adequate national security to the United States. The policy may have succeeded in the past, it may prevent some U.S. friends and allies from going nuclear today, but it is failing to prevent the spread of nuclear weapons capabilities to hostile states in the very regions in which U.S. military forces are most likely to become engaged in war.

Aspin provided a straightforward explanation of the consequence of this failure.

The new nuclear danger we face is perhaps as little as a handful of nuclear weapons in the hands of rogue states. . . . [O]ur commanders in the field have to assume that U.S. forces are threatened. . . . So the threat is real, and the threat is upon us

today; not in the future; it's here and now.[20]

Coping with the Gap between the Reality of Proliferation and the Ideal of Nonproliferation

The Moral Tone of U.S. Nonproliferation Policy

At a June 1991 Heritage Foundation seminar, Daniel Poneman, the National Security Council staff member in charge of nonproliferation in both the Bush and Clinton administrations, characterized U.S. nonproliferation policy as a declaration of "global norms that essentially it is a bad thing to obtain these sorts of weapons."[21] This tone was echoed by President Clinton in remarks at the Los Alamos National Laboratory, the birthplace of the atomic bomb, less than four months after taking the oath of office.

There are still too many nations who seem determined to define the quality of their lives based on whether they develop a nuclear weapon . . . that can have no other purpose but to destroy other human beings. It is a mistake and we should try to contain it and to stop it.[22]

There is a strong moralistic quality to U.S. nonproliferation policy that inhibits realistic appraisal of the state or prospects of nuclear proliferation. The sentiment expressed by Poneman and the president is reminiscent of arguments that abstinence should be the basis of domestic policies toward AIDS, teen pregnancy, and drug use. Those who accept this approach tend to argue against efforts to mitigate the effects of these ills by promoting, for example, safe sex, the abortion option, or the use of clean needles. Ameliorating the consequence of evil is taken to suggest that society will "allow" the ills to continue. By signaling that it will allow the evil, it is argued, society ultimately encourages it.

Efforts to deal with the problem of proliferation by focusing on the immorality of nuclear weapons have had a similar effect on U.S. national security policy. The policy of prevention by denial finds it practically impossible to openly recognize the reality of nuclear possession. Thus, India, Israel, and Pakistan are officially unacknowledged nuclear powers. In the face of ongoing proliferation, a nonproliferation policy starting with the proposition that it is morally unacceptable for countries other than the acknowledged nuclear powers of the NPT to obtain nuclear status is driven either to deny that such a process is occurring, or to consider extreme means to halt its progress. Both tendencies can be seen in the Clinton administration's approach to nuclear proliferation in North Korea.

Coping with the Gap: Focusing on the Past Success of Nonproliferation

Confronted with the growing evidence of strong demands for nuclear arsenals and expanding sources of supply, advocates of prevention struggle to resolve the gap between the actuality of proliferation and the supposed norm of nonproliferation. Perhaps the foremost technique has been to discuss nonproliferation as history, and in the abstract, global terms of "international security," rather than in the context of foreseeable and concrete military threats to U.S. national security. Thus, nonproliferation has been touted as a great success for the world, and so for the United States, because Argentina, Brazil, and South Africa have apparently denied themselves their nuclear weapons programs. At

the same time, the widely acknowledged nuclear weapons programs of those nations the United States is most likely to engage in war—Iraq, Iran, and North Korea—are characterized as a few problem cases.[23]

A similar approach is taken by U.S. government officials when they refer to the failure of early predictions that many more states would become nuclear powers than have actually done so as evidence of the nonproliferation regimes' success. Poneman took this tack in his remarks to The Heritage Foundation when he stated:

> I will not belabor the famous predictions from back in the '60s . . . 25 powers by year X. Needless to say, we are not anywhere near that stage, and I think, it is due to the fact that we have addressed what I would call the demand side of the equation in nuclear weapons through such norms as the Nonproliferation Treaty.[24]

The historical approach would have the United States judge the efficacy of nonproliferation policy by looking to what it has done for the nation in the past, rather than its relevance to the present.

Coping with the Gap: Considering Forcible Nonproliferation

As North Korea threatened to completely shatter the illusion of a nonuclear norm in late fall 1993, the Clinton administration attempted to close the gap between ideals and reality by demanding the troublemaker's compliance with the NPT and threatening to enforce it. The failure of a policy of prevention by denial momentarily yielded to a policy of denial by force.

In a November 7, 1993, interview from the Oval Office televised on *Meet the Press*, the president insisted that:

North Korea cannot be allowed to develop a nuclear bomb. We have to be very firm about it. I spend a lot of time on this issue. . . . We have got to stop the proliferation of nuclear weapons, and in particular North Korea needs to stay in the control regime.[25]

On November 17, Secretary of State Warren Christopher warned North Korea that the United States had "options other than negotiation" if it did not submit to inspections of its suspected nuclear weapons facilities.[26] Given U.S. actions in the war over Kuwait, such "options" were widely understood to include war.

In early December, Clinton told reporters,

I hope we are not headed toward a full blown crisis. I hope that we can avoid one, but I am not positive that we can. . . . I am confident that if, God forbid, any kind of a conflict should come we could do what we need to do.[27]

On December 11, while appearing on *Meet the Press*, Secretary Aspin agreed with *Washington Post* correspondent Bob Woodward that President Clinton had given the North an "ultimatum."

Woodward: Just so we make this clear. The president issued an ultimatum, didn't he? He said, like George Bush in the Iraqi invasion of Kuwait, this will not stand. We will not let them get the bomb.
Aspin: We will not let the North Koreans become a nuclear power, yes.
Woodward: Period.
Aspin: I believe that's correct.
. . . .
Aspin: . . . We have a policy that has been consistent from the very beginning, and that is, as I just outlined to Bob Woodward here, is the policy that says, look, nuclear weapons in the

hands of North Korea is not acceptable.[28]

Taken as a whole, the remarks strongly suggest that the administration was willing to consider the pursuit of nonproliferation on the Korean peninsula by means of war.[29]

The Option of Forcible Nonproliferation Is Generally Unrealistic

Translated into the narrowest possible military objective, President Clinton's demand that "North Korea cannot be allowed to develop a nuclear bomb" requires the destruction of North Korea's weapons grade material and its means of producing such material. At a minimum, this calls for destruction of the reactor at Yongbyon, assuming that it is the sole facility for the production of weapons grade material and that it is also the only location where any materials already produced are stored. It is certainly possible to destroy the reactor site and, if it constituted the entire nuclear weapons production complex, to at least delay North Korea's nuclear program.

So narrowly defined, this is an operation the U.S. military can accomplish unilaterally, quickly, and stealthily, with sea-launched cruise missiles and long-range bombers. The promise of no U.S. casualties would be very credible. But there would be Korean and, in the long run, Japanese casualties. An attack on the reactor could spew radioactive material across parts of North Korea. It could send a radioactive cloud over Japan. It could result in a nuclear disaster analogous to Chernobyl.

The attack could also start a second Korean War. Even without nuclear weapons, North Korea might well take Seoul, destroy substantial portions of South Korea, and kill many American

183

soldiers. Of course, the strike on the North Korean facility could be preceded by a substantial buildup of U.S. forces in the region, as Operation Desert Shield preceded Operation Desert Storm in the war with Iraq. A buildup of U.S. forces, however, might also lead the North to invade South Korea, rather than wait for the United States to attack at full strength.

Moreover, such a buildup would give the North warning to disperse its nuclear materials and to dismantle and disperse equipment, if it has not done so already. The United States could respond by expanding the target set to include the places North Korea might hide its nuclear program and suspected missile production facilities, storage sites, and dispersed field locations. Given the uncertainties surrounding the assumption of a single North Korean nuclear weapons production facility and materials storage site, considerations of military prudence are likely to lead operational planning in that direction in any event. But many of these facilities are likely to be deeply buried. One Defense Intelligence Agency estimate reportedly claimed the North's underground facilities are "virtually invulnerable to allied air attack."[30]

At the end of this analysis of move and countermove, which could go many steps beyond the points made here, a president considering military options against even a small nuclear program is likely to find that although virtually every uncertainty or problem can be answered to some extent with an additional increment of U.S. military power, forcible nonproliferation will quickly take on the character of a substantial military operation, involving enormous costs and risks.

In the case of North Korea, the operation will not be "surgical"; it may precipitate a preemptive attack on South Korea and eventually require the United States to invade and occupy the North. It will not be quick; finding and destroying the North Korean nuclear weapons infrastructure will take time. It will not be stealthy or unilateral; it will certainly require the active cooperation of South Korea and Japan, and the acquiescence of China and Russia. There is a substantial risk of significant U.S. casualties. Unless he is prepared to follow up even the limited attack with an invasion leading to removal of the regime and occupation of the country, President Clinton will also have to accept the risk of an eventual nuclear revenge against the United States, perhaps delivered by unconventional means. And there is one uncertainty for which no amount of U.S. military power can compensate; the possibility that North Korea has developed one or more nuclear weapons and put them on its missiles.

These costs and risks must be weighed against the consequences of a successful military operation. They might be acceptable if the result is that potential proliferators see the futility of pursuing the nuclear weapons option and give up their programs. But no one can say with any certainty that by attacking North Korea in the name of nonproliferation, the United States will actually reverse the international trend toward further proliferation. Israel's highly successful raid on the nuclear facility at Osirak did not convince Iraq to abandon its nuclear weapons program. On the contrary, the Iraqis subsequently enlarged their program and dispersed and hid their nuclear facilities. Even a highly successful U.S. attack is as likely to cause other would-be proliferators to redouble their efforts as it is to convince them to abandon their programs. A less successful attack could remove from the calculations of these onlookers a nagging fear that might otherwise tend to discourage pursuit of the nuclear option.

It is unlikely that the president will choose to risk war when he has no reason to believe that, absent his threat to destroy North Korea's nuclear program, North Korea is likely to start a war on its own. The cause of nonproliferation is simply not worth that risk. But having threatened at least implicitly to consider such an attack on North Korea, if the president fails to make good on that threat, other potential proliferators will tend to be emboldened to follow in North Korea's footsteps.

Coping with the Gap: Sidestepping the Question of a Proliferator's Nuclear Status

The most frightening way to close the gap between the reality of proliferation and the ideal of preventing proliferation would be to create circumstances that foster an impression that a proliferator is complying with the no-nuclear norm and to avoid actions that tend to contradict that impression. Unfortunately, elements of this approach can be found in the Clinton administration's dealings with North Korea.

To understand the problem it is important to recall how the North Korean crisis began. In March 1993, just a few months after coming to office, the new administration became so concerned about North Korea's nuclear weapons program that it insisted that routine inspections of the North's nuclear facilities by the IAEA were completely inadequate to monitor compliance with the NPT.[31] The United States convinced the IAEA to demand intrusive inspections, particularly of nuclear disposal sites, that would enable

nuclear engineers to better determine whether the North had processed weapons grade materials in violation of the treaty. The North refused, withdrew from even the limited inspections, and the crisis ensued.

In the following months the administration declared it would not allow North Korea to become a nuclear power; that it was "not acceptable" to the United States for the North to acquire nuclear weapons. The clear implication of U.S. policy pronouncements was that the North was not adhering to the no-nuclear norm and that special inspections were necessary to prove it to the world. When the North remained intransigent, the administration implied it might well be prepared to resolve the impasse by force.

The administration then reviewed the military options and apparently found them wanting.[32] Instead, the administration considered canceling Team Spirit, an annual joint U.S.–South Korean military exercise of plans to reinforce and protect the South in times of crisis, and offering economic incentives to North Korea, if it would return to the inspections regime considered unacceptable just a few months earlier.[33] By January 1994, the administration had abandoned plans to increase pressure on North Korea by various economic sanctions, perhaps including a blockade, because it seemed highly likely to move the United States closer to the unthinkable war option. Instead, it came to a settlement with North Korea. The North agreed to at least a one-time inspection of its declared sites, with the details to be worked out with the IAEA.[34]

According to Under Secretary Davis, the United States reportedly agreed to cancel Team Spirit and is "prepared to help bring North Korea

185

into the family of nations, but only if they meet our conditions" in their negotiations with the IAEA.[35] Davis reportedly also claimed that the agreement would permit international inspectors to "tell the rest of the world that there are no dangerous activities occurring in North Korea with respect to nuclear weapons."[36] As this article goes to print, something like a return to the previously unacceptable inspections regime seems a tolerable outcome to the Clinton administration.[37] There has been no suggestion from the administration that it is prepared to resume its position that routine inspections are unacceptable and return to the crisis atmosphere of 1993.

By arriving at a compromise with the North, the administration avoided the stark choice between starting down the road to war and stepping away from its commitment to nonproliferation. More important for the purpose of this article, the evidence necessary to prove that more likely than not the North has nuclear weapons, or at least the material to make them, will remain out of reach. As described in a January 1994 *Washington Post* editorial, the administration's policy "pushes into a foggy future the previous and prime American thrust to ensure that North Korea builds no bombs at all."[38] Thus, the compromise with North Korea enables the administration to continue to treat proliferation as a possibility rather than something to be faced today.

Allowing the nuclear status of states like North Korea to remain ambiguous amounts to pretending that they are not nuclear powers. Psychologists call the phenomenon "avoidance." A policy of avoidance enables potential proliferators to continue to proceed with their nuclear weapons programs in the dark. It also discourages the United States from taking actions urgently needed to deal with the military consequences of regional nuclear adversaries.

The U.S. Military Is Unprepared for Operations against a Regional Nuclear Adversary

A second obstacle to clear thinking about the consequences of nuclear proliferation for U.S. national security lies in the U.S. military. The DOD's civilian leadership, Democrat and Republican, has recognized the threat a regional nuclear adversary could pose to future U.S. military operations. Secretary Cheney spelled it out in testimony before the House Foreign Affairs Committee in March 1992.

> There are a growing number of nations in the world that have ballistic missile capability, it's going to expand significantly between now and the end of the century and increasingly there will be nations that will have nuclear warheads to put on those missiles. Our biggest loss in the Gulf, 28 people in one event, was when a SCUD, a very crude 1950s technology missile, hit one of our barracks in the rear area in Dhahran. Now that was a small scale but it represents the kind of problem that we have got to deal with long term. The next time we deploy forces like we did against Saddam Hussein, we have got to anticipate it will be in an environment in which our adversaries will be able to launch more sophisticated missiles, better guidance systems, bigger payloads and maybe weapons of mass destruction deployed on that.[39]

Former Secretary Aspin also recognized the danger posed by regional nuclear adversaries. In February 1992, while chairman of the House Armed Services Committee, he stated: "The proliferation of nuclear weapons is now the chief threat we face in the post–Soviet era." Reflecting on the aftermath of the war with Iraq, Aspin pointed out that:

proliferation . . . has continued for the last 20 years, largely obscured by the shadow of superpower competition. The extent of Saddam Hussein's nuclear ambitions, and near success in achieving them, should be a wake up call not just about Iraq, but about other countries as well.[40]

In his speech of December 7, 1993, Secretary Aspin outlined the message in that "wake up call" and put it in historical perspective.

During the Cold War, our principal adversary had conventional forces in Europe that were numerically superior to the West. For us during those years nuclear weapons were the great equalizer. . . . Now today . . . nuclear weapons can still be the equalizer against conventional forces . . . but today, the United States . . . is the biggest kid on the block when it comes to conventional military forces, and it is our potential adversaries who may attain nuclear weapons. So nuclear weapons may still be the great equalizer; the problem is the United States may now be the equalizee.[41]

Aspin's bottom line was that "the policy of prevention through denial won't be enough to cope with the potential of tomorrow's proliferators."[42]

Nevertheless, and despite the fact that the countries violating the supposed global norm of nonproliferation are the very nations the U.S. military is most likely to fight, the uniformed military has not joined the DOD's civilian leadership in challenging the preeminence of "prevention through

denial." Nor has it challenged the viability of prevention by forcible denuclearization. The reason is a post–cold war trend in U.S. military thinking that has devalued nuclear weapons as an element of U.S. military strategy in particular, and of military strategy in general. As a result, the United States is not preparing seriously for conflicts with regional nuclear adversaries.

The U.S. Military Is Getting out of the Nuclear Business

From fall 1991 to summer 1993, Roger Molander, Peter Wilson, and this author ran a RAND study examining the emerging debate within the U.S. government over the consequences of nuclear proliferation for U.S. national security policy.[43] The focus of "The Day After . . ." study was a series of case-study defense planning exercises on regional nuclear warfare assuming U.S. force postures similar to those later proposed in the Pentagon's *Bottom-Up Review* (to be discussed below). Roughly 240 people from throughout the U.S. government participated, including nearly 50 active duty officers drawn primarily from various defense planning staffs in the Pentagon.

Two of the scenarios dealt with U.S. military interventions against regional adversaries armed with small arsenals of nuclear-tipped mobile missiles, specifically Iran and North Korea. Observing the exercises, this author was impressed by the widespread confidence of military participants in the efficacy of the advanced conventional weaponry employed with such success in the war with Iraq against the forces of a regional nuclear adversary.[44] This impression was not contradicted when the Iranian exercise

187

was rerun with hundreds of officers attending the National War College.

Apparently Operation Desert Storm has left many in the U.S. military convinced that nuclear weapons are largely unnecessary in the post–cold war world. Conventional weapons are considered able to destroy virtually every military target that used to be assigned to nuclear weapons, from buried command centers to hardened aircraft shelters, and even large concentrations of armor. Military planners point out that the precision of modern conventional weapons allows the user to reduce civilian casualties to incredibly low levels, particularly compared to nuclear weapons. This capacity for discrimination gives commanders far greater operational flexibility than nuclear weapons could ever offer. The ability to reduce the collateral damage of attacks to adjacent populations also promises to minimize the "interference" of American civilian officials during the course of a war. Apart from recognition of a need to retain some number of warheads on U.S. land- and submarine-based ballistic missiles to balance those of whoever remains in charge of the former Soviet Union's intercontinental nuclear arsenal, there is a widespread belief in the military that U.S. armed forces can do without a nuclear capability.

These attitudes are consistent with changes to the nation's nuclear force posture made over the last several years. Aside from strategic forces, nuclear weapons are on their way out of the U.S. arsenal. And with the Clinton administration's agreement not to automatically target the former Soviet Union, even strategic nuclear weapons lack an immediate and compelling military rationale. Nuclear weapons have been withdrawn from U.S. ground forces. It is no exaggeration to say that the U.S. Army is out of the nuclear business. It is only a slight exaggeration to say that the U.S. Navy and Marines are out. Nuclear weapons have been withdrawn from U.S. surface ships and attack submarines. It would take weeks to rearm those vessels and the navy appears eager to rid itself of the cost of maintaining that option. The Strategic Command retains control of U.S. intercontinental nuclear forces, but the U.S. European Command is the only combatant command with nuclear forces at the ready, roughly 1,000 air-delivered weapons dedicated to the North Atlantic Treaty Organization (NATO). Because NATO has no adversary, the weapons have no mission, and the U.S. Air Force is seriously contemplating the option of returning them to the continental United States.

At a breakfast meeting of defense journalists on September 23, 1993, on the eve of his retirement as chairman of the Joint Chiefs of Staff (JCS), General Colin L. Powell looked back on the role of the military in the dismantlement of the U.S. nuclear arsenal with great pride.

I'm enormously pleased to sort of put it in the column for the four years I've been chairman that we have put in place arms control agreements and we have done unilateral things within the armed forces reflecting the post–Cold War environment that has resulted in us reducing in due course our nuclear weapons level by about 70 percent. I mean, it was the United States armed forces without a whole lot of prompting from anybody that decided let's get rid of artillery-fired projectiles in the Army. It was within the leadership of the armed forces that we bit the bullet on taking tactical nuclear weapons off our ships at sea. . . . [Y]ou know, the Navy, the Marine Corps, and the Army now totally rely on the Air Force for any potential future nuclear weapons they need in the battlefield. . . . So I'm very pleased that the JCS has stayed ahead of the curve with respect to nuclear weapons. In fact, they've been in the forefront of getting rid of capability that is no longer needed in the post–Cold War environment and that was costing us money to keep.[45]

With the ongoing disassembly of the theater nuclear stockpile, and the de facto closure of much of the nuclear weapons production complex, the United States will find it difficult to get back into the nuclear weapons business quickly in a time of crisis. As a consequence, the guarantee of security the United States extends to its regional allies is based increasingly on conventional military power. This author's experience with "The Day After . . ." study implies that this prospect worries few in the U.S. military. In place of nuclear deterrence they suggest that the United States offer its allies a promise to repeat Operation Desert Storm if they are attacked.

The U.S. Military Is not Planning to Fight Nuclear MRCs

Accompanying the U.S. military's belief that its own military strategy no longer requires nuclear forces is a more general sense that nuclear weaponry is essentially obsolete and unusable. In December 1992 General Powell reflected this attitude in remarks following a speech at American University: "I also think nuclear weapons have much less political utility than anyone thinks they do, particularly those who are trying to develop them."[46] This position was not new to the chairman. In January 1992 he was also quoted

disparaging the value of nuclear weaponry.

> I think there is far less utility to these weapons than some Third World countries think there is. What they hope to do militarily with weapons of mass destruction I can increasingly do with conventional weapons, and far more effectively.[47]

These remarks also reflect a widespread attitude among military planners we encountered in "The Day After . . ." study that because nuclear weapons have less value to the United States than they did during the Cold War, they ought to be of less value to potential proliferators as well. Many in the military reject Secretary Aspin's notion that if nuclear weapons fall into the hands of its regional adversaries the United States may become the "equalizee." Instead, they see nuclear weapons as weapons of the Cold War and, because the Cold War is over, the rationale for nuclear weapons has ended.

The results of this attitude can be found in the DOD's *Bottom-Up Review* (BUR), a study initiated almost at the outset of the Clinton administration and released in October 1993.[48] The review was intended to provide coherence to the administration's military strategy and guidance for downsizing the U.S. force structure under a reduced defense budget. The Joint Staff, under General Powell, played a substantial role in the effort, and the report was unveiled to the press at a joint conference by Aspin and Powell.

The most disturbing aspect of the BUR report is the disconnect between its review of the threat posed by the proliferation of nuclear weaponry, on the one hand, and its discussion of force-sizing scenarios and their implications for the U.S. force structure on

189

the other. The threat and policy-oriented sections are consistent with Secretary Aspin's perspective, but the force-sizing scenarios and force structure implications are more in line with the views of Chairman Powell.

The Report Reflects a Clear Conception of the Regional Nuclear Threat. The briefest review of Operations Desert Storm and Desert Shield suggests that future power projection operations based on that experience will be seriously vulnerable to even a small nuclear arsenal. The coalition flew thousands of sorties against a handful of Iraqi mobile SCUD missile launchers without a single confirmed kill.[49] The Patriot antiballistic missile system destroyed far too few SCUD warheads.[50] As President Clinton said in his speech before the United Nations General Assembly in September 1993, Iraqi missile attacks "would have been far graver in their consequences if they had carried nuclear weapons."[51]

The BUR report's review of the proliferation threat discussed some of the larger consequences of a potential conflict with a regional nuclear adversary. Specifically, "a hostile nuclear-armed state could threaten . . . its neighbors, perhaps dissuading friendly states from seeking our help to resist aggression[;] concentrations of U.S. forces deployed in the region[;] regional airfields and ports critical to U.S. reinforcement operations[; and] American cities—either with covertly delivered weapons or, eventually, ballistic or cruise missiles" (p. 5). Thus "weapons in the hands of a hostile power not only threaten U.S. lives but also challenge our ability to use force to protect our interests" (p. 5).

In keeping with this assessment, the BUR establishes a requirement to "ensure that U.S. armed forces can successfully carry out operations in a [regional] conflict involving the use of nuclear . . . weapons" (p. 73). The report describes the demanding requirements of military operations designed to assure a successful intervention against a regional nuclear adversary. It highlights some of the force structure implications of these requirements, including improvements to intelligence in support of battlefield operations against nuclear adversaries; the ability to seize, disable, and destroy nuclear arsenals; and the development of nuclear and conventional forces to assure a credible threat of retaliation to nuclear attack (pp. 6, 73).

The report also implies the possibility of war with a nuclear-armed Iran or North Korea. Indeed, it explicitly states that "chief among the new dangers is . . . aggression by regional powers" (p. iii) described elsewhere in the report as "set on regional domination through military aggression while simultaneously pursuing nuclear, biological, and chemical weapons capabilities" (p. 1). The BUR concludes that "countering proliferation is central to addressing . . . regional dangers in the Post–Cold War world. Strengthening the U.S. military's capabilities for meeting the threat of . . . proliferation . . . is one of the Department's most important responsibilities in the new security environment" (p. 74).

The Threat Is not Reflected in the Analysis of Force Posture. When he presented the BUR to the public, Secretary Aspin noted that the most important factor in sizing and shaping the future U.S. military posture is the prospect of simultaneously fighting two MRCs against such states as Iran and North Korea. The report's initial discussion of MRCs is consistent with the more general policy sections noted above. It describes a "potential regional aggressor" armed with "100–1,000 SCUD-class ballistic missiles, some possibly [armed] with nuclear . . . warheads" (p. 13). It notes the need to protect friendly forces from missile attacks and to "destroy high-value targets, such as weapons of mass destruction" (p. 16).

But beyond this verbal nod in the direction of a power projection operation fought under a nuclear shadow, the quantitative analysis of MRCs assumes the adversary does not employ nuclear weapons. The MRC operation is portrayed as a repeat of Desert Shield and Desert Storm. As a result, aside from a decision to retain the theater missile defense component of the otherwise defunct Strategic Defense Initiative, the report makes no mention, and there is no evidence of, any serious effort to focus resources on the capabilities required to fight nuclear MRCs.

The unmistakable implication of the BUR's analysis of MRCs is that a version of the force structure employed in the war against Iraq is sufficient for operations against regional nuclear adversaries. This conclusion is completely at odds with the rest of the report. It is also at odds with Secretary Aspin's December 7 remarks that U.S. military commanders must assume they are threatened by nuclear weapons, that the threat is "upon us today," that "it's here and now." The disconnect between the discussion of the consequences of nuclear proliferation and the analysis of essentially nonnuclear MRCs suggests that while some in the DOD have recognized the nature of the threat posed by regional nuclear adversaries, the department as a whole has been unable to respond decisively.

An Adequate Response May Be Perceived as too Expensive. One reason for this failure may be the cost of a military

capability to fight a credible nuclear MRC. In military campaigns against regional adversaries, U.S. defense planners contemplating the next Desert Storm face what Roger Molander and Peter Wilson call "a tyranny of small numbers."

For example, as noted in the BUR, a handful of nuclear weapons can destroy the few ports and airfields U.S. contingency plans now rely upon to reinforce a threatened ally. During Secretary Perry's confirmation hearing, Senator William S. Cohen (R–Maine) suggested that even with the nuclear weapons it might already have, North Korea could seriously undermine U.S. plans to defend South Korea.

[Given] the limited number of ports and airfields that the United States would be required to [use to] reinforce [South Korea], I would respectfully suggest that even one or two nuclear weapons would constitute a militarily-significant arsenal in the region.

Secretary Perry agreed. "We are very concerned about the possibility that North Korea has even one nuclear weapon. We're not sanguine about that at all."[52]

Assuring the survival of U.S. forces arriving in theater and the success of power projection operations requires a combination of highly effective defensive and offensive capabilities. Given its experience against Iraqi mobile SCUDs, the U.S. military understands that guaranteeing the destruction of a small arsenal of nuclear-tipped, mobile, medium-range missiles like the Nodong is likely to be a very expensive undertaking. Yet even under BUR assumptions, the DOD is reportedly underfunded by $40 to $50 billion over the next five years.[53] A U.S. military establishment attempting to adjust to a massive downsizing may be psychologically unable to contemplate the additional cuts to the traditional force structure that will undoubtedly be necessary to rapidly develop and field entirely new capabilities to conduct nuclear MRCs. Declaratory policies denying the reality of proliferation or relying on forcible denuclearization may be more palatable.

Regional Nuclear Proliferation Places U.S. Alliance Structure in Jeopardy

The result of the Clinton administration's failure to accept the emergence of nuclear arsenals in the states most likely to threaten U.S. vital interests and recognize that the U.S. military is not prepared to deal with a regional nuclear adversary could be disastrous.

The most dangerous consequence is that the most important regional allies of the United States may be taking the first tentative steps toward reconsidering their decisions to forswear nuclear arsenals and rely on U.S. security guarantees. Japan, South Korea, Germany—indeed almost any of the nations considered U.S. allies—have the capacity to acquire a nuclear arsenal in a matter of months. Given their industrial capabilities, technological expertise, financial strength, organizational capacity, and military sophistication, U.S. policymakers would do well to think of these allies as "virtual" nuclear powers. The only thing standing in the way of their acquiring an actual nuclear arsenal is their decision not to do so.

Again the North Korean crisis provides us with a view of the future. Close observers of Japan sense the first signs of what might become a serious debate over the nuclear option. Beginning with outgoing Foreign Minister Kabun Muto in July 1993, senior offi-cials in Japan have openly, albeit somewhat indirectly, raised the possibility that North Korea's nuclear weapons capability may require Japan to follow suit. "If it comes down to a crunch, possessing the will that we can do it is important," Muto said.[54] On January 30, the London *Sunday Times* reported that the British Defence Ministry had informed the prime minister that "Japan has acquired all the parts necessary for a nuclear weapon and may even have built a bomb which requires only enriched plutonium for completion."[55] Japan has enormous stockpiles of plutonium for its nuclear power program.[56] On February 4, 1994, Japan launched its H–2 rocket, a missile capable of carrying large satellites into orbit and a potential nuclear weapons delivery vehicle.[57] This is the stuff of virtual nuclear power. Only a political decision is needed to make it real.

Allied nuclear weapons options have acquired a certain degree of legitimacy as a response to the emerging reality of regional nuclear adversaries.[58] Secretary Perry admitted as much at his confirmation hearing. "[If] North Korea becomes a nuclear power—not as defined by us but as defined by the Japanese and the South Koreans and the Taiwanese—there is every possibility that they will then want to become nuclear powers as well." U.S. policymakers are beginning to realize that decisions to formalize, preserve, or move ahead with the nuclear weapons option could soon enter the mainstream of policy debate in allied capitals.

The Credibility of Extended Deterrence Is in Decline

A critical factor in allied decisions about nuclear weapons options is the credibility of U.S. security guarantees.

No country is predisposed to place its survival in the hands of another. During the Cold War the United States convinced its allies to place much of their hope for security in its hands, convincing them that their local problem was also part of the U.S. global strategic problem. U.S. treaty commitments were of course couched in phrases that left Congress with its constitutional right to declare war. But the United States built an integrated structure of coalition defense, placing hundreds of thousands of U.S. soldiers along its allies' borders with the Soviet bloc, basing thousands of nuclear weapons that could reach Soviet territory on allied soil, sharing responsibility for the release and delivery of those weapons with its allies' political authorities, and interlocking U.S. plans for intercontinental nuclear warfare with the theater nuclear plans. In so doing, the United States created a situation in which for all practical purposes, regardless of how a war against U.S. allies might start, it was automatically committed to their defense. Through these efforts it created a unique situation, in which in any debate over national security in any allied capital the burden of proof was placed on those who argued against relying on U.S. security guarantees.

With the end of the Cold War that situation has changed. U.S. leaders do not view today's threats as being on the order of that posed by the Soviet Union. Regional security problems are now treated by the United States more as local problems of secondary concern, particularly when compared to domestic issues such as the economy, health care, and the federal budget deficit. Against the backdrop of a much reduced U.S. military presence overseas, Americans must take care not to exacerbate fears among the allies that the United States is becoming disconnected from their own perceptions of their security requirements.

With this admonition in mind, the apparent desire of many in the U.S. military to replace extended nuclear deterrence with a promise to repeat Desert Storm is likely to be taken as a sign of a declining U.S. commitment to their security. However effective Desert Storm was as a military campaign from the U.S. perspective, Kuwait was first entirely overrun and pillaged by Iraqi forces.[59] The fact that the United States is offering this conventional deterrent as the answer to wars that its allies must assume will be conducted against adversaries armed with at least small nuclear arsenals is even less reassuring. And when U.S. officials suggest that they might give up the military exercises that give operational plausibility to U.S. promises to reinforce those allies, as the Clinton administration did when it suggested that Team Spirit could be canceled, U.S. credibility is eroded still further.[60]

On the other hand, and as the earlier reactions of South Korean and Japanese officials to Secretary Aspin's November 1993 trip to the Far East show, hints by U.S. officials of policies that might well lead to strikes on the nuclear facilities of the neighbors of U.S. allies raise the possibility that the United States might start a regional nuclear war.[61] This fear can only be reinforced when U.S. defense analysts voice their own concerns about the vulnerability of allied conventional forces to a short-warning attack by the North, and about the prospect of losing Seoul. Suggestions that U.S. leaders lack prudence and good judgment undermine allied confidence in U.S. leadership.

On reflection, allies of the United States may find the intensity of the administration's reaction to North Ko-

193

rea's nuclear program even more unsettling. There is no question that the United States has the military power to defeat North Korea in a nuclear war, perhaps even while refraining from nuclear use. But as Senator Cohen suggested, U.S. political leaders consider even two North Korean weapons to be "militarily significant." Even two nuclear weapons could not save North Korea from utter defeat, but their use would be a political disaster of enormous proportions for the United States and its president. The prospect of that disaster may be a source of deep fear on the part of U.S. leaders. Recognition that this fear can be manipulated—as perhaps it has been by North Korea—could become a powerful factor motivating nuclear proliferation. And if U.S. allies come to believe that a fear of nuclear conflict may cause the United States to hesitate at some moment when they must depend absolutely on its support to assure their own survival, the credibility of U.S. security guarantees will suffer tremendously.

If the allies of the United States come to believe that it no longer shares their view of regional security, is no longer automatically committed to their defense, can no longer be counted as prudent, and may suffer from a paralytic fear of nuclear conflict, the burden of proof in any debate over national security in any allied capital will shift to those who argue for continuing to rely on U.S. security guarantees. Decisions to pursue national nuclear weapons programs may not be far behind.

The Disintegration of U.S. Alliances Will Exacerbate Regional Military Instability

The lack of credible security assurances will push allies of the United States toward nuclear arsenals of their own to restore the military equilibrium upset by their local nuclear adversaries or by more general regional nuclear instabilities. These allies may well see a realization of their virtual nuclear arsenal as the only alternative to losing all influence over their own national security. This development, however, would lead down a worrisome path, with dangerous implications for regional stability and ultimately for the security of the United States itself.

One lesson U.S. defense decision makers should take from the growing understanding of U.S.–Soviet crises is that nuclear stability is not automatic. By the end of the Cold War nuclear stability was practically an institution; in the beginning it was barely a concept. As historians report their findings on such events as the Cuban missile crisis, it is becoming apparent that the superpowers learned to create stability on the basis of trial and error.[62] Reading the results of this research it is difficult not conclude that, particularly in the early days of U.S.–Soviet competition, luck played an uncomfortably significant role in avoidance of nuclear war.

It is possible that the new nuclear powers will learn from the history of U.S.–Soviet nuclear crises, just as they have learned to take advantage of U.S. technological innovations in the development of their own nuclear weapons programs. Perhaps the relatively rapid development of a stable regional nuclear balance is feasible. On the other hand, U.S. leaders should be concerned that nations with widely varying values, thought processes, and cultures may go through the learning experience without their own good fortune. It is hard to know where any nuclear war might end, or what lessons onlookers will take away from it.

It is doubtful that anyone is eager

to run a real world experiment on the universality of the superpowers' nuclear logic. Indeed the vision of experimental failure on a massive scale has probably influenced U.S. decision makers to give prevention its privileged role in the national response to the proliferation threat. But now that regional adversaries of the United States are going nuclear, the experiment will begin if U.S. allies follow suit. As perhaps several of these experiments play themselves out, the odds increase that one will lead to nuclear war.

When U.S. leaders come to recognize that these experiments are out of their hands, they will face the question of what to do with the remaining forward presence of their forces on allied territories. If they stay, the United States runs the risk of being sucked into nuclear wars that are not of its making against its will. If they leave, the United States will lose any hope of regional influence, but may at the same time precipitate a crisis that may itself increase the risk of nuclear conflict. Neither choice is appealing; both hold grave risks for U.S. national security. Preventing the need of future leaders to confront that choice should be the goal of U.S. policy.

U.S. National Security Policy Must Counter the Consequences of Proliferation

National security decision makers must recognize that the United States and its allies will face several regional nuclear adversaries in the next decade. They must focus on the need to reassure regional allies that the best counter to this threat lies in defense arrangements with the United States, rather than in pursuing their own nuclear options. To succeed, U.S. leaders must back up their security assur-

ances by giving regional nuclear conflict the highest priority in defense planning. Countering the consequences of proliferation should replace nonproliferation, and particularly the ideal of prevention, as the focus of U.S. policy to deal with the new nuclear threat.

A New National Policy Should Move Prevention from Center Stage

The first step toward a counterproliferation policy is to recognize that, however successful it may have been in the past, the policy of prevention is now failing to protect U.S. national security. Regional nuclear adversaries are emerging. Appeals to idealism, moral suasion, trade controls, and preventive strikes cannot continue to be the centerpiece of a strategy to deal with ongoing proliferation. A presidential decision directive should be promulgated, describing the reality of proliferation and placing the development of military means and alliance plans to conduct nuclear MRCs at the center of a national counterproliferation program.

The directive must also address the NPT, and particularly the 1995 Review Conference. That treaty has some value as the embodiment of an ideal, but maintaining it inviolate should not be the U.S. goal if the price is denying the reality of ongoing proliferation. At a minimum the United States should not seek an indefinite extension of the treaty, which remains the administration's position.[63] Such an objective is simply too much at odds with the reality of ongoing proliferation and reflects a blindness to that reality that can only undermine U.S. credibility.

A policy is needed that allows U.S. decision makers—and forces the U.S.

195

bureaucracy—to recognize the emergence of regional nuclear powers. The United States must relate to the new nuclear powers as nuclear powers, not pariahs. Perhaps they will have to be admitted to the NPT as nuclear weapon states. This would at least allow U.S. policymakers to begin to develop the kind of dialogue they engaged in with the Soviets. This dialogue would tend to enhance a U.S. ability to predict the behavior of these new powers. It might also speed up their acculturation to the responsibility of nuclear power, a responsibility that even radical states like the Soviet Union eventually came to accept. It would also form the basis for formal negotiations to promote nuclear stability that might lead, for example, to meaningful arms-control treaties. Without recognition of the nuclear status of these new nuclear powers, no such negotiations are possible.

As for export controls, the president's directive must openly recognize the rising tide of global technological sophistication and the extent to which advanced and dual-use technologies are vital to the export strategy to fuel the economic growth of the United States itself and provide Americans with quality, high-wage employment. In these circumstances, the best U.S. leaders can hope for is that national and multilateral export controls will slow the spread of some uniquely nuclear weapons-related technologies and at least provide a mechanism for warning intelligence and defense analysts of the acquisition strategies of potential proliferators.[64]

Of far greater importance to U.S. policy than NPT renewal or export controls is the expression of an unambiguous intention to help U.S. allies defend themselves against regional nuclear predators. Indeed, the directive should make clear a policy determination by the president that a serious effort by the United States and its allies to reduce the military value of small nuclear arsenals is the best means of deterring regional nuclear adversaries from employing their arsenals for political benefit and of dissuading potential proliferators from pursuing the nuclear option. Admittedly, this is a far less ambitious policy than prevention by denial or force. It recognizes that some countries will acquire nuclear arsenals, despite U.S. best efforts. But given the ongoing proliferation of nuclear weapons capabilities, the limited goal is realistic; prevention is not.

The Defense Component of Counterproliferation Requires Planning for Nuclear MRCs

The second and most important step is to convince the allies of the United States that its leaders understand the strategic threat regional nuclear adversaries present to their survival and consider it to be an equivalent threat to U.S. security. The United States must renew the faith of its allies in its promises to assure their security.

The *Bottom-Up Review* constituted the first of three opportunities Secretary Aspin created for the DOD to address the consequences of proliferation for the U.S. military establishment and move forward with programmatic responses. The second was the Counterproliferation Initiative (CPI), an effort initiated in spring 1993 to identify programs that might address the proliferation threat. Some of the CPI's early findings must have been folded into the BUR effort before the report was released in October, but the initiative's results were not announced until Secretary Aspin's December 7 speech.

In his speech, Aspin listed five elements of the DOD's counterproliferation policy: the adoption of counterproliferation as a new DOD "mission"; plans to "fight wars differently"; plans to change "what we buy to meet the threat"; changes in "how we collect intelligence and what intelligence we collect"; and "do[ing] all of these things with our allies."[65] Less than two weeks after launching this initiative, Aspin was forced from office. Given the strong tendency in the Clinton administration to downplay the emerging reality of regional nuclear adversaries and the military's preference to downplay the threat of regional nuclear conflicts, the CPI's future is questionable. In the wake of Aspin's resignation, the burden of turning words into action falls on his successor, William J. Perry.

Planning for Nuclear MRCs. Convincing regional allies of the credibility of U.S. security guarantees necessitates a major revision of U.S. operational planning. The United States must be prepared to conduct MRCs under the nuclear gun. The DOD must reanimate policy and operations analysis of the consequences of proliferation for U.S. defense planning. Aspin noted that the department was "preparing guidance for dealing with this new threat—fighting a Desert Storm kind of war with the opponent actually having a handful of nuclear weapons." He also stated that the JCS and regional commanders in chief were "developing a military planning process for dealing with adversaries who have weapons of mass destruction."[66]

The most important near-term response to the regional threat of a small nuclear arsenal is in the area of operational planning. Even as part of a high-priority effort, U.S. military capabilities tailored to the threat may take years to develop and deploy; the

threat is here and now. At a minimum, the U.S. military must be able to deny a potential regional nuclear adversary the military advantages that Iraq would have had if its SCUDs had been tipped with nuclear warheads.

In future power projection operations, the United States cannot rely on a few local ports and airfields to receive reinforcements as it did in Desert Shield, or as it would today to reinforce South Korea. Nor can it rely on a small number of airfields relatively close to enemy lines to conduct a massive air offensive as it did in Desert Storm, or as it would today to defend South Korea. The survival of any such facility cannot be guaranteed and its loss could be an enormous blow to any U.S. military effort planned along the lines of Desert Shield and Desert Storm. In power projection operations fought under the nuclear shadow, U.S. military planners must seek to limit the importance of any one potential target to the success of the mission and to increase the number of nuclear warheads the adversary must use to destroy that facility.

The objective of these changes to operational planning should be to limit the damage a regional nuclear predator can do to U.S. and allied military capabilities in the theater with its small arsenal, and to deny the adversary the advantages that might accrue to him from first-use early in the conflict. In general terms, the near-term operational response to the new nuclear threat requires:

- the dispersal of allied facilities, logistics support, and forces in the theater, in order to reduce the military effect of a successful nuclear attack on any one target;
- an increase in the number of nuclear-hardened facilities such as aircraft shelters, in order to increase

the number of warheads required for a successful nuclear strike; and

- at least a limited ability to preferentially defend military targets, in order to increase the uncertainties facing an enemy attack planner.

A regional nuclear adversary facing this problem would be unable to do what Iraq might have done if it had possessed a handful of nuclear weapons. Operational planners must assure that two nuclear weapons in the hands of North Korea are not "militarily significant," as Secretary Perry and Senator Cohen believe they are today.

Acquiring New Means to Defeat a Regional Nuclear Adversary. Aspin also stated that "acquisition . . . has to be readjusted in the light of the new emphasis."[67] In keeping with this admonition, Secretary Perry should reopen the BUR by initiating a thorough study of nuclear MRCs. The results of the revised BUR should inform decisions on changes to force structure and the reallocation of defense resources to accelerated development of military forces specifically designed for regional nuclear contingencies.

In particular, the DOD must begin to redirect substantial defense resources to the research, development, and acquisition of weapon systems that will give U.S. leaders a high-confidence, conventional, damage-limiting capability against regional adversaries. This capability should consist of intelligence collection and analysis systems directed particularly at the location of mobile missiles and concealed facilities, highly responsive and accurate offensive weapon systems to destroy enemy nuclear forces and deeply buried facilities, missile defense systems that in combination permit only a small percentage of warheads to leak through, and the command and control arrangements

necessary to coordinate the employment of these systems in time-sensitive operations.

The capability must be of high confidence and damage-limiting because the consequences of nuclear attack are so devastating. Perfection is not possible and probably not necessary to deter regional adversaries from aggression, but the U.S. Air Force must do far better in attacking mobile missile launchers than it did against the SCUD carriers during the war with Iraq, and the follow-ons to the U.S. Army's Patriot missile defense must be far more capable of intercepting incoming warheads. The capability must be conventional, because U.S. leaders may be forced to use it in the early hours of a regional war. They should not be self-deterred from using the capability because they or their allies are unwilling to conduct nuclear operations.

Elements of this capability exist in various stages of development in each of the armed services. What is missing from these programs is overall coherence and a sense of urgency. As the *Economist* noted in late 1993, in the area of acquisition, the CPI "is still, as yet, a collection of hitherto disparate ideas rather than big-budget innovations."[68]

A Meaningful Line Item for Counterproliferation. Adequate funding of counterproliferation is a critical issue facing Secretary Perry. The DOD requested only $40 million specifically for counterproliferation in 1994: $9.5 million to support the Defense Technology Security Assistance Agency; $25 million to support improved export control activities in the former Soviet bloc; and $9 million for studies[69]—in short, nothing for the research, development, and acquisition of counterproliferation capabilities described in

198

Secretary Aspin's speech. Indeed, that particular budget request predates Aspin's remarks by months and is largely derivative of the prevention approach to nonproliferation the former secretary decried.

Aspin thought of the $40 million as the first step in developing a serious line item for counterproliferation. "It's just the beginning," he told House Armed Services Committee chairman Ronald V. Dellums (D–Calif.).[70] Secretary Perry should work to create a meaningful counterproliferation line item for future defense budgets.

A Counterproliferation Organization. The conventional damage-limiting capability must be thought of as a comprehensive system of systems. It needs unified command and control to operate in war. It needs its own concept of operations. It also needs a substantial budget, which, in the current fiscal environment, will have to come from elsewhere in the DOD. This will probably result in further cuts to the traditional force structure of air wings, carrier battle groups, and divisions and will probably be resisted by the military.[71]

To achieve programmatic and budgetary coherence, the secretary of defense must create an organizational structure dedicated to that objective. Currently, responsibility for pulling together the programmatic information on counterproliferation lies with the assistant to the secretary of defense for atomic energy, the official responsible for the reliability of the U.S. nuclear stockpile and the secretary's principal adviser on matters related to nuclear weapons. That arrangement may be appropriate for information gathering, but the assistant's charter is too narrow to cover development of the conventional damage-limiting capability.

A better option would be to reorient the staff and resources once devoted to the Strategic Defense Initiative and now to the reduced Ballistic Missile Defense Organization (BMDO) to this new mission, under the leadership of someone with the confidence of the secretary, Congress, and the uniformed military. An even more radical option, suggested by Roger Molander, would be to merge the activities and resources of the BMDO and the Defense Nuclear Agency to create a Defense Strategic Weapons Agency. This new agency would combine the DOD's sources of technological and organizational expertise most relevant to development of counterproliferation capabilities.

Reinterpreting the ABM Treaty. Secretary Aspin noted that development of the defensive portion of the damage-limiting capability requires a reinterpretation of the Anti-Ballistic Missile (ABM) Treaty.[72] That artifact of the Cold War prohibited the development of systems capable of intercepting strategic missile payloads under the guise of "theater" missile defense programs in order to close off a "back door" route to nationwide strategic missile defenses, thus maintaining the condition of mutual assured destruction between the superpowers and containing their arms race. To limit the damage from such medium-range ballistic missiles as North Korea's Nodong, ballistic missile defense systems must be developed to specifications that give them capabilities against some classes of former Soviet submarine-launched ballistic missiles. The Clinton administration is contemplating changes in its interpretation of the treaty's requirements that would allow one such system—the Theater High-Altitude Area Defense—to be developed and deployed beginning in 1996.[73] The political conditions that underlay the

199

ABM treaty no longer exist, and Secretary Perry should push the administration to change its interpretation of the treaty, preferably with the approval of the nuclear successor states of the former Soviet Union, but without their leave if necessary.

Reevaluating the Role of U.S. Nuclear Forces. The third opportunity Secretary Aspin created for the DOD to address the consequences of proliferation for the U.S. military establishment and move forward with programmatic responses is the Nuclear Policy Review, a reexamination of the U.S. nuclear posture initiated in fall 1993. Unfortunately, it appears that this effort will examine nuclear proliferation only to the extent that it has implications for U.S. nuclear forces.[74] Work on the CPI should be coordinated with the Nuclear Policy Review to assure that the United States has the combination of nuclear and conventional weapons programs necessary to counter the regional nuclear threat. The critical problems cutting across the two efforts are the extent to which conventional defense can serve as a military and political substitute for nuclear deterrence in the perception of U.S. adversaries and allies and, to the extent it cannot, a definition of the nuclear forces required to meet U.S. extended deterrence commitments. As discussed below, this analysis should be a joint venture with U.S. allies.

The Diplomacy of Counterproliferation Is Collective Defense

Developing U.S. military capabilities that improve prospects of U.S. victory in nuclear MRCs is only part of the answer to nuclear proliferation. Reorienting the alliances of the United States to address the consequences of proliferation should be seen as a cru-

cial task of U.S. diplomacy in the coming years. To reassure its allies of its commitment to their security, the United States must reconsider—from a political perspective—the matter of forward presence and the extent to which conventional deterrence can substitute for nuclear deterrence.

The allies must be intimately involved in this review, for only they can judge what kind of local U.S. military presence will meet their needs and whether they prefer the threat of nuclear retaliation to aggression to the promise of Desert Storm. Certainly the United States cannot allow its allies to blackmail it into protecting them by even an implicit threat to go nuclear, nor can it afford to bear the brunt of the financial burden as it did throughout the Cold War. But it must recognize that its allies will respond to the nuclear threat posed by regional adversaries or unstable neighbors. If the United States does not accept their problem as its own, the allies will be forced to go it alone.

Sharing the Risk of Regional Nuclear Conflict. For the United States to accept the allies' problem as its own demands more than declaring a state of "deterrence" that is somehow inherent in the mere existence of the U.S. strategic nuclear arsenal. The fact that the United States is capable of utterly destroying any of its regional nuclear adversaries is well known to Iraq, Iran, and North Korea. It did not deter them from pursuing their nuclear arsenals. The United States must take active measures to dispel any perception they may have that by threatening a regional nuclear war they can separate the United States from its allies.

Thus, a successful counterproliferation policy requires more than a theoretical ability to dominate the escalation ladder. It requires that the

United States share the risk of war with its allies in such a way that both they and U.S. regional adversaries are convinced that the United States is unequivocally committed to allied defense. Conceptualizing this structure and seeing that it is implemented is a task that combines diplomacy and defense analysis. As noted above, the United States was highly successful in building a physical and organizational structure of collective defense during the Cold War that deterred its adversaries and reassured its allies. Finding a way of recreating the character of that commitment to allies and giving it physical qualities should be the central focus of U.S. alliance institutions in the post–cold war era.

Joint Development of Counterproliferation Capabilities. Part of the answer probably lies in collective development and deployment of the high-confidence, conventional, damage-limiting capability, building on the theater ballistic missile defense systems Secretary Aspin proposed to NATO, South Korea, and Japan in November 1993, and again at NATO in December.[75] Commenting on the possibility of joint development in his December 7 speech, Aspin recognized that U.S. "allies and security partners around the world have as much to be concerned about in these areas as we do."[76] Aspin also emphasized the economies of an alliance initiative during his visit to NATO.

The advantage of cooperation, of course, is that it reduces the cost to any one member but is able to spread the benefits. . . . We could cooperate, for example on research and development in methods to counter weapons of mass destruction, we could cooperate on intelligence efforts, we could cooperate on missile defense.[77]

Secretary Perry should continue the push for joint activities, because it makes U.S. expressions of allied solidarity concrete.

Theater Nuclear Forces. Part of the answer also may lie in maintaining some U.S. theater nuclear capability that can be deployed to allied territory in time of crisis and over which U.S. and allied political authorities would share control.[78] Such a deployment could send a strong message to a potential military foe that the United States and its ally are unified in their resolve to resist nuclear intimidation. It would also give a regional nuclear adversary pause if it knew that its local opponent also had access to nuclear weapons. And the option raises the specter of a proportionate retaliation in kind. Perhaps allied planning for the deployment of theater nuclear warheads to bolster deterrence against nuclear predator states ought to begin. Whatever its form, effective reassurance requires the United States to shoulder real risks on behalf of its allies.

Summary and Conclusion

The threat posed by North Korea's ballistic missile and nuclear weapons programs offers U.S. policymakers insights into an emerging reality. Efforts to deny even minor, isolated countries nuclear weapons capabilities are becoming problematic as the world catches up to the level of technological sophistication achieved by the United States in the 1950s and 1960s, the sources of nuclear weapons-related supplies expand, and modern dual-use technologies become a ubiquitous feature of the global economy. Similarly, there is little reason to believe in the efficacy of forcible nonproliferation. For military and political reasons, the prospects of destroying even a small nuclear weapons program before it yields a nuclear arsenal are not good. As a result, small survivable arsenals of nuclear weapons in the hands of regional adversaries are likely to become an important obstacle to U.S. military operations in the post–cold war world.

There is little evidence that the United States takes this new threat seriously. The Clinton administration has largely denied the emerging reality of regional nuclear adversaries with high-minded statements about an international "norm" of nonproliferation, stern warnings to those who violate the norm, tough talk about military strikes on nascent nuclear arsenals, and redefinitions of nonproliferation that accommodate the actuality of ongoing proliferation.

The U.S. military has largely cooperated in this refusal to accept the possibility of regional nuclear war because of an assessment that nuclear weapons are an obsolete vestige of the Cold War. The only serious statement that the U.S. military establishment might actually have to be prepared to fight regional nuclear adversaries has been former Secretary of Defense Les Aspin's December 7 speech to the National Academy of Sciences. Little has been said on the matter before or since those remarks, and Aspin is now gone from office.

The outcome of this refusal to face the emerging reality of regional nuclear adversaries is that the United States is not preparing seriously for the possibility of having to fight in a regional nuclear war. If it continues down this path, it will be unable to cope with the potential threat of nuclear aggression against its allies. If it cannot assure the security of its allies against this threat, the result is likely to be further proliferation among these allies, highly unstable regional military

situations, a severe reduction of the United States' international influence, and a growing probability of regional nuclear wars involving U.S. forces.

Proliferation by regional allies of the United States is not inevitable. If it first recognizes that the threat of regional nuclear war threatens its own survival in ways no less meaningful than the threat presented to its allies by the Soviets and then convinces its allies that it understands this fact, the United States can dissuade them from deciding to follow their regional adversaries down the nuclear path. If the United States takes these steps, it has some hope of steering its way safely through the uncertain times ahead.

U.S. policy should embrace Aspin's analysis of the proliferation problem. It should proceed from the assumption that the United States will face several regional nuclear adversaries in the next decade, emphasize the need to reassure regional allies that the best counter to this threat lies in collective defense arrangements with the United States, and give regional nuclear conflict high priority in U.S. military planning. This approach would reduce the prospect of proliferation by regional allies of the United States, improve regional military stability, maintain U.S. influence, and reduce the chances of U.S. military forces being dragged into a regional nuclear conflict. Turning Aspin's words into action requires a serious effort on the part of Secretary Perry, and even his efforts will be effective only if President Clinton changes national policy.

The author would like to thank Marten Van Heuven, Jonathan Pollack, Chris Bowie, Paul Davis, and Brad Roberts for their comments on earlier drafts of this paper. He would also like to thank Roger Molander and Peter Wilson for the many hours of spirited debate that drove him to write it. The views expressed here are the author's and are not intended to reflect those of The RAND Corporation or any of its sponsors.

Notes

1. "Remarks of Defense Secretary Les Aspin to the National Academy of Sciences Committee on International Security and Arms Control," Federal News Service, December 7, 1993, available in LEXIS, Nexis Library, Current News File. The speech was entitled "The Defense Department's New Nuclear Counterproliferation Initiative: Dealing with the Spread of Weapons of Mass Destruction in the Post–Cold War, Post–Soviet Era."

2. John Dunn, "The Ukrainian Nuclear Weapons Debate," *Jane's Intelligence Review*, August 1993, pp. 339–342.

3. "United States Will not Have Veto Power in New Export Control Regime, Official Says," *International Trade Reporter*, Current Reports, November 17, 1993, p. 1923; Jack Kelley, "Nuclear Program in the Works," *USA Today*, January 4, 1994, p. 6.

4. Mark Matthews and Charles Corddry, "U.S. Warns North Korea over Nukes," *Baltimore Sun*, November 18, 1993, p. 1 (quoting Gates).

5. Jon Swain and James Adams, "Kim Goes to Brink on Frontier of Hate," *Sunday Times* (London), March 21, 1993 (quoting Woolsey).

6. Stephen Engelberg with Michael Gordon, "Intelligence Study Says North Korea Has Nuclear Bomb," *New York Times*, December 26, 1993, p. 1.

7. "Newsmaker," *The MacNeil/Lehrer News Hour*, Educational Broadcasting and GWETA, December 7, 1993, Tuesday Transcript # 4814, available in LEXIS, Nexis Library, Current News File.

8. "Hearing of the Senate Armed Services Committee; Confirmation of William Perry to be Secretary of Defense," Federal News Service, February 2, 1994, available in LEXIS, Nexis Library, Current News File.

9. See Paul Beaver, "Nodong–1 Details Fuel New Fears in Asia," *Jane's Defence Weekly*, January 15, 1994, p. 4; John Fialka, "Check of North Korea Nuclear Sites Won't Provide Comfort Clinton Wants," *Wall Street Journal*, January 31, 1994, p. 14.

10. "Remarks by Defense Secretary Les Aspin."

11. "Hearing of the Senate Armed Services Committee: The START Treaty and the US–Russia Joint Understanding on Further Reductions in Strategic Offensive Arms," Federal News Service, July 28, 1992, available in LEXIS, Nexis Library, Current News File.

12. Kevin Rafferty, "Iran and North Korea 'to Test Missile,'" *Guardian*, October 26, 1993, p. 20.

13. "Hearing of the House Foreign Affairs Committee, Foreign Military Aid," Federal News Service, March 4, 1992, available in LEXIS, Nexis Library, Current News File.

14. "Remarks by Defense Secretary Les Aspin."

15. *Technology for Economic Growth: President's Progress Report* (Washington, D.C.: The White House, November 1993).

16. *Ibid.*, pp. 34–35.

17. "Mixed Signals on Proliferation," *Middle East Defense News*, March 22, 1993 (quoting Perry).

18. Henry Sokolski, "Unseen Dangers in China," *Armed Forces Journal International*, February 1994, p. 25; Andrew Lawler, "Lawmakers Rap Clinton's Policy on Missile Sales," *Defense News*, October 10, 1993, p. 3; "U.S. Will Continue to Ease Export Controls on China Despite Nuclear Test, Official Says," *International Trade Reporter*, Current Reports, October 13, 1993, p. 1709; John Mintz, "The Satellite Makers' China Card: Martin Marietta Warn U.S. Sales Ban Will Cause Massive Layoffs," *Washington Post*, October 20, 1993, p. C–11; Elaine Sciolino, "U.S. Will Court China in a Sale of Big Computer," *New York Times*, November 19, 1993, p. 1.

19. "Remarks by President Bill Clinton and Vice President Al Gore to a Group of Business CEO's," Federal News Service, September 29, 1993, available in LEXIS, Nexis Library, Current News File.

20. "Remarks by Defense Secretary Les Aspin."

21. "Heritage Foundation Asian Studies Center Panel Discussion: Missile and Nuclear Weapons Proliferation in East Asia," Federal News Service, June 24, 1991, available

in LEXIS, Nexis Library, Current News Library.

22. Ronald A. Taylor, "Clinton: U.S. Will Block Nukes Abroad," *Washington Times,* May 18, 1993, p. 3 (quoting Clinton).

23. This approach is most openly taken by those with a long-standing interest in the cause of nonproliferation. A typical example is "NPT 1995: Time to Shift Gears," an article in the November 1993 issue of *Arms Control Today* by Lewis Dunn, a former assistant director of the Arms Control and Disarmament Agency, and U.S. ambassador to the 1985 NPT Review Conference. Assessing the effectiveness of the NPT, Dunn wrote "The overall record is very good and getting better, but not untarnished" (p. 15). China's unwillingness to adopt tight export controls, and the position of North Korea, Ukraine, India, and Pakistan are referred to as "wild cards," as exceptions to the rule, and certainly not indications of any trend (p. 17).

24. "Heritage Foundation . . . Missile and Nuclear Weapons Proliferation in East Asia."

25. Martin Walker and Kevin Rafferty, "US Warns Off North Korea," *Guardian,* November 8, 1993 (quoting Clinton).

26. Matthews and Corddry, "U.S. Warns North Korea over Nukes."

27. Quoted in Carl P. Leubsdorf, "Clinton Somber about Impasse on N. Korea Nuclear Program," *Dallas Morning News,* December 9, 1993, p. 1–A.

28. "Broadcast Interview With Defense Department Personnel," Federal News Service, December 11, 1993, available in LEXIS, Nexis Library, Current News File.

29. The concept of forcible denuclearization may go well beyond rhetoric. Maj. Gen. Robert Linhard, director of plans and policy at the Strategic Command, is an important player in the development of military responses to proliferation. In an unclassified briefing given at a conference on emerging nuclear actors against the backdrop of the escalating crisis with North Korea, and drawing on administration statements as potential guidance, he identified "rollback of proliferation where it has occurred" as one of the DOD's "counterproliferation objectives." Linhard noted the department's "unique responsi-

bility to develop plans/options involving direct military action, especially preemptive military action." These military options would support political objectives including to "punish illegal proliferation and eliminate acquired capabilities" and "preemptively destroy capabilities." Among the administration pronouncements Linhard drew on was a statement made by Secretary of State Warren Christopher in January 1993. In it, the secretary outlined a general approach to nonproliferation in which "we must work assiduously with other nations to discourage proliferation through improved intelligence, export controls incentives, sanctions, and even force when necessary." Robert Linhard, "Counterproliferation Strategies," Appendix A (briefing charts), in *Counterproliferation: Deterring Emerging Nuclear Actors,* Compendium of Proceedings of the Strategic Options Assessments Conference held at U.S. Strategic Command, Offutt AFB, Nebraska, July 7–8, 1993, and sponsored by the Defense Nuclear Agency (Arlington, Va.: Strategic Planning International, Inc., 1993).

30. Barton Gellman, "Trepidation at Root of U.S. Korea Policy; Conventional War Seen Catastrophic for South," *Washington Post,* December 12, 1993, p. A–1 (quoting the Defense Intelligence Agency monograph, "North Korea: The Foundations for Military Strength").

31. Swain and Adams, "Kim Goes to Brink on Frontier of Hate."

32. Secretary of State Christopher suggested as much on ABC television on November 21, when he cautioned that Israel's raid on Osirak might be "too easy an analogy" to possible strikes on Yongbyon. David Sanger, "U.S. Revising North Korea Strategy," *New York Times,* November 22, 1993, p. 5. Gen. Merrill McPeak, chief of staff of the air force, told reporters that "a preemptive attack would not be totally successful, because American intelligence could not locate North Korea's hidden caches of plutonium and because attacks on North Korea's . . . nuclear reactor core with conventional bombs could cause radioactive pollution." Quoted in Michael Gordon, "Pentagon Begins Effort to Combat More Lethal Arms in Third World," *New York Times,* December 8, 1993, p. 15. But McPeak was even more concerned about the conventional defense of South

Korea. "The worst nightmare," he said, "is that Seoul would come under attack almost immediately. . . . I just can't answer whether we could stop them before they got to Seoul or not." Quoted in Gellman, "Trepidation at Root of U.S. Korea Policy."

33. Thomas L. Friedman, "U.S. and Seoul Differ on Offer to North," *New York Times*, November 2, 1993, p. A–16.

34. Steven Greenhouse, "U.S. Backs Off on Atomic Sites in North Korea," *New York Times*, January 5, 1994, p. A–1.

35. Lynn Davis, "Korea: No Capitulation," *Washington Post*, January 26, 1994, p. A–21.

36. John J. Fialka, "Check of North Korean Nuclear Sites Won't Provide Comfort Clinton Wants," *Wall Street Journal*, January 31, 1994, p. 14 (quoting Davis).

37. On February 15, after some stalling, the North once again agreed to IAEA inspection of its seven declared sites, but not of the suspect sites so important to determining whether the North has been developing nuclear weapons. Carol J. Williams and Jim Mann, "N. Korea Agrees to Inspection of 7 Nuclear Sites," *Los Angeles Times*, February 26, 1994, p. 1.

38. "No North Korean Bomb?" *Washington Post*, January 6, 1994, p. A–16.

39. "Hearing of the House Foreign Affairs Committee, Foreign Military Aid," Federal News Service, March 4, 1992, available in LEXIS, Nexis Library, Current News File.

40. Les Aspin, "From Deterrence to Denuking: Dealing With Proliferation in the 1990s" (monograph), February 18, 1992, p. 5.

41. "Remarks by Defense Secretary Les Aspin."

42. *Ibid.*

43. The results of this research are documented in Marc Dean Millot, Roger Molander, and Peter A. Wilson, *"The Day After . . ." Study: Nuclear Proliferation in the Post–Cold War World*, vol. 1, *Summary Report* (MR-266-AF); vol. 2, *Main Report* (MR-253-AF); vol. 3, *Exercise Materials* (MR-254-AF) (Santa Monica, Calif.: RAND, 1993).

44. *Ibid.*, vol. 2, pp. 39–110, and particularly 69–70, 109; vol. 3. At least one former senior civilian official also appears to accept this line of argument. See Paul H. Nitze, "Is it Time to Junk Our Nukes?" *Washington Post*, January 16, 1994, p. C–1.

45. "Defense Writers Group Breakfast Meeting," Federal News Service, September 23, 1993, available in LEXIS, Nexis Library, Current News File.

46. "Joint Chiefs of Staff Chairman Gen. Colin Powell Address Sponsored by American University's Kennedy Political Union," The Reuters Transcript Record, December 1, 1992, available in LEXIS, Nexis Library, Current News File.

47. Stephen Budiansky and Bruce Auster, "Tackling the New Nuclear Arithmetic," *U.S. News and World Report*, January 20, 1992, p. 38.

48. Les Aspin, *Report on the Bottom-Up Review* (Washington, D.C.: Department of Defense, October 1993) (hereinafter referred to as BUR).

49. On some of the problems of "SCUD-hunting" see Rick Atkinson, *Crusade: The Untold Story of the Persian Gulf War* (Boston, Mass.: Houghton Mifflin, 1993), pp. 145–148.

50. On the debate over Patriot operations see, "Playing Patriot Games," *U.S. News and World Report*, November 22, 1993, p. 16.

51. "President Bill Clinton Addresses the General Assembly of the United Nations, the United Nations, New York," Federal News Service, September 27, 1993, available in LEXIS, Nexis Library, Current News File.

52. "Hearing of the Senate Armed Services Committee; Confirmation of William Perry to be Secretary of Defense."

53. "Clinton to Complete '95 Budget Meetings with Cabinet, Agency Heads by This Week," Daily Report for Executives (Bureau of National Affairs), December 13, 1993, p. A–237.

54. Selig S. Harrison, "A Yen for the Bomb?" *Washington Post*, October 31, 1993 , p. C–2.

55. Nick Rufford, "Japan to 'Go Nuclear' in Asian Arms Race," *Sunday Times* (London), January 30, 1994, p. 1.

56. See generally, Harrison, "A Yen for the Bomb?"

57. Andrew Pollack, "Japan Launches Rocket, Cutting Reliance on U.S.," *New York Times*, February 4, 1994, p. A–17.

58. See Ken Adelman, "The Nuclear Domino Threat," *Washington Times*, October 20, 1993, p. 21.

59. The comment concerning the outcome of another Korean conflict attributed to Gen. Gary Luck, a veteran of the war with Iraq and commander of U.S. forces in Korea, that "I can win a war, I just can't do it right away" is unlikely to make South Koreans feel more secure. Gellman, "Trepidation at Root of U.S. Korea Policy."

60. Friedman, "U.S. and Seoul Differ on Offer to North."

61. The headline of one newspaper article on the trip read, "Seoul's Big Fear: Pushing North Koreans Too Far," as a North Korean buildup along the DMZ reportedly placed 70 percent of its forces within range of the South. David Sanger, *New York Times*, November 7, 1993, p. 16. See also R. Jeffrey Smith, "North Korea Bolsters Border Force," *Washington Post*, November 6, 1993, p. 19.

62. See James G. Blight and David A. Welch, *On the Brink: Americans and Soviets Reexamine the Cuban Missile Crisis* (New York, N.Y.: Hill and Wang, 1989). One interesting means of accessing this record is the *Cold War International History Project Bulletin* (Woodrow Wilson International Center for Scholars, Washington, D.C.). For example, the fall 1993 issue contains a fascinating debate over the extent of the local Soviet military commander's authority to initiate the use of tactical nuclear weapons in Cuba during the missile crisis.

63. "State Department Regular Briefing," Federal News Service, December 8, 1993, available in LEXIS, Nexis Library, Current News File.

64. Indeed, this appears to be the likely outcome of multilateral talks to replace the West's export control Coordinating Committee (COCOM) with a regime (including the former Soviet republics) to control the spread of technologies associated with weapons of mass destruction. "Eagleburger Says Allied Pressure Will Force End to COCOM Relatively Soon," *International Trade Reporter*, Current Reports, September 29, 1993, p. 1609. In her November 1993 testimony to Congress, Under Secretary Davis noted that the United States had been unable to retain the right of CO-COM members to veto proposed exports. "United States Will not Have Veto Power in New Export Control Regime, Official Says," *International Trade Reporter*, Current Reports, November 17, 1993, p. 1923. Members of the new system will be able to approve exports after notifying the other members. Consequently, export controls are likely to be a marginal component of counterproliferation.

65. "Remarks by Defense Secretary Les Aspin."

66. *Ibid.*

67. *Ibid.*

68. "Cold War II," *Economist*, December 11–17, 1993, p. 29.

69. Statement of Walter B. Slocombe, principal deputy under secretary of defense (policy), before the Senate Armed Services Committee hearing on Arms Control Treaty Verification, Nunn–Lugar Programs, and Counterproliferation, June 23, 1993 (mimeograph), p. 26.

70. "Hearing of the House Armed Services Committee, Fiscal Year 1994 Defense Authorization Bill," Federal News Service, March 30, 1993, available in LEXIS, Nexis Library, Current News File.

71. For one example of the continuing competition between the services over a more integrated defense against ballistic missiles see "Army Stands by Status Quo for Its Role in Air Defense," *Defense Daily*, November 5, 1993, p. 195.

72. "Remarks by Defense Secretary Les Aspin."

73. Jeffrey Smith, "Officials Say U.S. Wants to Change ABM Treaty to Buttress Missile Defense," *Washington Post*, December 4, 1994, p. A–22.

74. "Press Briefing With Secretary of Defense Les Aspin; Ash Carter, Assistant Secretary of Defense for Counter-Proliferation; Lieutenant General Barry McCaffery Regarding Defense Nuclear Posture Review, The Pentagon," Federal News Service, October 29, 1993, available in LEXIS, Nexis Library, Current News File.

75. See generally, "Aspin Pitches TMD to Japanese, S. Koreans," *BMD Monitor*, November 5, 1993, p. 297.

76. "Remarks by Defense Secretary Les Aspin."

77. Charles Aldinger, "Aspin Urges Allies to Develop New Nuclear Defenses," Reuters, December 9, 1993, available in LEXIS, Nexis Library, Current News File.

78. In remarks before the Indianapolis Press Club on December 6, which were subsequently broadcast on C-SPAN, Senator Richard G. Lugar (R–Ind.) proposed a return of U.S. nuclear artillery shells to South Korea. On February 1, 1994, the Senate passed a nonbinding amendment to State Department legislation, urging the United States to "enhance the defense capability of United States forces by preparing to reintroduce tactical nuclear weapons in South Korea," if the North refused to submit to inspections. "Senate Calls For Isolation Of North Korea," Reuters, February 1, 1994, available in LEXIS, Nexis Library, Current News File.

Peacekeeping and U.S. Interests

John Gerard Ruggie

DO UNITED NATIONS (UN) peace operations serve the interests of the United States? When, where, and how? Only a few short years after the Bush administration basked in "new world order" euphoria, President Bill Clinton's decision directive on peacekeeping (PDD–25) has evoked a mixture of dispirited disappointment from those who had hoped for more, and dismissive criticism from those who want still less.[1] This steep downward slope suggests that the remaining political base for redefining the UN's role in U.S. thinking about post–cold war international security policy is shrinking fast. The present article frames these issues within a broader historical and conceptual context, in the hope that doing so will deepen and sharpen current policy discourse.

The language of interests is an instrumental language. The views of U.S. policymakers about the UN, in contrast, are all too often shaped by preset postures. One of these is liberal internationalism, which originated with Woodrow Wilson and currently includes the self-styled "pragmatic Wilsonianism" of Anthony Lake, Pres-

ident Clinton's national security adviser. This view tends instinctively to favor international organization, based ultimately on the belief that it expresses the essential interdependence of humankind. A second is conservative unilateralism, the position of Henry Cabot Lodge, Wilson's nemesis in the League of Nations ratification fight, as well as of the current Senate minority leader Robert Dole (R–Kan.), author of the highly restrictive "peace powers act." They view international organization as inevitably constraining rather than enabling the pursuit of U.S. interests. Finally, practitioners of realpolitik, such as former secretary of state Henry Kissinger, who are normally a natural constituency for instrumentalism in international politics, typically reject out of hand the idea that international organization can make any significant difference in a world driven by self-seeking power politics.

If the subject of possible U.S. interests in UN peace operations is to be discussed fruitfully, therefore, it must first be rescued from the orthodoxies that frequently capture it, wherein answers are given before questions are asked. Although it may look like a bit of a stretch, I begin by describing briefly the views on this subject held by Franklin Roosevelt. Why? Because Roosevelt was chiefly responsible for the creation of the UN, because his views stayed clear of pre-

John Gerard Ruggie is dean of the School of International and Public Affairs at Columbia University.

Copyright © 1994 by The Center for Strategic and International Studies and the Massachusetts Institute of Technology
The Washington Quarterly • 17:4

vailing orthodoxies, and because he was the last U.S. president who had to devise an overall framework for the conduct of U.S. foreign policy, including a role for the UN, before the Cold War became its animating force. With Roosevelt's pre–cold war heterodoxy as a backdrop, I then address more specifically the relationship between current U.S. interests and the peace operations of the UN.

Roosevelt and the Founding Rationale

Historians have found it extraordinarily difficult to accurately capture Roosevelt's views about the United Nations he helped to create. Some have depicted him as a closet Wilsonian, others as pursuing traditional power politics in liberal internationalist disguise. In fact, neither interpretation does him justice. Here as elsewhere, Roosevelt was a tinkerer—"the juggler," as he once described himself.[2] Three elements of Roosevelt's thinking about the UN were especially critical and remain instructive even today.

First, Roosevelt did not value the creation of the UN as an end in itself, nor primarily as a means to transform the traditional conduct of international relations, which is how Wilson had viewed the League. Roosevelt felt that a universal security organization in which the United States was the leading member was needed to ensure the timely, active, and sustained engagement by the United States in postwar international security affairs. He deeply appreciated how the country's geographic isolation and abundance of natural wealth had fostered its traditional aversion to "entangling alliances." He sensed, therefore, that a case-by-case interest calculus of whether or not the United States should get involved in any particular

threat to international peace and security was unlikely in most instances to prove persuasive to the U.S. Congress and the public—until it was too late and the United States faced a far more difficult situation than it would have at an earlier stage or, even worse, was dragged yet again into a major war that it had done little to prevent. Needless to say, the origins of World War II were foremost in his mind. Thus, Roosevelt above all else saw in the UN an institutional trip wire, as it were, that would force U.S. foreign policy makers to take a position on potential threats to the peace and then justify their actions or inaction to the body politic.

Although Roosevelt had originally favored a regional spheres-of-influence approach to organizing postwar security relations, he came to fear that this "four policemen" scheme, as it was known, might be used by Congress and the public as a pretext for the United States to shirk involvement beyond its own hemisphere, especially in Europe. Consequently, Roosevelt reached the conclusion, as he explained to Anthony Eden in 1943, that "the only appeal which would be likely to carry weight with the United States public . . . would be one based upon a world-wide conception."[3]

Second, Roosevelt believed that a stable postwar international security order also required, in the words of John Lewis Gaddis, the eminent cold war historian, "offering Moscow a prominent place in it; by making it, so to speak, a member of the club."[4] Gaddis calls this the strategy of "containment by integration"—in contrast to the subsequent U.S. strategy of containing the Soviets by exclusion and exhaustion. But this strategy required a club to which both Washington and Moscow belonged. Roosevelt hoped that the UN Security Council would perform that function. Thus, Roosevelt envisioned a hybrid design for the UN: a universal security organization grafted onto a concert of power. In effect, he was trying to reconcile Wilson at Versailles with Metternich at the Congress of Vienna.

Finally, Roosevelt believed that the UN had to have "teeth" and be able to enforce its decisions by military means if others failed. Without teeth, it would neither provide deterrent value vis-à-vis potential aggressors nor would it possess the credibility required for the geopolitical objectives of engaging the United States while constraining the Soviet Union. At the same time, Roosevelt assured the American people, "we are not thinking of a superstate with its own police force and other paraphernalia of coercive power." Instead, the United States and the other major powers, he said, planned to devise a mechanism for "joint action" by national forces.[5] Roosevelt's proposal enjoyed strong approval in public opinion polls and had overwhelming support in the Congress.[6]

Contrary to subsequent criticism, Roosevelt did not assume that the great powers would maintain their unity after the war. He did assume, as historian William Widenor has put it, "that the U.N. plan would work if, and only if, they did."[7] When it did not work other means would simply have to be fashioned. Moreover, the basic parameters of the postwar security order were placed well beyond the writ of the UN in the first place, by the permanent member veto and by explicit provisions for the direct occupation of the Axis powers. Finally, the Security Council veto also ensured that the United States could not be compelled to commit forces or funds to international security objectives it did not support.

That Roosevelt's views were heterodox is clear. But do they shed any light on the situation today?

Contemporary Relevance

U.S.-instigated, UN-based negotiations concerning the levels of, and the means by which to coordinate, possible joint national forces were abandoned in 1947, victims of the Cold War.[8] Today, the issue of UN forces has resurfaced and is the source of great controversy in the United States. Proponents are accused of seeking to subcontract U.S. foreign policy to the UN; opponents are dismissed as neoisolationists. Both sides exaggerate and distort. Both sides also treat the issue almost entirely as a favor that the United States should or should not bestow upon the rest of the world. This is an impoverished view when compared with Roosevelt's conception, wherein the issue of joint military forces and action was informed by a larger vision of the United States' own geopolitical objectives. Are there any such links today between the United States' broader geopolitical aims and possible roles for the UN?

Surely the most central need today is to redefine the fundaments of the international security order, now that the overriding impulses of the Soviet military threat and Communist ideological challenge have dissolved. When the Cold War marginalized the security role of the UN, and with it Roosevelt's strategy for ensuring sustained U.S. engagement in international security affairs, Harry Truman discovered that it also provided an even more effective substitute. By invoking the Communist menace, *Newsweek* wrote at the time, the Truman Doctrine "had clearly put America into power politics to stay."[9] And so it did for the duration of the Cold War. But where does the United States go from here? What puts it into power politics to stay today? À la carte interest calculations are no more likely to suffice today than they have in the past. But what are the "grander" alternatives? Fears of a Russia gone mad? The clash of civilizations? The doctrine of "enlargement"? Jobs, jobs, jobs? In the absence of a compelling alternative, it may be worth pondering what a Rooseveltian strategy of institutionalized engagement would look like.

Let us assume that the United States remains leery of entangling alliances and weary of foreign quagmires. Let us also assume, however, that sooner or later the United States will be drawn into seeking to counter particularly egregious acts of aggression or violations of civility—which, if the first premise holds, it will have done little to prevent or contain. This was Roosevelt's dilemma in a nutshell. Avoiding it suggests, at a minimum, that the United States should try to build on past institutional successes and promising institutional models.

The most important institutional success story in postwar U.S. security policy is the North Atlantic Treaty Organization (NATO). Today, the United States can either endeavor to extend the security framework of NATO to include key East European countries in a meaningful way—or watch them renationalize their defense efforts and rebuild independent military capabilities, thereby detracting from economic reforms while posing the danger of future regional instability and conflict. Similarly, the United States can either help to deepen the West European pillar of NATO and thus facilitate the emergence of a greater political and security component in the European Union— or watch Western Europe continue to flounder, flail, and fail on international

security issues, worsening unstable situations for all concerned, including the United States. In both contexts, possible links between the military arm of NATO and the political apparatus of the UN, haphazardly operationalized in Bosnia, need to be more clearly articulated and more effectively rationalized.

The most promising institutional model from the past is that of a concert of power—or perhaps overlapping concerts of powers—performed, at least in part, through the UN. Take the case of Russia. The outbreak of the Cold War rendered irrelevant Roosevelt's attempt to contain the Soviets by integration. But what of the post– cold war world? The United States has been trying to define a viable Russia policy, thus far without striking success. The policy preferences of Washington officials and Beltway mavens have oscillated between the close embrace of "partnership," which Russia as an independent great power is obliged to resist, and isolation, which is likely to produce self-fulfilling prophecies of uncooperative behavior by Russia. For its part, Russia has been most consistently constructive when it has been "a member of the club"—which, after some false starts, is now the case with regard to Bosnia.

It may be worth thinking along analogous lines with regard to parts of what Russia calls its "near abroad." The West would like to see Russia's behavior constrained. But neither the United States nor anyone else is likely to undertake direct action to prevent Russia from doing pretty well as it pleases in the Caucasus and the former Central Asian republics—as well as in Moldova and possibly even Crimea. The Russians, in turn, want to protect their local interests while containing regional conflicts, yet would prefer to do so in a manner that does not seriously jeopardize their relations with the West. How can these diverse objectives be reconciled? Although far from ideal, one of the few practical means available is to transform Russia's ongoing military involvement in Georgia and Tajikistan, for example, into a broader UN peacekeeping framework—requiring Security Council authorization and review, including troops from out-of-area countries, and coupled with an internationally supervised process of political negotiations.

In the Asia-Pacific region, the central longer-term task of post–cold war reconstruction in the security arena is to achieve the "normalization" of Japan's security policy and forces without, at the same time, deepening regional rivalries and amplifying the already rapid pace of arms acquisition—even as the United States gradually scales down its own military presence there. This task is inherently difficult. Moreover, European models of regional community formation have little appeal in Asia-Pacific. And even though measures to enhance transparency and otherwise build mutual confidence have been proposed by Australia, among others, their significance is likely to remain relatively modest. Under these circumstances, it may be worth also exploring an unorthodox UN angle: for example, permanent membership on the Security Council for Japan as part of a broader initiative by Japan to multilateralize its security relations, perhaps going so far as to sign an article 43 agreement with the UN, which would put some of Japan's defense forces at the disposal of the Security Council.

These are but a few illustrations of a contemporary strategy of institutionalized engagement. Other prospects could be explored, including possible links between effective mechanisms of international conflict resolution and

reductions in weapons proliferation. Obviously, such a strategy would not constitute the totality of U.S. security policy, or even its primary thrust. But it would be linked directly to core U.S. foreign policy interests. Admittedly, a presidential decision directive on the subject of improving UN peace operations is not the place to discuss in detail the potential broader geopolitical roles of the UN in U.S. foreign policy. Nevertheless, one would expect the document to reflect such concerns. PDD–25 does not. As the *Washington Post* noted editorially, the strategy paper portrays UN peace operations strictly as "a sometime tool for third-level American interests."[10]

UN Peace Operations Today

UN peace operations will lack credibility unless the mechanisms themselves deliver. That is why Roosevelt insisted that the UN have teeth. Some of the newer, more "assertive" forms of UN peace operations, however, have not functioned at all well. Writing in the *International Herald Tribune* in September 1992, I observed that "it is a miracle of no small magnitude that disaster has not yet befallen one of these peacekeeping missions."[11] Since then, alas, the UN has run out of miracles. The setbacks in Somalia, Bosnia, and Haiti are, in fact, the key drivers behind the Clinton initiative for more "selective," "effective," and "less expensive" UN peace operations.

Oddly, the administration's strategy paper ignores one, and only touches on the other, of the two fundamental defects that have afflicted these UN missions: a complete doctrinal void and nightmarish command and control arrangements.

Doctrine. The most basic problem with the recent, more muscular peace operations is that neither the UN, nor its member states, strictly speaking know what they are doing or how to do it. Peacekeeping is not mentioned in the UN Charter, having been invented at the time of the 1956 Suez crisis.[12] But in its classical form, peacekeeping has evolved a rationale, and training manuals have been written describing it in detail. It is premised on the consent of the parties. Given the interpositionary or "umpire" role peacekeepers play, they fight against neither side in a dispute but remain impartial. They are a device to create transparency, to assure each side that the other is carrying out its promises. To that end, they observe and report. They carry only light arms and shoot only in self-defense. Unlike fighting units, then, peacekeeping forces are not designed to create on the ground the conditions for their own success; those conditions must preexist for them to be able to perform their task. In short, theirs is essentially a noncombatant mission carried out by military personnel. Accordingly, the combat effectiveness of such units and the adequacy of UN headquarters and field support operations have not had to be major issues of concern in the past.

To this classical peacekeeping portfolio the UN, starting in the late 1980s, began to add monitoring and sometimes conducting elections, supporting and sometimes performing tasks of civil administration as well as related services facilitating transitions to stable government. To ensure the future viability of these activities, the UN requires increased levels and more timely provision of financial resources, better trained personnel, and more sophisticated logistical support and communication systems. But neither the classical peacekeeping portfolio nor its civilian offshoots require any fundamental doctrinal or institutional innovations.

Enforcement is also well understood. An aggressor is identified by the Security Council and subjected to an escalating ladder of coercive measures until its aggression is reversed. Ultimately, enforcement involves flat-out war-fighting—the "all necessary means" of resolution 678, authorizing what became Operation Desert Storm. War-fighting of that sort is everything that peacekeeping is not: the decisive, comprehensive, and synchronized application of preponderant military force to shock, disrupt, demoralize, and defeat opponents. Military enforcement will remain the province of a small number of countries that have the requisite capabilities, with the UN performing, at most, political legitimation and some coordination functions.

It is in the gray area of conflict between classical peacekeeping and all-out war-fighting that the UN has gotten into trouble. The trouble stems from the fact that the UN—the secretariat and Security Council alike—has tried simply to ratchet up and project a perfectly good instrument into highly unstable and potentially lethal environments for which it was not designed and in which it cannot succeed. Inevitable failure has produced inevitable backlash.

There is no agreed doctrine to inform operational planning and common training for missions in this gray area.[13] The most extensive doctrinal work seems to have been done by the British army.[14] But after exploring all known options with the aim of devising a comprehensive formulation that makes sense on the ground, the British team concluded that the endeavor was doomed, that—other than outright military enforcement—there was no viable alternative to consent-based, impartial, interpositionary UN intervention, involving minimum force. Because nearly half of all ongoing UN peace operations find themselves in this gray area between classical peacekeeping and enforcement, however, they are currently condemned to making things up as they go along. PDD–25 is silent on this critical issue.

Command and Control. According to the UN Charter, under article 47(3) a Military Staff Committee, comprising the chiefs of staff of the five permanent members of the Security Council, was to have been responsible "for the strategic direction of any armed forces placed at the disposal of the Security Council." The drafters could not resolve questions related to the actual command of such forces, however, leaving them to be "worked out subsequently." These charter provisions have never been operative. UN-authorized military enforcement in Korea and in Desert Storm delegated command to the United States. In classical peacekeeping, governments vest operational control for employing and deploying military personnel in the secretary general. Because no peacekeeping mission other than the Congo operation ever saw extensive combat, this arrangement has posed few problems.

The in-between gray area, however, does pose serious problems. Because consent is sporadic, as in Bosnia, or civil authority has collapsed altogether, as in Somalia, such UN operations have much greater requirements than their antecedents for force protection, force mobility, possibly armed deterrence, and some capacity for neutralizing the use of force by local combatants. Quite apart from equipment and logistical needs, which the UN can ill afford to meet, the

existing command and control arrangements of these operations become progressively more problematical the more they are called upon to perform these tasks. The UN secretariat has made major strides in reorganizing itself, centralizing and rationalizing functions within the Department of Peacekeeping Operations. But the problems run deeper. Civil-military relations are poorly defined in the UN, the political objectives and military missions of operations are unreliably linked, force commanders control too few of the assets that are ostensibly under their command, and tactical intelligence is episodic at best.[15]

PDD–25 exhibits some awareness of these problems, promising to assist the UN in augmenting its communication, logistics, and management capabilities. Its proposed solution to the underlying structural defects of UN command and control arrangements, however, is simply to opt out. That is to say, U.S. troops are less likely to be placed under UN operational control, the document states, the higher the probability that a mission will encounter combat, and the greater the anticipated U.S. role in the mission. On close inspection, however, this is no solution at all. It approximates what was actual U.S. policy in Somalia. And any objective telling of that story will conclude that the policy made matters worse for everyone affected by it, including U.S. troops.[16]

The only U.S. forces that were ever under direct operational control of the UN in Somalia comprised a roughly 3,000-strong logistics component. The U.S. Quick Reaction Force (QRF) remained under the command of US-CINCCENT, the U.S. commander in chief, Central Command, although for each of a series of raids on Mohamed Farah Aideed's clan the QRF came under the temporary tactical control of

215

Maj. Gen. Thomas Montgomery of the U.S. Army. General Montgomery also served as UN deputy force commander, in which capacity he reported to the UN force commander, Lt. Gen. Cevik Bir, a Turk. Finally, the U.S. Army Rangers remained entirely under the direct command of Special Operations Command in Florida, bypassing both the UN command and control structure and General Montgomery, even in his U.S. role.

The Rangers who were ambushed in Mogadishu on October 3, 1993, then, operated fully under U.S. command and control. Retired U.S. admiral Jonathan Howe, who, as special representative of the secretary general in Somalia, was responsible for overall coordination of all in-theater activities, did not learn of the Rangers' raid until after it began. General Bir and General Montgomery were not informed until shortly before it got under way. With no advance warning, let alone joint planning, and lacking interoperable communications equipment, it took Malaysian and Pakistani UN forces several hours to come to the Rangers' assistance.[17] In short, having U.S. troops in Somalia serve under U.S. command amid a UN operation whose own command and control structure was already cumbersome and tangled manifestly contributed to the problem.

The October 3 tragedy in Mogadishu, more than any other factor, turned the Clinton administration away sharply from its earlier declaratory commitment to "assertive multilateralism." Hence, it is singularly perplexing that the presidential directive proposes one of the causes of failure in Somalia that day as the solution governing future U.S. participation in combat-prone UN peace operations. More viable options will have to be considered: either working with the UN and other countries to create effective UN command and control arrangements, or altogether excluding U.S. ground troops from potential combatant roles in UN gray area peace operations.

The two most serious shortcomings of the recent UN peace operations in semipermissive contexts, characterized by sporadic consent and greater likelihood of violence, are a doctrinal void and erratic command and control arrangements. The Clinton strategy paper does not address the first, and its proposed solution to the second threatens to compound the problem. When coupled with the fact that its analysis is largely detached from core U.S. geopolitical objectives, it is not surprising that the document elicited little enthusiasm from across a broad spectrum of political and editorial opinion.

A Concluding Word about Interests

The United States is not now and has never been a relative equal on a continent densely populated by potential adversaries—the European context for which balance-of-power theory and the principle of *raison d'état* were first invented. For a power so great as the United States, interests, therefore, are rarely determined by external exigencies alone. More often than not, it enjoys the luxury of defining the content of its interests and choosing how best to pursue them. In the post–cold war world as before, the Americans' sense of who they are as a people and what kind of world they aspire to must inform the United States' choice of ends and means.

This ideational and aspirational dimension is missing almost entirely from foreign policy discourse in the United States today. It will be hard to redefine the nation's interests for the post–cold war world without it. One might think that an administration of self-proclaimed multilateralists and pragmatic Wilsonians would draw on that tradition to give it a try. But in its peace operations directive, the Clinton team failed to take the opportunity. Ironically, Henry Kissinger—the canonical U.S. figure in the pantheon of realpolitik—has risen to the challenge. He concludes in his recent magnum opus,

> In traveling along the road to world order for the third time in the modern era, American idealism remains as essential as ever, perhaps even more so. But in the new world order . . . [t]raditional American idealism must combine with a thoughtful assessment of contemporary realities to bring about a usable definition of American interests.[18]

Roosevelt could not have put it better.

An earlier version of this article was prepared for a conference of the Aspen Institute's Congressional Program on "The United Nations, Peacekeeping and U.S. Policy in the Post–Cold War World," St. Croix, Virgin Islands, April 4–9, 1994. The author thanks the MacArthur Foundation for funding the research on which the article draws, and Sandrine Teyssonneyre for research assistance.

Notes

1. The unclassified text of the presidential decision directive has been released as "The Clinton Administration's Policy on Reforming Multilateral Peace Operations" (The White House, Washington, D.C., May 1994). For a sampling of initial reactions, see Ann Devroy, "Clinton Signs New Guidelines for U.N. Peacekeeping Operations," *Washington Post*, May 6, 1994, p. A–30, and Elaine Sciolino, "New U.S. Peacekeeping Policy De-emphasizes Role of the U.N.," *New York Times*, May 6, 1994, p. A–1.

2. The term is used as the title of Warren F. Kimball's study, *The Juggler: Franklin Roo-*

sevelt as Wartime Statesman (Princeton, N.J.: Princeton University Press, 1991).

3. Cited in *ibid.*, p. 96.

4. John Lewis Gaddis, *Strategies of Containment* (New York, N.Y.: Oxford University Press, 1982), p. 9.

5. Cited in Robert C. Hilderbrand, *Dumbarton Oaks: The Origins of the United Nations and the Search for Postwar Security* (Chapel Hill: University of North Carolina Press, 1990), p. 65.

6. For evidence, see Robert A. Divine, *Second Chance: The Triumph of Internationalism in America During World War II* (New York, N.Y.: Atheneum, 1967), chaps. 9–10.

7. William C. Widenor, "American Planning for the United Nations: Have We Been Asking the Right Questions?" *Diplomatic History* 6 (Spring 1982), p. 251.

8. To put some perspective on current debates, it is worth recalling the final U.S. and Soviet positions on the proposed size and composition of joint forces. The United States favored a combined total of 20 ground divisions or around 200,000 men, 1,250 bombers, 2,250 fighters, 3 battleships, 6 carriers, 15 cruisers, 84 destroyers, and 90 submarines. The Soviets advocated a smaller combined force, consisting of 12 ground divisions, 600 bombers, 300 fighters, 5 to 6 cruisers, 24 destroyers, and 12 submarines. By the time negotiations were formally discontinued, however, these differences reflected political jockeying more than technical assessments of collective security needs. See D. W. Bowett, *United Nations Forces: A Legal Study* (New York, N.Y.: Praeger, 1964), pp. 12–18.

9. Cited in David McCullough, *Truman* (New York, N.Y.: Simon and Schuster, 1992), p. 549.

10. "Peace-Keeping Guidelines," *Washington Post*, May 8, 1994, p. C–6.

11. John Gerard Ruggie, "No, the World Doesn't Need a United Nations Army," *International Herald Tribune*, September 26–27, 1992.

12. Once the concept of peacekeeping was articulated, the UN discovered that, like Molière's Monsieur Gentilhomme, it had been speaking prose all along. The truce supervisory organization established in

Palestine in 1948 as well as the observer team stationed on the Kashmir border of India and Pakistan in 1949 thereafter came to be seen as antecedents to peacekeeping.

13. For one attempt to sketch out a possible logic behind such a doctrine, see John Gerard Ruggie, "Wandering in the Void: Charting the U.N.'s New Strategic Role," *Foreign Affairs* 72 (November/December 1993). Also see John Mackinlay and Jarat Chopra, *Draft Concept of Second Generation Multinational Operations* (Providence, R.I.: Watson Institute, Brown University, 1993).

14. I base this judgment on, among other sources, the papers presented at the symposium on "Military Coalitions and the United Nations: Implications for the U.S. Military," National Defense University, Fort McNair, Washington, D.C., November 2–3, 1993. See, in particular, Maj. Gen. M. A. Willcocks, "Peace Operations: What the United Kingdom Is Doing." A complete British army field manual, entitled "Wider Peacekeeping," has since been circulated in draft form.

15. For useful surveys, see Mats R. Berdal, "Whither UN Peacekeeping?" *Adelphi Papers* 281 (London: Brassey's for IISS, 1993), and William J. Durch, ed., *The Evolution of UN Peacekeeping* (New York, N.Y.: St. Martin's Press, 1993).

16. A good account may be found in Mats R. Berdal, "Fateful Encounter: The United States and UN Peacekeeping," *Survival* 36 (Spring 1994). I have supplemented it with interviews in New York and Washington.

17. A U.S. Marine colonel with Somalia experience subsequently commented at a Washington meeting I attended how glad he was that the UN forces that finally came to the Rangers' assistance did not invoke any right to disobey orders from their UN commander that they viewed as subjecting them to "needless risk" or simply being "imprudent"—a right an earlier draft of PDD-25 claimed for U.S. troops—because the rescue order might well have been so regarded.

18. Henry Kissinger, *Diplomacy* (New York, N.Y.: Simon & Schuster, 1994), p. 834.

Religion and Peace: An Argument Complexified

George Weigel

BEIRUT, AND INDEED all of Lebanon, the Golden Temple of Amritsar, Kashmir, Belfast, Tehran, the Temple Mount in Jerusalem. These being the typical reference points for most discussions of "religion and peace," it is little wonder that Western elites—our academic institutions, the prestige press, our governments—tend to think of religion, in its impact on international public life, as a source of, rather than a remedy for, violent conflict.

But the fact that these are taken to be the primary reference points, however, is not itself an accident, because it reflects the broader inclination of elite Western opinion to view religion as an irrational, premodern phenomenon, a throwback to the dark centuries before the Enlightenment taught the virtues of rationality and decency and bent human energies to constructive, rather than destructive, purposes. Nor should it be considered a secret that this elite Western suspicion of religion frequently involves a caricature of religious conviction.

It would be foolish for people of faith to deny that religion can be a source of violent conflict. It has been; it is today; it will be in the future. But it would be imprudent, unwise, and just plain wrongheaded for both religious skeptics and statesmen to ignore

George Weigel is president of the Ethics and Public Policy Center and the author of several books on ethics and international affairs.

the fact that religious conviction has also functioned as a powerful warrant for social tolerance, for democratic pluralism, and for nonviolent conflict resolution. This essay will explore the latter, often uncharted, territory in the conviction that, as religion is not going to fade from the human landscape, it is important to understand how religious faith, and the personal and social values that derive from it, can serve the cause of peace.

The Unsecularization of the World

Although rarely recognized, the "unsecularization" of the world is one of the dominant social facts of life in the late twentieth century.

This is true of the United States which, despite the predictions of two generations of secularization theorists, remains an incorrigibly religious society.[1]

It is true of central and eastern Europe; indeed, the revolution of 1989 would not have taken the form it did, and might possibly never have happened at all, without the efforts of the Roman Catholic church in Poland and Czechoslovakia and the Evangelischekirche in the late German Democratic Republic.[2] One could also mention in this regard the roles played by various Orthodox churches in Romania, Bulgaria, and throughout the republics of the Soviet Union.[3]

"Unsecularization" aptly describes

the situation in Latin America, where the traditional Roman Catholic religiosity of the population is being forcefully challenged not merely, or even primarily, by secularization but by forms of evangelical and fundamentalist Protestantism whose social impact could be supportive of economic liberalization and political democratization.[4]

"Unsecularization" also characterizes the Asian subcontinent, where Hinduism, Buddhism, and Islam, and variants on each, remain powerful social (and indeed political) forces.

Finally, "unsecularization" characterizes much of the Arab world, in which a particularly militant form of Islam is a powerful (some would argue, the most powerful) social and political dynamic.

The social, political, and geopolitical impacts of man's persistent yearning for communion with the divine are, of course, diverse in the extreme, as these examples of "unsecularization" indicate. That modernization puts great stress on traditional communities—familial, ethnic and tribal, religious—is, further, an empirically established fact.[5] But that modernization inevitably leads to radical secularization of the Scandinavian sort is a much more dubious proposition with little empirical warrant. The world is not going to become Sweden (or Cambridge, Massachusetts, or the CBS executive dining room) in the foreseeable future. Religion is, so to speak, here to stay. The task, then, is to discern the theological and political conditions under which religion serves the cause of nonviolent conflict resolution.

Religion and Cultures of Tolerance

The political *structure* of societies is a function of the political *culture* of societies. The forms and functions of governance are not the result of a kind of social virgin birth. Rather, they express the fundamental, constitutive self-understandings and values of a people—understandings and values that are frequently religious in origin and nature.

How, then, does religion contribute to the evolution of societies that prize social tolerance, that cherish pluralism, that prefer nonviolent to violent means of resolving conflicts over public life: societies that, by the values and dynamics of their own political cultures, will be likely to prefer nonviolent means for resolving conflicts among, as well as within, political communities?

The case with which we are most familiar is, of course, that of the West. Western democratic societies are the result of a complex process of cultural, economic, social, and political evolution, and it would be a prime example of the fallacy of *pars pro toto* (confusing a part with the whole) to ascribe to religion the sole place as a causal force in the development of Western democracy. Greek philosophy, Roman law, feudalism, and the Enlightenment each played a key role in shaping Western democracy—and its preference for legal and political, that is, nonviolent, conflict resolution—as we know it today. But Judaism and Christianity made essential contributions to the political *culture* of the West, the culture from which the democratic structures of our societies have grown.

How did this happen? Three dynamics in the history of this culture-forming process should be noted.

First, the ethical monotheism of Judaism, spread throughout the Western world by the Jewish diaspora and by Judaism's child, Christianity, taught that "there are universal ethical principles which stand over the action of individual human beings and societies as a whole."[6] The debate over the content of those principles and their applicability to public life has, of course, been continuous for over two millennia. But "immediate agreement" on the content and implications of these universal principles "was taken to be less important than the common conviction that all parties are under the same truth," and the parallel conviction that, in this debate, "revelation and reason, faith and experience, all count as evidence."[7]

Jews and Christians believed, and taught, that these universal ethical principles were based on God's nature and God's will for His creation, but several of the key forms of Judaism and Christianity also taught that knowledge of these principles was discernible through a disciplined moral reflection on the structure of creation itself, a reflection sometimes described as the "natural law" method of moral reasoning.

This teaching had a tremendous, if usually unappreciated, social or public impact on the political culture of the West. For if ethical monotheism teaches that "all persons in principle have access to [the universal moral norms],"[8] then it follows that "all have certain responsibilities, and all in principle may, indeed ought to participate in the edification and evaluation of others and of the society at large."[9] Jewish and Christian understandings about the universal "availability" of moral insight were an important cultural factor in opening up the possibility of a politics of persuasion in which all men would have a moral claim to participate.

Second, Judaism and Christianity also occasioned a profound shift in the social structures of Western societies.

Because these great religious traditions insisted that the key communities of identity were the synagogue or the church, they radically altered the force of claims made by other contending communities: the family or tribe and the polis. Societies in which the family or tribe or the polis is the dominant locus of personal and social identity are centripetal in nature: they tend toward cultural, social, and political monism. The claims of the synagogue and the church, on the other hand, desacralize politics and clear the social space for pluralism, thus further enhancing the prospects of a politics based on persuasion and consent rather than on divinely sanctioned coercion.[10]

To be sure, the monistic impulse has never been expunged from some forms of Christianity (particularly, although not exclusively, in the worlds of Eastern Christianity), and it is also evident today in various types of what is usually termed "ultra-Orthodox" Judaism. Nevertheless, the logic of Judaeo-Christian ethical monotheism drives toward pluralism rather than monism in the construction of societies and polities, and thus the political logic of the "Judaeo-Christian ethic" was an important building block of democratic *culture*.

Third, the process described in the two points above also had a kind of feedback mechanism within it. The evolution of pluralistic democracy over the past two centuries and the 70-year struggle between the West and the monism of Marxism–Leninism have not only been influenced by Judaism and Christianity, they have themselves influenced Jewish and Christian theological understandings. Catholicism's experience of a liberal democratic society in the United States, for example, was an important element in the 190-year evolution of Catholic theological understanding that eventually yielded the Second Vatican Council's 1965 "Declaration on Religious Freedom."

Religious conviction and democratic culture have, therefore, experienced a dialectical or reciprocal relationship in the West. Yet the key point to grasp is that tolerance in Western societies is frequently grounded, even today, in religious conviction. Or, as Richard John Neuhaus has nicely put it, Jews and Christians in the West have come to understand that "it is the will of God that we be tolerant of those who disagree with us about the will of God."[11] This religious warrant for domestic social tolerance and civil amity has, in turn, been one of the cultural factors mitigating the more bellicose instincts in Western societies and predisposing Western democracies to prefer nonviolent to violent means of conflict resolution in international public life. Societies whose political cultures prize tolerance and teach the importance of civilized conversation as a means of resolving differences even in matters of (to borrow from Paul Tillich) "ultimate importance" would seem, ipso facto, more likely to look toward other than violent means of redressing grievances and settling disputes among nations. In any event, that seems to have been the way things have worked out empirically.[12]

To sum up, Judaism and Christianity have made three seminal contributions to the evolution of relatively pacific democracies in the West, societies in which (and for which, in their encounter with the world) nonviolent means of conflict resolution are understood to be morally, as well as pragmatically, preferable: the concept of a universal moral law that is in principle knowable by all men; the concept of the independent integrity and moral

priority of the religious community as the key community of identity, a claim that desacralized politics and cleared the ground for pluralism and the politics of consent; and, more recently, the *religious* affirmation of religious freedom and social tolerance, which is an important building block of a political culture capable of sustaining an experiment in democratic pluralism, itself the world's most successful example of nonviolent conflict resolution.[13]

The Just War Tradition and the Pursuit of Peace

On the narrower question of religion and the problem of war, I would also argue—in what will perhaps strike some as a paradoxical fashion—that Christianity in particular has made an important contribution to nonviolent conflict resolution through the evolution of the just war tradition and Christianity's gradual acceptance of that tradition as its mainstream normative framework for reflecting on problems of war and peace.

The classic just war criteria of the *ius ad bellum* (by which it is determined that the resort to armed force is morally justifiable) and the *ius in bello* (by which morally justifiable conduct within war is assessed) have, of course, been abused throughout history. But they have also served as a restraint on political officials and military personnel, and they continue to shape both the U.S. policy debate (as in the 1984–1986 exchange between George Shultz and Caspar Weinberger on the use of U.S. military forces abroad) and the U.S. Uniform Code of Military Justice.[14]

More broadly, the *ius ad bellum* principles (just cause, right intention, proper authority, likelihood of success, last resort) have been an important cultural current in shaping international law and international organizations, even though the central "non-intervention" principle of modern international law is, in some respects, in tension with the understanding of the international system found in classic just war theorists.[15]

Moreover, the religiously informed just war tradition has had an important moral and cultural impact on Western democratic societies and their approach to problems of international conflict. The just war tradition assumes that we live in a morally coherent universe in which all human actions, even in extremis, are susceptible of moral judgment. In other words, and according to the just war tradition, we do not live in hermetically sealed, separated compartments labeled, respectively, "morality" and "politics" (or "war"). Rather, just war theorists, rejecting the moral simplifications of both pacifism and what we might call bellicism (the holy war or crusade tradition), argue for the possibility of rational moral judgment even under duress. John Courtney Murray described the public impact of the evolution of the just war tradition in these elegant terms:

The [political] community is neither a choir of angels nor a pack of wolves. It is simply the human community which, in proportion as it is civilized, strives to maintain itself in some small margin of safe distance from the chaos of barbarism. For this effort the only resources directly available to the community are those which first rescued it from barbarism, namely, the resources of reason, made operative chiefly through the processes of reasonable law, prudent public policies, and a discriminatingly apt use of force. . . .
The necessary defense against

barbarism is, therefore, an apparatus of state that embodies both reason and [armed] force in a measure that is at least decently conformable with what man has learned, by rational reflection and historical experience, to be necessary and useful to sustain his striving toward the life of civility. The historical success of the civilized community in this continuing effort of the forces of reason to hold at bay the counterforces of barbarism is no more than marginal. The traditional [just war] ethic, which asserts the doctrine of the rule of reason in public affairs, does not expect that man's historical success in installing reason in its rightful rule will be much more than marginal. But the margin makes the difference.[16]

Father Murray's reflections may help us to understand, moreover, that the just war tradition is more than a set of moral guidelines for determining when the resort to armed force is justified, and more than a catechism of rules setting boundaries on the use of military force once war has been entered upon. Rather, the just war tradition contains within itself what I have called a *ius ad pacem*: a theory of statecraft that is religiously and morally supportive of nonviolent legal and political approaches to conflict resolution. Just war theory points, in other words, toward a concept of peace while determining the ways and means in which discriminate and proportionate armed force can contribute to the pursuit of that peace.

The "peace" in question is thoroughly worldly; it is not the peace of the Kingdom of God, where the lions lie down with the lambs, nor is it the secular utopia of a world without conflict. Rather, the peace envisioned by just war theory—the peace that

223

functions as a kind of moral and intellectual horizon against which the use of force may be measured and toward which the use of force ought to be ordered—is the peace that St. Augustine called *tranquillitas ordinis,* "the tranquillity of order," or, as I have interpreted it, the peace of "dynamic and rightly-ordered political community."[17] The peace of just war theory, in other words, is the peace of politics and law as nonviolent means of conflict resolution. Far from being an obstacle to the nonviolent resolution of conflict, then, the just war tradition, in its formal criteria (especially the *ad bellum* criterion of "last resort") and in its logic, gives a highly developed moral warrant to conflict resolution through other than military means, even as it holds open the moral possibility that the defense of innocents and the pursuit of a lasting peace may, at times, require the proportionate and discriminate use of armed force.

This concept of a *ius ad pacem* will continue to play an important role in the moral culture of the West as we face the necessity of refining the traditional *ius ad bellum* ("war-decision law") and *ius in bello* ("war-conduct law") criteria under the impact of new forms of international conflict by both state and nonstate actors and new military technologies. The current situation in the Persian Gulf, which would have been even more potentially disastrous without Israel's energetic exercise in nuclear nonproliferation vis-à-vis Iraq's Osirak reactor in 1981, has brought to the fore crucial questions involving the ethics of preemption, the proscription of violence against noncombatants (e.g., in the case of "human shields" surrounding legitimate military targets), and the nature of "proportionality." Questions of the morality of deterrence, this time around in terms of chemical weapons,

are also being pressed upon us. In a sense, the issues engaged in the Gulf are a dramatic magnification of the stress put on traditional understandings of the just war criteria by the phenomenon of contemporary terrorism—stresses felt, for example, during the U.S. confrontation with Libya during the early 1980s, stresses that are daily part and parcel of political life in Israel.

The just war tradition is, then, in need of what theologians would call a "development of doctrine." Such a development might usefully take place, at least in part, in conversation with those international legal scholars who have come to understand the inadequacy of the nonintervention principle as the sine qua non of contemporary international law. But in its capacity to restrain violence, in its broader understanding of how the use of military force has to be ordered to the pursuit of peace, and in its concept of statecraft, the just war tradition remains an invaluable resource for developing both the moral culture and the political actors capable of sustaining efforts to broaden the sphere of nonviolent conflict resolution.[18]

Religion and Peace: A Brief Global Survey

The following survey of current arenas of conflict may help illustrate some of the dynamics of the complex relationship between religious conviction and the nonviolent resolution of conflict within and among nations.

Central and Eastern Europe. The impact of religious conviction and religious organizations on the revolution of 1989 in central and eastern Europe remains the least-reported facet of that astonishing and heartening complex of events. And yet, as Timothy Garton

Ash has demonstrated in his reportage from the region, the political revolution of 1989 was preceded by a moral and cultural revolution, one of whose ignition points was the "most fantastic pilgrimage in the history of contemporary Europe"—the visit of the newly elected pope, the Pole John Paul II, to his homeland in March 1979:

> In a beautiful, sonorous Polish, so unlike the calcified official language of communist Poland, [John Paul II] spoke of the "fruitful synthesis" between love of country and love of Christ. At Auschwitz he gave his compatriots a further lesson in the meaning of patriotism, recalling, with reverence, the wartime sacrifices of the Jews and Russians, two peoples whom few Poles had learned to love. He spoke of the "inalienable rights of man, the inalienable rights of dignity.". . .Invoking the romantic messianism of Adam Mickiewicz, he spoke of the special lesson which Christian Poland had to teach the world, and the special responsibility which this laid on the present generation of Poles. "The future of Poland," he declared from the pulpit of his old cathedral, "will depend on how many people are mature enough to be non-conformists."[19]

According to Garton Ash, the pope's pilgrimage was more than a "triumphant articulation of shared values"; it also engendered a mass "popular experience of—there is no better word for it—solidarity. . . . That intense unity of thought and feeling which previously had been confined to small circles of friends—the intimate solidarity of private life in eastern Europe—was now multiplied by millions." The result would loom large in political history:

> For nine days the state virtually ceased to exist, except as a censor doctoring the television coverage. Everyone saw that Poland is not a communist country—just a communist state. John Paul II left thousands of human beings with a new self-respect and renewed faith, a nation with rekindled pride, and a society with a new consciousness of its essential unity.[20]

Perhaps the most remarkable dimension of the Polish revolution lay in the linkages forged between that mass, religiously derived sense of national unity and purpose, so evident in the worker-based trade unionism of the Gdansk Solidarity leadership, and the political activism of secular (and often Jewish) intellectuals in the Committee for Social Self-Defense (usually known by its Polish initials, KOR). In any event, the result was a revolutionary impulse with staying power (it is difficult to imagine the Polish revolution surviving the martial law period from 1981 to 1983 without the motivation and discipline provided by the Church)[21] and with a commitment to nonviolence. For the intellectuals in the KOR group, nonviolence was a commitment derived primarily from a sense of the possible (the other side had all the weapons), but also from intense historical study and moral reflection, particularly during the martial law period.[22] Garton Ash in fact stresses the moral component of the Poles' commitment to nonviolence against those who would reduce it to a merely pragmatic calculation: "It was a statement of how things should be. They wanted to start as they intended to go on. History, said Adam Michnik, had taught them that those who start by storming bastilles will end up building their own."[23] For the masses, though, it seems likely that the commitment to nonviolence was most powerfully warranted by the continual preaching of this theme by a pope who had, in the Latin American context, vigorously rejected those currents in the theologies of liberation that seemed to favor revolutionary violence against the "first violence" of oppressive social systems.

The same dynamics and actors—intellectuals, workers, Church—shaped the "velvet revolution" of Czechoslovakia, where Václav Havel's motto, "living in the truth," provided a splendid parallel to the pope's exhortation to "call good and evil by name."[24] Indeed, President Havel's magnificent New Year's Day address to his countrymen on January 1, 1990, was a compact, highly charged statement of the priority of the moral revolution over the political revolution and a clarion call to cleanse the "devastated moral environment" of Czechoslovakia so that the seeds of a democratic political culture might take root in fertile ground.[25] That religious conviction might have a key role in that process of democratic consolidation was presaged by the importance among the Prague intellectuals of the Catholic priest Václav Maly and by the mass impact of the petition for religious freedom initiated in 1988 by a Moravian peasant, Augustin Navrátil, vigorously endorsed by the octogenarian Catholic primate, Cardinal František Tomášek, and eventually signed by over a half-million Czechoslovaks.[26] At the time, the Navrátil petition looked like a brave act of defiance without a discernible public impact; in retrospect, it was an important step in teaching the people of Czechoslovakia that they could, in fact, live "in the truth."

Similarly, in the late, unlamented German Democratic Republic, the Lutheran Evangelischekirche pro-vided, throughout the 1980s, an organizing ground for the civic opposition to the regime, an opposition that first formed around the issue of religious conscientious objection to conscription and that took its inspiration from the life and death of the theologian Dietrich Bonhoeffer, a martyr to Nazi tyranny.

We may also note that the countercase to nonviolence, during the revolution of 1989, was Romania, where religious leaders (such as Laszlo Tokeş) were key figures in the agitations that led to the downfall of Nicolae Ceauşescu, but where the hierarchy of the Romanian Orthodox Church had been thoroughly coopted by the regime and was thus in no position to aid in the creation of a parallel or alternative "civil society" from which a nonviolent revolution might have sprung.

No doubt the relationship between religious and political conviction and between religious and political institutions in the new democracies of central and eastern Europe will shift during the process of democratic consolidation. Friction along these lines is already evident in Poland, especially in terms of the church's role in education.[27] But if one is looking for striking examples of how certain forms of religious conviction can provide powerful warrants for nonviolent approaches to conflict resolution, even under the most strained circumstances, one need not look much further than to the revolution of 1989 and its antecedent movements throughout the 1980s in Poland, Czechoslovakia, and the former German Democratic Republic.

The Soviet Union. The highly disciplined and nonviolent nature of the Lithuanian revolution of 1990 was due in no small part to the role of the Catholic resistance in Lithuania over the past 15 years and to the ideas that have informed that activism on behalf of religious freedom. Indeed, one can argue that the ground on which the current independence movement and its nonviolent character were formed was initially tilled in the mid-1970s by the Lithuanian Catholic Committee for the Defense of Believers' Rights and its remarkable samizdat publication, the *Chronicle of the Catholic Church in Lithuania*. Before Vytautas Landsbergis and Kazimiera Prunskiene, so to speak, there were Father Alfonsas Svarinskas, Father Sigitas Tamkevicius, and Sister Nijole Sadunaite. Moreover, the continuing importance of Catholicism in the life of the Lithuanian people makes it likely that the Lithuanian revolution will remain (as it did despite massive Soviet provocations in the spring of 1990) nonviolent because of the commitment to nonviolence repeatedly urged by John Paul II.

The role of religion in several of the other restive republics of the Soviet Union has been, of course, far more complex. The emergence in the Russian Republic of a Christian Democratic movement, led by former Russian Orthodox dissidents and with some affinities to the Christian Democratic movement in Western Europe, suggests the possibility that a revolutionary political force committed on religious grounds to nonviolent change could emerge and make common cause with those secular radical democrats whose choice for the nonviolence of politics and legal change has different warrants. Conversely, in Ukraine, the nationalism and corruption of the russifying Russian Orthodox patriarchate of Moscow, on the one hand, and the intense linkage between Eastern-rite Catholicism and nationalism in western Ukraine on the other, have combined to produce scuffles, some attacks on people, and a general atmosphere of confrontation rather than reconciliation. Were this situation to get even more precarious, one might expect that the current Soviet leadership would be prepared to make virtually any concessions in order to have John Paul II make a pastoral visit to Ukraine.

The relationship between religion and nonviolent conflict resolution during the dismantling of Lenin's Soviet Union is thus likely to be as complex as the Union itself. Leaning toward a religiously grounded preference for nonviolence are those parts of Catholicism most directly linked to John Paul II and to the Polish experience, together with those reformist elements in Russian Orthodoxy that have distanced themselves from the machinations of the patriarchate of Moscow for some years now.

Latin America. The picture in Latin America is as complex as the region. The romance with revolutionary violence (heavily influenced by Franz Fanon) in which some Latin American theologians of liberation indulged themselves from the late 1960s through the early 1980s has been blunted by Vatican interventions at the level of both ideas and personnel,[28] and by the evident preference of "the people," in whose name liberation theology claimed to speak, for the rule of law and for democracy: in short, for nonviolent means of resolving conflict and pressing urgent claims for social change. Moreover, the hierarchy of the Catholic church has shown itself to be an adept midwife to democracy in certain countries (most prominently, in Chile), and a strong, if sometimes lonely, voice for nonviolence in other nations (Nicaragua, El Salvador).

Nevertheless, as suggested above, the most dynamic force in Latin American religion and politics over the next decade may well be the new evangelical and fundamentalist (more accurately, pentecostal) Protestants. Viewed historically and theoretically, this "Protestantization" of Latin America may, as one observer has suggested, follow the pattern of social impact of its immediate antecedents— the Wesleyan revolutions in eighteenth-century England and the nineteenth-century United States: "Protestantization" will involve the *embourgeoisment* of the affected populations and will provide religious and moral warrants for both entrepreneurship and democracy, thus leading to a kind of pacification of social life.[29] Viewed through the lens of present-day politics, however, the situation may be rather more complicated than that. Guatemala, which will become the first country in Latin America with a Protestant majority during the 1990s, has also witnessed a disturbing linkage between evangelical Protestantism and the far from nonviolent activities of former president Efraín Ríos Montt. "Protestantization," in other words, is no guarantee of a future in which nonviolent forms of conflict resolution prevail, although on balance, and speaking in broad generalities, the pentecostal phenomenon in Latin America could prove good news for those interested in the nonviolent resolution of conflict.

South Africa. The picture is extremely complex in South Africa as well. Some South African blacks have flirted with local variants of liberation theology and have endorsed revolutionary "second violence" against the "first violence" of the apartheid system. Other black South African religious leaders have been steadfast in their condemnation of violence; Archbishop Desmond Tutu is a primary example.

Of perhaps greater significance for the long haul, however, are two religious groupings in South Africa that have received relatively little attention from the Western press and from Western policy analysts. The first is the Dutch Reformed Church which, under the leadership of Dr. Johan Heyns, has disentangled itself from the ideology of apartheid associated with Hendrik Verwoerd, and has in fact condemned the system as biblically unwarranted. This "development of doctrine" has already had a great impact in the Afrikaner community and was certainly one stream of influence shaping the post-apartheid policies of the government of F. W. de Klerk. Moreover, should the Afrikaner community begin to unravel, with racial radicals turning to violence as a means to curb the de Klerk initiatives, the Dutch Reformed Church could play a key role in depriving the rejectionists and their resort to violence of moral legitimacy.

The second religious grouping that may have an impact on nonviolent forms of conflict resolution in South Africa is comprised of the various African Indigenous Churches, often called the "independent black churches" or the "Zionist" churches. Although census figures are not very reliable here, the best estimate is that some one-third of South African blacks (i.e., 6.3 million people) belong to these churches, whose theological conservatism has led to a largely apolitical stance toward the social order.[30] The independent or Zionist churches would not, therefore, provide the kind of positive, religiously grounded, moral warrants for nonviolent approaches to social change that, say, the Catholic church provided in Poland. But these churches may, by the very fact of their existence and by their theological disinclination to engage in political strife, provide an important black counterweight to those forces, aligned with either the African National Congress (ANC) or the Inkatha Movement, which are increasingly turning to violence in the run-up to a post-apartheid South Africa.

The Islamic World of the Middle East. Islam is poorly understood in the West, with various stereotypes competing for media and political attention. It is, therefore, important to remember, with Bernard Lewis, the significance of Islam for millions of lives over a period of many centuries:

> Islam is one of the world's great religions. . . . Islam has brought comfort and peace of mind to countless millions of men and women. It has given dignity and meaning to drab and impoverished lives. It has taught people of different races to live in brotherhood and people of different creeds to live side by side in reasonable tolerance. It inspired a great civilization in which others besides Muslims lived creative and useful lives and which, by its achievement, enriched the whole world.[31]

This is not the Islam with which most Americans, indeed most Westerners, are familiar. Nor are Western commentators and policy analysts sufficiently aware of the complexity of the jihad tradition within Islam and the important work that has been done in developing the Islamic just war tradition in ways that parallel the Western equivalent's effort to restrain political violence.[32] And it would doubtless come as a surprise to many Westerners to be told that there are, today, Islamic scholars who are working to develop a Qur'anic theory of

religious tolerance, and even a Qur'anic theory of what we in the West would call "civil society." On the basis of these realities, one should not prematurely dismiss Islam as a potential religious ally in the pursuit of peace and the development of nonviolent means of conflict resolution within and among nations.

Even so, where is the modern Islamic society in which pluralism is legitimated, where nonviolent means of political succession are institutionalized, where religious liberty is protected for all? One can concede, as indeed one should on the basis of empirical evidence, that what is often (and loosely) termed "Islamic fundamentalism" is not the predominant form of Muslim belief in the modern world. But one must still confront the countervailing empirical evidence that militant forms of Islam play an extraordinarily important role in regional and world politics, even as other, less bellicose, Islamic currents of thought struggle for a hearing in those regions.

Might one look, without minimizing present difficulties or romanticizing the past, toward what in Western terms would be called a "development of doctrine" in Islam on this matter of religion and peace? Perhaps the crucial determinant of the future of the intra-Islamic debate on the relationship between religious conviction and the proper ordering of society will be the fate of recent attempts to ground the right of religious freedom within Islamic-dominated societies on the Qur'an. For religious freedom is, arguably, the first of human rights and an essential foundation for a polity committed to giving priority to the nonviolent resolution of conflict.[33]

The Sudanese scholar and activist Mahmoud Mohamed Taha (executed by President Ja'far Mohamed Numeiri in January 1985) worked for some 30 years to develop what he termed the "second message of Islam," which included an Islamic jurisprudence "that allows for the development of complete liberty and equality for all human beings, regardless of sex, religion, or faith."[34] One might also cite, as an important contribution to this discussion, the work of Abdulaziz Sachedina, who has tried to develop a Qur'anic argument for religious freedom from within a self-consciously Shiite perspective.[35] Mahmoud Mohamed Taha was not, to be sure, an advocate of the Western, secular polity, and his call was for tolerance within an Islamic state; in that sense, one can say that the discussion as he formulated it paralleled Roger Williams, but not James Madison. And Taha's translator, Abdullahi Ahmed An-Na'im, concedes that the development of an Islamic theory of religious freedom would necessarily involve a kind of "reformation" in Islamic approaches to the interpretation of sacred texts. But the very fact of that admission presumes the possibility of such a pathbreaking new hermeneutic of Islamic law.[36]

The conversation with Islam that is just beginning on these issues will be short-circuited at the outset if it ignores either of two realities that, it should be freely admitted, are in tension with each other. On the one hand, modern Islamic societies exhibit a pronounced tendency toward monism: they link family or tribe, polis, and religious community into a unity that is, by definition, antipluralistic. And insofar as the cultural affirmation of pluralism as a positive social good seems an important element in the evolution of societies committed to a preference for nonviolent conflict resolution within and among political communities, there are problems that simply have to be faced on this front.

On the other hand, there is the historic experience of Islam in the Middle Ages, which testifies to the capacity of Islam to accord religious legitimation to societies that display considerable tolerance. There is, further, the contemporary fact of what we may call, on the central and east European model of the 1980s, "dissidents" within the Islamic world, whose potential influence on the future of Islamic self-understanding ought not be prematurely gainsaid. These include not simply religious leaders like Mahmoud Mohamed Taha and scholars like Abdulaziz Sachedina and Abdullahi Ahmed An-Na'im, but cultural leaders like the Egyptian Nobel laureate Naguib Mahfouz and major political figures like Anwar Sadat. These men, and others like them, are, clearly, a minority in the Islamic world. For precisely that reason, though, locating, supporting, and engaging such "dissidents" in active conversation ought to be a priority for Western scholars and policy analysts concerned about Islam's relationship to the pursuit of a post–cold war world order in which nonviolent conflict resolution plays an increasingly important role.

Indeed, Sadat's personal odyssey may be taken as a kind of paradigm of possible development in the Islamic world. The Sadat who began his public career in sympathy with the Muslim Brotherhood, and who argued on a Qur'anic basis for a policy of refusal to negotiate with Israel, eventually came to justify his peacemaking efforts in explicitly Qur'anic terms. That this led, finally, to Sadat's assassination is an important warning against excessive optimism about the short-term possibilities of development here. But the facts of Sadat's evolution cannot be denied. The model is there, for those who wish to emulate, and indeed amplify, it. I am not optimistic that such an amplification will soon reshape the politics of the Islamic Middle East. All the more reason, then, to get the needed conversation started—and precisely on the level of theology and moral theory.

Postlude

Politics is a function of culture, and at the heart of culture is religion: so thought Paul Tillich, and so have I argued in this paper. Whatever else may or not happen in the last decade of this millennium, it is as certain as anything can be in this contingent world that religious conviction will continue to play a crucial role in the politics of nations. If that is a surprise to some, then so be it.

Religious conviction is today, as it has ever been, a source of conflict within and among political communities. But it should also be remembered that it has not been religion that has made an abattoir of life in the twentieth century. Lenin, Stalin, Hitler, Mao Tse-tung, and Pol Pot maimed and murdered on an unprecedented scale, in the name of a politics which explicitly rejected religious or other transcendent reference points for judging its purposes and practices. Radical secularization, therefore, is no guarantee of peace, just as vibrant religious conviction is no guarantee of war. These are simple points. Unhappily, U.S. academics and policymakers seem to have no end of trouble grasping them. That intellectual failure is itself an obstacle to effective religious support for the nonviolent resolution of international conflict.

From Conflict Resolution in the Post–Cold War Third World *(Washington, D.C.: United States Institute of Peace, forthcoming). Used by permission of the publisher. The views expressed in this article are those of the author alone and should not be taken as representing the opinion of the Ethics and Public Policy Center, the United States Institute of Peace, or any other agency.*

Notes

1. See Richard John Neuhaus, ed., *Unsecular America* (Grand Rapids, Mich.: Eerdmans, 1986), pp. 115–158, for useful summaries of the research data.

2. See Timothy Garton Ash, *The Uses of Adversity: Essays on the Fate of Central Europe* (New York: Vintage Books, 1990), and *We the People: The Revolution of 1989 Witnessed in Warsaw, Budapest, Berlin, and Prague* (Cambridge: Granta Books, 1990).

3. The complexity of the interaction between religion and the pursuit of peace with freedom and justice is, of course and as noted below, illustrated by the current tensions between Ukrainian Catholics and the two forms of Orthodoxy in Ukraine.

4. See David Martin, *Tongues of Fire: The Explosion of Protestantism in Latin America* (London: Basil Blackwell, 1990).

5. See Peter L. Berger, *The Capitalist Revolution: Fifty Propositions About Prosperity, Equality, and Liberty* (New York: Basic Books, 1986).

6. Max L. Stackhouse, "Democracy and the World's Religions," *This World* 1 (Winter/Spring 1982), p. 108.

7. *Ibid.*, pp. 108–109.

8. *Ibid.*

9. *Ibid.*

10. One key episode in this historical development was the exchange in 494 between Pope Gelasius I and the Byzantine emperor Anastasius I, in which the pope wrote, "Two there are, august emperor, by which this world is ruled on title of original and sovereign right—the consecrated authority of the priesthood and the royal power." By asserting the independence of the Church from the sovereign authority of the emperor, the pope also asserted (deftly, to be sure) a radical limit on the emperor's authority: the emperor was incompetent in certain areas (in fact, the most important areas), which belonged by God's will to another sphere of power.

And thus a small step toward the religious legitimation of pluralism was taken.

11. Richard John Neuhaus, "What the Fundamentalists Want," *Commentary*, May 1985, p. 43. That this understanding arose, perhaps paradoxically or perhaps providentially, in a line of development that followed the European wars of religion does not diminish the force of the point. In one sense, it could be argued that the Peace of Westphalia and the political arrangements that historically followed that attempt at the desacralization of politics were a matter of Western Christianity catching up with St. Augustine.

12. This phenomenon is not without its dangers, of course. Societies which prize tolerance, dialogue, and civility in domestic life may come to think of conflict as somehow epiphenomenal, a matter of bad communication or misunderstanding—particularly when personalist psychology has begun to function as a weltanschauung or all-purpose explanatory framework for discerning the truth of things. This seems to have been the case in certain elite and activist circles in the West during the 1980s. Other possible outcomes notwithstanding, recent events in the Persian Gulf have provided an important check to this temptation.

13. This is not to argue, of course, that religious warrants are the only culturally available norms for legitimizing religious freedom and social tolerance, a claim that would be historically and empirically absurd. Other moral legitimations of democratic pluralism are clearly in play in the United States and indeed throughout the Western world. On the other hand, it is the religious warrants for religious tolerance that are least accounted for in much of the contemporary scholarly and media debate.

14. For a discussion of the Shultz/Weinberger exchange and other issues of the reception of the just war tradition in modern U.S. life, see James Turner Johnson, "The Just War Idea and the American Search for Peace," in *The American Search for Peace: Moral Reasoning, Religious Hope, and National Security*, George Weigel and John Langan, SJ, eds. (Washington, D.C.: Georgetown University Press, 1991).

15. See J. Bryan Hehir, "Intervention and International Affairs," in Weigel and Langan, *American Search for Peace*.

16. John Courtney Murray, *We Hold These Truths: Catholic Reflections on the American Proposition* (Garden City, N. Y.: Doubleday Image Books, 1964), p. 275.

17. See George Weigel, *Tranquillitas Ordinis: The Present Failure and Future Promise of American Catholic Thought on War and Peace* (New York: Oxford University Press, 1987).

18. Pacifism has, of course, made important contributions to the idea that nonviolent means of conflict resolution are to be preferred to armed force. On the other hand, it must be noted that contemporary pacifists have found themselves, on more than one occasion in recent years, sanctioning violent responses to what is often termed the "first violence" of "unjust social structures." For a discussion of this phenomenon, see Guenter Lewy, *Peace and Revolution: The Moral Crisis of American Pacifism* (Grand Rapids, Mich.: Eerdmans, 1988). Lewy's thesis is debated in Michael Cromartie, ed., *Peace Betrayed? Essays on Pacifism and Politics* (Washington, D.C.: Ethics and Public Policy Center, 1990). My own "theses for a pacifist reformation" are included in the latter volume.

19. Timothy Garton Ash, *The Polish Revolution: Solidarity* (Sevenoaks, U.K.: Hodder and Stoughton, 1985), pp. 28–29.

20. *Ibid.*, pp. 29–30.

21. See Garton Ash's analysis in his *Uses of Adversity*, pp. 47–60.

22. On this point, see Bronislaw Geremek, "Postcommunism and Democracy in Poland," *The Washington Quarterly* 13 (Summer 1990), pp. 125–131.

23. Garton Ash, *We the People*, pp. 139–140.

24. Václav Havel, "The Power of the Powerless," in *Living in Truth*, Jan Vladislav, ed. (London: Faber and Faber, 1987), pp. 36–122, and Garton Ash, *Uses of Adversity*, p. 48.

25. It is interesting (to say the least) that the *Washington Post* saw fit to edit out of the lengthy excerpt of Havel's address that it reprinted on its op-ed page the Czechoslovak president's explicitly religious warrant for the kind of society he wanted to see emerge from under the rubble of the to-

talitarian state. Said Havel, "Our first president wrote 'Jesus and not Caesar.'. . . This idea has once again been re-awakened in us. I dare say that perhaps we even have the possibility of spreading it further, thus introducing a new factor in both European and world politics. Love, desire for understanding, the strength of the spirit and of ideas can radiate forever from our country, if we want this to happen. This radiation can be precisely what we can offer as our very own contribution to world politics" (Foreign Broadcast Information Service document FBIS-EEU-90-001, January 2, 1990).

26. On the Navrátil petition, see Garton Ash, "The Yeoman and the Cardinal," in *Uses of Adversity*, pp. 214–221.

27. See Adam Michnik, "The Two Faces of Eastern Europe," *New Republic*, November 12, 1990, pp. 23–25.

28. See the two seminal statements from the Congregation for the Doctrine of the Faith, "Instruction on Certain Aspects of the 'Theology of Liberation'" (August 6, 1984) and "Instruction on Christian Freedom and Liberation" (March 22, 1986). The first instruction offers a powerful critique of politicized religion; the second describes the multiple ways in which Christianity contributes to the moral—and political—liberation of man.

29. See Martin, *Tongues of Fire*, pp. 205–232.

30. The figures are from *South Africa 1989/90*, the official yearbook of the Republic of South Africa.

31. Bernard Lewis, "The Roots of Muslim Rage," *Atlantic*, September 1990, p. 48.

32. On the jihad tradition and its complexity, see Rudolph Peters, *Jihad in Medieval and Modern Islam* (Leiden, Netherlands: E. J. Brill, 1977) and Mehdi Abedi and Gary Legenhausen, eds., *Jihad and Shahadat: Struggle and Martyrdom in Islam* (Houston: Institute for Research and Islamic Studies, 1986). Nonviolence as a means of political action is also being discussed in an Islamic context, albeit with many of the difficulties that have plagued Western nonviolent and pacifist thought over the past 20 years; see Ralph Crow, Philip Grant, and Saad E. Ibrahim, eds., *Arab Nonviolent Political Struggle in the Middle East* (Boulder: Lynne Rienner, 1990). For an argument developing what the author believes is the "striking similarity" between the formal structures of Islamic just war theory and its Western counterpart, see John Kelsay, "Islam and the Distinction Between Combatants and Non-Combatants," in *Cross, Crescent, and Sword*, James Turner Johnson and John Kelsay, eds. (Westport, Conn.: Greenwood Press, 1990).

33. See George Weigel, "Religious Freedom: The First Human Right," *This World* 21 (Spring 1988), pp. 31–45, and "Catholicism and Democracy: The Other Twentieth-Century Revolution," *The Washington Quarterly* 12 (Autumn 1989), pp. 5–25.

34. Abdullahi Ahmed An-Na'im, "Introduction," in Mahmoud Mohamed Taha, *The Second Message of Islam*, translated by Abdullahi Ahmed An-Na'im (Syracuse, N.Y.: Syracuse University Press, 1987), pp. 21–22.

35. Abdulaziz Sachedina, "Freedom of Conscience and Religion in the Qur'an," in David Little, John Kelsay, and Abdulaziz Sachedina, *Human Rights and the Conflicts of Culture: Western and Islamic Perspectives on Religious Liberty* (Columbia, S.C.: University of South Carolina Press, 1988), pp. 53–90.

36. See Abdullahi Ahmed An-Na'im, "Human Rights in the Muslim World: Socio-Political Conditions and Scriptural Imperatives," *Harvard Human Rights Journal* 3 (Spring 1990), pp. 13–52.

Transnational Criminal Organizations: Strategic Alliances

Phil Williams

ORGANIZED CRIME HAS traditionally been seen as a domestic problem bedeviling a relatively small number of states such as Italy, the United States, and Japan. In the last few years, however, there has been a recognition that the problem is no longer limited to a few states and can no longer be treated as something that falls within a single jurisdiction. The rise of a global market for illicit drugs, the end of the Cold War and the breakdown of the barriers between East and West, the collapse of the criminal justice system in Russia and the other states of the former Soviet Union, the development of free trade areas in Western Europe and North America, and the emergence of global financial and trading systems have fundamentally changed the context in which criminal organizations operate and encouraged what had been predominantly domes-

tic groups to develop into transnational criminal organizations (TCOs).

The threat posed by these organizations has been dramatized by a variety of developments: the struggle of the Colombian cartels to change the government's extradition policy; the attack by the Sicilian Mafia on the Italian state and the killing of judges such as Giovanni Falcone; the emergence of Russian criminal organizations not only in the Commonwealth of Independent States but also in Western Europe and the United States; the vast upsurge in money laundering; and, perhaps most dramatically, the revelations about trafficking in nuclear material, have all helped to imprint the new threat on the consciousness of policymakers and publics alike. Congressional hearings in the United States during the latter half of 1993 and much of 1994 revealed that the problem has also evoked the attention of national intelligence agencies, with testimony being provided not only by representatives from the Drug Enforcement Administration and the Federal Bureau of Investigation but also by the Director of Central Intelligence.

This upsurge of attention is, in most respects, very welcome. The problem of transnational organized crime is a

Phil Williams is director of the Ridgway Center and professor in the Graduate School of Public and International Affairs at the University of Pittsburgh.

The Washington Quarterly • 18:1

real one that demands both more careful investigation and greater resources than have so far been devoted to dealing with it. It is clear that the Chinese triads, Russian criminal organizations, Colombian cartels, Japanese Yakuza, Sicilian Mafia (as well as the other Italian groups such as the Neapolitan Camorra, 'Ndrangheta, and Sacra Corona Unita), Nigerian criminal organizations, and Turkish drug-trafficking groups engage in extensive criminal activities on a regional and often a global basis. Developments at the national level have provided new opportunities to exploit and have enabled TCOs to attain a level of prominence that threatens national and international security in a variety of ways. These organizations violate national sovereignty, undermine democratic institutions even in states where these institutions are well established, threaten the process of democratization and privatization in states in transition, and add a new dimension to problems such as nuclear proliferation and terrorism.

As the policy community begins to get a handle on the issue, however, it is essential to conceptualize the threat posed by TCOs as accurately as possible. Without a valid assessment of the challenge posed by these organizations, the prospects for effective action against them are minimal. Unfortunately there are some indications that the assessment is moving in directions that are not completely warranted, and that could lead to inappropriate and ineffective policies.

Part of the problem is a form of threat inflation. Dramatizing the challenge can be understood largely as an effort to galvanize public attention, mobilize support, and generate the resources necessary to deal with a problem that traditionally has had a relatively low profile—at least at the international level. Treating transnational crime as some kind of monolithic global conspiracy is particularly appealing because it suggests—implicitly at least—that a threat to international security may be emerging that is a worthy successor to the challenge posed by the Soviet Union during the Cold War. This has special resonance for intelligence agencies used to dealing with a centrally controlled enemy and finding it difficult to adjust to a world where there is no overwhelming threat to provide either intellectual rationale or budgetary legitimacy.

The irony is that an assessment of this kind is not only misleading and, therefore, pernicious in its consequences, but may, paradoxically, underestimate the threat. It is misleading because it lumps together different kinds of threat and fails to distinguish clearly between those TCOs, for example, that exploit the openness of the global financial system through money laundering and those that want to disrupt the system through terrorist actions. Most TCOs are concerned about profit rather than politics, and are unlikely to want to undermine a system that they are able to exploit and abuse for their own purposes. A few other groups, especially those linked to "pariah states," may have more disruptive goals. Treating these very different organizations as part of a single global challenge is not only misleading conceptually, but could encourage a policy response that is as ineffective as it is undifferentiated.

The notion that there is a relatively small number of global conglomerates linked in a vast criminal conspiracy also underestimates the threat. An assessment of organized crime that focuses exclusively on large organizations such as those mentioned above implies that the problem is relatively straightforward, and that if enough resources are devoted to dismantling a few organizations then transnational organized crime will be virtually eliminated. The reality is not only more messy but also more unsettling—and less susceptible to simple solutions. Large, fixed, monolithic, strictly hierarchical structures are relatively easy targets. They are vulnerable to decapitation and other forms of dismantling. Looser, less formal network structures, in contrast, are resistant to such efforts and actually more difficult to contain. The problem was neatly encapsulated by a British customs officer who commented that a smuggling organization is like a

> plate of spaghetti. Every piece seems to touch every other, but you are never sure where it all leads. Once in a while we arrest someone we are sure is important. Well he may have been up to that moment, but once we get him, he suddenly becomes no more than a tiny cog. Someone else important pops up in his place.[1]

Moreover, the fluid network organizations of various sizes engage in a mixture of cooperation and competition not only with each other but with governments and other nongovernmental actors. The diversity of these organizations, their symbiotic relationships with legitimate businesses, their capacity to exploit (rather than disrupt) legitimate trading activities and financial institutions, and their ability to corrupt governments and law enforcement agencies, make efforts at decapitation somewhat moot to say the least. And even if government actions do lead to the indictment or elimination of the top leadership, this simply provides new opportunities for internal promotion unless the organization itself is destroyed. And even in those cases where the organizational structure itself is compromised or dismantled, this merely allows other organizations to make up the shortfall in the supply of illicit goods and services. The way in which the Cali cartel succeeded its Medellín counterpart as the dominant force in cocaine trafficking is indicative of the kind of succession that can take place in transnational organized crime. Indeed, the succession issue highlights the need to consider very carefully the consequences of one's strategy, especially in the event that it might prove effective.

Even without a clear succession, however, the cocaine-trafficking industry would have continued to operate, albeit in a less centralized form. This suggests that transnational organized crime is constantly evolving in ways that make it particularly difficult to counter. Low entry barriers combined with ease of international travel and communication have helped to create an entrepreneurial free-for-all with potentially high payoffs that outweigh the risks associated with law enforcement and regulatory efforts. As a result, small businesses and individual entrepreneurs flourish alongside their larger and more extensive counterparts. Although the Cali cartel may have devised the perfect blend of corporate and criminal cultures, even smaller criminal organizations display considerable business acumen as well as a high level of operational sophistication and organizational adaptability. Moreover, the sheer number and diversity of criminal organizations is part of the challenge facing governments and law enforcement agencies. The beginning of wisdom in dealing with TCOs, therefore, is to recognize that fashionable and relatively straightforward labels not only hide enormous complexity but can seriously mislead policymakers.

Such complexity is not fully captured by labels such as global organized crime or "Pax Mafiosa." Even if these labels carry the wrong connotations, however, they do help to draw attention to the growing linkages among TCOs that make them an even more formidable challenge than they are in isolation. The main purpose of this article is to identify the nature of these linkages and to assess their implications for law enforcement efforts to respond to the challenges posed by TCOs. As it stands, the connections among criminal organizations are not well understood. This is partly because of the paucity of evidence but also because little effort has been made to conceptualize the nature of the linkages. Indeed, the linkages have developed with such rapidity and are so novel, especially for criminologists who have a primarily domestic focus, that they have outrun efforts both to delineate the phenomenon and to explain it.

In attempting to provide a solid conceptual foundation to enhance our understanding of the nature of these linkages among TCOs, it is possible to draw on the literature about how transnational corporations cooperate and compete, and in particular how they form and maintain strategic alliances. Because organized crime is essentially enterprise crime, the motivating principles underlying the activities of TCOs are usually very similar to those of transnational corporations. The differences between legitimate and illegitimate enterprises are not insignificant, but the fact that criminal enterprises operate in illicit markets conditions their behavior in ways that accentuate rather than obviate the driving forces of economic principle and good business practice, especially the need to respond to market conditions and demands. Although it is important not to ignore the distinctive

features of TCO behavior that stem from illegality, these features are generally aimed at circumventing law enforcement and regulatory efforts in ways that enable the organization to increase its profits. The activities of TCOs in this respect differ in degree rather than kind from other transnational organizations that also seek a high degree of autonomy from state control.[2] The overall effect of illegality may be to provide additional motivations for the development of strategic alliances.

In spite, therefore, of the differences between the licit and the illicit business worlds, an analysis of strategic alliances among licit corporations should facilitate greater understanding of the conditions and considerations that lead to strategic alliances among TCOs, make it easier to elucidate the nature of these alliances, and provide insights into the problems that can arise in their operation and management.

Transnational Corporations and Strategic Alliances

Business linkages can take many forms, but they often revolve around what has been described as the global commodity chain.[3] The chain from raw material to final product tends to encourage the development of a series of supplier relationships as well as the emergence of links with companies providing ancillary specialized services. Such linkages form an integral part of the normal operation of the market. They also underline the fact that forms of vertical cooperation are central to the effective operation of even very competitive markets.

This is not to say that all the firm's interactions are regularized. In thinking about cooperation it is important to recognize that there is a continuum from complete mergers between companies at the one extreme to independent spot market transactions on a one-off basis at the other.[4] Strategic alliances among companies tend to be at the more regularized end of the spectrum and generally involve systematic forms of cooperation that have a high degree of regularity and predictability. These alliances can take many forms, including operating linkages, licensing or franchise agreements, and joint ventures.[5]

Some analysts have suggested that the essence of a strategic alliance is cooperation to exchange technology and goods and services across national and company boundaries, an exchange that can be accomplished through informal agreements, contractual collaborations, joint ventures, and minority equity alliances.[6] Another commentator has contended that the requirements for cooperative strategies to encompass strategic alliances are more stringent.[7] In this view, strategic alliances involve tight operating linkages, with the participants having a vested interest in each other's future, long-term time horizons, and significant competitive advantages.[8] Tactical arrangements are not strategic alliances because they lack the expectation of long-term cooperation.

With this understanding of strategic alliances, it is necessary to examine the reasons why companies form alliances. In general terms, the development of strategic alliances can be understood as a response by individual firms to the business environment and as an attempt to overcome their own limitations. Within this overall framework, however, it is possible to delineate several more specific reasons why firms engage in such alliances.

In the first place, strategic alliances are a rational response to the emergence of global markets, and in particular to what might be described as the global-local nexus. A global market can be understood, in one sense at least, as simply a composite of local markets that have become increasingly homogenized. Yet these local markets are extremely important to companies. As one commentary has pointed out, the strategic management literature emphasizes that firms seek to maximize long-term profits through improving their competitive position vis-à-vis rivals. One of the most important ways of accomplishing this is by aggressively gaining access to new markets; expanding market share in existing markets is another.[9] Firms often find it easier to enter local markets that have hitherto been outside their purview or range of activity if they cooperate with those firms that are already entrenched in these markets, have greater knowledge of local conditions, and are more attuned to local problems, rather than trying to insert themselves as competitors on unfamiliar territory. Linking with host-nation companies to facilitate access to new markets is a major reason why transnational firms form strategic alliances.

Closely related to this is a second consideration, involving the desire to neutralize and even co-opt actual or potential competitors. Paradoxically, cooperative strategies offer a rational and effective response to a highly competitive situation. Cooperation through the development of a strategic alliance, for example, could facilitate the neutralization of major competitors. As one analyst has noted, "A strong competitor that already enjoys a profitable position in its own market can become a fierce ally. Better to fight the competitive battle alongside an ally than to face this same competitor in open combat."[10] Obviously the firms already in the market have to be offered something substantial in return. This might be a share in a market that is made more lucrative through the introduction of more diverse products, the promise of greater profit through the creation of an entirely new market, or some other form of reciprocity. Whatever the case, it is the promise of mutual benefit that underlies the formation and maintenance of strategic alliances.

Strategic alliances can also provide an effective means of circumventing restrictions and can pave the way for entry into strictly controlled markets.[11] Where government regulations make it difficult for foreign corporations to enter a market, the formation of an alliance with a firm that already has access to the market is an attractive means of overcoming obstacles.

Another closely related consideration is that a strategic alliance can be an indispensable means of spreading or minimizing risk. Attempts by transnational corporations to expand their activities or to enter new markets often require new investments of resources with uncertain payoffs. A strategic alliance offers an opportunity to minimize these investments and to spread or reduce risks. In effect, it enables companies "to tackle opportunities that might otherwise be too risky."[12] The synergy means that the participants in a strategic alliance are able to do things that neither one could do alone, at least not with anything like the same effectiveness or confidence.

Synergy is central to strategic alliances. Such alliances effectively enhance the resource base available to the participants, whether it be in terms of capital, technology, the capacity to develop new markets, or simply greater access to a more extensive set of interorganizational networks. The opportunities for organizational learning through the exchange of informa-

tion and expertise among the partners may also be important. Accordingly, a strategic alliance may enable the individual firm to close what has been termed a "strategic gap"—the difference between what that corporation would like to achieve and what it has the resources to achieve.[13] This is particularly the case when the strategic alliance involves specialization and complementary expertise, and each side therefore brings to the alliance something that the other lacks.

Another reason for forming strategic alliances is that they can be a useful means of reducing the unpredictability of the free market and of regularizing relationships. Strategic alliances offer a means of ensuring specialization and division of labor, often in relation to suppliers. By allying with a firm that supplies raw materials, it is possible for a corporation to obtain both better financial terms and to guarantee that supplies of necessary materials will always be available. This form of strategic alliance is perhaps best encapsulated in the Japanese *keiretsu*, a set of arrangements in which suppliers are bound very closely to those firms that depend on their product for their own manufacturing processes.

Although it is possible to identify several distinct reasons why firms engage in strategic alliances, in practice more than one consideration is usually involved. Strategic alliances promise multiple benefits: they "enable partners to share financial and operating risks and costs, obtain benefits associated with scale economies and operating synergies, and increase market share."[14]

Not surprisingly, these alliances can take many different forms. One type is the franchise alliance, which generally involves an alliance between a larger, more developed company and numerous independent, smaller, more tightly managed companies.[15] A second form is what might be termed the compensatory alliance, in which two companies recognize that each one acting alone has inherent weaknesses that can be offset by the other's strengths. A variation on this is what could be described as a specialization alliance, in which one company forms an alliance with another that can fulfil specialized tasks beyond the existing capacity of the first organization. This results in a kind of contractual relationship as regards specific tasks and responsibilities. Another form of strategic cooperation occurs through what are sometimes described as countertrade alliances, in which goods are exchanged for goods. Yet another variant is the supplier alliance, in which there are regularized relations between the suppliers of basic raw materials and firms that transform these materials into consumer products.

This is not a comprehensive description of the infinite variety of strategic alliances, but it does highlight some of the most important forms of these alliances. It does nothing, however, to explain why some strategic alliances succeed and others fail. The starting point for considering this issue is a recognition that the basis for strategic alliance is mutual need. Each firm has something that the other needs or wants. Yet, even if the selection of allies is appropriate and there is a basic mutuality of interest underlying the initial impulse for cooperation, this is no guarantee either of continued harmony or that the alliance will be successful. Strategic alliances between transnational corporations encounter many problems. The strategy, chemistry, and operations must all be right.[16] At the outset it may appear that this is the case, but unforeseen problems can all too easily arise. The participants in strategic alliances usually come from different cultures, operate according to different precepts and principles, and, in spite of their common interest, may have different needs and priorities. Clash of cultures, discrepant and incompatible operating procedures, and divergence of interests and priorities are all inherent possibilities in strategic alliances among transnational corporations from different home nations.

Another consideration is that the alliance may result in unequal or asymmetrical gains. This can lead to resentment on the part of the firm that believes its benefits are not commensurate with what it has put into the alliance. Even if this does not occur, the possibility that the partner may defect—for example, after assistance with the initial market penetration one of the firms might conclude that it is now capable of going it alone—can create an aura of suspicion that can undermine continued cooperation. As one analyst has argued, when one of the participants engaged in cooperation can obtain considerable short-term advantage by defecting, then the possibility for the breakdown of the alliance is ever present.[17]

Another cause of alliance breakdown may be unauthorized actions by subordinates or particular divisions within the corporation. The effective functioning of an alliance generally requires that the top-level management have strong internal control.[18] Actions taken by subordinates that are not congruent with top-level directives can prove particularly disruptive, especially in instances where companies remain competitors in spite of their strategic alliance. If one transnational corporation, for whatever reason, continues to engage in independent marketing activity, for example, even though it has an agreement with another on joint marketing or selling, this could provoke a reappraisal of the alliance. Yet another possibility is that the alliance simply does not live up to expectations. In counter-trade alliances, for example, late delivery of goods or the supply of inferior products can erode the level of trust and may lead one of the partners to seek an alternative ally.

In short, strategic alliances may be easier to create than to maintain. Expectations that were very high will often be disappointed as performance falls short of promise. Disappointed expectations can result in lack of trust and the erosion of effective communication. The result is that although strategic alliances are very popular initially they often lose some of their luster. In the words of one observer, "Although the number of international cooperations appears to be increasing dramatically, they are notoriously unstable, prone to failure, and at best, difficult to govern."[19]

TCOs and Strategic Alliances

Because TCOs are essentially profit-maximizing and risk-reducing entities, it is hardly surprising that they too engage in strategic alliances. Cooperation among these organizations is a natural activity, particularly because they share the common problem of circumventing law enforcement and national regulations. As suggested above, there is an added incentive for cooperation that stems from the illicit nature of the activity. Whereas transnational corporations have to negotiate with governments in order to obtain access to new markets, TCOs have to negotiate with the illicit power structure. This again may encourage a propensity to create strategic alliances.

From this perspective it is clear that at least some of the alliances among TCOs can be understood as risk-reduction alliances. There are several kinds of risk that criminal organizations are anxious to reduce: the risk of interdiction or seizure of the illicit product they are supplying; the risk of apprehension of members of the organization; the risk of infiltration of the group; and the risk that their profits will be seized. A very good example of a risk-reduction alliance, at least from the perspective of one of the partners, is that between the Colombian cartels and Mexican drug-trafficking families.

In many ways, this is a very natural alliance that can also be understood as a contractual relationship in which the Mexicans perform a highly specialized task for the Colombians. Mexican criminal groups, often with a family basis, have long had a well-developed smuggling infrastructure for the transport of goods and services across the extensive frontier with the United States. The Sinaloa drug-trafficking organization led by Joaquin Guzman Loera (who was arrested in 1993) is one of the best connected of these groups but there are several others that have extensive and systematic linkages with Colombian drug-trafficking organizations. The Mexican groups understand the *frontera* and what is required to ensure the viability of smuggling activities. For the Colombian cartels, therefore, allowing the Mexican families to do something in which they are extremely experienced and skillful makes eminent sense. The strategic alliance with Mexican smuggling organizations is an important means of risk sharing or even risk avoidance for the cartels in one of the most high-risk aspects of the business—crossing the border into the United States. And for the Mexicans, the alliance is important in allowing them significant participation in the cocaine industry—an industry that has higher profit margins than the marijuana industry that has traditionally been the preserve of Mexican smugglers. Although the risks are certainly not negligible in cocaine smuggling, they are outweighed by the very substantial economic benefits that come from both the contractual arrangements and the fact that Mexican organizations control much of the cocaine distribution in California. Elsewhere, the cocaine, once in the United States, is returned to Colombian traffickers who dominate the wholesale trade.

Another intriguing alliance has developed between Mexican smugglers and Chinese criminal organizations involved in trafficking illegal immigrants into the United States. Once again, the Mexicans are able to provide a major service because they possess the ability to smuggle migrants across the border into the southwestern United States with minimum risk of detection. The result has been what the *Los Angeles Times* described as "a clandestine corridor linking the villages of Fujian, the shores of Mexico and Central America, and suburban safe houses in heavily Chinese enclaves of the San Gabriel Valley."[20] The scale of the enterprise became clear during the first six months of 1993 when the Border Patrol arrested over 500 Chinese, over 400 of them in San Diego, and acknowledged that for every captured illegal alien two others escape detection. The implication is that when trafficking routes and methods of proven effectiveness are available not only is the product (drugs or people) virtually irrelevant so far as the criminal organizations are concerned, but these organizations are willing to engage in any kind of alliance that facilitates their illegal enterprise.

Another kind of alliance is that between some of the Nigerian drug-trafficking organizations and the Co-

lombian cartels. The Nigerian criminal organizations are classic free-market entrepreneurs. Engaged in both cocaine and heroin trafficking, they have progressed from being couriers for others to being major players in their own right. They have developed an alliance of sorts with the Colombians based on product exchange. In several instances Nigerian trafficking organizations have supplied heroin to Colombians in return for cocaine. This has helped the Colombians to develop their own heroin market, while also offering opportunities for the Nigerians to sell cocaine in Western Europe. How extensive this form of counter-trade actually is remains uncertain. Nevertheless, there is some evidence that it is not insignificant.

Another important motive for the development of strategic alliances has been the desire to enter new markets. This has been perhaps most evident in the relationship between the Colombians and the Sicilians. During the late 1980s and the early 1990s it became clear that linkages were growing between the Colombian cartels, especially the Cali cartel, and the Sicilian Mafia. These linkages can be explained in large part by the desire on the part of the Colombians to enter the European market. Such an entry was necessary because of the saturation of the cocaine market in the United States, and highly desirable because cocaine could be sold for higher prices in Europe and therefore offered higher profit margins. In some respects Europe was also an area in which the product was less likely to be seized: European law enforcement was not as engaged in counter-narcotics activity as the authorities in the United States, which had even mobilized the U.S. military in the war against drugs. At the same time, Europe was not risk free, especially for Colombians, who generally had a higher profile and greater visibility than was desirable. Although the Colombians had developed their own marketing and trafficking strategies for Western Europe— with access mainly through Spain and Portugal—the costs had been relatively high in terms of the number of arrests. In 1991, 2,048 cocaine traffickers were arrested in Western Europe, 27 percent of whom were Colombians.

Against a backdrop of this kind, alliance with the Sicilians had a dual payoff. The Cosa Nostra not only had well-established distribution networks for heroin that could also be used for cocaine, but also had excellent knowledge of local conditions and was able to go further than the Colombians in neutralizing law enforcement authorities through bribery and corruption. If marketing considerations drove the alliance, therefore, it can also be understood as an attempt by the Colombians to overcome limitations in their indigenous capacity to penetrate the European market. Alliance with the Sicilians, in effect, compensated for the lack in Europe of a counterpart to the Colombian ethnic network that had been central to the success of Colombian drug-trafficking activities in the United States.

From the Sicilian perspective, there was also considerable benefit to be gained from alliance with the cartels. The Sicilian role in the heroin market in the United States had been superseded to a large extent by the Asian suppliers themselves. What at one point had been predominantly an alliance in which the Chinese supplied the opium and the processing was done in Sicily, was transformed as the Chinese began to integrate forward and do much of the processing and trafficking for themselves. The results were evident in the way in which Southeast Asian heroin came to domi-

nate the U.S. heroin market in the latter half of the 1980s. And even in Europe, Turkish criminal organizations, trafficking heroin from Southwest Asia, made great inroads into the heroin market. For the Sicilians, therefore, alliance with the Colombians offered opportunities to recoup some of the ground that had been lost in other areas.

Although the needs of the two organizations were very different, they were sufficiently compatible to lead to a strategic alliance. The effects of this alliance can be seen in the way in which the cocaine market has developed in Europe. U.S. law enforcement officials had been warning their European counterparts for some time about the impending cocaine blitz on Western Europe, but it was not until 1993 and 1994 that the blitz materialized. Although seizures alone are not necessarily an accurate indicator of supply levels (because they can also be explained by greater law enforcement effectiveness in interdicting supplies), they do tend to reveal broad trends. In this connection, the number of seizures went up so dramatically between 1993 and 1994 as to suggest that there had been a qualitative leap in trafficking cocaine to Western Europe. In the first three months of 1993 around 2,300 kilograms of cocaine were seized (counting seizures over 100 kilograms each). In the first three months of 1994 that figure had risen to almost 12,000 kilograms.

Another kind of relationship has arisen reflecting the need for specialized services on the one side and the capacity to provide them on the other. Once again, it appears that the Sicilian Mafia and the Colombian cartels have developed arrangements in which the Sicilians engage in money laundering on behalf of their Colombian allies. There have also been agreements between the Sicilians and some of the Russian organized crime groups to engage in money laundering. The Cali cartel has also been laundering money through an illegal numbers racket in Rio de Janeiro that may be closely linked to the activities of the American Mafia.

The notion of neutralizing potential competition through alliances, or at least through tacit agreement on limiting competition, has also been discernible. A good example of this occurred in the Czech Republic.[21] In October 1992 members of the Italian and Russian mafias met in Prague and decided on the areas of their respective operations. Italian gangs use the Czech Republic as a place for recreation and support, while the Russians use it for money laundering as well as arms dealing, drug trafficking, blackmail, and prostitution. Even if this agreement does not qualify as a strategic alliance, it does highlight one means of limiting conflict among TCOs.

Other important relationships, especially those in the drug-trafficking industry, can be understood as franchise alliances. There are many well-established relationships of this kind, with African-American groups, Dominicans, Puerto Ricans, and others involved as retailers for Colombian wholesalers of cocaine and Chinese and Nigerian wholesalers of heroin.

It is clear even from this brief survey that strategic alliances among TCOs have become increasingly common. Some observers have seen this as the development of a Pax Mafiosa and argued that it involves an attempt to carve up the globe into criminal fiefdoms.[22] The analysis here, however, suggests that these linkages can be understood in less grandiose and more prosaic terms. They are essentially alliances of convenience based on strictly economic considerations rather than part of a global criminal conspiracy. This is not to denigrate their importance, because it is clear that they greatly enhance the capacity of TCOs to circumvent government controls.

Moreover, it has to be recognized that alliances are only one of the many instruments used by TCOs to further their activities. There are several alternatives to fully fledged alliances. Criminal organizations sometimes reduce their vulnerability by co-opting non-criminals. The Nigerian organizations have been particularly good at this and have succeeded in recruiting couriers (especially American women) who did not fit a profile that would immediately arouse suspicion on the part of customs or law enforcement officials.

It is also clear that fully fledged alliances between large criminal organizations such as the cartels and Sicilian Mafia provide only part of the picture. Many smaller, more tactical alliances flourish alongside strategic alliances between large organizations. A good example of this was uncovered in January 1994, when Mexican authorities seized 52 kilograms of heroin and arrested four Thais, a Laotian, and four Mexicans in Ensenada, a port city 70 miles south of San Diego. The scheme was an ingenious one in which heroin was sent into the United States by mail. It was operated by criminals who had infiltrated the postal services in both Mexico and Thailand. Initially bath products were sent to Thailand to false addresses. They were then stuffed with heroin and sent back as undeliverable. Because they had not originated in Thailand they were not inspected by Mexican customs.[23]

In many respects such activities seem to be typical of a significant part of the drug-trafficking industry, that is, they are carried on by small, independent organizations that have come together to exploit a particular trafficking route and a specific way of circumventing customs and law enforcement. Not only are there many of these small tactical alliances based on transnational networks, but when they are effective they have an inherent capacity for growth. At the same time, their loose, fluid nature makes it equally plausible that they will be disbanded and their constituent elements reformed in different constellations. Tactical alliances are made for specific purposes and are often followed by a search for other partners to make shipments to different locations using different modes of concealment.

In attempting to place strategic alliances in perspective, it is also necessary to keep in mind that TCOs also make alliances with governments, either through corruption or coercion or, more often, a mix of both. Corruption can reach such a level in some cases that the government can be regarded as collusive (that is, hand in glove with the criminal organizations). High-ranking members of the government may benefit directly from the actions of TCOs, receiving large payoffs in return for facilitating trafficking activities and providing protection and safe havens.

Links are also increasing between TCOs and terrorist organizations. Indeed, the distinction between terrorist groups pursuing essentially political objectives and TCOs pursuing economic goals is likely to be become increasingly blurred. The loss of state sponsorship for terrorist organizations means that they are likely to seek alternative sources of financial support for their activities. Drug trafficking and other forms of enterprise crime are obvious means of doing this. On the other side, criminal organizations may find that the opportunities for large-scale extortion through the possession

of smuggled nuclear material encourages them to use the threat of terror for business purposes. This process of convergence is likely to make cooperative linkages more frequent.

Another point that needs to be made about strategic alliances, particularly if the parallels with corporate alliances are accepted, is that although these alliances can be very effective means of enhancing the capacity for criminal activity, both their initial development and their continued maintenance may encounter significant problems. The desire to circumvent the common enemy of law enforcement provides an underlying incentive for sustained cooperation. Even so, alliances may encounter significant problems. These can stem from different criminal cultures and codes of honor among thieves, from different priorities, and from concerns over relative gains and who is benefiting most from the collaborative ventures. In addition, the lack of total control over operatives and the inability to prevent independent actions may cast doubt on the validity of the cooperative agreement. Continued independent marketing operations outside the alliance may also be seen by one of the partners as inconsistent with any accord that has been reached.

Some of the problems that can arise are revealed by even a brief examination of the evolution of the relationship between the Medellín and Cali cartels. During the early 1980s there was a close working relationship between drug-trafficking organizations in Medellín and those in Cali. The cartels themselves were formed partly because of a recognition of the benefits of cooperation but there was also an element of serendipity. The kidnapping of Martha Ochoa, daughter of a leading drug lord, led to a meeting of traffickers in which they agreed to form a paramilitary arm to take action against the kidnappers. This marked the beginning of a period of intense collaboration, joint ventures in transportation, and the common underwriting of large cocaine loads into the United States. It was also a period of rapid market expansion in which profits burgeoned. During this period the relationship between the Cali and Medellín cartels was exceptionally good. The two cartels shared risks, sometimes used the same airstrips and processing facilities, and appeared to have agreed on market shares in the United States. By the end of the 1980s, however, this relationship had deteriorated almost completely, and although elements of cooperation still lingered, the two cartels were, in effect, at war with one another.

The breakdown of cooperation was rooted partly in the regional rivalries that have made Colombia particularly difficult to govern. Regional tensions were accentuated by what was virtually a difference of social class: members of the Cali cartel were, in some cases, businessmen who had moved into narcotics but who still acted as legitimate businessmen; the Medellín leadership consisted of petty hoodlums from the slums who had become major traffickers. Not surprisingly the latter group was more publicly flamboyant and used violence more extensively than did its counterpart in Cali. The different attitude to violence was also rooted in divergent investment strategies.[24] The Cali cartel invested in legitimate business, while Medellín invested in land and then developed paramilitary groups to protect its holdings. It was a natural extension of this for the Medellín cartel to adopt a confrontational strategy toward the government, whereas the Cali cartel adopted a strategy of co-option, corruption, and assimilation. The unwill-

ingness of the Cali cartel to join Medellín in a frontal assault on the Colombian state was also a source of tension between the two organizations and may have contributed significantly to the split.

These structural and strategic differences between the two cartels were exacerbated by personal rivalries. Moreover, once the conflict began, it appeared to take on its own momentum. Pressure from the government led to allegations by Pablo Escobar that the Cali cartel had provided the information that led to the killing of one of his partners in the Medellín cartel, Rodriguez Gacha. The familiar problems of trust and concern over relative gains also took on a new dimension with concern over relative losses by the two cartels in the struggle with the government. The tensions were exacerbated by the fact that the cocaine-trafficking industry was also coming under intense pressure in the United States. With market saturation in Miami and the Bahamas and a significant drop in prices as a result, the Medellín cartel tried to enter the New York market, which had hitherto been the almost exclusive preserve of Cali. This represented a major escalation of the conflict and led to press reports in the latter half of 1988 that the struggle between the cartels was over the control of a New York wholesale cocaine trade worth about $1 billion a year. Although the reports themselves may have been too narrowly focused, the market share issue was certainly of great significance.

The implication of this brief survey of the conflict between Medellín and Cali is that even where cooperation between TCOs appears to be well established (and does not even involve problems of different nationalities), it retains a certain fragility. If this is extrapolated, it suggests that some of the other strategic alliances identified above might be less robust and resilient than expected. There may even be a life cycle of cooperation in which the initial benefits from cooperation appear to outweigh any negative consequences, but which is followed either by a phase of consolidation or a period in which the difficulties and costs of cooperation come to the fore. The implications of all this for government and law enforcement agencies must now be considered.

Implications for Policy

The development of strategic alliances among TCOs is clearly a cause for considerable concern on the part of governments. Strategic alliances augment the capacity of these organizations to circumvent law enforcement and implement strategies central to the success of their illicit enterprises. Although this problem has to be put in perspective and seen in terms of many alliances among small-scale organizations as well as a small number of alliances among major TCOs, it does present a new challenge to law enforcement. It also offers some opportunities.

The first challenge is for national governments, partly through more systematic and careful integration of law enforcement intelligence and information from intelligence agencies, to develop better predictive intelligence about the formation (and the demise) of strategic alliances among TCOs.

The second challenge is for governments and law enforcement agencies to develop cooperative strategies to match those of the TCOs. Such cooperation would include more extensive exchanges of information and personnel, a greater emphasis on judicial assistance to those states that lack an effective criminal justice system, and

more widespread use of both Mutual Legal Assistance Treaties and extradition treaties. The formation of multinational task forces to go after TCOs and their activities, including money laundering, should be given high priority. Such task forces, especially those involving U.S. and Italian law enforcement agencies, have had striking successes.

Many problems inhibit more extensive cooperation of this kind, however, most of which come down to the familiar issue of preserving national sovereignty. Governments have to realize, though, that unless they are willing to sacrifice some of the formalities of sovereignty they will be unable to take effective action against criminal organizations whose cross-border activities erode the foundations of real sovereignty.

The third challenge is to recognize that the development of strategic alliances not only presents dangers but also offers opportunities for law enforcement. Given the problem of establishing and maintaining trust in an area that depends on mutual confidence regarding the ally's reliability rather than formal agreements and legal contracts, the potential for creating suspicion and sowing discord is very considerable. Consequently, strategic alliances could become a source of weakness for TCOs. Law enforcement activities can help to create discord where there is none and exploit problems that arise naturally between organizations engaged in cooperation. Strategic alliances offer many opportunities for the development of a counter-competitive strategy by intelligence and law enforcement agencies. It might be possible, for example, to interdict supplies of drugs but somehow make it look as if one of the organizations involved is betraying its partner for short-term gain. Alliances

nology is certainly a risk that Singapore knows it runs as it moves ahead with its ambitious plan to network its island for the twenty-first century. Singapore already has one of the highest per capita rates of cellular phones in the world and with its IT2000 plan it hopes to take itself to the forefront of information technology. But the paradox of Singapore's love affair with technology and planning is its knowledge that the technology will empower individuals, bring in unwanted ideas and values, and, in the eyes of government officials, thereby threaten long-term stability. Singaporean officials are aware that to succeed with IT2000 they will need to encourage the messy individualism of cutting-edge research, but that to do so requires a less ordered and controllable Singapore. Some reports suggest that Singapore has even tried to sweep through personal computers searching for pornography, but what seems far more likely is that Singapore will tolerate insubordination by individuals, so long as they do not try to pass on illegal material to others in large numbers.[16] Singapore has licensed the two gateways to the 'Net for the public, and although the authorities have negotiated "locks" on access to certain sites, it is easy to get around the locks, if only because the business community demands a very flexible system.

Singapore, especially given its tiny size, remains a special case. Japan, which has far fewer fears about the new technology, has nevertheless been much slower in wiring its islands. Despite Japan's success with robotics and its much-hyped program of "informatization" by the Ministry of International Trade and Industry, it remains remarkably badly plugged in to the Infobahn and remains even more closed to foreigners trying to access Japanese databases than it is to foreign

exports.[17] In 1991 only 46 percent of Japanese state schools had any computers, although the plan is to get full coverage by 1997. But Japan will not have a fiber-optic system until 2015. This tardiness contrasts with current images in the Atlantic world of a Pacific Century led by Japanese doyens of computer technology. The reality is that the new information technology depends on, and interacts with society. In order to succeed in the information age, Japan needs to inculcate and tolerate far more individualism. With time, modernization in East Asia is changing social values in this direction. As Asians catch up to the Atlantic world's levels of application of new technology, they will be affected by many of the same social, economic, and political forces that have been at work in Europe and North America.

Crime in Cyberia

The challenge posed by information technology to East Asia, as to other parts of the world, is also how to cope with the vast new potential for cyber-crime. Indeed, East Asia may even be particularly vulnerable to the new technologies of crime, and certainly so if its governments continue to trust in their ability to prevent the advent of greater transparency. As even users of by now humble credit cards know, financial fraud can be easily perpetrated, even in developed states with sophisticated electronic defenses. Hackers, or to give them a more trendy name, "crackers," have become a major problem with no obvious long-term solution. Defense in this high-technology cat-and-mouse game is difficult enough in the most highly developed countries, but it poses even greater challenges for the rapidly developing countries of East Asia. Most computer crime has so far focused on the developed world of North America and Europe, largely because the pickings are richest in these regions. But as East Asians grow rapidly rich, all the hype about new wealth and new opportunities also lures the criminals. A major attraction of the East Asian market is that because they are relative newcomers to high technology, Asians have had less time to build sophisticated defenses or train skilled personnel able to take on and track down the hackers. An important problem faced by law enforcement authorities, even in the most developed world, is the lack of sufficient expertise in dealing with criminal gangs. As crime syndicates develop in Latin America or even the Caucasus or Central Asia, the police cannot even speak the languages of the criminals.[18] The resources of East Asians are even more stretched by the new criminals.

Another vulnerability of East Asians derives from the fact that they tend to have more authoritarian regimes. More stress is placed on means of control over society, and in an age of new technology, these means are increasingly electronic and therefore vulnerable to subversion. The harshness of the regimes also tends to encourage more determined opposition with a deeper grudge that can be satisfied by attacking the regime in its electronic underbelly.

Although a major assault on East Asian states by computer criminals and computerrorists has yet to begin in earnest, it is possible to identify obvious areas of weakness. One objective of such criminals is to steal information. Spy stories of the late days of the Cold War included computer and counter-computer operations by both East and West. In the less clear-cut conflicts after the Cold War, information is now stolen, and then sold on to whomever might be interested. In the United

States the antihacker struggle is led by the U.S. Secret Service, and in the United Kingdom by MI5. But despite the involvement of even the most capable of counterintelligence services, weaknesses have been exposed. In the United Kingdom in 1994, a hacker broke into government computers with sensitive intelligence information about senior leaders and intelligence sources and then provided the information to the media.[19]

Perhaps the most spectacular recent case of cybercrime involves East Asia in a major way. A 16-year-old British hacker (his Internet name was "datastream") broke into South Korea's nuclear secrets via the Air Development Center at Griffith Air Force Base in Rome, New York. He also obtained data on North Korea's missile firing sites, aircraft design, and U.S. agents in North Korea. The material was posted on open bulletin boards on the 'Net and in the end compromised over 1 million government passwords. U.S. officials admitted that military readiness in Northeast Asia was affected by this case.[20]

Yet another risk comes from computerrorists who are out to wreak havoc. A favorite tool is to spread viruses and to poison information systems. Some modern viruses can lie dormant until specified events such as the anniversary of the Tiananmen massacre of June 4, 1989. One virus making the rounds in China pops up to ask if you like the hated Premier Li Peng, and if you say yes, the virus trashes your hard disk. So far these operations have mainly been the work of deranged people or former employees settling grudges, but as the Chinese cases show, the scope for determined sabotage by political opponents is obvious. In the last days of the Cold War the North Atlantic Treaty Organization allies took seriously the risk that their war-fighting systems were increasingly vulnerable to such sabotage. As warfare grows more electronic and dependent on modern information systems, the risks of sabotage also grow. Asia's most accomplished hackers, at least for the time being, appear to be Australians with a special fixation on the resources of the U.S. National Aeronautics and Space Administration. The terrorists might simply be a group opposed, say, to Indonesia's policies in East Timor, and out to sabotage government resources either as a form of punishment or a way to get the government to change policy. As radical defenders of the environment grow more willing to use force, bloodless operations on computer networks will have special appeal. Could the Taiwanese or Japanese government be subjected to such tactics over their policies on whaling or tuna fishing? It is already clear that those opposed to the Chinese government's policies are accomplished computerrorists.

There is also a link between criminal computer activities and the growing international crime syndicates. The digital underground is going the same way as the drug underground from the 1960s on, becoming more hard-edged, better organized, and larger. Internet crime is up 77 percent in 1994 over 1993. Asia has more than its fair share of criminal actors in postmodern international affairs, most notably the Yakuza in Japan, the Chinese secret societies, and the Vietnamese gangs that operate in immigrant communities around the world. As these groups learn from the Latin American drug cartels, and in turn teach the new Central Asian gangs, the size of criminal operations grows apace. These criminal gangs operate in all states in East Asia, and especially those with ethnic Chinese, who provide the "sea" in which the criminal "fish" can swim.

Chinese and Japanese gangs are negotiating closer collaboration with Latin American drug cartels on a wide range of fronts, including even an effort to launch their own satellite to ensure more secure communications.

As with most criminal and terrorist operations, computer crime depends to an overwhelming extent on having clever people and having them in the right place at the right time. Figures from the U.S. National Security Agency showed that in 1989 up to 90 percent of known security breaches were the work of corporate or government insiders. What is crucial is to avoid having spies within institutions, because dissidents and rival governments will seek such people as the most effective operatives in crimes of information. The presence of overseas Chinese communities throughout East Asia is likely to be a focus for those concerned with the risks presented by clever, computer-literate insiders. The failure of the war on drug cartels is instructive in part because the strength of ethnic-based cartels such as the Chinese or Vietnamese gangs has been a particular problem.[21]

There are no simple solutions to the challenges posed by criminals in Cyberia. Authoritarian Asian states are not protected from cybercrime simply because they are authoritarian. The fact that they rule more by fear than do pluralist political systems will only encourage opponents to seek out their weak spots. Asian states might begin by getting to grips with ethnic crime syndicates operating in and through their territory. Given the known linkage between computers and the likes of the Yakuza or the Chinese or Vietnamese gangs, there is much that Asian states could do to contain the problem before it grows out of control as it has in Latin America. As the existence of Asian criminal networks shows, neither should Asian states believe that somehow their culture protects them from computerrorism. The computer criminals are white-collar, often highly trained, specialists schooled in increasing numbers in the hothouse technological education available in East Asia. Asians often make much of the difference between their societies and the more violent societies in the Atlantic world. Because computer crime is often seen as "victimless" and certainly not violent, it may prove to be a particularly Asian form of crime or an Asian strategy for undermining regimes.

Broadcasting and Narrowcasting

The ability of any society, including those in East Asia, to respond to the challenges of the new information technology depends essentially on the strength of the society concerned. East Asian leaders like to think that they have strong states because they trust in the firm smack of authoritarianism and have a core of relatively unchanging, conservative Confucian values. But much like Victorian values a century ago, the neo-Confucianist impulse is soon overwhelmed by the juggernaut of modernization that forces society to adopt and adapt new ideas. Thus many East Asian states are not as strong as they think. Some states, especially in Southeast Asia, are new creations and lack deep social coherence. Some of these states also have important ethnic divisions. Nearly all states in the region are facing major challenges simply because they are modernizing so quickly. When their leaders become so agitated about retaining their values, one suspects that they know they are losing control. Acute criticism by these leaders of Western intellectuals and the media is

a sign that the information revolution is overwhelming their defenses.

The resulting attitude—that of an outraged ostrich protesting loudly but mostly keeping its head in the sand— is odd for an East Asia that adopted and then adapted Western economic practices with such success. If only East Asians would acknowledge that they cannot hold back the tide of information technology and instead join in adapting it from the inside. The success of Asian films and food in the West suggests there is much that a more positive Asian approach can achieve to change Western culture in this sphere as well.

Nevertheless, there is no avoiding the fact that the information technology revolution is already forcing major changes in East Asian values. Part of the challenge to Asian values and the authority of the state comes from what can be called "broadcasting"—the transmission of values that come from the wider world. Most dangerous are the values born of the Age of the Enlightenment in the Atlantic world— the belief in individual rights and satisfactions. A particularly hazardous feature of these values is not so much concern with individual human rights, but rather concern with satisfying an individual's desire for a better style of life—consumerism. As East Asians grow rich, they demand the satisfactions of wealth. It is illuminating that although wealthy East Asian firms such as Sony or Nintendo have captured Western entertainment markets, they have done so without transmitting any particularly Asian consumer values. The result of creeping consumerism is that so-called Confucian values of thrift and self-effacement are fading—witness modern Japan and more recently South Korea and Taiwan. Confucian values, like Victorian values before them in the Atlantic world, are more a product of a specific stage of development than of a specific culture.

Another part of the challenge of information technology to the authority and values of East Asia is transmitted through what can be called "narrowcasting"—the ability of the new technology to reach and empower smaller subgroups in society and therefore fragment social structures. The empowerment of tiny groups, whether it is on the Information Superhighway or in television, enhances sectarian interests and cynicism about big government. That is no doubt part of the reason why U.S. politics are as sectarian and cynical as they are. Weak societies in East Asia are certainly vulnerable to the effects of narrowcasting, and East Asians are deluding themselves if they believe that their Confucian values protect them from the impact of new technology and the "culture of complaint" that has so affected North America and Western Europe.[22] Japanese, and to some extent South Koreans and Taiwanese, already realize that their own versions of Victorian values are fading.

Thus if Japan, South Korea, and Taiwan are harbingers of the future for East Asia, there may be a deepening recognition among Asians that the culture of complaint, with its attendant problems of irresponsibility and excessive individualism, is a real challenge that cannot go unmet. Perhaps the growing understanding that they share with Europeans and Americans a problem concerning the breakdown of state authority and national values is part of the explanation for the unusual appeal in Asia, as in the Atlantic world, of the Victorian values embodied in Walt Disney's *Snow White* or the *Lion King*. It would be a pity if East Asians, in their flawed attempt to hold back the tide of the information revolution, missed the opportunity to work with Europeans and Americans in finding new values and new sources of legitimate authority.

Notes

1. Henry Petroski, *The Evolution of Useful Things* (New York, N.Y.: Vintage, 1994).

2. *Wired*, January 1995, p. 102, with details of the usefulness of modems in making the revolution in Czechoslovakia in 1989.

3. *Time*, January 24, 1994; *U.S. News and World Report*, March 28, 1994; *Business Week*, December 19, 1994. George Yeo, Singapore's minister of information, called STAR "a splash of cologne in the face."

4. *Reuters*, January 18, 1995. (Now that these wire services are easily available on-line, they will be quoted more often in footnotes. Of course, they are difficult to trace unless your on-line service includes these specific services.)

5. In February 1995, STAR agreed with NBC to carry its CNBC Asia channel, which essentially provides only "business news."

6. *Financial Times*, December 22, 1994.

7. *Asian Wall Street Journal*, January 27, 1995.

8. *Far Eastern Economic Review*, August 18, 1994, and November 24, 1994; *International Herald Tribune*, December 16, 1994; *Financial Times*, December 22, 1994.

9. *Reuters*, January 18, 1995, and also *International Herald Tribune*, December 16, 1994, and *Economist*, October 8, 1994.

10. *Business Week*, December 19, 1994, on Singapore; *International Herald Tribune*, December 3, 1994, on Japan; and *Reuters*, January 25, 1995, on Australia. See the formal position from Singapore as presented by the ever-challenging Kishore Mahbubani, "The Pacific Way," *Foreign Affairs* 74 (January–February 1995), pp. 100–111.

11. *Economist* Surveys on October 23, 1993, February 12, 1994, and September 17, 1994. See also the changing pattern of registration of new Internet domains, which is available on the Internet at ftp.isoc.org/isoc/charts/hosts3.ppt and at www.nw.com/zone/www/report.html. (This is in effect a "virtual footnote" because the material it cites regularly

changes, but that will be true of most citations of Internet resources. Yet another challenge to old-fashioned academic authority.)

12. Use the URL on the Web to reach www.cnd.org for *China News Digest* in its various forms.

13. *Economist,* June 4, 1994, noted that there were then 100,000 callbacks a day.

14. *Economist,* January 7, 1995.

15. *Far Eastern Economic Review,* November 10, 1994, pp. 17–18.

16. *Financial Times,* February 25, 1995, and *Internet and Comms Today,* February 1995, p. 10.

17. *International Herald Tribune,* November 29, 1994. On the access to databases in Japan see Stephen Anderson's paper on the sub-ject posted on fukuzawa@ucsd.edu, an Internet discussion list (yet another Internet resource impossible to track in normal academic fashion).

18. For an exploration of related difficulties, see Phil Williams, "Transnational Criminal Organizations: Strategic Alliances," *The Washington Quarterly* 18 (Winter 1995), pp. 57–72.

19. *Independent* (London), November 24, 1994.

20. *Independent* (London), January 3, 1995.

21. Bruce Sterling, *The Hacker Crackdown* (London: Penguin, 1994), and Douglas Rushkoff, *Cyberia* (London: Flamingo, 1994).

22. See Robert Hughes, *The Culture of Complaint* (London: Harvill, 1994).

III. Geopolitics versus Geoeconomics

Looming Collision of Capitalisms?

Erik R. Peterson

ACCELERATING GLOBAL economic integration is bringing national economic policies into sharper competition, especially among the advanced capitalist economies. How these competing domestic policies are managed through the turn of the century and beyond will have profound implications not only for the international economy but also for broader international security and political relations. The risk is that increasingly nationalist economic policies, fanned by deteriorating economic conditions and social pressures, will propel the preeminent economic powers—and the rest of the world with them—into an era of *"realeconomik"* in which parochial economic interests drive governments to pursue marginal advantage in an international system marked by growing interdependencies.

The conclusion in December 1993 of the General Agreement on Tariffs and Trade (GATT) Uruguay Round, the culmination of seven years of tortuous negotiation by governments to strip away more of their own policy prerogatives, refuted the proposition that the major economic powers—the United States, the European Union

(EU), and Japan—were leading the collective effort to break down traditional trade barriers and trade-distorting domestic policies globally. Although it culminated in agreement, the process revealed the extent to which those powers were disinclined to do the "heavy lifting" in liberalizing their policies that many of the less prominent economies had already done to advance the round. In effect, the protracted negotiations highlighted the thresholds of national tolerance among the predominant economies beyond which the political costs for the respective governments were unacceptably high.

There is little doubt that the current economic troubles confronting Washington, Brussels, and Tokyo were a major factor in limiting the scope of the final GATT agreement. Those troubles have also elevated the levels of economic nationalism and unilateralism, both of which can be expected to intensify further as longer-term structural problems in all three economies generate additional political and economic dislocations in the years ahead.

Because of the increasingly binding constraints placed on national economic policy-making by the process of global economic integration, the temptation for the major economies to engage in defensive strategies by supporting national "strategic" industries—especially high-technology indus-

Erik R. Peterson is director of studies at CSIS.

dustries—could bring the major capitalisms into collision. The operative question is whether the governments concerned will succumb to the growing tendency to "pursue relative gains at the expense of mutual gains [and] political power at the expense of economic welfare,"[1] or whether they will be able to devise a system of rules and an appropriate institutional vehicle to defuse the potential for escalating economic clashes between respective "national champions."

Accelerating Economic Globalization

It has long been recognized that the traditional line of demarcation between domestic and international economic policy-making is fading. Economic shocks ranging from the oil embargo by the Organization of Petroleum Exporting Countries to the "Black Monday" international stock market crash in October 1987 have underlined the susceptibility of national markets to developments abroad. For governments worldwide, the internationalization of the world economy has also meant the progressive deterioration of their capacity to manage their economies. Macroeconomic policies have been increasingly undermined by the offsetting effects of international responses; an increase in interest rates to decelerate economic growth, for example, is more likely than ever before to be countered by an increase in interest-sensitive capital flows from abroad.[2]

But international trade and investment linkages have expanded to such an extent that sensitivities of economies to decision making in other economies are now substantially more pronounced. Advances in communication and information technologies, the pursuit by multinational enterprises (MNEs) of complex cross-border strategies, the formation and development of regional trading blocs, the GATT process, economic liberalization undertaken in a host of developing economies, and ongoing efforts at marketization in former command economies are metamorphosing the international economic and financial system. As these elements bring about higher levels of global integration, constraints on national economic policy-making will continue to grow—and with them the potential for wider conflict over national policies.

The real-time capabilities offered by new communication and information technologies have already had a tremendous impact on international capital flows. Daily global capital movements have increased to well over $1 trillion in 1992. The implications of these movements for national macroeconomic policy-making are profound. Alan Greenspan, chairman of the Federal Reserve, noted in August 1993 that the internationalization of finance and the reduction in constraints on international capital flows "expose national economies to shocks from new and unexpected sources, with little if any lag."[3] As a result, he stressed the importance central banks should attach to developing new ways of assessing and limiting risk. But those ways remain to be identified.

Nowhere has the impact on policy-making of these cross-border capital flows been more obvious recently than in the EU, where international speculative pressures played a significant role in the partial collapse in the European Monetary System in 1992. Those forces contributed to the circumstances that led London and Rome to withdraw from the semifixed exchange rates under the Exchange Rate Mechanism (ERM); since the British and Italian withdrawal, they have also forced the Spanish to devalue the peseta and brought the Belgian franc under extreme stress. As the *Economist* noted in October 1993, "[t]he financial markets have discovered, in a way they are unlikely to forget for years, their power to crack the system."[4] In short, we have entered a new stage in the development of international finance in which financial markets—and even some individuals—can dramatically influence the outcome of policy decisions by states.

MNEs are another major driver of global economic integration. By virtue of increasingly complex strategies involving multitier networks of firms that are geographically dispersed and through strategic alliances with other firms, MNEs are establishing unprecedented linkages among economies worldwide. According to the United Nations Conference on Trade and Development (UNCTAD), the strategies of MNEs have generally moved beyond a "simple integration" approach involving strengthened links with their foreign affiliates and with independent firms serving as subcontractors or licensees; the new strategy, which UNCTAD characterizes as "complex integration," provides for heightened geographical distribution of the value-added chain.[5] That MNEs account for a staggering one-third of world private productive assets suggests how important the ramifications of such a shift of strategy are.[6]

According to UNCTAD, sales by MNEs outside their countries of origin were $5.5 trillion in 1992—as opposed to total world exports for the same year of about $4.0 trillion; furthermore, the stock of foreign direct investment (FDI) worldwide reached $2 trillion in 1992, as opposed to one-half that amount in 1987.[7] These data reflect the substantial role that MNEs are playing in integrating the world econ-

omy and suggest the extent to which private-sector forces have become a factor in national economic decision making. As discussed in greater detail below, a number of countries with policies that were previously anathema to MNEs have refashioned their approaches so that attraction of foreign investment is a key component of their economic development strategies.

The development of regional trading blocs has also generated higher levels of economic interdependence and by definition represents the voluntary acceptance by the respective member states of constraints on national policy prerogatives. Because the EU, the North American Free Trade Agreement (NAFTA), and the emerging trading framework in Asia are based on political as well as economic considerations, the trend toward regionalism transcends the surrender of policy prerogatives for purely economic reasons.[8] Nevertheless, the impact is to advance economic integration between member states. In the case of the EU, where the impact of German monetary policy clearly transcends the national economic challenges inherent in reunification, the linkages may be more pronounced than some member states would want.

The GATT process, of course, has also steadily broken down barriers between international and domestic policy-making. The GATT is no longer the vehicle through which only tariff barriers are broken down; the non-tariff barriers that were the focus of the Tokyo Round and the issues at the fore of the Uruguay Round—trade in services, trade-related investment measures, intellectual property protection, price supports and subsidies, countervailing duties, dumping, and dispute settlement—have exposed the nerves of national economic interests

279

as never before. The demonstrations from Brussels to Tokyo attested to the degree to which GATT negotiations have become (and should be) a major domestic political issue. By definition, the GATT process and the Uruguay Round—in the event it is ratified—represent "another stake in the heart of the idea that governments can direct economies."[9]

Economic and financial liberalization in developing economies represents another stimulus to growing integration. A select number of developing countries with liberalized investment environments are now primary targets of portfolio and foreign direct investment flows.[10] Over the past 10 years, international portfolio investment in developing countries has mushroomed. Market capitalization has grown by a factor of 11, from $67 billion in 1982 to $770 billion in 1992. As a percentage of world equity market capitalization, developing countries increased their share over this period from 2.5 percent to 7 percent. The trend can be expected to continue as secondary markets in developing countries widen and deepen. Simply put, the key reason for this rapid growth in developing-country capital markets is profitability. According to the International Finance Corporation, emerging stock markets took 8 of the top 10 positions as best performing markets last year.[11] Gains of over 20 percent were registered in markets stretching from Mexico City to Amman to Bangkok. In addition, over the past eight years emerging markets as a group have significantly outperformed their counterparts in developed countries.[12]

The pattern of FDI to developing countries has been no less extraordinary. According to UNCTAD, FDI flows to developing countries increased from $25 billion in 1991 to $40

billion in 1992; if high growth is sustained in Asia and Latin America, annual flows could double in real terms to $80 billion by the end of the century.[13] What is behind this trend? Simply put, economic liberalization has replaced statism, trade liberalization has followed protectionism, and privatization has replaced nationalization. For these countries, the necessity of conforming their national economic decision making to the realities of the international system is now a matter of record. In many cases, those adjustments have extended beyond actions to attract FDI inflows to include fundamental policy shifts such as imposing discipline on fiscal deficits, developing clear legal and commercial systems, streamlining bureaucracies, simplifying taxation systems, and liberalizing trade policies.[14]

Although they are not yet as fully integrated into the world economic system, the former command economies that are seeking to marketize their systems are another driver of international integration. For the first time since the beginning of the century, they are opening their economies to the world economic system and enacting national policies designed to encourage the development of market forces.

Integrating Markets Versus Integrating Policies

It should be stressed that there are fundamental differences among these forces driving international economic integration. Some can be referred to as "organic" integration—the private cross-border flows of capital, goods and services, technology, and information driven in large part by MNEs. Others promote "inorganic" integration—the formal and politically oriented trade agreements forged among countries to reduce tariff and non-tariff barriers and harmonize trade-relevant domestic economic policies.

Organic integration is the result of strategies enacted by international private-sector actors to maximize the efficiency of their operations in the light of increasing global competition. As noted above, to an ever greater extent MNEs are distributing their operations internationally regardless of political institutions and frameworks to seek innovation or to achieve cost savings at various stages in the value-added chain. Although the pattern of this distribution of economic activity may be (and often is) influenced by regional economic blocs such as the EU and the NAFTA, it will be influenced only to the extent that such frameworks can be incorporated into prevailing global strategies. Increasingly, however, that activity is falling outside the regional blocs and generating higher levels of more global economic integration in the process.

These kinds of private-sector-driven economic dependencies must be differentiated from the "inorganic" or formalized efforts at economic cooperation undertaken among and between states. Such arrangements are based by definition on perceived mutual gains from economic cooperation, but generally they also represent a mixture of economic and political concern. The EU is clearly grounded in political and security objectives advanced in the period immediately after World War II; for its part, the NAFTA also has a strong political character. As a result, the inorganic integration fostered by regional blocs may not necessarily reflect the market fundamentals that are driving the interdependence now created by the private sector. Furthermore, the political nature of regional blocs suggests the possibility that they might be

tempted to engage in aggressive trade policies that could generate a protectionist equivalent of an arms race.[15] They could ultimately become the means by which organic integration is resisted.

Together, these organic and inorganic forces driving economies into heightened interdependence can be compared to a set of tightening constraints in a linear programming model that serve to progressively limit the area in which national economic policy-making is feasible. It follows that governments are likely to resist the restrictions this kind of global convergence places on their policy prerogatives, especially when they are facing acute short-term economic challenges or when the adjustments forced by growing integration entail profound economic or social change. In short, integration of policies is lagging behind integration of markets.

Capitalisms in Collision?

The salient question is how governments can protect their national economic interests in an increasingly integrated global economic and financial framework. More and more, the preeminent economic powers in particular are finding the answer in drawing lines beyond which they will resort to defensive strategies grounded in parochial interests. The result is the development of political conditions that encourage the outbreak of economic nationalism.

The current political and economic environments in the United States, Europe, and Japan do not augur well for the level of cooperation necessary to avoid the neomercantilist confrontation that could flow from competing national policies. The overarching security concerns generated by the common threat from the erstwhile Soviet

Union are a thing of the past, and immediate economic concerns now overshadow residual security ties. It is a time of fundamental redefinition of security, political, and economic relations—but the process of redefinition is proceeding in the absence of the international leadership and corresponding institutions necessary to meet the challenges of escalating economic rivalry.

The trauma that Washington experienced in fall 1993 in deciding on whether to adopt a free-trade agreement with Mexico—an economy only 4 percent of the U.S. gross national product and with a $5.5 billion trade deficit—amounted to a highly visible demonstration of U.S. attitudes about trade. Although of course the NAFTA was adopted, the emotional and sometimes vacuous debate served to highlight the extent to which economic nationalism threatens the historic role of the United States as leader of the global economic system. But apart from the NAFTA debate, there are other symptoms of this uncertainty. Regular calls in the U.S. Congress and elsewhere for unilateralist approaches to trade and foreign investment issues suggest that the concepts of "fair" rather than "free" trade and "reciprocal treatment" rather than "national treatment" in international capital flows are steadily gaining ground.

These warning signs are the result of the growing perception in the United States that new approaches are necessary to ensure fair access for trade and investment by U.S. firms. The perception is grounded in the view that what was recently referred to as "unilateralist national treatment"[16]—namely, the position on international investment that Washington has maintained for decades—is not being reciprocated by many of its investment partners. Of course, the recent domestic economic difficulties have thrown fuel on the fire.

In Europe, where the economic problems at present are even more pronounced,[17] where the partial collapse of the ERM has generated profound doubts about the outlook for a single European currency, and where the tenuous ratification process of the Maastricht agreement has left leaders searching for ways to advance the integration agenda, attention is predominantly inward. The seriousness of the challenge was underlined in October 1993 when the president of the European Commission, Jacques Delors, warned that the then European Community was drifting toward becoming a free-trade zone that could break up in as little as 15 years.[18] The EU is clearly in a period of intense consolidation and restructuring.

Japan is also engaged in political and economic soul-searching. The Hosokawa coalition has embarked on a program of political reform with potentially important longer-term implications for Tokyo's position in the international economic system. The outcome, however, is by no means assured. To sustain the reform process that it initiated immediately prior to the November 1993 meeting of the members of APEC (the Asia–Pacific Economic Cooperation), the government must continue to pass through the political thicket of its own eight-party coalition before contesting with the opposition Liberal Democratic Party to push through its initiatives. It must also do so against the backdrop of stagnating or declining growth, severe volatility in the financial markets, less than promising longer-term growth projections, and a highly resistant bureaucracy.

When considered together, these

developments in the United States, Europe, and Japan have led some analysts to revisit arguments advanced in the 1970s about the ungovernability of democracies.[19] But there is also reason to question whether relations between the capitalist countries themselves will be governable. It is no exaggeration to suggest that the political agendas in all three major economic powers are predominantly inward-looking and focus primarily on reviving national economic growth and employment. All three are engaged in economic triage. Evidence of economic parochialism in the pursuit of those objectives appears to be growing on a day-by-day basis. In short, they could be on a course that suggests the potential for the rise of neomercantilism.

"Strategic" Trade at Issue

In particular, there is the possibility of an escalation of industrial policies that would bring "national champions" and "strategic" industries—especially those in high technology—into sharper conflict. The magnitude of the threat has been set out by the Organization for Economic Cooperation and Development (OECD):

> Government support for economically strategic industries could become a major source of international dispute in the 1990s. The move over the last decade towards subsidies and other forms of state assistance for important technologically advanced sectors is set to accelerate. The proliferation of such policies, which affect a relatively narrow band of often identical sectors, could well develop into a keenly competitive "subsidy race," with harmful and far-reaching implications for the

international system of trade, investment and technology.[20]

Despite the predominately unfavorable—or, at best, mixed—experience with allocating government resources in support of strategic industries,[21] the temptation for governments is to engage in "picking winners" because of the political benefits they engender and the rationale under "strategic trade" theory that "technology trajectories" have a clustering effect of positive externalities extending throughout a wider part of the economy.[22] Some advocates of this theory suggest that such interventionist national policies can be advanced without undermining the pursuit of an open, integrated world economy.[23] Others point to the impending competition for "national futures."[24] That this new genre of thought on competition theory is predicated on results with pronounced sensitivities to changes in assumptions has not prevented it from assuming rising political currency.[25] Nor have the new political advocates of strategic trade been deterred by steadily mounting empirical evidence suggesting that protection and subsidization of industries can actually weaken their competitive position.[26]

Whatever the underlying explanations, from the standpoint of competing national policies the advancement of strategic trade objectives can be achieved through a wide array of policy measures—including but not limited to trade-related policies such as "orderly marketing agreements," industrial and technology policies that provide subsidy, research and development support and other "cover," discriminatory procurement practices, and exemption of relevant sectors from antitrust law.

Assuming such strategic trade policies are adopted more fully by all three major world economic powers, it follows that competition between the respective "beggar-thy-neighbor" approaches could mount quickly because they are based on zero-sum thinking. As Michael Porter has noted,

> [i]f the rate of innovation slows because an "us versus them" attitude leads to subsidy, protection, and consolidation that blunts incentives, the consequences for advanced and less advanced nations alike are severe.[27]

Government intervention in a host of sectors has been a long-established practice in the EU. From ESPRIT to EUREKA, from Concorde to Airbus, from the TGV rail initiative in France to aircraft production in the Netherlands, industrial policy is already a part of the European economic topography. In Japan, where the connection between the government and the private sector is also well established, decision makers have a less visible but nevertheless significant role in promoting industries through a variety of policies. And in the United States, where sector support has been less prevalent, momentum is mounting for a shift to a higher profile for the government in selected strategic industries. The shift is in response to the perception that "our competitors close off their markets to American firms while looking for ways to tap into our rich market . . . and we let them."[28] A senior Clinton administration official recently put it this way: "If no one else wants to play the game [our way], we'd look pretty silly [doing nothing] while they clean our clock."[29]

These divergent positions on industrial policy serve to highlight the more general differences between the capitalisms of the United States, the EU, and Japan. At issue is the differing relationship between government and business in each of the major economic powers and how those relations translate into national policies that have international repercussions. At one end of the spectrum is the consumer-oriented system of capitalism in the United States, where linkages between government and business have been loose and sometimes at odds as a result of the tradition of limiting the extent to which market concentrations occur; at the other end is Japan, which by fostering a producers-oriented form of capitalism is marked by substantially closer ties between the public and private sectors; and in the middle is the EU, where government intervention—traditionally based on social welfare criteria—is more pronounced than in the United States.[30]

A Multilateral Response?

A common approach by the three preeminent economies to defining acceptable limits to industrial policy is necessary if spiraling competition for marginal advantage is to be averted. The prospect for the negotiation of multilateral rules governing industrial policy is, however, remote at best. No international framework is in sight that could represent a release valve for the emerging pressures associated with these competing policies. The Group of Seven (G–7) falls substantially short of representing a forum through which a detailed agreement could be reached. Despite its past attention to the issue, the OECD is not likely to become the forum for the United States, the EU, and Japan to seek to reconcile their differences because of the large membership involved, although the OECD could take an active role in defining more specifically how the highly industrialized economies might proceed more generally in fashioning an approach to the issue. The experience of the Uruguay Round suggests that the next stage of negotiations under the Multilateral Trade Organization will be equally if not more arduous as differences in competition and investment policies come to the fore.

Furthermore, no single economic power seems predisposed to spearhead an effort to defuse the potential of conflicting industrial policies. In the meantime, "competition between governments [is progressively replacing] competition between companies as industrial activities become more and more global."[31]

It is an irony that at this critical historical juncture—when many of the former command economies are embarking on transitions to market systems and a number of developing countries have substantially liberalized their economies after decades of failed statist policies—the highly industrialized powers are in economic distress and embroiled in efforts to reinvigorate their domestic economies. If, as expected, the macroeconomic difficulties in the United States, Europe, and Japan persist or intensify, the attempt at integration into the world economy by significant parts of the second and third worlds—a historically unprecedented development that for decades has been the lodestar of the highly industrialized states themselves—will have been unassisted by the major global economic players and in some ways impeded by their paralysis.

Another fundamental irony of the immediate post–cold war period is that with the decline of the threat from Moscow, the emphasis is shifting from the clash between capitalism and communism to the differences between the "capitalisms" of the highly industrialized economies. The threat is that traditional political and security link-

ages will be recast as subordinate features of a competition for industrial advantage—or supremacy.[32]

In the face of rising domestic economic problems and accelerating global economic integration, the manner in which the major economic powers manage their relations through the turn of the century and beyond will have an enormous impact on the world economy. A descent into a period of *realeconomik*, pitting government against government in a global competition for markets, would have a deleterious effect on the capacity of those same governments to meet future national and international economic challenges. Such a descent would also threaten the integrity of political and security relations in a highly uncertain period. To avoid this outcome, policymakers need to heed the advice of Akio Morita, who in an open letter to the G–7 heads of state in June 1993 argued:

> You, as political leaders, have the power to take the steps necessary to make the increasing de facto globalization of business the most creative, positive, and beneficial force it can be, rather than the source of new international conflict.[33]

The author gratefully acknowledges the research assistance of Marcus Castain in the preparation of this article.

Notes

1. Theodore H. Moran, "An Economics Agenda for Neorealists," *International Security* 18 (Fall 1993), p. 211.

2. See, for example, Marina von Neumann Whitman, "The State of Business: Global Competitiveness and Economic Nationalism," *Harvard International Review* 15 (Summer 1993), pp. 5–6.

3. Speech presented at meeting on "Changing Capital Markets: Implications for Mon-

etary Policy," Jackson Hole, Wyoming, August 19, 1993.

4. "Europe's Monetary Future: From here to EMU," *Economist*, October 23, 1993, p. 25.

5. UNCTAD, *World Investment Report 1993: Transnational Corporations and Integrated International Production* (New York, N.Y.: United Nations, 1993), pp. 4–5, 115–133.

6. *Ibid.*, p. 13.

7. *Ibid.*, pp. 13–14.

8. See Paul Krugman, "Regional Blocs: The Good, the Bad and the Ugly," *International Economy* 6 (November/December 1992), pp. 54–56.

9. "The World Wins One," *Wall Street Journal*, December 15, 1993, p. A–16.

10. Argentina, Brazil, the People's Republic of China, Egypt, Hong Kong, Mexico, Nigeria, Singapore, Taiwan, and Thailand. See UNCTAD, *World Investment Report*.

11. International Finance Corporation, *IFC Emerging Stock Markets Factbook 1993* (Washington, D.C.: IFC, 1993), p. 3.

12. *Ibid.*, p. 3. The report notes that from the end of 1988 to the end of 1992, markets in Argentina, Chile, Colombia, Mexico, Pakistan, Thailand, and Venezuela rose more than 100 percent in dollar terms as compared with 51 percent in the United States.

13. UNCTAD, *World Investment Report*.

14. DeAnne Julius, "Liberalisation, Foreign Investment, and Economic Growth," *Shell Selected Papers*, March 1993, pp. 4–5.

15. Krugman, "Regional Blocs: The Good, the Bad and the Ugly," p. 55.

16. See Office for Technology Assessment, *Multinationals and the National Interest: Playing by Different Rules* (Washington, D.C.: OTA, 1993).

17. See, for example, Arnaud de Borchgrave, "Eurogloom Foreshadows Social Upheaval," *Washington Times*, October 4, 1993, p. A–12.

18. Despite ratification of the Maastricht treaty, Delors states that "What I see is European construction drifting towards a free-trade zone, that is to say an English-style Europe, which I reject." See "Delors Fears EC Drifting towards Break-up," *Fi-*

nancial Times*, October 18, 1993, p. 2. See also "Delors Bloodied but Unbowed," *Financial Times*, October 23, 1993, p. 3.

19. See, for example, the articles on ungovernability by Michel Crozier, Samuel P. Huntington, and Joji Watanuki in *American Enterprise* 4 (November/December 1993), pp. 28–41. The three authors originally addressed the issue in a research effort in the early 1970s sponsored by the Trilateral Commission, chaired by Zbigniew Brzezinski, which culminated in the book entitled *The Crisis of Democracy* (New York, N.Y.: New York University Press, 1975).

20. OECD, *Strategic Industries in a Global Economy: Policy Issues for the 1990s* (Paris: OECD Publications, 1991).

21. See inter alia "When the State Picks Winners," *Economist*, January 9, 1993, pp. 13–14; "Europe's Technology Policy: How Not to Catch Up," *Economist*, January 9, 1993, pp. 19–21; Daniel Malkin, "Industrial Policy in OECD Countries," *International Economic Insights* 4 (March/April 1993), pp. 22–23; Barrie Stevens, "Strategic Industries: What Policies for the 1990s?" *OECD Observer*, no. 172 (October/November 1991), pp. 4–7; and Candice Stevens, "Industrial Internationalisation and Trade Friction," *OECD Observer*, no. 173 (December 1991/January 1992), pp. 27–30.

22. See Wayne Sandholtz et al., *The Highest Stakes: The Economic Foundations of the Next Security System* (New York, N.Y.: Oxford University Press, 1992).

23. See Peter F. Cowhey and Jonathan D. Aronson, *Managing the World Economy: The Consequences of Corporate Alliances* (New York, N.Y.: Council on Foreign Relations Press, 1993).

24. Sandholtz, *Highest Stakes*, p. 182.

25. Michael E. Porter, *The Competitive Advantage of Nations* (New York, N.Y.: The Free Press, 1990), p. 812, n. 46.

26. For a recent comparison of selected manufacturing industries in the United States, Germany, and Japan, see McKinsey Global Institute, "Manufacturing Productivity" (Washington, D.C., October 1993). See also Paul Betts, "Penalties for Excess Baggage," *Financial Times*, December 1, 1993, p. 13.

27. Porter, *The Competitive Advantage*, p. 682.

28. Scott Gibson and Saul Goldstein, "The Plane Truth: How European Deals Are Killing U.S. Jobs," *Washington Post*, October 10, 1993.

29. Hobart Rowen, "A Little Boost from Washington," *Washington Post*, October 7, 1993, p. A–23. Rowen was quoting President Bill Clinton's science adviser, John H. Gibbons.

30. Whitman, "The State of Business," p. 7.

31. Stevens, "Industrial Internationalisation," p. 30.

32. For a provocative account of the role of the United States in the emerging international economic system, see Edward N. Luttwak, *The Endangered American Dream: How to Stop the United States from Becoming a Third-World Country and How to Win the Geo-Economic Struggle for Industrial Supremacy* (New York, N.Y.: Simon & Schuster, 1993). See also Luttwak's related article, "From Geopolitics to Geo-Economics: Logic of Conflict, Grammar of Commerce," *National Interest*, no. 20 (Summer 1990), pp. 17–23.

33. Akio Morita, "Toward a New World Economic Order," *Atlantic Monthly*, June 1993, pp. 88–89.

Economics and National Strategy: Convergence, Global Networks, and Cooperative Competition

James R. Golden

THE UNITED STATES needs a national strategy that responds to the central post–cold war political, economic, and military realities: the end of East–West confrontation, economic parity across the developed regions of the West, the information technology revolution, the proliferation of weapons with enormous lethality, and the growing importance of intrastate war. In the emerging environment the threats to national security are real, but they are more diffuse and less likely to provide a clear focus for standing alliances or to justify the subordination of economic issues to security concerns. Instead, national strategy will have to balance economic and security interests and support approaches that develop international consensus: cooperation will be essential in providing institutions that promote international economic stability and effective crisis management. At the same time the United States must

James R. Golden, Colonel, U.S. Army, was a senior staff economist on the President's Council of Economic Advisers and now serves as professor and head of the Department of Social Sciences at the U.S. Military Academy.

meet the economic challenge of sustaining high and rising levels of national income in the face of intense regional competition. The national strategy, in short, must blend cooperation and competition in ways that respond to the new environment.

The world's new political structure centers on a triangle of competing regions that have achieved economic parity—Europe, North America, and Japan[1]—loosely tied to developing regions on their peripheries. The three developed regions are integrated by the globalization of production and finance and by the network structures of the information technology revolution, but they are separated by differences in culture and by regional markets and institutions that tie various industries to their respective home bases. The combination of convergence in economic performance and the new structure of global networks has altered the nature of regional competition in ways that have profound strategic implications.

If the first industrial revolution can be characterized by a focus on steam, iron, and railways in national firms, and the second by electricity, chemistry, automobiles, and consumer durables in increasingly multinational firms, the third centers on microelectronics, biological engineering, and new materials in internationally networked firms. The transforming power of the third revolution lies in the impact of information technology in integrating related technologies, reducing transactions and processing costs, and changing industrial structures.

The information technology revolution is having repercussions for strategy at many levels. One of the most significant has been in the changing structure of industrial organizations and corporate networks. The growing access to and importance of information flows is transforming traditional hierarchical firms into more horizontal organizations that emphasize flexibility, coordination, on-time production, and long-term relationships with suppliers and customers. In the information technology industry in particular, research and development (R&D) relationships extend across firms through horizontal information networks that have redefined traditional corporate boundaries. Perhaps ironically, the same firms that cooperate in R&D activities then compete aggressively in product markets. Corporate strategy now requires *cooperative competition*, a framework that simultaneously enhances mutual performance and shapes the form of competition. In this sense cooperation and competition are not alternative approaches to relationships; both elements are always present to some extent. The cooperative component enhances the competition by making both parties more effective, and at the same time the structure of cooperation limits the scope of acceptable competition.

That insight—that competitors must also cooperate in research networks in order to compete effectively in product markets—captures the essential impact of the information rev-olution for other levels of strategy as well. The new network relationships are redefining regional power balances, altering patterns of economic growth, and shifting the structure of potential alliances that will come into play in dealing with the proliferation of sophisticated threats. In this setting, national strategy must balance cooperation and competition to achieve national objectives. I use the term cooperative competition in a strategic sense to stress the importance of building cooperative networks that will permit the United States to pursue objectives in concert with other nations while still competing with them for the location of high-value economic activities. The cooperative element of the strategy recognizes the need to create the public goods, or infrastructure, needed to provide the stability essential for efficient interaction.[2] The competitive component recognizes that national objectives still differ, that the distribution of wealth, income, and power will continue to be a national concern, and that, sadly, political and economic competition may occasionally spill over into armed conflict.[3] National strategy must recognize both components by working to create a network of infrastructure relationships to keep the international competition within acceptable limits and by developing the capacity to respond effectively when the competition exceeds those limits.

A National Strategy

Before we examine the new economic environment and the components of a strategy of cooperative competition in more detail, we need to address the possibility of sustaining *any* U.S. national strategy. By a national strategy, I mean a vision of the process through which national resources will be used to achieve national objectives. National strategies may be distinguished by the relative roles given to the private and public sectors, the emphasis given to different policy instruments, and the importance assigned to various possible outcomes. National strategies are seldom explicit, and the implementation of strategy rarely flows from objectives to resource allocation. Objectives, concepts, and means normally evolve together.

In modern mixed-market economies national strategy starts from the premise that a wide range of national objectives will be pursued through decentralized economic markets in which firms and consumers are relatively free to make informed decisions that influence their own welfare. The rationale for government action results from market failures, in the sense that some distortion in information or incentive structures is producing the "wrong" signals for private actions, or from a desire to alter the distribution of income that results from private decisions. Judgments on what constitutes a market failure or an unacceptable distribution of income are obviously intensely political decisions, and those judgments and the extent and form of intervention to correct perceived failures differ substantially from country to country. Japan and France intervene in that process with a structure of indicative planning to coordinate public and private actions in selected industries. The U.S. government has traditionally rejected such explicit industrial planning, although its regulatory framework and its large intervention through defense research, development, and procurement have large sectoral impacts.

In theory U.S. national strategy would begin with a structure of private activities based on the operation of free markets and then provide a framework for modifying the use of the nation's resources to achieve national objectives derived from enduring national interests. In practice national objectives conflict, and consensus on how to achieve them is limited. The actual allocation of public resources is settled in an often heated political process that is constitutionally designed to balance competing interests. Policy formulation is rarely driven by overarching strategy: instead there is an overlapping web of public policies fashioned by a broad array of agencies that compete for resources in the political arena, urged on by many private interest groups with divergent concerns. Effective coordination of those policies in ways that preserve the vitality of the private sector and eliminate the most egregious inconsistencies in public programs is difficult because the costs of identifying and obtaining the right information and overcoming the frictional problems of defining and implementing policies are enormous. The government's energy and resources are limited, so at best the nation might be able to coordinate the use of a subset of national resources in pursuit of its most important national interests.

As a result the central role of strategy is to elevate a narrow set of policies to prominence for more careful coordination. In the post–World War II period the analytical device for narrowing national strategy to a manageable scale has been to focus on "security" strategy, based on an assessment of national interests that are at risk in the international arena. Economic policy rarely entered explicitly into this framework, aside from the economic constraints imposed in the budget process. The National Security Act of 1947 institutionalized the security strategy framework in a system centered on the integrating functions of the National Security Council and its staff. Since 1986 the staff has drafted the president's *National Security Strategy of the United States* each year, typically beginning with lists of national interests such as national survival, economic strength, cooperative relations with allies and friendly nations, and a stable world in which democratic institutions can flourish.[4] National security policy attempts to integrate economic, diplomatic, and military policies to deal with threats to those national interests.[5] This post–World War II emphasis on the peacetime coordination of national power to achieve security objectives applies the basic ideas of wartime "grand" strategy to the cold war setting.[6]

The "security" framework for strategy is ultimately based on a system of threat and coercion justified by the importance of preserving vital national interests. Thus security strategy is distinct from other government policy because of the vital importance of the issues involved and the sensitivity of the policy instruments. In the security framework, elements of national "power" become instruments for achieving security objectives. From this perspective economic "power," a term used by security analysts but rarely by economists, can be used directly to influence states and other international actors or indirectly as a foundation for generating other elements of power, such as military forces.

The advantages of focusing on national security strategy rather than broader national strategy are manifest. Threats to national security interests provide a clear focus for coordination across relevant agencies, particularly the Departments of State and Defense, in the realm of "high policy," which is less susceptible to partisan bickering. At least to some extent, the security strategy helps to identify capabilities needed to meet the threats, informs analysis of trade-offs across alternative military force structures and weapon systems, and ultimately influences strategic plans and budget decisions. The security focus also emphasizes the distinction between long-term planning and what many analysts feel is the sine qua non of strategy—the presence of an adversary—and reinforces the concept of "strategic thinking" with its web of moves and countermoves.

The disadvantages of the emphasis on security strategy are also clear, and they have become more obvious in the post–cold war era. When external threats become ambiguous and more remote, the logic and cohesion of the security strategy formulation is less compelling. The "threat" no longer provides a clear orientation for budget and force structure decisions, and the distinctions between security and other policies break down. Moreover, as economic issues become relatively more important, casting them in a security framework could actually be harmful. In practice, economic policy is not formulated by the actors in the national security system and it is not driven by national security strategy in any meaningful sense. By focusing on the narrow range of economic policy issues that are influenced by security strategy, the system deemphasizes such key issues as productivity and competitiveness that are handled in other agencies. Moreover, by focusing on threats to national interests in the international arena, an emphasis on economic security could incorrectly stress coercion against economic competitors rather than domestic policies to enhance competitiveness.

Although economics and security are clearly linked, the idea that economic policy is or should be driven by security interests is inconsistent with the post–cold war environment. More precisely, the security framework places economic relationships in a power balance perspective that may seriously distort the economic agenda by emphasizing zero-sum relationships, in which one actor gains at the other's expense, over the normal non-zero-sum relationships of economic exchange, in which both actors gain. The security framework is inappropriate for dealing with relationships when vital national interests are not directly challenged and the primary policy instruments do not involve threats and coercion. As the relative scope of issues involving military confrontation declines, the security framework provides a less compelling approach for organizing national strategy. Indeed, by making clear threats to national interests, or future capabilities to mount such threats, the organizing principle for strategy, the security framework may lead decision makers to miss the key point that U.S. national interests are increasingly defined in terms of managing competition within the context of cooperative processes.

In the evolving environment we need a new orientation on economics and security issues. Although the security framework and machinery will remain essential for dealing with direct threats to vital U.S. interests, that framework can no longer provide the sole organizing principle for national strategy. Samuel Huntington argues that the United States needs to move beyond the "national security state" of the postwar period to what he calls the "competitive state," whose goal would be "to enhance American economic competitiveness and economic strength in relation to other countries."[7] He notes that economic strength is needed to sustain defense outlays and that interaction in international markets is becoming a relatively more important means of achieving security goals. As he correctly argues, strong growth, productivity, and technological innovation generate international influence through world product, capital, and currency markets. Those markets provide the major forms of interaction among world powers and with the declining importance of military power in great power relationships they are increasingly important means for influencing international behavior.

Huntington correctly identifies the required shift away from a purely security framework for organizing national strategy, but his emphasis on the "relative" economic performance of the United States casts national strategy in a primarily competitive context. In the highly integrated global economy, however, too narrow an emphasis on competition might lead to policies that reduce efficiency and lower national welfare. An analysis of economic convergence and global industrial networks suggests that cooperation must also be a key element of national strategy. Indeed competitive steps that serve to isolate the U.S. economy from those networks would actually weaken relative U.S. economic performance.

The Economic Environment

The two dominant trends in the international economic environment are convergence in levels of income, growth, and productivity among North America, Europe, and Japan, and the evolution of global industrial networks with highly integrated, but remarkably stable, regional nodes. Although convergence in economic performance will not mean equality in economic power because of the differences in scale of national economies, it will mean that U.S. strategy must increasingly involve other major economic powers. That is not to say that the United States has lost its position among world economic leaders, or that it is destined to fall behind other industrial powers in the coming century. It will still be a hegemon in terms of its overall share of world markets, but it will not and should not be expected to dominate every industrial area.

The evolution of global industrial networks, in which firms in related industries develop long-term R&D as well as trade relationships, means that the three major industrial regions will be tied more and more closely together, enhancing convergence. That does not mean that regional policies will become less effective in the future. On the contrary, regional factors that determine the concentration of niches of particular industries may well become more, not less, important. The combination of convergence and global networks suggests new patterns of specialization that will alter the nature of regional cooperation and competition.

Convergence

Over the past decade a growth industry has developed around studies of the decline of the U.S. economy. Paul Kennedy's *The Rise and Fall of the Great Powers* published in 1987—with its thesis that "imperial overstretch" leads to excessive defense spending that crowds out private investment, lowers economic growth, and brings down great powers—came at the crest of a wave of writing on the decline in U.S. productivity growth, the apparent triumph of Japanese corporatism, and the emergence of twin U.S. budget and trade deficits.[8] Improved U.S. economic performance in the mid-

1980s muted some of this criticism, but low-growth concerns returned in force with the recession of 1991 and its impact on the 1992 presidential campaign. The facts do not support the thesis of U.S. economic collapse, but they do show that convergence in economic standards and growth rates across Europe, Japan, and the United States is proceeding. That convergence does not imply a sharp reversal in the central position of the U.S. economy, but it does suggest that the extent of U.S. hegemony will decline and that the brief period of U.S. dominance in most key technologies has ended.

The record of U.S. output per hour worked, or labor productivity, presented in table 1 shows that U.S. workers became the most efficient in the world around the turn of the century. After World War II the United States briefly held a dominant position, but by 1984 the gap had closed considerably. The precise size of the gap is subject to a number of problems in computing and comparing international productivity figures, but a range of comparisons using different exchange rate benchmarks and labor input concepts suggest that by 1990 France and Germany had moved even with the United States, while Japan and the United Kingdom had reached roughly 70 to 75 percent of the U.S. level, respectively.[9] The surprisingly weak showing of Japanese workers reflects a wide range of productivity across industries, with levels in some industrial sectors equal to the best in the world, but with other sectors trailing far behind.

There has been enormous confusion over interpreting the economic record, primarily because of a lack of precision in differentiating among the concepts of slowing rates of growth, falling behind, deindustrialization, industrial

Table 1
Comparisons of Productivity Levels Across Countries, 1870–1984

(in each year the leader's productivity is set to 100)

Country	1870	1913	1950	1984
France	49	49	42	98
Germany	53	56	34	90
Japan	17	18	14	56
United Kingdom	100	80	59	81
United States	90	100	100	100

Source: Computed from Angus Maddison, "Growth and Slowdown in Advanced Capitalist Economies: Techniques of Quantitative Assessment," *Journal of Economic Literature* 25 (June 1987), p. 683.

Note: Maddison estimates gross domestic product per hour worked and converts to dollars using purchasing power parity exchange rates. This table divides the estimates for each year by the figure for the leader, the United Kingdom in 1870 and the United States in other years, and multiplies by 100 to estimate each country's percentage of the leader's productivity.

leadership, and convergence.[10] Productivity growth rates in table 2 show that output per worker rose faster in other developed economies than in the United States after 1950, and the pace of productivity improvement fell off sharply in each of the countries listed after 1973. The slower productivity growth in the United States does mean that others are catching up to U.S. levels, but it does not mean that the United States will inevitably fall behind. Growth rates in gross domestic product (GDP) in table 3 show that while each country but the United Kingdom was catching up to the United States in the period from 1950 to 1973, the United States has held its own since then, with France growing at about the same rate and only Japan, the country furthest behind in productivity, growing more rapidly. The de-

Table 2
Comparisons of Average Annual Growth Rates in Productivity Across Countries in Selected Periods, 1870–1990

(percent per year)

Country	1870–1913	1913–1950	1950–1973	1973–1984	1984–1990
France	1.7	2.0	5.1	3.4	2.4
Germany	1.9	1.0	6.0	3.0	1.9
Japan	1.8	1.7	7.7	3.2	3.4
United Kingdom	1.2	1.6	3.2	2.4	1.4
United States	2.0	2.4	2.5	1.0	1.0

Sources: 1870–1984: Maddison, "Growth and Slowdown," table 2, p. 650. 1984–1990: computed from Organization for Economic Cooperation and Development, *Economic Outlook Statistics on Microcomputer Diskettes* (Paris, June 1992).

Table 3

Comparisons of Average Annual Growth Rates in Gross Domestic Product Across Countries in Selected Periods, 1870–1990

(percent per year)

Country	1870–1913	1913–1950	1950–1973	1973–1984	1984–1990
France	1.7	1.1	5.1	2.2	3.8
Germany	2.8	1.3	5.9	1.7	3.0
Japan	2.5	2.2	9.4	3.8	4.7
United Kingdom	1.9	1.3	3.0	1.1	3.0
United States	4.2	2.8	3.7	2.3	3.5

Sources: 1870–1984: Maddison, "Growth and Slowdown," table 1, p. 650. 1984–1990: United Nations, Department of International Economic and Social Affairs, *World Economic Survey, 1991* (New York: United Nations, 1991), p. 210.

cline in productivity growth in all of the countries after 1973 suggests that the root cause is not unique to the U.S. economy. Moreover, the growth rates fall together from earlier levels in the period from 1973 to 1984, and they rise together in the subsequent period, suggesting a convergence in growth patterns.

Kennedy's thesis concerns the proposition of moving ahead and falling behind and argues from historical example that great empires lose economic steam from trying to sustain military hegemony too long. Growth rates in the United States and elsewhere, however, have little to do with military outlays. GDP growth rates in table 3 show that the slowdown after 1973 was quite uniform across the major economic powers, and indeed the slowdown in the 1970s occurred at a time of declining, not rising, defense shares of total GDP. As Huntington has argued so effectively, there is little evidence to support Kennedy's view as a description of current U.S. experience. Defense outlays in the United States never reached the share of GDP in Kennedy's other examples, and his other hegemons never reached the level of economic dominance achieved by the U.S. economy. Although sav-

ings and investment are lower in the United States as a share of GDP than in Europe and especially Japan, that is because of the much higher share of GDP that goes to consumption, not to the share that goes to defense. In Huntington's words:

> Consumerism, not militarism, is the threat to American strength. The declinists have it wrong; Montesquieu got it right: "Republics end with luxury; monarchies with poverty."[11]

Another version of the United States in decline emphasizes the loss of U.S. economic leadership, the idea that the nation is losing its position among the leaders in industrial technology. It is certainly true that the United States has lost the dominant technology position it held after World War II, but it still ranks first in most technology areas. In spite of a popular misconception that the decline in overall U.S. productivity growth has resulted from a loss of competitiveness in manufacturing, the growth rate in manufacturing productivity has not declined. Productivity growth in manufacturing per year averaged 3 percent from 1950 to 1973, fell to just over 1 percent for 1974 to 1982, and then soared to 5 percent from 1983 to 1989.[12] The United States still leads the world in output per worker, whether output is measured by GDP, as in table 1, by industrial products in general, or by manufacturing in particular. By one estimate, in 1989 manufacturing productivity in Japan and Germany stood at 80 percent of the U.S. level.[13] It is certainly true that Japan now leads the United States in productivity in some key manufacturing categories including transport equipment, machinery, and electrical equipment, but the overall record would still make the U.S. economy the world's industrial leader by any reasonable standard.

Another related misconception is that the United States is becoming deindustrialized by low manufacturing productivity growth, which is reducing the U.S. share of world manufacturing markets and driving workers to the lower-wage, slow productivity-growth services sector. But from 1965 to 1980 service sectors grew more rapidly as a share of total employment overseas than they did in the United States. In fact the service sector share of real national output in the United States has not been increasing, nor has the industrial sector share been declining. The apparent shift has been caused by the increase in the relative prices of services, and in fact the relative wage of service workers has been rising, not falling. In other words, workers are not being forced out of manufacturing by declining market share, they are being pulled into services by higher wages there. Deindustrialization is not a real phenomenon in terms of output; it is an illusion created by shifting prices and wages.[14] It is certainly true that while the shares of real output remained constant, the portion of the labor force employed in industry and manufacturing declined from 1980 to 1990, but that decline coincided with higher rates of productivity growth in those sectors than in other sectors of the economy. In short, U.S. productivity problems do not originate in the manufacturing and high-technology areas. In fact, the United States maintains its lead in the share of high-technology exports in world markets, and the major shift in the last two decades has been the improved position of Japan relative to Europe.[15]

A more persuasive interpretation of the data is that while the United States is not falling behind or deindustrializing, the economies of Japan and Europe have converged on U.S. productivity levels. We would expect growth rates to converge over time because followers have advantages in being able to borrow best industrial practices, often embodied in new capital, while the leader must absorb the costs and risks of developing new technologies.[16] Tables 1 and 2 suggest that other economies have in fact been converging on levels of U.S. productivity. The puzzle is not why convergence is occurring, but why the United States held out so long as a distant front-runner.

Before we race to implement policies to reverse the decline in U.S. productivity growth, we need to understand the sources of the productivity leadership the United States displayed earlier. It has been suggested that the U.S. surge to industrial supremacy after 1900 was based on an integrated internal market, the growth of transportation infrastructure, and the simultaneous development of resource extraction and specialization in industrial technologies that complemented those natural resources. Although the U.S. cost advantage in world mineral markets subsequently faded, the accumulated base of an educated work force and science-based technologies gave the United States a dominant position in a wide range of industries after World War II.[17] From that perspective, the unique advantages that sustained relatively high productivity growth in the immediate postwar period may now have faded. In particular, integration of world markets permitted other countries to gain the advantages of mass production, and large Japanese and European investments in education and R&D created the social conditions required for convergence.[18]

The point is not that the United States is destined to remain the world's productivity leader forever. It would be naive to assume that would be the case, but it is equally naive to expect that the United States will fall behind as other industrialized countries surge past it. Others will encounter problems in sustaining high productivity growth as they lose the advantages of technological followers and are forced to deal with lagging agricultural and services sectors.

Certainly large U.S. budget deficits constrain U.S. public and private investment, and policies to reduce the size of those deficits are clearly in order. U.S. trade imbalances and the loss of competitiveness in some key industries also pose serious challenges for economic policy. But while these are important issues that require attention, they have often been linked with broader arguments about U.S. decline. Convergence in economic performance across regions, however, has far different implications than a systematic process of falling further and further behind. Proponents of reform must, of course, show that U.S. problems are serious in order to stimulate action, and that may lead well-meaning analysts to exaggerate U.S. decline. There is also a danger, however, that excessive alarm could trigger unwarranted and counterproductive intervention in national and international markets. Indeed, the continuing growth of the U.S. economy depends on access to dynamic global networks.

Global Networks

Convergence in economic performance among the major economic powers has been reinforced by the emergence of global industrial networks that, driven by the revolution in information technologies, are transforming international markets, shifting traditional patterns of industrial organization, changing the specialization of labor, altering patterns of research, development, and innovation, and accelerating the integration of global capital and product markets. The competition that will determine future U.S. economic performance, living standards at home, and the ability to influence events abroad, will be waged in those global networks. Although the competition begins with the United States still in an economic leadership position, sustaining that lead will require an understanding of how globalization is proceeding and how regions can influence the process.

Global networks spring from regional home bases that provide competitive advantages to industries, or niches within industries, based on economies of scale and scope and the unique characteristics of local markets. Some standardized activities are footloose, shifting from one region to another in response to fluctuations in the costs of labor and capital or tax incentives. Other high-value, specialized activities concentrate in network nodes, or regions that contain firms linked to several intersecting networks. As a result, regions still matter, but they matter in ways that differ from the classical model of trade based on resource endowments. The key in the new competition is the ability to create the specialized resources that develop nodes in the global network. Economic strategy must therefore come directly to grips with the dynamic nature of "factor creation" and its impact on the location of high-value activities in global networks. Before proceeding to the full implications of convergence and global networks for national strategy, we need to examine how global networks are evolving and how the location of network nodes might be influenced by public policy.

Networks. Network concepts are transforming the global workplace and creating new forms of interaction across traditional enterprises. The key aspects of the new network structures include shifts from hierarchical to more horizontal relationships and a growing emphasis on long-term cooperation, both driven by the need and possibilities for more complete and timely communication. As Anthony Carnevale, reporting on the work of the Hudson Institute's Workforce 2000 project, argues, the workplace is being transformed by networks that build from individual work teams through links across organizations:

> Network structures grow from within and eventually extend beyond the boundaries of traditional organizational structures. . . . The whole organization becomes a network of working teams. In turn, the organization is a member of a network made up of other organizations that are its suppliers, customers, regulators, and financial backers.[19]

As a result, jobs are being redefined by the requirements for greater coordination, both within and outside the enterprise. The core corporation is itself a network linking strategic insight

at the center to more autonomous points on the periphery that are in turn connected to other networks.[20] The critical tasks of the network involve the exchange and processing of information, creating a new set of critical skills and increasing the services component of total output. Robert Reich makes this point:

> In such global webs, products are international composites. What is traded between nations is less often finished products than specialized problem-solving (research, product design, fabrication), problem-identifying (marketing, advertising, customer consulting), and brokerage (financing, searching, contracting) services, as well as certain routine components and services, all of which are combined to create value.[21]

The new networks extend beyond the traditional exchange of goods and services across enterprises to include expanding cooperation in R&D.[22] The number of interlocking research agreements among corporations in the information technology industry has been exploding over the last decade. Separate clusters of arrangements across information technology firms are dominated by regional groups of Japanese, European, and U.S. companies, although the linkages also extend across regions.[23] This same transfer of technology across horizontally linked Japanese firms goes beyond the traditional *keiretsu*, or business group structure. Ken-ichi Imai calls the new configurations "network industrial organizations" to emphasize the central role given to creating and exchanging information in such enterprises.[24]

Although the use of the term *network* is widespread, its precise meaning varies in applications across fields from electronics to sociology. In a

299

sense, everything is "networked" to everything else: more precision is needed to make the concept useful. Shumpei Kumon has provided the most precise formulation to date by classifying social systems according to the dominant form of interaction among actors in the system, which he divides into three categories: threat-coercion, exchange-exploitation, and consensus-inducement. In this framework the nation-state is an organization dominated by a threat-coercion orientation based on international law; the modern industrial organization based on property rights would be in the exchange-exploitation category; and organizations featuring consensus-inducement relationships based on information rights would be "modern network organizations." The new organizations evolve from the growing importance of shared information:

> The sharing of information and knowledge—about recognition and evaluation of facts, the setting of goals, and action to achieve those goals—is the prime concern of networks in general and network organizations in particular.[25]

Kumon has identified the key aspect of the new network relationships: the critical importance of communications flows. Of course, multinational firms have existed for a long time, but the essential difference is that the new network arrangements are not based on the ownership of subsidiaries in a hierarchical structure, nor on the arms-length impersonal interaction of the market, but on shifting patterns of personal interaction across firms based on information exchange. As a result the key players in the new system are the strategic brokers who are constantly creating and editing global networks. Vertically structured, hierarchical firms, with clear divisions of

responsibility across different corporate levels and a top-down centralized information flow, are being overwhelmed by new organizations structured around a more horizontal flow of information within and across traditional corporate boundaries. These network industrial firms are winning the information technology competition.

Individual firms cannot afford the enormous costs nor bear the high risks of remaining at the cutting edge of all the technologies that are integrated in new products, but they also cannot miss a breakthrough that could create whole new product lines. Sharing proprietary information has enormous risks, but the risks of isolation from new technologies may be even greater. Network structures permit the development of trust needed for balancing exchanges over an extended period without the inflexibility that creeps into hierarchical organizations.

The emergence of global networks provides a clear challenge to traditional ways of thinking about national strategy. If firms are no longer national champions whose profits are closely tied to national markets but brokers linked in global networks, the pursuit of national economic interests through the support of "national" firms becomes problematic. If the exchange of value occurs by electronic transmission rather than the transfer of products, traditional commercial policies may be less important than policies that influence the location of network nodes. The new network structures are changing the organizing principles for the analysis of power. Albert Bressand makes this point:

> In such an environment, power will tend to reside in the capacity to influence interconnection and access rather than in the capacity

to enforce borders, a change that obviously is not confined to the economy but has deep repercussions for the national and international society.[26]

From this network perspective, national strategy will depend less on confrontation with opponents and more on the art of cooperation with competitors. National neomercantilist policies that attempt to shield "national" firms from "international" competition might simply isolate domestic workers from the high-value jobs available through global networks.

Network Nodes. How can public policy influence patterns of network "interconnection and access"? Global networks are transforming politics and economics by altering the national identity of products, technologies, corporations, and industries.[27] As a result, international competition will increasingly depend on the relative competence of the one resource that does not flow freely across borders in international markets—people. In Reich's terminology "high-value" businesses, based on specialized problem-solving skills provided by "symbolic analysts," are needed to ensure competitive advantage against "high-volume" foreign firms, because it is not products but skills that are traded in the global webs.[28] One dimension of national strategy must address the education of a labor force with the skills needed in the global economy. From a network perspective, labor with the appropriate skills will create network nodes of high-income activities.

Other factors are also important in capturing high-value network activities, and a substantial literature emphasizes the multiple sources of stability of regional network nodes.[29] For example, Michael Porter shows that data on 10 nations and over 100

industries indicate that leading industrial firms have stable ties to specialized regions. Porter argues persuasively that successful firms become masters of their "value systems," which include the firm's suppliers, distributors, and customers. Operating from a "home base" where the firm defines its strategy, develops its core products and process technologies, and maintains its most sophisticated production, the global firm reaches out through a "global network" of activities. The location of the home base is determined by a "national diamond" composed of factor conditions, demand conditions, related and supporting industries, and firm strategy, structure, and rivalry.[30] Porter's analysis correctly focuses on the new reality that competitive advantage lies not in the nation's endowment of resources, but in the pressure the environment places on the firm to invest and innovate. Sustainable competitive advantage in high-value products and technologies comes from the creation of "advanced" factors—such as communications infrastructure, graduate engineers, and research institutes—and "specialized" factors that are tailored for use in particular industries. The private sector creates those factors in response to constantly shifting international standards.[31]

Network nodes, then, depend on labor skills that evolve in a broader context of factor creation driven by education and training systems, public and private R&D, adaptation of innovations into commercially successful processes and products, and an environment of supporting services. National characteristics such as social and political stability, the definition of property rights, the structure of factor, product, and financial markets, labor-management relationships, the science and technical infrastructure, the

Labour Skills

education system, and attitudes toward innovation, all constrain a nation's approaches to factor creation and thus limit the industries in which the nation can successfully compete. Within that national environment, the complex processes of innovation and factor creation help to determine the structure of industry competitive advantage and hence the rate of productivity growth.

The synergies among the determinants of competitive advantage produce advantages to industrial concentration that cause the structure of competitive advantage, and hence the location of network nodes, to persist over time. The processes of concentration are "path-dependent" in the sense that early events change costs of future production, so network nodes tend to endure. A textile mill, for example, might be located on any of several different rivers in a region, but after the first mill is established, others might gain significant cost advantages from locating on the same river. Transitory advantages become locked into particular regions through the development of a pool of specialized labor, supporting trade and services, and the sharing of technological ideas.[32] The most spectacular current examples of concentration are in the industries that trade services, such as Hartford's insurance, Chicago's futures trading, entertainment in Los Angeles, and even Silicon Valley and Route 128, which are more centers for technological services than of production.[33] Improved communications and the reduction in transportation costs and trade barriers that have facilitated global markets have arguably increased the importance of these regional concentrations, because firms can leverage their local competitive advantages into wider and wider markets.[34]

The persistence of network nodes,

or home bases, suggests a potential for strategy to influence the location of economic activity despite the prevalence of globalization. Regional distinctions persist in part because global firms must operate from and sustain large positions in their home markets. Moreover, despite the globalization of wholesale finance, regional differences in capital costs persist, perhaps because retail banking practices differ and exchange rate risks vary across regions. As a result, trade and technology policy differences sustain separable regions centered on the United States, Europe, and Japan, in which the rate of intraregional trade is growing faster than interregional trade.[35]

This analysis of the factors that influence the location of network nodes suggests a potential role for national or regional "strategic trade" policies to gain market share, lower production costs, and alter competitive advantage.[36] Japanese encouragement of the semiconductor industry might provide an example of success with such a policy. European subsidies have allowed Airbus to achieve a growing share of the commercial aircraft market, although it is not yet clear that Airbus will ever be profitable without the subsidies. At this point the evidence suggests that the short-term gains from government intervention in noncompetitive markets remain small.[37] Nonetheless, the strategic trade arguments make the superiority of free markets, particularly in high-technology areas, an empirical rather than a purely theoretical issue. Moreover, when the strategic trade arguments are linked with technology policies the dynamic impacts could be significant.

Competing technological policies across regions provide a potential realm for strategic efforts to capture network nodes, particularly in industries with broad impacts on other industrial sectors. If innovation and the creation of advanced and specialized factors are the keys to competitive advantage, many analysts argue that government assistance to promote innovation and factor creation might be in order. The central problem with such assistance is that market competition provides the driving force for innovation and creativity geared to commercial applications, and without that market test it is difficult to assess the future returns to government programs. Government intervention might, however, be useful if it is geared to correcting market failures, such as the private sector's reluctance to pursue projects not all of whose benefits can be appropriated by the firm. For example, if the project benefits all companies in an industry equally, no single company may have sufficient incentive to pursue the investment. In addition, the scale of some forms of R&D and the risks of failure to produce productive innovations may be so high that the private sector cannot pursue projects for which public benefits may outweigh public costs. Although there are clear theoretical justifications for some government support of innovation and factor creation, the precise level and form of that intervention remain controversial, and differing policies across various nations remain a source of friction. Writing on "national systems of innovation" has emphasized the justifications for alternative approaches to innovation across regions, although there is controversy over whether or not national borders are still important given the structure of internationally networked technology markets.[38]

The strategic trade and technology arguments become more persuasive when they are combined, because it is conceivable that a strategy for capturing critical technologies through strategic trade policies could have large dynamic effects. Some argue that there are strategic industries with large, long-term impacts on other sectors; that capturing them requires domestic production of components as well as products (semiconductors as well as computers); that technological development is path-dependent so you cannot just jump in at the next technological level; and that while the short-run gains from strategic trade policies are small, their long-term impact by capturing strategic technologies may be very large.[39] Those arguments provide a foundation for the use of government policy to attract and defend regional network nodes containing high-value activities with the potential for influencing long-term technological patterns. John Zysman correctly identifies technology policy and the regional competition for strategic industries as central issues for national strategy:

> Individually the components of a policy of technological development are already difficult international issues—intellectual property and anti-dumping or subsidy policies are examples—but when taken together as a matter of how to generate and retain advantage in technologies and industries on which future development will rest they are the basis of real conflict amongst the three regions of the Western economy.[40]

In sum, convergence in economic performance among the major economic powers does not mean that the United States is destined to fall behind new industrial leaders, but it does mean that future competition will occur on a more equal footing. That competition will center on efforts to capture the nodes of global networks that have resulted from the revolution in information technology. Earlier

U.S. advantages from an abundance of natural resources, a large integrated national economy that permitted mass production, and then a large lead in science-based R&D, have faded. In the new competition for network nodes, the United States will have to rely on other sources of competitive advantage by promoting the creation of the advanced and specialized factors valued in emerging global networks. The tactics to be used in the competition remain controversial, but the evidence is that the competition is already well under way and that it will focus on attempts to capture nodes of high-value activities in the context of global networks. As a result national strategy must reconcile cooperation in building global networks with the competition for network nodes.

Cooperative Competition

Theodore Moran argues that the United States is in decline but that the process is reversible, and that there are two competing grand strategies for achieving this: "sophisticated neomercantilism" and "transnational integration." Sophisticated neomercantilism would include managed trade to ensure market share for "national" firms in critical industries and swift reprisals against unilaterally defined unfair practices in U.S. markets, such as dumping goods below the cost of production or foreign subsidies for exports. Foreign investment in the United States would be carefully reviewed, public investment funds would be targeted on "national" champions, and transborder corporate alliances would be scrutinized to ensure U.S. firms could sustain favorable market positions.

The cluster of policies aimed at transnational integration, on the other hand, would feature trade liberalization along multilateral lines, generally open investment policies with performance requirements to enmesh foreign firms in the U.S. industrial base, the use of R&D credits for both domestic and foreign firms to promote the development of critical technologies, and a general presumption in favor of global alliances. In Moran's view the ultimate choice of a grand strategy depends not only on technical assessments of the effectiveness of the different policy components but also on an evaluation of the international repercussions of the regional confrontation implicit in the sophisticated neomercantilist approach and of the burdens of international leadership implicit in the transnational integration approach. He correctly notes that the appeal of the transnational integration strategy would be enhanced if U.S. budget deficits were reduced and the macroeconomic house were in better order.[41]

Although Moran overstates the extent of U.S. decline, his presentation of the two alternatives for grand strategy is compelling. The cluster of policies he calls "transnational integration" comes very close to what I have defined as "cooperative competition." Cooperative competition is superior to sophisticated neomercantilism on many counts. In the context of global networks that are increasingly the source of dynamic technological change, the economic risks of isolation implicit in sophisticated neomercantilism are enormous. Moreover, the sophisticated neomercantilist approach is inconsistent with the nature of the broader political and military challenges national strategy must also address, including arms proliferation, internal wars, the AIDS epidemic, environmental decay, drug traffic, and humanitarian relief efforts. The complexity of those challenges, and the limitations of national resources and approaches for dealing with them, mean that cooperation in political and security networks will be essential. The idea of networks is relevant here because of the increasing importance of the coordination of information flows in dealing with those sophisticated problems and because the precise set of countries willing to cooperate on a given issue will vary over time. As a result, international organizations will require greater flexibility in organizing themselves for specific tasks. Global political and security networks will perform the same kinds of functions as economic networks, providing an infrastructure that will enhance cooperation and constrain the nature of competition. From that perspective neomercantilism, sophisticated or otherwise, would constitute a set of economic policies that are inconsistent with the broader requirements of grand strategy.

Convergence in the economic performance of the three leading economic regions and the emergence of global networks underscore the importance of cooperative competition. Cooperation across those regions will be essential to avoid confrontations over the location of network nodes that could undermine the advantages of global networks. A narrow focus on "relative" U.S. economic performance might well miss the point that the level of economic well-being increasingly depends on the ability to operate in integrated world networks. Although it may well be possible to influence the location of network nodes, the form of the competition must be consistent with the need to cooperate in constructing and sustaining global political, security, and economic net-

works. In contrast to the zero-sum nature of cold war military confrontation with clear winners and losers, the creation of cooperative global networks is a non-zero-sum exercise in which all competitors can gain, albeit to differing degrees. In short, in the new environment the "competitive state" must promote cooperative competition.

The essence of the cold war strategy was economic and political isolation of the Soviet Union, bilateral nuclear deterrence, forward deployment of U.S. forces in standing alliances based on containment, economic and technological leadership by U.S.-dominated multinational firms, and catch-up growth in Europe and Japan. The new strategy of cooperative competition would be defined more in terms of networks of information flows among equals that provide for enhanced cooperation on technological developments and potential responses to international crises in a framework of shifting ad hoc coalitions and intense economic competition.

More broadly, the strategy of cooperative competition recognizes the key role of technological innovation and economic growth in meeting broad national goals, including internal well-being as well as external security. The economic dimension of the strategy stresses the reality that while the United States and its allies are building an international infrastructure that will improve the well-being of all the participants, they will still be competing with each other for markets. Although the United States needs to cooperate in providing the essential public goods that make international markets operate effectively and permit the mobilization of resources in response to common interests, it also needs to ensure that domestic firms

305

are not disadvantaged in those markets.

Implications of Cooperative Competition

Cooperation. In the post–cold war era, the legitimacy for international action will increasingly derive less from narrowly defined security interests and more from international consensus on common approaches to key global problems such as the environment, the AIDS epidemic, drugs, the proliferation of weapons of mass destruction, the destabilizing consequences of internal wars, and humanitarian relief efforts. The complex problems of economic restructuring and defense conversion in the states of the former Soviet Union, "ethnic cleansing" in Yugoslavia, and starvation in Somalia suggest the scope of problems that will clearly be beyond the resources of any great power, including the United States. Cooperative international networks that can develop consensus and coordinate responses will be essential in dealing with those challenges. Local and regional political factors will inevitably change the coalition of potential actors in any given instance, so the international networks must be flexible enough to accommodate a changing cast of players in each instance. International burden sharing will then be measured in national contributions not to any one effort, but to the longer-term record of cooperation and commitment of resources in those instances permitted by unique national conditions.

The strategy of the United States, then, would be to play the role of strategic broker, forming, sustaining, and adjusting international networks to meet a sophisticated array of challenges. Charles Kindleberger stresses the importance of U.S. leadership in providing the essential public goods of what might be defined as network creation and maintenance.[42] Others lament the passing of U.S hegemony and the absence of a new hegemon that could take on these burdens, although coordination among a small group of states might provide those public goods as the relative U.S. position declines.[43] U.S. leadership should be focused on creating networks that will allow coalitions to act in concert because in the new global environment unilateral actions will be increasingly ineffective. Although the relative U.S. economic position has declined, it remains the only superpower and it still brings a unique array of advantages to the task of strategic broker, including economic influence, strategic military mobility, advanced communications, ethnic diversity, political stability, a strong democratic tradition, diplomatic alliances, and an established record of assuming an impressive share of the burdens of international responsibility. In short, U.S. strategy would be to help forge an array of international networks that would permit the international community to act in concert without the United States itself being forced to commit a disproportionate share of resources.

Ironically, from this perspective organizations such as the North Atlantic Treaty Organization (NATO) that now appear to some analysts as cold war relics are actually invaluable international networks for coordinating common responses in a host of situations. NATO provides precisely the kind of command, control, communications, intelligence, and logistics networks required for cooperative security or humanitarian efforts. Whether that particular organization will be the instrument for intervention is less im-

Institution [handwritten annotation]

portant than the network relationships that will make cooperative efforts more feasible and efficient. Although NATO played a relatively minor direct role in Desert Shield and Desert Storm as an organization, the political and military networks it helped create were invaluable. Cooperative regimes on nonproliferation, the United Nations, the General Agreement on Tariffs and Trade (GATT), the World Bank, the International Monetary Fund, and other similar organizations provide established networks in which the United States has enormous influence and through which it can pursue cooperative competition. This does not suggest a surrender of U.S. sovereignty to international organizations: regional competition will remain intense and the United States has important regional interests. It does, however, imply that U.S. strategy should seek to extend leverage through cooperation in international organizations to shape and restrain the form of regional competition.

Competitiveness. Cooperative competition underscores the importance of economic strength as the foundation of national strategy, and economic strength depends on sustaining high and growing levels of productivity among U.S workers in the face of intense international competition. Despite the short-term dislocations of international integration, the United States should welcome the competition because it will induce the creation of the specialized and advanced factors of production needed for competitive advantage. Indeed, international networks will channel information, technology, and resources to those economies that provide the best home bases for each industrial sector. The key issue then is how each region is positioned for success in the home

base competition, and what ground rules will be followed in competitive trade, industrial, and technology policies.

Virtually all analysts begin with the need for reform of education as a first step in improving U.S. competitiveness.[44] Next comes lowering the cost of capital through increased national savings, deficit reduction, and tax incentives for productive investment. The solutions here seem clear, although the short-run political problems will be enormous.

The next tier of potential reforms deals with coordination of strategic trade, industrial, and technology policies that are more controversial, particularly when they involve replacing market forces in picking the winners of the future. Policies toward particular industries can easily be distorted by special interests, and the record of industrial policies in other countries has been mixed at best.[45] The global network framework also makes it difficult to define national firms or to anticipate the full ramifications of any purely domestic policy. The approaches with the most promise, like education reform, deal with the processes of innovation and factor creation at a level above individual industries, focusing on compensation for market failures and emphasizing the need for competition within global networks. Instead of attempting to block the operation of global networks, effective strategy should center on steps to enhance efficiency within the new global structures.

Consensus is growing on two points that can enhance U.S. competitiveness in this new environment. First, government policies in a wide variety of areas—from health care, to the environment, to product safety, to antitrust, and a host of others—do affect productivity and hence competitiveness, but these policies are not centrally coordinated so as to assess those consequences. The role of national strategy is precisely to highlight the impact of policies on issues with the highest national interest and to force coordination and an assessment of trade-offs within that strategic context. That function should now be performed by the newly organized National Economic Council.[46]

Second, looking across the continuum of trade, industrial, and technology policies, the latter appear to offer the most fruitful areas for strategic review. The international trade framework is established in the GATT process, and although progress on the tough issues of agriculture and international property rights has been slow and painful, there is at least consensus on what constitutes "sin" in the trade area even if states have not yet agreed to sin no more. Regional progress and pressure through the North American Free Trade Agreement (NAFTA) should provide additional pressure within GATT to help open regional markets.[47] Similarly, industrial policies targeted on specific industries do not look any more promising now than they have for the last decade. In the contest between bureaucrats and the market in picking the winners of the future, the market appears to be the clear winner.[48]

Technology policies, however, at least warrant careful review as strategic instruments for several reasons. First, the reduction in defense research, development, and procurement means that the de facto technology policy of the United States is changing in important ways, and its government will need to decide if technology programs should be supported more explicitly.[49] Second, the interaction between government laboratories, research universities, and the private sector can have

important synergies if it is tied to reaction to market forces, particularly at the level of "pre-competitive research" where there are applications in several industries.[50] New steps to integrate government laboratories with the private sector may suggest future patterns of cooperation. Third, focus on the innovation climate in general, rather than the promotion of specific technologies, provides the potential for enhancing productivity growth with the least downside risk. Policies such as tax incentives to encourage factor creation most closely match the results of research on the development of home bases for competitive advantage, and they are somewhat less susceptible than commercial or industrial policies to political pressure from particular interests.

Conclusion

Cooperative competition is a strategic framework for examining options, not a list of specific policy proposals. It does not propose a new world order in the sense of a desired set of outcomes or a fixed set of institutional relationships. Instead, it recognizes that international networks are an integral part of the new economic and political environment and that their structure will be modified by the strategic brokers of the future. The network perspective provides a flexible format for viewing emerging global regions that have less to do with geographic distinctions than with shifting patterns of interconnection.

Convergence and global networks have changed the economic landscape just as the end of the Cold War has changed the political and military environment. Regional competition for the home bases of global networks poses a challenge for U.S. strategy, and there is a real risk that the com-

The Business Response to the Global Marketplace

Murray Weidenbaum

THE GLOBAL MARKETPLACE had surely arrived when villagers in the Middle East followed the Gulf War on Cable News Network (CNN), via Soviet government satellite and through a private subsidiary of a local government enterprise. Both public and private businesses were involved, and they were located on three different continents. This increasing globalization of the marketplace is forcing individual enterprises to pay more attention to international developments and to adjust their structure and methods of operations to a broader and more rapidly shifting economic environment.

A number of other more quantitative indicators give a sense of the global marketplace. A rising share of the products manufactured in the United States (perhaps one-half or more) have one or more foreign components. Ford's Crown Victoria has a foreign content of 27 percent, while 25 percent of Honda's U.S.-manufactured Accord is made overseas.[1] This development was nicely summed up in a recent conversation. The customer asks the auto dealer, "Is this car made in the United States?" The

Murray Weidenbaum is Mallinckrodt Distinguished University Professor and director of the Center for the Study of American Business at Washington University in St. Louis. He also serves as cochairman of the CSIS International Research Council.

salesman responds with another question, "Which part?"

A second way of looking at the global marketplace is to consider that one-half of all imports and exports—what governments label foreign trade—is transacted between domestic companies and their foreign affiliates or foreign parents. That is true in the United States, the European Community (EC), and Japan. From the viewpoint of political geography, the activity is classified as foreign commerce. But from an economic viewpoint, these international flows of goods and services are internal transfers within the same company.[2] That is the global enterprise in full operation.

One final indicator: Despite the massive and well-known U.S. trade deficit, U.S. companies sell to and in other nations as much as, if not more than, "foreign" companies sell in and to the United States.[3] This leads to a related set of questions on which experts answer differently: Is Honda USA part of the U.S. economy? What about IBM in Tokyo? What is clear is that the consequences of the internationalization of business are profound for many firms. Half of Xerox's 110,000 employees work on foreign soil. Less than one-half of Sony's employees are Japanese. More than half of Digital Equipment's revenues come from overseas operations. One-third of

GE's profits arise from its international activities.[4]

Technology and economics are outpacing traditional ways of thinking about international politics. The standard geopolitical map is out of synchronization with the emerging business and economic map. Economic and technological forces are powerful agents for change.

A dramatic example is the Kuwaiti bank that was moved by facsimile machine. The day of the Iraqi invasion, the manager set up three open telephone lines with his office in Bahrain. Over two he transmitted all of the bank's key documents via fax. Over the third, he checked to make sure that each page was being received. From time to time, the shooting around him slowed the process. But, before the end of the day, the necessary transmissions were complete. The next morning the bank opened up as a Bahraini institution neither subject to the freeze on Kuwaiti assets nor to Iraqi control.[5]

On a more aggregate level, business planning must increasingly be geared to the fundamental shifts that are occurring in national positions in the international economy. There are likely to be three regions of dominant economic power far into the twenty-first century. One is North America, led by the United States. Another is Japan and the other vibrant Asian rim economies. The third is the reinvigorated European Community, where change is taking place on an unprecedented scale. Business support for a North American free trade area arises in good measure in response to the competitive developments in Europe and Asia.

From all indications, the countries along the Asian rim will continue to grow rapidly during the 1990s. Japan and the four "little dragons" (Hong Kong, Singapore, Taiwan, and South Korea) are being joined by Thailand, Malaysia, and Indonesia as the newest members of the club of industrialized nations. Even so, radical changes in government policy toward business in the decade ahead will most likely occur, not across the Pacific Ocean, but across the Atlantic in Western Europe.

EC '92

The key structural shift in Western Europe is the economic integration of the 12 members of the European Community, scheduled to be completed in its essential elements by the end of 1992.[6] This phenomenon is usually referred to as EC '92 even though the actions being taken constitute an ongoing process that is likely to continue into 1993 and beyond. These governmental developments will have profound long-term effects on business productivity and international competitiveness.

Many discussions of EC '92 get mired in details and overlook the main points. The big positive about EC '92 is that the 12 countries are reducing restrictions on business, trade, and labor. People as well as goods and investments will be able to move readily from one of the Common Market nations to any other. That will tend to make industries more efficient as they achieve greater economies of scale and as standardization replaces 12 varieties of many products and services.

Not all of the changes will be beneficial to companies located outside of the community, however. A large negative, from the viewpoint of other nations, is that the trade wall around the EC is not coming down. Actually, the EC is toughening its external barriers to commerce. Enlightened economists are not supposed to use pejorative terms such as Fortress Europa, so let us cite some numbers instead. In 1960, before the Common Market gained momentum, more than 60 percent of the foreign trade of the 12 EC members was outside of the EC. Now over 60 percent of their trade stays in the EC—a complete reversal.[7] That ratio is bound to rise further as a result of EC '92.

This development toward a larger but more inward-looking community serves as a powerful reminder to companies headquartered elsewhere of the benefits of having strong European-based operations in order to take advantage of what is known as "national treatment." In effect, the EC is adopting the economic version of the U.S. driver's license rule, under which each state honors the licenses issued by the other states no matter how great the variation in the rules of qualification. The results will be similar.

Some of the freedoms that will contribute to the integrated market of Europe may not, however, be extended fully to U.S. firms doing business in the EC, in part because of restrictions imposed by U.S. regulatory authorities themselves. An example is "mutual recognition," meaning that each member of the EC recognizes the laws of the other members. Under this concept, European banks whose home nation permits underwriting and dealing in securities (i.e., investment banking) can provide that service in other member nations, even those that prevent their own banks from doing so. As European banks begin to provide such services beyond the borders of their home countries, the more restrictive regulations of other member nations are likely to loosen.

This regulatory convergence, however, could prove to be a competitive stumbling block for many of the U.S. banks in Europe because of more restrictive U.S. regulatory standards.

For example, the Federal Reserve System prevents foreign subsidiaries of U.S. banks from offering nonfinancial services "that could present undue financial risk or otherwise potentially harm the safety and soundness of the banking institution." As the Europe of the 1990s develops, the legal ability of large European banks to own nonfinancial companies and to provide more services than U.S. banks could substantially reduce the competitiveness of U.S. financial institutions operating in Europe.

The biggest negative coincident with the movement to EC '92 is that a more inward-looking Community is toughening its barriers to external commerce. The 1985 White Paper, which outlines the basic approach to the economic integration of the European Community, contains only a single sentence relating to the effects on relations with non-EC countries:

> In addition, the Community's trading identity must be strengthened, so that other trading partners will not be offered the benefits from the enlarged Community market without themselves being forced to make concessions.[8]

The French government, for example, has announced new regulations on TV programming (an important service export for the United States and one of the relatively few favorable items in its balance of trade). In the guise of promoting EC-wide TV programming, the French are limiting non-EC programming to 40 percent of total air time.

In private conversations, the Europeans tell U.S. companies not to worry, that most of their trade restrictions, such as reciprocity and domestic content rules, are aimed at Japan. It is, however, far more than a mere riposte for the United States to say that it does not know how good their aim is. The same restrictions that adversely affect Japan can keep out U.S. goods. This may especially be the case for the automobile "transplants," which are built in the United States by Japanese-owned companies. Moreover, if the products of the Asian rim countries are kept out of Europe, the Western Hemisphere is their major alternate market.

EC '92 will produce winners and losers, on both sides of the Atlantic. Likely winners will include strong U.S. firms with an established presence in Western Europe. High-tech, well-capitalized U.S. companies are accustomed to competing on a continentwide basis. They can use one EC country as a base to sell to the other eleven. General Motors and Ford have more Europe-wide strength than such European automakers as Volkswagen, Fiat, Peugeot, and Renault. The same holds true for computer manufacturers such as IBM, Digital Equipment, Unisys, and Hewlett Packard compared to their European counterparts.

The winners will also include the stronger, high-skilled European companies that will be enjoying the economies of scale and growing domestic markets. They should emerge larger than ever.

One category of losers from EC '92 will be the high-cost European firms that have been sheltered within their national markets. These tradition-bound companies will be hurt by continentwide competition. Cheap labor and tax incentives will no longer be key competitive factors. The backward areas, such as Italy's Mezzogiorno, will fall further behind. Realistically, not all barriers to business will be down. The French are not going to make a stampede for German wine, no matter how great the reduction of formal obstacles to intra-European trade.

Finally, many U.S. businesses are likely to be losers from European economic unification. They will find it more difficult to export to Europe. They will also face tougher competition in their domestic markets from stronger EC enterprises. The losers will include many companies that have not yet awakened to developments across the Atlantic. One recent survey found that less than one-half of all U.S. corporations had even heard about Europe '92. Only a small fraction of U.S. firms are responding to that strategic change.[9]

Beyond 1992

By the end of 1992, the economic integration of the present members of the European Community will be far advanced. Of the 300 actions sanctioned in a general way by the EC in 1987, about 250 have been presented as formal proposals, and 130 of them have been adopted by the EC Council of Ministers. Thus far, many of the measures that have passed are difficult, major items. For example, German and Italian regulations covering ingredients of beer and pasta, respectively, have been outlawed as policies that impede imports from other member countries that abide by the EC regulations.[10]

Although the member nations of the EC are expected to be working in harmony much of the time, each will continue to have individual values, cultures, and needs. Despite the substantial amount of progress being made toward full integration, each of the 12 countries will still retain its own currency (at least for the next few years), its own tax system, and, of course, its ultimate sovereignty. Perhaps even more fundamental are the differing national traditions, especially the nine languages that are spoken in the Community.[11]

The EC is not a static concept. It started with 6 countries—Germany, France, Italy, Belgium, the Netherlands, and Luxembourg. Gradually, it has expanded to 12—adding the United Kingdom, Ireland, Denmark, Greece, Spain, and Portugal. That is not the end of the line. Many other European nations are seeking admission. They have been told to wait until 1993 or later.

Austria is a logical candidate for early entry into the EC. Although its economy is modest in size, its admission could be a strategic move, especially since Vienna often views itself as a gateway to Eastern Europe. Most likely, Hungary would then be close behind in the waiting line in Brussels. Czechoslovakia and Poland might be next or, at the least, they could apply to become "associate members."

With Denmark already a member, the other Scandinavian countries are prime candidates for EC membership—Iceland, Sweden, Finland, and especially Norway. With the end of the Cold War, the traditional neutrality of some of these nations should no longer be a barrier to entering into a formal relationship with the EC. In any event, the trade barriers between the EC and the European Free Trade Association or EFTA will be disappearing soon (EFTA includes Norway, Sweden, Finland, Iceland, Austria, and Switzerland). The EC and EFTA are joining forces to form a "European economic space" free of trade barriers.

Looking beyond the initial adjustment period, an economically united Europe will become a political and economic superpower early in the twenty-first century if not sooner. As Stanley Hoffmann, chairman of the Center for European Studies at Harvard, notes in his comment on the European Community:

> Clearly, the purpose of the whole effort is not merely to increase wealth by removing obstacles to production and technological progress, but also to increase Europe's power in a world in which economic and financial clout is as important as military might.[12]

Consider the implications if and when the EC expands from 12 members to 16 or 20. Adding all those gross national products (GNPs) together shows that, in the 1990s, Western (and Central) Europe will become the world's largest market area, with concomitant economic and political power. Despite all the protestations of openness and friendship, the nations in Asia, Africa, and the Americas—and many of their business firms—will be on the outside looking in. Nor is the economic unification of Western and Eastern Europe a foregone conclusion.

Business Potentials in Eastern Europe

Four decades of Communist rule have left the economies of Eastern Europe in extremely poor shape. They are experiencing great difficulty converting their inefficient nationalized industries into competitive private enterprises. Because of the Marxist cliché that unemployment does not exist under communism, East European enterprises are notoriously overstaffed. One steel mill in Poland employs 30,000 workers to make the same amount of steel a U.S. company would make with 7,000.[13]

To make matters worse, Eastern

Europe lacks a business infrastructure, which is something so basic to the efficient functioning of a modern economy that Western nations take it for granted. These basic requisites for a private enterprise system include:

- a body of commercial law that is enforced;
- a credible accumulation of cost accounting data that can be used both for setting prices and making valuations of assets;
- personnel who can perform financial analyses;
- banks to provide credit on the basis of financial valuations rather than political determinations; and
- organizations to provide insurance for normal business risks.

In light of the criticism often hurled at these professions in the United States, it is fascinating to consider that Eastern Europe is a world with a shortage of lawyers, accountants, and insurance agents! From a positive viewpoint, that large area may provide a major new client base for many service enterprises headquartered in the more advanced economies.

Eastern Europe also needs generous supplies of capital from the United States and other capitalist nations. This is brought home by Lech Walesa's response to the numerous (and perhaps patronizing) statements by Americans that it is only proper for the United States to repay the moral debt it incurred when so many Poles—such as General Kazimierz Pulaski and General Tadeusz Kosciuszko—helped it during its critical formative period. Walesa on occasion has answered, "OK, so now send us General Electric, General Motors, and General Mills."

Attracting foreign capital in substantial amounts will not be easy. The recent credit history of the East European nations is abysmal. The East Europeans were brought up to hate greedy capitalists and their profiteering. But the move to capitalism (which seems to be an almost universal desire in those nations) will be difficult without capital and capitalists.

It also will be necessary for the rank-and-file employees of the East European nations to do a 180-degree turn in their attitude toward work. They must abandon their universal slogan, "They pretend to pay us and we pretend to work." Consider the thousands of East Germans who have been fired by their new West German employers because they were not in the habit of returning to work after lunch.

Not all East European nations are likely to make the transition to democratic capitalism; the most promising cases are Hungary, Czechoslovakia, and perhaps Poland. Some of the other countries, such as Bulgaria and Romania, may go the authoritarian route. Of course, it would be most heartening if several in fact demonstrate that a nation can return from communism to capitalism—a move that has yet to be accomplished anywhere.

Those countries that succeed could be tough competitors for the low-tech, high-labor-cost industries in the more advanced economies. They could, however, also become subcontractors and suppliers to established Western firms hard pressed by low-cost competitors. The high school education of East European workers is quite good as measured by standardized math and science tests.

The Soviet Union is conspicuously absent from this discussion of ascending economic powers. It is still very much a military superpower, but its economy—aside from the military sector—remains primitive, even if the current political and social instability can be overcome. According to the Soviet Academy of Sciences, Soviet computer capacity is less than one one-thousandth of that of the United States.[14]

Threats and Opportunities for Business

For the individual business firm, the rapid changes in the international economy offer both threat and opportunity. The opportunity arises as more of the developing countries enter the status of industrialized nations. Advanced economies are the best customers of other advanced economies. For example, Bangladesh is not an important customer of U.S. jet airplanes and grain, but Japan is. Yet at the same time home markets will become increasingly vulnerable to foreign competition.

Patterns of Business Adjustment. There is great similarity between the domestic threat of hostile takeovers and the loss of market position due to new foreign competition. In both cases, the firm is forced to review its strengths and weaknesses and to rethink its long-term strategy. Streamlining, downsizing, accelerating product development, and organizational restructuring are often responses to both internal takeover threats and foreign competition.

Stepping back and taking a longer-term perspective makes it clear that fundamental changes are occurring in the very nature of the private business enterprise. The most domestic-oriented firm is increasing its geographic reach as its suppliers and customers are, with increasing frequency, located on a variety of continents. Joint ventures are no longer an obscure legal form. To cite one example among many, over one-half of Corning Glass's profits come from joint ventures. Two-thirds of these cooperative endeavors are with a wide range of foreign companies, including Siemens and Ciba Geigy in Europe and Samsung and Asahi Glass in Asia.

Strategic alliances are no longer just a theoretical possibility; they, too, increasingly involve companies located on different continents. Philips N.V., the Dutch producer of consumer electronics, has cooperated extensively with Matsushita of Japan in developing new products such as compact discs and VCRs.[15]

Sweden's Volvo and France's Renault also have established a strategic alliance, with an explicit division of labor. Renault is doing diesel-engine development, while Volvo is handling advanced emissions controls. The two enterprises are also moving to coordinate parts purchasing, transportation and communication, and new-product strategy.[16] An interesting variation is the collaboration between the U.S. firm Digital Equipment Corporation and Italy's Olivetti & Co. The two companies are funding and sharing the results from Olivetti's research laboratory in Cambridge, England.[17]

Mergers and acquisitions increasingly involve crossing national boundaries and dealing with two or more national governments, as well as a variety of state, provincial, and local authorities. In 1985, business mergers within the United States accounted for 85 percent of global merger activity. By 1990, U.S. domestic mergers accounted for less than half of the worldwide volume. Most of the U.S. companies operating in Europe do so through subsidiaries resulting from acquisitions.[18]

Partially owned subsidiaries, associated firms, licensing, and correspondent relationships are also on the rise. Often the same companies engage in joint ventures to develop new products, coproduce existing products,

319

serve as sources of supply for each other, share output, and compete. There is no set pattern. Various companies—in the same nation and often in the same industry—are responding to ¯he global marketplace differently.

United Technologies exemplifies the use of geographic diversification on a global scale in developing new products. For its new elevator, its French division worked on the door systems; the Spanish division handled the small-geared components; the German subsidiary was responsible for the electronics; the Japanese unit designed the special motor drives; and the Connecticut group handled the systems integration. International teamwork cut the development cycle in half.[19]

IBM is often cited as the role model for foreign firms focusing on high-technology markets. Potential imitators note that the corporation's basic research laboratories are in Switzerland and Japan, as well as the United States. Its 30-odd research divisions are located around the world. Thus, the process of international technology transfer at IBM is often internal to the firm. Xerox Corporation is another interesting example of global production. Xerox has introduced some 80 different office copying machines in the United States that were engineered and built by its Japanese joint venture, Fuji Xerox Company.

The automobile industry provides a fascinating array of examples of interfirm and intercontinental endeavors. General Motors has joint ventures with Japan's Toyota and Suzuki and partial ownership of Sweden's Saab, Korea's Daewoo, and Japan's Isuzu and Suzuki. Volkswagen reports joint ventures with America's Ford and Japan's Nissan and Toyota, and has a stake in Czechoslovakia's Skoda.[20] Virtually all of these companies compete

with their partners and investors, at least to some degree.

The computer industry is not to be outdone in this regard. For example, Unisys is a customer of, a supplier to, and a competitor of IBM and Honeywell in North America, Fujitsu and Hitachi in Asia, and Phillips, Siemens, and BASF in Europe.[21] The trend is accelerating. In June 1991, AT&T, British Telecommunications, France Telecom, and Kokusai Denshin Denwa joined forces to provide large customers with a global communications network capability.[22]

Business Lessons for the Future. Some lessons can be learned from the experience of companies that do well in international markets. First, they change their basic corporate goals to conform to a global marketplace; for the most successful, top management leads that process of adjustment.[23]

Second, they translate a domestic advantage to create overseas opportunities by adapting their established home products to the local markets in other nations. Pall Filters, the major U.S. producers of wine filters, penetrated the sophisticated French market by designing a new French version of its filters. The company then went on to enter the Italian wine market with a second variation of its product.

In the service area, U.S. financial institutions compete internationally primarily by building on strengths developed in their domestic markets. Financial institutions in the United States and the United Kingdom have developed a high degree of technical expertise in constructing, managing, and marketing complex financial products and services used around the world. This expertise involves both the development of physical capital—primarily computer systems and software—and trained professionals and support staff with both technical and market knowledge.

For example, banks participate heavily in foreign exchange "swaps" related to balance sheet management because of their expertise in managing interest rate risks. U.S. investment bankers, in contrast, are more prevalent in the market for swaps related to new issues of securities. There is a broader sense in which financial institutions have sought competitive advantage in international markets through product specialization that mirrors their strength in domestic markets.[24]

Japanese banks, in contrast, initially penetrate an overseas market by serving the Japanese firms doing business there. Subsequently, they broaden their customer base (after learning more about the local market) to win local clients.[25]

The third lesson is that the successful global firms do not set up large international bureaucracies. One recent survey reported that the cost of the international staff rarely exceeds 1 percent of sales. Moreover, most overseas operations are run by foreign nationals who understand the local markets. Further, they start their foreign operations when the company is still of moderate size, contradicting the widespread notion that only giant companies can succeed overseas.

But it takes massive resources to provide a universal presence. Toyota, IBM, Phillips, DuPont, Bayer, Sony, and Unilever have expanded into almost all of the world's major markets.[26] A global economy, however, does not mean that every company should try to cater to every global market. Many small and medium-sized firms are learning the hard way to focus on specialty products and market niches where they have special advantages. For example, Sweden's L. M.

Ericsson sells very specialized state-of-the-art components for communications equipment in approximately 70 countries.[27]

Local offices provide a company with a built-in laboratory for developing new programs and servicing techniques that can be adapted throughout the global network. Moreover, the power of modern communications means that Manchester, England, and Louisville, Kentucky, are as much a part of the international marketplace as London and New York. A mix of smaller and medium-sized locations is part of a pattern that gives the modern corporation diversification and stability during periods of rapid growth and recession alike.

Finally, global successes encourage foreign subsidiaries to make innovations that can also be used in the home market. Dunkin' Donuts established its reputation in the United States by always having fresh doughnuts and coffee prepared on the premises. In Tokyo, however, land was too expensive for that procedure, so the company started preparing the doughnuts and coffee on the trucks bringing in supplies. The company is now starting to follow this practice in some of its domestic sites in central cities.

Clearly, there will be winners and losers as business adjusts. Not every company is going to be a grand success in the global marketplace of the 1990s. All this illustrates an earlier point: In change, there is both threat and opportunity—and the global marketplace is surely changing rapidly.

Important Public Policy Implications

The current legislative battles over trade protectionism and foreign investment restrictions are only the most obvious manifestations of the rising tension between domestic political forces and transnational economic influences. Although private enterprise is increasingly global (in purchasing, financing, research, and production as well as marketing), government policy remains parochial. Understandably, voters still care about jobs in their country, province, state, and locality, and politicians react to those sentiments.

Business and National Governments. The tension between business and government is nothing new. It has traditionally existed between large private enterprises and the rulers of developing countries. In fact, most countries restrict foreign investments in defense, public utilities, and the media. Quite a few governments require that a majority of the capital of local firms be owned by their own nationals. [28]

The tension between governments generally (both those with developing and those with more advanced economies) and the business firm is being exacerbated by the rapid rate of economic, social, and technological change. Fortunately, there is another force involved that is ultimately likely to carry the day—the citizen as consumer. Consumers vote every day of the week—in dollars, yen, deutsche marks, pounds, francs, and lira. The same protectionist-oriented voters, as consumers, purchase products made anywhere in the world. They give far greater weight in spending their own money to price and quality than country of origin. And they increasingly travel to, and communicate with, people in virtually every land.

Thus, without thinking about it, consumers are adapting to the global economy. After all, if consumers were not so globally oriented, the pressures for restricting international trade would not arise in the first place. In

the years ahead, the power of economic forces and technological change will increasingly force voters and government officials to adjust to the realities of the international economy. [29]

Meanwhile, some of the former *multinational* companies with large headquarters operations and a number of overseas subsidiaries are becoming *transnational* enterprises with activities and responsibilities spread more evenly around the world. For an increasing number of transnational companies, profits and revenues from abroad surpass those of the country of origin. Because the interests and stakeholders of these transnational businesses are located all over the globe, some of their leaders contend that they are losing their national identities and becoming "global citizens." [30]

Business and International Agencies. The transnational business firms also develop relationships with the international economic organizations established by governments. They participate actively in the business advisory committees of the Organization for Economic Cooperation and Development (OECD), the European Community, and the specialized agencies of the United Nations (UN), such as the Economic and Social Council and the International Labor Organization.

The rise of international regulatory agencies, in many ways, is an expected response of political forces to the global economy. Some types of supranational regulation are traditional, going back to the nineteenth century. For example, the forerunner of the International Telecommunications Union was established in 1865 as the International Telegraph Union. It dealt mainly with technical standards.

Some of the specialized agencies of the UN have moved ahead with the formulation of codes and guidelines. Examples range from the World Health Organization's Infant Formula Code, to the Food and Agricultural Organization's International Code of Conduct in the Distribution and Use of Pesticides, to the over 300 labor standards promulgated by the International Labor Organization. The latter in the aggregate have resulted in more than 5,000 government ratifications.

The UN's Economic and Social Council is developing a code governing multinational corporations. However, the effort has bogged down, given the complexities arising from the great variety of international business relationships (as described above). Also, the governments of the developing nations, in many cases, see a more activist role for the UN agencies than do the representatives of the more advanced economies, who are oriented to private-sector decision making in less regulated marketplaces.[31]

In a far more basic sense, the mobility of enterprises—of their people, capital, and information—is reducing the power of government at all levels. Some economists maintain that public-sector decision makers around the world are being forced to understand that in a very new way they have to become competitive in the economic policies they devise. Domestic policies that impose costs without compensating benefits or that reduce wealth substantially in the process of redistributing income undermine the competitive positions of domestic enterprises. The result is either the loss of business to firms located in other nations or the movement of the domestic company's resources to more hospitable locations.

Political scientists and economists have long since understood that people vote with their feet, leaving regions and nations with limited opportunity in favor of those that offer a more attractive future. In a day of computers, telephones, and facsimile machines, enterprises are far more mobile than that. Thus, the fear of losing economic activity to other parts of the world can be expected to reshape domestic political agendas in fundamental ways.[32] Moreover, more open economies characterized by governments that have less influence over private decision making will generate an unexpected side effect—the promotion of international harmony simply because of the growing economic incentives to avoid the devastation of war.

There is a positive role for government in dealing with the global marketplace and it is well known: Enhance the productivity and competitiveness of the enterprises located in the government's jurisdiction by reducing tax and regulatory burdens and lowering the real cost of capital through curbing deficit financing.

Also, antitrust laws need to be updated. It took decades for the U.S. Justice Department to acknowledge the role of imports in the domestic marketplace. Yet the "relevant market" (a key concept in antitrust enforcement) often now extends beyond the borders of the United States. Likewise, the geographic restrictions on U.S. banks, limiting them to a single state or region, prevent them from attaining the economies of scale and market positions that would match the now dominant power of Asian and European financial institutions.

Economic education at present faces the challenging task of helping citizens (consumers/taxpayers) to understand the increasingly global nature of economic life. It is true that it is easier to see the impact of foreign money in the domestic economy than it is to visualize the role of one country's investment in other nations. Yet the effects flow in both directions.

A quarter of a century ago, the citizens of Western Europe were complaining that the United States was making the world one big Coca-Cola franchise. The "American challenge" was a popular topic for public debates overseas. The U.S. reply was that U.S. investment benefited foreigners by creating employment, income, and tax collections in their countries. Although the shoe is now on the other foot, the results are very similar. Foreign investment is creating jobs, income, and tax revenue in the United States. Because the financing of outsized budget deficits drains off so much of U.S. domestic savings, that foreign money is a key factor in the continued prosperity of the United States.

In a positive way, U.S. public policy should focus on the government's area of primary responsibility: the education of the future work force. Given the international economy in which the next generation will be competing, it is sad to report that, compared to the students of most other industrial nations, U.S. students know less biology, chemistry, and math, understand little of foreign cultures, and rarely speak or read foreign languages.

The low literacy rates and high dropout rates cannot be blamed on foreigners. Dealing with domestic educational shortcomings is the unique responsibility of Americans. A well-educated citizenry is vital to the future of a democracy; it is also the key to achieving greater productivity and global competitiveness.

Work for this paper was supported by a grant from the William H. Donner Foundation.

Notes

1. Alex Taylor III, "Do You Know Where Your Car Was Made?" *Fortune*, June 17, 1991, pp. 52–53.

2. "America and Japan: The Unhappy Alliance," *Economist*, February 17–23, 1990, pp. 21–24; Jane S. Little, "Intra-Firm Trade," *New England Economic Review*, May–June 1987, pp. 46–51.

3. De Anne Julius, *Global Companies and Public Policy* (Rotterdam: RIIA/Pinter, 1990); Kenichi Ohmae, "The Interlinked Economy," *Chief Executive*, October 1990, p. 50.

4. Jeff Shear, "Foreign Investment Is Making a Borderless Corporate World," *Insight*, July 1990, p. 40.

5. Sandra Feustel, "How a Fax Machine Saved GIC," *Institutional Investor* 24 (September 1990), p. 78.

6. This section draws on Murray Weidenbaum and Mark Jensen, *Threats and Opportunities in the International Economy* (St. Louis: Washington University, Center for the Study of American Business, 1990).

7. Wilhelm Nolling, *Fortress Europe? The External Trade Policy of the European Communities* (Frankfurt, 1988), p. 31; *Basic Statistics of the Community*, 26th ed. (Luxembourg: Eurostat, 1989).

8. Cited in Nolling, *Fortress Europe?* p. 31.

9. "Calls Japan the One to Beat in Europe After 1992," *Electronic News*, September 1989, p. 37; see also Kenneth Oehlkers, "Are Top U.S. Executives Slow to Develop a Global Outlook?" *A. Gary Shilling's Insight*, June 1990, p. 5.

10. Michael Emerson, "The Emergence of the New European Economy of 1992," *Business Economics* 24 (October 1989), pp. 5–9.

11. Nolling, *Fortress Europe?* p. 26. The EC nations are trying to move toward a common value added tax rate, such as 15 percent, to expedite trade across the Community.

12. Stanley Hoffmann, "The European Community and 1992," *Foreign Affairs* 68 (Fall 1989), p. 43.

13. Murray Weidenbaum, "Poland: Another Middle Way?" *Society* 28 (November/December 1990), pp. 51–55.

14. Yuri N. Maltsev, "When Reform Collides

With Ideology," *American Enterprise* 1 (March/April 1990), p. 89.

15. David Lee, "Strategies for Global Competition," *Long Range Planning* 22, no. 1 (1989), p. 102.

16. Robert Simison and Stephen D. Moore, "Volvo Defends Alliance With Renault, Saying the Logic Will Soon Be Evident," *Wall Street Journal*, June 17, 1991, p. A–7.

17. Richard L. Hudson, "Digital and Olivetti Plan to Collaborate on Research Project at British Facility," *Wall Street Journal*, June 17, 1991, p. A5A.

18. Roy C. Smith and Ingo Walter, *The First European Merger Boom Has Begun* (St. Louis: Washington University, Center for the Study of American Business, 1991), p. 3.

19. "The Stateless Corporations," *Business Week*, May 14, 1990, p. 101.

20. Christopher Sawyer, "The Global Village," *Autoweek*, January 28, 1991, pp. 20–21.

21. Michael Blumenthal, "Macroeconomic Policy," in *International Economic Cooperation*, Martin Feldstein, ed. (Cambridge, Mass.: National Bureau of Economic Research, 1987), p. 16.

22. Robin Gareiss, "Carriers Set Global Plan," *Communications Week*, June 3, 1991, p. 1.

23. William Lilley, "How U.S. Companies Succeed in International Markets," *National Economists Club Summary*, December 1, 1987, pp. 1–3; Booz-Allen Hamilton survey reported by George Anders, "Role of Chief Is Seen Crucial in Going Global,"

Wall Street Journal, November 30, 1990, p. A–9.

24. Beverly Hirtle, "Factors Affecting the Competitiveness of Internationally Active Financial Institutions," *Federal Reserve Bank of New York Quarterly Review*, Spring 1991, pp. 38–51.

25. Rama Seth and Alicia Quijano, "Japanese Banks' Customers in the United States," *Federal Reserve Bank of New York Quarterly Review*, Spring 1991, pp. 79–82.

26. W. Chan Kim and R. A. Mauborgne, "Becoming an Effective Global Competitor," *Journal of Business Strategy* 9 (January/February 1988), p. 34.

27. Jordan D. Lewis, *Partnerships for Profit: Structuring and Managing Strategic Alliances* (New York: Free Press, 1990), p. 26.

28. Thomas N. Gladwin and Ingo Walter, *Multinationals Under Fire: Lessons in the Management of Conflict* (New York: John Wiley & Sons, 1980), p. 265.

29. Richard McKenzie and Dwight Lee, *Quicksilver Capital: How the Rapid Movement of Capital Has Changed the World* (New York: Free Press, 1991).

30. Wisse Dekker, "The Rise of the Stateless CEO," *CEO/International Strategies*, March/April 1991, p. 17.

31. Murray Weidenbaum, *Business, Government, and the Public*, 4th ed. (Englewood Cliffs, N.J.: Prentice-Hall, 1990), pp. 307–311.

32. Richard McKenzie, *The Global Economy and Government Power* (St. Louis: Washington University, Center for the Study of American Business, 1989), pp. 17–18.

The U.S. Leadership Role in World Trade: Past, Present, and Future

Ernest H. Preg

THE CRITICAL ROLE of leadership within the international trading system has been studied extensively. The United Kingdom's leadership role from the mid-nineteenth century to 1914 is widely recognized. The impact of the lack of leadership during the Great Depression of the 1930s, when world trade collapsed, is more controversial. Charles Kindleberger concluded that the depression was "so wide, so deep, and so long because the international economic system was rendered unstable by British inability and U.S. unwillingness to assume responsibility for stabilizing it." Even more pointed is his "main lesson of the interwar years . . . that for the world economy to be stabilized, there has to be a stabilizer—one stabilizer." For the trading system, the stabilizer had, inter alia, "to keep the import market open in periods of stress."[1]

From 1945 to 1980, the United States was the unquestioned leader in world trade. U.S. initiative led to the creation of the General Agreement on Tariffs and Trade (GATT) in 1947,

dedicated to nondiscrimination among trading partners and a mutual lowering of trade barriers. The timing and agenda of successive GATT "rounds" of negotiations were orchestrated by the United States, and they led to a dramatic reduction in tariffs for manufactured products. The almost continuous GATT rounds were also designed to repress protectionist pressure and were based on the "bicycle theory," whereby trade liberalization needs to move forward or else, like a bicycle, it will fall down. Finally, the United States played the stabilizer role by keeping its import market open in periods of stress, although with a significant lapse in 1971 when a temporary import surcharge was levied in conjunction with the break of the linkage between the dollar and gold.

The 1980s, however, were a period of important change in the world economy, including change in the U.S. leadership role. Globalization of markets was accompanied by an ideological consensus on the benefits of market-oriented national economies and open trade that swept away the old economic dichotomies of North versus South and East versus West. At the same time, industrial development, investment, and trade tended strongly

Ernest H. Preg holds the William M. Scholl Chair in International Business at CSIS and is currently writing a book on the Uruguay Round and the future of the international trading system.

to polarize regionally in Western Europe, North America, and East Asia (see table 1). About half of world trade now takes place within these three regions, and another quarter among them. The U.S. share of world trade did not change greatly, but the trade balance turned sharply negative, with the result that the United States shifted from largest creditor to largest debtor nation during the decade. Even more fundamental, the United States lost its heretofore commanding technological lead, especially vis-à-vis Japan, and thus its hegemonic position in industrial trade and investment.

The impact of these developments on the U.S. leadership role, and vice versa, can be assessed in terms of three distinct yet interacting aspects of trade policy leadership: (1) the role as stabilizer in periods of stress; (2) the GATT leadership role to strengthen the multilateral system; and (3) the

management role for transition to a "three-track" trading system.

The Stabilizing Role in Periods of Stress

The U.S. market remained surprisingly open to imports during the 1980s despite the surging trade deficit that peaked at $170 billion in 1987. The import surge came principally from Japan and other East Asian countries, but aside from voluntary export restraints on automobiles from Japan, which had become ineffective by the decade's end, and a few lesser restrictions, the United States provided the principal market for the extraordinary East Asian export-led growth of the 1980s. Even in the textiles and apparel sector, which is cluttered with bilateral quotas, U.S. imports rose from $8.9 billion in 1980 to $19.8 billion in 1985 and to $31.9 billion in 1990.

Table 1
The Tripolarization of World Trade
(Percentage of world imports of goods)

	1980	1990
I. Within the Three Poles		
OECD Europe	28.0	33.2
North America[a]	5.9	6.5
East Asia[b]	6.1	9.5
Subtotal (within)	40.0	48.2
II. Among the Three Poles		
Europe-North America	7.7	8.0
East Asia-North America	7.1	10.5
Europe-East Asia	4.6	8.8
Subtotal (among)	19.4	26.5
III. All Other	40.6	25.3

Sources: International Monetary Fund, Bureau of Statistics, *Direction of Trade Statistics Yearbook*, 1981 and 1991 (Washington, D.C.); Republic of China, Ministry of Finance, Department of Statistics, *Preliminary Statistics on Exports and Imports,* Taiwan area, December 1980 and 1990 (Taipei).

[a] U.S., Canada, Mexico
[b] Japan, South Korea, China, Taiwan, Hong Kong, ASEAN

Nevertheless, in the 1980s, the long-standing U.S. stabilizing role in world trade was severely challenged by the most wide-ranging domestic debate over trade policy since the 1930s. A plethora of congressional initiatives for import restrictions to counter the trade deficit were put forward. A domestic content requirement for automobiles received widespread support in 1986. A number of variations of a bilateral trade balance approach, with the implied threat of U.S. import restrictions if targets were not met, followed. The most prominent was the amendment to the Trade Act of 1988 put forward by Congressman Richard Gephardt, which won congressional approval but was later modified into what became the section known as "Super 301."

The issue is whether in periods of "market stress," or more precisely when imports are rising sharply into a depressed domestic market, the policy response should be through macropolicy actions, including exchange rate adjustment, or through selective import restrictions. The United States, thus far, has more or less followed the former course and avoided import restrictions, but the policy has been subject to more serious question than in the past. In any event, one change during the 1980s in the U.S. role was a definitive shift away from being the "one stabilizer," as predicated by Kindleberger, to being one of three stabilizers, in uneasy concert with the European Community (EC) and Japan. The critical point was the Plaza Accord in September 1986, in which exchange rate and other macropolicy adjustments were adopted as the preferred and necessary means to deal with destabilizing trade imbalances.[2]

The question remains how much "in concert" the three largest trading partners will be during the 1990s in achieving trade balance adjustment without protectionist actions. Following the Plaza Accord, the U.S. trade deficit has declined from 3.8 percent of gross national product (GNP) in 1987 to a projected 1.1 percent in 1991, a considerable achievement of concerted action. Japanese trade surpluses, however, which also declined after 1986, are rising again, with both the European Community and the United States. There is also a broader East Asian surplus emerging, based in part on the "triangular trade" whereby Japanese investment elsewhere in Asia results in exports to the United States and Europe.

It is likely that we are approaching a new period of "market stress," and the leadership role for trade stabilization is by no means clearly defined. Despite the concerted approach among the largest trading nations, as in G–7 meetings, the United States may well emerge as primus inter pares. The European Community is already moving to limit imports of Japanese automobiles, consumer electronics, and other "destabilizing" products, while many Community political leaders are prone to pursue the protectionist route with respect to import surges from Asia. Japan, as the surplus country, will face less domestic pressure to act, and indeed its export industries will resist exchange rate adjustment.

Under these circumstances, the United States is likely to need to assume the leadership, largely by default, for trade stabilization or risk severe new protectionist pressures at home. The precise modalities for leadership to this end are beyond the scope of this paper, but the conclusions of a 1989 CSIS study group, cochaired by Senator William Bradley

329

and former U.S. Trade Representative William Brock, remain a promising point of departure:

> We should not seek to remedy the current unacceptable deficit relationship by attempting to balance trade bilaterally with each country. Rather, we should seek agreement that multilateral balance of the overall current account—which includes trade in goods and services and income from financial assets abroad—is the central target. Persistent large surpluses or deficits on this account should trigger prompt adjustment of internal policies or exchange rates. We should seek an agreed target for the United States.[3]

This formula would still appear to be a forceful and sound approach for dealing with destabilizing trade imbalances as long as it is clear that reaching common goals for current account balances should be achieved through macropolicy adjustment and not through selective trade restrictions. The management of such a trade adjustment strategy in the 1990s, however, would have to continue to rely on principal initiative and leadership from the United States.

The GATT Leadership Role to Strengthen the Multilateral System

The U.S. leadership role in the GATT also changed markedly during the 1980s. In a positive sense, the United States foresaw the need for a fundamental broadening of the GATT mandate in keeping with changes in the world economy. Earlier GATT rounds were limited to tariff cuts and codes for some non-tariff barriers, but the new Uruguay Round, at U.S. insistence, went much further, including trade in services, intellectual property rights, and trade-related investment measures. Other U.S. objectives were to integrate newly industrialized countries more fully into the GATT and to bring the agricultural sector within the GATT norms for market-oriented trade.

There is no question that U.S. leadership has been dominant and critical throughout the Uruguay Round period—more than 10 years since the initial U.S. proposal for a new round in 1981—in establishing the agenda and keeping political minds focused on the need to achieve substantial results if the GATT multilateral system is to remain a credible foundation for world trade. Some question about the U.S. commitment to a major Uruguay Round agreement was raised in the summer of 1990, in connection with U.S. willingness to negotiate seriously on such issues as textiles, antidumping, and even services, but by the time of the Brussels ministerial meeting in December these doubts were largely dispelled.

The most controversial act of U.S. leadership in the Uruguay Round was the decision to challenge the protectionist European agricultural policy frontally as a necessary step toward maintaining the cohesion and credibility of the GATT trading system. Shortly after the Punta del Este meeting of September 1986, the United States proposed to eliminate all trade-distorting measures in the agricultural sector. This initiative provoked a showdown with the Community that delayed and almost destroyed the round. The proposal was based on the U.S. assessment that the circumstances of agricultural trade in the 1980s were so greatly different from those of the 1960s and 1970s that a major change was necessary. In particular, the Community, as a result of internal price supports two to three times higher than world prices, had shifted from a net importer of between 12 and 22 million tons of grains per year in the mid-1970s to a net exporter of 23 to 27 million tons in 1988–1991 (see table 2). This had led to an escalating export subsidy war between the European Community and the United States beginning in 1985, just before the Uruguay Round officially got under way, which caught up other grain exporting countries in a ruinous cross fire. An unbridled export subsidy war between the two largest traders is antithetical to everything the GATT stands for, and its resolution became a vital U.S. objective; failure meant that the GATT system would not emerge from the round with its credibility intact.

Thus, in contrast with the U.S. role for the "trade stabilizing" objective, which could rely on a reasonably well-functioning trilateral structure for concerted action, the relationship within the GATT between the United States and the European Community became largely adversarial. This was especially the case after the stalemated ministerial meeting in Montreal in December 1988. Moreover, the predominant U.S. leadership role in the

Table 2
EC Net Imports of Grains and Agricultural Export Subsidies

	(1) EC Net Imports of Grains[a] (million metric tons)	(2) EC Export Subsidies (in million U.S. $)		(3) U.S. Export Subsidies (in million U.S. $)	
		Total	Grains	Total	Grains
1974	12.3	739.5	95.9		
1975	11.7	1,277.7	453.1		
1976	21.8	1,857.5	479.9		
1977	11.5	2,764.9	303.8		
1978	6.5	3,696.3	1,304.7		
1979	2.7	6,483.0	1,623.0		
1980	−3.8	7,517.1	1,632.8		
1981	−5.5	6,840.1	1,351.1		
1982	−10.0	4,668.9	1,043.6		
1983	−11.1	4,698.5	1,372.5		
1984	−19.6	4,901.2	725.2		
1985	−17.1	5,007.6	818.3	22.6	22.6
1986	−18.6	7,094.2	1,677.8	247.2	213.8
1987	−18.8	10,520.2	3,630.3	818.1	750.8
1988	−25.7	10,837.0	3,638.0	989.7	914.4
1989	−26.6	10,678.9	2,926.7	335.0	319.6
1990	−22.5	11,969.3	3,790.1	311.0	288.9
1991	−27.2	11,986.4	4,051.6	916.6	880.6

Sources: Column 1: 1974–1985, Dale E. Hathaway, *Agriculture and the GATT: Rewriting the Rules* (Washington, D.C.: Institute for International Economics, 1987), p. 10; 1986–1991, U.S. Department of Agriculture, Economic Research Service, *Western Europe Agriculture and Trade Report, 1991* (Washington, D.C.). Column 2: EEC, *The Agricultural Situation in the Community*, EEC annual reports 1975–1991 (Brussels). Column 3: U.S. Department of Agriculture, *Background for 1990 Farm Legislation* (Washington, D.C., 1990); 1990–1991, internal USDA figures.

[a] For crop year ending in listed year

GATT reflects, even more than elsewhere, the relative incapacity or unwillingness of the other two major participants—the European Community and Japan—to take major trade-liberalizing initiatives. The Community has been preoccupied by internal priorities and, especially since 1989, by historic opportunities within Europe, that can conflict with Uruguay Round objectives.[4] The protracted nature of decision making within the Community structure also tends to inhibit trade-liberalizing initiatives. Japan, on the defensive about impediments to access to its market and unwilling to negotiate any relaxation of its ban on rice imports, has played a basically passive role in the Uruguay Round. This attitude also reflects broader cultural and bureaucratic constraints on Japanese leadership in international organizations.

The perseverance of U.S. leadership in the GATT Uruguay Round negotiations has been offset to some extent, however, by other actions the United States has taken in the trade field that tend to weaken its overall commitment to the multilateral trading system. One important change in U.S. trade policy has been the increased prominence of bilateral or unilateral actions, initiated outside the GATT, to deal with trade issues. The United States carried on an almost continuous bilateral trade negotiation with Japan throughout the 1980s that culminated with the Structural Impediments Initiative (SII) agreement in 1990. This interaction dealt with a wide range of important issues that often affected third countries as well. The widespread use by the United States of unilateral requests under section 301 to open markets to U.S. exports in selected countries, although it often produced trade-liberalizing results, is nevertheless contrary to the GATT approach based on reciprocal actions. Frequent recourse to antidumping actions, sometimes as leverage to achieve export restraints, has highlighted the inadequacy of this GATT "trade remedy" provision.

The credibility of the GATT multilateral system was weakened during the 1980s by this strong U.S. tendency toward bilateralism, whose scope in the future will be largely dependent on the final outcome of the Uruguay Round and how the associated agreements are implemented. Negotiations on a revised safeguards procedure (article XIX) and a more tightly defined GATT antidumping agreement encompassed much of the scope of bilateralism during the 1980s. Extending the GATT mandate to trade in services, intellectual property protection, and trade-related investment measures could bring most of U.S. section 301 activity within the GATT purview. Perhaps most important, the little publicized Uruguay Round negotiating group on dispute settlement could play a pivotal role. In its customary proactive fashion, the United States threw down the gauntlet for a more expeditious and effective GATT dispute settlement procedure, including change in the consensus rule for adoption of panel recommendations. Others had to respond to the U.S. challenge and then hold the United States to the new GATT procedures if they wished an alternative to U.S. bilateralism in the post–Uruguay Round period.

An even more far-reaching change in U.S. policy toward the GATT that evolved during the 1980s has been the official view that, under certain circumstances, the United States might turn away from the multilateral approach and restructure its trade relations based on regional trading blocs. President Ronald Reagan, for instance, said in 1985 that

> If these [new GATT Round] negotiations are not initiated or if insignificant progress is made, I am instructing our trade negotiators to explore regional and bilateral agreements with other nations.[5]

In 1988, James A. Baker III, then secretary of the Treasury, stated:

> If possible we hope this follow-up liberalization [to the U.S.-Canada free trade agreement] will occur in the Uruguay Round. If not, we might be willing to explore a "market liberalization club" approach, through minilateral arrangements or a series of bilateral agreements.[6]

A year later, Carla Hills, U.S. trade representative, testified before the Congress:

> Our strategic goal is to open markets . . . we much prefer to use multilateral negotiations to achieve this end, but we will engage in bilateral and plurilateral efforts and take selective unilateral action where such can be effective.[7]

In December 1990, at the time of the failed Uruguay Round ministerial meeting in Brussels, Secretary of Commerce Robert Mosbacher explained:

> We could be okay either way [multilateralism or regionalism]. The U.S. always could make regional or other agreements. In all truth, we're doing this now.[8]

The statements, usually in the form of quasi-ultimatums if others were not more forthcoming in the Uruguay Round, might be viewed primarily as a negotiating ploy. The fact remains, however, that such statements would simply not have been made in the 1960s and 1970s, when the GATT multilateral system, despite its shortcomings, was the essential warp and woof of U.S. trade policy. Moreover, the United States has, in parallel, been negotiating free trade agreements in North America, with the intent of creating a single free trade region for the entire Western Hemisphere.

The "either-or" approach to U.S. participation in the GATT that might be read into such statements is an oversimplification of the underlying changes that have been evolving in U.S. leadership in the trade field. Part of the problem, however, as described in the following section, is that the new approach has not been fully formulated or adequately articulated.

The Management Role for Transition to a Three-Track Trading System

During the 1980s, the United States fundamentally changed its trade policy orientation from an overriding commitment to the GATT multilateral system, based on nondiscrimination and reciprocal reduction in trade barriers, to a three-track approach. Track one remains the GATT multilateral foundation. Track two is the negotiation of free trade agreements, principally on a regional basis. Track three consists of unilateral initiatives to open highly restricted markets to U.S. exports and thus to achieve an "even playing field."

This change in policy evolved over the decade and was not the result of a comprehensive, clearly defined initiative, such as the creation of the Bretton Woods system, including the

333

GATT, after World War II. The policy evolution, moreover, reflected conflicting views within the U.S. government and changing circumstances abroad. In 1980, Reagan spoke privately of a North American free trade area, was counseled by his political advisers to be less specific in public, and was opposed by State Department multilateralists. Actual negotiation of free trade agreements with Canada and Mexico was a result of the reaction of the latter countries to the perceived closing of markets in Europe and East Asia. Section 301 unilateralism was a negotiated compromise to meet earlier administration opposition to the Gephardt amendment. In the spring of 1991, the administration's rationale for free trade with Mexico was tailored largely to obtain legislative authority from a skeptical Congress.

As a result, other nations are not clear what the United States is seeking for the world trading system over the longer run and are suspicious about U.S. motives. Such perceptions tend to detract from U.S. leadership capability. A number of basic questions need to be more fully addressed, including: Are regional free trade agreements "building blocs" toward global free trade or are they strategic economic groupings designed to become more competitive vis-à-vis other blocs? If the latter (and the United States used this line of argumentation in support of "fast track" legislation for a North American free trade agreement), how should East Asians and others not part of a major bloc respond? As for track three, what precisely needs to be done in the GATT or elsewhere in order to bring U.S. unilateral and bilateral initiatives within the multilateral (or regional) framework?

If the United States is to exercise firm leadership in the trade policy field

in the 1990s, a more clear and complete trade strategy based on the convergence of these three tracks needs to be formulated, in which actions in each of the tracks reinforces the others in working toward well-defined longer-term goals.[9] Such a strategy has been evolving through U.S. trade policy implementation over the last several years, but some gaps remain.

The most important gap in U.S. trade strategy pertains to the Asia–Pacific relationship, which has urgency because of the ominous and growing U.S. trade deficit with East Asia noted earlier. The Asia–Pacific economic relationship and the U.S.–Japan relationship in particular are clearly three track in concept, but they are ill-defined in practice and lacking in direction. The GATT multilateral track is important to all in the region, but even a successfully implemented Uruguay Round would not resolve all U.S.–Japan and broader Asia–Pacific trade problems. At the regional level, a ministerial-level framework established in 1989—Asia Pacific Economic Cooperation, or APEC—has yet to define its substantive agenda, and thus has little credibility, while Malaysian Prime Minister Mahathir bin Mohamad is calling for an East Asian economic grouping to counter the European and North American trade blocs. The U.S.–Japan bilateral trade relationship, since the conclusion of the SII talks a year and a half ago, has been ad hoc, responding to trade problems only as they approach the political boiling point.

A more structured three-track response to the dynamic Asia–Pacific relationship is contained in a CSIS report that appeared in May 1991.[10] The report warns of a possible "drift apart into regional economic blocs" and calls for a more comprehensive policy framework. It offers a specific substantive agenda for APEC, including a regional policy framework for international investment, an integrated trade/aid approach for economic infrastructure projects, an Asia–Pacific Economic Policy Committee to achieve more prompt and effective macropolicy adjustment, and an action agenda for environmental issues of a regional character. The report also proposes a more structured U.S.–Japan bilateral framework that can anticipate and resolve trade and investment problems before they become publicly contentious, and that would deal with such issues as competition policy, government support for new technology development, and public procurement.

The American Challenge Ahead

The leadership challenge in world trade will continue to confront the United States during the 1990s, but under greatly changed—and continually changing—circumstances. Questions are being raised about U.S. self-interest in an open trading system, and a ground swell of post–cold war isolationism has strong protectionist overtones. In any event, U.S. leadership will no longer be based on the strength of a dominant creditor position and a commanding technological superiority.

There are even stronger arguments to support continued U.S. leadership for liberal trade, however, that hopefully will prevail. U.S. economic interests, and U.S. ability to improve living standards within the United States, are increasingly based on global trade and investment relationships. The domestic debate over international competitiveness is wide-ranging, but an inward-directed "Fortress America" approach is not a credible option.

The exercise of U.S. leadership in the period ahead will be facilitated by a broad international consensus on an economic strategy of open trade and market-oriented national economies. The economic liberalism consensus, however, is ill-defined in specific areas of trade policy and potentially conflictive. The central challenge is to reconcile the momentum toward regional integration, and the corresponding economic bloc formation, with the underlying multilateral policy structure, principally the GATT. More precisely, the regional tendency is toward a predominant tripolar relationship between Western Europe, North America, and East Asia. Trade policy deliberations center on the U.S.–EC–Japan relationship, with a second echelon of regional partners more and more likely to align with the primary regional economic power, and a third tier of many nations, mostly of relatively small trade significance, not yet part of any major grouping.

U.S. leadership capability reflects to some extent its more balanced export interests, as shown in chart 1: a 25 to 30 percent share each in Western Europe, North America, and East Asia, and the remaining 16 percent scattered elsewhere. More important, trade leadership continues to be thrust on the United States by default, as the alternative to the leadership vacuum of the 1930s. The European Community remains preoccupied with regional priorities and its capacity for initiative is constrained by its internal decision-making process. Japan has yet to assert itself in international forums, as shown in the Uruguay Round. This highly asymmetric leadership capability may change over time, but for the relevant policy horizon of at least five years, if not until the end of the decade, the challenge of defining the new world trading order will remain principally an American challenge.

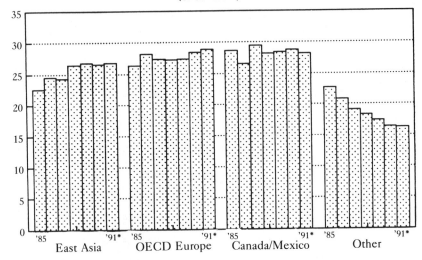

Chart 1
U.S. Exports (%)
(1985–1991)

East Asia   OECD Europe   Canada/Mexico   Other

Source: U.S. Department of Commerce
*January–September

In this dynamic context, the "bicycle theory" is no longer an adequate concept. Reliance on prolonged GATT negotiations to keep protectionist pressures in check lost force as the Uruguay Round dragged on and as the momentum for trade liberalization shifted to the regional level. The increasingly wobbly bicycle needs to be replaced, in fact, by a tricycle, reflecting the tripolar orientation of the world economy. A tricycle, among other things, has greater stability and does not fall over if it should stop for a while. Unfortunately, and to push visual imaging to its limit, the central trade policy configuration of the early 1990s appears to be a tricycle, two of whose wheels are square.

An earlier version of this article was presented at the CSIS-sponsored conference, "Global Forum: Leadership 2000," Washington, D.C., October 18, 1991.

Notes

1. Charles P. Kindleberger, *The World in Depression: 1929–1939*, rev. & enl. ed. (Berkeley: University of California Press, 1986), p. 289.

2. A related element of this concerted approach has been pursued in the Uruguay Round, where a priority objective of the United States, the European Community, and Japan has been to restrict greatly the use of GATT article XVIIIB, which permits selective import restrictions for developing countries for balance-of-payments reasons. Achieving this objective would bring the newly industrialized countries of East Asia and Latin America into a supportive sharing of the macropolicy trade adjustment strategy. Significantly, South Korea early in 1991 announced it would no longer utilize article XVIIIB, and Brazil recently stated likewise.

3. Ernest H. Preeg, *The American Challenge in World Trade: U.S. Interests in the GATT Multilateral Trading System*, CSIS Significant Issues Series 11, no. 7 (Washington, D.C.:

CSIS, 1989). The quotation is from the Steering Group statement, p. xii.

4. A major conflict of this kind was the July 1991 EC–Japanese agreement to freeze Japanese imports of automobiles at their current level for seven years and to put informal limits on foreign direct investment in the sector as well. This agreement was part of the EC '92 program to unify the Community market, but its effect was to undermine the key Uruguay Round objective of a revised safeguards clause (article XIX) that would involve tighter disciplines for "temporary" quotas, such as a three-year maximum time, minimum import growth during the three years, an adjustment assistance program by the importing country, and consultation with affected third countries. The new European Common Automobile Policy violates all of these proposed disciplines.

5. In a speech at the White House to business and congressional leaders, September 22, 1985.

6. From a speech before the National Cotton Council of America in Memphis, Tennessee, February 8, 1988.

7. Statement before the Senate Finance Committee, June 27, 1989.

8. Quoted in Clyde Farnsworth, "Brussels Talks Not the Only Trade Game Around," *New York Times*, December 4, 1990, sec. 4, p. 7.

9. The conceptual framework and a detailed policy program for a three convergent track trade strategy is contained in Preeg, *American Challenge*, chaps. 4–7.

10. The report contained the conclusions and policy recommendations of a U.S.–Japan working group cochaired by Ambassador Yoshio Okawara and former Undersecretary of State William D. Rogers and was titled "A Policy Framework for Asia–Pacific Economic Cooperation." It will be published as part of *The U.S.–Japan Economic Relationship in East and Southeast Asia*, CSIS Significant Issues Series 14, no. 1 (Washington, D.C.: CSIS, 1992).

the negative externalities of business and financial enterprise.

The Firm and the State System

Industrial and financial managers are, above all, realists and pragmatists. They interpret with great care the environments in which enterprises are located, and they make strategic decisions based on their analyses and evaluations. Thus, during the last several decades, international firms have responded to pressures exerted by national governments in ways such as the following:

(1) *Indigenization of managers,* such that corporate affiliates everywhere are increasingly in the hands not of expatriate managers but, rather, of citizens of each respective host country. As this transformation proceeds, companies have had to modify earlier concepts of a single "corporate culture," or of a single, undifferentiated sense of "corporate citizenship."

(2) *Conformance to national regulations* that reduce the proportion of equity shares in local affiliates that the parent company may hold. In some instances, these proportions actually fall under 50 percent. The era of the wholly owned subsidiary is a thing of the past; and even U.S. multinational companies, which tended to be highly resistant to equity sharing, have adapted to this newer climate.[10] This change has in turn led to modified forms of corporate organization; revised systems of communications; as well as radically revised formats for personnel training and human resources management.

(3) *Greater propensity to enter into joint ventures* with local firms or financial institutions. This change is in part a logical consequence of the new regulations as to equity sharing. International firms have now, however, discovered the utilities that derive from the direct involvement of local partners in overseas operations.[11]

(4) *Willingness to enter into joint-venture relations with state-owned industries.* International firms, once highly suspicious of and antagonistic toward state-owned industries, have recast many of these views as well. Not only have they discovered that the ownership of an enterprise is immensely less important than the quality of its managers; they have found that the managers of indigenous state-owned firms can be very effective partners when it comes to having to confront a wide range of regulations—and other business matters—that bring local and national governments into the picture.[12]

(5) *Acceptance of host country laws* as the basis for adjudicating disputes that may arise regarding the local operations of foreign companies—even in those instances where international arbitration may be an option. This transformation is most apparent regarding the so-called NICs (newly industrializing countries), which are highly attractive sites for foreign direct investments and are increasingly present in international markets with multinational corporations of their own nationality.[13]

(6) *Willingness to accept local content and export quotas* as conditions for doing business in a given country. These particular changes are strongly induced wherever a developing country, for example, shifts its economic policies from the import-substitution to the export-driven model. Although negotiations as to local content requirements are often complex, and sometimes acrimonious, it is noteworthy that they are now widely accepted (as they were not earlier) as a normal aspect of doing business in today's international economy.

(7) *Acceptance of the inevitability of the "obsolescent bargain,"* wherein, when it

suits the needs, or interests, or even the whim, of the national authorities of host countries, the terms of the original contracts, under which the foreign investor entered a country in the first place, can be renegotiated. Today's newspapers carry daily stories of confrontations of this kind between foreign investors and local authorities in Asia and eastern Europe. Beyond the acrimony and legal and diplomatic fencing, however, lies a more basic reality: the relationship between the international firm and host country governments is not as unbalanced as in decades past; and, in any case, whatever excessive advantage may be squeezed out today may carry a higher price tomorrow, when circumstances change.

This list might easily be expanded. Perhaps the most significant indicator of the basic point I am making is the organizational changes that now come increasingly to characterize the international firm. The global firm is no longer a single pyramid, managed from a single apex in its worldwide operations. Increasingly—and not merely for reasons of internal efficiency—decision-making authority has been delegated to the firm's affiliates located abroad.

With the possible exceptions of strategic planning, capital budgeting, and particularly corporate finance, the structure of the international enterprise comes to look less like a pyramidal or monolithic structure and more like a confederal system, in which affiliates located abroad enjoy considerable autonomy.[14]

These structural changes are dictated not only by the kinds of national regulations regarding foreign investors summarized above; they also grow out of the corporate community's recognition that national cultural differences demand that enterprise, if it

wishes to succeed, must adapt to these local cultural nuances. For all of these reasons, the recent history of the global enterprise reflects a near-universal understanding on the part of managers that the nation-state will for many decades remain a major factor to be reckoned with by business.

This being so, the question then arises as to how best to deal with aspects of international business and finance that are less than salutary and even inimical to the health and wealth of nations and of their inhabitants. The solution does not lie in supranational organizations like the EC. It will be time enough to turn to them if and when they actually emerge as real wielders of effective powers. In the meantime, it will remain for individual nation-states to bring the more unacceptable business and financial practices under better control.

It will not be easy to achieve this end. But bilateral and multilateral negotiations on specific problems will turn out to be much more rational than, for example, waiting around for a company law to materialize within the EC or for the United Nations or the Organization for Economic Cooperation and Development to provide effective policing of business or financial practices. The so-called codes of conduct of business practices abroad produced by such bodies have been, at best, very weak instruments.[15]

Even less efficacious is the form of "self-policing" that businesses engage in when they produce their own internal codes of conduct. Such steps should not be discouraged; but, for many years to come, the only effective way to deal with the unwanted aspects of international financial and business operations will be through parallel national legislation and ad hoc agreements among nation-states.[16]

Some progress along these lines has already been achieved. One might cite the areas of taxation, capitalization and local content requirements, royalty payments, and the like. It is probable that more parallel regulations will begin to emerge that address aspects of enterprise that have negative environmental effects or that subject consumers to dangerous products and workers to unacceptable levels of risk.

But there remains much to be done. Transfer pricing, for example, is a universal practice that not even the most developed and experienced authorities in advanced industrial countries have been able to bring reasonably under control. Consolidated balance sheets may have their utility, but they do not begin to reflect the extent to which the transfer-pricing mechanism is utilized by international enterprises. More nation-by-nation attention to this problem is required.[17]

The matter of antitrust remains, at best, in a somewhat chaotic state, and steps might be taken to ensure, for example, that the European Commission's directives and regulations in this important area are formally incorporated into the national legislation of the EC's member states. What I have said above about the unlikelihood that a supranational state will emerge in Europe should not be misunderstood to mean that, in the economic regulatory sphere, the Commission at Brussels is without teeth. Were this the case, fewer international firms would have established contacts or opened up offices there! But the Commission's decisions regarding competition would be immensely more effective if members of the EC established their own internal, and parallel, antitrust norms.

In this same regard, the European Commission should be pressed to abandon its efforts to come up with a comprehensive "company law" in favor of getting agreement among its members regarding such specific and fundamental issues as information disclosure by industrial enterprises and financial institutions. At the national level, the need for parallel regulations regarding the operation of stock exchanges should by now be painfully apparent.

It is also essential that national governments recognize and come to grips with another reality, namely, that some of their own institutions, including those with specific public responsibilities, do not always act in the national interest or for that matter, in conformance with national economic policies.

We witnessed a dramatic example of this, the full story of which remains to be told, in fall 1992, when the European Monetary System (EMS) began to fall apart. As the run against sterling and the Italian lira got under way in September of that year, the world press reported that speculators were responsible for this maneuver, which drove Britain out of the EMS and forced Italy first to devalue its currency and then to leave the EMS as well. The reading public was left with the impression that this crushing defeat of the EMS, and concomitantly of the Maastricht agreement, was engineered by the cynical barons of international finance.

But the key players in this gigantic multi-billion dollar maneuver were not the speculators per se, but rather the so-called corporates, the major banks and the largest international firms in Germany, Italy, France, Britain, and elsewhere, which made the correct judgment that neither Britain nor Italy could continue to support its own overvalued currency, even with outside help, against a massive sell-off in favor of the deutsche mark.[18]

These hardheaded managers of international business—and of major banks—correctly assumed that the EMS-dictated parity levels of these currencies simply did not reflect the underlying economic realities of Britain, Italy, and (a few months later) France. And so they made their fateful decisions. The speculators, however, did not lead this rout; they jumped on the bandwagon (as they usually do) only after they learned, privately, what the big banks and the big industries would do.

It goes without saying that central banks were also intimately involved in this process, and that some of them at least were not at all interested in following, or shoring up, the policies pursued by their own prime ministers or finance ministers. Such a problem is compounded by the fact that, when governments act (as in setting monetary targets, interest rates, and currency parities), these acts are quintessentially transparent, whereas the intentions and decisions of those who manage the immense pool of international capital are not. And even when these investors and speculators act, they can change course instantly, unlike governments—and just as instantly have their buy and sell orders implemented through a worldwide network of computerized and telecommunicated financial transactions.

To conclude on a somewhat despondent note, we live in a world in which those who manage international business will, for hardheaded economic reasons and without any compunction, "bet" against their own national governments. When national governments and the financial markets clash with each other, the latter are likely to win. Not because these money managers are "without nationality" or lack patriotism, but, rather, because they lack the conviction that political managers can manage economies.

One correct way to deal with this dilemma was well understood by those who drafted the economic integration sections of the Maastricht agreement. They calculated that the monetary unification of the EC would bring to heel at least some of the devastating effects of the 1992 EMS maneuvers. But if Germany itself, as now seems apparent, is no longer interested in the monetary unification aspects of Maastricht, the internationalization of monetary policy must remain a pyrrhic hope.

Looking to the Future

The globalization of business and finance will permit these organizations to remain outside the effective control of any single national government.[19] The question is whether nationalism will continue to stand in the way of even modest efforts, at least by the national governments whose industries and banks control most of the massive international capital pool, to bring this system under better control. The answer to this question will not be found in Brussels. It will be provided by the postures assumed by political leaders in Washington and Tokyo, in Berlin, London, Paris, and Rome. If the post-Maastricht events are an indication of the narrow, erosive, and self-defeating forms that economic nationalism can take, the prospects for the future are anything but reassuring.

The views expressed in this article are strictly and entirely those of the author. They should therefore not be attributed to either Yale University or any other organization with which he is affiliated. An earlier version of the article was presented to the 19th International Conference of the Pio Manzu'

Research Center on "The Third Round: The Global Enterprise in a World Torn between Neo-Tribalism and the Challenge of Trans-National Solidarity," Rimini, Italy, October 16–19, 1993.

Notes

1. On the complex matter of nationalisms, old and new, see Benedict R. Anderson, *Imagined Communities: Reflections on the Origin and Spread of Nationalism* (New York, N.Y.: Verso, 1991); Eric J. Hobsbawm, *Nations and Nationalism Since 1778* (Cambridge: Cambridge University Press, 1990); Eric J. Hobsbawm and Terence Ranger, eds., *The Invention of Tradition* (New York, N.Y.: Cambridge University Press, 1984); Ernest Gellner, *Nations and Nationalism* (Ithaca, N.Y.: Cornell University Press, 1983); William Pfaff, *The Wrath of Nations: Civilization and the Furies of Nationalism* (New York, N.Y.: Simon and Schuster, 1993); and Hans Kohn, *The Age of Nationalism: The First Era of Global History* (Westport, Conn.: Greenwood Press, 1976).

2. The intellectual community of the West easily developed the credo that the follies and tragedies of nationalism would be overcome once and for all by the emergence of the supranational state, first in Europe and perhaps later elsewhere. For a sampling of this earlier writing, see Ernst Haas, *The Uniting of Europe* (London: Stevens and Sons, 1958); Leon Lindberg and Stuart Sheingold, eds., *Regional Integration: Theory and Research* (Cambridge, Mass.: Harvard University Press, 1971); and James A. Caporaso, *The Structure and Function of European Integration* (Pacific Palisades, Calif.: Goodyear, 1974).

3. This is, alas, exactly the view of things that has been diffused after the termination of the Cold War, the disintegration of the Soviet sphere of influence, and the breakup of the Soviet Union itself. Leading newspapers, diplomats, political leaders, distinguished economists, and others who should know better beat the drums for the mistaken idea that economics drives politics. Events of recent months have given some of these reason for pause and reflection.

4. It must be said that enthusiasms die hard, particularly when they involve one's ideological and intellectual proclivities. Thus, books published before the Maastricht ratification included such items as Clifford Hackett, *Cautious Revolution: The European Community Arrives* (Westport, Conn.: Greenwood Press, 1990); Nicholas Colchester and David Buchan, *Europower: The Essential Guide to Europe's Transformation in 1992* (New York, N.Y.: Random House, 1990); and David Burstein, *Euroquake: Europe's Explosive Economic Challenge Will Change the World* (New York, N.Y.: Simon and Schuster, 1991). Cf. Nicholas Colchester and David Buchan, *Europe Relaunched: Truth and Illusions on the Way to 1992* (London: Hutchinson, 1992).

5. See Jeffrey Anderson, "Skeptical Reflections on a 'Europe of Regions: Britain, Germany and the European Regional Development Fund,'" *Journal of Public Policy* 10 (October-December 1990), pp. 414–447.

6. Foreign direct investment in manufacturing, mining, and service industries now approaches $1.5 trillion in book value. Internationalization of enterprise, in one form or another, is the single most important organizational aspect of the modern industrial world. See Mark Casson, ed., *The Growth of International Business* (London: Allen and Unwin, 1983). Cf. Norman J. Glickman and Douglas P. Woodward, *The New Competitors* (New York, N.Y.: Basic Books, 1989).

7. See Richard J. Barnet and Ronald Muller, *Global Reach* (New York, N.Y.: Simon and Schuster, 1974), for the most sweeping claims about the implications of the internationalization of business. See also Raymond Vernon, *Sovereignty at Bay: The Multinational Spread of U.S. Enterprises* (New York, N.Y.: Basic Books, 1971). Cf. Raymond Vernon, "Sovereignty at Bay: Ten Years After," in Theodore H. Moran, ed., *Multinational Corporations: The Political Economy of Foreign Direct Investment* (Lexington, Mass.: D. C. Heath and Co., 1985), pp. 247–259.

8. On the adaptive capacities of the multinational corporation, see Robert Gilpin, *The Political Economy of International Relations* (Princeton, N.J.: Princeton University Press, 1987), pp. 231–262. Cf. J. S. Lizondo, "Foreign Direct Investment," Working Paper WP/90/63 (Washington, D.C.: International Monetary Fund,

1990); F. C. Schuller, *Venturing Abroad: Innovation by U.S. Multinationals* (New York, N.Y.: Quorum, 1988); and Allen J. Morrison, *Strategies in Global Industries* (New York, N.Y.: Quorum, 1990).

9. It is, of course, not always the case that a keen sense of ethics and/or law-abidingness characterize the behavior of managers. See, for example, Thomas Donaldson, *The Ethics of International Business* (New York, N.Y.: Oxford University Press, 1989); and Irwin Ross, *Shady Business: Confronting Corporate Corruption* (New York, N.Y.: Twentieth Century Fund, 1992).

10. See Joseph LaPalombara and Steven Blank, *Multinational Corporations in Developing Countries* (New York, N.Y.: Conference Board, 1979); Denis Encarnation, *Dislodging Multinationals: India's Strategy in Comparative Perspective* (Ithaca, N.Y.: Cornell University Press, 1989); and Thomas Biersteker, *Multinationals: The State and Control of the Nigerian Economy* (Princeton, N.J.: Princeton University Press, 1987).

11. For a succinct, insightful commentary on new approaches to business ventures abroad, see Harvey S. James, Jr., and Murray Weidenbaum, *When Businesses Cross International Borders: Strategic Alliances and Their Alternatives* (Westport, Conn.: Praeger, 1993). Cf. Paul Beamish, *Multinational Joint Ventures in Developing Countries* (London: Routledge, 1988).

12. See Raymond Vernon, *Exploring the Global Economy: Emerging Issues in Trade and Investment* (Boston, Mass.: University Press of America, 1985), pt. 3, "The State-Owned Enterprise."

13. See Graeme C. Hughes, *Foreign Investment Law in Canada* (Toronto: Carswell, 1983); L. R. Kumor and K. V. Iyer, *Foreign Investment and Collaboration: Legal Parameters* (New Delhi: L. R. Kumor Associates, 1986); A. K. Ho, *Joint Ventures in the People's Republic of China* (New York, N.Y.: Praeger, 1990); Attila Andrade Junior, *Guidelines on Brazil's Foreign Investment Law* (Rio de Janeiro: Interinvest Editora, 1980); Jack Behrman, *International Business and Governments: Issues and Institutions* (Columbia, S.C.: University of South Carolina Press, 1990); and P. E. Bondzi-Simpson, *Legal Relationships between Transnational Corporations and Host States* (New York, N.Y.: Quorum, 1990).

14. The pressures driving international firms to effect organizational changes are multifarious, and they obviously include considerations that have less to do with the social or political environment than with the existential conditions of doing business in a competitive world. See, for example, Michael Best, *The New Competition: Institutions of Industrial Restructuring* (Cambridge, Mass.: Harvard University Press, 1990); Kenichi Ohmae, *Triad Power: The Coming Shape of Global Competition* (New York, N.Y.: Free Press, 1985); and Michael Porter, *The Competitive Advantage of Nations* (New York, N.Y.: Free Press, 1990).

15. See Kwamena Acquaah, *International Regulation of Transnational Corporations: The New Reality* (New York, N.Y.: Praeger, 1986).

16. See Bart S. Fisher and Jeff Turner, eds., *Regulating the Multi-National Enterprise: National and International Challenges* (New York, N.Y.: Praeger, 1983).

17. On transfer pricing, see G. F. Mathewson and G. D. Quirin, *Fiscal Transfer Pricing in Multinational Corporations* (Toronto: University of Toronto Press, 1979); Robert Tang, *Transfer Pricing in the United States and Japan* (New York, N.Y.: Praeger, 1979); Sylvain Plasschaert, *Transfer Pricing and Multinational Corporations* (Farnsborough, U.K.: Saxon House, 1979); and Organization for Economic Cooperation and Development, *Transfer Pricing and Multinational Enterprises* (Paris: OECD, 1984).

18. I am indebted to Richard Medley for a number of acute insights regarding this crisis. Medley is at work on a study that will provide sobering confirmation regarding the intractability of problems of the kind described here.

19. Raymond Vernon asserts that the international firm, by its very nature, develops global interests of its multinational network as a whole, and "hence can never respond single-mindedly to the requirements of any one national jurisdiction" (emphasis supplied) (*Exploring the Global Economy,* pp. 51–52). He also observes: "Nations are no longer very manageable as economic units. Their external economic links have become vital to their national existence; and these economic links are beyond their control to manage, except jointly with other nations. The problem is seen just as

vividly in monetary and countercyclical economic policies as in trade" (p. 25).

Cf. John Robinson, *Multinationals and Political Control* (New York, N.Y.: St. Martin's Press, 1983). For a broad overview of trends in the relationships between multinationals and public authorities in both developing and developed countries, see Theodore Moran, "Introduction," in Moran, ed., *Governments and Transnational Corporations* (London and New York, N.Y.: Routledge, 1993), pp. 1–26.

A Capital-Starved New World Order: Geopolitical Implications of a Global Capital Shortage in the 1990s

Penelope Hartland-Thunberg

FEARS ARE MOUNTING that George Bush's New World Order may founder on a much-bruited global capital shortage. Indeed, the international community is very likely to be starved of capital to varying degrees in the decade ahead. But at the core of the issue is a fundamental paradox: the New World Order is threatened less by what happens to capital availability than by the circumstances that would prevent the emergence of a capital shortage. These circumstances include principally the failed development of the conditions necessary for peace, prosperity, and cooperation in the world, especially in key areas such as Europe and the Middle East. The consequences would be political instability within countries, political tensions between countries, and a slower growth of the world economy. Thus whether or not the shortage materializes, its implications for geopolitical relations in the world arena are serious and merit attention. In what follows the outlook for the supply-demand balance in international capital markets is examined first and then the geopolitical implications of a relative shortage or plenty of global capital.

In an economic sense a shortage of capital is important because of its significance for interest rates and inflation. Excess demand will either force real interest rates to rise, thereby dampening economic growth, or, if interest rates are kept artificially low through monetary policy, will result in inflation—or both. These consequences of course are important for the outlook for world economic growth and development. But because of the nature and direction of the anticipated excess demand for capital, the consequences of a global shortage during the 1990s are also important to geopolitical relations.

Evidence adduced in support of the capital shortage thesis rests on shifts in international capital flows first observed in the late 1980s and expected to continue during most of the 1990s. These shifts involve a change in the position of some areas of the world from that of a net capital exporter to a net importer (e.g., Europe and Latin America). They also involve a shift from a position of balanced capital flows (or very small net movements) to a net import status (the Middle

Penelope Hartland-Thunberg is a senior associate at CSIS. Her most recent book is *China, Hong Kong, Taiwan and the World Trading System* (New York: St. Martin's Press, 1990).

East); a shift from a net import position to an even larger net import position (Asia, excluding Japan); and a shift from a sizable net export flow to a significantly smaller export surplus (Japan). The United States is likely to remain a major capital importer, although during the first half of the decade the decline in the net import position of the United States that commenced in 1988 may counterbalance these movements to some degree.

The Outlook in International Capital Markets: Near Term

Since the mid-1980s global capital markets have been dominated by the dramatic shift in the position of the United States from a net capital exporter to a net importer of unprecedented amounts of foreign capital. Where previously the United States had typically invested abroad a few billion dollars more than foreigners had invested in the United States, in 1985 that position was reversed. Between 1985 and 1990 the United States imported on average every year nearly $125 billion more of capital than it exported.

Foreign individuals and institutions worldwide increased their purchases of dollar assets. On balance, however, most other countries were in the same position as the United States; they were net capital importers. Only a handful exported capital on balance. Chief among these were Japan, Germany, Switzerland, and Kuwait. For the last five years of the 1980s, according to the International Monetary Fund (IMF), their net capital export averaged, respectively, $72 billion, $42 billion, $7 billion, and $5.5 billion.[1] Among others exporting smaller amounts were the Netherlands, Belgium, Korea, and South Africa. Despite data inadequacies, it is clear that the United States hogged the market for international capital because, for good reasons or bad, it was perceived as more credit-worthy than its competitors.

From the evidence available today, it appears likely that the United States will continue as a net capital importer through the 1990s and that it will confront increasing competition in its demand for foreign capital. Demand increases are likely in traditional importing areas like Asia, Latin America, and the Middle East, and also in the shift of traditional export areas to the net import list—notably in Europe.

Economists generally agree that for the United States to eliminate its dependence on foreign capital it must drastically reduce the government budget deficit (federal, state, and local combined). To make the United States self-sufficient in capital requires an increase in national saving; recently savings in the private sector from individuals and corporations have been increasingly offset by negative savings (excess expenditure) in the public sector. Even in the late 1980s when the federal deficit dropped, that improvement was offset by a declining budget surplus at the state and local level with the consequence that government saving remained constant at -2 percent of gross national product (GNP).[2] A recent probing study by the Federal Reserve Bank of New York concludes that even if the budget were balanced by 1995, the net inflow of capital into the United States would continue through the end of the decade, although at a declining rate. Even if the national savings rate by mid-decade were to increase by 5 percentage points (as a share of GNP), either through a decrease in the public deficit or an increase in private savings (a scenario that appears lacking in feasibility), the dependence on foreign capital would continue through the end of the century.[3] In other words, even on the basis of highly optimistic assumptions about the requirement for public-sector borrowing during the 1990s, the United States will continue to rely on foreign capital; the amounts will depend on the national savings rate,[4] and private domestic investment.

During the second half of the 1980s competition for international capital confronting the United States was subdued because various potential claimants were perceived as relatively poor credit risks compared with the United States. The experience of creditors with many of the debt-impacted developing countries had previously been so disastrous that new funds were almost totally unavailable. The consequence was that developing countries as a group became net capital exporters as interest and amortization payments exceeded new inflows. In addition, EC '92, the concerted effort by the European Community to develop community-wide free movement in goods, services, people, and capital (hopefully by 1992 but realistically by the turn of the century), only began to capture the attention of investors at the end of the decade. As it did so, international capital increasingly turned toward Europe. Similarly the attraction of the "Little Tigers" in Asia (Thailand, Malaysia, Indonesia) grew into boom proportions only late in the decade, as did the Japanese investment boom at home.

Meanwhile, the Middle East was a capital deficit area. Despite popular perceptions to the contrary, the larger oil exporters of the region rapidly increased their expenditures abroad after oil price rises but were slow to reduce expenditures following price declines. Only Kuwait and the United Arab Emirates (UAE) sustained net capital exports in every year of the last five years of the 1980s.[5] The Communist countries as a group were capital importers, the largest importer being China. "The poorest of the poor," namely most of the developing world, of course were small capital importers.

Although a global capital shortage is not imminent, international capital markets may become increasingly tight as the 1990s progress. In the immediate future (i.e., for the next 12 to 15 months or so) demand may be sluggish; two factors account for the near-term outlook. First, relatively low economic growth in the industrial countries, a consequence of recession in the United States, Canada, Britain, and Australia, and tight monetary policies in Europe and Japan, will continue to affect investment into next year. Slow growth in the Organization for Economic Cooperation and Development (OECD) is reflected in less buoyant exports from the developing countries with the consequence that even growth rates in the lively industrializing economies of Asia are relatively depressed.

Second, although the total capital requirements implicit in converting Eastern Europe to a free private market system from one of central planning and government ownership and in raising its productivity to the levels of the West are immense, certain basic legal and functional institutions and practices must be replaced before recovery there can take hold. Revising laws in a democracy and dramatically altering such functions as banking practices and accounting definitions inevitably take time. The essential institutional changes are currently in train, although to differing degrees in each country, but it will take more time for practices to change effectively and for the region to be perceived as credit-worthy by investors.

Similarly the total capital requirements implicit in restoring the economies of Kuwait and Iraq to their pre-war levels are huge. The same is true of those implicit in even moderately raising growth rates and living standards in the many poor Middle Eastern countries. Only in Kuwait is it likely that much progress will be made in the next year or two. Meanwhile, with the threat of political instability deterring foreign private investors, war-related costs in the Gulf area will remain sufficiently high that the region will be in capital deficit for at least the first half of the decade.

Outlook for International Capital Markets: Long Term

By the end of 1992 or thereabouts world economic activity is likely to quicken and with it the global demand for capital. Although growth in the United States is likely to be close to the bottom of the list of OECD countries, U.S. reliance on international capital will rise because of governmental funding requirements and low private savings rates. U.S. recovery will be retarded until about mid-decade by the high level of corporate and personal debt, by excess capacity in the financial sectors, by the huge overhang of empty commercial buildings on the real estate market, and by the just-in-time inventory policy of business. In the public sector it will be retarded by constraints on state and local governments forced to reduce expenditures and by the federal government's need to finance off-budget items like the savings and loan rescue (which will add to its borrowing requirements but provide no fiscal stimulus), the war, recession, and such. In addition, the

low deficits forecast by the budget accord of 1990 were based on several optimistic assumptions that are unlikely to be realized. All of this suggests that unemployment will fall only moderately until later in the decade, private sector savings will remain substantially below their level of the 1970s, and relatively high interest rates and slowly dwindling excess capacity will depress private investment until mid-decade. The one buoyant sector in the U.S. economic outlook for the entire decade of the 1990s will be the export industries that will benefit from more vigorous growth in the rest of the world. Private investment should recover around 1995, resulting in a larger inflow of capital in the second half of the decade.

Europe will be increasingly energized as the EC '92 program moves toward completion in the next century both by rising foreign investment as U.S., Japanese, and Asian businesses seek to benefit from positions inside the Community, and by rising consumption and investment in the new Germany, which will make the Federal Republic an engine of growth for Europe.

Also, as institution-building in Eastern Europe is completed and as training programs become increasingly effective in the area, Poland, Czechoslovakia, and Hungary will offer more and more attractive opportunities for foreign investors. When the USSR will be able to attract foreign investment will depend on when its political crisis is resolved and when the warring internal factions come to agree on what kind of economic system will replace their current chaos. The country's potential for absorbing foreign capital later in the decade is significant. Meanwhile, the European Bank for Reconstruction and Development (EBRD), which opened its doors on

April 15, 1991, will be increasingly able to provide financing to the area and to find projects worthy of support. Although the Bank's annual transfer of capital through the end of the decade may not amount to more than one or two billion dollars, its activities are likely to encourage and support (through market research, joint investments, and such) investment in the area by others from Eastern Europe, Western Europe, and the rest of the world. As the decade continues, Europe's credit-worthiness is likely to be perceived as brighter and brighter and its ability to absorb international capital will expand.

How much capital investment the East will attract will of course depend crucially on developments within the Soviet Union. Bloodshed in the USSR with or without a return to a centralized authoritarian regime would depress investment in Eastern Europe and probably in Western Europe too. On the other hand, higher defense spending that would follow such a contingency would compensate to some degree for the otherwise recessionary consequences. One should not forget that the New World Order assumes that the Cold War will not return, but that assumption has not yet been proven valid.

If during the 1990s Eastern Europe successfully initiates and makes progress on the transition to free private enterprise and the market system while the USSR is unable to do so (or vice versa), global capital markets would still be tight but the capital shortage would not be as acute as if both parts of the East were competing for capital. Estimates of the amount of Western capital "required" are almost as varied as the people making them. In 1991, a year when the "trickle" of Western capital into Eastern Europe was only beginning, it has been esti-

mated at $15 to $20 billion (excluding the former East Germany). It seems reasonable to assume that as the transition moves forward that sum will increase by 50 percent or more, a significant amount when combined with other potential sources of demand. In addition, it has been estimated that in 1991 the German government will spend about $80 billion on the eastern sector, an awesome figure suggesting the magnitude of the task all of these countries are undertaking.

Whether the Middle East remains a capital-deficient area throughout the decade will depend primarily on the course of oil prices, which in the past have been notoriously difficult to forecast. A consensus of informed observers foresees a tightening of oil markets through the 1990s, how tight depending on a variety of factors. IMF forecasts assume that world oil consumption will increase at 1 to 2 percent annually, that real oil prices will remain roughly constant until middecade (as production is resumed in Kuwait and Iraq, it will be reduced elsewhere in the region) and then will increase at about 3 percent a year. Assuming a small current account deficit for Iraq (with funds primarily provided by international institutions), larger deficits for Iran and Saudi Arabia, and a rough balance for Kuwait after middecade implies at best only a negligible capital surplus for the region in the second half of the 1990s. Moreover, as Iran rejoins the world community and undertakes reconstruction after its decade of war and destruction, opportunities for foreign investment there could boom. Saudi Arabia's appetite for arms and industrial construction is likely to be expansive; indeed, the entire area appears addicted to arms that the Chinese and North Koreans at least are willing to provide.[6] The commitment of Saudi Arabia (and the other countries of the Gulf Cooperation Council) to those countries in the region and elsewhere that supported its war effort together with its interest in moderate oil prices seem likely to insure that the Saudi balance of payments will show little surplus for investment elsewhere. If, moreover, political developments within Iraq appear favorable to foreign investors, public and private capital could flow to that country in sizable amounts. All oil-producing countries in the region (and elsewhere) are seeking to expand or upgrade their facilities for production and refining, both highly capital-intensive operations. In short, from the vantage point of the present, the Middle East is unlikely to be a net supplier of any significant amounts of capital during the 1990s and could be a significant absorber.

In contrast to the other traditional sources of capital, only Japan seems likely to continue as a substantial net capital exporter during the 1990s. The pattern of Japan's capital exports, however, has been shifting and these shifts are likely to be maintained during the forthcoming decade. Other countries in Asia like Taiwan, Singapore, and Korea are likely to export more capital on balance as the decade advances; also the rapidly growing emerging countries will save more as their incomes increase and will be able to provide a larger share of their own capital requirements as the next century gets closer.

Until the late 1980s, Japan's appetite for U.S. assets appeared insatiable—indeed, in the United States the complacent rhetorical question was often repeated, "Where else are they going to put their money?" The answer came in earnest in 1990, although the shift began in the previous year. An investment boom at home caused Japan's private domestic fixed investment as a share of GNP to jump by 3 percentage points between 1988 and 1990, while capital exports declined by nearly 40 percent. At the same time, East Asia's economic growth and the imminence of EC '92 made investment in those areas more attractive than in the United States. The consequence was disinvestment by the Japanese in U.S. securities at the turn of the decade and a shrinking of its purchases of U.S. real estate.

The outlook for the 1990s is controversial only in regard to the size of Japan's international capital availabilities, not in regard to the greater diversification of its geographic destinations. The greater attraction of potential yields in Europe and Asia will continue to be strengthened by Japanese concerns over protectionism in North America and the desire to make up for lost time by investing in Europe. Although to date Japanese businesses have been highly cautious about investing in Eastern Europe, they have monitored events there carefully. When they consider the time to be ripe they will be ready to invest. This is not to say that Japanese institutions and businesses are likely to withdraw from U.S. investment activity, but the annual volume is likely to be significantly below the average of the mid-1980s.

There are reasons to expect that Japan's net capital outflows may decline in volume during the decade. Demographic trends indicate that the labor shortage that has recently plagued Japanese industry will continue, thereby stimulating high domestic investment in Japan in labor-saving equipment and techniques. In addition, personal savings in Japan are in a long-term decline, a movement that will be furthered by demographics. Moreover, ongoing institutional changes in the country's financial sector, in raising the level of interest rates internally to international levels, will lessen the attraction of lending abroad.

Competitors for Japanese international capital will include, in addition to the emerging countries of Asia, Western and Eastern Europe, and the United States (probably in that order of credit-worthiness in Japanese perceptions), China, and a few Latin American countries. Total foreign investment in the People's Republic of China will remain subdued until a new regime once again embracing economic reform is installed in Beijing. That may not be until the twenty-first century. Meanwhile, new market-oriented regimes in Mexico, Chile, Venezuela, and possibly Argentina and Brazil will offer more and more attractive opportunities for foreign investors. Israel, which has a moral claim on the investable funds of Jews and Jewish institutions around the world, is overwhelmed by an influx of Soviet immigrants and anticipates foreign borrowing requirements for the next five years at $20 billion. Even Vietnam and the rest of Indochina are likely to be in the market for capital in the 1990s. Beyond a select few, however, the developing countries will find private capital mostly beyond their reach.

Demands on public aid funds and on the facilities of the international financial institutions, the World Bank Group—the International Bank for Reconstruction and Development (IBRD) and its associated agencies—and the IMF, are mounting as are proposals for new institutions or facilities within or outside of the existing ones. The Gulf Cooperation Council (comprising Saudi Arabia, Oman, Qatar, Bahrain, Kuwait, and the United Arab Emirates) has already established its own $10 billion development program to aid war-affected countries and other supporters of the Gulf War effort and

is urging developed countries to contribute. The EBRD has only $12.4 billion in capital provided by 39 industrial countries, but its president hopes that its activities will stimulate with a multiplier effect more than $100 billion in new public and private capital for Eastern Europe and the USSR. The Bush administration has proposed a five-year "Enterprise for the Americas" plan of $1.5 billion, urging Japan and the EC to join as equal partners, again with the hope that the plan will stimulate private investment in the area. The World Bank is seeking an increase of $1.3 billion in the capital of its private sector affiliate, the International Finance Corporation. Although during the late 1980s both the IBRD and the IMF became net receivers of funds because repayments exceeded new loans, their lending activities have recently been increasing, especially to Eastern Europe. Indeed an Asian Development Bank (ADB) report in April 1991 worried that new demands from Eastern Europe and the Gulf could drain funds from Asia and increase the cost of capital to the region. The loan activities of the ADB have also been slowing and budget constraints on its donors will probably result in no real growth in ADB resources through the first half of the 1990s.[7] The British meanwhile have been pushing for international support for a plan, known as the "Trinidad Terms," to ease the debt burden of the poorest developing countries by a cancellation of their debts to creditor governments.

Together these plans, hopes, and prayers rest on a shrunken base of capital availabilities compared with the salad days of the 1970s. Many are bound to be disappointed, all will find the costs high. The potential for world inflation is significant as all parts of the world in aggregate strive to consume

357

and invest more than the world as a whole is producing; the Bundesbank, the Bank of Japan, and the Federal Reserve Board will have their work cut out for them.

Geopolitical Implications

It is useful to speculate about the factors that might forestall the development of a global capital shortage. This expectation rests heavily on the conversion of Europe to the status of a net capital importer, which in turn depends primarily on a mounting flow of funds, public and private, into Eastern Europe and the Soviet Union from Western Europe and the rest of the world. It also rests on the assumption that oil prices will remain moderate. The capital inflow will fail to develop to any significant degree if political stability in the East is viewed as precarious or if rising costs there make the bottom-line calculus unattractive. Either would be bad news. Investment would be discouraged by the danger of the political instability that would probably be the consequence of a strong internal faction's advocacy of political independence. Such instability would hamper the fashioning of national economic policies (e.g., in the USSR or Czechoslovakia). In addition the retention of extensive government ownership of business would similarly delay the formation of new market-oriented policies. Neither of these contingencies would cause investment to cease, but it would delay and diminish the flow of capital and the recovery of the economies of Eastern Europe.

The very fact that the word *balkanization* has become part of the West's lexicon suggests that the danger of political fragmentation has strong historical precedent in Eastern Europe. Long-suppressed nationalistic forces can quickly resurface after the removal of authoritarianism and may lead to the creation of sovereign states too small to be viable economic entities.

The strength of liberal and conservative political factions internally varies from country to country. Either, moreover, can wane, surge, split, or recombine as has recently happened in the USSR and Hungary. Investment shrinks as uncertainty rises.

The greatest unknown in Eastern Europe lies in the degree of political patience that the citizenry can summon in the face of the austerity and unemployment that temporarily must accompany the wrenching experience of shifting from a planned, widely subsidized economy to one based on individual initiative, profit, and bankruptcy. What is involved is essentially a shift from a secure, riskless society to an environment offering the opportunity for individual betterment but at relatively high risk. The more severe and prolonged the period of austerity, the more the enthusiasm for the new system is likely to wane and the more comfortable the old will appear.[8] An articulate, populist leader claiming that he can solve the problems of unemployment and living standards without austerity may have great appeal.[9] This, however, is the Latin American solution that has often resulted in authoritarian regimes as well as hyperinflation and general economic deterioration as the countries struggle in vain to consume more than they produce.

The danger of insufficient patience to stay the course toward a new society will be enhanced if the European Community is niggardly in admitting exports from the East to its protected market. In this regard EC agricultural policies are of special importance because of the large role of agriculture in the economies of Poland and Hungary as well as Rumania, Bulgaria, and Albania. Thus far the Community has not been forthcoming in response to appeals from the East for some kind of associate membership. If the EC's reluctance persists, capital investment in the East can be seriously retarded.

Political instability in Eastern Europe and/or the USSR, whether the result of economic or political causes, would be likely to lead to increased defense spending in both the East and West. In the East, defense spending could be a tool of economic policy (to help solve unemployment problems) and security policy (to help maintain the existing regime in power). In Western Europe it would follow from the perception of heightened dangers on the eastern borders. In either case rising defense expenditures would be likely to retard the flow of investment resources to Eastern Europe as national savings rates declined.

Slow growth and prolonged austerity in Eastern Europe and the USSR would undoubtedly be accompanied by a rising volume of migration from East to West, legal and illegal. Since the collapse of the iron curtain, European Community members have been agitated by the danger of a mounting flood of foreign workers seeking employment in the EC and the political dissension and internal resentment in the West that could follow. This potential has made the EC '92 goal of a free flow of labor within the Community vastly more difficult to implement. By the same token the immigration potential is an important factor in EC reluctance to admit East European countries to associate membership.

Foreign capital alone cannot ensure a successful transformation within the decade of Eastern Europe and the USSR into growth economies with a rising standard of living because the capital requirements are beyond the capacities of the West to provide. At the margin, however, a rising inflow of foreign investment can buoy the hope and sustain the confidence of the East, encouraging the citizenry to stay the course of sacrifice and hard work that is essential to the transformation. Western capital, moreover, cannot compensate for political or geographic fragmentation in the area, for the failure of the EC to open its markets, for the failure to establish institutions that provide the foundation of a successful market economy, or for the unwillingness of a majority to sustain the declining living standards and great insecurities involved in the early years of the transformation process.

Thus if Europe as a whole does not become a net capital importer during the 1990s, the consequences are likely to entail enhanced political instability in the entire area. The New World Order, with its hope for peace, justice, and prosperity, could be aborted. For Eastern Europe the lost opportunity could be irreplaceable. If much of Eastern Europe or the USSR should follow the Latin American option, they would slip yet farther behind the West, thereby making the task of catching up even more difficult. If a diaspora of East Europeans were to follow and become concentrated in Western Europe, it could delay or obliterate the completion of EC '92. In addition, it could divert Europe's attention from larger, worldwide issues to solely Eurocentric concerns. The world as a whole would have lost an opportunity for growth and amity unequaled in the century.

The appearance of a global capital shortage in the 1990s could also be forestalled by the development of a sizable and sustained net capital export from the Middle East. Such an eventuality would be most likely to

359

occur as a result of a large increase in the real price of oil (e.g., above $30/barrel in today's prices). A sustained oil price hike would come about only if the Saudi Arabian regime were to initiate a dramatic shift in its long-term oil price policy. Since the early 1970s the Saudis have argued for a moderate oil price policy in order to avoid the stimulus to conservation and the development of oil substitutes that high real oil prices induce. Saudi petroleum reserves are so immense that such a pricing policy maximizes the aggregate long-term revenue attainable from them. Although the House of Saud may change its price policy temporarily for political reasons, a long-term sustained high oil price policy seems improbable during their tenure.

Any sustained change would imply the replacement of the royal family by a regime committed to maximizing present, not long-term, oil revenues. Such a regime would probably have different geopolitical goals than those of the Saud family. If the new regime represented a radical Arab group, higher current oil revenues could be desired for welfare payments to the poorer Arab states, for economic development in those states, for war preparations (including nuclear and missile capabilities) against perceived external enemies, for subversion, propaganda, and espionage abroad, or any combination of the above. The geopolitical map of the world would be vastly altered; growth rates in the oil-importing countries would collapse, at least temporarily; the effects on Eastern Europe could be disastrous; even with oil prices in the moderate range, East Europeans have been struggling to find the convertible currency now required for their oil imports from the USSR. The USSR would benefit, but unless the leadership of that country had committed itself to economic re-

form, the higher foreign exchange earnings would probably be squandered.

High oil prices (above $30/barrel in 1991 prices) if sustained for a number of years would almost certainly obliterate the New World Order. Resentment in oil importing countries against the regime instituting such a policy could become virulent. The danger of another armed conflict in the Gulf would be high. This danger in fact would be likely to give pause to any regime contemplating such a pricing policy shift.

Although from a rational viewpoint a sustained high oil price policy in the Middle East appears unlikely, the many long-standing enmities lacerating the region endure; its commitment to violence and retribution appears little altered. Bitterness between the haves and the have-nots can only be heightened by the policy of the rich Gulf states to aid solely those who offered support in the war. While Saddam Hussein remains in power, political instability will be rife, and if Iran should engineer his replacement by one of its supporters, nascent cooperation between Iran and Saudi Arabia would return to competition. A coup in Saudi Arabia cannot be ruled out, nor can the chance of high oil prices.

The appearance of a global capital shortage could also be forestalled if investment opportunities in Asia cease to be attractive. Once again the most likely cause of such an eventuality is political; potential economic causes do not have a high probability. For example, a sharp spike in real oil prices in the first half of the decade could have such an effect, but oil-consuming countries have had a good bit of experience in learning how—and how not—to cope successfully with high real oil prices. Moreover, Asia is an oil producer and thus would benefit somewhat from higher prices. Although temporary high oil prices would reduce the volume of world trade and redirect it, the competitive strength of the Asian economies implies that they would suffer less than other parts of the world. Investment, except in the oil producers, would decline and the global capital shortage would at least be postponed but less because of the decline in the demand for capital in Asia than from its decline elsewhere.

Whether a collapse in the U.S. market for Asian exports would by itself be sufficient to reduce Asia's growth and demand for international capital is not clear. Japan and the rest of the Pacific Rim could remain prosperous and growth in South and East Asia could continue, although at a slower pace, if policy changes in Japan successfully encouraged a large increase in Japanese consumption. Such a drastic change in Japanese policy appears improbable but not impossible.

A collapse in the U.S. demand for Asian goods could flow from virulent protectionism introduced in the United States. Such a development would affect world trade in the aggregate and could effectively eliminate the possibility not only of a global capital shortage but of the continuing U.S. role as the world leader. The New World Order would have no hope of surviving.

Investment in South and East Asia could be depressed by political developments in the area, perhaps in the form of renewed Chinese or Soviet threats to the stability of the region. A military crackdown by the People's Republic of China (PRC) in Hong Kong (to suppress alleged subversion there) or an attack on Taiwan (because of a declaration of independence there) would probably be highly destabilizing because, rightly or wrongly,

it would be perceived as an expansionary move on the part of the PRC. The return of an authoritarian regime in the USSR, especially if it resulted in enhanced Soviet influence in Indochina, would also be threatening. None of these now appears to present a threat to Asia in the 1990s. The most likely source of political instability seems to lie in the Korean peninsula, where an aging leader in the North will in due course move on. Events in North Korea after Kim Il-Sung are unpredictable, but rumors of a nuclear capability there are rife. A nuclear-armed North Korea under Kim or his successor could be highly destabilizing, not only to the area, but also to the entire world.

In summary, a global capital shortage in the sense defined above would reflect successful reconstruction and development in parts of the world mostly untouched by economic growth since World War II. As such it should be welcomed. The high interest rates that are implicit would allocate private capital to the most credit worthy; bilateral and multilateral foreign aid could ensure that countries of greater perceived risk are not totally excluded.

Dangers of inflation could be awesome. Pressures on governments to provide more help to eminently worthy countries, groups, and institutions may be irresistible. Efforts to expand the abilities of the multinational institutions to offer aid to the poorest of the poor as well as emerging economies will mount. In any year, however, the resources of the world are limited; the world cannot consume and invest more than it produces. World inflation would redistribute income toward rentier classes, further impoverishing the poor and contributing to political instability all over the world.

361

Inflationary dangers could be managed by appropriate monetary and fiscal policies. Such management would by no means be easy but it is not impossible. If, however, the worldwide demand for resources does seriously outstrip increases in world output—whether or not because of policy mismanagement in one important area—bitter recriminations over policy are likely. In these the United States will certainly be called to task for competing ("unfairly" will be implicit if not explicit) with struggling young democracies valiantly attempting to change their ways in the face of a greedy, recalcitrant, arrogant behemoth.

For the United States, a global capital shortage in the 1990s implies increasing competition for U.S. goods, services, and companies around the world. Trade will follow capital flows; thus although U.S. exports will benefit from growth in Asia and Eastern Europe, exports from Japan and Western Europe (respectively) will benefit most. More rapid growth in Europe and Japan implies that U.S. economic leadership will steadily diminish. It is not inconceivable that the Japanese economy could equal the U.S. economy in size at the turn of the century. By the twenty-first century the United States may be the world leader—a world leader or an also-ran.

Implications for the New World Order and the United States

The New World Order has been defined in summary as post–cold war responsibility-sharing. President George Bush defined it more fully during a speech in Alabama in April 1991. He spoke of his vision of new ways to achieve peace and prosperity in the world based on "a responsibility imposed by our successes." He based his hopes on commitments shared by large and small nations to four principles: peaceful settlement of disputes; solidarity against aggression; reduced and controlled arsenals; and just treatment of all peoples. He took the occasion to warn that in an interdependent world "no industrialized nation can maintain membership in good standing in the global community without assuming its fair share of responsibility for peace and security."

The leadership of the New World Order, however, remains ambiguous. The United States has seized the leadership role in this, as in the Gulf War, by default. U.S. military strength and its commitment to international agreements were put to the test and proven in that war (although some would doubt the accuracy of this statement). Unlike its ability to lead by example in the military realm, however, U.S. ability to set an example in the economic realm has been emasculated by a decade of economic excess. Not only does the United States lack the resources necessary to support its vision of the New World Order, but it is competing for those resources with the very nations it wants to help. The United States seeks to lead by exhortation, but with little or no leverage. Its geopolitical priorities are not necessarily those of Europe and Japan, for whom "responsibility-sharing" equates to "burden-sharing." Many in Europe and Japan resent what they see as a U.S. demand that they foot the bill for U.S. initiatives in which they have no voice. Disputes over priorities are simmering; the resolution of the burden-sharing versus the responsibility-sharing issue is not in sight. To a large degree this resolution awaits a definition by both Japan and Europe of what their proper role in the post–cold war world should be and whether it should be regional or global. In the past each has been content to confine its world role to international commerce, leaving leadership in geopolitical decisions to the United States. Now they are being asked to dilute their pursuit of profit by the broader interests of world peace and political stability. The ambiguity of their responses to the Gulf War indicates that they are not yet committed to a world role.

The opportunity for constructive harmony in geopolitical relations has never been so great since World War I when sharp ideological differences first began to shape the world. Today the degree of consensus on the principles of a market economy, democracy, and pluralism is truly astonishing, embraced not only by the industrialized democracies but by most of the developing world and the formerly centralized, one-party authoritarian states. This consensus developed Topsy-like during the 1980s as the failure of communism was acknowledged by its practitioners and while the rapid growth of export-based Asian economies, most of whom claimed without justification to be free markets, attracted attention in the import-replacement, closed economies in most of the developing world. The awesome victory of the United Nations coalition during the Gulf War served to consolidate the consensus. That consensus encouraged the industrialized countries to believe that fledgling market economies and emerging democracies merited financial help.

Just as the opportunities contained in this new consensus are immense, so are its hazards. The terms *democracy* and *market-mechanism* have been grasped by citizens of failing systems as an incantation, often without any real comprehension of what is entailed or what sacrifices will be necessary to make the shift to the newly embraced

system. There is the danger that the amulet can be discarded as quickly as it was grasped.

The greatest contribution that the United States can make during the 1990s toward the success of the New World Order lies in strengthening its own economy. Only by increasing the productivity of its own resources can it once again raise its own standard of living, eliminate its dependence on foreign capital, and generate the resources necessary to support its foreign policy by example rather than exhortation. If the promise of the New World Order fails to materialize, the blame will fall in large measure on the United States.

Notes

1. Data on international capital flows are ambiguous and unreliable. They are statistically hard to measure because they exist in such magnitude, because of exchange rate changes and other valuation problems, because of the desire for secrecy on the part of many borrowers or lenders, and because statistical techniques employed in many countries leave much to be desired. As a consequence of the resulting errors and omissions, IMF data show aggregate payments of international capital exceed receipts, which for the world cannot happen. Figures cited in the text should be viewed only as rough orders of magnitude, even for the United States and other developed countries. It should be noted that the consistent direction of the errors gives a bias toward gloom in the IMF data.

2. Federal Reserve Bank of Boston, *New England Economic Review*, September–October 1990, p. 44.

3. Ethan S. Harris and Charles Steindel, "The Decline in U.S. Savings and Its Implications for Economic Growth," Federal Reserve Bank of New York, *Quarterly Review* 15, no. 3–4 (Winter 1991), p. 14.

4. It is interesting to note that in most industrial countries private savings (as a share of GNP) are relatively constant with changes in corporate savings moving in the opposite direction from changes in personal savings. "Savings Trends and Behav-

ior in OECD Countries," *OECD Working Paper No. 67* (Paris, 1989).

5. Robert Mabro, "Surplus Economies: Middle East Oil Producers," *International Economic Insight* 2 (March/April 1991), p. 4.

6. *Far Eastern Economic Review*, May 23, 1991, p. 16.

7. *Financial Times* (London), April 24, 1991, p. 4; *Far Eastern Economic Review*, April 25, 1991, p. 51.

8. See "Old Regime Comforts Many East Germans," *Financial Times* (London), May 24, 1991, p. 3.

9. In Poland after only about six months of austerity following the shift to a market system an astonishing number of Poles voted for a Canadian businessman (for president) who was promising such wonders.

IV. Toward a New World Order?

The New World Order: A Historical Perspective

Paul W. Schroeder

THE NEW WORLD order (NWO) is a term that burst onto the scene with the outrage accompanying Iraq's annexation of Kuwait and seems to have passed as rapidly from the scene as its creator, George Bush. As a rallying cry it certainly has fallen from favor, but as a kind of conceptual shorthand it continues to engage anyone interested in the character of the post–cold war world.

Most of the writing about the NWO has been done by policy specialists, but the rest of us should not allow them to coopt entirely the discussion of post–cold war order. After all, they are usually preoccupied with the present, looking little beyond the immediate task of defending or criticizing specific policy initiatives by the United States on the world scene. Questions of order and disorder in the international system cannot be brought into focus in this fashion. Here the historian has something unique to offer, not narrowly in the

Paul W. Schroeder is professor of history and political science at the University of Illinois and specializes in the history of international politics. His most recent book is *The Transformation of European Politics, 1763–1848* (Oxford: Clarendon Press, 1994).

Copyright © 1994 by The Center for Strategic and International Studies and the Massachusetts Institute of Technology
The Washington Quarterly • 17:2

sense of useful analogies that shed light on specific decisions, but more broadly on how to think about larger questions, issues, and trends.

This historian's perspective on the NWO debate is that the policy pundits have it wrong. A new disorder has not replaced the new world order. The historic moment has not passed. Something important remains in the discussion of the NWO, something that will help the United States and the international community to get their bearings in this period of uncertainty, to chart a course away from the anarchic tendencies of the moment and toward a world more orderly in its affairs.

The most basic questions about the NWO—does one exist? how substantial is it?—cannot in fact be answered without a fairly long historical perspective. Such a perspective is essential for understanding the nature of the contemporary international system by revealing how it developed and how it differs from previous counterparts—and thus for understanding where and how to invest the intellectual and political energies of the United States, to say nothing of national blood and treasure.

This article offers one such historical perspective. Admittedly, my task is to paint a big, complex picture inside a very small frame—the short page length of a journal article. By necessity, this means omitting and

nplifying a great deal and mak-
few assertions that a lengthier
it would permit me to explain
and defend. But the point here is to
craft a cogent, albeit sketchy line of
argument that makes possible some of
these other tasks.

The Current Definition

The phrase "new world order" is com-
monly used without explicit definition
and ideas on it doubtless vary. Yet one
can elicit a working definition from the
kinds of measures carried out or called
for in its name since the end of the
Cold War, most of which involve peacemaking actions of various kinds in
different world trouble spots—actions
intended to preserve or restore law and
order; deter, stop, and punish war,
aggression, and oppression; relieve civilian suffering; and promote civil and
human rights. One therefore could define the NWO as an international system in which the United States and
like-minded friends and allies act together, preferably under the aegis of
the United Nations (UN), to preserve
or establish peace by upholding international law and order against aggressors, lawbreakers, and oppressors.
The definition, if the NWO is to survive and work, implies that the international community in some cases will
have to proceed beyond persuasion,
mediation, and conciliation to deterrence and compellence, that is, the
use of force, to make certain actors
stop certain actions and perform
others. Again, this fits common usage.
According to many, including former
President Bush, the NWO was
founded by the Persian Gulf War, a
UN-sanctioned collective war against
Iraqi aggression. Actions taken since
by the United States and other states

in Iraq and Somalia, like those often
proposed in regard to Bosnia, involve
the use of armed force. Coercive actions against other supposed aggressors and lawbreakers are often urged
in the name of the NWO, and the
humanitarian and prudential arguments used in favor of such measures
assume that there is an NWO that
mandates such peacemaking actions
by the international community.

Few Americans condemn the idea
of such an NWO on principle or oppose all U.S. participation in international efforts to promote peace and
humanitarian causes. Disagreement
arises, however, over using force (especially U.S. force) to uphold the
NWO, namely, to bring supposed aggressors and lawbreakers into line with
some law or code of international conduct supposedly set by the international community through compellence and deterrence. Often the
concerns are practical (the operation's
sustainability, limits, chances of success, costs, risks, precedents, unintended consequences, etc.). But other
challenges go to issues of principle.
Who is to decide who is right among
the parties in conflict, and by what
right or principle? What gives UN resolutions the sanctity and force of law?
Why should some resolutions be rig-
orously enforced and others not, some
international crimes punished and
others ignored?

Thus Americans may agree tacitly
on the definition of the NWO, but
sharply disagree over its reality, prac-
ticability, and desirability. The split
can be seen as one between "idealists"
and "realists" (by which I do not mean
the two schools in international relations theory, but simply those who believe that certain norms, rules, and
laws can and should be enforced in
international relations, as opposed to

those who believe that conflicting state interests and balance of power politics still prevail). Idealists, noting the spread of civil, ethnic, and interstate conflict in the world since the end of the Cold War, argue that a failure now to uphold the rule of law in critical areas will encourage lawlessness and aggression, undermine the NWO, ruin a historic opportunity to promote peace and justice, and promote new violence and conflict throughout the world. Realists, recognizing the same world trends, stress different problems and dangers—the difficulties, risks, and unpredictable consequences of intervention, the limited resources of the United States and its allies and their frequent divergences of views and interest, the shaky juridical basis and controversial nature of claims about international law and justice, and so on. This leads them to an opposite conclusion about the NWO: that it is a mirage, that historical patterns of power politics, national conflict, and great-power rivalry still govern world politics, and that the goals of limiting war and preserving general world peace are better served if U.S. force is used solely for clearly defined and strictly limited U.S. national interests.

Frequently in debates like this, key assumptions are shared by both sides without their being fully aware of it. These assumptions, left unarticulated and unchallenged, distort and stultify the debate. This essay contends that this holds true here, with paradoxical effects. Where the two sides openly disagree, on the likely consequences of acting or failing to act according to the NWO's supposed mandates and requirements, they are both correct; but where they tacitly agree, in how they define and conceive of the NWO, they are both wrong.

How Both Sides Are Right about the NWO

To start with the idealists: they are right to insist that a genuinely new and effective NWO has emerged in the last 50 years, especially the last decade, and further right in believing that this NWO, if not sustained and developed, may break down at great cost and risk to the United States and the whole international community. One need not be an international historian to see that a new era in international relations has emerged since World War II. In fact, the evidence of it is by now so familiar that Americans take it for granted and fail to see how startling it is in historical perspective. The signs include:

- the conversion of Germany and Japan in one generation from militarist, imperialist aggressors to stable, democratic industrial giants ambitious for trade and prosperity rather than military or political power;
- the economic and political integration and permanent pacification of Western Europe;
- the dismantling of the great European colonial empires, largely peacefully and voluntarily;
- the expansion of the UN to worldwide scope, the recognition of official juridical equality among its members, and its growth in reach and effectiveness for practical peacekeeping;
- the preservation of general peace (i.e., no system-wide wars and no all-out wars between major powers) through four decades of intense ideological and political competition between rival blocs, even while new powers were emerging and dangerous regional conflicts and rivalries constantly flared up;
- the gradual development of re-

straints on the arms race and the cooling of ideological rivalry even while this competition went on;[1]

- the admission of a host of new or transformed states into the world community; and, finally,

- the end of the Cold War and the (until now, at least) generally peaceful dismantling and transformation of the Soviet empire.

The point is not that this has yielded a brave new world free of war and upheaval. No one claims that; few if any think that such a world will ever come about. The point is rather that accomplishments such as this were unheard of and impossible in previous eras of history. When one adds to these developments others perhaps less spectacular or more disputable but nonetheless hopeful and progressive (e.g., democratization in Spain and Portugal, the end of apartheid in South Africa, progress toward Arab–Israeli peace, the astonishing economic and political development of the western Pacific Rim, and the decline of dictatorships and rise of democracies in Latin America and elsewhere), the case for the existence of the NWO, that is, a genuine new order of international politics, becomes overwhelming.

The historian's contribution to understanding this remarkable change is not to try to show that the more things have changed, the more they have stayed the same. This is the line some so-called realists take, insisting on the unchanging dominance of power politics and the primacy of the balance of power. The historian should know better. Granted that grave international problems and dangers still exist or will arise, what sensible person would exchange the current problems for those of 10, 50, or 100 years ago, or insist that they are really still the

same? The international historian can indeed identify certain roots and antecedents of the NWO in history, can even (in my view) show that it is not solely the product of the last 20 or 50 years, but the climax of a long historical development stretching back to the sixteenth and seventeenth centuries. Yet the very historical insight that sees the NWO as the fruit of a long evolution highlights the contrast between this era and the past, emphasizing how the NWO now enables statesmen to manage problems and maintain a stable international order in ways that statesmen of previous eras could only dream of. Denying the fundamental differences between the world orders of previous centuries and that of today is like denying the changes in the capitalist system over the same period.[2]

Yet, on the other side, the realist critics are right to claim that current ways of using and sustaining the NWO are not working well, and if pursued much longer may harm both the NWO and world peace. Once again special historical knowledge is not required to see this or understand the reasons; in fact, political and social science, international relations theory, practical experience in international politics, and plain common sense work as well or better. The special contribution of historians is first to point out that the idea of preserving peace and establishing a new international order through collectively enforcing international law against violators or imposing certain norms of international conduct on all actors—an old idea that goes back at least to the high Middle Ages and figures in most peace plans developed in the centuries since[3]—has regularly failed in history, proving ineffective and utopian at best and productive of even greater violence and wider war at worst. Second, historians then help show why the reasons for this persistent failure still prevail under the NWO today. The central reason, familiar to all scholars, is that making international politics into a confrontation between alleged lawbreakers and supposed enforcers of the law runs counter to the core of the international system that originated in Europe between the fifteenth and the seventeenth centuries and now embraces the whole world. That system, as the term "international politics" implies, presupposes the coexistence of independent states in juridically coordinate rather than superordinate and subordinate relations with each other, each claiming sovereignty, that is, the sole right to proclaim and enforce the law within its own domains, and demanding recognition of that sovereignty from the others. Carried to its logical conclusion, the concept of the NWO as the collective enforcement of international law against transgressors fundamentally challenges and undermines this order, still the only one available, and therefore must tend to provoke resistance and heighten conflict.

This shows up in international affairs in various ways, obvious and commonplace yet often overlooked. Tactically, this concept of "law enforcement" makes international confrontations and conflicts into something like a gunfight between the sheriff and the outlaws in a movie Western. Yet for purposes of limiting conflict and promoting peace in international affairs, force, if it is unavoidable, should be used as in judo rather than as in a gunfight. The object in judo, to use an aggressor's own force combined with a minimum effort of one's own to overbalance and disarm rather than destroy him, is better not only because it results in less violence and destruction, but also because a key assumption in an international system is that all essential actors should be preserved, because even an aggressive opponent, once curbed, has a necessary role to play. Psychologically, when sanctions imposed by the international community are portrayed as enforcing the law against violators, the honor as well as the interests of the accused party are impugned, giving it additional incentives to resist (for a government that cannot defend its honor often quickly loses its power) and effective propaganda to rally domestic support against outsiders. (Precisely this has happened in the former Yugoslavia and Somalia.) Strategically, this outlook pulls the international community into pursuit of a vague, almost undefinable goal (when is the law sufficiently enforced, the lawbreaker adequately punished?). This raises the stakes for the international coalition in terms of its prestige and credibility, while leaving its means of enforcement limited and the concrete interests of its various members in the quarrel divergent—a sure prescription for disunity and defections. Juridically, it encourages challenges to the legitimacy of the action that an aggressor can easily exploit. Practically, it engenders disputes over meeting and sharing the costs and burdens of enforcement, and fears that enforcing the law will result in more suffering and damage than did the original alleged violation.

All this, added to the fundamental reluctance of states to acknowledge an authority higher than themselves and thereby implicitly surrender their right to judge and defend their own cause, makes it clear that the NWO, so long as it is conceived as a collective effort to enforce compliance with international law or the will of the international community, faces grave obstacles.

The conclusion seems to represent an impasse. The NWO is real and vitally important, as its defenders insist; yet the measures it apparently requires are unworkable, counterproductive, and dangerous, as its critics claim. The way out calls for rethinking the NWO.

The NWO: Not Compellence-Deterrence, but Association-Exclusion

This rethinking begins with seeing that the NWO did not basically arise from successful compellence and deterrence, and does not mainly require these means to survive and work today. The account offered here of how the NWO was actually born and has worked is, like the whole essay, brief, oversimplified, and doubtless controversial, but it rests on well-known historical facts. The NWO as it emerged after World War II was principally the product of a durable consensus among a sizable number of major states and smaller powers, mostly West European and well developed politically and economically, that certain kinds of international conduct (direct military aggression and threats, the undermining of foreign governments by subversion, economic practices considered tantamount to economic warfare, and even some forms of civil war or internal oppression) had to be ruled out as incompatible with their general security and welfare. They formed various associations based on this consensus, designed both to deter external actions or threats of this kind and to promote a different kind of international conduct among themselves, namely, to encourage political and economic cooperation and integration, expand trade and communication, resolve conflicts peacefully, and promote broad political participation, civil and human rights, and the economic and social welfare of the member states. The various associations and institutions created for these purposes (the Western European Union, Benelux, the North Atlantic Treaty Organization [NATO], the European Coal and Steel Community, the European Community [EC], the European Free Trade Area, and others) proved over time not only durable, able to withstand external challenges and internal disintegration, but also successful in promoting prosperity, political stability, and democratic freedoms among the members themselves. As a result, these kinds of association promoting these patterns of conduct became a leading model for international politics in the developed world and much of the developing world, tending to pull other states toward it and to undermine associations and practices hostile to it.

The story is familiar; the historian's contribution is again to emphasize how new and unprecedented this development was and remains. A rough rule of thumb on alliances and associations in European international history is this: in the seventeenth century, all alliances worked almost purely as instruments of power politics (i.e., self-defense, war, and territorial expansion), even when ostensibly created for other purposes (e.g., religion or dynastic unions), and all were highly unreliable, no matter how solemnly sworn and guaranteed or expensively purchased with subsidies and bribes— so much so that it was impossible to calculate when or under what circumstances an ally was likely to defect. By the eighteenth century, alliances and associations, although still oriented almost exclusively to power politics, had grown more reliable, but not much more durable. They lasted only so long as they served the special interests of the contracting parties and so long as other more profitable alliances

the Cold War" means. Even where a confrontation in some form still persists, with Cuba, China, North Korea, and elsewhere, the best hopes for change and means to promote it are those of association-benefits/exclusion-denial. Although the new methods cannot work quickly to end fighting already begun or control parties already locked in mortal combat over irreconcilable positions, as in the former Yugoslavia and parts of the former Soviet Union, even here they are not useless. Ultimately the only kind of pressure and coercion helpful in producing a durable settlement is one that induces all parties to recognize that violent solutions do not work in the long run, and that another way is open. (Witness the recent signs of a break in the Israeli–Palestinian and Israeli–Arab impasse.) This is what the NWO sanctions of association and exclusion are designed to do; the NWO not only enables the United States to use them, but almost compels it to do so.

Some Implications for Policy

Changing the way Americans think about the NWO and its operation affects their goals, priorities, and expectations in its regard. If the NWO is developed and works, not by enforcing international law and punishing violators, but by forming and maintaining associations that reward those who conform to group norms and exclude those who do not, then the main goal of policy under the NWO should be sustaining this process of association and exclusion. This sounds like a mere truism, but it has specific, important implications. It means that the prime concern in regard to the NWO should not be how it can be used in particular problem areas to advance

particular ends, values, and interests, even vital ones like peace, democracy, and human rights, but rather to make sure that the NWO itself is preserved and developed, for its own sake. The NWO, in other words, must finally be seen as an end in itself, the necessary means and condition for other vital ends and values. Americans accept this logic in other contexts. They understand, for example, that even in the hurly-burly of domestic politics they must be concerned to uphold the Constitution and the democratic process, so that politics can remain free. They know that agreements and institutions like the General Agreement on Tariffs and Trade (GATT), the International Monetary Fund (IMF), the World Bank, the Group of Seven, and others are needed not just to promote economic stability and prosperity for themselves and their friends, but to maintain a viable world economic system generally. The same principle applies to international relations. If the NWO's working principle of association-exclusion enables the international community to accomplish important tasks better and more safely than can be done without it, then that system itself deserves support as something of intrinsic and not mere instrumental value. The descriptive analysis must have prescriptive implications.

This applies a fortiori to the associations that produced the NWO and make it effective. The UN, which once could be dismissed as merely a useful talking shop or meeting place handy for certain purposes, has become valuable in its own right as an integral part of the NWO. This is even more true of the narrower associations that in recent decades have succeeded in keeping their members in line and making others wish to join them. The end of the Cold War has made them not less but more important in a practical, immediate way, at the same time presenting them with major challenges of reorientation, consolidation, and expansion. The most vital task in the NWO today is not stamping out conflict and enforcing international law everywhere in the world, but preserving and consolidating gains already made and in danger of being lost—not putting out brush fires in remote areas, but securing and expanding the homestead and the corral as a place of refuge from them. This means keeping the EC cohesive and attractive, NATO intact and functioning as a vehicle of integration and cooperation, the Japanese–American economic and political relationship stable, the progress of the Pacific Rim going, the world system of relatively free world trade working, and the road to freedom and prosperity in eastern Europe and Russia open in the long run.

If one recognizes that the NWO, thus understood, has intrinsic value and is best maintained by preserving and developing the associations and mechanisms that support it, this suggests in turn a simple, practical rule of thumb for policy. Each proposal that the UN, the EC, the United States and its allies, or some other international group should carry out some mission or measure in the name of the NWO must face an initial question: Is this action compatible with the special nature, mission, and methods of the NWO, primarily those of association and exclusion? If so, and if the action is also desirable and practical per se, then it is worth considering; if not, then not. In other words, Americans must stop expecting and demanding that the NWO perform tasks it was not designed to do, which would wreck it if seriously tried, and then denouncing it or despairing of it when these mis-sions are not undertaken or the effort fails.[6]

This happens repeatedly—whenever, in fact, the UN and/or some other international community or authority is called on to intervene in civil wars and ethnic conflicts, restore civil order, alleviate starvation, break illegal blockades, settle territorial disputes, impose armistices, stop governmental oppression and violations of civil rights, establish war-crimes tribunals and judge war criminals, punish countries for defying UN resolutions or supporting terrorism, and so on—all without asking whether the way the NWO actually works makes these tasks necessary or possible. Name any international evil or problem, and it is a safe bet that someone has called on the world community to solve it, and denounced it or proclaimed the demise of the NWO for its failure to do so. Much of the current cynicism and despair about the NWO derives from the inevitable disappointment of unrealistic expectations. Although, as already noted, such proposals are frequently opposed on practical grounds, little attention is given to the danger of ruining the NWO by burdening it with assignments unsuited to its mission and methods.

This perspective also calls for some faith in the NWO, patience with the process of association and exclusion by which it works, and allowing it sufficient time and steady application to work. It is unreasonable to argue, for example, that if there were a real NWO the international community would long since have acted to bring the fighting in Bosnia to an end, stop "ethnic cleansing" and other atrocities, relieve the suffering of civilians, settle the territorial and other disputes there, and establish a viable Bosnian state. Whether one believes that more could have been done earlier to achieve these ends through diplomacy or other means, or believes (as I do) that these goals were largely unattainable from the outset given the circumstances and the attitudes and aims of the various parties involved, and regardless of the inherent desirability or undesirability, feasibility or unfeasibility of these ends, achieving them is not now and never was the kind of task the NWO is designed or suited to carry out, and they must not be made the test of its existence and worth.

This does not mean that the NWO is useless or irrelevant in situations like Bosnia. It rather means that the real task of the NWO in Bosnia and the Balkans as a whole, and the real test of the efficacy of its principle of association-exclusion, still lie ahead of it, after the current conflict, which Serbia and Croatia have already effectively won, is over. The vital question, once the fighting is ended and some sort of "peace settlement" is patched up, will be whether the international community decides to forget the manner in which the newly independent states of Serbia and Croatia were founded and the integral-nationalist ideologies on which they are based, and receives them back into Europe and the world as full, normal partners. Should this happen, it would constitute weighty evidence that there is no real NWO; for this would represent the old politics pure and simple, even if it were defended as a way to forget the past and promote peace and reconciliation among former enemies. It was characteristic of previous eras that successful aggression usually paid. States could generally expect, once they had made their gains and got them sanctioned in some sort of treaty, to be treated once more as a normal member of the family of states; this is

exactly what Serb and Croat nationalist leaders are counting on now. If, however (as could relatively easily be done), the international community chooses to exclude Serbia and Croatia after the "peace settlement," that is, to ban them from full membership and participation in the UN and its constituent agencies and above all from the EC, until and unless these two states give concrete evidence of change in their fundamental outlook toward other states and people, especially Muslims, Albanians, and Macedonians, this would be evidence of the NWO in operation. Moreover, this kind of isolation and confrontation would have every chance of success, given the sorry state of the Croatian economy and the still worse condition of Serbia's—success of course being defined not as the destruction of either state but a realization in both, by leaders and peoples, of what their victory and the policies of aggression and ethnic cleansing used to achieve it has cost them in terms of European and international recognition and status, commerce, technology, academic and cultural exchanges, tourism, foreign investment, international sports, and more. Such long-term pressures of exclusion-denial would have a far better chance of bringing about the needed changes in attitude and political culture in Serbia and Croatia (above all, the realization that prosperity and security in today's Europe and the world cannot be based on aggression, ethnic cleansing, and authoritarian nationalist programs) that using external force for deterrence and compellence could not produce, even in the unlikely case that force was successful in a military sense. This is said merely to illustrate how the NWO could work. Rather than prescribe a policy, it suggests an idea for one, as part of an argument

379

that the NWO makes strategies and outcomes possible now that were futile and utopian even a few decades ago.

Some Objections

There are some likely objections to this view that deserve brief discussion, less to refute them (the answers have mostly already been indicated) than to avoid misunderstandings and correct wrong impressions.

One is that this view of international politics is soft and sentimental, ignores its harsh realities, and relies on reason and moral suasion for peace and stability. Surely, however, a view that gives the maintenance of an impersonal system and process in international politics priority over all other goals, including the promotion of justice, civil and human rights, international law, the relief of innocent suffering, and even the prevention of local wars, is not sentimental. Nor is it soft to call for excluding successful aggressor states from the international community, and making their peoples pay the heavy political and economic price for that exclusion.

Another objection is that this proposal reflects too academic a concept of how human beings learn and the world works. It expects history to teach peoples and states their errors and induce them to change, when in fact people generally learn what they want to from history, mostly the wrong things or nothing at all, and many leaders are totally indifferent to "lessons of history" and the costs of their failures so long as they can keep their state machines and essential followers under control, make the masses pay, and deceive them into blaming the outside world for their sufferings. This is largely true, but irrelevant.

This view of the NWO *does not propose to let* history teach Saddam Hussein or Slobodan Milosevic, or their peoples, that aggression does not pay. True, history left to itself can and does "teach" almost any lessons one wants it to, including the lesson that aggression does pay. This is instead an argument that the NWO enables the current generation, unlike past generations, to control the "lessons" of history in some measure, by affording it means other than external armed force, and better than armed force, to make governments and peoples recognize that certain courses fail and have negative results and that others are unavoidable and more profitable. Certainly peoples often resist learning from history, clinging stubbornly to a familiar version of the past that validates their collective image and self-view and justifies their actions. The historian Lewis B. Namier's comment that Freud's definition of neurosis, to be "dominated by unconscious memory, fixated upon the past, and unable to overcome it," is the regular condition of historical communities,[7] points exactly to a big part of the current problem, especially in the Balkans. But the strategy of exclusion and denial is a good way of helping states and peoples to get over their history, to break out of it. Repeated, long-term experience of failure is a powerful teacher, especially in teaching that one must break with one's past to have a tolerable future.

The most important criticism, however, is the charge of ineffectiveness: that the incentives and sanctions of association-benefits and exclusion-denial are too weak to produce a stable world order. They will be ineffective with dictators like Saddam Hussein or against dedicated or desperate peoples, groups, and organizations of all kinds, and will fail to stop civil wars, settle serious territorial disputes, or curb terrorism. They also act too slowly, and therefore cannot prevent or quickly stop developments too dangerous or horrible to be tolerated—aggressions like the invasion of Kuwait, the acquisition of weapons of mass destruction by rogue governments or terrorist organizations, the spread of aggression, conflict, and ethnic cleansing from one region to another, or genocide and mass starvation. In other words, even if the so-called NWO and its methods may work with reasonably mature, developed, peaceful states, they cannot handle the real problems of a world still violent, hostile, and chaotic. These problems call for either the old instruments of individual state action and power politics, or newer ones in the form of effective forcible sanctions imposed by the international community through the UN, or a combination of the two.

Much of this is true, and has already been admitted; this essay has emphasized that there are tasks the NWO cannot do, and should not be expected or asked to. One can go further: forcible sanctions are still needed in cases where a particular evil or danger so clearly and directly threatens the general peace and the continued existence and operation of the whole international system that it must be averted promptly at almost any cost. But this does not annul the case for the NWO as presented here, or even weaken it. To believe in the reality and efficacy of the NWO does not mean to suppose that everything in international politics is new, that coercive force, including military force, need no longer ever be used, or anything of that sort. Any "new order" in history (even where this much-abused term is legitimate) is never wholly new; the term means only that a corner has been turned, a trend set, a new way of doing things

become dominant, and an old one recessive. So, here, the claim made about the NWO means only (but this is a great deal) that the principal hopes and chances for durable, general, relative peace in the world (all the adjectives are important) rest now on a world order operating primarily by association-exclusion rather than deterrence-compellence. This certainly implies that the rewards and sanctions of association-benefits and exclusion-denial must be in general more effective for more of the required purposes of general world order and peace than deterrence-compellence. That claim, however, can be sustained despite exceptions.

To be sure, NWO-style rewards and sanctions will not achieve some desired ends in international politics—but neither will armed force. The question of which is more useful under more circumstances for more important goals, moreover, must include an analysis of costs. A historic trend in international politics, rapidly accelerating in this century, has been the steep rise in costs attached to the use of armed force, both absolutely and in ratio to the benefits achieved, and a corresponding diminution in what it can usefully accomplish. To the old familiar escalating costs—possible failure and defeat, blood, lost treasure, diverted resources, ancillary destruction, lasting alienation and bitterness—the emergence of the NWO has added an important opportunity cost: that ends conceivably attainable by association-exclusion become impossible once force is used. Using armed force against an international transgressor like Serbia or Iraq is not a more quick and effective way of teaching it the same lessons about international association and cooperation as are intended by the tactics of association-benefits and exclusion-denial. Instead, trying to "teach" these lessons by armed force obstructs teaching or learning them by the other route at all, as current U.S. experiences in Iraq, Bosnia, and Somalia indicate and many historical examples attest. The more the lesson desired is inflicted by external armed force, the less the experience of defeat and failure is likely to be internalized in a useful way and lead to the kind of durable change desired. Furthermore, every resort to armed force willy-nilly teaches both the participants and the bystanders the retrograde lesson that the NWO and its methods cannot be trusted in critical cases to get the job done—which becomes a self-fulfilling prophecy.

Another major element in the cost-benefit analysis is the consideration that many of the proposed aims in international politics for which NWO methods are admittedly ineffective—enforcing international law, reversing historic wrongs, stopping civil wars, imposing territorial settlements in hotly disputed cases, punishing international crimes and criminals and compensating their victims—are unattainable by any means and incompatible with any working international system. The truth is that many evils and injustices in the world are too deeply rooted to be undone; that, as the nineteenth-century publicist Friedrich von Gentz said, "All historic rights are wrongs, sanctioned by time"; and that the only sane response to historic wrongs is often, as Prince Metternich of Austria argued, to "outlive the evil." Recognizing and accepting the NWO means, among other things, coming to terms with these commonplace truths, accepting that some goals possibly desirable in themselves cannot be pursued under it and are not worth pursuing at the cost of the system as a whole. At the same time, association and exclusion are not in-

effective in achieving the goals most central and important to the NWO, namely, rewarding international cooperation and inducing aggressors and troublemakers to recognize failure and change course. To see this, one need only look at the long list of states that since 1945 have been excluded, or have excluded themselves, from the mainstream of international commerce, industry, technology, communications, travel and tourism, exchange of information, international capital, and so forth. None of these states has found peace and prosperity; most have tried or are trying to escape from that exclusion, often changing the policies the international community objects to in the attempt.

Naturally this learning process required to bring states and peoples into the NWO takes time. Important, durable changes in collective mentality and political culture cannot happen overnight—which means (to reiterate) that some threats may require a different, speedier response, despite the strictures and reservations discussed above. Yet one of the important things making the NWO new is the fact that now such changes can develop much faster and be more predictable, even controllable, than in the past. International history used ironically to illustrate the Old Testament saying that the sins of the fathers are visited upon the children to the third and fourth generation. Generations usually passed before leaders and peoples became aware of the real consequences of past policies, or even recognized past follies and crimes as such. Prussians tasted the full fruits of Frederick the Great's militarism and aggression only in Napoleon's time; only in 1919 and 1945 did the full consequences of Bismarck's founding of the Second Reich in 1871 become clear. This still is often the case, of course; but much speedier learning has now become possible. Germans and East Europeans, for example, have judged and decided between two competing systems in one generation. In the NWO, with history accelerated and the speed and ease of communication enormously increased, it is no longer unreasonable to expect children to see and repudiate the sins of the fathers while the fathers are still around.

There is a further objection to this view of how the NWO works and should be used that, if true, cannot be answered by rational argument. It is that this way of conceiving and managing the NWO does not fit the U.S. character and political system. It requires patience, steady attention to the long view, a willingness to wait for results, and the ability to adjust to changed reality and to accept blurred, complex, uncertain outcomes and live with them if they are the best attainable—all virtues that the U.S. public does not possess and the U.S. political system, focused on domestic concerns, immediate issues, simple solutions, and clear-cut moral dichotomies, neither teaches to citizens nor rewards in politicians.

It is not clear to me that so sweeping an indictment of the U.S. political culture and its effects on international politics is justified. Americans, both leaders and the public, have over the last 50 years or so shown in some instances a striking ability to learn, adjust, stay the course, and adapt to change in the international arena—witness their support of Israel, commitment to NATO, general maintenance of free trade, and acceptance of relative failure and the limits to U.S. power in Korea, Vietnam, and elsewhere. Yet it may be that calling on Americans to accept this version of the NWO and lead it (for who else can?) means calling for a United States dif-

ferent from the existing one—less prone to violence at home and abroad, less shortsighted about its own interests and those of other states, less provincial and ignorant about the rest of the world, and less insistent that in dealing with any crisis it call the shots and that, if it decides to get in, other states must help it get the job done quickly and get out. Clearly the NWO cannot work under this kind of leadership or these conditions. Even more important, this attitude on the part of many Americans is incompatible with the ongoing transformation of international politics through a collective learning process, a change in collective mentalities and political cultures involving whole nations and peoples, enabling them to adjust to each other successfully in a new order. Americans need to be part of this learning process as much as other people, perhaps in some respects more. Americans deny this cardinal need and responsibility whenever they say in effect, "The United States cannot follow this or that policy in international affairs, even though it is necessary and legitimate, because the American people will not support it and the American political system makes it impossible to sell it to them." What they really say by this is that they want to run the NWO and enjoy its benefits, but not belong to it, or change and grow with it—that they are stupid and inconsistent, and prefer to stay that way. A nation that uses that excuse for very long must sooner or later excuse itself into disaster.

The author first wrote this essay as a Jennings Randolph Peace Fellow at the United States Institute of Peace, whose support he gratefully acknowledges. He also wishes to thank Jack Snyder of Columbia University's Institute of War and Peace Studies for his comments. The views expressed in this article are the author's own and do not necessarily reflect the views either of the University of Illinois, or of the United States Institute of Peace.

Notes

1. Roger Kanet and Edward A. Kolodziej, eds., *The Cold War as Cooperation* (Baltimore, Md.: Johns Hopkins University Press, 1991).

2. In a forthcoming book, *The Transformation of European Politics, 1763–1848* (Oxford: Clarendon Press, 1994), I argue that the Congress of Vienna transformed international politics in 1814–1815, producing a new international system much more peaceful and stable than any previous one, resembling the current NWO in certain respects. I would argue just as strongly, however, for the superiority of the current NWO over the Vienna system in providing solutions to various problems that the Vienna system only dimly foreshadowed.

3. See, for example, Jacob van Meulen, *Der Gedanke der Internationalen Organisation in seiner Entwicklung 1300–1800* (The idea of international organization in its development 1300–1800) (1917; The Hague: M. Nijhoff, 1968), or F. H. Hinsley, *Power and the Pursuit of Peace* (Cambridge: Cambridge University Press, 1963).

4. Even the two most important exceptions really prove the rule. The German Confederation of 1815–1866 was originally founded both to provide for the common defense of its members, the various independent German states, and to promote their joint welfare in various ways. Yet its leaders, especially Austria, quickly stultified its potential for advancing the general welfare, for particular Austrian reasons, and after 1848 it could no longer even serve for common defense and for reconciling power-political differences between its members, especially Prussia and Austria. Similarly, the European Concert worked well from 1815 to 1853 to preserve international peace, but mostly failed as a way of promoting a common approach to more general European political and social problems.

5. See Norman Rich, *Why the Crimean War? A Cautionary Tale* (Hanover, N.H.: University Press of New England, 1985); Anselm Doering-Manteuffel, *Vom Wiener Kongress zur Pariser Konferenz* (From the Congress of Vienna to the Conference of Paris) (Göttingen: Vandenhoeck and Ru-

precht, 1991); Winfried Baumgart, *Der Friede von Paris* (The Peace of Paris) (Munich: R. Oldenbourg, 1972); and my own *Austria, Great Britain and the Crimean War* (Ithaca, N.Y.: Cornell University Press, 1972).

6. This view rejects, to be sure, the widespread condemnation of the international community for not stopping the current fighting and atrocities in Bosnia. István Deák, a renowned historian at Columbia University, for example, concluded a series of review articles on recent works on the Holocaust in the *New York Review of Books* by remarking that the undertaking had left him with "a sense of hopelessness" at the refusal of states and peoples to learn from the Holocaust—a refusal that the "international failure to act" in the face of ethnic cleansing and other horrors in Bosnia demonstrates. "Holocaust Heroes," *New York Review of Books*, November 5, 1992, p. 26.

Deák and others are entirely right to remind us that human beings are still capable of bestial conduct, and that many individuals and groups have refused to learn from the Holocaust and other acts of genocide, or learned the wrong things. To ascribe the ongoing tragedy in Bosnia simply to an "international failure to act," however, is a mistake. It misunderstands the nature of the NWO and its methods, as already argued; it underestimates the real, formidable obstacles to any kind of international action capable of preventing or ending this kind of warfare in this region as in many others; and above all it ignores the huge difference between the international response to these particular Balkan horrors and the historic responses to all earlier ones. Central to all previous international responses to internecine Balkan conflicts has been the primary concern of the great powers to safeguard their individual great-power interests, spheres of influence, and positions of power within the region. Even where, as often happened, the great powers did not mainly try to exploit the conflicts for selfish ends but cooperated to regulate and end them, they were always concerned to preserve a favorable balance of power.

The most obvious feature of the current international response is that this long-dominant motive has almost totally disappeared. States that formerly would never have allowed the Balkan balance to shift fundamentally against them—Britain,

France, Italy, Germany, Austria, Russia— now would prefer to ignore the struggle entirely and intervene, if at all, primarily for peacekeeping and humanitarian reasons. A frequent argument for forcible intervention in Bosnia is that the conflict should be stopped to prevent it from spreading into a wider Balkan conflict that could trigger another wider war like World War I, touched off precisely in this area. The danger of a Balkan ripple effect is no doubt serious and important; the danger of another 1914 has virtually disappeared, because the general outlook prevalent in 1914 among all the powers, great and small, that the Balkans were vital to the general European and world balances has disappeared. It is one thing to emphasize the tragedy of the current situation for Bosnians and many others on all sides; another to claim that unless the international community under the NWO does something immediately effective to fix it, the NWO is useless and the world has learned nothing. This very situation, for all its horrors, proves that the international community, especially in Europe, has learned something, changed for the better.

7. Lewis B. Namier, "History," in Fritz R. Stern, ed., *Varieties of History: From Voltaire to the Present* (Cleveland, Ohio: World Publishing Co., 1956), p. 375.

Power, Principles, and Prospects for a Cooperative International Order

Alberto R. Coll

In 1943, as the eventual outcome of World War II was becoming clear, but well before the Cold War had begun, the historian Carl Becker wrote an essay with the apt title *How New Will the Better World Be?*[1] In it he took a hard look at the world around him and tried to dampen some of the more utopian enthusiasms of his contemporaries about the new age of peace that the collapse of fascism and the founding of the United Nations (UN) supposedly would mark. Today, Americans have a similar challenge before them, to discern whether the period of international relations ahead will be either new or better.

One thing seems certain. The prospects for a cooperative world order will depend to no small extent on the degree to which the United States has a sober appreciation for the role of both power and principle in international politics. Such an appreciation is not foreign to the American tradition. The American presidents most successful in the conduct of foreign affairs have been well aware of the indissoluble connection between power and prin-

Alberto R. Coll is principal deputy assistant secretary of defense for Special Operations and Low-Intensity Conflict. He has taught previously at the Naval War College and Georgetown University.

ciple, of the necessity for shaping U.S. policies with due regard for both realities of power and the constraints and possibilities posed by moral principles. As president, Washington, Jefferson, Monroe, Lincoln, Wilson, the two Roosevelts, Truman, Eisenhower, Kennedy, and Reagan were all realists determined to safeguard U.S. power. But they also appreciated the importance of grounding and articulating their policies and strategies in terms of moral principles congruent with the character of the American polity.

Americans often think of the relationship of power to principle as one of tension and even conflict. It is important to remember that it can also be one of mutual reinforcement. U.S. principles need U.S. power every bit as much as U.S. power needs U.S. principles. Without power to back them up, those principles wither in the harsh environment of international politics. Yet, without principles to energize and impart a guiding vision to it, U.S. power either lies dormant or drifts purposelessly or misdirected. Moreover, the principles are in themselves a source of power, as Americans discovered repeatedly in both world wars and throughout the Cold War. Besides infusing Americans with vitality, their principles attract others around the world who share them, joining their resources to those of the United States in a common purpose. As Americans seek to construct a cooperative world order in the 1990s and beyond they will have to exercise their power in the world while remaining faithful to their principles. And they will have to develop policies and strategies that reflect a dynamic interaction between the requirements of their power and those of their principles.

Two opposite dangers loom ahead. The first is that Americans will overestimate the capacity of principles unaided by power to shape a more decent international order. The second is that, in a fit of cynicism and despair over their mounting domestic problems, Americans will succumb to the temptation of assuming that raw economic or military power is all that matters in today's world. Either outcome reflects a false understanding of the true character of politics and human nature and would bode ill for cooperative security.

The Requirements of Power

Promoting a cooperative international order will require Americans to pay attention simultaneously to the requirements of both their power and their principles. With regard to the requirements of U.S. power, it is possible to sketch two policy objectives that, while promoting U.S. security, will also encourage the development of a more cooperative international system. These are to nurture and strengthen U.S. alliances in Europe and the Pacific Basin and to integrate multilateral institutions and practices more thoroughly into the fabric of U.S. foreign and defense policy.

The first of these objectives has been widely accepted to this day and may seem prosaic enough, but it is in danger of being gradually discarded as a result of economic squabbles among the allies and of weariness among the American people with the responsibilities it implies. The second objective is far from accepted today, yet will be vital to a constructive U.S. role in the future ordering of international politics and economics along lines beneficial to U.S. interests. Both of these objectives must be pursued at a difficult time when U.S. economic resources will be limited as a result of the current U.S. fiscal crisis.

Nurturing and Strengthening U.S. Alliances in Europe and the Pacific Basin. Secretary of Defense Richard B. Cheney has rightly emphasized that the network of alliances of which the United States is a part is its single most important political-military asset, more valuable than any weapon or military unit it possesses. Those critics who urge the United States to withdraw from its existing alliances forget that those alliances are a series of partnerships through which the United States significantly leverages its investments in security, enabling the nation to protect and promote its global interests far more extensively and cheaply than it could standing alone. Over the next few years the alliances will be under great strain as a result of economic tensions and the belief of some that, with the Soviet threat no longer a stimulus, the alliances are neither sustainable nor desirable. The United States must not yield to such pressures.

In truth, the U.S. alliances with Europe and Japan embody long-term U.S. interests that go well beyond the containment of Soviet or Russian power. Although the Soviet threat provided the initial impetus for their formation, the alliances have nurtured over the last half century a community of economic and political interests that now has a life of its own and that provides ample justification for preserving the alliances as its political-military backbone. This community of interests will be as important to Americans in the future as it was during the cold war years, if not more so.

By the second decade of this century, long before the outbreak of the Cold War and the formation of the North Atlantic Treaty Organization (NATO), it had become clear to many thoughtful Europeans and Americans that Great Britain was no longer capable of maintaining the European balance of power and that without an active U.S. political and military role in European affairs Europe would be torn by the traditional rivalries of such great powers as Germany and Russia and might become dominated by one of them, with harmful consequences for U.S. interests. To varying degrees, Theodore Roosevelt, Alfred Thayer Mahan, and Elihu Root shared this view. At the end of World War I the United States's greatest mistake was not its refusal to join the League of Nations; by itself, U.S. membership in the League, absent any willingness to use American power in support of the League's policies, would not have averted the coming of World War II. Its greatest error was, rather, to refuse France's request for an Anglo–American military guarantee in the event of future German aggression. Such a guarantee, if embodied in effective military arrangements among the three countries, would have given France the requisite security with which to pursue a conciliatory policy toward Weimar Germany in the 1920s and later a firmer policy toward Nazi Germany in the 1930s.

The implications of that failure are history, and they weighed heavily in the minds of the American and European architects of NATO. Within the protection afforded by NATO, European states have for several decades been able to lay aside their traditional security anxieties, even as far as accepting German reunification with much less opposition than would have seemed possible. It is also because of NATO that Europe and the United States are free to follow a magnanimous policy of friendship and assistance toward the former Soviet republics today.

Although it is natural to expect that over time the U.S. contribution to NATO will decline from its cold war levels, NATO can and should survive. Its maintenance and strengthening will be immensely useful to American and European interests for several reasons. First, NATO will continue to have a stabilizing effect on European affairs, calming security anxieties and deterring any future forces that may seek to overturn Europe's current status as a peaceful, democratic community of free peoples. Under NATO's roof, European integration will continue, ancient interstate rivalries will be moderated, and separatist tendencies within major European states will not be as difficult to accommodate as they would be in a system without an overarching security framework.

Second, NATO will act as a magnet, drawing toward the European–Atlantic security community states at present outside it. It is not inconceivable that some day most East European states and many of the former Soviet republics will join NATO. NATO then would have an effect on them similar to its eventual effect on Portugal, Spain, and Greece: by drawing them toward Europe it would also draw them more firmly toward democracy and free markets, eroding old authoritarian and statist traditions.

The U.S.–Japanese alliance is also rooted in common interests that go well beyond the containment of Soviet or Russian power. By the end of the nineteenth century U.S. interests as a Pacific power were already being affected by the growing rivalries among Russia, Japan, China, and Korea. In the future, the stability of the Pacific Basin and a strong U.S.–Japanese relationship will be more important to the United States than ever before. The U.S. economy needs the vast markets of the Pacific Rim, and it benefits enormously from Japanese investment capital and technology and the impetus toward greater productivity provided by Japanese competition. By making it unnecessary for Japan to maintain large offensive military capabilities, and by reassuring other regional powers about the U.S. commitment to a peaceful, stable Pacific Basin, the alliance helps to hold in check traditional rivalries among Asian powers that otherwise could unravel into unrestrained military competition, conflict, and aggression.

By anchoring German and Japanese security in a broader multinational security community, the Atlantic and Pacific alliances respectively play a key role in discouraging what has been described as the "renationalization" of both countries' security policies. Such a renationalization is not desired by most Germans and Japanese or by their neighbors. Preventing it is a signal contribution to international order.

Integrating Multilateral Institutions and Practices More Thoroughly into the Fabric of U.S. Foreign and Defense Policy. Fiscal realities will dictate considerable reductions in U.S. military forces and in the economic resources available to the United States for foreign assistance. This means that the nation will have to use its available assets more imaginatively and with greater versatility. The United States will need to

look for ways to enhance its diplomatic and political leverage by joining its resources to those of others in pursuit of common objectives. Multilateral institutions and practices provide such an opportunity.

At the height of the Cold War the usefulness of certain multilateral institutions such as the United Nations was limited by the hostility of the Soviet bloc and of a group of third world states that, emboldened by Soviet support, felt confident in obstructing U.S. policy. On some occasions, such as with the infamous "Zionism is racism" resolution, the UN actually helped to inflame rather than calm the tensions of international politics. For the time being, however, Russia is following a pro-Western course, the People's Republic of China is too eager for Western economic ties to act as an obstructionist power, and many third world states have little incentive to alienate the United States and its allies gratuitously.

While these conditions last, the UN is potentially more useful than ever before for promoting both international cooperation and Western security. This is neither a call for multilateralism for its own sake, nor another incantation of the supposed goodness and efficacy of the United Nations. It is simply an acknowledgment that, as long as the core of the UN leadership is a concert of states with which the United States has considerable common interests, the institution can be useful in promoting policies that benefit both Americans and the larger international community. Such a hardheaded realist as Winston Churchill had a similar outlook toward the League of Nations up until the mid-1930s.

It goes without saying that this argument is true as well of other multilateral institutions that traditionally have been friendlier than the UN to Western interests. With regard to at least three important issues the United States can accomplish far more through multilateral efforts than by acting on its own: (1) encouraging the integration of the former Soviet Union into the community of democratic and capitalist states loosely known as the West; (2) slowing the proliferation of ballistic missiles and nuclear, chemical, and biological weapons; and (3) organizing peacekeeping and peace-enforcement operations to defuse selected conflicts around the world.

As former President Richard M. Nixon has reminded us, helping the former Soviet republics to join the family of liberal democratic nations is not only in accordance with the highest principles of the United States, it is also in its national interest. Although the United States has much to offer the new republics in the way of political-military incentives such as arms reduction arrangements, much of the investment capital and economic assistance will have to be provided through multilateral efforts in which the United States joins its resources to those of others. Such investments in a democratic, capitalist order in the heart of Eurasia will enhance both future U.S. security and future prospects for a more cooperative international order.

Enough can never be said about the horrendous perils posed to contemporary democratic civilization by the rapid worldwide spread of weapons of mass destruction. It is only a matter of a few years before numbers of such weapons will be in the hands of regimes willing to use them. An effective U.S. strategy to slow down and disrupt proliferation will require a multilateral effort on the diplomatic, economic, political, and military fronts. The acquisition of these weapons is a long and complex process with numerous stages, each of which is vulnerable to disruption and obstruction through diplomatic pressures, carefully targeted economic sanctions and regulations, and covert as well as overt military operations. Only with the support of other interested parties and under the legitimacy and moral authority provided, however loosely, by multilateral institutions, can the United States hope to succeed.

The third area in which multilateralism can pay generous dividends for the United States is in peacekeeping and peace-enforcement operations. The United States cannot afford to become involved everywhere with substantial military resources, but there are conflicts in which, for a relatively small investment of political capital and military power, it can encourage constructive settlements that benefit its long-term interests. Two such kinds of conflicts come to mind.

In one, the security of the United States is not threatened directly but its interests are affected considerably, as they would be by a conflict between Russia and Ukraine or between Greece and Turkey that threatened to escalate to major war. In the second kind of conflict, such as Serbia's war against its Balkan neighbors, or a possible future civil war in Peru, U.S. interests may not be affected immediately in substantial ways, but the long-term consequences can be highly corrosive to the fabric of regional stability and eventually undermine important U.S. objectives. In neither of these cases should the United States intervene unilaterally, yet it is not in its interests to remain indifferent.

The ongoing war in the old Yugoslavia is a case in point. For almost a whole year, as the war among Serbia, Croatia, and Bosnia widened, many insisted that it was peripheral to U.S.

391

interests and that, beyond offers of support to the European Community's mediation efforts, U.S. policy should not exercise any forceful leadership to settle or contain the conflict. Eventually, and perhaps too late, it was realized that, as a matter of practical realism, the United States could not afford to remain on the sidelines. First, American indifference to Serbian aggression and Serbian atrocities would send a dangerous signal to potential would-be imitators in Eastern Europe and the former Soviet Union about the will of the United States and the Atlantic Alliance to shape Eastern Europe's political future. The prospects for orderly democratic reform and peaceful interstate relations in this region would suffer a severe setback if Serbia's policies were not sharply reined in. Second, if allowed to burn uncontrollably, the war might spread and draw into it outside parties such as Greece, Bulgaria, Turkey, Germany, and Russia, imperiling European peace and NATO's cohesiveness in highly dangerous ways. Finally, the threatened migration of millions of refugees from the conflict to Austria and Hungary posed an urgent humanitarian and political challenge requiring not merely a regional, but an international solution. In retrospect, with the hindsight rarely available to statesmen, it appears that the United States should have taken a more vigorous lead in defusing the conflict, in a multilateral context, in the fall of 1991 instead of waiting for others to do so. The war's human and economic costs would have been lower, and a settlement acceptable to all parties and to the long-term interests of the United States and the Atlantic Alliance would have been more feasible than it is now.

There will be other conflicts of this kind where it will be desirable for the United States to be engaged, while limiting the extent and risks of its engagement. By joining others in a peacekeeping or peace-enforcement effort, the United States can leverage its political and military power considerably and reduce the risks and costs of its involvement. As we move into an era of ever deadlier military technologies and virulent ethnic and religious struggles, multilateral peacekeeping and peacemaking operations that can defuse conflicts and promote settlements will become increasingly relevant to both U.S. security and international order.

The Requirements of Principle

The requirements of principle also present opportunities for policies that will benefit U.S. security while encouraging a more cooperative international order. Two sets of principles drawn from the American tradition offer such an opportunity. They are an appreciation of the value of international order and the prudent encouragement of liberal, capitalist democracy.

All great American statesmen have recognized that the United States exists in a particular kind of international society or order that, by facilitating the peaceful conduct of relations among states, benefits the United States considerably. The institutions and practices of diplomacy, of international law or what the Founding Fathers called "the Law of Nations," and of international morality, however blurred their boundaries and substance sometimes are, are intrinsic elements of such an order. Formal respect for them has always been part of the American tradition, even at the height of such intense struggles as the Cold War.

One of the greatest U.S. assets in international politics is the credibility of the United States as a power that succeeds more often than not in paying attention to the concerns and interests of its allies and friends and the rules and customs of international society. The value of such credibility is incalculable, especially at a time when, contrary to popular misperceptions, the United States will need its allies and friends more, not less, in the arduous task of shaping the international security environment. As the global conventional forces of the United States shrink and its economic resources become relatively less dominant, its credibility in Europe and Asia as a power that can be trusted to act responsibly will become proportionately more important as an asset. And key to that credibility's strength will be the kind of international order, including the framework of international principles and practices, that the United States supports.

Defining such an international order brings one close to three core prohibitions that U.S. foreign policy has supported over the last eight decades and that serve to strengthen both U.S. security and the prospects for a more cooperative international order. They are the impermissibility of armed aggression as an instrument of foreign policy, of war crimes, and of human rights violations egregious enough to classify as crimes against humanity. An international order grounded in these prohibitions is one in which the United States will be more secure.

These prohibitions, though formally embodied in international law since the Nuremberg trials, have been part of the Western moral tradition for several centuries. They are a set of minimalist norms that prevent pluralism from degenerating into chaos and unrestrained violence. They place restraints on the conduct of states, but they do not seek to uproot established cultural traditions or political systems.

Indeed, they presuppose a pluralistic world of different cultures, religions, and political and economic systems.

As a practical matter, the United States will have to act in concert with other states to enforce the prohibitions when they are violated. Such enforcement will be problematic, and often the norms will be honored more in the breach than in the keeping. What is important is that the United States and other interested parties summon the requisite will and resources to articulate and enforce the prohibitions on enough occasions to maintain them alive as generally authoritative norms whose violation carries significant costs, thereby raising the threshold at which potential violators consider it convenient to disregard them.

Enforcing the prohibitions against aggression and egregious human rights violations may require U.S.–led and coordinated multilateral peace-enforcement operations in which military force is used against the will of some of the warring factions to facilitate or impose a particular kind of diplomatic settlement. Such operations are extremely complex politically and militarily, and the United States should be highly selective in undertaking them. But they should be part of the armory of political instruments through which the United States, in a multilateral context, helps to shape the international political and security environment in ways that are favorable to its long-term interests and values.

The U.S. military is likely to resist involvement in peace-enforcement operations, citing the specter of Vietnam and similar "quagmires." Although such protestations deserve a fair hearing, they should be treated as useful warnings rather than inviolate counsels. The U.S. military will tend to be wary of any use of military power that falls short of the Desert Storm paradigm, which Gen. Colin Powell has approvingly described as "overwhelming force." In the world ahead, however, the requirements of shaping the international security environment will often call for the use of force at levels far short of, and in ways quite different from, "overwhelming force."

Although the prohibitions against aggression, war crimes, and egregious human rights violations embody positive human values to which Americans are strongly attached, they do not capture the whole range of principles to which the United States has been committed since its founding. One would have to add a principle that, though highly desired by many around the world, is still far from universally cherished. It is the principle of freedom, both in its political dimension of democracy and in its economic dimension of capitalism. It is in the interests of the United States to promote freedom and to help it take root in those societies where it can flourish, even while recognizing that not all societies are either capable of it or want it.

In the aftermath of the cold war victory we must not succumb to the temptation of ascribing to freedom a historical inevitability and triumphal universality that, historically, it has never had. Most philosophers and historians, including some within the liberal tradition itself, would warn us that freedom requires a delicate balance between the enjoyment of rights and the exercise of responsibilities, between creativity and restraint, between the desires of the individual and the needs of the community, that few societies are able to achieve for more than a flickering historical moment. The implication of this warning should be to instill in U.S. foreign policy a degree of modesty and circumspection at odds with the natural enthusiasm of Americans. The United States should support freedom around the world, but always in the context of this modesty and of a prudential appraisal of the kind of world in which Americans live. The history of U.S. foreign policy since 1914 represents an effort to strike such a prudential balance.

Prospects for a Cooperative World Order

It is difficult to predict how successful the United States will be in building a more cooperative international order. The world is being shaped simultaneously by forces of integration and disintegration. Viewed from one angle, modern communications, technology, trade, and the appeal of political and economic freedom have the potential to create a global democratic capitalist society where international cooperation will be more successful than in the past. But from another perspective, the post–cold war world does not look as comforting.

In addition to the current intensification of international economic competition, which sooner or later could have political ramifications destructive of international cooperation, the new world is facing an unexpected development. From California to Czechoslovakia, old ethnic and cultural identities are surfacing with vigor, threatening to overwhelm the integrating processes of democracy and technology with the disintegrating effects of ethnicity and tribalism. In a manner eerily reminiscent of Fyodor Dostoevsky's "underground man," many people are rebelling against the depersonalized, desacralized character of modern society by searching for new sources of identity and meaning, in the process discovering some very ancient ones. Throughout history, ethnic and tribal politics have been peculiarly resistant to either an ethic or statecraft of prudence. Its norm has been instead total annihilation of the enemy—not a reassuring prospect in an age of weapons of mass destruction.

Meanwhile, democratic societies everywhere—not only the new ones in Eurasia and in the Third World but also more established ones such as the United States—are facing a complex array of problems that are diminishing their governability or capacity to provide effective government. First, modern democracies have dangerously shifted the ground of their legitimacy from the principle of freedom to the guarantee of perpetually greater economic prosperity. It is questionable, however, whether a political arrangement based on the promise of ever rising living standards can endure for long. Long recessions and depressions have always been part of the economic cycle, and there is no reason to think it will be otherwise in the future. At some point there could be a major economic global contraction, and modern mass democracies will be vulnerable to authoritarian leaders or ideologies that artfully promise renewed prosperity.

Second, democratic legal systems are gradually evolving into enormously complex and burdensome institutions for facilitating individual fulfillment rather than simply protecting life and liberty. The long-term durability of a legal order whose prevailing maxim is to get for yourself the most that the law allows you to have is also questionable. As Thomas Jefferson pointed out, as soon as everyone tries to push the law to its uttermost limits, the social foundation that makes possible a legal system in the first place begins to crumble.

Third, Charles Krauthammer and others have reminded us that Western democratic society is the first in history to combine individual liberty with mass hedonism.[2] The result has been the creation of a democratic, capitalist mass culture whose dominant values—unrestrained individualism, consumerism, and the rejection of authority—paradoxically undermine the very virtues of self-discipline, hard work, and thrift necessary for the long-term viability of both capitalism and political liberty. As we look at the decline of that society over the last 30 years—a decline that has been masked by economic prosperity and the spectacular collapse of communism—we need to ask ourselves how long a society combining the liberty of democracy with an ethic of mass hedonism can endure.

Regarding all these vulnerabilities of democracy, it is also useful to note that, like its rival political systems, democracy has failed to address thus far the most pressing social and economic problems generated by modern urban society and technology, including the widespread alienation, loneliness, and sense of futility pervading much of our collective life.

Although democracy, in Churchill's words, may be the worst system of government except for all the others, it is possible that over the long run some democratic societies will collapse under the weight of their inadequacies and revert to forms of traditional authoritarianism that offer a degree of social discipline and economic security in exchange for limits on individual freedom. Such authoritarianisms, of which there remain plenty in the 1990s, do not augur well for peaceful international relations. It is thus an open question whether a global democratic society will take root long or deeply enough to advance significantly the prospects for international cooperation.

It is not clear today, any more than it was to Carl Becker in 1943, whether we are entering a world that is either new or better. In the face of these uncertainties, the United States must remain hopeful yet sober. As incurable optimists, Americans must not allow their hopes to outrun their prudence. They will have to balance the requirements of their power with those of their principles, for their strength will lie precisely in the way in which they can relate principles to power for mutual reinforcement. But Americans must also remember that international society remains anarchical, and that the best way to construct a cooperative international order is not to place their hopes in such institutions as collective security or the United Nations as if they had a life of their own apart from the values, direction, and effective strength that nations bring to them. A much sounder way to improve the prospects for international cooperation is to look for ways in which the United States and its allies, who together wield enormous power, can put that power behind policies that further U.S. national and common security while simultaneously strengthening the fabric of that international society to which Americans are inexorably tied and upon whose stability and welfare they so heavily depend.

The views in this article are the author's alone and do not necessarily represent those of the U.S. Department of Defense.

Notes

1. Carl Becker, *How New Will the Better World Be? A Discussion of Post-War Reconstruction* (1944; Freeport, N.Y.: Books for Libraries Press, 1971).

2. Charles Krauthammer, "The Issue-Thin Campaign," *Washington Post*, September 11, 1992, p. A–23.

Antidote to Anarchy

John Stremlau

PREVENTION HAS BECOME a buzz word among diplomats seeking to stem anarchy in Africa, the Balkans, the new states of the former Soviet Union, and elsewhere.

At the United Nations (UN) it means "action to prevent disputes from arising between parties, to prevent existing disputes from escalating into conflicts, and to limit the spread of the latter when they occur."[1] Washington's version is more political. Everybody gains—at home and abroad—if somehow conflicts can be resolved before they become costly disasters that distract attention from domestic priorities and require major expenditures of financial and political capital.

Prevention has always been the goal of balance of power politics, to maintain peace among rival states in the absence of world government. But conflicts today typically arise not out of the foreign policy failures of governments but the failures of domestic policy. Balance of power has proved its worth as a mechanism for conflict prevention *among* states; we now need

new mechanisms for conflict prevention *inside* them. The object of foreign policy, however, remains the same: some semblance of world order.

Three harsh realities are common to the scourge of deadly conflicts following the Cold War: in 1992 nearly all— 29 out of 30—military actions were taking place inside states;[2] modern weapons are pervasive and available to practically any state or faction; and 90 percent of the casualties are not soldiers but civilians caught up in local conflicts where battle lines blur and issues of ethnic, racial, and religious self-determination often become non-negotiable demands for sovereign independence.

Although none of these conflicts immediately threatens world order, the proliferation of local disasters, as Robert Kaplan has noted, suggests deeper ills and raises fundamental questions about the future for international peace and security in an era of rapid political, economic, social, and technological change.[3] To solve the growing list of global economic, environmental, nonproliferation, population, health, and public safety problems of the twenty-first century will require unprecedented international cooperation. This will not be possible if more small states fail and larger ones become increasingly ungovernable.

Reforming rather than replacing the interstate system looms as the greatest political challenge facing the world

John Stremlau, adviser to The Carnegie Commission on Preventing Deadly Conflict, was deputy director of the Department of State's Policy Planning Staff from 1989 to 1994.

The Washington Quarterly • 18:1

community well into the twenty-first century. If deadly domestic conflicts proliferate, the cumulative effects could undermine the political and economic foundations of the modern interstate system that has been evolving since the mid-seventeenth century. Further democratic reform within and among states would become impossible. Prevention, in this broader context, is an essential step forward on the long road of building a more stable and democratic international order, from the bottom up.

The obstacles to effective prevention are daunting. The frequency, diversity, simultaneity, and unpredictability of domestic conflicts impede early diagnosis, prescription, and application of effective preventive measures. Moreover, the concepts, doctrines, and prerogatives of sovereignty that have been developing over three centuries to prevent interstate conflict continue to impede timely initiatives to prevent conflicts inside states. Resistance to foreign involvement tends to be highest in states that most need help, and the United States and other democracies with the means to undertake preventive measures lack the domestic consensus to use them until it is too late.

President Bill Clinton and his foreign policy team have repeatedly declared their intention to pursue preventive diplomacy. The many difficulties the administration has had in dealing with conflicts have made prevention more attractive, but also more elusive. Presidential Decision Directive 25 on reforming multilateral peace operations, for example, does not address prevention.[4]

A broad foreign policy debate is overdue about the immediate and long-term threat to the national interest of mass violence inside states. In the late 1940s the United States set a new course for national security, one based on a military alliance system and solid bipartisan support. Today's challenge is much more diffuse and less military than political, economic, and cultural. As always, however, broad domestic and international coalitions will be vital if the foreign policy to meet this challenge is to be credible and effective. Such coalitions can build upon the history of conflict prevention among states and a nascent consensus about the purposes, parameters, and principles for collective engagement to prevent deadly conflict inside states.

Conflict Prevention among States

Preventive diplomacy in international relations is an old idea. As early as 1623 the French scholar Émeric Crucé published a treatise calling for a standing group of sovereigns or their delegates to resolve conflicts peacefully.[5] Following major wars, world powers have gathered to ratify peace and negotiate arrangements to enable their diplomats to prevent future conflict. Historians may one day ask why there was no peace conference following the Cold War. After all, the strategic realignment that has just occurred is no less significant than those that produced the treaties of Westphalia (1648), Vienna (1848), Versailles (1918), or San Francisco (1945).

The geopolitical landscape of the 1990s is, however, fundamentally different from the landscape of even 1945. Power politics is not what it used to be. None of today's major states threatens the others. Each is primarily concerned with issues of internal governance and economic growth. The last great empire, the Soviet Union, has dissolved remarkably peacefully and no new imperial threats loom. The most successful states—the United States, Japan, and the European states—have finally overcome three centuries of war and fragile power balances and now comprise a community within which war is unthinkable.

The permanent members of the UN Security Council not only pursue peaceful relations with each other, they have also ceased testing each other's resolve and capabilities through surrogates in regional conflicts. When balance of power diplomacy failed they demonstrated a new willingness to cooperate against Iraq's open aggression. Elsewhere, policies of "regional solutions for regional problems" have helped to eliminate the interstate dimensions of conflicts in southern Africa, Central America, Southeast Asia, and other places where the legacies of the Cold War lingered on.

Regional organizations such as the Partnership for Peace of the North Atlantic Treaty Organization, the Organization of American States, the Organization of African Unity, and the ASEAN (Association of Southeast Asian Nations) Regional Forum have further lowered the risk of interstate conflict. Even in the few places that the risk of interstate war remains high, notably between India and Pakistan, early warning and other conflict prevention mechanisms are highly developed, proving their worth in 1990 when Indo–Pakistani conflict once again seemed dangerously close.

The UN also has also assumed a greater role in preventing conflicts among states, and Secretary General Boutros Boutros-Ghali aspires to do much more. With UN financial and management resources already stretched to meet current humanitarian and other peace operations, everyone is in favor of strengthening the relatively inexpensive UN prevention capabilities. But the main challenge facing Boutros-Ghali and other peacemakers is how to reinforce and build on the extraordinary degree of stability in relations among states in order to prevent anarchy inside them.

Politics of Prevention inside States

When European statesmen concocted norms of sovereign equality and territorial integrity 300 years ago as a way to bring order to the anarchical world of independent states, they surely never imagined the extent to which these ideas would be put into practice. Today the UN comprises some 184 sovereign states and very few of them—including tiny ministates—fear external threats to their physical safety. Ironically, this success has had the unintended consequence of inspiring a growing number of dissident forces inside states to seek sovereignty, by force if necessary.

Shifting Terms of Reference

Article 2.7 of the UN Charter still prohibits intervention in the internal affairs of member states, except when the Security Council detects a threat to international peace and security. The Charter never stopped the major powers from intervening when they deemed it in their vital interests, although their international lawyers and diplomats often showed great ingenuity in justifying such actions. With the Cold War over, however, the major powers have yet to demonstrate comparable creativity in interpreting new threats to international peace and security so as to justify expanding the scope for intervention to prevent deadly domestic conflicts.

Successful statecraft of the future will require not only restraining the powerful from forcibly dominating the weak internationally, but the far more complex task of containing the abuse of power and chaos inside states.

The Self-Determination Challenge

In August 1992 Boutros-Ghali referred to the dangers self-determination can unleash in a special report, *An Agenda for Peace*, requested by the first-ever heads of government meeting of the UN Security Council. The secretary general suggested ways to improve the capacity of the UN for preventive diplomacy, peacemaking, and peace-keeping. In the introductory overview Boutros-Ghali draws attention to the vital links between domestic and world political order:

> If every ethnic, religious or linguistic group claimed statehood there would be no limit to fragmentation, and peace, security and economic well-being for all would become ever more difficult to achieve. (para. 17)

As to prescriptions that could inform prevention efforts, Boutros-Ghali observed that:

> the time of absolute and exclusive sovereignty has passed . . . [and] it is the task of leaders of States today to understand this and to find a balance between the needs of good internal governance and the requirements of an ever more interdependent world. Respect for democratic principles at all levels of social existence is crucial. (para. 17)

This is not idealism but democratic realism. The internal character of states has become a legitimate international concern that is no longer tied to cold war ideological alignments. Boutros-Ghali now posits that unless

multiethnic states respect human rights and develop according to democratic principles they will lack the resilience to withstand the self-determination challenge. Allowed to proliferate unchecked, such forces of fragmentation could eventually undermine the UN system.

General reaction among developing countries to this aspect of the secretary general's report is important because this huge block of some 130 multiethnic states has long been vociferous in opposing any hint of infringement on their sovereignty. Surprisingly, *An Agenda for Peace* was well received at the September 1992 summit of the non-aligned states in Jakarta. Efforts by a handful of radical states to condemn the report failed. Rather, in keeping with Boutros-Ghali's message, the Jakarta summit called upon the UN to assist a return "to constitutional rule and sustainable democracy without which development of the country would be impossible."[6] This encouraging response, and subsequent calls from developing countries for earlier and more effective international engagement to prevent disasters like that in Rwanda, reflect a growing appreciation of the need for collective action.

Demands for greater self-determination are being made on an unprecedented scale. Over 900 million people belong to 233 increasingly assertive groups that were identified in the U.S. Institute of Peace's 1990 *Minorities at Risk* study.[7] These are groups whose members have either experienced systematic discrimination or have taken political action to assert their collective interests against the states that claim to govern them. The study's estimates show the greatest concentration in Africa south of the Sahara—74 groups comprising more than 42 percent of the population. But it concludes that ethnic tensions are rising practically everywhere, with many potential problems lurking in the large developing and formerly Communist countries. Preventing deadly conflicts from destroying the small states now might one day contribute to conditions and capabilities that could facilitate peaceful domestic transitions in these larger states.

The Globalization of Communications and Trade

In an era of instant mass communications the costs of repression are rising for governments that use it and those that tolerate it. Diplomats may still be reluctant to interfere in the internal affairs of other states but the reports and photographs of human rights abuse make policies of neutrality increasingly difficult to sustain. There are also consequences beyond the immediate danger that such abuse could lead to costly humanitarian disasters. Access to foreign economic aid, trade, and investment are also jeopardized. This may not be of great consequence to militant factional leaders of small states close to collapse, but it should be of increasing concern to larger states in transition.

Expanding foreign trade and investment now rank high on the national security agenda of most developing countries, virtually all of them multiethnic states. Across the developing world 3 billion people are now rapidly integrating into the world economy, an event that Lawrence Summers, under secretary of the U.S. Treasury, compares in economic *and* political significance to the Renaissance and the Industrial Revolution.[8] One price of their success is that they have had to accept highly intrusive policy advice

from the World Bank and the International Monetary Fund. They have also had to realize that the rule of law is essential for developing a market economy and expanding trade and investment ties abroad. A collateral effect is that law-based systems can aid those seeking greater political protection.

As the United States looks increasingly to the 10 "Big Emerging Markets" (BEMs) to provide the margin of growth in U.S. exports, high-skill jobs, and the domestic economy for at least the next two decades, the importance of preventing inevitable tensions within these evolving states from escalating into civil conflict will also increase.[9] The 10 BEMs—China (including Taiwan and Hong Kong), Mexico, Indonesia, India, South Korea, Turkey, Poland, South Africa, Brazil, and Argentina—comprise nearly one-half the world's population, have economies that are among the most rapidly growing in the world, and are expected to buy more U.S. products than Europe and Japan combined by 2010.[10] Yet virtually all have national political institutions that are still fragile and undergoing fundamental changes. The BEMs and their major trading partners—most notably the United States—appear to have a convergence of interests that could lead them toward greater cooperation in achieving mutually acceptable ways for preventing conflict inside the BEMs, while also cooperating to prevent ethnic conflict elsewhere that could inspire insurrections close to home.

Thus, with unusually stable relations among the major powers and the absence of major ideological cleavages along either East–West or North–South axes, there may be a historic opportunity to shift the focus of world

401

the dangers of war among ...eventing conflicts inside

Parameters of Intrastate Prevention

Identifying a common danger is one thing, but doing something about it is obviously a much bigger challenge, particularly if voluntary international cooperation is required to solve primarily domestic problems.

A New Call for "Realism"?

There is, as yet, no set of norms or body of international law to give authority and legitimacy to intervention for the sake of preventing conflicts inside states. But realist theory, which purports to explain politics among nations as the pursuit of interests defined in terms of power, may be of use in understanding rising anarchy inside states. Recent outbreaks of ethnic conflict in the former Yugoslavia, Somalia, Rwanda, and other failed or failing states appear to be less the result of primordial antagonisms or the struggle between good and evil than a reaction to changes in the distribution of power.

In failing states insecurity reigns. Absent a central authority to arbitrate and/or enforce imbalances of power among factions, the logical response of their leaders is to fear the worst and to act accordingly. With each group potentially threatened by every other in a failing state, there is no other remedy for their insecurity than to take up arms in their own defense. Unless this cycle can be broken, conflict and war are the inevitable by-products.

The realist theory of international conflict also holds that the striving for power is not affected by an actor's inherent nature, good or evil. Because everyone is a potential enemy, even the most decent must, in self-defense, assume many of the attributes of the more bloodthirsty. Just as leaders of states use ideologies to mask their immediate goal of gaining or retaining power, factional leaders often seek to expand their base of power under the guise of ethnic nationalism. In the Balkans, Rwanda, and elsewhere, ethnic differences, often in combination with economic and other insecurities, are being exploited by political leaders to mobilize support for separatism, irredentism, or hegemonism.

Extending realist theory to internal conflict might lead to prevention policies that would worry less about the intentions of factional leaders than their relative power. The objective would be to diffuse and balance power in pursuit of the longer-term goal of institutionalizing the separation and sharing of power. There are obviously many practical problems with such an approach, particularly when one faction is a recognized government. But the failure to build power-sharing into the terms of the Angolan elections of September 1992 may explain the return to war in that country. Power-sharing also appears to be key to progress toward peace in Cambodia, Central America, South Africa, and elsewhere.

Building on Limited Experience

Whatever concepts emerge to guide policy obviously need to be grounded in political reality. At this stage experience is still very limited and the debates about how to implement conflict prevention are not very advanced. John Kornblum, recently U.S. ambassador to the Conference on Security and Cooperation in Europe (CSCE), has worked creatively on the front lines of conflict prevention within and among multiethnic states at risk. He notes that U.S. and West European prevention policies still reflect cold war habits of "late prevention": they are activated primarily by the warning signs of unusual troop movements, the acquisition and deployment of weapons, surges of refugees, and other indications that conflict is imminent.[11] To be effective in this new environment requires much earlier prevention, by essentially political rather than military means.

Kornblum argues that successful diplomatic strategies for conflict prevention should no longer be compared to a game of chess because they are:

> more likely to resemble those of a stock market trading floor, where many conflicting interests are competing with each other at one time. Even more confusing will be the fact that several different sets of rules are likely to be followed by various participants at any given point. (p. 7)

He adds that diplomats do not even have an agreed vocabulary for discussing early prevention efforts inside troubled states.

Harold Saunders, former assistant secretary of state and a veteran of the Camp David peace process, has been experimenting for several years with the role of nongovernmental organizations (NGOs) in preventive diplomacy. His work has included information-gathering, confidence-building, and unofficial U.S.–Russian assessments of conflict avoidance and measures to resolve problems in Tajikistan and other conflicted states of the former Soviet Union.

Like Kornblum, Saunders also calls for a different conceptual framework for conflict prevention, noting that:

> we no longer concentrate mainly on conflicts between states—dangerous as they will still be—but also on deep-rooted human conflicts embroiling whole bodies politic. These conflicts are often beyond the reach of governments and the instruments governments traditionally deploy . . . policies that respond must be policies that operate in the whole political arena.[12]

Opening Political Space

Conventional diplomatic practice relies on secrecy, leading to agreements that can be imposed from above. Preventive diplomacy, as it applies to possible conflicts inside states, is an ongoing process that is more open, flexible, low-key, and inclusive.

Early prevention requires detailed knowledge of local history, recent changes in ethnic relations, economics, land use, the growth and movements of population, environmental degradation, and the distribution of political power. Conflict prevention, in this wider context, often becomes a matter of finding ways to open political space for governments and the increasingly alienated forces demanding greater self-determination so that they can reach accommodation.

A search for ways to encourage early political compromise is getting under way at the Development Cooperation Directorate of the Organization for Economic Cooperation and Development (OECD), which advises the foreign assistance agencies of Western governments. According to its director, Bernard Woods, "successfully managing competing interests and loyalties in societies is the vital prerequisite for both achieving successful development, and for containing disputes and conflicts." Woods tells donors that "placing primacy on good governance and participation will bring peace and development closer together."[13]

Starting such a process, as Saunders and others have shown, does not require huge expenditures or direct involvement by foreign governments. In Eastern Europe, where states are not at risk from outside aggression but goals of irredentism linger and ethnic grievances are long-standing and easily aroused by ambitious politicians, the Project on Ethnic Relations based in Princeton, New Jersey, seeks to reduce tensions between the government of Romania and leaders of the Hungarian minority and promote efforts to counter violence against the Roma populations throughout the region. This experiment of grassroots efforts to lower barriers to accommodation among groups may provide practical lessons for other international NGOs that try to reduce the risk of factional conflict elsewhere.

The sensitivities of incumbent governments are another reason why concerned foreign powers and international organizations are likely to depend increasingly on the work of NGOs, at least in early phases of the process. The number of internationally active NGOs has grown to some 5,000.[14] Although most work in economic and social development, more and more have associate status with the UN and are engaged in all stages of peace operations.[15]

The close working relations that governments of smaller liberal democracies, such as Norway, Canada, and Australia, enjoy with NGOs are also contributing to early and sustained conflict prevention because these states have been extensively involved in UN peace operations.

Prevention Principles

Several rules of thumb are available to guide international efforts to prevent internal conflicts.

Promote Civic Nationalism

At the heart of the problem of how to end sectarian violence is a conundrum: Are peace and justice better served by fitting the state to the people, or by fitting the people to the state? In the first option, the state is created according to a principle frequently referred to as "ethnic nationalism," that is, the state is defined by a group of people rooted in a shared culture and a belief in their common ancestry. This was the definition that Woodrow Wilson drew on when he called for full rights of self-determination and majority rule for any "people" demanding them.

The second option, based on the principle of "civic nationalism," subsumes all groups within a territory into one state. Membership in the national group is generally open to everyone who is born or permanently resident within the national territory, without regard to race, language, or culture. In a democracy, the most advanced form of civic nationalism, the rights of minorities to self-determination are usually circumscribed by constitutional requirements for due process. The heart of Lincoln's argument in his First Inaugural, for example, was not a denial of the South's right to secede but that it was illegal for it to do so unilaterally, without the consent of the rest of the nation. Today, Boutros-Ghali defends civic nationalism as a more rational and stable basis than ethnic nationalism for developing international cooperation and for avoiding an unmanageable proliferation of new states within the UN.

Any prevention strategy for the 1990s should take as its central purpose active support of civic nationalism: majority governments must be held accountable for constructing credible political guarantees for the rights of individuals and ethnic minorities within their territory. Forcing people to remain in a state against their will carries many risks that in rare instances may require changing borders. But the overall desirability of promoting political accommodation within existing frontiers should be clear.

In Russia and South Africa, two countries of great interest to the United States, civic nationalism is developing under very difficult conditions. Few issues are more vital to the United States than stability in Eurasia and to maintain that stability it will be essential for the Russian government to continue its policy of giving no encouragement to secessionist movements among the large Russian minorities in other states, and, indeed, to make no attempt to create a greater Russia. In South Africa, the new government's accommodation of Zulu and Afrikaner minorities within a framework of constitutional guarantees is also important for national stability. Its continuation will help maintain confidence abroad in prospects for investment in South Africa, as well as give an example to Africa and the rest of the world of the advantages of civic nationalism.

The strategic goal of preventive diplomacy, in Russia, South Africa, and elsewhere, is to ensure that the positive-sum game of political pluralism prevails over the zero-sum politics of ethnic nationalism. The bilateral, multilateral, and nongovernmental cooperation programs that the United States and its partners are undertaking with important transforming nations are as vital to international security in this new era as the Marshall Plan, the Berlin airlift, and alliance formation were to the early stages of the Cold War.

Develop Early Warning Mechanisms

Early warning about deteriorating power balances within states is vital to conflict prevention. Boutros-Ghali has shown leadership, once again in *An Agenda for Peace*, by directing attention to the most vital warnings of trouble—decline in a government's "commitment to human rights with a special sensitivity to those of minorities, whether ethnic, religious, social or linguistic."[16] The denial of human rights and adequate protection for minorities in this preventive context should be regarded as a tool of analysis, an early indicator that a state is in trouble.

Early warning cannot work without the political will to act in time. Alexander George, who has carefully analyzed the warning and response problem in preventive diplomacy, has identified three important factors in its application: the strength of the warning signal, the expectations of the listener, and the "rewards and costs" associated with correct recognition of the signal.[17]

The vital warning signals that Boutros-Ghali identified can too easily be overlooked by the United States and other major Western powers that are distracted by other concerns, unaccustomed to dealing with human rights as an analytic or early warning tool, and reluctant to pay the political costs of offending another government when the immediate rewards seem slight. The large and growing number of multiethnic states that could slip into conflict makes it important for governments interested in early prevention to delegate greater authority to those who have field experience in the region and are therefore best suited to develop integrated warning and response strategies that can be carried out quickly and flexibly.

The world is currently suffering from too many examples of the failure to defend the rights of minorities. Recognition of Croatia by European countries following its declaration of independence without first ensuring guaranteed protection for the rights and interests of its large Serbian minority was a major missed opportunity for preventive diplomacy.

Recent work by Max van der Stoel, minority rights commissioner of the CSCE, further suggests the importance and the cost-effectiveness of paying attention to minority-related disputes before they become destabilizing.[18] Although the success of CSCE monitoring teams in Estonia, Latvia, Moldova, Tajikistan, and elsewhere has not been total, these teams are plowing important new ground for preventive engagement. On a broader plane, the UN's newly created special representative of the secretary general on the human rights issues related to internally displaced persons is monitoring the plight of 24 million people forced to leave their homes but still within the borders of their own countries. This office could develop important—if not very early—warning mechanisms to identify states at risk.

NGOs, too, are playing important roles in early warning and prevention. These NGOs include traditional human rights groups such as Amnesty International and Human Rights Watch, as well as nontraditional advocacy groups such as Common Ground, which is working to prevent conflict in Macedonia.

Forge Collective Actions

The authority and legitimacy of foreign involvement in conflict prevention within states will vary directly with the size of the coalition willing to play a role. Strength in numbers is even more important when sanctions are required to punish misbehavior. For democracies, notably the United States, acting in concert with others also greatly improves the chances for gaining domestic political support for whatever preventive measures are required.

But engaging the help of those who are geographically and culturally closest to a problem places a special burden on ad hoc coalitions and the more established subregional and regional organizations. UN oversight is necessary to ensure that in cases, such as Rwanda, where cross-border ethnic ties are a complicating factor, more neutral actors lead prevention efforts.

Prevention coalitions cannot be neutral about the values at stake, even as they seek to broker for compromise among local factions. Civic nationalism must be their goal. Building coalitions for this purpose is a more complex political process than forming a military alliance to meet a common threat or undertaking impartial peacekeeping operations. There are as yet no blueprints for building civic nationalism and a host of competing interests have to be accommodated. Many deep differences, even within the community of liberal democracies, remain regarding the role of the state and the institutions of government. Reconciling these differences will not only make the coalition more effective in dealing with troubled states but will also strengthen the community of liberal democracies.

Promote Economic Well-Being

A broader view of conflict prevention also entails more than political and military instruments. Economic factors are at least as important in building and holding nations together. Law-rence Summers pointed to the critical role of the International Monetary Fund in fostering domestic stability when he asserted that in the case of Russia democracy would not survive hyperinflation.[19]

More generally, majority and minor-ity groups within states need to be given a vision of the practical benefits of peaceful accommodation. Economic support, various forms of technical as-sistance, help in managing common water, land, and other resources, and other measures can be geared to conflict prevention by showing in very practical ways that a bargain can be struck to maintain the territorial status quo that will be to the advantage of all factions.

Scholars have long and inconclu-sively debated the relationship be-tween economic inequality and politi-cal conflict. But common sense points to the importance of linking economic incentives and disincentives to pre-vention efforts. Asian experience sug-gests that interethnic accommodation becomes far easier with prosperity. The recent prevention success in Es-tonia also correlates with relative eco-nomic well-being.

Boutros-Ghali's *Agenda for Develop-ment*,[20] a recent follow-on to his *Agenda for Peace*, and a major policy paper by the World Bank entitled *Governance*[21] reflect an important post–cold war convergence within the UN system that links promotion of economic de-velopment, human rights, and democ-racy to conflict prevention.

The multilateral groups on eco-nomic development, trade, water, the environment, and arms control that the United States has organized to aug-ment the Middle East peace process are intended to help prevent conflict by providing the antagonists with a vi-sion of the mutual benefits of collec-tive restraint. This formula may be replicated on a smaller scale to support prevention strategies in many other situations.

Make Process a Priority

Conflict prevention has to be an on-going effort. Specific institutional outcomes are less important than re-sponsible ways and means of getting there. This also applies to the difficult issue of territorial adjustments as a last resort. Although prevention strategies seek to encourage civic nationalism, as noted earlier, avenues to democracy are wide and varied.

When the Soviet Union was dissolv-ing, the United States and its partners took a flexible but principled position toward recognition that stressed the importance of due process. In Septem-ber 1991, the secretary of state an-nounced a set of broad criteria, consis-tent with the position of the CSCE, that would guide any decisions to rec-ognize and cooperate with successor states. These were:

- explicit acceptance of the provisions of the Helsinki Final Act, including respect for human rights and the equal treatment of minorities;
- respect for existing borders, internal and external, with changes made only by peaceful consensual means consistent with CSCE principles;
- support for democracy and the rule of law internally; and
- respect for international law and ob-ligations.

Failure to abide by these criteria by some states has been costly. Had Croa-tia, for example, not been recognized by Western governments until Zagreb had satisfied such criteria, the course of conflict in the Balkans might have been very different. Ironically, West-ern representatives now working to stabilize Croatia's relations with the Serbian-held areas of the country are proposing constitutional changes to grant Serbian residents the full rights of citizenship that were precluded in the independence constitution.

Efforts to revitalize these criteria should extend to the European Bank for Reconstruction and Development (EBRD), which applies similar principles as conditions for lending under its articles of agreement. The bank's willingness to make borrowers uphold these criteria appears to be weakening, which is unfortunate at a time when ethnic tensions are heightened in several key countries across Eurasia. The EBRD was the first multilateral financial institution to adopt such criteria, and the success of this experiment could, like the CSCE's, have an important impact on conflict prevention efforts in other regions.

When Necessary, Apply Force Majeure

Preventive measures cannot help states that have failed or are in advanced crisis. But a credible threat to use force can certainly contribute to success in prevention. Expanding the criteria for humanitarian intervention would put factional leaders on notice of the dangers to their own freedom of allowing internal violence to escalate. Given the UN's current budget crisis, however, this may be unrealistic.

Gareth Evans, the Australian foreign minister, has published a study of peace operations that outlines several conditions to guide UN peace enforcement measures, among them clear evidence of extreme human rights abuse and failure of non-forcible measures as signals to intervene, and the designation of sufficient resources to carry out the operations.[22] Whenever successful military operations are undertaken, developing a postconflict peace-building strategy to render the peace process irreversible becomes conflict prevention by another name.

Role of the United States

Any U.S. campaign of prevention of intrastate conflict will have to be supple, accommodate a diversity of states, and have access to a wide range of political, economic, and cultural instruments.[23] It would operate very differently from the highly secretive and centralized military doctrine still required to meet U.S. traditional defense needs but would complement it.

At the level of a Presidential Decision Directive, national security policy could be clarified along two lines. One would reiterate the military defense posture set forth in the *Bottom-Up Review* of 1993.[24] A second conflict prevention strategy for U.S. foreign policy would cover essentially nonmilitary foreign policy measures to prevent conflicts.

In developing a more inclusive prevention strategy the United States can draw on the enormous comparative advantages that it enjoys in world affairs but that normally do not feature in national security strategy reviews. For example, U.S. political institutions, values, and traditions are not just assets to defend but are resources that U.S. representatives can draw on to advance civic nationalism and build stable, democratic, market-oriented societies. The United States is the only power that still thinks and acts globally. More than any other nation, it has made human rights an integral part of its foreign policy, providing an important comparative advantage in developing effective early warning procedures for a new prevention strategy.

Already, U.S. missions to the new states of the former Soviet Union and many developing countries often function more as forums to discuss civic values than traditional embassies. U.S. diplomats are being drawn into local mediation and civic education efforts for which they were not trained but where their work could be very helpful in conflict prevention. Further reforms in the training, organization, funding, and delegation of authority to field missions abroad may be required if this second line of conflict prevention is to succeed.

U.S. foreign assistance programs and policies in multilateral institutions could also be geared more to conflict prevention around the world. U.S. foreign assistance programs are small, less than 1 percent of the federal budget. The entire foreign affairs budget of about $20 billion equals only 7 percent of the defense budget. In the future, bilateral foreign assistance funds should be directed more exclusively to urgently needed prevention efforts.

If direct military threats to U.S. vital interests continue to ebb, reallocating Department of Defense funds to support more effective diplomatic, economic, multilateral, and nongovernmental instruments of intrastate conflict prevention would be a sound investment. Relatively modest resources can also be effectively redeployed to consolidate the enormous comparative advantages that the United States still enjoys in the UN, the Bretton Woods financial institutions, and other regional and multilateral bodies. The national security dimensions of these investments need to be made clearer. Making foreign assistance accounts more flexible may also

be necessary. Small amounts of assistance, if used quickly, can leverage ad hoc preventive coalitions.

Another low-cost U.S. asset for advancing a new prevention strategy is the U.S. Information Agency and other U.S. public education capabilities. Adapting these instruments to post–cold war foreign policy is already under way, but much more could be done to target states and populations at risk. One way for public diplomacy to promote moderation on local issues is by providing information about how conflicts have been avoided or resolved peacefully in other parts of the world.

Engaging the public's interest in this foreign policy strategy of prevention would be especially important and probably not as difficult as suggested by those who emphasize the U.S. preoccupation with domestic priorities. Peace as a goal and activity of U.S. diplomacy has always been popular and more comprehensible than vague commitments to enlarge the community of democratic nations. Few have questioned the wisdom of the extraordinary and sustained U.S. commitment to preventing further war in the Middle East, or the many other efforts in which U.S. leadership has been essential to resolving conflict.

An early, more comprehensive, and active commitment to preventing intrastate conflict—if successful—would obviate the need for military peacekeeping operations. But it would also inform decisions about where, when, and how force is necessary and cost-effective. By engaging early to prevent conflict, both policymakers and the public would be better informed and better prepared for contingencies. The difference between popular reaction to the October 1993 killing of U.S. soldiers in Somalia, where the mission was unclear to the public, and the lack of a similar reaction to the tragedy of two downed Blackhawk helicopters in northern Iraq a few months later is striking.

An expanded prevention strategy would take advantage of the incomparable richness of the civic society of the United States. U.S. NGOs are at the forefront of emerging global networks of nongovernmental cooperation that, as already noted, contribute to opening up political space and create other conditions conducive to civic nationalism. Not only do such networks advance U.S. interests abroad, they enrich U.S. civic society at home because they create important domestic constituencies in support of this kind of foreign policy.

Finally, the very nature of this new security doctrine, and the coalitions and operations necessary to carry it out, will draw foreign policy makers closer to the dynamics of pluralism in the United States. By the middle of the next century, the majority of Americans will have ethnic ties to Africa, Asia, and the Hispanic world. Many of these citizens will seek to influence U.S. foreign policy much as those with special ties to Ireland, Greece, Turkey, Armenia, Israel, and a host of other countries have done historically. Ensuring that ethnic conflict abroad does not trouble ethnic relations at home will be in the highest national interest of the United States for decades to come.

Conclusion

Prevention, as a "new" concern of U.S. foreign policy, is focused primarily on states where humanitarian disasters appear imminent or are already under way. In the aftermath of Rwanda, the Department of State and the U.S. Agency for International Development

(USAID) each launched efforts, with the help of the intelligence community, to forecast similar humanitarian disasters. Whether and how such mechanisms work have not been addressed in this article. Nor have the merits of USAID's appeal for prevention funds to deal with the "root causes" of this anarchy—poverty, overpopulation, and environmental degradation—been considered.

Instead, this article has put the challenge of prevention in a broader historical and political context, one that points to the need for a strategic shift in foreign policy—from a predominant concern with politics among nations to politics inside nations. Chaos in failed or failing states, transitions inside countries of the former Soviet Union or the "Big Emerging Markets," and factionalism in liberal democracies are all major elements in this complex equation.

Looking ahead, four assumptions should frame the quest for a post–cold war foreign policy and a more durable and democratic international order:

- world politics, like world economics, is increasingly a seamless process of continuous interactions as traditional distinctions between foreign and domestic affairs lose salience in the formulation and implementation of national policy;
- the role of governments will be vital in determining the rights and obligations that define these interactions, and in developing the necessary regimes to secure them;
- governments of states, big and small, share a growing interest in maintaining and strengthening the international legal order so as to contain forces that could lead to further fragmentation; and
- the most prevalent threat to the integrity of the international legal or-

der arises less from the threat of aggression between states than from the abuse of fundamental human rights inside them.

Protection of fundamental human rights, as Boutros-Ghali now frequently stresses, is critical to keeping communities from breaking apart and a precondition for their coming together nationally and internationally. For in the long run, integration, derived from and protected by democratic means, is the best antidote to anarchy and the surest foundation for sustainable peace and development.

The views expressed in this article are those of the author and not necessarily of the Carnegie Corporation of New York or its Commission on Preventing Deadly Conflict.

Notes

1. Boutros Boutros-Ghali, *An Agenda for Peace* (New York, N.Y.: United Nations, 1992), para. 20.

2. Ramses Amer et al., "Major Armed Conflicts," *SIPRI Yearbook 1993* (London: Oxford University Press, 1993), p. 81.

3. Robert Kaplan, "The Coming Anarchy," *Atlantic Monthly,* February 1994, pp. 44–76.

4. "Executive Summary: The Clinton Administration's Policy on Reforming Multilateral Peace Operations," Presidential Decision Directive 25, unclassified document (Washington, D.C., May 3, 1994).

5. Émeric Crucé, *Le Nouveau Cynée* (1623), Eng. trans., *The New Cyneas of Émeric Crucé* (1909).

6. David Cox, *Exploring an Agenda for Peace: Issues Arising from the Report of the Secretary-General* (Ottawa, Canada: Center for Global Security, October 1993).

7. Ted Robert Gurr, *Minorities at Risk* (Washington, D.C.: United States Institute of Peace, 1993).

8. Lawrence Summers, Address to the Institute for International Economics, Washington, D.C., May 20, 1994.

9. For a fuller discussion, see the present author's forthcoming article in *Foreign Policy,* no. 97 (Winter 1994–95).

10. Jeffrey E. Garten, "The Big Emerging Markets: Changing American Interests in the Global Economy" (address to the Foreign Policy Association, New York, N.Y., January 20, 1994).

11. John Kornblum, "Strategies for Conflict Prevention" (paper presented at a seminar on "Early Warning and Preventive Diplomacy," Warsaw, Poland, January 1994).

12. Harold Saunders, "Enlarging U.S. Policy toward 'Ethnic' Conflict: Rethinking Intervention" (paper presented at a National Defense University Symposium, Washington, D.C., November 11, 1993), p. 1.

13. Bernard Woods, "Peace, Conflict, and Development: Linkages and Policy Issues" (paper presented at an International Development Research Center Forum, Ottawa, Canada, April 6, 1994), p. 7.

14. Leon Gordenker and Thomas G. Weiss, "Non-State Actors in International Organization: The Democratization of Global Governance," Draft (Brown University, Providence, R.I., May 1994), p. 1.

15. See Peter J. Spiro, "New Global Communities: Nongovernmental Organizations in International Decision-Making Institutions," in this issue of *The Washington Quarterly,* pp. 45–56.

16. Boutros-Ghali, *An Agenda for Peace*, para. 18.

17. Alexander George, "The Warning-Response Problem in Preventive Diplomacy" (paper presented to the United States Institute of Peace Study Group on Preventive Diplomacy, Washington, D.C., January 1994).

18. See Konrad J. Huber, "CSCE's New Role the East: Conflict Prevention," *RFE Research Report* 3 (August 12, 1994).

19. Summers, Address, May 20, 1994.

20. Boutros Boutros-Ghali, *An Agenda for Development* (New York, N.Y.: United Nations, May 8, 1994).

21. Operations Policy Department, IBRD, *Governance: The World Bank's Experience* (Washington, D.C., November 29, 1993).

22. Gareth Evans, *Cooperating for Peace* (St. Leonards, Australia: Allen and Unwin, 1993).

411

23. For a full discussion of the changing U.S. role, see Michael S. Lund, "Preventive Diplomacy and American Foreign Policy," Draft (United States Institute of Peace, Washington, D.C., 1994).

24. Les Aspin, *The Bottom-Up Review: Forces for a New Era* (Washington, D.C.: Department of Defense, 1993).

The Once and Future Security Council

Jose E. Alvarez

THE POST–COLD WAR revival of the United Nations (UN) Security Council has come with a price: many UN members are questioning the Council's legitimacy and calling for its restructuring. Oddly enough, the possible restructuring of what is potentially the most powerful supranational organ in the world has not generated much political heat in Washington. Council restructuring is not part of the Republicans' "Contract with America" or the Democrats' response. To the extent the UN is discussed in official Washington, the focus is more parochial: how best to contain the cost of UN peace operations and how best to preserve constitutional separation of powers when resorting to them. These were the live issues animating Senator Bob Dole (R–Kan.) and his proposed Peace Powers Act,[1] as well as the administration's response in its much-revised presidential directive on peace operations.[2] Lost somewhere in the

Beltway rhetoric over "duty to the U.S. taxpayer" and "fidelity to the constitutional separation of powers" has been any thorough discussion of the changing role of the Security Council and how the United States should handle the change.

The U.S. government is acting almost as if Council decisions, membership, and procedures were parts of a jurylike black box whose contents cannot be examined. To date, the United States has cautiously responded to calls for Council restructuring with minimalist suggestions largely reflective of cost containment concerns. Essentially on the grounds that the participation of Germany and Japan would lessen the pressures on the United States for peacekeeping funds, the administration, with barely a partisan counter, has quietly indicated that it favors permanent Council membership for those countries. It has let others carry the ball with respect to proposals for additional new permanent members or with respect to proposed changes in Council procedures. The U.S. government has not even taken a position on whether the new status for Germany or Japan should be accompanied by the veto.

Few in Washington seem to inquire about the reasons for the growing dissatisfaction of other UN members with the Council. Cursory analysis rests on the assumption that the criterion for

Jose E. Alvarez is professor of law at the University of Michigan Law School. This article is adapted from a speech originally presented to the Council on Foreign Relations and reprinted in University of Michigan Law School, *Law Quadrangle Notes* (Ann Arbor, Mich.) (Fall 1994).

permanent membership ought to be expanded beyond military capability to include economic prowess. The solution—the addition of Germany and Japan—is usually accompanied by realpolitik considerations. It is assumed that some developing state or states, possibly Nigeria, Brazil, or India, may have to be given permanent or other enhanced status as a necessary accommodation. The post hoc justification for increasing the Council's membership is usually some vague reference to the need to "democratize" the organization, to parallel democratic trends among its membership. The last is sometimes cast in politically correct terms designed to appeal to certain domestic constituencies. Thus, restructuring is said to bring needed "diversity" to the present Western-dominated Council.[3] Both sides of the aisle in official Washington appear to assume that now that the Council is finally working "as intended" is not the moment to drastically alter its composition or the way that it operates.[4] The accepted wisdom appears to be that the Security Council "runs" and ought to continue to run the UN and that, with the use of the veto largely a thing of the past, members ought to only tinker with the Council, not dramatically alter it. This article challenges these views.

Is the Council Out of Control?

Contrary to popular wisdom, the newly energized Council is *not* working as originally intended. The institutional innovations wrought by great power unanimity (or at least great power acquiescence) have turned the post–cold war Council into something far different than that conceived in 1945. The collective security scheme established then was simple enough: the chief aim was to prevent a reprise of World War II. To this end, the UN Charter prohibited *inter*state aggression—the use of force by one state against another.[5] The Council, including the five police powers, was given, in chapter VI of the Charter, recommendatory and investigatory powers designed to encourage (but not require) the pacific settlement of disputes likely to endanger the international peace. Chapter VII gave the Council additional powers to impose legally binding sanctions short of armed force (article 41) and, if these were inadequate, to use force (article 42) in those cases where the Council found an existing "threat to the peace, breach of the peace, or act of aggression."[6] The force anticipated was *UN* force, pursuant to special agreements (article 43) and supervised by a Military Staff Committee (article 45).

The scheme has *never* worked precisely as intended. When, in the absence of the then Soviet Union, the Council managed to authorize force in Korea and delegated that authority to forces under the command of the United States,[7] legal purists questioned whether the invasion by North Korea of the South was truly an instance of interstate aggression or was in reality an intervention in a civil war. Others demurred on the grounds that use of the UN flag was too easily delegated to the United States, without special agreements committing troops to the UN and without real supervision by the Military Staff Committee.[8] Similarly, when the Council imposed sanctions on Rhodesia in 1966 and 1968, Dean Acheson, among others, demurred on the grounds that controversy over the legitimacy of the then Rhodesian government did not constitute a threat to the "international peace" and that therefore the Council's action was an illegal intervention in a state's domestic affairs.[9]

But the cold war exercise of the veto

meant that few had to worry about these legal qualms. Today the almost defunct organ largely unable to react to the most direct breaches of the international peace during the Cold War has become an entity capable of finding an "international threat to the peace" or "breach of the peace" in unexpected, not to say strange, places: in the context of conflicts *within* states (e.g., Somalia and, some would say, at least initially in the former Yugoslavia); because of ostensible threats to the human rights of a state's own citizens (e.g., the Kurds in Iraq); because of a state's refusal to surrender its own nationals accused of terrorism (Libya); or because a military elite has failed to respect the results of a UN-supervised election (Haiti).[10] Further, the entity that had only rarely in 45 years authorized the use of force, has now, in the few years since the end of the Cold War, managed to delegate away the authority to use force in its name on several occasions—explicitly in Haiti and on the occasion of the Persian Gulf War—and implicitly in Somalia, post–Gulf war Iraq, and the former Yugoslavia. Yet, despite the increasing resort to force and its variants (such as the use of "peacekeepers" to track down a warlord in Somalia), articles 43 to 45 in the Charter remain effectively unimplemented: special agreements to allocate forces to the organization are not in place and neither is there an effective Military Staff Committee to oversee UN use of force.[11]

Indeed, it is impossible to understand the complaints about the legitimacy of the Council without a closer look at some of its more recent actions and the questions they provoke.

Post–Gulf War Sanctions on Iraq

Although some have questioned aspects of the Council's initial authorization to use force in defense of Kuwait,[12] more widespread have been the doubts evoked by the Council's actions since the end of the Gulf war. Serious doubts began with resolution 687 of April 3, 1991, the "mother of all resolutions" and the most complex adopted in the Council's history. In this resolution, and in many since relating to Iraq, the Council exercised sweeping powers over a defeated aggressor state.[13] Ostensibly licensed by its power to "restore" international peace and security (article 39), the Council effectively put Iraqi sovereignty under UN receivership. For the first time, the UN told a supposedly sovereign state what its borders are supposed to be, what proportion of its export earnings it is entitled to keep, what financial liability it has incurred and to whom, what kinds of observers it must admit into its militarily most sensitive areas, what types of weapons it may possess, and even what treaties it must ratify.

These determinations have been imposed as if by a legislature or a court, subject to no time constraint and indeed, some of them, such as with respect to boundaries, presumably to apply in perpetuity. Although Iraq's renewed threats of October 1994 with respect to Kuwait might suggest that all of these Council actions were, in hindsight, justified, this fails to satisfy those who question whether these onerous sanctions, all backed by the threat of renewed force against Iraq, were justified when they were adopted by a threat to the international peace. There are doubts about the Council's good faith. It is suspected that the post–Gulf war resolutions were in reality attempts to bring down a particular regime in pursuit of well-known U.S. foreign policy goals (i.e., to stifle a powerful regional enemy of democracy, encourage nuclear nonproliferation, and secure regional stability).

Others have questioned the Iraqi sanctions on moral or humanitarian grounds. Under existing Council decisions, Iraq remains liable, for example, for all Gulf war liabilities as determined by the Council and the Compensation Commission it has created to deal with claims against Iraq. Unless these Council resolutions are modified or terminated, in principle the people of Iraq remain liable, if necessary in perpetuity, for what is estimated to be over $170 billion to cover the 2,335,000 claims filed to date.[14] The Council has presumably decided that a "just" peace in the region requires the infliction of economic pain on a people living within a totalitarian state not amenable to bottom-up pressures for change. One need not be a friend of Iraq to be troubled by the Council's assumption of a judicial power purportedly more vast than any wielded by any national or international court in history.[15] Doubts about the wisdom of such a course are only heightened by the suspicion that, unlike any court, the Council has not established any clear rules of general applicability on when comparable actions will be taken for other culprits or the scope of the precedents being set.[16] Certainly the Council has not visited such a plight on all those who have violated the Charter or international law.

Council resolution 688 of April 5, 1991, another in the line of post–Gulf war resolutions, whereby the Council compelled Iraq to grant access to international humanitarian organizations to assist its internal Kurdish population, illustrates another set of concerns about legitimacy. Advocates of self-determination for the Kurdish people as well as others have criticized this institutional innovation, considered by many international lawyers to be the UN's first real attempt to legitimize the doctrine of humanitarian intervention.[17] Advocates of Kurdish self-determination note that this resolution fell far short of the Council's full-throttle response to Iraq's invasion of Kuwait and was a betrayal of the UN's responsibilities to a population that had been encouraged to put itself at risk by the organization's own actions. On the other hand, there were those, such as Chinese representatives to the UN, who were reluctant to establish even this modest precedent, arguing that a state's treatment of its own nationals lies at the heart of a member's untrammeled "domestic jurisdiction."[18] Both sides see the Council's resolution as legally incoherent: it bows to the principle of noninterference in domestic jurisdiction in article 2(7) but then proceeds to interfere, without making an explicit determination that the situation constitutes a breach of the international peace.[19]

Libya

Security Council resolution 748, imposing economic and other sanctions on Libya to force it to surrender for trial in the United States or the United Kingdom two Libyans accused of masterminding the Lockerbie bombing, poses numerous issues. The criticism most often heard in the halls of Congress, inspired by empathy for the families of the Lockerbie victims, was that the Council's action was unforgivably weak, far short of its response to aggression against Kuwait. But the more telling critique is the one given very short shrift in the West because of its source: Libya. As Libya argued before the International Court of Justice (ICJ), the Council acted in that instance while Libya's complaint against the legality of compelled extradition was being heard by that Court.

Libya argued that under relevant treaty law, it had the right to extradite or prosecute and that, at a minimum, it had the right to have its nationals tried by an impartial international body rather than domestic courts in the United States or Scotland. Once the Council had acted under chapter VII, however, a majority of the members of the Court, with trepidation among some judges who concurred or dissented, dismissed Libya's request for provisional relief on the grounds that Council determinations trumped any existing treaty rights Libya might have enjoyed.[20] That case is now proceeding to a full hearing concerning the merits of Libya's claims. That the arguments against the United States' position are coming from a renegade state should not blind onlookers to the serious legal and policy questions that Libya is raising. As all lawyers know, sometimes even the most notorious defendants manage to raise serious questions.

As was made abundantly clear by several concurring and dissenting opinions in the ICJ's provisional measures order in the Libyan case, as well as by scholarly commentary since, not everyone is comfortable with a precedent that the Council, without benefit of trial, can compel State A to turn over its own national to State B on the basis of State B's mere allegations of wrongdoing and without any specific warrant in existing treaties between the two states. But for the U.S. veto on the Council, the United States itself would probably reject such a proposition out of hand. And the law's need for consistency and impartial application raises other doubts. Is every state accused by a permanent Council member of international terrorism now subject to Council sanction? If not, is the Council creating and applying post hoc a rule against an outlaw regime under the pretext of an existing "threat to the international peace"?

More broadly, the Libyan case casts some doubts on the efficacy and/or wisdom of the Council's ever more frequent resort to economic sanctions to get its way. The tools available to the Council under articles 41 and 42—sanctions or use of force—seem in this instance ill-suited to the end sought to be achieved. They are both too blunt and too weak. Broad economic sanctions extremely costly to both the economies of innocent third parties and the lives of Libyans not responsible for their government's defiance seem a very blunt instrument with which to compel a small ministerial act: the transfer of two individuals. As with Iraqi sanctions, they prompt suspicions about the Council's real objectives. But from another perspective, the Council's hesitation to apply the one type of sanctions that might prove effective—a total ban on oil imports from Libya—suggests that it lacks credibility as an objective enforcer of the law. If the terrorist act over Lockerbie was in fact a "threat to the international peace" when it occurred, and if Libya's failure to surrender those accused of that act constitutes a continuing threat to the peace, why should the Council's application of the law be affected by such blatantly political considerations as the impact on the price of oil in certain states?

Haiti

The Council's recent authorization to use force to dislodge the military regime in Haiti has prompted concerns both within the United States and in the greater membership of the UN. As with respect to other Council authorizations of force—Korea and Iraq—the Council acted without standing agreements from members to contribute forces and without a fully functioning Military Staff Committee to oversee the action. It again overcame such handicaps through the simple expedient of delegating to the United States the role of coordinating and undertaking military action. Although this delegation was arguably permissible under the Charter, doubts remain. Is it tactically wise to cast the military action of select states charged with doing the UN's bidding as UN action? What is the cost to the organization's future ability to collectively legitimize such action? Does the UN want to be held accountable for all that is done in its name, especially when the Council delegation is given in such expansive terms ("all necessary means")?

Further, although the cases of Korea and Iraq were relatively easy to portray as "aggression," posing clear threats to the international peace and therefore licensed under chapter VII, just exactly what was the "threat to the international peace and security" posed by Haiti?[21] If waves of refugees, standing alone, are enough, the Council's license to authorize force has now expanded exponentially. No less potentially expansive is the alternative criterion in the Clinton administration's presidential directive on peace operations, which would permit the United States to vote in favor of UN intervention if this is intended to address a "sudden interruption of established democracy or gross violation of human rights coupled with violence, or threat of violence."[22] That a military coup, because of its threat to an emerging right to democratic governance, is sufficient to trigger chapter VII action is not comforting to those states whose histories are strewn with the wrecks of successful and unsuccessful coups. It is an especially questionable precedent to establish in the context of Haiti, a country whose history of "established democracy" is essentially limited to one presidential election. It is also not a precedent that the UN is likely to follow with any lawyerly consistency—as is suggested by the Council's total inaction with respect to Alberto Fujimori's undemocratic actions within Peru.

Establishment of a War Crimes Tribunal in the Former Yugoslavia

Although numerous questions continue to be raised about the efficacy and wisdom of Council actions in the former Yugoslavia, probably the least criticized has been the Council's establishment of an international tribunal to prosecute persons responsible for war crimes committed in that region.[23] On the contrary, this development has been hailed as a great achievement and has won extravagant bipartisan and scholarly praise.[24] After all, the tribunal is expected to affirm and enforce hard-won principles established by the Nuremberg and Tokyo tribunals and, better still, will have greater legitimacy than either of those former efforts because, unlike them, the new tribunal, established by multilateral action, cannot be disparaged as "victors' justice." The international community is affirming through the new tribunal that certain acts will not be tolerated.

In the face of such noble goals, criticism of the tribunal is necessarily muted but there are real concerns. Is it any more legitimate for the Council, acting under chapter VII, than for victorious states after a war, to establish such a court? The drafters of the Charter would be surprised to discover that in giving the Council a license to take action against aggressor states they had also authorized creation of a standing international court capable of trying and convicting individuals. Further, after a war, with some assurance that culprits will be captured, a war crimes tribunal is more than a symbolic gesture. In this instance, even assuming that its creation is legally permissible under the Charter and is a desirable precedent, creating such a tribunal in the face of likely refusal by Serbia and perhaps others to give up those accused is merely "imagined justice, which is to say no justice at all."[25] Even assuming that any future peace agreement in the region somehow—miraculously—does not include a provision exempting those who signed it from being convicted of war crimes, establishing a war crimes tribunal in the absence of military victory may still undermine the substantive rules of law sought to be upheld. As one writer has starkly put it:

> substantive justice, and not merely the symbolic justice of Nuremberg or any tribunal, can come for the millions of people affected by ethnic cleansing only by massive outside intervention—war, in other words, and making sure that the just side wins. To establish a symbolic tribunal—even if it did get its hands on the defendants, try them, and punish them, without simultaneously taking the massive military action on the ground to make good on the promise of real justice . . . is a mockery and a hoax. . . . Nuremberg was a lovely hood ornament on the ungainly vehicle that freed Europe from the Nazis; it was not, however, a substitute for D-Day.[26]

There are other questions about the compatibility of the tribunal with existing law. As a report by the American Bar Association on the statute of the Yugoslav tribunal has, somewhat timidly, suggested, there are some doubts about whether its envisioned procedures and rules of evidence will be applied consistent with the rights of the criminal defendant recognized under international human rights law or under national constitutions, including that of the United States.[27] The Council's hastily drafted statute for the tribunal left to the judges' discretion important issues concerning the right of confrontation, the right to counsel, and the right against double jeopardy, and, despite the tribunal's subsequent release of its rules of evidence and procedure, it is not yet clear how these difficult questions will be resolved in practice. On the other hand, those concerned with the rights of victims, particularly the rights of rape victims, have understandable concerns about how these victims' stories will be told, consistent with defendants' confrontation rights, in a way that does not invade victims' privacy and dignity.

Moreover, the crimes over which the tribunal has jurisdiction reflect the UN's confusion over the nature of the dispute in the former Yugoslavia. The new war crimes tribunal departs from judgments rendered at Nuremberg in one significant respect: the tribunal has no jurisdiction to try persons for the waging of aggressive war. Yet the judges at Nuremberg specifically found such charges to be the linchpin for all convictions.[28] The omission is probably due in part to the UN's hesitation in branding the conflict in the former Yugoslavia as either "civil war" or "interstate aggression." Notwithstanding the admission of Bosnia and Herzegovina to UN membership and notwithstanding the UN's attempt to oust Serbia and Montenegro from its membership, there has been considerable equivocation on the part of the organization with respect to these issues.[29] This equivocation is understandable at the political level but may further wreak havoc with the legal goals that inspired the creation of the tribunal. It was established to buttress existing laws of war and of human rights, to confirm to the world that what constitutes a "war crime" is well understood under customary international law (and includes, for example, the crimes of mass rape and "ethnic cleansing"). These goals are undermined to the extent the tribunal is perceived as not following precedents established at Nuremberg, and to the extent its own legal legitimacy is questioned, particularly if, in practice, the tribunal fails to indict or convict those high officials most responsible for the gravest atrocities in the former Yugoslavia.

These doubts invite criticism that the tribunal exists merely to soothe the consciences of those lacking the political will to prevent further horrors in the former Yugoslavia. These doubts are doubly significant in that the Yugoslav tribunal is now being seen as a model to be replicated elsewhere, as in Rwanda.

The UN's Emerging Democratic Deficit

Joseph Weiler has suggested that the making of law by international bodies, as in the European Union, appears to follow a peculiar dynamic: successful international organizations evolve into effective lawmaking institutions when members forgo their sovereign option to "exit" (either totally or selectively) and opt instead to correct the organization's inadequacies by exercising a greater "voice" in that organization's decision-making processes. Weiler argues that the more an international organization successfully "legislates," in the sense of the promulgation of rules that are binding both on and within states, the more members become conscious of the need to assert themselves in the organization's ways of making law, for instance, by keeping tighter "democratic" control over their executive branch representatives to that organization.[30]

Although the UN is a long way from becoming the effective lawmaking institution that the European Union now is, the Council is issuing purportedly binding edicts on a regular basis and other parts of the UN are also showing signs of waking up from their cold war quiescence.[31] And the more the organization "legislates," the more its members, particularly those without the veto, see possible threats to their "sovereignty." Recent claims within the UN for greater "democratic accountability" replicate, at a modest level, Weiler's exit and voice dynamic. Such demands, like those from states whose economies are dramatically affected by the UN's penchant for economic sanctions targeting their trading partners, stem from an increased realization that what the organization, and especially the Council, is doing *matters* to them.

Such demands also originate from pressures internal to governments—from nongovernmental interest groups and others affected by UN action. Council decisions are beginning to have a direct impact on individuals and corporations and not merely on their governments. An individual charged with a crime before an international tribunal created by the Council, the business whose contract for exports of goods to Iraq or Libya is breached at the Council's direction, the consumer who cannot get an imported product because of a decision by a sanctions committee, or the corporation whose claim against Iraq is dismissed because of a decision by the Compensation Commission, all have an interest in the Council's decisions and are beginning to articulate those interests—just as environmental groups offended by a report by a panel of the General Agreement on Tariffs and Trade (GATT) that disapproved of U.S. efforts to protect dolphins in the tuna industry suddenly developed an interest in the formerly esoteric topic of GATT dispute settlement and its impact on domestic environmental law.[32]

Concerns about the Council's emerging democratic deficit are only heightened by the Council's increasing tendency, on the one hand, to delegate responsibility to other UN bodies in some instances, while, on the other hand, failing to cooperate with others, such as other international organizations, to maintain international peace. Quite apart from the ultimate delegation of use of force, it is not clear that the Council should have delegated to the secretary general the task of drafting a statute for the Yugoslav war crimes tribunal or of determining what portion of Iraq's oil revenues should be allocated to the Compensation Commission to pay for claims against Iraq. Nor is it clear that sanctions committees operating in the absence of the veto should be permitted to issue binding interpretations of the often vague sanctions regimes authorized by the Council, or that a Compensation Commission should be able to determine the eligibility of many types of claims under the Council's open-ended liability scheme for postwar Iraq. In these and other instances, although the Council retains ultimate responsibility, institutional precedents are being established and law and policy are being made in ways scarcely foreseen by the Charter. Bodies to which these functions have been delegated, exercising ever more responsibility, prompt fears of lack of effective accountability. These fears are not addressed in Washington, which, to the extent it focuses on the international civil service at all, only seems to care about traditional management and cost concerns.[33] Yet at a time when the Council is delegating ever more of its power, and involving a greater number of actors as either targets of its action or participants in its measures—from the secretary general to sanctions committees to other international organizations—more and more members are likely to feel the need to assert their own right to participate, as will significant interest groups within the members themselves.

The Council's traditional reluctance to involve others in its "peace and security" efforts further aggravates these concerns. As credible observers of peacekeeping have long maintained, the most effective and least costly peacekeeping is that which never occurs: that is, effective preventive action prior to any breach of the peace. But preventive action does not simply consist of Macedonia-type troop deployments. It requires serious attention to the underlying social and economic problems that are the root causes of violence. The Council, which focuses on violence and the threat of violence, is not adept at identifying or equipped to handle the root causes of violence. Other entities—including the World Bank, the International Monetary Fund, private enterprise, and nongovernmental organizations—are better able to handle these issues and need to be consulted if the Council is to be a more effective preventer of warlike threats and not merely an expensive mechanism for enforcing peace.[34]

A similar need to coordinate and work with others is becoming clear in other parts of the Council's work, particularly with respect to the varied tasks that fall under modern "peacekeeping." (Thus, the Council has found it necessary to enter into coop-

421

erative arrangements with regional organizations, such as the Organization of American States in connection with Haiti, the Conference on Security and Cooperation in Europe [CSCE], and the North Atlantic Treaty Organization in connection with former Yugoslavia, the Economic Community of West African States in connection with Liberia, and the CSCE in connection with Azerbaijan and the Republic of Georgia.) But even when the Council involves other organizations in its tasks, it clearly reserves to itself ultimate calls on peace and security questions. Council decisions seem undemocratic, then, not merely because only a select number of members are involved in Council decisions, but because it is the Council alone—whatever its representation—that is asserting power, with no check or balance by any other institution or organ.

Amelioration of the emerging democratic deficit problems will, over the long term, require something more than the addition of two or three members to the Council. The United States needs to seriously consider some of the procedural changes now emerging from that most representative of UN organs, the General Assembly, including proposals for greater coordination and consultation with the Assembly both prior to and after significant Council action.[35] These proposals have a respectable lineage. It was, after all, the United States that, near the beginning of the Cold War, helped redefine the role of the General Assembly with respect to these issues through the Uniting for Peace Resolution, under which the Assembly can authorize peacekeeping in the face of Council deadlock. The United States, which then helped convince UN members that the Council's "primary" responsibility for international peace and security did not confer on it "exclusive"

power, must be prepared to cope with the institutional precedent it helped establish. It is hardly in a position to complain about proposals to increase the General Assembly's role with respect to peace and security.

One approach, suggested by Michael Reisman, would be the formation of a "Chapter VII Consultation Committee" of 21 members of the Assembly.[36] Under Reisman's proposal, the Council would immediately notify this committee whenever it planned to move into a chapter VII mode. The secretary general and the president of the Council would promptly meet with the committee to share information and solicit its views. Throughout the crisis, the Council and committee would remain in constant contact in the best tradition of "consultation" as understood in international law and practice. The Assembly would not have a veto over Council action, but at the same time its participation would extend beyond a right to mere notification. Such institutionalized give-and-take would facilitate a greater sense of participation and endow final Council decisions with the imprimatur, the legitimacy, of the larger world community. (Any similarities with, for example, joint congressional–executive consultations under the War Powers Act are presumably intentional.)

Less radical but no less useful may be more modest changes to the Council's now overly secretive "informal consultations." The Council, which did not hold a single meeting during the first four weeks of the 1991 air war over Iraq, needs to consider, as do all public bodies, the need for public accountability. Although much that goes on within the Council may need to remain confidential, especially in the midst of an ongoing crisis, at a minimum, states particularly affected by the imposition of economic sanctions or states that would be expected to contribute troops to a contemplated mission should be invited to Council deliberations before decisions are made—as is anticipated in articles 44 and 50 of the Charter. The Council also needs to take more seriously its duty to report to the Assembly; such reports should be more timely and include substantive discussions of the issues. They should not merely list Council decisions. After a crisis is over, the Council could seek the advice of others as to controversial issues likely to arise again.

The Security Council's Normative Deficits

But the Security Council and the United States need to address not only *how* the Council undertakes decisions, but *what* decisions it undertakes. What is in doubt is the substance of its decisions, not only the procedures behind them.

The purported legal justifications offered for the Council's involvement in the Haiti situation suggest one major substantive issue: the Council has not come up with an alternative to interstate aggression as a raison d'être likely to be coherent over the long term. To date it has given no principled answer—apart from realpolitik—to those who would ask why the Council chose to act in some cases falling short of manifest interstate aggression but not in other cases of arguable violation of the Charter. Why Libya and Haiti but not Israel, Cuba, or North Korea? Particularly to those unable to exercise a veto over these decisions, these Council actions—not to mention cases of Council inaction—pose increasingly difficult issues of normative justification.

The scope of recent peace operations suggests another set of normative

gaps. Even official Washington is becoming aware that the UN appears to be floundering when it comes to adapting traditional peacekeeping to current conflicts.[37] As the second stage of UN operations in Somalia showed, increasingly today "peacekeepers" are being sent where there is no peace to keep, where there is no host state to give consent to their presence, and where the rules of engagement anticipate the use of force in instances other than self-defense. Although the Council's peacekeeping failures are sometimes due to a failure of political will, at least part of the problem is a failure to clearly delineate the requisites and limitations of modern peace operations. At times the Council embarks on "peacekeeping with teeth" without an express chapter VII determination, without a clear vision of the outcome sought, and without even a clear notion of whether what the Council is doing is "enforcement action" and therefore an exception to the Charter's prohibition against interference in the domestic jurisdiction of states. Peacekeeping has become yet another terrain of fast and dirty institutional innovation by the Council, intended to address immediate crises without regard to longer-term consequences.

More generally the United States needs to recognize the implications of the fact that the Council is a lawmaking institution as well as a facilitator of U.S. foreign policy. When it acts under chapter VII, the Council is authorized to make binding law that can be invoked against members of the UN and even non-members.[38] In the cases discussed above and in others the Council purports to act to enforce the rule of law and purports to be subject to the rule of law. It also purports to act in a judicial manner. Council decisions "determine" that Iraq, Libya, Serbia, and Montenegro have violated international law in specific ways, invoke treaty authority to render judgment, and invite the international community to judge the Council as if it were a court or legislature. States are encouraged to judge the Council's actions—which after all constitute precedents for the interpretation of the Charter—in the same way all laws are judged: by their textual clarity, consonance with other rules of general application, the match between deed and sanction, and the impartiality of application. When on close examination the Council's actions fail to meet these requisites, when no rule emerges to explain what the Council is doing or how its action comports with the Charter, including its principles, states are entitled to legalistic doubts.

Much of the criticism directed at the Council seems to suggest that it is doing too little, too late, as with respect to Bosnia. Such concerns evoke concerns about consistency and "double standards"—as when Libya is sanctioned for state-sponsored terrorism but Israel is not. These worries are legitimate because the Council is supposed to act consistently with the Charter's principle of sovereign equality set out in article 2(1). But the Council also prompts concerns when it undertakes too much, too quickly—not only because what it is doing is exceeding its operative capabilities but also because it is trying to accomplish what others might do better, albeit more slowly.

Today the Council sometimes goes beyond the immediate need to defuse a threat to international peace and security. At times it is attempting to adjudicate legal disputes and impose long-term legal solutions (as with Iraq on weapons, financial liability, and boundaries); trying to alter (or progressively develop) established law (as with the regime to "extradite or prose-cute" terrorists and possibly with respect to war crimes); or trying itself to apply (or create) principles of international law (as through its delegated body to adjudicate claims against Iraq). Arguably nothing in the Charter precludes these actions. Indeed, back in 1945, the United States argued that the Council had two functions: the "political function" of taking enforcement action and a "quasi-judicial" function of settling disputes. It argued that the veto applied only to the first type of action and that every nation "large or small" should abstain from voting on disputes to which it was a party. Although the United States' promise not to deploy its veto and to abstain from voting all but died with the Cold War, the premise that the Council can successfully carry out this dual role is with us yet again.

Revival of the no-veto/abstention promise might yet make the Council's claim to "quasi-judicial" status credible, but this is dubious. The Council is preeminently a reactive, political forum apt to act on the basis of short-term needs, not long-term judicious (or judicial) perspective. Council representatives do not necessarily consider the broader legal consequences of what they do. This is probably as it must and should be, because the enforcer of the international peace must be political. A decision to act or to refuse to act in a case like Bosnia needs to consider factors other than the establishment of legal precedents pleasing to law professors. Council decisions are often the product of political horse-trading and compromise. No amount of tinkering in its membership is likely to turn the Council into an impartial court or a deliberative "law-making" body like the International Law Commission.

Yet, if at least some of the doubts now entertained about the Council are due to its tendency to assume a greater quasi-judicial role than is warranted by the existing threat to the peace, there are ways to defuse these doubts. The Council cannot and should not avoid taking legally binding decisions. The Council's legal determination that Iraq's purported annexation of Kuwait is "null and void," for instance,[39] is part of its job. It can, however, consciously exercise some restraint and leave to more appropriate bodies the task of defining and applying the law. In other instances, when the Council has either no or only a dubious normative justification for doing what it is doing, it should reconsider the wisdom of doing it.

The Council could, for example, have attempted to settle the boundary and treaty interpretation disputes between Kuwait and Iraq in the way such disputes have been more traditionally settled: through submission to the ICJ or arbitration. An imposed solution to such legal disputes is not exactly foreseen by those parts of the Charter that address such disputes, namely chapter VI. Similarly, although the Council may have needed to condemn specific acts by Iraq during its occupation of Kuwait, it need not have definitely concluded either their legality under existing treaties or the scope of Iraq's consequent liability. The Council could have accepted the possibility of an international forum for the trial of the accused Libyans in which Libya's claims based on the Montreal Convention would also have been aired. In certain cases, it could have included "sunset" provisions or disclaimers on certain of its actions to limit the legal effect to the crisis at hand.[40] For example, a determination that the continuation of the arms embargo in Bosnia or continued weapons inspections in Iraq would be reexamined either by the Council or by some impartial body in

one year's time would have shown the Council's acceptance of some limits to its power and helped to distinguish its actions from those of a court or a general lawmaking body. Rather than delegate to the secretary general the drafting of a rushed statute for a new and possibly ineffective war crimes tribunal for the former Yugoslavia, it might have turned to UN fact-finding processes such as a "Truth Commission" on the model of El Salvador. Such an approach might have reaffirmed the Nuremberg principles pending the creation of an international criminal tribunal through a more deliberative process or pending results in the greater peace process.

The legitimacy concerns relating to substance might also be met, as was recently suggested by Colombia, by recourse to some concept of constitutional review over Council decisions, to "strengthen the sense of responsibility of United Nations organs in exercising the powers delegated to them . . . and to avoid abuses of power while at the same time legitimizing the measures taken by the Council."[41] This proposal is not as radical as it sounds. Even back in 1945, when it (perhaps naively) believed that the Council could act in a quasi-judicial capacity, the United States stressed that legal aspects of disputes should be referred to the ICJ for advice, as is contemplated by article 36(3) of the Charter.

Today, with at least two cases pending before the ICJ that pose challenges to Council decisions, the Court may find it difficult to avoid a decision that at least suggests that it has the power to review the legality of the Council's action. Such cases should prompt the Council to reconsider its role vis-à-vis the Court. Indeed, the Council may have no choice, because any decision by the Court is likely to provoke debate, and future challenges to the Council's actions appear inevitable. Libya's arguments before the ICJ, directed at the United States and the United Kingdom for their role in imposing UN sanctions, have already tempted individual judges on the Court into saying (however obliquely) that the Council is either violating international law or acting beyond the scope of its authority. Similarly, Bosnia's plea before the ICJ for the lifting of the UN's arms embargo, however resolved by the Court, puts the Council potentially at odds with the "inherent" right of self-defense and with an alleged duty under international law to assist the victims of genocide—to the discredit of the Council, the UN, and international law.

Anticipating, encouraging, and accepting the assistance of the ICJ on those issues appropriate for judicial resolution would reduce the likelihood of such embarrassing spectacles before the Court and may be in the long-term interest of the Court, the Council, and the rule of law.

Conclusion

UN Security Council decisions, like all of international law, are ultimately made effective by collective legitimation. Council sanctions have not always been faithfully enforced, and unless measures are taken to expand the sense of participation there may well be a progressive deterioration in the effectiveness of these and other Council decisions or, at a minimum, direct conflict between institutional organs—as is suggested by General Assembly resolutions that have criticized the Council's continued arms embargo for Bosnia.[42] To avoid the fate of its illustrious but failed predecessor, the League of Nations, the UN needs to shore up its floundering legitimacy.

Restructuring the Council is part of that task, but such restructuring must be pursued with a broader vision of the final goal.

From a Western lawyer's perspective, the Council's current dilemma is predictable. A Charter that puts at the helm unreviewable political authority with no competing political or judicial check may indeed be the basis of a workable system but it is not, as has been suggested, a constitution worthy of the name.[43] Yet if there is to be a "new world order" based on the rule of law, it is difficult to see how that world can come about except through some approximation of such a constitutional system.

In its stead, the Council is flexing its legal muscles, and no other entity—certainly not the General Assembly and not the ICJ—has yet emerged as an acceptable check or balance on Council action. No organ exists that can call the Council to account under the rule of law to protect the interests of members, or to protect other persons with no voting power, or to protect the long-term interests of law itself. The result is fear—fear that power that is accountable to no one is only coincidentally power pursuant to law and fear that any peace achieved at the expense of the rule of law may be short-lived. Reducing these fears, the cumulative result of the Council's emerging democratic and normative deficits, will require leadership from Washington. And it will require that the U.S. government consider seriously possibilities that go beyond mere tinkering with Council membership.

Notes

1. See Bob Dole, "Peacekeepers and Politics," *New York Times*, January 24, 1994.

2. Although the presidential directive is a classified document, the administration released a detailed "white paper" on the

issue. See "Administration Policy on Reforming Multilateral Peace Operations, May 1994," *International Legal Materials* 33 (1994), p. 705.

3. See, e.g., Barbara Crossette, "At the U.N., a Drive for Diversity," *New York Times,* October 24, 1994, p. A–5.

4. Even the UN's harshest critics have tended to assume that the post–cold war Council is now "empowered to revert to the very mission intended by those who adopted its Charter in 1945." See, e.g., Dick Thornburgh, "Report to the Secretary General of the United Nations" (United Nations, New York, N.Y., March 1, 1993), p. 1.

5. See UN Charter, article 2(4), prohibiting the use of force directed at the territorial integrity or political independence of any state.

6. See articles 25, 39, and 48.

7. See Security Council resolution 84 (July 7, 1950).

8. See, e.g., questions raised in a basic international law casebook used in law schools: Joseph M. Sweeney, Covey T. Oliver, and Noyes E. Leech, *The International Legal System,* 3d ed. (Westburg, N.Y.: Foundation Press, 1988), p. 1308.

9. See, e.g., Frederic L. Kirgis, *International Organizations in Their Legal Setting,* 2d ed. (St. Paul, Minn.: West Publishing, 1991), pp. 628–629.

10. See, e.g., Security Council resolutions 733 (January 23, 1992) (Somalia), 794 (December 3, 1992) (Somalia), 713 (September 25, 1991) (former Yugoslavia), 688 (April 5, 1991) (Iraq), 748 (March 31, 1992) (Libya), 940 (July 31, 1994) (Haiti).

11. Compare Brian Urquhart, "Who Can Stop Civil Wars?" *New York Times,* December 29, 1991 (proposing a permanent UN strike force created under article 43 agreements).

12. See, e.g., Burns Weston, "Security Council Resolution 678 and Persian Gulf Decision Making: Precarious Legitimacy," *American Journal of International Law* 85 (July 1991).

13. See, e.g., Security Council resolutions 688 (April 5, 1991), 689 (April 9, 1991), 692 (May 20, 1991), 699 (June 17, 1991), 705 (August 15, 1991), 706 (August 15, 1991), 707 (August 15, 1991), 712 (September 19, 1991), and 715 (October 11, 1991).

14. This estimate, by Kuwait's U.S. attorneys, does not include environmental damages for which the Council also found Iraq liable. Although Iraq's refusal to sell oil on the international markets has, to date, made the actual payment of such claims nearly impossible, the Compensation Commission remains in operation and its determinations purport to constitute legal obligations for which Iraq remains liable.

15. Prior to establishment of the Compensation Commission to handle claims against Iraq, it was said that the largest international claims tribunal ever established in terms of absolute number of claims or amount of potential liability had been the Iran–United States Claims Tribunal. By any measure, the Compensation Commission dwarfs the Claims Tribunal.

16. To cite just one issue: Just exactly what legal precedent is being set with respect to a state's liability for environmental damage?

17. See, e.g., Kirgis, *International Organizations,* pp. 852–867.

18. Article 2(7) provides that "[n]othing in the present Charter shall authorize the United Nations to intervene in matters which are essentially within the domestic jurisdiction of any state or shall require the Members to submit such matters to settlement under the present Charter, but this principle shall not prejudice the application of enforcement measures under Chapter VII."

19. Compare article 2(7) permitting an interference in domestic jurisdiction in the case of enforcement actions under chapter VII.

20. Case Concerning Questions of Interpretation and Application of the 1971 Montreal Convention Arising from the Aerial Incident at Lockerbie, Interim Measures Order, April 14, 1992, 1992 ICJ Rep. 114. See especially, Separate Opinion of Judge Mohamed Shahabuddeen and Dissenting Opinions of Judges Mohammed Bedjaoui, Christopher G. Weeramantry, Bola Ajibola, and Ahmed Sadak El-Kosheri.

21. See, e.g., "A U.N. License to Invade Haiti," *New York Times,* lead editorial, August 2, 1994 (arguing that Washington "recklessly stretched the boundaries of

what constitutes a threat to international peace and security under Chapter Seven of the Charter"). As usual, most of official Washington ignored that issue and focused instead on a different question, namely whether an invasion of Haiti was in the U.S. national security interest.

22. "Administration Policy on Reforming Multilateral Peace Operations," p. 803.

23. Security Council resolution 827 (May 25, 1993).

24. See, e.g., Payam Akhavan, "Punishing War Crimes in the Former Yugoslavia: A Critical Juncture for the New World Order," *Human Rights Quarterly* 15 (1993).

25. Kenneth Anderson, "Illiberal Tolerance: An Essay on the Fall of Yugoslavia and the Rise of Multiculturalism in the United States," *Virginia Journal of International Law* 33 (Winter 1993), p. 405, n. 55.

26. *Ibid.*

27. See ABA Special Task Force, *Report on the International Tribunal to Adjudicate War Crimes Committed in the Former Yugoslavia* (1993). (The author was on the task force that drafted this report.)

28. Judgment of the International Military Tribunal, Nuremberg, Germany, 1946, 22 I.M.T., Trial of the Major War Criminals, 411, 427 (1948).

29. Thus, despite Security Council resolution 777 of September 19, 1992, and General Assembly resolution 47/1 (1992), both of which seemingly compel the Federal Republic of Yugoslavia (Serbia and Montenegro) to reapply for UN membership, the organization has not expelled the Federal Republic from the UN and has only denied it the right to participate in the Assembly.

30. This vastly oversimplifies a rich and complex argument. See J.H.H. Weiler, "The Transformation of Europe," *Yale Law Journal* 100 (June 1991).

31. For a survey of recent legal issues raised within the organization, see, e.g., the "Legal Issues" chapters of *A Global Agenda: Issues Before the 49th General Assembly of the United Nations* (New York, N.Y., 1994) and prior annual volumes. Apart from the Assembly itself, the most active UN bodies

with potential "lawmaking" effects include the International Law Commission, the UN Commission on International Trade Law, and, of course, the ICJ.

32. See United States, Restrictions on Imports of Tuna from Mexico, 39th Supp. BISD 155 (1993)(Panel Report not adopted by the GATT Contracting Parties).

33. Hence Washington's inordinate concern with the need for an "Independent Inspector General's Office" at the UN. See, e.g., Foreign Relations Authorization Act, 1994–95, P.L. 103–236, 103d Cong., sec. 401.

34. See, e.g., Erskine Childers, "Old-Boying," *London Review of Books*, August 18, 1994.

35. For surveys of some of these see, e.g., annual reports of the Special Committee on the Charter of the UN and on Strengthening of the Role of the Organization, A/47/33 (1992) and A/48/33 (1993).

36. W. Michael Reisman, "The Constitutional Crisis in the United Nations," *American Journal of International Law* 87 (January 1993), p. 99.

37. See, e.g., George Melloan, "Facing the Realities of UN Peacekeeping," *Wall Street Journal*, April 12, 1993.

38. See articles 2(6), 25, and 48.

39. Security Council resolution 662 (August 9, 1990).

40. Instead, the Council rejected one amendment to resolution 687, proposed by six nonaligned members of the Council, which would have added a paragraph stressing the unique circumstances and suggesting that the Council's actions were not intended to "set undue precedents." *Internal Documents Revision*, April 8, 1991, p. 4, quoted in Kirgis, *International Organizations*, p. 676. Compare, for example, Council resolution 748 (March 31, 1992), in which the Council undertook to review Libyan sanctions every 120 days.

41. A/C.6/48/SR.7.

42. General Assembly resolution, A/Res/47/121.

43. Reisman, "Constitutional Crisis," p. 95.

The South and the New World Order

Shahram Chubin

THE INTERNATIONAL SYSTEM of the last 50 years, one dominated and framed by the bipolar superpower rivalry, has been replaced by something more regionally fragmented and multifaceted, more plural and varied. Within this new system, the perspectives, interests, and security needs of the states of the South play an increasingly significant role. For lack of a better term, the "South" is used here to describe that diverse collection of countries in varying degrees developing, nonaligned, and heretofore peripheral to the centers of world politics. Whether they will contribute toward the emergence of a new order, or reinforce the drift toward anarchy, remains to be seen. The developed world is ill-prepared for this fact, both conceptually and as a matter of policy.

This article surveys the perspectives and attitudes of leaders in states of the South concerning the emerging international agenda. It is an explication, not a defense, and a partial one at best. There is no such thing as a coherent worldview of the South. But the failure to understand the South and to translate such understanding into effective diplomatic, economic,

political, and military strategies will have profound consequences. Partnership between North and South remains a possibility, although arguably an improbable one. Antipathy and confrontation are also possible, and made more likely by Northern complacency.

The article begins with a review of the state of the South in the 1990s, evaluating the problems of security and development faced by these countries and the changing international context in which leaders of these states make choices. The analysis then turns to the key issues of world order on the North–South agenda, namely proliferation, arms control, and collective security. The aim of the paper is not to justify proliferation in the South or the repressive domestic policies of some of these states, but to argue that a U.S. policy style more sensitive to a broader consensus will be more effective in achieving its proper ends than a peremptory style that Americans might find congenial in an era of limited attention to and patience with the South.

The State of the South

Most scholars in the North appreciate that the South faces large challenges of economic development. But this is hardly enough. In writing about "the end of history," Francis Fukuyama has helped to broaden common under-

Shahram Chubin is a specialist in Middle East politics and security studies who is based in Geneva, Switzerland.

standing of the South by describing it as pre-historical and still embroiled in "struggle, war, injustice and poverty" even while the North moves on to a new level of historical development.[1] Even this fails to capture the enormity of the challenge. The South faces, in fact, a daunting set of interconnected problems in the economic, political, social, and security domains. Many Southern countries are also corrupt, unrepresentative, and repressive. Because these problems coexist with rapidly rising expectations, these countries cannot develop at the more leisurely pace enjoyed by the now developed world, where progress toward the current level of development is measured in centuries, not decades. Thus, in some fundamental sense, the circumstances of the South are without precedent. Moreover, the South is under siege—from an international community impatient to meddle in its affairs. States of the South are losing their sovereignty, which in many cases was only recently or tentatively acquired.

The problems of development confronting the South do not require recitation here. The large gap in living standards between South and North is well known. Less well known is the fact that in many parts of the South population pressures, chronic misgovernment, political insecurity, and conceptual poverty combine to drive countries backward, not forward—so the gap widens. The revolution of expectations, both political and economic, is putting governments under new stresses to perform and to direct the myriad processes of change.

Northerners are now engaged in a debate about whether the essence of power is military or political, but for most Southern states this debate is immaterial—they are unable to achieve either. The rentier states of the Persian Gulf after two decades of respectable oil revenues have been unable to achieve sustained development, transform their economies to guarantee results without oil, cooperate meaningfully on regional security, or move toward democracy, which some of them deny to be compatible with their traditions. As for military power, the accumulation of arms has been an empty and futile policy gesture except as a means of buying into Western security by recycling oil money to the West—a modern form of subvention.

Even where the economy is growing, as in Indonesia, there is no respite from concern for security. There, as elsewhere in the South, this is mainly defined in terms of internal security and unity. This implies controlling government institutions and securing the people's loyalty, which in turn implies cultivating the "values" of the country as well as developing its national resources. In areas where national polities are fragile, state institutions new, weak, or under attack, ethnic balances unstable or poorly structured, the tendency to emphasize the center, and to hope that it will "hold," is commonplace and understandable. People concerned about keeping the country together find intrepid researchers looking for clues of civil society or embryonic pluralism a nuisance. In many places, the state is under pressure from corrupt oligarchies (whether traditional, governmental, or business) and international institutions dispensing advice about structural adjustment. No wonder, then, that there are countries in which the state has simply broken down, unable to deal with demands and stresses.

In an era of growing global interdependence states of the South remain more vulnerable than their counterparts in the North and more sensitive to forces beyond their borders. Consider the sliding commodity prices over the past decade, or even the much weakened position of oil producers, a relatively privileged group. Consider, too, the issue of the environment, where Southern states are being asked to meet standards and to consider the question cooperatively and in terms of interdependence. Yet as Maurice Strong, former director general of the United Nations (UN) Environment Program, has said: "The absorptive capacity of the eco-system is being preempted by the North," which should accept the responsibility of "making space" for the others.[2]

Furthermore, in much of the South, states and frontiers are relatively artificial, and the forces keeping them intact have weakened. The end of the Cold War and bipolarity undermined a framework that had favored the territorial status quo and made international intervention difficult. The end of the Communist empire has set off fissiparous tendencies long latent in the multinational composite bloc and simultaneously sapped and delegitimized authoritarianism everywhere.[3]

Moreover, the developing states are undergoing change at a time of maximum exposure to political pressures: "A crucial difference between the nation building of Western Europe and that of Africa and much of Asia," we are reminded, "was that the processes in Europe occurred well before the rise of popular demands for democratic rights: nations already existed as relatively cohesive citizenries."[4] It is no comfort to these countries that sovereignty has been, or is being, redefined in the home of the nation-state, with a turn toward smaller communities and intermediate institutions between government (the market) and the individual.

All of this has undermined traditional notions of state sovereignty in the South. As one scholar has put it, international law now protects "the people's sovereignty rather than the sovereign's sovereignty." Sovereignty can no longer be considered an exclusively domestic issue, or "used as an all-purpose excuse or wall by states to exclude external interest" or intervention. States like the People's Republic of China (PRC), which continue to try to emphasize noninterference in the internal affairs of others, are thus considered "wholly anachronistic."[5] In the words of the secretary general of the UN, "the time of absolute and exclusive sovereignty . . . has passed; its theory was never matched by reality." He called for "a balance between the needs of good internal governance and the requirements of an ever more interdependent world."[6]

The North's weakening commitment to the sovereignty of states of the South is evident in the increased concern about human rights as an international rather than strictly domestic concern, and the concomitant increased willingness to intervene in a state's internal affairs in defense of ostensibly international standards. This has made leaders of states of the South fearful. Their fear grows even more sharp when well-meaning analysts argue that as an antidote to the excesses and disintegrative tendencies of self-determination, minority (communitarian) or individual human rights should be stressed.

It is, of course, one thing to observe the drift toward weakening sovereignty, and entirely another to encourage it as an unmitigated good in itself, castigating the backsliders who resist. The PRC is a favorite whipping boy here: "Many states, especially China in recent years, have sought to hide behind 'sovereignty' to shield themselves from international criticism of their abysmal human rights records."[7] Western policy appears to have exacerbated the problems of sovereignty facing the South with little consideration of ultimate objectives. Chester Crocker has it right: "We in the post-industrial north are encouraging an across-the-board challenge to the political and territorial status quo."[8]

To be sure, the human community appears to have reached a stage "in the ethical and psychological evolution of Western civilization in which the massive and deliberate violation of human rights will no longer be tolerated."[9] Criteria have been defined whereby intervention will occur only if human rights violations constitute a threat to international security. Nonetheless, it is easy to see that a right to intervention is an implicit challenge to states if not a direct threat, especially if broadened as an excuse for intervention to unravel and make over states. What the Islamic Republic of Iran disarmingly calls "international arrogance" can be precisely that. On these issues its views are not far from those of India, the PRC, and many other states of the South. Few are sufficiently homogenous or confident of their policies toward their minorities to be unaffected by the cultivation of the right or duty to intervene that has been promulgated in recent years.

Advocates of the right of intervention would do well to note that despite all the global forces promoting cultural convergence or standardization, homogenization has not (yet) been achieved. Regrettably or not, nations remain different and determined to pursue their own ideas about politics, the role of the state, religion, independence, equality, and cultural liberation.

Cultural differences among states influence their perceptions of international relations. Many states of the South believe that existing international legal rules were not only made by the European or Western powers but "were also substantially made *for* them" (emphasis in the original).[10] Within the non-Western world, international relations are shaped by forces not evident in Europe today. As one expert has written: "One of the main shared themes in the non-Western realms . . . is the reaffirmation of traditional religious beliefs as ultimate norm-setting principles of identity in politics and culture."[11] The resurgence of religiosity is stronger in Islam than in any other religious tradition, although it is hardly confined to it. In the Middle East this has been given an additional twist by the proximity of Christianity, with which it has battled for some 14 centuries.

By and large, Western values have been imposed on societies that have ritualistically admired or accepted them. But as one observer has written: "the alien laws, not being rooted in deep convictions and old customs, were simply not accepted by the people as the necessary regulative principles of society." Rather the central issue for them was "how to preserve the community and make it strong by generating dynamism and common will."[12] As Adda Bozeman notes, religion and identity gravitate toward the past,

And since the glory of the past is forever associated with Islam, it is the road back to the Koran that is being fervently sought not only in the Near East but throughout the commonwealth of *c.* 600 million believers. This means, *mutatis mutandis*, a near total refutation of the West's Promethean civilization which earlier generations had accepted as the most promising source of guidelines for the recovery of success in history.[13]

Among other things, the concept of "state" does not have the legitimacy or currency in Islam as elsewhere, especially as it applies to the idea of a "community of states" as opposed to traditional Islamic concepts. Ayatollah Ruhollah Khomeini used to say that he had not promised democracy but Islam, which is what his followers had clamored for. In Algeria in 1993 the same issue is raised—Islam or democracy—for the two are not identical, nor, given the latter's emphasis on pluralism, necessarily compatible.

In a multicultural world, life may be richer but disputes harder to resolve. Combined with inequalities and political resentments, cultural differences and incomprehension can exacerbate North–South relations in a profoundly negative way.

During the Cold War, the states of the South were able to partially compensate for their weaknesses by banding together under the rubric of nonalignment. But this political device is now lost to them. Nonalignment died with the Cold War. More than that, the way the East–West rivalry ended, with the values and systems of the West vindicated and triumphant, undermined the very basis of the nonaligned movement, which had adopted as its foundation a moral neutrality between the two blocs.

For the erstwhile nonaligned, the end of the Cold War has had cataclysmic results. The old uncertainties of the cold war structure, which tended to nurture the status quo and play to the strengths of authoritarian regimes, have given way to a more fluid world in which the assets of the South, whether individually or collectively, are transformed. No longer proxies, clients, and strategic bases, these states are judged by their adherence to standards, values, and procedures that are now generally and unabashedly seen as full international responsibilities. These states now face strong pressures to adhere to various norms (human rights and democratic procedures) and policies (adherence to nonproliferation of nuclear and other mass destruction weapons and limitations on military spending), which some may find difficult or undesirable.

On the other hand, the end of the Cold War has freed the North to indulge its basic antipathy toward the poorer South, to dictate to it without delicacy or dialogue, and to dispense with the appearance of soliciting its views or the pretense of equality. Given today's domestic preoccupations of the North, it may be difficult to generate sympathy for a South that seems mired in problems attributable to bad governance, corrupt elites, and docile and work-shy populaces more eager to resort to rhetoric, excuses, and feuds than to build the foundations for a better future. Indeed it is not clear that the South or the developing countries generally merit sympathy. They exploited the Cold War, used it as an excuse, pampered bloated armed forces, and in some cases acted as clandestine proliferators and shameless regional predators.

However much the postindustrial world may wish it, insulation from this other, more populous and turbulent, world is simply not possible. These worlds intersect most obviously in the former USSR, where the fate of Russia and its neighbors could weigh heavily in the balance between North and South. In other respects, too, the fate of the South inexorably impinges on that of the North. Due to the globalization of economies and the growth of interdependence (including the rise of transnational issues) areas cannot simply be insulated from the rest of the world. This is most evident with respect to political instabilities, in the presence of which uncertainty, repression, or persecution can give rise to large-scale migration into adjacent areas, perhaps disturbing the ethnic or national balance in the host country. It is even more clear when "domestic" issues like ethnic balance or policy toward minorities may give rise to civil wars spilling over into neighboring states and increasing the risks of "interstate war" and "outside" power intervention. (The very categories appear archaic and forced.) In the most obvious case, interstate conflicts spur migration and damage the economic prospects of belligerent states.

There are still other reasons to pay attention to the South. At the most obvious level, population pressures compel attention. Moreover, many of the new security issues such as environment and migration directly concern the South, and its fate and policies in this respect will inevitably affect those of the North. In much of the South the wave of democratization, however dimly sensed or remote from traditional culture, is welcomed by the populace and provides hope for their future. Furthermore, any world order, whether it is underpinned by balance of power, collective security, or unilateral or ad hoc interventions, must, if it is to become durable, eventually be seen to be legitimate. For this it must solicit the support of the widest number of states possible.

The United States will be a principal determinant of the character of North–South relations on these issues in the new international system. This fact alone has generated concern in the South. Especially after the Iraqi crisis, the United States appears to feel not only that its capabilities have been tested but also that its judgment has

been validated. From a distance at least a whiff of uncharacteristic hubris and querulousness is discernible. This translates into "no apologies" take-it-or-leave-it attitudes, especially evident in relations toward the South, which is either ignored or subjected to the Marines—Somalia being a vivid case. The South is often depicted as the "new threat," and some of its members characterized as "rogue" states.

Li Peng, the PRC's prime minister, in a visit to India at the end of 1991 referred to the "emerging international oligarchy," hinting that no one country should be allowed to be in a position to dictate to others. Feeling "excluded from the new world order," the two Asian powers found solace in a convergence and criticism of U.S. "hegemonism." Each was and remains concerned about the degree to which Soviet disintegration has left the United States unchecked and in some senses unbalanced.[14]

The United States has translated its episodic interest in the external world and in the South into new pressure on those states to adhere not just to existing standards of international politics but to higher ones. It has enshrined human rights as a centerpiece of its global engagement, and in postwar Iraq it has used military force to partially dismember a state that failed to meet the new norm.

It has also enshrined nonproliferation. States of the South are now expected to exercise restraint in arms expenditures, to imitate the North (Europe and the superpowers) in arms control and disarmament, cultivate transparency, and practice "cooperative security." Whether or not they feel their security has been enhanced by the end of Cold War, they are being told to get into step with the North or else risk a cutback in development assistance. In emphasizing weapons proliferation as a new priority the United States appears to be targeting an issue that it feels can generate domestic concern and consensus; but it is arguably a false or exaggerated issue, and a crusading policy style that tends to unilateralism is the exact reverse of what is called for if the aim is to establish meaningful restraints rather than temporary obstacles to the spread of these weapons.

Thus, the South struggles not only with its own problems of political and economic development, domestic stability, and regional antagonisms, but also with a changing international system that promises it little in the way of assistance or relief. On the contrary, the South faces many international pressures well beyond its control, not least the actions of some leading actors in the international system to define and enforce new standards of behavior for which a common basis of international understanding does not exist. Unless North and South are able to arrive jointly at ordering concepts for the new international system, the possibility of conflict between them grows more likely. This is a shame, because it is avoidable and unnecessary.

World Order: A View from the South

Whatever else the new world order portends, it does not mean the end of international hierarchies or a new age of equality. Nor is it clear, whatever its shape, how—or whether—it will incorporate the needs and demands of the South into its priorities or agenda. What is the new order? From the South, it looks like a new form of Western dominance, only more explicit and interventionist than in the past. In some Western states a shrillness is detectable when the South is discussed, as if the enemy has shifted there. Consider the following:

- New rationales for intervention appear to be minted daily—human rights, democracy, drugs, environment, and weapons proliferation (while unilateral application of laws extraterritorial and seizures of foreign citizens are upheld by U.S. courts);[15]
- Armed forces structures and sizes are being configured and geared to contingencies in the South;
- The North Atlantic Treaty Organization (NATO) has designated a rapid-reaction force for "out-of-area" contingencies;
- An antitactical ballistic missile (ATBM) system against limited strikes—GPALS, or Global Protection Against Limited Strikes—has an explicitly Southern orientation and it is on these terms that it has been offered to and considered by Russia;
- Even nuclear targeting is being reassessed, justified, and recalibrated for contingencies involving Southern states;
- The Coordinating Committee for Multilateral Export Controls (COCOM) is being reconfigured for use and application against the South;
- A host of regimes to control and restrain suppliers are in place or soon will be, all designed to deny certain technologies to Southern states (the London Club or Nuclear Suppliers Group, the Australia Group in chemicals, the Permanent Five [P–5] of the UN Security Council on conventional arms transfer registers, the Missile Technology Control Regime [MTCR] on missile technology); and
- Arms-control initiatives, whether nuclear, chemical, biological or con-

ventional, strategic or tactical/theater, are now planned and assessed for their impact on the South. Consideration of a total nuclear test ban (CTB), verification mechanisms, reduced reliance on nuclear weapons, elimination of missiles of a certain range, and possible missile test bans, are now all considered in terms of their impact on the South. The Strategic Arms Reduction Treaty (START) is now presented as an important nonproliferation tool.

The North makes no apologies about being more demanding and is not timid about asserting its values since their vindication by the outcome of the Cold War. Illustrative is the North's increasing tendency to insist that there is a definite positive connection between democracy and economic development and democracy and international stability.

Economic assistance is being tied to reduced expenditure on arms. Barber Conable (president of the World Bank 1986–1991) argues that when military expenditures are above 5 percent or in excess of health and education combined "it is hard to see the good sense of lending to such countries."[16] Robert McNamara argues that the West should link economic aid to the former Soviet republics with progress in shifting priorities from military to economic development.[17] The recipient states (the G–24) have been reluctant to accept conditions imposed by the International Monetary Fund and World Bank that would establish a certain ceiling for military expenditures above which no aid would be forthcoming.[18]

Such proposals appear to the South as earnest cant. Money is of course fungible. It is also arguable whether defense is the business of the Bretton Woods institutions. Military spending is simply another excuse, after human rights and the environment, not to transfer resources to poorer countries, to avoid a candid admission that the poorer countries are no longer of strategic interest.[19]

Military spending in the South appears especially wasteful to Americans and Europeans now destroying, transferring, or converting arms. The costliness and futility of the past arms race appears to them all too apparent. Yet it is significant that there is no consensus on the role of arms and especially nuclear weapons in the Cold War: Did they deter a Soviet conventional attack? Were they instrumental in keeping the peace on the Continent? Would deterrence have been as effective at much lower levels of nuclear weapons? Were nuclear weapons essential? Without serious evaluation of the past role of nuclear weapons in the North it seems premature to deride their utility elsewhere. Also it may be noted by the states of the South that even in this phase of enthusiasm for arms control in the North, although some suggest a minimum deterrent posture, scarcely anyone suggests complete nuclear disarmament. Even nuclear weapons still retain a role in the security of the North, however residual. Why, it may be asked, can they not play a similar role in the South?[20]

The fluidity of the current period has not made predictions any easier, yet it is evident that the hierarchy of power has been blurred as other forms of power have become more relevant. Although this blurring may have led to the "obsolescence of major war" in the North, as some suggest, this is less evidently the case elsewhere. Even in an interdependent world competition and rivalry will drive an interest in relative as opposed to absolute standing. States will still be concerned about their relative power positions. Traditionally war has been the means by which power and status have been defined and change has occurred. Choices about war and peace will depend on the alternatives and these choices are not always the same in the South as in the North. The South lacks a security community as a nucleus for order that is present in the North. The mechanisms for peaceful change in the South are not yet designed or constructed.

Weapons Transfers and Proliferation

Since the end of the Cold War the United States has been free to define arms transfers as an arms-control rather than foreign policy problem. This is logical for purely selfish reasons, for as the superpowers reduce their nuclear inventories, the salience of others' nuclear weapons increases. Indeed, at a certain point (not yet reached) the incentives for cheating or breaking-out may increase considerably.[21]

The encounter with Iraq's arsenal provided an additional incentive. The "lessons" of the Persian Gulf War will provide grist for many varied mills for the foreseeable future. Iraq gave reality to a looming apprehension: a regional predator with a whole panoply of advanced arms—possibly soon to include nuclear weapons—that had shown itself unready to be bound by restrictions on their use and has shown a parallel reluctance to be limited in its employment of chemical weapons (CW) by using them in a war with its neighbor. Western concern, of course, was stimulated only when the risk was seen to affect Westerners, for the silence was deafening when Iranians were the victims.

The Iraqi "lesson" unleashed American activism. There was much talk of "coercive disarmament" or what Rolf Ekéus refers to as "arms control by imposition." Some argued that one lesson was that prevention is easier than cure. The new world order could scarcely be jeopardized by a few bad eggs like Iraq. The United States, some implied, might simply have to decide for others what was permissible and define their legitimate defense needs.

As the risks of proliferation of new arms have become more apparent, Northern states have begun to consider ways of limiting arms and technology transfers to the South. As the developing countries now account for some 75 percent of arms traded, their military expenditures have grown at three times the pace of that of the North and now account for between two to three times their expenditures on health, education, and welfare. Apart from the distortion to their societies, such spending constitutes a potential threat to neighbors as well as the more distant North.

This Northern concern is, however, selective. Where states are poor and unable to pay for arms, Northern states advocate reduced military spending. Where there is a large market for arms, Northern suppliers compete to get orders for their shrinking defense industries (as in the Persian Gulf and East Asia). Little systematic consideration has been given to the types of arms that are particularly destructive, whether stabilizing or destabilizing; often this distinction corresponds to what you are selling as opposed to what your competitor is selling. The issue is difficult enough without commercial competition and hypocrisy, because all too often such definitions depend as much on the recipient's military doctrine as on the intrinsic characteristics of the weapon systems.

Equally little thought has been given to the relationships among various categories of arms and the reasons for proliferation. Focusing on particular weapon systems like missiles makes little sense out of context. In terms of destructive power and practical military effectiveness missiles do not (yet?) compare to advanced strike aircraft. Nor does an attempt to ban missiles treat the question of motivation in its context. Iran's quest for missiles, for example, came as a result of an inability to acquire parts for its air force (due to the embargo) and its need to counter the much larger and more varied stock of missiles of its adversary (Iraq).[22] For Syria and others, missiles are a psychological comfort or equalizer, guaranteeing some penetration against a foe with a much superior air force.

Nonetheless, in the fight against weapons proliferation the United States in particular has singled out missiles and weapons of mass destruction. Concern about them seems to focus on the following: Under certain conditions they could increase incentives for preemption. Given their relative inaccuracy, population centers may be targeted; moreover, low accuracy may lead to a preference for mass destruction weapons over conventional ones. Some categories of unconventional weapon systems, like chemical weapons, that may be intended to deter an opponent's nuclear arms may complicate deterrence and blur thresholds. Missiles also to some extent decouple a capacity to damage or destroy an opponent from underlying industrial and societal sources of military power.

These concerns are too simplistic. Mating unconventional warheads to ballistic missiles is not easy. The effects of biological warheads are difficult to predict. An international treaty banning chemical weapons should make the deployment and use of these particular weapons more difficult. In any case, the effort to ban only missiles with specified range and weight (300 km and 500 kilograms) tends to obscure the problem of improving accuracies. Even missiles with ranges shorter than 300 km, if forward-deployed and capable of delivering a strike against an opponent's military arsenal, increase the incentive to strike preemptively. As accuracies increase, more missiles may be used for counterforce strikes, and as ranges increase, they could pull into conflict a wider circle of states.

The direct military threat of these and other weapons to the North is as yet remote. But the potential threat is significant as delivery ranges increase. By one report, by the end of this decade, eight states of the South will have the ability to produce nuclear weapons, while six will have an intercontinental ballistic missile (ICBM) capability, presumably capable of reaching the United States.[23] A larger number of countries will have the ability to build or acquire chemical and biological weapons and other missiles—perhaps as many as 50 states. Of course, the North faces a more immediate although more remote threat in terms of its access to certain regions or the possibility that regional conflicts will erupt under the nuclear umbrella it extends to a few allies in the South.

In a world where distances are shrinking while the capacity to wreak devastation is dispersing, it is not surprising that the Northern states should be inclined to do something. This impulse has translated into energetic efforts to restrict the trade and transfer of technologies that might increase these military capabilities. But this approach runs counter to much of the liberal and open exchange of information and the spread of technology that is part of the modern world. It also risks seeking to restrict dual-use technology for which Southern states may have legitimate commercial or developmental needs.[24]

Are there alternatives to these strategies of technology denial? The control regimes could be improved by expanding membership beyond the Western club, adopting a more comprehensive approach that tries not to segregate technologies, and working toward universal, not discriminatory, standards. But arms control based on denial alone tends only to delay programs and will ultimately contribute to security only if the time gained is used to reduce the motivations for acquisitions. This requires active, constructive diplomacy in regions of endemic rivalry and conflict, notably the Middle East, the Korean peninsula, and South Asia. Moreover, reducing the rhetoric and volume on the subject of missiles would also be useful; their military importance has been overstated and has doubtless stimulated and misguided some Southern policymakers into acquiring them.[25]

Nuclear Proliferation

After the end of the Cold War no issue appears to threaten global stability more or evokes as immediate a response as the prospect of nuclear proliferation. It conjures up images of direct attacks on the homeland of states of the North as well as a kind of global anarchy. Nuclear nonproliferation has been rediscovered with an intensity and vigor that suggest either blind neglect in the past or frenzied displacement of energy at present, for it cannot be justified by any evidence that more states are energetically looking toward nuclear weapons. It is also an issue around which the inchoate fears

of the threat from the South can coalesce.

"Nuclear Saturday night specials" are a growing preoccupation in the United States, where there is a perceived need to "spur a new coalition for . . . elimination [of] the existing or would-be arsenals of South Africa, Syria, Israel, China, India, Pakistan, Argentina, Brazil, the two Koreas and Iran as well as Iraq."[26] Even relatively civilized voices talk tough: "If you can't beat them the gentlemanly way, biff them. That should be the motto for the bomb-busters from the International Atomic Energy Agency (IAEA)."[27] Others refer to nuclear inspections, arguing that it is "time for hardball."[28] The inference is that the United States should no longer be "Mr. Nice-guy." The experience with Iraq has seemingly resulted in putting the onus on states to show that they are not even thinking about "going nuclear." As one senior official monitoring North Korea put it: "We don't even believe our eyes—especially when it looks like nothing is there."[29]

In the United States, this combative "show me" attitude is particularly strong. Americans appear on the brink of unilaterally redefining the bargain entailed in the Nuclear Non-Proliferation Treaty (NPT). As one journal put it:

> The nuclear have's promise to work toward disarmament. The have-not's promise not to acquire weapons and in return are given help with their civilian nuclear industries. Both sides can gain more if they persist with this bargain than if they abandon it.[30]

The price they may well pay for attempting a redefinition of this bargain is its unraveling. There is justifiable concern that much of the expertise and training that can be attained in a "peaceful" program is in fact indistinguishable from that needed for a weapons program. But the United States now seeks (with some success) to stop the transfer of any nuclear technology to countries like Iran whether or not they have ratified the NPT, negotiated safeguards agreements, and accepted special inspections. The United States may demand much more stringent conditions about that country's intentions, but precisely what it would take to reassure Washington is not yet clear apart, perhaps, from a change in regime.

This position frankly discriminates between friendly and unfriendly states, focusing on signatories (and possible cheats) like Iran but ignoring actual proliferators like Israel. It is perforce more intelligible in the North than in the South. The discrimination is especially unpalatable for countries that accept special IAEA inspections, knowing that these are "targeted inspections" relying on U.S. intelligence sources. As the IAEA has noted: "Intrusive inspections make some countries nervous: We need to maintain political support."[31]

This is not an argument for nuclear weapons proliferation. The North also fears that its own experience, in which nuclear weapons and deterrence stabilized the East–West confrontation, is unlikely to be replicated elsewhere. The geostrategic circumstances of the East–West nuclear standoff may prove in retrospect to have been highly unusual. In other areas, the political, situational, and technical prerequisites for establishing stable deterrence might not be present.[32] Politically, stable deterrence requires established lines of authority, civil peace, and clear criteria for use. Most developing countries are prey to civil strife, coups, and struggles for power, making un-

authorized use more likely. Outside of Europe, multiple axes of conflict (consider India, Pakistan, and the PRC) are likely to shape the propensity for conflict rather than a bimodal context. This makes doctrine, targeting, and so on more problematic. In addition the superpowers were not neighbors, had no bilateral territorial disputes, were not traditional adversaries, and above all had time to develop, or let evolve, their deterrent relationship. The superpowers' technical situation will also be difficult for others to match. Its most important aspect is the need for secure second-strike forces, the foundation of a stable system of deterrence. Without this the incentives for preemption or early use will be great, inviting crisis instability. Technical deficiencies will make possible unauthorized use, accidents, theft, leakage, and deterioration. In sum, nuclear deterrence is neither automatic nor universal and there are grounds for suspecting that it will not have the same robust qualities as it did in the East–West context.

There are other considerations. The new nuclear weapon states are not likely to be as satisfied with the international order as the two superpowers, nor will they act as status quo powers.[33] There is also the potential impact that proliferation in the South might have on the North. Japan or Germany might come to see such proliferation as detrimental to their own security and requiring the acquisition of their own nuclear weapons. Another serious consequence could come from the use of nuclear weapons; the global taboo, the "tradition of non-use," has created a threshold for nuclear weapons that separates them from other weapons. If the threshold were to be (frequently) broken, so too would the taboo. A buildup of nuclear weapons in the South would also probably halt or reverse the ongoing nuclear arms reductions in the North.[34]

Although there are many good reasons to suspect that more nuclear weapon states would contribute to global insecurity, these and other arguments do not fully satisfy skeptics, largely in the South. The recently revived crusade against proliferation suggests to some not a new threat, but a new need to focus on a threat—any threat—preferably one in the guise of an Islamic foe. In general, the poorer states find it difficult to stomach the patronizing, rueful air surrounding the subject of nuclear weapons. Despite McGeorge Bundy's conclusion that "in the long run, possessing nuclear weapons is hard work and in the absence of a threat, these weapons have little or no day-to-day value,"[35] the original nuclear powers are fated, it seems, to keep theirs because "they can't be disinvented." So the nuclear states of the North modernize their nuclear forces, even as the threats for which they were constructed have disappeared, while also pressing the South on the nuclear nonproliferation agenda.

The Southern skeptic asks why the argument of France and Britain that nuclear weapons are important for the "seat at the table" they ensure is not equally valid and just for nuclear-capable states of the developing world. They also ask why the North pursues a policy of "selective" proliferation rather than nonproliferation. Some Southerners find it difficult to understand why their major security threats cannot be met by nuclear weapons when they have little capacity to provide for a sophisticated conventional defense or deterrent.

Skeptics also take issue with the argument that stable deterrence cannot emerge outside of the "civilized" North. Their views echo those of one Western scholar, who a dozen years ago argued that the nuclear military revolution itself, because of the destructive power of such weapons, compels a refashioning of political relations.[36] He has gone on to ask more recently whether the fact that the nuclear weapon states have been less involved in conflicts than was traditionally the case with the great powers has something to do with the nuclear weapons they possess.[37]

Concern about possible nuclear weapons use in the South is also difficult to understand for those who have endured many years of war on their territory. If conventional deterrence is less effective than nuclear deterrence, and the threat of nuclear war can deter conventional attacks, then, it is argued, perhaps nuclear deterrence might rid the South of repeated wars. As for irresponsibility, it is difficult to imagine a more dangerous policy than the "extended deterrence" that was the cornerstone of the Western alliance; prudent states would be reluctant to seek to widen the utility of nuclear weapons in this fashion.

None of this means that countries of the South are queuing up for nuclear weapons, or that the benefits of nuclear status are uppermost in their minds. Wars, conflict, and instability regrettably have been the lot of many of these states. Many have not had the means to assure their security unilaterally or through access to arms or alliances. Nor have they been able to fashion a diplomatic compromise.

Moreover, their security has not automatically been improved by the passing of the Cold War. Regional concerns persist. Yet these states are usually only noticed, or taken seriously, if they look as if they are interested in nuclear weapons. Otherwise they are ignored or marginalized.

Those states that *are* interested in nuclear weapons have, for the most part, specific motivations. It is difficult to define the prestige, status, or self-image dimension of India's motivation, which might have led it toward the bomb anyway, but its national security motivation vis-à-vis the PRC and Pakistan cannot be denied. In the Middle East there is little question that Israel's understandable quest for a "last resort" device as insurance against the superior numbers of its foes has created an asymmetry that has stimulated the development of chemical, and possibly biological, weapons and missiles by Syria, Iraq, and possibly Egypt. Attempts to contain one without the other are unrealistic, yet given the short distances and the number of parties that could be involved (among them Saudi Arabia and Iran), any attempt to deal with proliferation here becomes an exercise in managing, if not actually settling, a host of problems from the Persian Gulf through to North Africa.

Iraq's experience in the Persian Gulf War will have an impact on nuclear weapons proliferation. No doubt states of the North hope that potential proliferators will appreciate the risks Saddam Hussein ran with his ambitions and the fear that galvanized the coalition into coercive action. Equally certain is the fact that states of the South will find other lessons as well, not least in Saddam Hussein's mistake in moving before he had nuclear weapons, and the fearsomeness of the North's conventional weapons, suggesting that states wishing to avoid such interventions may find it prudent to acquire other means to deter them.

Nuclear weapons will continue to hold a fascination for states in an insecure and fluid world. Whether as shortcuts, equalizers, status symbols, or simply as "options" to be kept against the possibility of need at a future date, they will be sought by states anxious about their security and/or keen to play a role in international affairs. States poor in resources or technical manpower will find it hard to acquire nuclear weapons and may not even consider them. Those states in a security environment that does not dictate their consideration, such as Latin America, may pass them by. Still others may find the original motivation for them reduced (e.g., South Africa). This will leave a number of states of some wealth, incentive, or capability that, whether from ambition, security, status incentives, or considerations of prudence, will want either to develop nuclear weapons or maintain the option of developing them quickly later.

If arms-control responses are to be found to this strategic reality, they must strive for universal, equal obligations. The extension of positive security guarantees for those states renouncing nuclear weapons that might come under nuclear threat should be considered. With the revival of the UN Security Council as an instrument for peace and security, and given its interest in proliferation issues, perhaps it might take such an initiative. Other measures, such as renunciation of use of nuclear weapons against nonnuclear states, a comprehensive test ban treaty, further cuts in nuclear arsenals, and the like, will all be helpful in giving the appearance of greater equality of treatment. These political incentives for nuclear weapons seem to be given shorter shrift these days when the focus is on denial of technology.

Technology- and weapons-denial strategies are not only morally unsustainable—they can scarcely be counted upon as a long-term solution. The nature of the world—technologically, scientifically, and economically—is such as to make diffusion inevitable. The real question is whether the time bought by such measures is well used to erect more effective barriers against the use of weapons of concern. A good way to do this might be to involve a large number of states in the enterprise that today are treated merely as objects of the control regime. As in other arms-control agreements, there is a trade-off between the rigor of the instrument and the need for the widest possible adherence; in this case surely a wide membership should be consciously sought in order to build a global norm. Technology-denial regimes such as the MTCR are one-way arrangements in which the South has to like it or lump it. This is hardly the stuff of a consensual world order.

The case of North Korea is illustrative. Here is a state with few resources, no allies, and a dim future. Neither the threat of sanctions nor a military strike is an adequate or plausible response. It may be too late for technology denial as well. A policy that combines engagement, dialogue, and positive inducements stands a greater chance of success.

Ukraine is another case. A state concerned about maintaining its new-found independence and deterring a nuclear neighbor—Russia—that seems erratic and unpredictable cannot be said to lack cogent reasons for delaying its renunciation of nuclear weapons. Ukraine needs reassurances and security guarantees if the military incentives for the retention of these weapons are to be weakened.

Iran is analogous to North Korea. It may or may not be moving toward nuclear weapons. If it is, this is due less to pressing or identifiable security concerns than to status considerations and possible bargaining leverage. Margin-

alizing Iran, denying it access to dual technology, and depicting its conventional military programs as a regional threat will do little to deal with the problem. It is simply not feasible in today's world to attempt to deny a country the size, weight, and location of Iran access to the fruits of modern technology for very long. Weak in other areas, Tehran may only redouble its efforts at depicting U.S. and Western hostility as the cause of its economic problems. Ultimately a U.S. policy of "sanctions only" can buy time and impose costs. But unless the time is used for diplomacy, it is wasted. Furthermore, this U.S. policy vis-à-vis Iran's alleged nuclear program risks unraveling, for it may well be seen as politically motivated.[38] To build global norms the United States will have to eschew favoritism, selective applications of norms, and build the broadest possible consensus.

States do not generally seek nuclear weapons, or seek to leave open the option to do so, for frivolous reasons. It would be helpful if the United States in particular attempted to consider the motivations in a balanced way. In seeking to address the motivations of potential proliferators, it would find that there is some relationship among the regional security context, the presence or absence of reliable sources of conventional arms, the availability or lack of allies, and the means for self-expression internationally. The reason why states like North Korea or Iran should not be cornered incessantly in every forum and on every front is precisely because it leaves so little room for dialogue. South Africa shows the way in which a change in political perceptions and regional politics can change incentives to acquire nuclear weapons. With the ebb and flow of time even rogue states can become responsible. Trying to get even the most recalcitrant states on board is worth the effort.

The issues raised by the quest for equality and the needs of order are not susceptible to easy solution. As Hedley Bull wrote of nuclear proliferation: "This is one area in which the goals of international order and of international justice or equal treatment are in conflict with one another."[39] It may be precisely for that reason that the foundations of international order need to be broadened to include more states, giving them a feeling of participation and a sense that their interests are also being accommodated.

Collective Security

If one primary element of the new world order agenda relates to the proliferation of advanced military capability, another relates to the rules and norms governing the use of force in international affairs. The term collective security has been used over most of the last half century to encompass the state of thinking about these matters that emerged at the end of World War II. Today, much hope is being placed by the North in a reinvigorated UN system, released from the fetters of the Cold War, to achieve the benefits of concerted international responses to aggression.

Unfortunately, the renovation of the UN system and of collective security is taking place in a haphazard and ill-defined way. Improvisation has perforce been the dominant motif. The risks of mistakes, incompetence, overload, and disappointment are real. Little effort has been made to clarify the criteria for UN intervention, whether to make, keep, or enforce the peace. This issue is especially salient for the states of the South—the likely target, after all, of such intervention. On the face of it, such matters are by defini-

tion under the jurisdiction of the Security Council, where the South has little or no say. The capacity of the Council to act coherently and forcefully has of course changed with the end of the Cold War, and today, in principle at least, threats to the peace, breaches of the peace, or acts of aggression that may constitute threats to international peace and security can be the basis for action by air, land, or sea forces. But the capacity to act is not exactly as UN advocates might envisage. The weakening and impoverishment of Russia and the agile diplomacy of a PRC that seeks to use its membership (votes and vetoes) for unilateral advantage has undermined the value of the Council as the locus of great power authority and will.

Ambiguity is the stuff of international politics, and it is far from clear how ambiguous circumstances in the South will be evaluated by the great powers of the North. Within the South, there is considerable skepticism that its interests will be taken into account. An obvious example is the fate of Bosnia's Muslims. In the former Yugoslavia, the complexities of peacekeeping are great, the parallels with Kuwait few, and the potential for spillover of conflict into Western Europe quite real, but it is nonetheless striking how many Islamic states have felt it necessary to suggest that UN reluctance to act stems from a double standard concerning the fate of Muslims. This accusation of a double standard emanates not just from Iran but also from Western friends such as Turkey, Saudi Arabia, and Egypt, whose leaders evidently share a view that Muslims are marginalized and treated differently, if not in fact actively discriminated against.[40]

A related concern of states of the South is that the Security Council today disproportionately reflects U.S.

The South and World Order

power. One need not agree with Mu'ammar Qadhafi that the UN Security Council risks becoming an extension of NATO to note that, with Russia in its present condition, the United States and its allies dominate the Security Council to an extraordinary degree. Moreover, talk among these countries of reforming the membership of the Council tends to focus on adding membership for Germany or Japan, and not any Southern state, except as a bogey or argument against reform.

It is true that the United States has much to contribute to the effective functioning of the UN system. It is the only great power with a global view of issues that is not mired in regionalism and parochialism. And when it comes to major or distant military operations, the United States and its NATO allies are the only entities able to provide the requisite logistics and airpower. But even U.S. allies cannot avoid the thought that this is too much of a good thing. How might such U.S. dominance be replaced? How might U.S. engagement be sustained in a way that promotes global stability without it assuming an impossible role as "guarantor of the globe's existing borders"?[41]

Talk of revitalizing the UN Security Council assumes a degree of consensus about the role of the United States that may not be present in today's still culturally diverse world. Collective security will continue to be defined selectively and unequally, reflecting limited resources among the great powers, different priorities among nations generally, and uneven commitment to underlying international norms. The Security Council will be only one of several possible candidates for involvement in crisis areas. The broadest possible consensus on and involvement in collective security is im-

portant for practical and moral reasons. It will protect the reputation of the UN when it decides *not* to act, where it acts unsuccessfully, and where it acts controversially. Situations in which the UN will need such support will surely occur in the future, if the cases of Bosnia and Cambodia are any indication. A broad and diverse constituency can thus act to undergird the UN's collective security effort; to act as proof against its trivialization (e.g., the assertion of the UN Security Council that the situation in Haiti constitutes a threat to international peace and security under chapter 7 of the charter); to enable it to retain its authority and legitimacy even in contingencies when it acts and is bogged down; and to protect it from the charge of selectivity or political bias. Collective security operationally may be a preserve of the great powers and cannot prudently be undertaken in the teeth of their opposition, but without broader involvement, it risks being more exposed and brittle politically than it need be.

Regional organizations might be one alternative. Responsibility might be devolved to them for the development of structures for conflict reduction and prevention, confidence-building, and the elaboration of regional norms. Of course, there are obvious difficulties where the region is riven by conflict, regional organizations resemble regional alliances not security communities, and transparency by definition is in short supply. But in some regional conflicts an outside power is essential as a catalyst, so long as it remains evenhanded. It may spark something that can then become self-sustaining or orchestrate harmony where local parties left to themselves would be stymied—witness the U.S. role in the Middle East peace negotiations.

The promise of regional organizations is limited, however. The Middle East case is an exceptional one unlikely to be replicated elsewhere. In the South generally disputes and instabilities are more likely to have to play themselves out unless local initiatives and self-restraint emerge. Regional organizations are generally weak and as polarized as the parties to the conflict—witness the absence of the Organization of African Unity in the tragedy in Somalia. Nonetheless, their efforts to elaborate norms dealing with border disputes, intervention in civil wars, treatment of refugees, and the like should be encouraged.

Some of the most promising responses are local. Because many parts of the South will continue to be neglected in the new world order, it will be better to count on local resources rather than to wait for others to bail them out. Perhaps the new wave of more representative governments will be more responsible than their authoritarian predecessors in struggling with these issues.

The theme for states of the South must be self-help. Southern states must devise their own organizations to replace those like the irrelevant nonaligned group to deal with their own affairs. In an era of compassion fatigue, domestic concerns, and competing demands, help from the North will only be forthcoming if the South is seen to be helping itself.

But even with Southern activism, there is no guarantee that the North will be able to engage the South in a coherent and progressive program to deal with questions of international security. With the sharp domestic economic concerns of the North and the turmoil in Eastern Europe and Russia, the North appears unable to look beyond short-term issues such as weapons proliferation.

This would be a tragic mistake. The gap between rich and poor is increasing. Problems of migration, which involve political stability and peace as much as economic motives, need to be tackled as a common security issue. If such questions are not dealt with constructively, if other cultures are not treated with respect, and if the populous weaker nations are not given a larger platform and coopted into the system of security management that purports to be global, the present happy juncture of hope and opportunity will be shattered by a deteriorating international security environment.

Conclusion

The issues dividing North from South today are numerous, ranging from the proliferation of nuclear, chemical, and biological weapons and missiles, to technology transfer, population growth, developmental inequality, migration, and environmental issues. None of them will be dealt with productively if conceived of, and treated as, North–South security issues. They are more accurately global security issues, requiring dialogue, compromise, and grand bargains.

The system of global order centered on the UN Security Council was based on the premise of great power collaboration. It languished for 45 years and now is being revived. That revival must go very far indeed—well beyond what the existing great powers now envisage—if it is to have a meaningful impact on the security agenda of the future.

As Hedley Bull observed, no international order sustained by the great powers can provide equal justice for all states, but much can be done to alleviate this perhaps necessary and inevitable inequality.[42] To provide "central direction in international affairs," the major powers need to "explain, prepare, negotiate, coordinate and create a consensus with other states . . . to involve [them] directly in the defence of the existing distribution of power." Bull argued that the fact that great power management of the international order may not "afford equal justice" to all did not necessarily make it intolerable, because the great powers might have a greater stake in that international order of which they became guardians. But these same powers "do, however, have a permanent problem of securing and preserving the consent of other states to the special role they play in the system."

This managerial role, Bull believed, is only possible "if these functions are accepted clearly enough by a large enough proportion of the society of states to command legitimacy." Inter alia, great powers should "seek to satisfy some of the demands for just change being expressed in the world," which include economic justice and nuclear justice among others. Where the demand cannot be met, great powers need to go through the motions of considering them: "A great power hoping to be accepted as a legitimate managerial power cannot ignore these demands or adopt a contrary position."

The states of the North, with only one-fifth of the world's population and a dynamic two-thirds of the global economy, have a long-term interest in framing a new order that is acceptable to the majority of the world's populace. A world of diffuse discontent surely cannot be an orderly one. In a world where nuclear proliferation cannot be frozen permanently and where science and technology spread quickly, it is important to involve all states in elaborating norms and to give them a stake in the more plural world order that is at once desirable and inevitable.

The views in this article are the author's alone and not those of any institution with which he is associated.

Notes

1. Francis Fukuyama, *The End of History and the Last Man* (New York, N.Y.: Free Press, 1992), p. 318.

2. David Lascelles, "Life, the Universe and Everything," *Financial Times*, March 21, 1992.

3. See Robert Cooper and Mats Berdal, "Outside Intervention in Ethnic Conflicts," *Survival* 35 (Spring 1993), pp. 119–120.

4. David Welsh, "Domestic Politics and Ethnic Conflict," *Survival* 35 (Spring 1993), p. 64.

5. John Chipman, "The Future of Strategic Studies: Beyond Even Grand Strategy," *Survival* 34 (Spring 1992), pp. 117–118.

6. Quoted in Gerald B. Helman and Steven R. Ratner, "Saving Failed States," *Foreign Policy*, no. 89 (Winter 1992–93), p. 10.

7. *Ibid.*

8. Chester Crocker, "Ad Hoc Salvage Work Won't Make for World Law and Order," *International Herald Tribune*, December 22, 1992.

9. The quote is from Pérez de Cuéllar cited by Steven S. Rosenfeld, "When There's Good Cause to Meddle," *International Herald Tribune*, October 12–13, 1991. See also Lionel Barber, "UN Takes First Hesitant Moves to Armed Intervention," *Financial Times*, September 27, 1991.

10. Hedley Bull, "The Revolt Against the West," in Bull and Adam Watson, eds., *The Expansion of International Society* (Oxford: Oxford University Press, 1984), pp. 217–220. See also editors' introduction, p. 9.

11. Adda Bozeman, "The International Order in a Multicultural World," in Bull and Watson, *Expansion of International Society*, p. 400.

12. Paraphrase of Albert Hourani, *A Vision of History* (Beirut, 1961), pp. 151ff., in *ibid.*, p. 402.

13. Bozeman, "International Order in a Multicultural World," p. 401.

447

14. See "China and India Reject US Primacy," *International Herald Tribune*, December 13, 1991; "New Delhi et Pékin critiquent la domination des Etats Unis dans les affaires mondiales," *Le Monde*, December 15–16, 1991; and Edward Gargan, "India and China: Much Said, Little Done," *International Herald Tribune*, December 14–15, 1991.

15. See Abraham Lowenthal, "Latin America: Ready for Partnership?" *Foreign Affairs 72, America and the World, 1992/93* (1993), p. 85, and Marc Weller, "The Invasion of the Bodysnatchers," *Independent*, March 13, 1992.

16. Barber B. Conable, Jr., "What the Third World Needs is Growth, Not More Weapons," *International Herald Tribune*, December 26, 1991.

17. Nicole Ball and Robert S. McNamara, "Make Aid Conditional on Demilitarization," *International Herald Tribune*, January 13, 1992.

18. See Stephen Fiddler and Peter Norman, "Survey of the World Economy," *Financial Times*, October 14, 1991.

19. See "Let Them Eat Guns," *Economist*, November 2, 1991, p. 67.

20. On this topic see Edward Mortimer, "Superpowers Move the Winning Post," *Financial Times*, February 2, 1992.

21. As Hans Blix has argued in these pages, this will increase the need for confidence in arms-control agreements and require correspondingly tighter safeguards. Blix, "Verification and Iraq," *The Washington Quarterly* 15 (Autumn 1992), p. 65.

22. This falls very much into the category of motivations noted by John Harvey in his thoughtful analysis "Regional Ballistic Missiles and Advanced Strike Aircraft: Comparing Military Effectiveness," *International Security* 17 (Fall 1992), especially p. 78.

Because ballistic missiles confer status on their owners, acquisition by one state may compel its adversary to do likewise, regardless of their military utility. The inability or unwillingness of a state to "maintain missile parity" may convey a perception of inferiority, or a lack of will, to defend itself. This dynamic can stimulate regional arms races.

23. Quoted by Thomas L. Friedman from a "recent administration study." *International Herald Tribune*, February 8–9, 1992.

24. For a discussion of the need for technology transfer from a different perspective, see Kenneth Keller, "Science and Technology," *Foreign Affairs* 69 (Fall 1990), pp. 123–138. See also Janne E. Nolan, *Trappings of Power* (Washington, D.C.: Brookings, 1991).

25. Some of these suggestions are found in Harvey, "Regional Ballistic Missiles," especially pp. 81–82. See also Steven Fetter, "Ballistic Missiles and Weapons of Mass Destruction: What Is the Threat? What Should Be Done?" *International Security* 16 (Summer 1991), pp. 5–42, especially pp. 34, 41–42.

26. Roger Morris, "For a New Foreign Policy That Forgets the Cold War," *International Herald Tribune*, February 6, 1992.

27. "Getting Tough with North Korea," *Economist*, February 27, 1993, pp. 16–17.

28. Stephanie Cook, "Nuclear Inspections: Time for Hardball," *International Herald Tribune*, July 30, 1992.

29. The "senior official" quoted was in the Pentagon. See *International Herald Tribune*, January 6, 1992.

30. "Bombs for All," *Economist*, March 14, 1992, p. 15.

31. IAEA spokesman David Kyd, quoted by Paul Lewis in "UN Nuclear Inquiry Exposes Treaties' Flaws," *New York Times*, November 10, 1991.

32. See Lewis Dunn, "Containing Nuclear Proliferation," *Adelphi Paper* 263 (London: Brassey's for IISS, Winter 1991).

33. Robert Jervis, *The Meaning of the Nuclear Revolution* (Ithaca, N.Y.: Cornell University Press, 1989), p. 26, n. 73.

34. Dunn, "Containing Nuclear Proliferation," p. 67.

35. McGeorge Bundy, *Danger and Survival: Choices about the Bomb in the First Fifty Years* (New York, N.Y.: Random House, 1988), p. 516.

36. Kenneth Waltz, "The Spread of Nuclear Weapons: More May Be Better," *Adelphi Paper* 171 (London: IISS, 1981).

37. Kenneth Waltz, "Nuclear Myths and Po-

litical Realities," *American Political Science Review* 84 (September 1990).

38. International Institute of Strategic Studies, *Strategic Survey 1992–1993* (London: Brassey's for IISS, 1993), p. 124.

39. Hedley Bull, *The Anarchical Society: A Study of Order in World Politics* (London: Macmillan, 1977), p. 243. For arguments along the same lines refer to Brad Roberts, "Arms Control and the End of the Cold War," *The Washington Quarterly* 15 (Autumn 1992), especially pp. 43–50, and Chris-

tophe Carle, "Proliferation and the New World Order" (Paper presented to the European Strategy Group–Aspen Strategy Group Annual Conference, Rome, Italy, October 28–30, 1992).

40. For a discussion of these views see Gassan Salame, "Islam and the West," *Foreign Policy*, no. 90 (Spring 1993), pp. 22–37.

41. James C. Clad, "Old World Disorders," *The Washington Quarterly* 15 (Autumn 1992), p. 148.

42. Bull, *Anarchical Society*, pp. 227–229.